Handbook on

Anti-Rape Laws in India

First Edition	2013
Second Edition	**2017**

Handbook on

Anti-Rape Laws in India

SECOND EDITION

PK Das

Author of

- Supreme Court on Rarest of Rare Cases
- Handbook on The Right to Information Act
- Handbook on Protection of Women from Domestic Violence
- Handbook on Hindu Succession – Property Rights of Women and Daughters
- Law Relating to Cruelty to Husband – Divorce and Maintenance to Wife
- Famous Murder Trials
- Handbook on The Food Safety & Standards Act
- Handbook on the The Limited Liability Partnership Act
- Rights of Divorced Wife and Widows

Universal Law Publishing

an imprint of LexisNexis

LexisNexis

This book is a publication of LexisNexis
(A Division of RELX India Pvt Ltd)
14th floor, Building No 10, Tower-B, DLF Cyber City, Phase-II,
Gurgaon-122002, Haryana, India.
Tel : + 91 124 4774444 Fax: + 91 124 4774100
Website : www.lexisnexis.co.in / E-mail : help.in@lexisnexis.com

---

P.K. Das: *Handbook on Anti-Rape Laws in India*, Second Edition 2017

ISBN: 978-93-5035-985-3

Printer: Sita Fine Arts Pvt. Ltd., New Delhi

Printed and bound in India.

Dedicated to

The Champion for the
cause for better laws for the
Victims of Rape

JUSTICE J S VERMA

18-01-1933 to 22-4-2013

25-03-1997 to 17-01-1998
(Chief Justice of Supreme Court of India)

04-11-1997 to 17-01-2003
(Chairperson of National Human Rights Commission)

"Rape is an ancient crime which has received penal punishment in the old Indian Penal Code of Macaulay. But this crime has escalated horrendously over the decades for the punishment remains static and has had no preventive impact on the community. There has been a sudden explosion of aggravated form of rape on such a larger scale that Indian womanhood as a class has begun to feel a grave danger to their safety and dignity and their very right to life".

Justice VR Krishna Iyer

PREFACE TO THE SECOND EDITION

The Offence of Rape has been dealt with under the Indian Penal Code not as a mere provision with a limited scope but has acquired a very wide dimension in terms of its definition as well as scope. The obvious reason is the challenge posed by the increasing number of instances of commission of such crimes in the society and a corresponding urgent need to re-impose the deterrent effect of our penal law. Even though the IPC was codified in the year 1860 *i.e.* about 157 years ago with provisions considered very stringent in terms of the punishments laid down for different offences therein, it has somewhere failed to achieve its purpose. The ever increasing number of such offences being committed in the society is the best evidence of its shortcomings. Perhaps, Indian societal humanitarian and ethical status are responsible for such uprise in criminal statistics.

The legislature, executive, judges and lawyers on the one hand and our legal system on the other are well aware and conscious of the menace posed by such crimes. However, there is hardly any control over the commission of such heinous crimes. Further, the voice raised by the social activists, NGOs, women interest organisations, time and again in India and abroad, has also failed to yield any fruitful results at the ground level though it cannot be denied that a fight against such a heinous crime has to be a continuous one and not a mere one-time affair.

Our judicial system even at the cost of being charged with 'judicial activism' has discharged its functions by acting in the most desirable manner not restraining itself from hearing the voice of conscience and thus delivered some landmark judgments going beyond the literal interpretation to the black letters of law. This has been done *inter alia* in the area of basic human rights of women.

Keeping the above aspects in mind, this second edition of the book has been prepared by including the recent landmark judgments delivered by both the Supreme Court of India as well as the High Courts along with some relevant foreign courts judgments.

Last but not the least, I thank Manisha Sharma, Legal Research Editor at LexisNexis India, for her immense contribution towards editing and updating this edition.

Moreover, this edition has been prepared and updated taking into account the pressing need of judges, lawyers, law students, research scholars and all other who are connected or otherwise interested in this field of law.

January 2017 **PK DAS**

PREFACE TO THE FIRST EDITION

"No one in the world is there who can understand the mental pain of a rape victim upto her last breath"

From a House on the Lawless Road.

The rape offence is so heinous that the victim, her family, her society and the country as a whole, sees with hatred eye. Since Macaulay's Indian Penal Code in 19th century the rape is an offence and punishable with either life imprisonment or upto 10 years imprisonment and/or with fine and compensation to rape victim. Still this did not show any deterrent effect on the offenders. In India there is no jail without convicts of rape offences.

In this first score of 21st century, every day and in every State in India the reports come to police about the rape. It is also true that every rape is not reported and all cases of rape in courts do not result in punishment.

Few months back particularly after Delhi gang rape case in Vasant Vihar on 16 December, 2012 the commission of offence of rape is increased particularly in Delhi itself and in NCR and NCT. It is a very shameful affair that within 24 hours 7 rapes was committed in Delhi and in NCT and NCR. It is witnessed that in North-India the rate of offence of rape is in increasing trend in comparison to other parts of India. If some one sees the data of National Crimes Record Bureau the rape related offences against women and girls and other offences against them also increase year to year in ascending order. This is only the data of reported offences of such nature.

The social activists throughout India agitated and activated more aggressively after Delhi Vasant Vihar gang rape case and it compelled the government of India to enact the Criminal Law (Amendment) Act, 2013 (13 of 2013) with effect from 3rd February, 2013 after two Committees Reports *viz.* Justice J.S. Verma Committee Report and Usha Mehra Committee Report of this year.

Taking all these views and for an awareness among civilians, social activists and police role to deter such type of most hated and heinous crime, this book is written keeping in view almost all the necessary factors.

This book is arranged in much more vivid manner with consequential arrangements of various parts for easy access to readers.

I am thankful to Mr. Dhrubojyoti Chakraborty of Assam who has helped me in structuring this book along with his editorial assistance.

It is hoped that this Book on Anti-Rape Laws will be useful for lawyers, Judges, law students, NGOs, social activists and general public in larger areas of subject.

April 2013 **PK DAS**

CONTENTS

Part 2

THE CRIMINAL LAW (AMENDMENT) ACT, 2013 (13 OF 2013)

Part 3

OLD STATUTORY PROVISIONS FOR OFFENCE OF RAPE

Part 4

SUPREME COURT GUIDELINES ON RAPE AND ALLIED ISSUES

Part 7

Rape and Murder – Judicial Activism

Part 8

Rape and Murder – Death Sentence – Rarest of Rare Cases

Part 9

Supreme Court on Rape Cases

Part 10

HIGH COURTS ON RAPE CASES

Part 11

CRIMINAL PLEADINGS, PETITIONS AND AFFIDAVITS

FIR AND CHARGE-SHEET

MODEL FORMS OF CHARGE

BAIL APPLICATIONS AND PETITIONS

TABLE OF CASES

A

B

C

D

E

F

G

H

I

J

M

N

O

P

Q

R

S

T

Part 1

INTRODUCTION

INTRODUCTION

BACKGROUND

Rape is not only a crime against the person (of a woman victim) it is a crime against the entire society. It destroys the entire psychology of a woman and pushes her into deep emotional crises. It is only by her sheer will power that she rehabilitates herself in the society which, on coming to know of the rape, looks down upon her in derision and contempt. Rape is therefore, the most hatred crime. It is a crime against basic human rights and is also violative of the victim's most cherished of the fundamental rights, mainly right to life and personal liberty enshrined under Article 21 of the Constitution of India and in its noble Preamble.[1]

The offence of rape is not a current coin. It has its existence since very dawn of civilisation. Even eighty thousand years back when the modern men left Kenian caves of African forest this kind of act was treated as heinous crime against girls and women. It is a continuous offence in every society which has its presence from ancient period. Though the sex is inherent part of both male and female, it is treated as an offence against women in every community because it is a well-known fact that Indian society is male dominated and the women is expected and commanded to stay behind curtains unlike male members of that society. The word shame was only used to be followed by female strata of society and out of many form of shame the rape is placed in number one pose. Even the history says the prosecutrix is discarded, bald-headed and displaced from her society and some of them could not marry and thrown to destitute and also sometimes commit suicide. The history also says the children born out of rape were to be fully treated as bastards with no place in society. But now in European Countries even in United States and Australia, there are various laws for the protection of illegitimate child and the provisions for their rehabilitations and shelters. Some countries have, in their social transfer, the provisions for rehabilitation of rape victims. Overall in present modern and civilised society the stringent anti-rape laws have been enacted to punish the offenders and to compensate rape victims. In Arabian countries and Canada, rape is treated as most heinous offence and the offender is awarded by jury or court the capital punishment. In India the punishment amounts to either life imprisonment or upto 10 years rigorous imprisonment and/or with fine. And in cases of rape and murder, the Supreme Court of India awards death penalty treating the offence as rarest of rare cases as was held in *Dhananjay Chatterjee* case[2] in West Bengal.

1. *Bodhisattwa Gautam* v. *Subhra,* AIR 1996 SC 922: 1996 AIR SCW 325.
2. *Dhananjay Chatterjee* alias *Dhana* v. *State of West Bengal,* (1994) 2 SCC 220: 1995 AIR SCW 510.

Declaring that the right to life included the "finer graces of human civilisation" the Supreme Court in *P. Nalla Thampy Terah (Dr.)* v. *Union of India*, AIR 1985 SC 1133: 1985 Supp SCC 189, virtually rendered this fundamental right under Article 21 of the Constitution of India a repository of various human rights thus it includes right to life with human dignity.

DEFINITIONS OF RAPE

The *Halsbury's Laws of England*, Vol. 11 (1), 4th Edn., p. 386 para 514 defines rape as "It is an offence for a man to rape a woman. For the purposes, a man commits rape *viz.* (1) he has unlawful sexual intercourse with a woman who at the time of the intercourse does not consent to it; and (2) at the time he knows that she does not consent to the intercourse or he is reckless as to whether she consents to it".

Further para 514 states that in a trial for a rape offence the jury has to consider whether a man believed that a woman was consenting to sexual intercourse. The presence or absence of reasonable grounds for such a belief is a matter to which the jury is to have regard in conjunction with any other relevant matter in considering whether he believed.[1]

The offence of rape means any of the following namely rape, attempted rape, aiding, abetting, counselling and procuring rape or attempted rape, incitement to rape, conspiracy to rape and burglary with intent to rape.[2]

A man who induces a married woman to have sexual intercourse with him by impersonating her, the husband commits rape.

Further a person guilty of rape or attempted rape is liable to conviction on indictment to imprisonment for life or for any other shorter term.[3]

The corroboration of evidence of the complainant, although not essential in law, is in practice always looked for.[4]

The *Black's Law Dictionary*, 7th Edn., p. 1267 defines the term "rape" as "Unlawful sexual intercourse with a person under the age of consent (as defined by statute), regardless of whether it is against that person's will. Generally only an adult may be convicted of this crime. A person under the age of consent cannot be convicted". Further the rape is "carnal knowledge of a child is frequently declared to be rape by statute and where this is true the offence is popularly known as "statutory" "rape, although not so designed in the statute".[5]

In Common Law of UK, rape is an unlawful sexual intercourse committed by a man with a woman not his wife through force and against her will. The

1. *See* UK Sexual Offcences Act, 1956 and UK Sexual Offcence (Amendment) Act, 1976. *See* also *DPP* v. *Morgan*, 1976 AC 182: 61 Cr App Rep 136 (HL); *R.* v. *Khan, R.*v. *Dhokia, R.* v. *Bomga, R.* v. *Faiz,* (1990) Times 3 (CA); *R.* v. *Kehal,* (1983) 78 Cr App Rep 149.
2. *See* UK Sexual Offences (Amendment) Act, 1976, section 1(2) and *R.* v. *Woods,* (1981) 74 Cr App Rep 312 (CA); *R.* v. *Fotheringham,* (1989) 88 Cr App Rep 206 (CA); *R.* v. *Woods,* (1981) 74 Cr App Rep 312 (CA); *R.* v. *Fotheringham,* (1989) 88 Cr App Rep 206 (CA).
3. UK Sexual Offences (Amendment) Act, 1985, section 3(2).
4. *R.* v. *Billam,* (1986) 1 All ER 985; *R.* v. *Roberts,* (1982) 1 All ER 609: 79 Cr App Rep 242 (CA).
5. Rollin M. Perkins & Ronald N. Boyce, Criminal Law, p. 198, 3rd Edn., 1982.

common law crime of rape required at least a slight penetration of the penis into the vagina. Also at common law, a husband could not be convicted of raping his wife. Further it occurs when unlawful sexual activity especially, intercourse is made with a person, usually a female without consent and usually by force or threat of injury.

Most modern country statutes have broadened the definition along these lines. Also it is termed in some statutes as "unlawful sexual intercourse", "sexual assault", "battery" and "sexual abuse".

"The offence, against the female part also of his majesty's subjects, but attended with greater aggravations than that of forcible marriage, is the crime of rape, *raptus muli-rum,* or the carnal knowledge of a woman forcibly and against her will".[1]

If force is to be declared an element of the crime of rape, it becomes necessary to resort to the fiction of "constructive force" to take care of those cases in which no force is needed beyond what is involved in the very act of intercourse itself.

A better analysis is to recognize that the requirement of force is simply a means of demonstrating that the unlawful violation of the woman was without her consent and against her will. Therefore, evidence of serious force need not be shown in many cases. Hence the better view is that "force" is not truly speaking an element of the crime itself, but if great force was not needed to accomplish the act the necessary lack of consent has been disproved in other than exceptional situations. The courts today frequently state the position that a woman's resistance need not be more than her age, strength, the surrounding facts and all attending circumstances make reasonable.[2]

SEXUAL ASSAULT

It is if there occurs that the threat or use of force on another that causes that person to have a reasonable apprehension of imminent harmful or offensive contact and also the act of putting another person in reasonable fear or apprehension of an immediate battery by means of an act assaulting to an attempt or threat to commit a battery, requiring the specific intent to cause physical injury.

Particularly the words "sexual assault" means sexual intercourse with another person without that person's consent. Several countries have repealed the offence of rape and replaced it with the "offence of sexual assault".

An assault carried out with the additional criminal purpose of intending to rape the victim is otherwise called "the assault with intent to commit rape".[3]

RAPE OF A MINOR GIRL OF SEVEN YEAR

The 19 year accused committed the crime of rape with a seven year old girl. He was convicted and sentenced to life imprisonment and to pay 20,000 – as an amount of fine. The sentence was modified to 10 years rigorous imprisonment as

1. William Blackstone Commentaries of the Laws of England, 1769, para 210.
2. Rollin M. Perkins & Ronald N. Boyce, Criminal Law, pp. 211-12, 1982 Edn.
3. Black's Law Dictionary, 7th Edn., p. 110.

the accused was poor agricultural labour. The amount of fine was also reduced to Rs 1000 only.[1]

SEXUAL INTERCOURSE WITH YOUNG LADY

The victim did not resist initially but escalated the matter after the incident. It was held that the sexual intercourse was not consensual. The accused convicted under section 376 of IPC and sentenced to 10 years of rigorous imprisonment.[2]

RAPE ON PROMISE TO MARRY

The accused committed sexual intercourse on promise to marry. Prosecutrix eloped with the accused. On complaint of father of prosecutrix, the accused was arrested and marriage was not solemnized. It was held that the accused was not guilty of rape.[3]

ATTEMPT TO RAPE AND MURDER OF NINE YEAR OLD GIRL

The accused made an attempt to rape on a nine year old girl and strangulated her to death when failed. Two of the witnesses stated in cross-examination that they had seen the blood on the spot, but the medical report showed that there was no oozing of blood from any part of the body of the deceased and further that there was no injury on private parts of the girl. It was held that it would not destroy the prosecution when other cogent evidence was available.[4]

RAPE AND MURDER OF 14 YEAR MINOR GIRL

Rape and murder committed by the accused on a 14 year minor girl by her neighbour. The accused was convicted for a minimum of 35 years in jail without remission.[5]

FATHER RAPED ON HIS 4 YEAR OLD DAUGHTER

The father committed rape on his four year old daughter and strangulated her to death when nobody was in house. The accused did not explain the reason of her death which was in his special knowledge. This was a strong incriminating circumstance against the accused. The accused was convicted on these similar grounds and was sentenced to life imprisonment in jail for 30 years without remissions.[6]

---

1. *Bavo* v. *State of Gujarat*, 2012 (1) SCC (Cri) 983: (2012) 1 MWN (Cri) 430: 2012 (2) Law Herald (SC) 1237: 2012 (1) RAJ 233: 2012 (1) Crimes 230; *State* v. *Harkesh*, 2016 (2) RAJ 111: 2016 (2) RCR (Cri) 273: 2016 (2) Law Herald (SC) 1151.
2. *State of Assam* v. *Ramesh Dowarah*, 2016 (158) AIC 11: 2016 (1) RCR (Cri) 799: 2016 (1) RAJ 342: JT 2016 (1) SC 195: 2016 (1) SCALE 258: 2016 Cr LJ 1125: AIR 2016 SC 341: 2016 (1) ACJ 326: 2016 (2) PLJR 85.
3. *Deepak Gulati* v. *State of Haryana*, 2013 (4) E Cr C 2010: 2013 (3) RCR (Cri) 96: 2013 (3) RAJ 558: 2013 (2) CCR 482: 2013 (2) KLT 762: 2013 (2) Ker LJ 810.
4. *Jugender Singh* v. *State of Uttar Pradesh*, 2013 (3) SCC (Cri) 129: 2012 (6) SCC 297: 2012 AIR SCW 3170: 2012 (4) RAJ 1: 2012 (115) AIC 25: AIR 2012 SC 1013 (Cri): 2012 Cr LJ 3005: JT 2012 (5) SC 374.
5. *Rajkumar* v. *State of Madhya Pradesh*, 2014 (2) RCR (Cri) 45: 2014 (3) SCALE 42: 2014 (1) CCR 540: 2014 (3) SCR 212: 2014 RAJ 290: 2014 (1) MLJ (Cri) 699.
6. *Neel Kumar* v. *State of Haryana*, 2012 (3) Cal LJ 58: 2013 (122) AIC 224: 2012 (2) RCR (Cri) 941: 2012 (3) RAJ 17: 2012 (3) RLW 2009; *see* also *Prithipal Singh* v. *State of Punjab*, 2011 (4) RCR (Cri) 791: 2011 (6) RAJ 61: (2012) 1 SCC 10.

REDUCTION OF SENTENCE NOT POSSIBLE IN OFFENCE OF RAPE

The offence of rape is the offence against the society. The sentence not to be reduced on basis of compromise. The offence of rape is non-compoundable.[1]

PLIGHT OF VICTIMS OF RAPE

The social stigma has a devastating effect on rape victim. The victims need physical, mental, psychological and social rehabilitation. Physically she must feel safe in society, mentally she needs help to restore her of loss of self-esteem. She needs to be accepted back in the social fold.[2]

REDUCTION OF SENTENCE IN RAPE CASE

The punishment of accused in rape case, has to be decided after considering all aggravating and mitigating factors and the circumstances in which the crime has been committed. The conduct and state of mind of the accused and the age of sexually assaulted victim and the gravity of the criminal act, are the factors of paramount importance.[3]

RAPE ON 15 YEAR OLD GIRL

The accused and his three accomplices took away the prosecutrix and brought her to Haridwar, where they were staying in a house. The accused and his three accomplices committed the rape with her. Defence version was that it was prosecutrix who allured the accused to marry her and elop with him to Haridwar and had consensual sex with accused and his accomplices. This defence version was not convincing.[4]

NO CONSENT OF PROSECUTRIX

The prosecutrix stated in her sworn testimony that she did not given consent for commission of rape. The accused failed to give satisfactory evidence to rebut the presumption under section 114A of Evidence Act. It was held that the sexual intercourse was without consent of prosecutrix. The accused was sentenced to 7 years rigorous imprisonment.[5]

MEDICAL AND OCULAR EVIDENCE IN OFFENCE OF RAPE

The accused convicted and sentenced to life imprisonment. It was prayed that the conviction should be quashed on the ground that as per medical evidence

---

1. *Shimbhu* v. *State of Haryana,* 2013 (5) RAJ 110: 2013 (3) CCR 547: 2014 Cr LJ 308: (2013) 10 SCALE 595: AIR 2014 SC 739; *Baldev Singh* v. *State of Punjab,* (2011) 13 SCC 705: 2012 (2) RAJ 59: 2011 (2) RCR 127; *Mohd. Imran Khan* v. *State (NCT of Delhi),* (2011) 10 SCC 192; *State of Madhya Pradesh* v. *Madanlal,* 2015 (3) ILR (Ker) 485: 2015 (3) PLJR 481; *State of Rajasthan* v. *Vinod Kumar,* 2012 (4) RCR 305: 2012 (4) RAJ 431: (2012) 6 SCC 770.
2. *Md. Iqbal* v. *State of Rajasthan,* JT 2013 (10) SC 53: (2013) 14 SCC 481: (2013) 3 CCR 555: 2014 (4) SCC (Cri) 271; *Narender Kumar* v. *State (NCT of Delhi),* 2012 (3) RCR (Cri) 66: 2012 (3) RAJ 138; *Vijay* v. *State of Madhya Pradesh,* 2010 (3) RCR (Cri) 794: (2010) 8 SCC 191.
3. *State of Rajasthan* v. *Heera Lal,* 2012 AIR SCW 3237: 2012 (78) A Cr C 167: 2012 (115) AIC 114: 2012 (3) Cr CC 422: 2012 (3) PLJR 121: (2012) 6 SCC 770.
4. *Jarnail Singh* v. *State of Haryana,* 2013 (2) NCC 431: 2013 (3) CCR 194: 2013 (4) RAJ 226: JT 2013 (9) SC 374; *Sunil* v. *State of Haryana,* 2010 (1) RCR (Cri) 166: 2009 (6) RAJ 594.
5. *Deepak* v. *State of Haryana,* 2015 (1) CCR 523: 2015 (2) RCR (Cri) 246: 2015 (2) RAJ 210: JT 2015 (3) SC 28: 2015 (2) Bom CR (Cri) 1: 2015 All SCR 1236.

there was no mark of sexual violence on the genital organs of the victim. It was not accepted by the Court on the ground that there was no reason to disbelieve the version of eye-witnesses which was corroborated by the witnesses.[1]

REFUSAL OF REDUCTION OF SENTENCE IN RAPE CASE

The sexual offence is not only an unlawful invasion of the right of privacy and sanctity of a woman but also a serious blow to her honour. It also indelibly leaves a scar on the most cherished possessions of a woman *i.e.,* her dignity, honour, reputation and last but not the least her chastity. And also the entire psychology of a woman and pushes her into deep emotional crisis.[2]

ATTEMPT TO RAPE

The statement of prosecutrix was that the accused undressed her and also undressed himself and tried to commit bad work with her. The prosecutrix resisted and suffered injuries on her breast but same was not corroborated by the medical evidence. Hence there was absence of attempt to rape and the accused was convicted under section 354 of Indian Penal Code.[3]

SEXUAL RELATIONS *V.* SEXUAL ACTIVITY

Sexual Relations and Sexual Activity relates to:

- sexual intercourse.
- physical sexual activity that does not necessarily culminate in intercourse.
- sexual relations usually involve the touching of another's breast, vagina, penis, or arms.
- both persons (toucher and the person touched) engage in sexual relations or sexual activity.

ANALYSIS OF INDIAN POSITION ON ANTI-RAPE LAWS

In India, at present days in comparison to whole of world, the occurrence of rape is so and so worse that it creates a negative attitude towards our present system of democratic governance and hatred heart towards executive set up. In the year 2001, the Decan Herald posed that out of 68 rapes only 1 case is reported (*i.e.* 1:68) and the sexual harassment case the ratio is 1:10,000. The National Family Survey reports that one to five women face domestic violence from their husbands. The Global statistic says between 20% to 50%.[4]

---

1. *Bhaikon* v. *State of Assam,* 2013 (Supp) Cut LT (Cri) 1766: 2013 (4) MR LJ (Cri) 415: 2013 (4) C CrC 184: 2013 (2) RCR (Cri) 952; *Chhote Lal* v. *State,* 2012 (2) RCR (Cri) 305; *Life Convict @ Khoka* v. *B.K. Srivastva,* (2013) SCC 425; *Mohinder Singh* v. *State,* 2013 (1) RCR 878: (2013) 3 SCC 294; *Rameshbhai* v. *State,* (2011) 2 SCC 764; *Sahib* v. *State,* 2013 (6) SCALE 219.
2. *Pushpanjali Sahu* v. *State of Orissa,* 2012 (4) RCR (Cri) 612: 2012 (5) RAJ 109: (2012) 9 SCC 705: 2012 (129) AIC 39: 2012 AIR SCW 5447.
3. *State of Rajasthan* v. *Sri Chand,* 2015 All MR (Cri) 2437: 2015 (2) Cr LR 623: 2015 (3) ALJ (Cri) 15: JT 2015 (4) SC 542: 2015 (152) AIC 134: 2015 AIR SCW 3293: 2015 (6) SCALE 224; *Azfar Ali* v. *State,* (2013) 10 SCC 31.
4. Naina Kapoor, Criminal Justice Reform: What is in it for women? Vol. 30. *See* also the Indian Advocate (2001-2002), p. 123.

It is a shame for our whole society irrespective of caste and creed to mention that in upper part of 2012 and early first quarter of 2013 and particularly after Delhi Vasant Vihar gang rape case on 16 December, 2012. Even if after such incidents Delhi and its NCT witnessed seven rape and gang rape within 24 hours. Many incidents of rape is noted in North India in respect to other part of India. But India does not sleep in a deep sleeps. Every spectrum of society, NGOs, social activities, judicial activism shouted against the increased trend of such herons crime of rape so that the government of India passed the Criminal Law (Amendment) Act, 2013 on 21 March, 2013 which followed and repealed the ordinance proclaim by the President of India on a new law and a new approach to the rape law. This new rape law is based on western approach of Sexual Offence Act particularly the new Sexual Offences Act of 2003 in England.

The Indian Penal Code, sections 375, 376 and 376A to 376D (old law, before Criminal Law (Amendment) Act, 2013 (13 of 2013) with effect from 3rd February, 2013) dealt with the offence of rape.

The offence of rape is an "unlawful sexual intercourse between a man and a woman without the woman's consent and against her will. The offence of rape requires both *mens rea* (motive of offender) and *actus reus* (act of offender). The offence of rape requires both these two elements. It furthers needs that the man intends to have sexual intercourse knowing that the woman does not consent to such intercourse. The *actus reus* refers to the penetration *per vaginam*[1] to constitute the offence of rape.

The case of *Phul Singh* v. *State of Haryana*[2] it was held that the offence of rape signifies in common terminology as the ravishment of a woman without her consent, by force, fear or fraud or the carnal knowledge of a woman by force against her will. In other words rape is a violation with violence of the private person of a woman, an outrage by all means.[3]

Section 375 of Indian Penal Code defines rape and section 376 prescribes its punishment. Section 376A makes husband punishable for intercourse with his wife during judicial separation and sections 376B to 376D provides punishment for custodial rape (old law before 2013 Amendment).

But in considering the inadequacy of rape law the Supreme Court of India concerned its view in the cases[4] for which the Parliament of India amended extensively in 1983 the rape law provisions by incorporating more stringent penal provisions.

The Supreme Court in case of *State of Punjab* v. *Gurmit Singh*[5] refused to question about the character of prosecutrix (victim of rape) in cross examination.

1. *Gaston*, (1981) 73 Cr App Rep 164.
2. (1979) 4 SCC 413: AIR 1980 SC 249: (1980) 1 SCR 589: 1980 Cr LJ 8: (1980) 2 SCJ 26: 1979 CAR 393.
3. *See* also Nelson's Pakistan Penal Code, 7th Edn., 1983, Vol. 2, p. 2014.
4. *Tukaram* v. *State of Maharashtra*, AIR 1979 SC 185: (1979) 2 SCC 143: (1979) 1 SCR 810: 1978 CAR 413: 1978 Cr LJ 1864; *Shideswari Gangul* v. *State of West Bengal*, AIR 1958 SC 143: 1958 SCR 749: 1958 SCJ 349: 1958 Cr LJ 273; *Bharwada Bhoginbhai Hirjibhai* v. *State of Gujarat*, AIR 1983 SC 753: (1983) 3 SCC 217: (1983) 3 SCR 280: 1983 Cr LJ 1096: 1983 CAR 343.
5. AIR 1996 SC 1393: (1996) 2 SCC 384: (1996): 1996 Cr LJ 1728: 1996 AIR SCW 998: (1996) 1 Crimes 37.

This court in a case[1] confirmed the admissibility of evidence by way of video-conferencing.

In another case the Supreme Court observed that in the judgments, be it of High Court or a Lower Court, the name of the victim should not be mentioned and the name should be replaced by "victim".[2]

The Supreme Court in case of *State of Karnataka* v. *Krishnappa*[3] held that in addition to strengthening the rape law, it was necessary to have a co-operative victim, professional investigation, diligent prosecution, expeditious trial and sensitive judges to ensure proper investigations, trial and conviction in sexual crimes.[4] Protection of society and deterring the criminal is the avowed object of law and that is required to be achieved by imposing an appropriate sentence. The sentencing courts are expected to consider all relevant facts and circumstances bearing on the question of sentence and proceed to impose a sentence commensurate with the gravity of the offence. Courts must here the loud cry for justice by the society in cases of such heinous crime of rape on innocent helpless girl of tender years, and respond by imposition of proper sentence; public abhorrence of the crime needs retention through imposition of appropriate sentence by the court.

The Supreme Court in a case[5] where three accused after abducting the victim, subjected her to sexual intercourse forcibly, held that the act was against her will and it amounted to rape within the meaning of section 375 of Indian Penal Code punishable with its section 376.

The word "consent" can change a shape of offence in case of rape or sexual assault.

In *Rao* case[6] it was observed that:

> "Consent is an act of reason accompanied by deliberation, a mere act of helpless resignation in the face of inevitable complaint in quiescence non-resistance and passive giving it cannot be deemed to be consent to exempt a man of the charge of rape".

In *Mango Ram's* case[7] the court held that:

> "Submission of body under the fear or terror cannot be construed as a consented sexual act, consent for the purpose of section 375 requires voluntary participation not only after the exercise of intelligence based on the knowledge of the significance and moral quality of the act but after

1. *Sakshi* v. *Union of India,* (2004) 6 SCALE 15: AIR 2004 SC 3566: 2004 AIR SCW 3449: 2004 Cr LJ 2881.
2. *Bhupinder Sharma* v. *State of Himachal Pradesh,* (1983) 8 SCC 551; 2003 AIR SCW 5493: AIR 2003 SC 4684 (2004) Cr LJ 1.
3. AIR 2000 SC 1470: 2000 Cr LJ 1793: 2000 AIR SCW 1040: (2000) 4 SCC 75.
4. *See* Kiren Bedi "What use is law if the victim herself does not want any Action Taken? Times of India, November 25, 2002.
5. *State of Punjab* v. *Gurmit Singh,* AIR 1996 SC 1393: (1996) 2 SCC 384: 1996 Cr LJ 1728: 1996 AIR SCW 998: (1996) 1 SCJ 566: (1996) 1 Crimes 37.
6. *Rao Harnarain Singh @ Shroji Singh* v. *State,* AIR 1958 Punj 123: (1958) Cr LJ 563.
7. *State of Himachal Pradesh* v. *Mango Ram,* (2000) 7 SCC 224.

having fully exercised the choice between resistance and ascent. Whether there was consent or not, is to be ascertained only on a careful study of all relevant circumstances."

Most importantly the Supreme Court in a case[1] held that:

1. Consent given by a woman believing the man's promise to marry her would fall within the expression "without her consent" *vide* clause (iii) to section 375 of Indian Penal Code, only if it is established that from the very and inception the man never really intended to marry her and the promise was mere hoax;
2. When prosecutrix had taken a conscious decision to participate in the sexual act only on being impressed by the accused's promise to marry her and the accused's promise was not false from its inception with the intention to seduce her to sexual act, clause (ii) to section 375 of this Code is not attracted and established. In such a situation the accused would be liable for breach of promise to marry for which he will be liable for damages under civil law;
3. False promise to marry will not *ipso facto* make a person liable for rape if the prosecutrix is above 16 years of age and impliedly consented to the act.

In case of *Uday* v. *State of Karnataka*[2] it was observed that the consent given by prosecutrix to sexual intercourse with a person with whom she is deeply in love on a promise that he would marry her on a later date, cannot be said to be given under a misconception of fact.

The consent procured by putting the woman under fear of death or hurt is no consent in law.[3]

Consent of a woman of unsound mind or under the influence of intoxication is no consent.[4]

The consent of mentally retarded woman is no consent.[5]

A woman under 16 is considered incapable of giving consent for sexual intercourse.[6]

---

1. *Deelip Singh @ Dilip Kumar* v. *State of Bihar,* (2005) 1 SCC 88: AIR 2005 SC 203: 2004 AIR SCW 6479: 2004 (8) Supreme 266; In Re *N. Jaladu,* ILR (1913) 36 Mad 453; *Jayanti Rani Pande* v. *State of West Bengal,* 1984 Cr LJ 1535; *Purshottam Mahadev* v. *State,* AIR 1963 Bom 74.
2. (2003) 2 SCALE 329: (2003) 4 SCC 46: 2003 Cr LJ 1539 (SC).
3. *State of Maharashtra* v. *Prakash,* AIR 1992 SC 1275: 1993 Supp (1) SCC 653; *Tukaram* v. *State of Maharashtra,* AIR 1979 SC 185: (1979) 2 SCC 143: (1979) 1 SCR 810: 1978 CAR 413; *Nanak Singh* v. *State of Uttar Pradesh,* 1984 All LJ 548; *R.* v. *Doe,* (1984) 15 Cox CC 579; *R.* v. *Jackson,* 1822 Russ & R 487: 169 ER 911; *State of Uttar Pradesh* v. *Chhotey Lal,* (2011) 1 Supreme 418. *See* also *Papadimitropoulos* v. *R.,* (1957) 98 CLR 249.
4. *Hall,* (1987) 86 Cr App Rep 159: 1987 Cr LR 831.
5. *Tulsidas Kanolkar* v. *State of Goa,* (2003) 8 SCC 590: 2003 AIR SCW 6581: AIR 2004 SC 978.
6. *Sideshwar Ganguli* v. *State of West Bengal,* AIR 1958 SC 143: 1958 SCR 749: 1958 SCJ 349: 1958 Cr LJ 273; *Yeswant Rao* v. *State of Madhya Pradesh,* AIR 1992 SC 1683: 1993 Supp (1) SCC 520; *Gurcharan Singh,* AIR 1972 SC 2661; *Harpal Singh* v. *State of Himachal Pradesh,* AIR 1981 SC 361: (1981) 1 SCC 560: 1981 Cr LJ 46 (SC): 1981 CAR 29; *Deelip Singh @ Dilip Kumar* v. *State of Bihar,* (2005) 1 SCC 88; *Bishrudayal* v. *State of Bihar,* AIR 1981 SC 39.

SEXUAL INTERCOURSE – MEANING OF

As per *Halsbury's Laws of England*[1] it is necessary to prove the completion of sexual intercourse by the emission of seed; intercourse is deemed complete[2] upon proof of penetration only.[3] The slightest degree of penetration is enough.[4]

If penetration cannot be satisfactorily proved, the accused may be convicted of attempted rape; if the intent is not proved, he may be convicted of indecent assault.

There is an irrebuttable presumption that a boy under 14 is incapable of sexual intercourse; evidence may not be adduced to show that he is capable.[5]

As per such English Law corroboration of the evidence of the victim is not essential in law but in practice is always looked for except where there is no dispute as to be commission of the offence, but only as to the identity of the offender.

UNLAWFUL SEXUAL INTERCOURSE WITH THE GIRL UNDER 16 YEARS OF AGE

As per *Halsbury's Laws of England*[6] it is an offence for a man to have unlawful sexual intercourse with a girl under the age of 16[7]; the consent of the girl is immaterial.

However, a man is not guilty of such an offence because he has unlawful sexual intercourse with a girl under the age of 16, if he is under the age of 24 and has not previously been charged with a like offence[8], and he believes her to be of the age of 16 or over and has reasonable cause for the belief.[9]

Where a marriage is invalid by reason of the girl being under the age of 16[10], the invalidity does not make the man guilty of such an offence because he has sexual intercourse with the girl if he believes her to be his wife.[11]

A prosecution for such an offence or an attempt to commit such an offence may not be commenced more than 12 months after the offence charged.[12] Corroboration of the evidence of the girl is not essential in law, but the general

1. 4th Edn. Vol. 11(1), p. 388, para 516.
2. *See* Sexual Offences Act, 1956 (it is necessary to prove sexual intercourse natural or unnatural).
3. *R.* v. *Cox,* (1832) 5 C&P 297 (CCR); *R.* v. *Allen,* (1839) 9 C&P 31; *Kaitamaki* v. *R.,* (1985) AC 147: 79 Cr App Rep 251 (PC).
4. *R.* v. *Hill,* (1781) 1 East PC 439; *R.* v. *Limes,* (1844) 1 Car and Kir 391; *R.* v. *Stanton,* (1844) Car & Kir 415; *R.* v. *Jordan and Cowmeadols,* (1839) 9 C&P 118.
5. *R.* v. *Philips,* (1839) 8 C&P 736.
6. 4th Edn., Vol. 11(1), p. 527, para 527.
7. *See* UK Sexual Offences Act, 1956.
8. *R.* v. *Rider,* (1954) 1 All ER 5: 37 Cr App Rep 209.
9. *R.* v. *Banks,* (1916) 2 KB 621: 12 Cr App Rep 74 (CA); *R.* v. *Harrison,* (1938) 3 All ER 134: 26 Cr App Rep 166 (CCA); *R.* v. *Forde,* (1923) 2 KB 400: 17 Cr App Rep 99 (CCA).
10. See *Mohamed* v. *Knott,* (1969) 1 QB 1: (1968) 2 All ER 563 (DC).
11. *See* UK Sexual Offences Act, 1956.
12. *R.* v. *West,* (1898) 1 QB 174 (CCR); *R.* v. *Shellaker,* (1914) 1 KB 414: 9 Cr App Rep 240 (CCA).

rule is as to warning the jury in case of sexual offence of the danger of convicting on the uncorroborated evidence if the victim applies. A person guilty of such an offence or an attempt to commit such an offence is liable of conviction on indictment to imprisonment for a term not exceeding two years, or on summary conviction to imprisonment for a term not exceeding six months or a fine not exceeding the prescribed sum, or to both.[1]

CHARACTER OF COMPLAINANT

If at a trial any person is for the time being charged with rape to which he pleads not guilty, then, except with the leave of the judge, no evidence and no question in cross-examination may be adduced or asked at the trial, by or on behalf of any accused at the trial, about any sexual experience of a complainant with a person other than the accused. The judge may not so give leave for any evidence or question except on an application made to him in the absence of the jury by or on behalf of an accused; and on such an application the judge must give leave if, and only if, he is satisfied that it would be unfair to that accused to refuse to allow the evidence to be adduced or the question to be asked.[2]

RAPE AND SEXUAL ABUSE

Black's Law Dictionary, 7th Edn., p. 10 defines – "sexual abuse" as an "illegal sex act, especially one performed against a minor by an adult" and it is also termed as carnal abuse and also includes a rape.

RAPE AND SEXUAL BATTERY

The *Black's Law Dictionary*, 7th Edn., p. 146 defines "sexual battery" as the forced penetration of or contact with another's sexual organs or the sexual organs of the perpetrator.

The case of *Anil Kumar Mahsi* v. *Union of India*[3] defines rape as although the modern usage of the word "rape" extends also to the trouble sexual intercourse by a woman with a man, the dictionary meaning of the said word as well as the offence of rape as defined in the Indian Penal Code speaks only a forcible sexual intercourse by a man with a woman. The latter meaning of the word is accepted in the context of Indian Divorce Act, 1869.

"Rape" is an offence under Common Law as unlawful sexual intercourse with a woman without her consent, by force, fear, fraud and as unlawful sexual intercourse with a woman who at the time of intercourse does not consent to it, where at that time the accused knows that she does not consent to the intercourse or he is reckless as to whether she consents to it.[4]

---

1. *R.* v. *Taylor,* (1977) 3 All ER 527: 64 Cr App Rep 182 (CA). *See* also UK Sexual Offences Act, 1956 and UK Magistrates Courts Act, 1980.
2. *R.* v. *Mills,* (1978) 68 Cr App Rep 327 (CA).
3. (1994) 5 SCC 704.
4. See *DPP* v. *Morgan,* (1975) 2 All ER 347; *Kaitamaki* v. *R.,* (1985) AC 147; *R.* v. *Satnam and Kewal,* (1984) 78 Cr App Rep 149; *R.* v. *Khan,* (1990) 1 WLR 815. For sentencing guidelines see *R.* v. *Billam,* (1986) 1 WLR 349; A-G's Reference No. 25 of 1990 (1991) Crim LR 924, No. 15 of 1991 (1992) Crim LR 454, No. 18 of 1991 (1992) Crim LR 455.

CONSENT FOR RAPE

"Consent" in rape covers states of mind ranging from actual desire to reluctant acquiescence; it is no longer necessary in proving rape to establish that intercourse took place as a result of fear, fraud or fork, but merely that it occurred without the woman's consent.[1]

OFFENDERS UNDER THE AGE OF EIGHTEEN – AN APPROACH TO NEW RAPE LAW

So far as the general principles are questioned, every court, in dealing with a child or young person who is brought before it, either as an offender or otherwise, must have regard to the welfare of the child or young person, and, in a proper case, must take steps for removing him from undesirable surroundings and for securing that proper provision is made for his education and training.

The principal aim of youth justice system is to prevent offending by children and young persons, and all persons and bodies carrying out functions in relation to that system are under a duty to have regard to that aim.

It is conclusively presumed that no child under the age of 18 years can be guilty of any criminal offence. There was formerly a rebuttable presumption of criminal law that a child is incapable of committing an offence which has now abolished in some countries.[2]

So far as the restrictions on proceedings against young persons, it is the duty of a person who decides to lay an information in respect of an offence in a case where he has reason to believe that the alleged offender is a young person to give notice of the decision to the appropriate local authority, unless he is himself is not that authority.

Further arrangements must be made for preventing a child or young person while detained in a police station or while being conveyed to or from any criminal court, or while waiting before or after attendance in any criminal court, from associating with an adult (not being a relative) who is charged with any offence other than an offence with which the child or young person is jointly charged. Arrangements must also be made for ensuring that a girl must while so to detained, being conveyed, or waiting, be under the care of a woman.

HUSBAND AND WIFE

As a general rule, a man cannot be guilty of rape upon his wife, for the wife is in general unable to restrict the consent to sexual intercourse which is a Part 1 of the contract of marriage.[3]

---

1. *R.* v. *Olugboja,* (1982) QB 320. See *R.* v. *Barton,* (1987) Crim LR 399. For assault with intent to rape (which is no longer known to the law). See *R.* v. *P,* (1990) Crim LR 323.
2. See *R.* v. *Secretary of State for the Home Department ex p Venables,* (1998) AC 407 HL (E); *R.* v. *Secretary of State for the Home Department ex p Thompson,* (1996) 40 Sol Jo LB 127: (1997) 1 All ER 327: (1997) 2 WLR 67 (CA): 1998 AC 407.
3. *R.* v. *Miller,* (1954) 2 QB 282: 38 Cr App Rep 1; *R.* v. *Kowalski,* (1988) 1 FLR 447: 86 Cr App Rep 339 (CA): 1 Hale PC 629; *Popkin* v. *Popkin,* (1794) 1 Hag ECC 765.

However, he may be guilty of rape upon the woman who is or was his wife if there is in force a separation order or a decree of judicial separation[1] or a decree *nisi* of divorce,[2] or an injunction restraining him from molesting his wife or an undertaking in lien of such an injunction.[3]

A husband is not entitled to exercise his marital rights by the use of force or violence and a wife's implied consent to sexual intercourse does not extend to other sexual acts performed against her will, whether or not they are preliminary to sexual intercourse.[4]

Again a husband, who is present and assisting another person to commit a rape upon his wife, may upon an indictment of rape be convicted of aiding and abetting[5], as may a boy under 14[6], or a woman under similar circumstances[7].

ADMINISTERING DRUGS TO OBTAIN OR FACILITATE INTERCOURSE

Any person who applies or administers to, or causes to be taken by, a woman any drug, matter or thing with intent to stupefy or overpower her so as thereby to enable any man to have unlawful sexual intercourse with her is guilty of an offence and liable on conviction on indictment to imprisonment for a term not exceeding two years.[8] A person may not, however, be convicted of such an offence on the evidence of one witness only, unless the witness is corroborated in some material particular by evidence implicating the accused.[9]

PRESUMPTION AND DETERMINATION OF AGE

Where a person, whether charged with an offence or not, is brought before any court otherwise than for the purpose of giving evidence and it appears to the court that he is a child or young person, the court must take due inquiry as to the age of that person, and for that purpose must take such evidence as may be forthcoming at the hearing of the case. However, an order or judgment of the court is not invalidated by any subsequent proof that the age of that person has not been correctly stated to the court, and the age presumed or declared by the court to be the age of the person so brought before it must, for the purpose of the law or statute, be deemed to be the true age of that person, and where it appears to the court that the person so brought before it has attained the age of 18 years, that person must be deemed not to be a child or young person.

Where, in any charge or indictment for any offence, it is alleged that the person by or in respect of whom the offence was committed was a child or young person or was under or had attained any specified age, and he appears

1. R. v. *Clarke,* (1949) 2 All ER 663; R. v. *Miller,* (1954) 2 QB 282: 38 Cr App Rep 1; R. v. *Roberts,* (1996) Crim LR 188 (CA).
2. R. v. *O'Brien,* (1974) 3 All ER 663; R. v. *Miller,* (1954) 2 QB 282: 38 Cr App Rep 1; R. v. *Roberts,* (1986) Crim LR 188 (CA).
3. R. v. *Steele,* (1977) Crim LR 290.
4. R. v. *Kowalski,* (1988) 1 FLR 447: 86 Cr App Rep 339 (CA).
5. R. v. *Lord Andley, Earl of Castelhaven's* case, (1631) 1 State Tr 401 (HL).
6. R. v. *Eldershaw,* (1828) 3 C&P 396.
7. R. v. *Lord Baltimore,* (1768) 1 Wim BL 648; R. v. *Ram and Ram,* (1893) 17 Cox CC 609.
8. *See* UK Sexual Offences Act, 1956, sections 4(1), 37(1), (3).
9. R. v. *Shillingfood,* (1968) 2 All ER 200: 52 Cr App Rep 188 (CA).

to the court to have been at the date of the commission of the alleged offence a child or young person; or to have been under or to have attained the specified age, as the case may be he must be presumed at that date to have been a child or young person or to have been under or to have attained that age, as the case may be, unless the contrary is proved.

Further where, in any charge or indictment of any offence, it is alleged that the person in respect of whom the offence was committed was a child or was a young person, it is not defence to prove that the person alleged to have been a child was a young person or the person alleged to have been a young person was a child in any case where the acts constituting it alleged offence would equally have been an offence if committed in respect of a young person or child respectively.

Where person is charged with an offence under statute in respect of a person apparently under a specified age it is a defence to prove that the person was actually of or over that age.

YOUNG PERSONS REACHING 18 YEAR OF AGE DURING PROCEEDINGS

Where proceedings in respect of a young person are begun for an offence and he attaining the age of 18 before the conclusion of the proceedings the court may continue to deal with the case and make any order which it could have made it had he not attained that age.

OFFENCE OF RAPE AND SEXUAL ASSAULT IN ENGLAND AND WALES

New Rape Law *i.e.* the Sexual Offences Act of 2003 which repealed the Sexual Offences Act of 1956 has been introduced in the United Kingdom in May 2004 by modifying the definition and meaning of "rape", "sexual assault" and "sexual activity with child". By this Act "offence of rape" became the offence against both male and female including the "sexual assault" *i.e.* against a male or female unlike India where rape can be committed by a male only.

As per data of rape and also of sexual assault in England and Wales from the years 2004-2005 to 2009-2010 after the so-called law of 2003 reveals that rape of female increased from 12,903 reported in 2004-2005 to 13,991 in 2009-2010 which is average of 10% increase and on the other hand in case of rape of a male increased from 1,139 to 1,175 during the same period which is approximately 10.3% increasing trend.[1]

But sexual assault in case of both female and male declined from 2004-2005 to 2009-2010. The female sexual assault reported 24,636 during 2004-2005 and reported 19,813 in 2009-2010 and in respect of male from 3,531 to 2,270 during such period *i.e.* decrement of 12.35% and 15.5%.

In England and Wales one victim from three victims never expressed any one about what happened to them. There was a greater willingness among

1. Crimes Records Bureau, Government of India, New Delhi, 2009, Chapter VI, p. 83. See www.ncrb.nic.in.

victims to report rape upon them in few years in recent past only about one in five rapes or sexual assault went to the attention of local police station.[1]

In England and Wales the rape is classified into two categories *viz.:*

- Real Rape;
- Acquaintance Rape.

The "real rape" means the "rape" in which the victim and the rapist are unknown to each other, mostly strangers.[2]

The "acquaintance rape" is offence where "rape" is committed by at least some degree of familiarity between the victim and the offender.[2]

Both these types also involve other categories of rape and sexual offences also.

As per the data position in United Kingdom only 7% of rape offence was reported to police and resulted in a conviction. Such figure includes the offence of attempted rape. Such statistics states that those most at risk are women aged between 16 to 24. These victims faced the occurrence were single women, students and women living in private rented accommodations. These also include the rape by strangers at public place.

Further in this country 92% of offenders are known to victims. The judicial approach to rape particularly in case of consent in relation to rape reveals that to constitute rape, intercourse must have taken place without the consent of the woman.[3] In the case of a girl under 16, the prosecution must prove either that she physically resisted, or if she did not, that her understanding and knowledge were such that she was not in a position to decide whether to consent or resist.[4] The consent after the act, or condonation affords no defence. As to counsel not putting forward an inconsistent defence alleging consent when requested by the accused to do so.[5] As to consent in relation to charge of unlawful sexual intercourse with a girl under a specified age the case[6] of 1865 is vital one.

A person accused of rape may raise the defence of consent without putting his own character in issue.[7]

Consent obtained by duress is in law no consent.

Where the woman is insensible by reason of intoxication the accused cannot successfully plead consent as a defence to a charge of rape.[8]

1. A. Myhill and J. Allen, Rape and Sexual Assault of Women – The extent and nature of the problem, Home Office Research Study (UK), 2002, Chapter 3.
2. Susan Estrich, Real Rape (Cambridge, Mass: Harvard University Press, 1987).
3. *R.* v. *Bradley,* (1910) 74 JP 247: 4 Cr App Rep 225 (CCA); *R.* v. *Harling,* (1938) 1 All ER 307: 26 Cr App Rep 127 (CCA).
4. *R.* v. *Howard,* (1965) 3 All ER 684: 50 Cr App Rep 56 (CCA).
5. *R.* v. *Donoel,* (1916) 85 LJ KB 1756: 12 Cr App Rep 49 (CCA).
6. *R.* v. *Beale,* (1865) LR 1 CCR 10; *R.* v. *Ryland,* (1868) 18 LT 538 (CCR).
7. *R.* v. *Turner,* (1944) KB 463; *Sevey* v. *DPP,* (1970) AC 304: 52 Cr App Rep 443 (HL); *R.* v. *Jones,* (1861) 4 LT 154.
8. *R.* v. *Camplin,* (1845) 1 Cox CC 220 (CCR) (Accused giving drink to girl with intent to excite her). See *R.* v. *Page,* (1846) 2 Cox CC 133; *R.* v. *Fletcher,* (1859) Bell CC 63; *R.* v. *Lang,* (1975) 62 Cr App Rep 50 (CA) (administering drugs etc. with intent to stupfy a woman so as to enable a man to have sexual intercourse with her.

Where the woman is asleep and thus incapable of consent, the accused may be convicted of rape if he knew that she was asleep even though he used no violence.[1] Submission owing to ignorance of, or to a mistake as to the nature of the act done or the person doing it, and induced by the fraud of the accused, does not constitute consent[2] nor does submission induced by fear, even though no violence was threatened.[3]

A person who has sexual intercourse without consent with a woman of unsound mind who is incapable of expressing consent or dissent is guilty of rape.[4] However, if such a woman consents to the act by reason of mere animal instinct, the act does not constitute rape.[5]

So far as the guidelines for conviction of rape is concerned, the Court of Appeal (CA) of England in the year 2003 pronounced its judgment giving some norms of conviction of rape in case of *R.* v. *Lackenby*[6] considering the issues *viz.:*

- degree of harm to victim.
- level of culpability of the offender.
- level of risk posed by the offender to society.

These three norms relates to "real rape" and "acquaintance rape" or "stranger rape", "consensual sexual relationship" and also "attempt to rape".

The provisions of rape law in England have been to drastically attend as it was before. The offence of rape is not in only confinement of women only. In this country a man can also be the victim of rape.[7]

ANTI-RAPE LAWS AND LAWS RELATED TO SEXUAL ASSAULT IN USA

In United States of America only 16% of rape case is reported to police or Law Enforcement Authorities, 84% are kept in hidancy. This is to so the offenders or accused persons always threaten to revictimise the victims and the another cause is psychological, sociological, physical and emotional harm to victims. In USA rape is defined as the carnal knowledge of a woman forcibly and against her will.[8]

In this country the law does not require that rape victim be a woman; although as per data of statistics rare, males are victims of rape.

Like any other countries law in USA rape is an offence when it attract sexual act without the consent of victim, a requirement satisfied when the victim is

1. *R.* v. *Mayers,* (1872) 12 Cox CC 311; *R.* v. *Young,* (1878) 14 Cox CC 114 (CCR).
2. *R.* v. *Case,* (1850) 4 Cox CC 220 (CCR) (For accused giving drink girl with intent to excite her see, *R.* v. *Page,* (1846) 2 Cox CC 133; *R.* v. *Camplin,* (1845) 1 Cox CC 220 (CCR).
3. *R.* v. *Olngboja,* (1982) QB 320: 73 Cr App Rep 344 (CA).
4. *R.* v. *Fletcher,* (1859) Bell CC 63; *R.* v. *Fletcher,* (1886) LR 1 CCR 39; *R.* v. *Baratt,* (1873) LR 2 CR 81.
5. *R.* v. *Fletcher,* (1866) LR 1 CCR 39.
6. (2003) 2 All ER 939. *See* also *R.* v. *Millberry, Director of Prosecution* v. *Morgan,* 1975 Cr App Rep 136: 1976 AC 182.
7. Sexual Offences Act, 1956, section (1).
8. William Blackstone, Commentaries, 1789 p. 210.

unconscious, asleep or mentally impaired, or when the sexual act was inducted by fraud.

ANTI-RAPE LAWS IN CANADA

The word is not used in Canadian Criminal Code. Instead law criminalises "sexual assault". Sexual assault is defined as sexual contact with another person without that other person's consent. Consent is defined under section 273-1(1) of criminal law as "the voluntary agreement to engage in the sexual activity in question": The punishment is stringent depending upon age, status, reputation and other circumstance of victim and his/her society.

ANTI-RAPE LAWS IN FRANCE

Articles 222 to 226 of the French Penal Code provide the provisions relating to rape.

Article 222 states any act of sexual penetration, whatever of its nature, committed against another person in violence, constraint threat or surprise, is rape which is punishable to 15 years of imprisonment. Rape is punished by a maximum of 20 years criminal imprisonment in certain aggravating factors (including under age of 15 years). In case death of victim is caused punishment may extend upto 30 years criminal imprisonment. (Article 225). Articles 222 to 226 punishes the offence of rape with life imprisonment when it is preceded, accompanied or followed by torture or acts of barbarity.

ANTI-RAPE LAWS IN CHINA

The Criminal Code of Peoples Republic of China, 1997 states, in its Article 236, on the offence of rape. It defines rape and provides for punishment. As per this provision anyone who rapes a woman by violence, coercion or other means shall be sentenced to fixed-term imprisonment of not less than 3 years and not more than 10 years.

But anyone who has sexual relations with a minor girl under age of 14 years shall be deemed to have committed rape subject to harder punishment. Anyone who rapes upon a woman or has a sexual relations with a minor girl in any of the following manner, shall be punished with imprisonment of not less than 10 years or sentence of death:

1. raping a woman having sexual relations with a minor girl in disgusting way; or
2. raping many women or having sexual relation with many minor girls; or
3. raping a woman before many people in a public place; or
4. raping woman in turn with another man or other men; or
5. causing a severe injury, death or other serious consequence to the victim.

In this country even death sentence is prescribed for rape and further a sexual relationship with a minor girl is considered rape and consent of such girl is immaterial.

ANTI-RAPE LAWS IN SWEDEN

In Sweden the offence of rape, is not considered to be a heinous offence as to maximum punishment provided for rape varies from 2 to 6 years of imprisonment.

In this country the provision in law states that a person who by violence or threat which involves, or appears to be threatened person to involve in imminent danger, forces another person to have sexual intercourse or to engage in a comparable sexual act, that having regard to the nature of violation and the circumstances in general, is comparable to enforced sexual intercourse, shall be sentenced for rape to imprisonment for at least 2 years and at most 6 years of imprisonment.

In this country so far as the legal provision of gross rape is concerned, if the violence involves danger to life or caused serious injury or serious illness rape will be termed as gross rape punishable to the extent of 4 to 10 years and both man and woman can be involved in the offence of rape in USA, UK and Sweden.

ANTI-RAPE LAWS IN RUSSIA

The "rape" is defined under Article 131 of Criminal Code of Russia as "heterosexual vaginal intercourse using violence or threaten of violence or if the victim is in a helpless state".

In this country the offence of rape is further defined as coercive sexual action *i.e.* (male-male, female-female, and non-vaginal male-female) and such offence is punishable under Article 132 of Criminal Code of Russia. These offences are punishable with 3 to 6 years imprisonment if the crime:

- was committed repeatedly;
- was committed by a group of criminal;
- was committed with a threat of murder or grievous harm to the health of victim;
- was committed with particular cruelty;
- was caused by HIV+ infection, then it is punishable with 4 to 10 years of imprisonment with possible subsequent restraint of liberty for upto 2 years *i.e.* criminal may not change or leave residence without permission and must register himself at local penal inspectorate 1 to 4 times a month; the court may also impose additional restrictions such as the criminal may not leave home in certain hours, visit certain locations, change work without permission.

If the crime is committed against a girl or woman under 18 years of age and if caused the grievous hurt to health, HIV+ infection or other grievous consequences then in Russia it is punishable with 12 to 20 years of imprisonment, mandatory restraint of liberty for upto 2 years and possible ban on certain occupation or employment positions for upto 12 years.

Further, in case of repeated rape or organised rape by a group of persons or with threat of homicide punishment may extend from 4 to 10 years and if death of the victim is caused punishment may extend from 8 years to 15 years.

PUNISHMENT FOR OFFENCE OF RAPE IN INDIA

In India in the year 1983 before the new rape law in 2013 a drastic change was brought about in punishment of rape so as to deter people from committing such a heinous crime. Section 376 of Indian Penal Code has been divided into two sub-sections to fix punishment taking into account the gravity and special nature of the case. In point of seriousness of such crime in sub-section (1) a minimum of 7 years and sub-section (2), the 10 years of imprisonment has been provided.

In detail sub-section (1) to section 376 of Indian Penal Code provides to a minimum sentence of 7 years of imprisonment that may extend to 10 years and fine. However, in case of a husband committing rape on his wife and if she is not under 12 years of age, the punishment may extend to 2 years, fine or with both.

Sub-section (2) to section 376 prescribes a minimum of 10 years of imprisonment, in case of custodial rape under clauses (a) to (d) where rape is committed under special circumstances, either by a police officer, or by a public servant, or by a person on the management or on the staff of the jail, remand home, or women's or children institution, or hospital, etc. under clauses (e), (f) and (g) where the woman is pregnant, or a child under 12 years of age or when a woman is gangraped.

It was marked in some quarters that a differential treatment sought to be meted out in case of custodial rape, etc., and other, render the law cumbersome, besides being discriminatory. Further, it is said that the provisions for minimum punishment for rape deprives the courts of the power of discretion as available in the case of other offences and this Indian Penal Code. Such a provision of minimum sentence may lead to injustice and hardships in many cases where a case is otherwise fit for a lenient punishment, such as juvenile offender and alike. However, such propositions have no substance in view of proviso clause to section that provides for a lesser sentence if the court considers appropriate in a particular case.

In case of *Santosh Moolya* v. *State of Karnataka,* AIR 2010 SC 2247 the Supreme Court dismissing the appeal of two accused, for raping on two victim sisters held that 42 days delay in lodging FIR when properly explained and corroborated by the mother of victims was not fatal. It showed a serious concern of our apex court about the sentiment of victims and society.[1]

In case of *Rajinder @ Raju* v. *State of Himachal Pradesh,* JT 2009 (9) SC 9: AIR 2009 SC 3022: 2009 Cr LJ 4133 (CC): 2009 AIR SCW 4858 it was held that the courts must, while evaluating evidence, remain alive to the fact that in a case of rape, no self-respecting woman would come forward in a court just to make a humiliating statement against her honour, such as, is involved in the commission of rape on her. In cases involving sexual molestation, supposed considerations which have no material effect on the veracity of the prosecution case or even discrepancies in the statement of the prosecutrix should not, asked

1. *See* also *State of Punjab* v. *Gurmit Singh,* AIR 1996 SC 1393: (1996) 2 SCC 384: 1996 Cr LJ 1728: 1996 AIR SCW 998: 1996 (1) SCJ 566: (1996) 1 Crimes 37.

the discrepancies are such which are of fatal nature, be allowed to throw out an otherwise reliable prosecution case.

The proviso to section 376, Indian Penal Code has given discretion to the courts to award a lesser sentence than minimum prescribed for rape when there exists "special and adequate reasons" so that injustice might not be done to an accused in a particular case. Whether there exists "any special and adequate reasons" would depend upon a variety of factors and the particular facts and circumstances of each case. No hard and fast rule can be laid down in that behalf of universal application.

In a case[1] the appellant was found guilty of raping a child of one and half years and sentenced to 10 years rigorous imprisonment.

In another case[2] the prosecutrix aged between 13 to 14 years was sexually assaulted by the respondent in day light. The prosecutrix was carrying lunch box for her father, who was grazing cattle in fields when the respondent all of a sudden cought hold of her and committed rape on her despite her protest.

The trial court sentenced 10 years rigorous imprisonment to the accused and in appeal the High Court reduced the sentence to 4 years and after State appeal in Supreme Court his sentence was enhanced to 7 years rigorous imprisonment which is minimum prescribed under section 376(1) of Indian Penal Code.

In another case[3] the Supreme Court observed that every case has to be approached with realistic diversity based on peculiar facts and circumstances of that case.

In case of *State of Madhya Pradesh* v. *Balu*[4] the Supreme Court held that section 376 of Indian Penal Code imposes an obligation on the part of the court to impose a minimum sentence to 7 years of imprisonment in case of rape, but for "adequate and special reasons" the court can reduce the sentence from minimum prescribed under this section.

In the language of Justice Krishna Iyer it is clear that:

> "Sentencing efficacy in cases of criminality cannot be simply assumed by award of long incarceration, for, often that remedy aggravates the malady....... . A hypersexed homo-sapien cannot be rehabilitated by humiliating or harsh treatment".[5]

In another case[6] it was that that rape is violation with on the private person of the victim, an abominable outrage by all canons. Considering the background

1. *T.K. Gopal @ Gopi* v. *State of Karnataka,* (2000) 3 Supreme 706: (2000) LRI 1045: AIR 2000 SC 1669: 2000 Cr LJ 2286 (SC). *See* also *State of Karnataka* v. *Krishmappa,* AIR 2000 SC 1470.
2. *State of Andhra Pradesh* v. *Borden Sundara Rao,* AIR 1986 SC 530: (1995) 6 SCC 230: (1995) 3 SCJ 511.
3. *State of Himachal Pradesh* v. *Raghubir Singh,* (1993) 1 SCALE 708: 1983 (1) Crimes 887: (1983) 2 SCC 622.
4. (2005) 1 SCC 108: AIR 2005 SC 222: 2004 AIR SCW 6507.
5. *Phul Singh* v. *State of Haryana,* (1979) 4 SCC 413: AIR 1980 SC 249: (1980) 1 SCR 589: 1980 Cr LJ 8: (1980) 2 SCJ 26: 1979 CAR 393.
6. *State of Andhra Pradesh* v. *Ghanshyam Singh,* AIR 2003 SC 3191: 2003 Cr LJ 4339: 2003 AIR SCW 4547: (2003) 8 SCC 13.

of what has been stated in a number of cases by the apex court the inevitable conclusion is that the High Court was not justified in restricting the sentence to the period already undergone. Which is 46 days. Leniency in matter involving sexual offences is not only undesirable but also against public interest. Such types of offences are to be dealt with serverity and with iron hands. Showing leniency in such matter would be really a case of misplaced sympathy. The acts, which led to the conviction of the accused, are not only shocking but also outrageous in their contracts.

In *Utpal Das* v. *State of West Bengal*[1] the Supreme Court set aside the acquittal of appellants by trial court and sentenced them to suffer rigorous imprisonment for 5 years and with fine of ₹ 2,000 each.

In *State of Uttar Pradesh* v. *Chhotey Lal*[2] the Supreme Court held that the accused was liable for kidnapping and rape under section 376 of Indian Penal Code, against prosecutrix. It is wrong to assume that in all cases of intercourse with the women against will or without consent, there would be some injury on the external or internal part of the victim.

The Supreme Court in case of *State of Karnataka* v. *Puttaraja*[3] said that a rapist not only causes physical injuries but more indelibly leaves a scar on the most cherished possession of woman *i.e.* her dignity, clarity, honour and reputation. The depravation of such animals in human form reaches the rock bottom of morality when they sexually assault children, minors and a woman in the advance stages of pregnancy also.

It is therefore, the duty of every court to award proper sentence having regard to the nature of the offence and the manner in which it was executed or committed etc.[4]

In *Dhananjay Chatterjee @ Dhana* v. *State of West Bengal*[5] it was observed that shokingly large number of criminals go unpunished thereby increasingly, encouraging the criminals and in the ultimate making justice to suffer by weakening the system's creditability. The imposition of appropriate punishment is the manner in which the court respondents to the societies' cry for justice against the accused persons.

In a very recent case in 2013[6] the court showed its concern on rape offence and observed that:

> "The primary concern at both national and international level is about the devastating increase in rape cases and cases relating to crime against women in the world. India is no exception to it. Although the statutory provisions provide strict penal action against such offenders, it is for the courts to ultimately decide whether such incident has occurred or not. The court should be more cautious in appreciating the evidence

1. AIR 2010 SC 1894.
2. 2011 (1) Supreme 418.
3. AIR 2004 SC 413: 2004 Cr LJ 579 (SC): 2003 AIR SCW 6429: (2004) 1 SCC 475.
4. *Sevaka Perumal* v. *State of Tamil Nadu*, AIR 1991 SC 1463: (1991) 3 SCC 471.
5. (1994) 2 SCC 221: 1995 AIR SCW 510: 1994 SCC (Cri) 358.
6. *State of Uttar Pradesh* v. *Munesh*, AIR 2013 SC 147.

and the accused should not be left scot-free merely on filmsy grounds. In the instant case accused had committed rape, which repels against moral conscience as he chose a girl of 11 years to satisfy his lust and subsequently murdered her."

In this case the court awarded life imprisonment to the accused.

SHOULD DEATH SENTENCE BE AWARDED FOR RAPE?

The judges are not blood-thirsty.

The death sentence is awarded in rarest of rare cases as was held in case of rape and murder.[1]

The death sentence is the law and the "Rarest of rare cases" is the policy of judiciary.[2]

According to Justice Arijit Pasayat "death sentence is imposed in rarest of rare cases. Life imprisonment is the rule and death sentence is the exception."

The day was there when the court had been criticised on the ground that:

> "The Court cannot give birth to a human being and hence how it can take away his life".

The social activists like Human Rights Activists and NGOs are against the death penalty given by court. But as the heinous crimes are in increasing rate the courts are being serious about the serious types of offences. Because the death penalty is not a principal mode of punishment rather it is a major deterrent effect to the future judiciary system and checks the preparing accused.

The Supreme Court in *Machhi Singh* v. *State of Punjab,* (1983) 3 SCC 470: AIR 1983 SC 957: 1983 Cr LJ 1457: 1983 SCC (Cri) 681: (1983) 3 SCR 413 held that the reasons why the community as a whole does not endorse the humanistic approach reflected in "death sentence in no case" doctrines are not for to seek.

In the first place the very humanistic edifice is constructed on the foundation of "reverence for life" principle. When a member of the community violates this very principle by killing another member, the society may not feel itself bound by the shackles of this doctrine.

Secondly, it has to be realised that every member of the community is able to live with safety without his or her own life being endangered because of the protective arm of the community and on account of the rule of law enforced by it. The very existence of the rule of law and the fear of being brought to book operates as a deterrent to those who have no scruples in killing others if it suits their ends. Every member of the community owes a debt to the community for his protection. When ingratitude is shown instead of gratitude by "killing a member of the community which protects the murderer himself from being killed, or when the community feels that for the sake of self-preservation the killer has to be killed, the community may well withdraw the protection by sanctioning the death penalty. But the community will not do so in every case. It

1. *Dhananjay Chatterjee @ Dhana* v. *State of West Bengal,* (1994) 2 SCC 220: 1995 AIR SCW 510.
2. Indian Penal Code, section 53 spells the death sentence as first category of punishment (brutal) for murder and heinous killing.

may do so in "rarest of rare cases", when its collective conscience is so shocked that it will expect the holders of the judicial power centre to inflict death penalty irrespective of their personal opinion as regards desirability or otherwise of retaining death penalty. The community may entertain such a sentiment, when the crime is viewed from the platform of the motive for, or the manner of commission of the crime or the anti-social nature of the crime *viz.*

1. Manner of commission of murder.
2. Motive for commission of murder.
3. Anti-social or socially abhorrent nature of the crime.
4. Magnitude of crime.
5. Personality of victim of murder.

1. Manner of Commission of Murder

When the murder is committed in an extremely brutal, grotesque, diabolical, revolting, or dastardly manner so as to arouse intense and extreme indignation of the community *i.e.*

(i) When the house of the victim is set in flame with the end in view to roast him alive in the house.

(ii) When the victim is subjected to inhuman acts of torture or cruelty in order to bring about his/her death.

(iii) When the body of the victim is cut into pieces or his body is dismembered in a fiendish manner.

2. Motive for Commission of Murder

When the murder is committed for a motive which evidences total depravity and meanness *viz.*

(i) when a hired assassin commits murder for sake of money

(ii) a cold-blooded murder is committed with a deliberate design in order to inherit property or to gain control over property of a ward or a person under the control of the murderer or *vis-à-vis* whom the murderer is in a dominating position or in a position of trust.

(iii) a murder is committed in the course for betrayal of the motherland.

3. Anti-social or Socially Abhorrent Nature of the Crime, *viz.*

(i) when murder of a member of a Scheduled Caste or minority community etc., is committed not for personal reasons but in circumstances which arouse social wrath. For instance when such a crime is committed in order to terrorise such persons and frighten them into fleeing from a place or in order to deprive them of, or make them surrender, lands or benefits conferred on them with a view to reverse past injustices and in order to restore the social balance.

(ii) in the cases of bride-burning and what are known as "dowry deaths" or when murder is committed in order to re-marry for the sake of extracting dowry once again or to marry another woman on account of infatuation.

4. Magnitude of Crime

When the crime is enormous in proportion *viz.*, when multiple murders say of all or almost all the members of a family or a large number of persons of a particular caste, community, or locality, are committed.

5. Personality of Victim of Murder

When the victim of murder is:

(i) an innocent child who could not have or has not provided even an excuse, much less a provocation, for murder.

(ii) a helpless woman or a person rendered helpless by old age or infirmity.

(iii) when the victim is a person *vis-à-vis* whom the murderer is in a position of dominion or trust.

(iv) when the victim is a public figure generally loved and respected by the community for the services rendered by him and the murder is committed for political or similar reasons other than personal reasons.

Aggravating circumstances where the court may award Death Sentence[1]

- If the murder has been committed after previous planning and involves extreme brutality, or
- If the murder involves exceptional depravity, or
- If the murder is of a member of any of the armed forces of the union or of a member of any police force or of any public servant and was committed:—
    - While such member or public servant was on duty; or
    - In consequence of anything done or attempted to be done by such member or public servant in the lawful discharge of his duty as such member or public servant whether at the time of murder he was such member or public servant, as the case may be, or had ceased to be such member or public servant, or
    - If the murder is of a person who had acted in the lawful discharge of his duty under section 43 of the Code of Criminal Procedure, 1973 or who had rendered assistance to a Magistrate or a police officer demanding his aid or requiring his assistance under section 37 and section 129 of the Cr.P.C., 1973.

Mitigating Circumstances for Death Sentence[2]

1. The offence was committed under the influence of extreme mental or emotional disturbance.
2. The age of the accused. If the accused is young or old, he shall not be sentenced to death.

---

1. *Furman* v. *Georgia*, 1976 USA SC decided on 29 June, 1976; *Bachan Singh* v. *State of Punjab*, AIR 1980 SC 898: (1980) 2 SCC 684: 1980 Cr LJ 636: 1980 SCC (Cri) 580.
2. Suggested by Dr. Chitaley.

3. The probability that the accused would not commit criminal acts of violence as would constitute a continuing threat to society.
4. The probability that the accused can be reformed and rehabilitated. The State shall by evidence prove that the accused does not satisfy the conditions 3 and 4 above.
5. That in the facts and circumstances of the case the accused believed that he was morally justified in committing the offence.
6. That the accused acted under the duress or dominion of another person.

The condition of accused showed that he was mentally defective and that the said defect impaired his capacity to appreciate the criminality of his conduct.

In *Jagmohan Singh* v. *State of Uttar Pradesh,* (1973) 2 SCR 541: AIR 1973 SC 947, the Constitution Bench, of Supreme Court held that:

> "The impossibility of laying down standards (in the matter of sentencing) is at the very Core of Criminal Law as administered in India which invests the judges with a very wide discretion in the matter of fixing the degree of punishment and that this discretion in the matter of sentence is liable to be corrected by Superior Court..... The exercise of judicial discretion on well recognised principles is, in the final analysis, the safest possible safeguard for the accused."

RAPE AND DOUBLE MURDER BY BURNING

The accused tried to commit rape on brother's wife. When she protested against it, the accused hit her on head with wooden rod. The deceased fell down unconscious. The accused committed rape. Thereafter, the accused punched 11 months old daughter who became unconscious. The accused poured kerosene oil and burnt both to death. The doctors ruled out the possibility of suicide. The accused was convicted to the life imprisonment.[1]

PUNISHMENT FOR RAPE: CIRCUMSTANTIAL EVIDENCE

The accused was last seen taking victim on a cycle, but returned alone after an hour. Accused made extra-judicial confession. The dead body of deceased was recovered. The opinion of doctor was that the victim was raped and murder. Hence under these circumstantial and medical evidence, accused was sentenced to life imprisonment.[2]

RAPE ON 12 YEARS OLD VILLAGE GIRL UNDER FEAR OF KILLING HER

The rape was committed on prosecutrix aged about 12 year by putting her under fear of killing her. It was held that the absence of injuries or mark of violence on the person of prosecutrix might not be decisive, particularly in a

1. *Kumar* v. *State of Tamil Nadu,* 2013 (4) E Cr C 203: 2014 (4) SCC (Cri) 492: (2013) 2 CCR 515: JT 2013 (7) SC 175: 2013 (2) Crimes 324: 2013 (3) MLJ (Cri) 187: 2013 AIR SCW 3708.
2. *Duryodhan Rout* v. *State of Orissa,* 2015 (2) SCC (Cri) 306: 2014 (4) AIR Jhar R 740: 2015 (2) SCC 783: AIR 2014 SC 3345: 2014 (3) RCR (Cri) 700: 2014 (3) JLJR 301: JT 2014 (8) SC 273: 2014 (8) SCALE 96.

situation where the victim did not offer any resistance on account of threat of killing. The accused was punished under section 376 of IPC.[1]

RAPE AND MURDER OF 18 YEAR OF GIRL

The death sentence was awarded to the accused by trial court. The High Court commuted death sentence to life imprisonment. It was held by the Supreme Court that no error was committed by the High Court.[2]

RAPE WITH MINOR GIRL: ACCUSED WORKING IN THE HOUSE OF PROSECUTRIX

The accused had been working in the house of prosecutrix as manson. One day the accused came to the house of prosecutrix and forcibly raped her. Then he attacked minor brother of prosecutrix with deadly weapon and killed him. Thereafter, accused inflicted injuries upon another minor girl who had also seen the occurrence. The lower court awarded death sentence. The Supreme Court commuted death sentence to life imprisonment.[3]

RAPE AND MURDER: PLEA OF JUVENILE

The plea of juvenile was raised by accused for the first time in Supreme Court. The accused was found juvenile when he committed the offence of rape. The accused was in jail since 14 years. The conviction of accused was upheld but he was set free from prison.[4]

RAPE BY POLICE OFFICERS IN CUSTODY

The prosecutrix was detained in Police Station at night and raped by the police officers. The prosecutrix was not medically examined. It was held that absence of medical examination was not significant as the prosecutrix was not young and her allegation were corroborated with her husband and neighbour. The accused persons were convicted.[5]

ABDUCTION AND RAPE OF PROSECUTRIX BY HUSBAND

The prosecutrix narrated every minute detail as to how her husband allured her by taking advantage of her contract, took her to Karnool where she was not acquainted with the local language of Telugu and ultimately, abused her physically for more than one month. He was convicted. It was held that no

1. *O.M. Baby* v. *State of Orissa,* 2012 (3) RAJ 447: 2012 (3) Cri CC 364: 2012 AIR SCW 4199: 2012 (117) AIC 59: 2012 (3) MLJ (Cri) 825: AIR 2012 SC (Cri) 1359: 2012 Cr LJ 3794.
2. *State of Uttar Pradesh* v. *Sanjay Kmar,* 2012 All MR (Cril) 3061: 2012 (8) SCC 537: 2012 (5) RAJ 199: 2012 (118) AIC 65: 2012 (5) Law Herald (SC) 3637; *Rajendra Singh* v. *State,* 2012 (2) RCR (Cri) 558; *Neel Kmar* v. *State,* (2012) 5 SCC 766.
3. *B. Kumar* v. *Inspector of Police, C.B. C.I.D.,* 2015 (2) SCC 346: 2015 (1) CCR 165: 2015 (146) AIC 140; *Md. Mannan* v. *State of Bihar,* (2011) 5 SCC 317; *Sunil* v. *State,* (2014) 1 SCC 129; *Yakub* v. *State of Maharashtra,* (2013) 5 RCR (Cri) 7.
4. *Durga Ram* v. *State of Rajasthan,* 2015 (88) A Cr C 634: 2015 (1) JLJR 414: 2015 (3) WLN 217: 2015 (1) MLJ (Cri) 224: 2015 (1) SCALE 132: JT 2015 (1) SC 57: 2015 (1) ALT (Cri) 402: 2015 (1) RCR (Cri) 978: 2015 (1) AIR SCW 699: 2015 (1) Bom CR (Cri) 446.
5. *Charanjit* v. *State of Punjab,* 2013 (4) E Cr C 97: 2013 (4) SCC (Cri) 717: 2013 (3) CCR 377: JT 2013 (10) SC 10: 2013 AIR SCW 4105: 2013 (10) SCR 688; *Sambhu Das* v. *State of Assam,* (2010) 10 SCC 374. *See* also *Rashmi Behl* v. *State,* 2015 (1) Law Herald (SC) 770: 2015 Cr LR 305: 2015 (2) Cal LT 67; *Doliben Kantilal Patel* v. *State,* 2014 (2) E Cr C 45: 2014 All SCR 249: 2014 (1) Cal Cr LR 8.

amount of cross-examination at the instance of the appellant could bring about any candid contradiction in her statement in order to disbelieve her deposition.[1]

RAPE AND MURDER OF 9 YEAR OLD GIRL

The accused was convicted and sentenced to death by lower courts but death sentence was converted to life imprisonment by the Supreme Court.[2]

REDUCTION OF SENTENCE IN GANG RAPE CASE

The accused was acquitted by the trial court in gang rape case. The High Court convicted the accused but awarded sentence of 7 years rigorous imprisonment which is less than the minimum prescribed as 10 years. It was unwarranted by Supreme Court.[3]

RAPE BY TWO ACCUSED PERSONS

The trial court convicted both the accused and sentenced them to 10 years relying on testimony of prosecutrix. The order of acquittal was set aside by the High Court without considering the detailed statement of prosecutrix before Magistrate. The case was remanded for reconsideration on merits. The Supreme Court observed that it would have gone through the entire evidence on record and decided whether the acquittal should be sustained or not. However, in the absence of analysis of the evidence by the High Court in first appeal, a right of appeal was available to accused would be taken away if the Supreme Court were to consider the case on its merits without the opinion of the High Court.[4]

Views of Abolitionists of Death Sentence

1. Death penalty is irreversible. Decided upon according to fallible processes of law by fallible human beings – it can be and actually has been-inflicted upon people innocent of any crime.
2. There is no convincing evidence to show that death penalty serves any penological purpose.
   (i) its deterrent effect remains unproven. It has not been shown that incidence of murder has increased in countries where death penalty has been abolished, after its abolition.
   (ii) Retribution in the sense of vengeance, is no longer an acceptable end of punishment.
   (iii) On the contrary, reformation of the criminal and his rehabilitation is the primary purpose of punishment. Imposition of death penalty nullifies that purpose.

---

1. *Mahadeo* v. *State of Maharashtra*, 2013 (4) CCR 365: 2013 (4) RAJ 580: 2013 (3) RCR (Cri) 932: (2013) 9 SCALE 568; *Lillu* v. *State of Haryana*, (2013) 2 RCR (Cri) 679: 2013 (3) RAJ 1.
2. *Selvam* v. *State*, 2014 (12) SCC 274: AIR 2014 SC 1911: 2014 AIR SCW 2574: 2014 (2) CCR 646: 2014 (5) SCC (Cri) 62: 2014 (3) RAJ 315: 2014 (2) RCR (Cri) 854: JT 2014 (5) SC 553: (2014) 6 SCALE 142.
3. *Ramesh Kumar* v. *State of Himachal Pradesh*, (2013) 3 RCR (Cri) 889: 2013 (4) RAJ 577: (2013) 9 SCALE 400: 2013 (14) SCC 110: 2014 (4) SCC (Cri) 114.
4. *State of Haryana* v. *Basti Ram*, 2013 AIR SCW 2010: 2013 (2) Bom CR (Cri) 512: JT 2013 (3) SC 622.

3. Execution by whatever means and for whatever offence is a cruel, inhuman and degrading punishment.

35th Report of Law Commission of India's view regarding the Deterrent Effect of Death Sentence

1. Basically every human being dreads death.
2. Death, as a penalty, stands on a totally different level from imprisonment for life or any other punishment. The difference is one of quality, and not merely a degree.
3. Those who are specifically qualified to express an opinion on the subject, including particularly the majority of the replies received from State Government Judges, members of Parliament and Legislatures and Members of the Bar and Police Officers are definitely of the view that the deterrent object of capital punishment is achieved in fair measures in India.
4. As to conduct of prisoners released from jail, it would be difficult to come to a conclusion, without studies extending over a long period of years.
5. Where any other punishment can possess all the advantages of capital punishment is a matter of doubt.
6. Statistics of other countries are inclusive on the subject. If they are not regarded as proving the deterrent effect, neither can they be regarded as conclusively disproving it.

Views of Lord Denning before British Royal Commission on Capital Punishment

The punishment is the way in which society expresses its denunciation of wrong-doing; and in order to maintain respect for law, it is essential that the punishment inflicted for grave crimes, should adequately reflect the revulsion felt by the great majority of citizens for them. It is a mistake to consider the objects of punishment as being deterrent or reformative or preventive and nothing else.... The truth is that some crimes are so outrageous that society insists on adequate punishment, because the wrong-doer deserves it, irrespective of whether it is a deterrent or not.

STATUTORY PROVISIONS IN INDIA IN RESPECT OF RAREST OF RARE CASES

(INDIAN PENAL CODE)

CHAPTER III

OF PUNISHMENTS

53. Punishments.—The punishments to which offenders are liable under the provisions of this Code are—

First.—Death;

Secondly.—Imprisonment for life;

Fourthly.—Imprisonment, which is of two descriptions, namely:—

(1) Rigorous, that is, with hard labour;

(2) Simple;

Fifthly.—Forfeiture of property;

Sixthly.—Fine.

CHAPTER VI

OF OFFENCES AGAINST THE STATE

121. Waging, or attempting to wage war, or abetting waging of war, against the Government of India.—Whoever, wages war against the Government of India, or attempts to wage such war, or abets the waging of such war, shall be punished with death, or imprisonment for life and shall also be liable to fine.

Illustration

A joins an insurrection against the Government of India. *A* has committed the offence defined in this section.

CLASSIFICATION OF OFFENCE

Punishment—Death or imprisonment for life and fine—Cognizable—Non-bailable—Triable by Court of Session—Non-compoundable.

132. Abetment of mutiny, if mutiny is committed in consequence thereof.—Whoever abets the committing of mutiny by an officer, soldier, sailor or airman in the Army, Navy or Air Force of the Government of India, shall, if mutiny be committed in consequence of that abetment, be punished with death or with imprisonment for life, or imprisonment of either description for a term which may extend to ten years, and shall also be liable to fine.

CLASSIFICATION OF OFFENCE

Punishment—Death, or imprisonment for life, or imprisonment for 10 years and fine—Cognizable—Non-bailable—Triable by Court of Session—Non-compoundable.

194. Giving or fabricating false evidence with intent to procure conviction of capital offence.—Whoever gives or fabricates false evidence, intending thereby to cause, or knowing it to be likely that he will thereby cause, any person to be convicted of an offence which is capital by the law for the time being in force in India shall be punished with imprisonment for life, or with rigorous imprisonment for a term which may extend to ten years, and shall also be liable to fine;

If innocent person be thereby convicted and executed.—and if an innocent person be convicted and executed in consequence of such false evidence, the person who gives such false evidence shall be punished either with death or the punishment hereinbefore described.

CLASSIFICATION OF OFFENCE

Para I: Punishment—Imprisonment for life, or rigorous imprisonment for 10 years and fine—Non-cognizable—Non-bailable—Triable by Court of Session—Non-compoundable.

Para II: Punishment—Death or as above—Non-cognizable—Non-bailable—Triable by Court of Session—Non-compoundable.

300. Murder.—Except in the cases hereinafter excepted, culpable homicide is murder, if the act by which the death is caused is done with the intention of causing death, or—

Secondly.—If it is done with the intention of causing such bodily injury as the offender knows to be likely to cause the death of the person to whom the harm is caused, or—

Thirdly.—If it is done with the intention of causing bodily injury to any person and the bodily injury intended to be inflicted is sufficient in the ordinary course of nature to cause death, or—

Fourthly.—If the person committing the act knows that it is so imminently dangerous that it must, in all probability, cause death or such bodily injury as is likely to cause death, and commits such act without any excuse for incurring the risk of causing death or such injury as aforesaid.

Illustrations

(a) *A* shoots *Z* with the intention of killing him. *Z* dies in consequence. *A* commits murder.

(b) *A*, knowing that *Z* is labouring under such a disease that a blow is likely to cause his death, strikes him with the intention of causing bodily injury. *Z* dies in consequence of the blow. *A* is guilty of murder, although the blow might not have been sufficient in the ordinary course of nature to cause the death of a person in a sound state of health. But if *A*, not knowing that *Z* is labouring under any disease, gives him such a blow as would not in the ordinary course of nature kill a person in a sound state of health, here *A*, although he may intend to cause bodily injury, is not guilty of murder, if he did not intend to cause death, or such bodily injury as in the ordinary course of nature would cause death.

(c) *A* intentionally gives *Z* a sword-cut or club-wound sufficient to cause the death of a man in the ordinary course of nature. *Z* dies in consequence. Here, *A* is guilty of murder, although he may not have intended to cause *Z*'s death.

(d) *A* without any excuse fires a loaded cannon into a crowd of persons and kills one of them. *A* is guilty of murder, although he may not have had a premeditated design to kill any particular individual.

Exception 1.—**When culpable homicide is not murder.**—Culpable homicide is not murder if the offender, whilst deprived of the power of self-control by grave and sudden provocation, causes the death of the person who gave the provocation or causes the death of any other person by mistake or accident.

The above exception is subject to the following provisos:—

First.—That the provocation is not sought or voluntarily provoked by the offender as an excuse for killing or doing harm to any person.

Secondly.—That the provocation is not given by anything done in obedience to the law, or by a public servant in the lawful exercise of the powers of such public servant.

Thirdly.—That the provocation is not given by anything done in the lawful exercise of the right of private defence.

Explanation.—Whether the provocation was grave and sudden enough to prevent the offence from amounting to murder is a question of fact.

Illustrations

(a) *A*, under the influence of passion excited by a provocation given by *Z*, intentionally kills. *Y*, *Z*'s child. This is murder, in as much as the provocation was not given by the child, and the death of the child was not caused by accident or misfortune in doing an act caused by the provocation.

(b) *Y* gives grave and sudden provocation to *A*. *A*, on this provocation, fires a pistol at *Y*, neither intending nor knowing himself to be likely to kill *Z*, who is near him, but out of sight. *A* kills *Z*. Here *A* has not committed murder, but merely culpable homicide.

(c) *A* is lawfully arrested by *Z*, a bailiff. *A* is excited to sudden and violent passion by the arrest, and kills *Z*. This is murder, in as much as the provocation was given by a thing done by a public servant in the exercise of his powers.

(d) *A* appears as witness before *Z*, a Magistrate, *Z* says that he does not believe a word of *A*'s deposition, and that *A* has perjured himself. *A* is moved to sudden passion by these words, and kills *Z*. This is murder.

(e) *A* attempts to pull *Z*'s nose, *Z*, in the exercise of the right of private defence, lays hold of *A* to prevent him from doing so. *A* is moved to sudden and violent passion in consequence, and kills *Z*. This is murder, in as much as the provocation was given by a thing done in the exercise of the right of private defence.

(f) *Z* strikes *B*. *B* is by this provocation excited to violent rage. *A*, a bystander, intending to take advantage of *B*'s rage, and to cause him to kill *Z*, puts a knife into *B*'s hand for that purpose. *B* kills *Z* with the knife. Here *B* may have committed only culpable homicide, but *A* is guilty of murder.

Exception 2.—Culpable homicide is not murder if the offender, in the exercise in good faith of the right of private defence of person or property, exceeds the power given to him by law and causes the death of the person against whom he is exercising such right of defence without premeditation, and without any intention of doing more harm than is necessary for the purpose of such defence.

302. Punishment for murder.—Whoever commits murder shall be punished with death, or imprisonment for life, and shall also be liable to fine.

CLASSIFICATION OF OFFENCE

Punishment—Death, or imprisonment for life, and fine—Cognizable—Non-bailable—Triable by Court of Session—Non-compoundable.

305. Abetment of suicide of child or insane person.—If any person under eighteen years of age, any insane person, any delirious person, any idiot, or any person in a state of intoxication, commits suicide, whoever abets the commission of such suicide, shall be punished with death or imprisonment for life, or imprisonment for a term not exceeding ten years, and shall also be liable to fine.

CLASSIFICATION OF OFFENCE

Punishment—Death, or imprisonment for life, or imprisonment for 10 years and fine—Cognizable—Non-bailable—Triable by Court of Session—Non-compoundable.

306. Abetment of suicide.—If any person commits suicide, whoever abets the commission of such suicide, shall be punished with imprisonment of either description for a term which may extend to ten years, and shall also be liable to fine.

CLASSIFICATION OF OFFENCE

Punishment—Imprisonment for 10 years and fine—Cognizable—Non-bailable—Triable by Court of Session—Non-compoundable.

Attempts by life convicts.—When any person offending under this section is under sentence of imprisonment for life, he may, if hurt is caused, be punished with death.

Illustrations

(a) *A* shoots at *Z* with intention to kill him, under such circumstances that, if death ensued. *A* would be guilty of murder. *A* is liable to punishment under this section.

(b) *A*, with the intention of causing the death of a child of tender years, exposes it in a desert place. *A* has committed the offence defined by this section, though the death of the child does not ensue.

(c) *A*, intending to murder *Z*, buys a gun and loads it. *A* has not yet committed the offence. *A* fires the gun at *Z*. He has committed the offence defined in this section, and if by such firing he wounds *Z*, he is liable to the punishment provided by the latter part of the first paragraph of this section.

(d) *A*, intending to murder *Z* by poison, purchases poison and mixes the same with food which remains in *A*'s keeping; *A* has not yet committed the offence defined in this section. *A* places the food on *Z*'s table or delivers it to *Z*'s servant to place it on *Z*'s table. *A* has committed the offence defined in this section.

CLASSIFICATION OF OFFENCE

Para I: Punishment—Imprisonment for 10 years and fine—Cognizable—Non-bailable—Triable by Court of Session—Non-compoundable.

Para II: Punishment—Imprisonment for life, or imprisonment for 10 years and fine—Cognizable—Non-bailable—Triable by Court of Session—Non-compoundable.

Para III: Punishment—Death, or imprisonment for 10 years and fine—Cognizable—Non-bailable—Triable by Court of Session—Non-compoundable.

396. Dacoity with murder.—If any one of five or more persons, who are conjointly committing dacoity, commits murder in so committing dacoity, every one of those persons shall be punished with death, or imprisonment for life, or rigorous imprisonment for a term which may extend to ten years, and shall also be liable to fine.

CLASSIFICATION OF OFFENCE

Punishment—Death, imprisonment for life, or rigorous imprisonment for 10 years and fine—Cognizable—Non-bailable—Triable by Court of Session—Non-compoundable.

The Criminal Law (Amendment) Act, 2013[1] (13 of 2013) which was specifically enacted after the Delhi Vasant Vihar gang rape case on 16 December, 2012 did not provide for death sentence for the offence of rape.

In a case in 2013[2] the Supreme Court in award of death sentence observed that the judges should not get swayed by personal notions or by ideas of continent jurist. The binding judgment should be Bible. The established principles should be guiding factor and there should not be any deviations.

The offence of rape does not appear to have been regarded as equally heinous at all periods of our history. Anciently, indeed, it appears to have been punishable with death, but this was afterwards thought too hard and in its stead another severe but not capital punishment was prescribed.

Justice J.S. Verma Committee Report, 2013 on Criminal Law (Amendment) is its Chapter of "Rape" did not provide death penalty for offence of rape.

---

1. W.r.e.f. 3-2-2013.
2. *Oma @ Omprakash* v. *State of Tamil Nadu*, AIR 2013 SC 825.

Part 2

THE CRIMINAL LAW (AMENDMENT) ACT, 2013 (13 OF 2013)

STATUTORY PROVISIONS FOR OFFENCE OF RAPE

THE CRIMINAL LAW (AMENDMENT) ACT, 2013

(13 of 2013)

[*2nd April, 2013*]

An Act further to amend the Indian Penal Code, the Code of Criminal Procedure, 1973, the Indian Evidence Act, 1872 and the Protection of Children from Sexual Offences Act, 2012.

BE it enacted by Parliament in the Sixty-fourth Year of the Republic of India as follows:—

CHAPTER I

PRELIMINARY

1. Short title and commencement.—(1) This Act may be called the Criminal Law (Amendment) Act, 2013.

(2) It shall be deemed to have come into force on the 3rd day of February, 2013.

CHAPTER II

AMENDMENTS TO THE INDIAN PENAL CODE

2. Amendment of section 100.—In the Indian Penal Code (45 of 1860) (hereafter in this Chapter referred to as the Penal Code), in section 100, after clause *Sixthly*, the following clause shall be inserted, namely:—

"*Seventhly.*—An act of throwing or administering acid or an attempt to throw or administer acid which may reasonably cause the apprehension that grievous hurt will otherwise be the consequence of such act.".

3. Insertion of new sections 166A and 166B.—After section 166 of the Penal Code, the following sections shall be inserted, namely:—

"*166A. Public servant disobeying direction under law.*—Whoever, being a public servant,—

(a) knowingly disobeys any direction of the law which prohibits him from requiring the attendance at any place of any person for the purpose of investigation into an offence or any other matter, or

(b) knowingly disobeys, to the prejudice of any person, any other direction of the law regulating the manner in which he shall conduct such investigation, or

(c) fails to record any information given to him under sub-section (1) of section 154 of the Code of Criminal Procedure, 1973 (2 of 1974), in relation to cognizable offence punishable under section 326A, section 326B, section 354, section 354B, section 370, section 370A, section 376, section 376A, section 376B, section 376C, section 376D, section 376E or section 509,

shall be punished with rigorous imprisonment for a term which shall not be less than six months but which may extend to two years, and shall also be liable to fine.

166B. Punishment for non-treatment of victim.—Whoever, being in charge of a hospital, public or private, whether run by the Central Government, the State Government, local bodies or any other person, contravenes the provisions of section 357C of the Code of Criminal Procedure, 1973 (2 of 1974), shall be punished with imprisonment for a term which may extend to one year or with fine or with both.".

4. Amendment of section 228A.—In section 228A of the Penal Code, in sub-section (1), for the words, figures and letters "offence under section 376, section 376A, section 376B, section 376C or section 376D", the words, figures and letters "offence under section 376, section 376A, section 376B, section 376C, section 376D or section 376E" shall be substituted.

5. Insertion of new sections 326A and 326B.—After section 326 of the Penal Code, the following sections shall be inserted, namely:—

'*326A. Voluntarily causing grievous hurt by use of acid, etc.*—Whoever causes permanent or partial damage or deformity to, or burns or maims or disfigures or disables, any part or parts of the body of a person or causes grievous hurt by throwing acid on or by administering acid to that person, or by using any other means with the intention of causing or with the knowledge that he is likely to cause such injury or hurt, shall be punished with imprisonment of either description for a term which shall not be less than ten years but which may extend to imprisonment for life, and with fine:

Provided that such fine shall be just and reasonable to meet the medical expenses of the treatment of the victim:

Provided further that any fine imposed under this section shall be paid to the victim.

326B. Voluntarily throwing or attempting to throw acid.—Whoever throws or attempts to throw acid on any person or attempts to administer acid to any person, or attempts to use any other means, with the intention of causing permanent or partial damage or deformity or burns or maiming or disfigurement or disability or grievous hurt to that person, shall be punished with imprisonment of either description for a term which shall not be less than five years but which may extend to seven years, and shall also be liable to fine.

Explanation 1.—For the purposes of section 326A and this section, "acid" includes any substance which has acidic or corrosive character or burning nature, that is capable of causing bodily injury leading to scars or disfigurement or temporary or permanent disability.

Explanation 2.—For the purposes of section 326A and this section, permanent or partial damage or deformity shall not be required to be irreversible.'.

6. Amendment of section 354.—In section 354 of the Penal Code, for the words "shall be punished with imprisonment of either description for a term which may extend to two years, or with fine, or with both", the words "shall be punished with imprisonment of either description for a term which shall not be less than one year but which may extend to five years, and shall also be liable to fine" shall be substituted.

7. Insertion of new sections 354A, 354B, 354C and 354D.—After section 354 of the Penal Code, the following sections shall be inserted, namely:—

'*354A. Sexual harassment and punishment for sexual harassment.*—(1) A man committing any of the following acts—

(i) physical contact and advances involving unwelcome and explicit sexual overtures; or

(ii) a demand or request for sexual favours; or

(iii) showing pornography against the will of a woman; or

(iv) making sexually coloured remarks,

shall be guilty of the offence of sexual harassment.

(2) Any man who commits the offence specified in clause (i) or clause (ii) or clause (iii) of sub-section (1) shall be punished with rigorous imprisonment for a term which may extend to three years, or with fine, or with both.

(3) Any man who commits the offence specified in clause (iv) of sub-section (1) shall be punished with imprisonment of either description for a term which may extend to one year, or with fine, or with both.

354B. Assault or use of criminal force to woman with intent to disrobe.—Any man who assaults or uses criminal force to any woman or abets such act with the intention of disrobing or compelling her to be naked, shall be punished with imprisonment of either description for a term which shall not be less than three years but which may extend to seven years, and shall also be liable to fine.

354C. Voyeurism.—Any man who watches, or captures the image of a woman engaging in a private act in circumstances where she would usually have the expectation of not being observed either by the perpetrator or by any other person at the behest of the perpetrator or disseminates such image shall be punished on first conviction with imprisonment of either description for a term which shall not be less than one year, but which may extend to three years, and shall also be liable to fine, and be punished on a second or subsequent conviction, with imprisonment of either description for a term which shall not be less than three years, but which may extend to seven years, and shall also be liable to fine.

Explanation 1.—For the purpose of this section, "private act" includes an act of watching carried out in a place which, in the circumstances, would reasonably be expected to provide privacy and where the victim's genitals, posterior or breasts are exposed or covered only in underwear; or the victim is using a lavatory; or the victim is doing a sexual act that is not of a kind ordinarily done in public.

Explanation 2.—Where the victim consents to the capture of the images or any act, but not to their dissemination to third persons and where such image or act is disseminated, such dissemination shall be considered an offence under this section.

354D. Stalking.—(1) Any man who—

(i) follows a woman and contacts, or attempts to contact such woman to foster personal interaction repeatedly despite a clear indication of disinterest by such woman; or

(ii) monitors the use by a woman of the internet, email or any other form of electronic communication,

commits the offence of stalking:

Provided that such conduct shall not amount to stalking if the man who pursued it proves that—

(i) it was pursued for the purpose of preventing or detecting crime and the man accused of stalking had been entrusted with the responsibility of prevention and detection of crime by the State; or

(ii) it was pursued under any law or to comply with any condition or requirement imposed by any person under any law; or

(iii) in the particular circumstances such conduct was reasonable and justified.

(2) Whoever commits the offence of stalking shall be punished on first conviction with imprisonment of either description for a term which may extend to three years, and shall also be liable to fine; and be punished on a second or subsequent conviction, with imprisonment of either description for a term which may extend to five years, and shall also be liable to fine.'.

8. Substitution of new sections 370 and 370A for section 370.—For section 370 of the Penal Code, the following sections shall be substituted, namely:—

'*370. Trafficking of person.*—(1) Whoever, for the purpose of exploitation, (a) recruits, (b) transports, (c) harbours, (d) transfers, or (e) receives, a person or persons, by—

First.—using threats, or

Secondly.—using force, or any other form of coercion, or

Thirdly.—by abduction, or

Fourthly.—by practising fraud, or deception, or

Fifthly.—by abuse of power, or

Sixthly.—by inducement, including the giving or receiving of payments or benefits, in order to achieve the consent of any person having control over the person recruited, transported, harboured, transferred or received,

commits the offence of trafficking.

Explanation 1.—The expression "exploitation" shall include any act of physical exploitation or any form of sexual exploitation, slavery or practices similar to slavery, servitude, or the forced removal of organs.

Explanation 2.—The consent of the victim is immaterial in determination of the offence of trafficking.

(2) Whoever commits the offence of trafficking shall be punished with rigorous imprisonment for a term which shall not be less than seven years, but which may extend to ten years, and shall also be liable to fine.

(3) Where the offence involves the trafficking of more than one person, it shall be punishable with rigorous imprisonment for a term which shall not be less than ten years but which may extend to imprisonment for life, and shall also be liable to fine.

(4) Where the offence involves the trafficking of a minor, it shall be punishable with rigorous imprisonment for a term which shall not be less than ten years, but which may extend to imprisonment for life, and shall also be liable to fine.

(5) Where the offence involves the trafficking of more than one minor, it shall be punishable with rigorous imprisonment for a term which shall not be less than fourteen years, but which may extend to imprisonment for life, and shall also be liable to fine.

(6) If a person is convicted of the offence of trafficking of minor on more than one occasion, then such person shall be punished with imprisonment for life, which shall mean imprisonment for the remainder of that person's natural life, and shall also be liable to fine.

(7) When a public servant or a police officer is involved in the trafficking of any person then, such public servant or police officer shall be punished with imprisonment for life, which shall mean imprisonment for the remainder of that person's natural life, and shall also be liable to fine.

370A. Exploitation of a trafficked person.—(1) Whoever, knowingly or having reason to believe that a minor has been trafficked, engages such minor for sexual exploitation in any manner, shall be punished with rigorous imprisonment for a term which shall not be less than five years, but which may extend to seven years, and shall also be liable to fine.

(2) Whoever, knowingly by or having reason to believe that a person has been trafficked, engages such person for sexual exploitation in any manner, shall be punished with rigorous imprisonment for a term which shall not be less than three years, but which may extend to five years, and shall also be liable to fine.'.

9. Substitution of new sections for sections 375, 376, 376A, 376B, 376C and 376D.— For sections 375, 376, 376A, 376B, 376C and 376D of the Penal Code, the following sections shall be substituted, namely:—

'375. *Rape.*—A man is said to commit "rape" if he—

(a) penetrates his penis, to any extent, into the vagina, mouth, urethra or anus of a woman or makes her to do so with him or any other person; or

(b) inserts, to any extent, any object or a part of the body, not being the penis, into the vagina, the urethra or anus of a woman or makes her to do so with him or any other person; or

(c) manipulates any part of the body of a woman so as to cause penetration into the vagina, urethra, anus or any part of body of such woman or makes her to do so with him or any other person; or

(d) applies his mouth to the vagina, anus, urethra of a woman or makes her to do so with him or any other person,

under the circumstances falling under any of the following seven descriptions:—

First.—Against her will.

Secondly.—Without her consent.

Thirdly.—With her consent, when her consent has been obtained by putting her or any person in whom she is interested, in fear of death or of hurt.

Fourthly.—With her consent, when the man knows that he is not her husband and that her consent is given because she believes that he is another man to whom she is or believes herself to be lawfully married.

Fifthly.—With her consent when, at the time of giving such consent, by reason of unsoundness of mind or intoxication or the administration by him personally or through another of any stupefying or unwholesome substance, she is unable to understand the nature and consequences of that to which she gives consent.

Sixthly.—With or without her consent, when she is under eighteen years of age.

Seventhly.—When she is unable to communicate consent.

Explanation 1.—For the purposes of this section, "vagina" shall also include *labia majora*.

Explanation 2.—Consent means an unequivocal voluntary agreement when the woman by words, gestures or any form of verbal or non-verbal communication, communicates willingness to participate in the specific sexual act:

Provided that a woman who does not physically resist to the act of penetration shall not by the reason only of that fact, be regarded as consenting to the sexual activity.

Exception 1.—A medical procedure or intervention shall not constitute rape.

Exception 2.—Sexual intercourse or sexual acts by a man with his own wife, the wife not being under fifteen years of age, is not rape.'.

376. *Punishment for rape.*—(1) Whoever, except in the cases provided for in sub-section (2), commits rape, shall be punished with rigorous imprisonment of either description for a term which shall not be less than seven years, but which may extend to imprisonment for life, and shall also be liable to fine.

(2) Whoever,—

(a) being a police officer, commits rape—

(i) within the limits of the police station to which such police officer is appointed; or

(ii) in the premises of any station house; or

(iii) on a woman in such police officer's custody or in the custody of a police officer subordinate to such police officer; or

(b) being a public servant, commits rape on a woman in such public servant's custody or in the custody of a public servant subordinate to such public servant; or

(c) being a member of the armed forces deployed in an area by the Central or a State Government commits rape in such area; or

(d) being on the management or on the staff of a jail, remand home or other place of custody established by or under any law for the time being in force or of a women's or children's institution, commits rape on any inmate of such jail, remand home, place or institution; or

(e) being on the management or on the staff of a hospital, commits rape on a woman in that hospital; or

(f) being a relative, guardian or teacher of, or a person in a position of trust or authority towards the woman, commits rape on such woman; or

(g) commits rape during communal or sectarian violence; or

(h) commits rape on a woman knowing her to be pregnant; or

(i) commits rape on a woman when she is under sixteen years of age; or

(j) commits rape, on a woman incapable of giving consent; or

(k) being in a position of control or dominance over a woman, commits rape on such woman; or

(l) commits rape on a woman suffering from mental or physical disability; or

(m) while committing rape causes grievous bodily harm or maims or disfigures or endangers the life of a woman; or

(n) commits rape repeatedly on the same woman,

shall be punished with rigorous imprisonment for a term which shall not be less than ten years, but which may extend to imprisonment for life, which shall mean imprisonment for the remainder of that person's natural life, and shall also be liable to fine.

Explanation.—For the purposes of this sub-section,—

(a) "armed forces" means the naval, military and air forces and includes any member of the Armed Forces constituted under any law for the time being in force, including the paramilitary forces and any auxiliary forces that are under the control of the Central Government or the State Government;

(b) "hospital" means the precincts of the hospital and includes the precincts of any institution for the reception and treatment of persons during convalescence or of persons requiring medical attention or rehabilitation;

(c) "police officer" shall have the same meaning as assigned to the expression "police" under the Police Act, 1861 (5 of 1861);

(d) "women's or children's institution" means an institution, whether called an orphanage or a home for neglected women or children or a widow's home or an institution called by any other name, which is established and maintained for the reception and care of women or children.

376A. Punishment for causing death or resulting in persistent vegetative state of victim.—Whoever, commits an offence punishable under sub-section (1) or sub-section (2) of section 376 and in the course of such commission inflicts an injury which causes the death of the woman or causes the woman to be in a persistent vegetative state, shall be punished with rigorous imprisonment for a term which shall not be less than twenty years, but which may extend to imprisonment for life, which shall mean imprisonment for the remainder of that person's natural life, or with death.

376B. Sexual intercourse by husband upon his wife during separation.—Whoever has sexual intercourse with his own wife, who is living separately, whether under a decree of separation or otherwise, without her consent, shall be punished with imprisonment of either description, for a term which shall not be less than two years but which may extend to seven years, and shall also be liable to fine.

Explanation.—In this section, "sexual intercourse" shall mean any of the acts mentioned in clauses (a) to (d) of section 375.

376C. Sexual intercourse by a person in authority.—Whoever, being—

(a) in a position of authority or in a fiduciary relationship; or

(b) a public servant; or

(c) superintendent or manager of a jail, remand home or other place of custody established by or under any law for the time being in force, or a women's or children's institution; or

(d) on the management of a hospital or being on the staff of a hospital,

abuses such position or fiduciary relationship to induce or seduce any woman either in his custody or under his charge or present in the premises to have sexual intercourse with him, such sexual intercourse not amounting to the offence of rape, shall be punished with rigorous imprisonment of either description for a term which shall not be less than five years, but which may extend to ten years, and shall also be liable to fine.

Explanation 1.—In this section, "sexual intercourse" shall mean any of the acts mentioned in clauses (a) to (d) of section 375.

Explanation 2.—For the purposes of this section, *Explanation 1* to section 375 shall also be applicable.

Explanation 3.—"Superintendent", in relation to a jail, remand home or other place of custody or a women's or children's institution, includes a person holding any other office in such jail, remand home, place or institution by virtue of which such person can exercise any authority or control over its inmates.

Explanation 4.—The expressions "hospital" and "women's or children's institution" shall respectively have the same meaning as in *Explanation* to sub-section (2) of section 376.

376D. Gang rape.—Where a woman is raped by one or more persons constituting a group or acting in furtherance of a common intention, each of those persons shall be deemed to have committed the offence of rape and shall be punished with rigorous imprisonment for a term which shall not be less than twenty years, but which may extend to life which shall mean imprisonment for the remainder of that person's natural life, and with fine:

Provided that such fine shall be just and reasonable to meet the medical expenses and rehabilitation of the victim:

Provided further that any fine imposed under this section shall be paid to the victim.

376E. Punishment for repeat offenders.—Whoever has been previously convicted of an offence punishable under section 376 or section 376A or section 376D and is subsequently convicted of an offence punishable under any of the said sections shall be punished with imprisonment for life which shall mean imprisonment for the remainder of that person's natural life, or with death.'.

10. Amendment of section 509.—In section 509 of the Penal Code, for the words "shall be punished with simple imprisonment for a term which may extend to one year, or with fine, or with both", the words "shall be punished with simple imprisonment for a term which may extend to three years, and also with fine" shall be substituted.

CHAPTER III

AMENDMENTS TO THE CODE OF CRIMINAL PROCEDURE, 1973

11. Amendment of section 26.—In the Code of Criminal Procedure, 1973 (2 of 1974) (hereafter in this Chapter referred to as the Code of Criminal Procedure), in section 26, in the proviso to clause (a), for the words, figures and letters "offence under section 376 and sections 376A to 376D of the Indian Penal Code (45 of 1860)", the words, figures and letters "offence under section 376, section 376A, section 376B, section 376C, section 376D or section 376E of the Indian Penal Code (45 of 1860)" shall be substituted.

12. Amendment of section 54A.—In section 54A of the Code of Criminal Procedure, the following provisos shall be inserted, namely:—

"Provided that, if the person identifying the person arrested is mentally or physically disabled, such process of identification shall take place under the supervision of a Judicial Magistrate who shall take appropriate steps to ensure that such person identifies the person arrested using methods that person is comfortable with:

Provided further that if the person identifying the person arrested is mentally or physically disabled, the identification process shall be videographed.".

13. Amendment of section 154.—In section 154 of the Code of Criminal Procedure, in sub-section (1), the following provisos shall be inserted, namely:—

"Provided that if the information is given by the woman against whom an offence under section 326A, section 326B, section 354, section 354A, section 354B, section 354C, section 354D, section 376, section 376A, section 376B, section 376C, section 376D, section 376E or section 509 of the Indian Penal Code (45 of 1860) is alleged to have been committed or attempted, then such information shall be recorded, by a woman police officer or any woman officer:

Provided further that—

(a) in the event that the person against whom an offence under section 354, section 354A, section 354B, section 354C, section 354D, section 376, section 376A, section 376B, section 376C, section 376D, section 376E or section 509 of the Indian Penal Code (45 of 1860) is alleged to have been committed or attempted, is temporarily or permanently mentally or physically disabled, then such information shall be recorded by a police officer, at the residence of the person seeking to report such offence or at a convenient place of such person's choice, in the presence of an interpreter or a special educator, as the case may be;

(b) the recording of such information shall be videographed;

(c) the police officer shall get the statement of the person recorded by a Judicial Magistrate under clause (a) of sub-section (5A) of section 164 as soon as possible.".

14. Amendment of section 160.—In section 160 of the Code of Criminal Procedure, in sub-section (1), in the proviso, for the words "under the age of fifteen years or woman", the words "under the age of fifteen years or above the age of sixty-five years or a woman or a mentally or physically disabled person" shall be substituted.

15. Amendment of section 161.—In section 161 of the Code of Criminal Procedure, in sub-section (3), after the proviso, the following proviso shall be inserted, namely:—

"Provided further that the statement of a woman against whom an offence under section 354, section 354A, section 354B, section 354C, section 354D, section 376, section 376A, section 376B, section 376C, section 376D, section 376E or section 509 of the Indian Penal Code (45 of 1860) is alleged to have been committed or attempted shall be recorded, by a woman police officer or any woman officer.".

16. Amendment of section 164.—In section 164 of the Code of Criminal Procedure, after sub-section (5), the following sub-section shall be inserted, namely:—

"(5A)(a) In cases punishable under section 354, section 354A, section 354B, section 354C, section 354D, sub-section (1) or sub-section (2) of section 376, section 376A, section 376B, section 376C, section 376D, section 376E or section 509 of the Indian Penal Code (45 of 1860), the Judicial Magistrate shall record the statement of the person against whom such offence has been committed in the manner prescribed in sub-section (5), as soon as the commission of the offence is brought to the notice of the police:

Provided that if the person making the statement is temporarily or permanently mentally or physically disabled, the Magistrate shall take the assistance of an interpreter or a special educator in recording the statement:

Provided further that if the person making the statement is temporarily or permanently mentally or physically disabled, the statement made by the person, with the assistance of an interpreter or a special educator, shall be videographed;

(b) A statement recorded under clause (a) of a person, who is temporarily or permanently mentally or physically disabled, shall be considered a statement in lieu of examination-in-chief, as specified in section 137 of the Indian Evidence Act, 1872 (1 of 1872) such that the maker of the statement can be cross-examined on such statement, without the need for recording the same at the time of trial.".

17. Amendment of section 173.—In section 173 of the Code of Criminal Procedure, in sub-section (2), in sub-clause (h) of clause (i), for the words, figures and letter "or 376D of the Indian Penal Code (45 of 1860)", the words, figures and letters "section 376D or section 376E of the Indian Penal Code" shall be substituted.

18. Amendment of section 197.—In section 197 of the Code of Criminal Procedure, after sub-section (1), the following *Explanation* shall be inserted, namely:—

"*Explanation.*—For the removal of doubts it is hereby declared that no sanction shall be required in case of a public servant accused of any offence alleged to have been committed under section 166A, section 166B, section 354, section 354A, section 354B, section 354C, section 354D, section 370, section 375, section 376, section 376A, section 376C, section 376D or section 509 of the Indian Penal Code (45 of 1860).".

19. Insertion of new section 198B.—After section 198A of the Code of Criminal Procedure, the following section shall be inserted, namely:—

"*198B. Cognizance of offence.*—No Court shall take cognizance of an offence punishable under section 376B of the Indian Penal Code (45 of 1860) where the persons are in a marital relationship, except upon *prima facie* satisfaction of the facts which constitute the offence upon a complaint having been filed or made by the wife against the husband.".

20. Amendment of section 273.—In section 273 of the Code of Criminal Procedure, before the *Explanation*, the following proviso shall be inserted, namely:—

"Provided that where the evidence of a woman below the age of eighteen years who is alleged to have been subjected to rape or any other sexual offence, is to be recorded, the court may take appropriate measures to ensure that such woman is not confronted by the accused while at the same time ensuring the right of cross-examination of the accused.".

21. Amendment of section 309.—In section 309 of the Code of Criminal Procedure, for sub-section (1), the following sub-section shall be substituted, namely:—

"(1) In every inquiry or trial the proceedings shall be continued from day-to-day until all the witnesses in attendance have been examined, unless the Court finds the adjournment of the same beyond the following day to be necessary for reasons to be recorded:

Provided that when the inquiry or trial relates to an offence under section 376, section 376A, section 376B, section 376C or section 376D of the Indian Penal Code (45 of 1860), the inquiry or trial shall, as far as possible be completed within a period of two months from the date of filing of the charge sheet.".

22. Amendment of section 327.—In section 327 of the Code of Criminal Procedure, in sub-section (2), for the words, figures and letter "or section 376D of the Indian Penal Code (45 of 1860)", the words, figures and letters "section 376D or section 376E of the Indian Penal Code (45 of 1860)" shall be substituted.

23. Insertion of new sections 357B and 357C.—After section 357A of the Code of Criminal Procedure, the following sections shall be inserted, namely:—

"*357B. Compensation to be in addition to fine under section 326A or section 376D of Indian Penal Code.*—The compensation payable by the State Government under section 357A shall be in addition to the payment of fine to the victim under section 326A or section 376D of the Indian Penal Code (45 of 1860).

"*357C. Treatment of victims.*—All hospitals, public or private, whether run by the Central Government, the State Government, local bodies or any other person, shall immediately, provide the first-aid or medical treatment, free of cost, to the victims of any offence covered under section 326A, 376, 376A, 376B, 376C, 376D or section 376E of the Indian Penal Code (45 of 1860), and shall immediately inform the police of such incident.".

24. Amendment of First Schedule.—In the First Schedule to the Code of Criminal Procedure, under the heading "I.–OFFENCES UNDER THE INDIAN PENAL CODE (45 of 1860)",—

(a) after the entries relating to section 166, the following entries shall be inserted, namely:—

1	2	3	4	5	6
"166A	Public servant disobeying direction under law	Imprisonment for minimum 6 months which may extend to 2 years and fine	Cognizable	Bailable	Magistrate of the first class
166B	Non-treatment of victim by hospital	Imprisonment for 1 year or fine or both	Non-cognizable	Bailable	Magistrate of the first class";

(b) after the entries relating to section 326, the following entries shall be inserted, namely:—

1	2	3	4	5	6
"326A	Voluntarily causing grievous hurt by use of acid, etc.	Imprisonment for not less than 10 years but which may extend to imprisonment for life and fine to be paid to the victim.	Cognizable	Non-bailable	Court of Session
326B	Voluntarily throwing or attempting to throw acid.	Imprisonment for 5 years but which may extend to 7 years and with fine.	Cognizable	Non-bailable	Court of Session.";

(c) for the entries relating to section 354, the following entries shall be substituted, namely:—

1	2	3	4	5	6
"354	Assault or use of criminal force to woman with intent to outrage her modesty.	Imprisonment of 1 year which may extend to 5 years, and with fine.	Cognizable	Non-bailable	Any Magistrate
354A	Sexual harassment of the nature of unwelcome physical contact and advances or a demand or request for sexual favours, showing pornography.	Imprisonment which may extend to 3 years or with fine or with both.	Cognizable	Bailable	Any Magistrate
	Sexual harassment of the nature of making sexually coloured remark.	Imprisonment which may extend to 1 year or with fine or with both.	Cognizable	Bailable	Any Magistrate
354B	Assault or use of criminal force to woman with intent to disrobe.	Imprisonment of not less than 3 years but which may extend to 7 years and with fine.	Cognizable	Non-bailable	Any Magistrate
354C	Voyeurism.	Imprisonment of not less than 1 year but which may extend to 3 years and with fine for first conviction.	Cognizable	Bailable	Any Magistrate

1	2	3	4	5	6
		Imprisonment of not less than 3 years but which may extend to 7 years and with fine for second or subsequent conviction.	Cognizable	Non-bailable	Any Magistrate
354D	Stalking.	Imprisonment up to 3 years and with fine for first conviction.	Cognizable	Bailable	Any Magistrate
		Imprisonment up to 5 years and with fine for second or subsequent conviction.	Cognizable	Non-bailable	Any Magistrate.".

(d) for the entries relating to section 370, the following entries shall be substituted, namely:—

1	2	3	4	5	6
"370	Trafficking of person.	Imprisonment of not less than 7 years but which may extend to 10 years and with fine.	Cognizable	Non-bailable	Court of Session
	Trafficking of more than one person.	Imprisonment of not less than 10 years but which may extend to imprisonment for life and with fine.	Cognizable	Non-bailable	Court of Session
	Trafficking of a minor.	Imprisonment of not less than 10 years but which may extend to imprisonment for life and with fine.	Cognizable	Non-bailable	Court of Session
	Trafficking of more than one minor.	Imprisonment of not less than 14 years but which may extend to imprisonment for life and with fine.	Cognizable	Non-bailable	Court of Session
	Person convicted of offence of trafficking of minor on more than one occasion.	Imprisonment for life which shall mean the remainder of that person's natural life and with fine.	Cognizable	Non-bailable	Court of Session

1	2	3	4	5	6
	Public servant or a police officer involved in trafficking of minor.	Imprisonment for life which shall mean the remainder of that person's natural life and with fine.	Cognizable	Non-bailable	Court of Session
370A	Exploitation of a trafficked child.	Imprisonment of not less than 5 years but which may extend to 7 years and with fine.	Cognizable	Non-bailable	Court of Session
	Exploitation of a trafficked person.	Imprisonment of not less than 3 years but which may extend to 5 years and with fine.	Cognizable	Non-bailable	Court of Session.";

(e) for the entries relating to sections 376, 376A, 376B, 376C and 376D, the following entries shall be substituted, namely:—

1	2	3	4	5	6
"376	Rape	Rigorous imprisonment of not less than 7 years but which may extend to imprisonment for life and with fine.	Cognizable	Non-bailable	Court of Session
	Rape by a police officer or a public servant or member of armed forces or a person being on the management or on the staff of a jail, remand home or other place of custody or women's or children's institution or by a person on the management or on the staff of a hospital, and rape committed by a person in a	Rigorous imprisonment of not less than 10 years but which may extend to imprisonment for life which shall mean the remainder of that person's natural life and with fine.	Cognizable	Non-bailable	Court of Session.

1	2	3	4	5	6
	position of trust or authority towards the person raped or by a near relative of the person raped.				
376A	Person committing an offence of rape and inflicting injury which causes death or causes the woman to be in a persistent vegetative state.	Rigorous imprisonment of not less than 20 years but which may extend to imprisonment for life which shall mean imprisonment for the remainder of that person's natural life or with death.	Cognizable	Non-bailable	Court of Session
376B	Sexual intercourse by husband upon his wife during separation.	Imprisonment for not less than 2 years but which may extend to 7 years and with fine.	Cognizable (but only on the complaint of the victim)	Bailable	Court of Session
376C	Sexual intercourse by a person in authority.	Rigorous imprisonment for not less than 5 years but which may extend to 10 years and with fine.	Cognizable	Non-bailable	Court of Session
376D	Gang rape	Rigorous imprisonment for not less than 20 years but which may extend to imprisonment for life which shall mean imprisonment for the remainder of that person's natural life and with fine to be paid to the victim.	Cognizable	Non-bailable	Court of Session

1	2	3	4	5	6
376E	Repeat offenders.	Imprisonment for life which shall mean imprisonment for the remainder of that person's natural life or with death.	Cognizable	Non-bailable	Court of Session,".

(f) in entry relating to section 509, in column 3, for the words "Simple imprisonment for one year, or fine, or both,", the words and figures "Simple imprisonment for 3 years and with fine" shall be substituted.

CHAPTER IV

AMENDMENTS TO THE INDIAN EVIDENCE ACT, 1872

25. Insertion of new section 53A.—After section 53 of the Indian Evidence Act, 1872 (1 of 1872), (hereafter in this Chapter referred to as the Evidence Act), the following section shall be inserted, namely:—

"*53A. Evidence of character or previous sexual experience not relevant in certain cases.*—In a prosecution for an offence under section 354, section 354A, section 354B, section 354C, section 354D, section 376, section 376A, section 376B, section 376C, section 376D or section 376E of the Indian Penal Code (45 of 1860) or for attempt to commit any such offence, where the question of consent is in issue, evidence of the character of the victim or of such person's previous sexual experience with any person shall not be relevant on the issue of such consent or the quality of consent.".

26. Substitution of new section for section 114A.—For section 114A of the Evidence Act, the following section shall be substituted, namely:—

'*114A. Presumption as to absence of consent in certain prosecution for rape.*—In a prosecution for rape under clause (a), clause (b), clause (c), clause (d), clause (e), clause (f), clause (g), clause (h) clause (i), clause (j), clause (k), clause (l), clause (m) or clause (n) of sub-section (2) of section 376 of the Indian Penal Code (45 of 1860), where sexual intercourse by the accused is proved and the question is whether it was without the consent of the woman alleged to have been raped and such woman states in her evidence before the court that she did not consent, the court shall presume that she did not consent.

Explanation.—In this section, "sexual intercourse" shall mean any of the acts mentioned in clauses (a) to (d) of section 375 of the Indian Penal Code (45 of 1860).

27. Substitution of new section for section 119.—For section 119 of the Evidence Act, the following section shall be substituted, namely: —

"*119. Witness unable to communicate verbally.*—A witness who is unable to speak may give his evidence in any other manner in which he can make it intelligible, as by writing or by signs; but such writing must be written and the signs made in open Court, evidence so given shall be deemed to be oral evidence:

Provided that if the witness is unable to communicate verbally, the Court shall take the assistance of an interpreter or a special educator in recording the statement, and such statement shall be videographed.".

28. Amendment of section 146.—In section 146 of the Evidence Act, for the proviso, the following proviso shall be substituted, namely:—

"Provided that in a prosecution for an offence under section 376, section 376A, section 376B, section 376C, section 376D or section 376E of the Indian Penal Code (45 of 1860) or for attempt to commit any such offence, where the question of consent is an issue, it shall not be permissible to adduce evidence or to put questions in the cross-examination of the victim as to the general immoral character, or previous sexual experience, of such victim with any person for proving such consent or the quality of consent.".

CHAPTER V

AMENDMENT TO THE PROTECTION OF CHILDREN FROM SEXUAL OFFENCES ACT, 2012

29. Substitution of new sections for section 42.—For section 42 of the Protection of Children from Sexual Offences Act, 2012 (32 of 2012), the following sections shall be substituted, namely:—

"42. *Alternate punishment.*—Where an act or omission constitutes an offence punishable under this Act and also under sections 166A, 354A, 354B, 354C, 354D, 370, 370A, 375, 376, 376A, 376C, 376D, 376E or section 509 of the Indian Penal Code (45 of 1860), then, notwithstanding anything contained in any law for the time being in force, the offender found guilty of such offence shall be liable to punishment under this Act or under the Indian Penal Code as provides for punishment which is greater in degree.

42A. *Act not in derogation of any other law.*—The provisions of this Act shall be in addition to and not in derogation of the provisions of any other law for the time being in force and, in case of any inconsistency, the provisions of this Act shall have overriding effect on the provisions of any such law to the extent of the inconsistency.".

CHAPTER VI

MISCELLANEOUS

30. Repeal and saving.—(1) The Criminal Law (Amendment) Ordinance, 2013 (Ord. 3 of 2013) is hereby repealed.

(2) Notwithstanding such repeal, anything done or any action taken under the Indian Penal Code (45 of 1860), the Code of Criminal Procedure, 1973 (2 of 1974) and the Indian Evidence Act, 1872 (1 of 1872), as amended by the said Ordinance, shall be deemed to have been done or taken under the corresponding provisions of those Acts, as amended by this Act.

Part 3

Old Statutory Provisions for Offence of Rape

INDIAN PENAL CODE
(Relevant Provisions)

Sexual offences

375. Rape.—A man is said to commit "rape" who, except in the case hereinafter excepted, has sexual intercourse with a woman under circumstances falling under any of the six following descriptions:—

First.— Against her will.

Secondly.— Without her consent.

Thirdly.— With her consent, when her consent has been obtained by putting her or any person in whom she is interested in fear of death or of hurt.

Fourthly.— With her consent, when the man knows that he is not her husband, and that her consent is given because she believes that he is another man to whom she is or believes herself to be lawfully married.

Fifthly.— With her consent, when, at the time of giving such consent, by reason of unsoundness of mind or intoxication or the administration by him personally or through another of any stupefying or unwholesome substance, she is unable to understand the nature and consequences of that to which she gives consent.

Sixthly.— With or without her consent, when she is under sixteen years of age.

Explanation.—Penetration is sufficient to constitute the sexual intercourse necessary to the offence of rape.

Exception.—Sexual intercourse by a man with his own wife, the wife not being under fifteen years of age, is not rape.

STATE AMENDMENT

Manipur.—In section 35,—

(a) in clause *sixthly*, for the word "sixteen" substitute the word "fourteen"; and

(b) in the *Exception*, for the word "fifteen" substitute the word "thirteen".

[*Vide* Act 30 of 1950, sec. 3 (w.e.f. 16-4-1950) (made earlier than Act 43 of 1983)].

376. Punishment for rape.—(1) Whoever, except in the cases provided for by sub-section (2), commits rape shall be punished with imprisonment of either description for a term which shall not be less than seven years but which may be for life or for a term which may extend to ten years and shall also be liable to fine unless the women raped is his own wife and is not under twelve years of age, in which cases, he shall be punished with imprisonment of either description for a term which may extend to two years or with fine or with both:

Provided that the court may, for adequate and special reasons to be mentioned in the judgment, impose a sentence of imprisonment for a term of less than seven years.

(2) Whoever,—

(a) being a police officer commits rape—

(i) within the limits of the police station to which he is appointed; or

(ii) in the premises of any station house whether or not situated in the police station to which he is appointed; or

(iii) on a woman in his custody or in the custody of a police officer subordinate to him; or

(b) being a public servant, takes advantage of his official position and commits rape on a woman in his custody as such public servant or in the custody of a public servant subordinate to him; or

(c) being on the management or on the staff of a jail, remand home or other place of custody established by or under any law for the time being in force or of a woman's or children's institution takes advantage of his official position and commits rape on any inmate of such jail, remand home, place or institution; or

(d) being on the management or on the staff of a hospital, takes advantage of his official position and commits rape on a woman in that hospital; or

(e) commits rape on a woman knowing her to be pregnant; or

(f) commits rape on a woman when she is under twelve years of age; or

(g) commits gang rape,

shall be punished with rigorous imprisonment for a term which shall not be less than ten years but which may be for life and shall also be liable to fine:

Provided that the Court may, for adequate and special reasons to be mentioned in the judgment, impose a sentence of imprisonment of either description for a term of less than ten years.

Explanation 1.—Where a woman is raped by one or more in a group of persons acting in furtherance of their common intention, each of the persons shall be deemed to have committed gang rape within the meaning of this sub-section.

Explanation 2.—"Women's or children's institution" means an institution, whether called an orphanage or a home for neglected woman or children or a widows' home or by any other name, which is established and maintained for the reception and care of woman or children.

Explanation 3.—"Hospital" means the precincts of the hospital and includes the precincts of any institution for the reception and treatment of persons during convalescence or of persons requiring medical attention or rehabilitation.

CLASSIFICATION OF OFFENCE

Para I: Punishment—Imprisonment for life or imprisonment for ten years and fine—Cognizable—Non-bailable—Triable by Court of Session—Non-compoundable.

Para II: Punishment—Imprisonment for two years or fine or both—Non-Cognizable—Bailable—Triable by Court of Session—Non-compoundable.

376A. Intercourse by a man with his wife during separation.—Whoever has sexual intercourse with his own wife, who is living separately from him under a decree of separation or under any custom or usage without her consent shall be punished with imprisonment of either description for a term which may extend to two years and shall also be liable to fine.

CLASSIFICATION OF OFFENCE

Punishment—Imprisonment for two years and fine—Non-cognizable—Bailable—Triable by Court of Session—Non-compoundable.

376B. Intercourse by public servant with woman in his custody.—Whoever, being a public servant, takes advantage of his official position and induces or seduces, any woman, who is in his custody as such public servant or in the custody of a public servant subordinate to him, to have sexual intercourse with him, such sexual intercourse not amounting to the offence of rape, shall be punished with imprisonment of either description for a term which may extend to five years and shall also be liable to fine.

CLASSIFICATION OF OFFENCE

Punishment—Imprisonment for five years and fine—Cognizable (but no arrest shall be made without a warrant or without an order of a Magistrate)—Bailable—Triable by Court of Session—Non-compoundable.

376C. Intercourse by superintendent of jail, remand home, etc.—Whoever, being the superintendent or manager of a jail, remand home or other place of custody established by or under any law for the time being in force or of a woman's or children's institution takes advantage of his official position and induces or seduces any female inmate of such jail, remand home, place or institution to have sexual intercourse with him, such sexual intercourse not amounting to the offence of rape, shall be punished with imprisonment of either description for a term which may extend to five years and shall also be liable to fine.

Explanation 1.—"Superintendent" in relation to jail, remand home or other place of custody or a women's or children's institution includes a person holding any other office in such jail, remand home, place or institution by virtue of which he can exercise any authority or control over its inmates.

Explanation 2.—The expression "women's or children's institution" shall have the same meaning as in *Explanation* 2 to sub-section (2) of section 376.

CLASSIFICATION OF OFFENCE

Punishment—Imprisonment for five years and fine—Cognizable (but no arrest shall be made without a warrant or without an order of a Magistrate)—Bailable—Triable by Court of Session—Non-compoundable.

376D. Intercourse by any member of the management or staff of a hospital with any woman in that hospital.—Whoever, being on the management of a hospital or being on the staff of a hospital takes advantage of his position and has sexual intercourse with any woman in that hospital, such sexual intercourse not amounting to the offence of rape, shall be punished with imprisonment of either description for a term which may extend to five years and shall also be liable to fine.

Explanation.—The expression "hospital" shall have the same meaning as in *Explanation* 3 to sub-section (2) of section 376.

CLASSIFICATION OF OFFENCE

Punishment—Imprisonment for five years and fine—Cognizable (but no arrest shall be made without a warrant or without an order of a Magistrate)—Bailable—Triable by Court of Session—Non-compoundable.

Of Unnatural Offences

377. Unnatural offences.—Whoever voluntarily has carnal intercourse against the order of nature with any man, woman or animal, shall be punished with imprisonment for life, or with imprisonment of either description for a term which may extend to ten years, and shall also be liable to fine.

Explanation.—Penetration is sufficient to constitute the carnal intercourse necessary to the offence described in this section.

CLASSIFICATION OF OFFENCE

Punishment—Imprisonment for life, or imprisonment for 10 years and fine—Cognizable—Non-Bailable—Triable by Magistrate of the first class—Non-compoundable.

STATE AMENDMENT

Madhya Pradesh.—In the entries relating to section 377, in column 6, for the words "Magistrate of the first class", substitute the words "Court of Session".

[*Vide* The Code of Criminal Procedure (Madhya Pradesh Amendment) Act, 2007 (Madhya Pradesh Act 2 of 2008), sec. 4 (w.e.f. 14-2-2008).]

THE PROTECTION OF CHILDREN FROM SEXUAL OFFENCES ACT, 2012

INTRODUCTION

Sexual Offences against children are not adequately addressed by the existing laws. A large number of such offences are neither specifically provided for nor are they adequately penalized. Such offences against children need to be defined explicitly and countered through adequate penalities as an effective deterence. This Act provides for protection of children from offences of sexual assault, sexual harassment and pornography with due regard for safeguarding the interest and well being of children.

STATEMENT OF OBJECTS AND REASONS

Article 15 of the Constitution, *inter alia,* confers upon the State powers to make special provision for children. Further, article 39, *inter alia,* provides that the State shall in particular direct its policy towards securing that the tender age of children are not abused and their childhood and youth are protected against exploitation and they are given facilities to develop in a healthy manner and in conditions of freedom and dignity.

2. The United Nations Convention on the Rights of Children, ratified by India on 11th December, 1992, requires the State Parties to undertake all appropriate national, bilateral and multilateral measures to prevent (a) the inducement or coercion of a child to engage in any unlawful sexual activity; (b) the exploitative use of children in prostitution or other unlawful sexual practices; and (c) the exploitative use of children in pornographic performances and materials.

3. The data collected by the National Crime Records Bureau shows that there has been increase in cases of sexual offences against children. This is corroborated by the 'Study on Child Abuse: India 2007' conducted by the Ministry of Women and Child Development. Moreover, sexual offences against children are not adequately addressed by the existing laws. A large number of such offences are neither specifically provided for nor are they adequately penalised. The interests of the child, both as a victim as well as a witness, need to be protected. It is felt that offences against children need to be defined explicitly and countered through commensurate penalties as an effective deterrence.

4. It is, therefore, proposed to enact a self contained comprehensive legislation *inter alia* to provide for protection of children from the offences of sexual assault, sexual harassment and pornography with due regard for safeguarding the interest and well being of the child at every stage of the judicial process, incorporating child-friendly procedures for reporting, recording of evidence, investigation and trial of offences and provision for establishment of Special Courts for speedy trial of such offences.

5. The Bill would contribute to enforcement of the right of all children to safety, security and protection from sexual abuse and exploitation.

6. The notes on clauses explain in detail the various provisions contained in the Bill.

7. The Bill seeks to achieve the above objectives.

ACT 32 OF 2012

The Protection of Children from Sexual Offences Bill having been passed by both the Houses of Parliament received the assent of the President on 19th June, 2012. It came on the Statute Book as THE PROTECTION OF CHILDREN FROM SEXUAL OFFENCES ACT, 2012 (32 of 2012) (*Came into force on 14-11-2012*).

AMENDING ACT

The Criminal Law (Amendment) Act, 2013 (13 of 2013) (w.r.e.f. 3-2-2013).

THE PROTECTION OF CHILDREN FROM SEXUAL OFFENCES ACT, 2012[1]

(32 of 2012)

[*19th June, 2012*]

An Act to protect children from offences of sexual assault, sexual harassment and pornography and provide for establishment of Special Courts for trial of such offences and for matters connected therewith or incidental thereto.

WHEREAS clause (3) of article 15 of the Constitution, *inter alia,* empowers the State to make special provisions for children;

AND WHEREAS, the Government of India has acceded on the 11th December, 1992 to the Convention on the Rights of the Child, adopted by the General Assembly of the United Nations, which has prescribed a set of standards to be followed by all State parties in securing the best interests of the child;

AND WHEREAS it is necessary for the proper development of the child that his or her right to privacy and confidentiality be protected and respected by every person by all means and through all stages of a judicial process involving the child;

AND WHEREAS it is imperative that the law operates in a manner that the best interest and well being of the child are regarded as being of paramount importance at every stage, to ensure the healthy physical, emotional, intellectual and social development of the child;

AND WHEREAS the State Parties to the Convention on the Rights of the Child are required to undertake all appropriate national, bilateral and multilateral measures to prevent—

(a) the inducement or coercion of a child to engage in any unlawful sexual activity;

(b) the exploitative use of children in prostitution or other unlawful sexual practices;

(c) the exploitative use of children in pornographic performances and materials;

AND WHEREAS sexual exploitation and sexual abuse of children are heinous crimes and need to be effectively addressed.

BE it enacted by Parliament in the Sixty-third Year of the Republic of India as follows:—

CHAPTER I

PRELIMINARY

1. Short title, extent and commencement.—(1) This Act may be called the Protection of Children from Sexual Offences Act, 2012.

(2) It extends to the whole of India, except the State of Jammu and Kashmir.

---

1. Published in the Gazette of India, Extra., Pt. II, Sec. 1, No. 34, dated 20th June, 2012.
2. Came into force on 14-11-2012, *vide* S.O. 2705(E), dated 9th November, 2012, published in the Gazette of India, Extra., Pt. II, Sec. 3(ii), No. 2250, dated 9th November, 2012.

(3) It shall come into force on such date[2] as the Central Government may, by notification in the Official Gazette, appoint.

2. Definitions.—(1) In this Act, unless the context otherwise requires,—

(a) "aggravated penetrative sexual assault" has the same meaning as assigned to it in section 5;

(b) "aggravated sexual assault" has the same meaning as assigned to it in section 9;

(c) "armed forces or security forces" means armed forces of the Union or security forces or police forces, as specified in the Schedule;

(d) "child" means any person below the age of [1][eighteen] years;

(e) "domestic relationship" shall have the same meaning as assigned to it in clause (f) of section 2 of the Protection of Women from Domestic Violence Act, 2005 (43 of 2005);

(f) "penetrative sexual assault" has the same meaning as assigned to it in section 3;

(g) "prescribed" means prescribed by rules made under this Act;

(h) "religious institution" shall have the same meaning as assigned to it in the Religious Institutions (Prevention of Misuse) Act, 1988 (41 of 1988);

(i) "sexual assault" has the same meaning as assigned to it in section 7;

(j) "sexual harassment" has the same meaning as assigned to it in section 11;

(k) "shared household" means a household where the person charged with the offence lives or has lived at any time in a domestic relationship with the child;

(l) "Special Court" means a court designated as such under section 28;

(m) "Special Public Prosecutor" means a Public Prosecutor appointed under section 32;

(2) The words and expressions used herein and not defined but defined in the Indian Penal Code (45 of 1860), the Code of Criminal Procedure, 1973 (2 of 1974), the Juvenile Justice (Care and Protection of Children) Act, 2000 (56 of 2000) and the Information Technology Act, 2000 (21 of 2000) shall have the meanings respectively assigned to them in the said Codes or the Acts.

CHAPTER II

SEXUAL OFFENCES AGAINST CHILDREN

A.—Penetrative Sexual Assault and Punishment Therefor

3. Penetrative sexual assault.—A person is said to commit "penetrative sexual assault" if—

(a) he penetrates his penis, to any extent, into the vagina, mouth, urethra or anus of a child or makes the child to do so with him or any other person; or

(b) he inserts, to any extent, any object or a part of the body, not being the penis, into the vagina, the urethra or anus of the child or makes the child to do so with him or any other person; or

(c) he manipulates any part of the body of the child so as to cause penetration into the vagina, urethra, anus or any part of body of the child or makes the child to do so with him or any other person; or

(d) he applies his mouth to the penis, vagina, anus, urethra of the child or makes the child to do so to such person or any other person.

4. Punishment for penetrative sexual assault.—Whoever commits penetrative sexual assault shall be punished with imprisonment of either description for a term which shall not be less than seven years but which may extend to imprisonment for life, and shall also be liable to fine.

COMMENTS

(Based on Notes on Clauses of the Bill)

This section provides for punishment for penetrative sexual assault. It provides that whoever commits penetrative sexual assault shall be punished with imprisonment of either description for a term which shall not be less than seven years but which may extend to imprisonment for life, and shall also be liable to fine

B.—Aggravated Penetrative Sexual Assault and Punishment Therefor

5. Aggravated penetrative sexual assault.—(a) Whoever, being a police officer, commits penetrative sexual assault on a child—

(i) within the limits of the police station or premises at which he is appointed; or

(ii) in the premises of any station house, whether or not situated in the police station, to which he is appointed; or

(iii) in the course of his duties or otherwise; or

(iv) where he is known as, or identified as, a police officer; or

(b) Whoever being a member of the armed forces or security forces commits penetrative sexual assault on a child—

(i) within the limits of the area to which the person is deployed; or

(ii) in any areas under the command of the forces or armed forces; or

(iii) in the course of his duties or otherwise; or

(iv) where the said person is known or identified as a member of the security or armed forces; or

(c) whoever being a public servant commits penetrative sexual assault on a child; or

(d) whoever being on the management or on the staff of a jail, remand home, protection home, observation home, or other place of custody or care and protection established by or under any law for the time being in force, commits penetrative sexual assault on a child, being inmate of such jail, remand home, protection home, observation home, or other place of custody or care and protection; or

(e) whoever being on the management or staff of a hospital, whether Government or private, commits penetrative sexual assault on a child in that hospital; or

(f) whoever being on the management or staff of an educational institution or religious institution, commits penetrative sexual assault on a child in that institution; or

(g) whoever commits gang penetrative sexual assault on a child.

Explanation.—When a child is subjected to sexual assault by one or more persons of a group in furtherance of their common intention, each of such persons shall be deemed to have committed gang penetrative sexual assault within the meaning of this clause and each of such person shall be liable for that act in the same manner as if it were done by him alone; or

(h) whoever commits penetrative sexual assault on a child using deadly weapons, fire, heated substance or corrosive substance; or

(i) whoever commits penetrative sexual assault causing grievous hurt or causing bodily harm and injury or injury to the sexual organs of the child; or

(j) whoever commits penetrative sexual assault on a child, which—

(i) physically incapacitates the child or causes the child to become mentally ill as defined under clause (b) of section 2 of the Mental Health Act, 1987 (14 of 1987) or causes impairment of any kind so as to render the child unable to perform regular tasks, temporarily or permanently; or

(ii) in the case of female child, makes the child pregnant as a consequence of sexual assault;

(iii) inflicts the child with Human Immunodeficiency Virus or any other life threatening disease or infection which may either temporarily or permanently impair the child by rendering him physically incapacitated, or mentally ill to perform regular tasks; or

(k) whoever, taking advantage of a child's mental or physical disability, commits penetrative sexual assault on the child; or

(l) whoever commits penetrative sexual assault on the child more than once or repeatedly; or

(m) whoever commits penetrative sexual assault on a child below twelve years; or

(n) whoever being a relative of the child through blood or adoption or marriage or guardianship or in foster care or having a domestic relationship with a parent of the child or who is living in the same or shared household with the child, commits penetrative sexual assault on such child; or

(o) whoever being, in the ownership, or management, or staff, of any institution providing services to the child, commits penetrative sexual assault on the child; or

(p) whoever being in a position of trust or authority of a child commits penetrative sexual assault on the child in an institution or home of the child or anywhere else; or

(q) whoever commits penetrative sexual assault on a child knowing the child is pregnant; or

(r) whoever commits penetrative sexual assault on a child and attempts to murder the child; or

(s) whoever commits penetrative sexual assault on a child in the course of communal or sectarian violence; or

(t) whoever commits penetrative sexual assault on a child and who has been previously convicted of having committed any offence under this Act or any sexual offence punishable under any other law for the time being in force; or

(u) whoever commits penetrative sexual assault on a child and makes the child to strip or parade naked in public,

is said to commit aggravated penetrative sexual assault.

6. Punishment for aggravated penetrative sexual assault.—Whoever, commits aggravated penetrative sexual assault, shall be punished with rigorous imprisonment for a term which shall not be less than ten years but which may extend to imprisonment for life and shall also be liable to fine.

C.—Sexual Assault and Punishment Therefor

7. Sexual Assault.—Whoever, with sexual intent touches the vagina, penis, anus or breast of the child or makes the child touch the vagina, penis, anus or breast of such person or any other person, or does any other act with sexual intent which involves physical contact without penetration is said to commit sexual assault.

8. Punishment for sexual assault.—Whoever, commits sexual assault, shall be punished with imprisonment of either description for a term which shall not be less than three years but which may extend to five years, and shall also be liable to fine.

COMMENTS
(Based on Notes on Clauses of the Bill)

This section provides punishment for sexual assault. It provides that whoever commits sexual assault, shall be punished with imprisonment of either description for a term which shall not be less than three years but may extend to five years and shall also be liable to fine.

D.—Aggravated Sexual Assault and Punishment Therefor

9. Aggravated Sexual Assault.—(a) Whoever, being a police officer, commits sexual assault on a child—

(i) within the limits of the police station or premises where he is appointed; or

(ii) in the premises of any station house whether or not situated in the police station to which he is appointed; or

(iii) in the course of his duties or otherwise; or

(iv) where he is known as, or identified as a police officer; or

(b) whoever, being a member of the armed forces or security forces, commits sexual assault on a child—

(i) within the limits of the area to which the person is deployed; or

(ii) in any areas under the command of the security or armed forces; or

(iii) in the course of his duties or otherwise; or

(iv) where he is known or identified as a member of the security or armed forces; or

(c) whoever being a public servant commits sexual assault on a child; or

(d) whoever being on the management or on the staff of a jail, or remand home or protection home or observation home, or other place of custody or care and protection established by or under any law for the time being in force commits sexual assault on a child being inmate of such jail or remand home or protection home or observation home or other place of custody or care and protection; or

(e) whoever being on the management or staff of a hospital, whether Government or private, commits sexual assault on a child in that hospital; or

(f) whoever being on the management or staff of an educational institution or religious institution, commits sexual assault on a child in that institution; or

(g) whoever commits gang sexual assault on a child.

Explanation.—When a child is subjected to sexual assault by one or more persons of a group in furtherance of their common intention, each of such persons shall be deemed to have committed gang sexual assault within the sexual meaning of this clause and each of such person shall be liable for that act in the same manner as if it were done by him alone; or

(h) whoever commits sexual assault on a child using deadly weapons, fire, heated substance or corrosive substance; or

(i) whoever commits sexual assault causing grievous hurt or causing bodily harm and injury or injury to the sexual organs of the child; or

(j) whoever commits sexual assault on a child, which—

(i) physically incapacitates the child or causes the child to become mentally ill as defined under clause (l) of section 2 of the Mental Health Act, 1987 (14 of 1987) or causes impairment of any kind so as to render the child unable to perform regular tasks, temporarily or permanently; or

(ii) inflicts the child with Human Immunodeficiency Virus or any other life threatening disease or infection which may either temporarily or permanently impair the child by rendering him physically incapacitated, or mentally ill to perform regular tasks; or

(k) whoever, taking advantage of a child's mental or physical disability, commits sexual assault on the child; or

(l) whoever commits sexual assault on the child more than once or repeatedly; or

(m) whoever commits sexual assault on a child below twelve years; or

(n) whoever, being a relative of the child through blood or adoption or marriage or guardianship or in foster care, or having domestic relationship with a parent of the child, or who is living in the same or shared household with the child, commits sexual assault on such child; or

(o) whoever, being in the ownership or management or staff, of any institution providing services to the child, commits sexual assault on the child in such institution; or

(p) whoever, being in a position of trust or authority of a child, commits sexual assault on the child in an institution or home of the child or anywhere else; or

(q) whoever commits sexual assault on a child knowing the child is pregnant; or

(r) whoever commits sexual assault on a child and attempts to murder the child; or

(s) whoever commits sexual assault on a child in the course of communal or sectarian violance; or

(t) whoever commits sexual assault on a child and who has been previously convicted of having committed any offence under this Act or any sexual offence punishable under any other law for the time being in force; or

(u) whoever commits sexual assault on a child and makes the child to strip or parade naked in public,

is said to commit aggravated sexual assault.

10. Punishment for aggravated sexual assault.—Whoever, commits aggravated sexual assault shall be punished with imprisonment of either description for a term which shall not be less than five years but which may extend to seven years, and shall also be liable to fine.

E.—Sexual Harassment and Punishment Therefor

11. Sexual harassment.—A person is said to commit sexual harassment upon a child when such person with sexual intent,—

(i) utters any word or makes any sound, or makes any gesture or exhibits any object or part of body with the intention that such word or sound shall be heard, or such gesture or object or part of body shall be seen by the child; or

(ii) makes a child exhibit his body or any part of his body so as it is seen by such person or any other person; or

(iii) shows any object to a child in any form or media for pornographic purposes; or

(iv) repeatedly or constantly follows or watches or contacts a child either directly or through electronic, digital or any other means; or

(v) threatens to use, in any form of media, a real or fabricated depiction through electronic, film or digital or any other mode, of any part of the body of the child or the involvement of the child in a sexual act; or

(vi) entices a child for pornographic purposes or gives gratification therefor.

Explanation.—Any question which involves "sexual intent" shall be a question of fact.

12. Punishment for sexual harassment.—Whoever, commits sexual harassment upon a child shall be punished with imprisonment of either description for a term which may extend to three years and shall also be liable to fine.

CHAPTER III

USING CHILD FOR PORNOGRAPHIC PURPOSES AND PUNISHMENT THEREFOR

13. Use of child for pornographic purposes.—Whoever, uses a child in any form of media (including programme or advertisement telecast by television channels or internet or any other electronic form or printed form, whether or not such programme or advertisement is intended for personal use or for distribution), for the purposes of sexual gratification, which includes—

(a) representation of the sexual organs of a child;

(b) usage of a child engaged in real or simulated sexual acts (with or without penetration);

(c) the indecent or obscene representation of a child,

shall be guilty of the offence of using a child for pornographic purposes.

Explanation.—For the purposes of this section, the expression "use a child" shall include involving a child through any medium like print, electronic, computer or any other technology for preparation, production, offering, transmitting, publishing, facilitation and distribution of the pornographic material.

COMMENTS
(Based on Notes on Clauses of the Bill)

This section defines the offences of use of child for pornographic purposes. It provides that whoever uses a child in any form of media (including programme or advertisement telecast by television channels or internet or any other electronic form or printed form, whether or not such programme or advertisement is intended for personal use or for distribution), for the purposes of sexual gratification, which includes (a) representation of the sexual organs of a child; (b) usage of a child engaged in real or simulated sexual acts (with or without penetration); or (c) the indecent or obscene representation of a child, shall be guilty of the offence of using a child for pornographic purposes.

It further clarifies that for the purposes of this section the expression "use a child" shall includes involving a child through any medium like print, electronic, computer or any other technology for preparation, production, offering, transmitting, publishing, facilitation and distribution of the pornographic material.

14. Punishment for using child for pornographic purposes.—(1) Whoever, uses a child or children for pornographic purposes shall be punished with imprisonment of either description which may extend to five years and shall also be liable to fine and in the event of second or subsequent conviction with imprisonment of either description for a term which may extend to seven years and also be liable to fine.

(2) If the person using the child for pornographic purposes commits an offence referred to in section 3, by directly participating in pornographic acts, he shall be punished with imprisonment of either description for a term which shall not be less than ten years but which may extend to imprisonment for life, and shall also be liable to fine.

(3) If the person using the child for pornographic purposes commits an offence referred to in section 5, by directly participating in pornographic acts, he shall be punished with rigorous imprisonment for life and shall also be liable to fine.

(4) If the person using the child for pornographic purposes commits an offence referred to in section 7, by directly participating in pornographic acts, he shall be punished with imprisonment of either description for a term which shall not be less than six years but which may extend to eight years, and shall also be liable to fine.

(5) If the person using the child for pornographic purposes commits an offence referred to in section 9, by directly participating in pornographic acts, he shall be punished with imprisonment of either description for a term which shall not be less than eight years but which may extend to ten years, and shall also be liable to fine.

15. Punishment for storage of pornographic material involving child.— Any person, who stores, for commercial purposes any pornographic material in any form involving a child shall be punished with imprisonment of either description which may extend to three years or with fine or with both.

CHAPTER IV

ABETMENT OF AND ATTEMPT TO COMMIT AN OFFENCE

16. Abetment of an offence.—A person abets an offence, who—

First.— Instigates any person to do that offence; or

Secondly.— Engages with one or more other person or persons in any conspiracy for the doing of that offence, if an act or illegal omission takes place in pursuance of that conspiracy, and in order to the doing of that offence; or

Thirdly.—Intentionally aids, by any act or illegal omission, the doing of that offence.

Explanation I.—A person who, by wilful misrepresentation, or by wilful concealment of a material fact, which he is bound to disclose, voluntarily causes or procures, or attempts to cause or procure a thing to be done, is said to instigate the doing of that offence.

Explanation II.—Whoever, either prior to or at the time of commission of an act, does anything in order to facilitate the commission of that act, and thereby facilitates the commission thereof, is said to aid the doing of that act.

Explanation III.—Whoever employ, harbours, receives or transports a child, by means of threat or use of force or other forms of coercion, abduction, fraud, deception, abuse of power or of a position, vulnerability or the giving or receiving of payments or benefits to achieve the consent of a person having control over another person, for the purpose of any offence under this Act, is said to aid the doing of that act.

17. Punishment for abetment.—Whoever abets any offence under this Act, if the act abetted is committed in consequence of the abetment, shall be punished with punishment provided for that offence.

Explanation.—An act or offence is said to be committed in consequence of abetment, when it is committed in consequence of the instigation, or in pursuance of the conspiracy or with the aid, which constitutes the abetment.

18. Punishment for attempt to commit an offence.—Whoever attempts to commit any offence punishable under this Act or to cause such an offence to be committed, and in such attempt, does any act towards the commission of the offence, shall be punished with imprisonment of any description provided for the offence, for a term which may extend to one-half of the imprisonment for life or, as the case may be, one-half of the longest term of imprisonment provided for that offence or with fine or with both.

CHAPTER V

PROCEDURE FOR REPORTING OF CASES

19. Reporting of offences.—(1) Notwithstanding anything contained in the Code of Criminal Procedure, 1973 (2 of 1974), any person (including the child), who has apprehension that an offence under this Act is likely to be committed or has knowledge that such an offence has been committed, he shall provide such information to,—

(a) the Special Juvenile Police Unit; or

(b) the local police.

(2) Every report given under sub-section (1) shall be—

(a) ascribed an entry number and recorded in writing;

(b) be read over to the informant;

(c) shall be entered in a book to be kept by the Police Unit.

(3) Where the report under sub-section (1) is given by a child, the same shall be recorded under sub-section (2) in a simple language so that the child understands contents being recorded.

(4) In case contents are being recorded in the language not understood by the child or wherever it is deemed necessary, a translator or an interpreter, having such qualifications, experience and on payment of such fees as may be prescribed, shall be provided to the child if he fails to understand the same.

(5) Where the Special Juvenile Police Unit or local police is satisfied that the child against whom an offence has been committed is in need of care and protection, then, it shall, after recording the reasons in writing, make immediate arrangement to give him such care and protection (including admitting the child into shelter home or to the nearest hospital) within twenty-four hours of the report, as may be prescribed.

(6) The Special Juvenile Police Unit or local police shall, without unnecessary delay but within a period of twenty-four hours, report the matter to the Child Welfare Committee and the Special Court or where no Special Court has been designated, to the Court of Session, including need of the child for care and protection and steps taken in this regard.

(7) No person shall incur any liability, whether civil or criminal, for giving the information in good faith for the purpose of sub-section (1).

20. Obligation of media, studio and photographic facilities to report cases.—Any personnel of the media or hotel or lodge or hospital or club or studio or photographic facilities, by whatever name called, irrespective of the number of persons employed therein, shall, on coming across any material or object which is sexually exploitative of the child (including pornographic, sexually-related or making obscene representation of a child or children) through the use of any medium, shall provide such information to the Special Juvenile Police Unit, or to the local police, as the case may be.

COMMENTS

(Based on Notes on Clauses of the Bill)

This section provides for obligation of media, studio and photographic facilities to report cases. It provides that if any personnel of the media or hotel or lodge or hospital or club or studio or photographic facilities, by whatever name called, irrespective of the number of persons employed therein, comes across any material or object which is sexually exploitative of the child (including pornographic, sexually-related or making obscene representation of a child or children) through the use of any medium, then he shall provide such information to the Special Juvenile Police Unit, or to the local police, as the case may be.

21. Punishment for failure to report or record a case.—(1) Any person, who fails to report the commission of an offence under sub-section (1) of section 19 or section 20 or who fails to record such offence under sub-section (2) of section 19 shall be punished with imprisonment of either description which may extend to six months or with fine or with both.

(2) Any person, being in-charge of any company or an institution (by whatever name called) who fails to report the commission of an offence under sub-section (1) of section 19 in respect of a subordinate under his control, shall be punished with imprisonment for a term which may extend to one year and with fine.

(3) The provisions of sub-section (1) shall not apply to a child under this Act.

22. Punishment for false complaint or false information.—(1) Any person, who makes false complaint or provides false information against any person, in respect of an offence committed under sections 3, 5, 7 and section 9, solely with the intention to humiliate, extort or threaten or defame him, shall be punished with imprisonment for a term which may extend to six months or with fine or with both.

(2) Where a false complaint has been made or false information has been provided by a child, no punishment shall be imposed on such child.

(3) Whoever, not being a child, makes a false complaint or provides false information against a child, knowing it to be false, thereby victimising such child in any of the offences under this Act, shall be punished with imprisonment which may extend to one year or with fine or with both.

23. Procedure for media.—(1) No person shall make any report or present comments on any child from any form of media or studio or photographic facilities without having complete and authentic information, which may have the effect of lowering his reputation or infringing upon his privacy.

(2) No reports in any media shall disclose, the identity of a child including his name, address, photograph, family details, school, neighbourhood or any other particulars which may lead to disclosure of identity of the child:

Provided that for reasons to be recorded in writing, the Special Court, competent to try the case under the Act, may permit such disclosure, if in its opinion such disclosure is in the interest of the child.

(3) The publisher or owner of the media or studio or photographic facilities shall be jointly and severally liable for the acts and omissions of his employee.

(4) Any person who contravenes the provisions of sub-section (1) or sub-section (2) shall be liable to be punished with imprisonment of either description for a period which shall not be less than six months but which may extend to one year or with fine or with both.

CHAPTER VI

PROCEDURES FOR RECORDING STATEMENT OF THE CHILD

24. Recording of statement of a child.—(1) The statement of the child shall be recorded at the residence of the child or at a place where he usually resides or at the place of his choice and as far as practicable by a woman police officer not below the rank of sub-inspector.

(2) The police officer while recording the statement of the child shall not be in uniform.

(3) The police officer making the investigation, shall, while examining the child, ensure that at no point of time the child come in the contact in any way with the accused.

(4) No child shall be detained in the police station in the night for any reason.

(5) The police officer shall ensure that the identity of the child is protected from the public media, unless otherwise directed by the Special Court in the interest of the child.

25. Recording of statement of a child by Magistrate.—(1) If the statement of the child is being recorded under section 164 of the Code of Criminal Procedure, 1973 (2 of 1974), (herein referred to as the Code), the Magistrate recording such statement shall, notwithstanding anything contained therein, record the statement as spoken by the child:

Provided that the provisions contained in the first proviso to sub-section (1) of section 164 of the Code shall, so far it permits the presence of the advocate of the accused shall not apply in this case.

(2) The Magistrate shall provide to the child and his parents or his representative, a copy of the document specified under section 207 of the Code, upon the final report being filed by the police under section 173 of that Code.

26. Additional provisions regarding statement to be recorded.—(1) The Magistrate or the police officer, as the case may be, shall record the statement as spoken by the child in the presence of the parents of the child or any other person in whom the child has trust or confidence.

(2) Wherever necessary, the Magistrate or the police officer, as the case may be, may take the assistance of a translator or an interpreter, having such qualifications, experience and on payment of such fees as may be prescribed, while recording the statement of the child.

(3) The Magistrate or the police officer, as the case may be, may, in the case of a child having a mental or physical disability, seek the assistance of a special

educator or any person familiar with the manner of communication of the child or an expert in that field, having such qualifications, experience and on payment of such fees as may be prescribed, to record the statement of the child.

(4) Wherever possible, the Magistrate or the police officer, as the case may be, shall ensure that the statement of the child is also recorded by audio-video electronic means.

27. Medical examination of a child.—(1) The medical examination of a child in respect of whom any offence has been committed under this Act, shall, notwithstanding that a First Information Report or complaint has not been registered for the offences under this Act, be conducted in accordance with section 164A of the Code of Criminal Procedure, 1973 (2 of 1974).

(2) In case the victim is a girl child, the medical examination shall be conducted by a woman doctor.

(3) The medical examination shall be conducted in the presence of the parent of the child or any other person in whom the child reposes trust or confidence.

(4) Where, in case the parent of the child or other person referred to in sub-section (3) cannot be present, for any reason, during the medical examination of the child, the medical examination shall be conducted in the presence of a woman nominated by the head of the medical institution.

COMMENTS

(Based on Notes on Clauses of the Bill)

This section provides for medical examination of a child. It provides that the medical examination of a child in respect of whom any offence has been committed under the Act shall be conducted in accordance with section 164A of the Code of Criminal Procedure, 1973 (2 of 1974) whether or not the First Information Report or complaint has been registered for the offence.

CHAPTER VII
SPECIAL COURTS

28. Designation of Special Courts.—(1) For the purposes of providing a speedy trial, the State Government shall in consultation with the Chief Justice of the High Court, by notification in the Official Gazette, designate for each district, a Court of Session to be a Special Court to try the offences under the Act:

Provided that if a Court of Session is notified as a children's court under the Commissions for Protection of Child Rights Act, 2005 (4 of 2006) or a Special Court designated for similar purposes under any other law for the time being in force, then, such court shall be deemed to be a Special Court under this section.

(2) While trying an offence under this Act, a Special Court shall also try an offence [other than the offence referred to in sub-section (1)], with which the accused may, under the Code of Criminal Procedure, 1973 (2 of 1974), be charged at the same trial.

(3) The Special Court constituted under this Act, notwithstanding anything in the Information Technology Act, 2000 (21 of 2000), shall have jurisdiction to try offences under section 67B of that Act insofar as it relates to publication or transmission of sexually explicit material depicting children in any act, or conduct or manner or facilitates abuse of children online.

29. Presumption as to certain offences.—Where a person is prosecuted for committing or abetting or attempting to commit any offence under sections 3, 5, 7 and section 9 of this Act, the Special Court shall presume, that such person has committed or abetted or attempted to commit the offence, as the case may be, unless the contrary is proved.

COMMENTS

(Based on Notes on Clauses of the Bill)

This section provides for presumption as to certain offence. It provides that where a person is prosecuted for violating any of the provisions under sections 3, 5, 7 and 9 of the Act, and where the victim is a child below the age of sixteen years, the Special Court shall presume that such person has committed the offence, unless the contrary is proved.

30. Presumption of culpable mental state.—(1) In any prosecution for any offence under this Act which requires a culpable mental state on the part of the accused, the Special Court shall presume the existence of such mental state but it shall be a defence for the accused to prove the fact that he had no such mental state with respect to the act charged as an offence in that prosecution.

(2) For the purposes of this section, a fact is said to be proved only when the Special Court believes it to exist beyond reasonable doubt and not merely when its existence is established by a preponderance of probability.

Explanation.—In this section, "culpable mental state" includes intention, motive, knowledge of a fact and the belief in, or reason to believe, a fact.

31. Application of Code of Criminal Procedure, 1973 to proceedings before a Special Court.—Save as otherwise provided in this Act, the provisions of the Code of Criminal Procedure, 1973 (2 of 1974), (including the provisions as to bail and bonds) shall apply to the proceedings before a Special Court and for the purposes of the said provisions, the Special Court shall be deemed to be a Court of Sessions and the person conducting a prosecution before a Special Court, shall be deemed to be a Public Prosecutor.

32. Special Public Prosecutors.—(1) The State Government shall, by notification in the Official Gazette, appoint a Special Public Prosecutor for every Special Court for conducting cases only under the provisions of this Act.

(2) A person shall be eligible to be appointed as a Special Public Prosecutor under sub-section (1) only if he had been in practice for not less than seven years as an advocate.

(3) Every person appointed as a Special Public Prosecutor under this section shall be deemed to be a Public Prosecutor within the meaning of clause (u) of section 2 of the Code of Criminal Procedure , 1973 (2 of 1974) and provision of that Code shall have effect accordingly.

CHAPTER VIII

PROCEDURE AND POWERS OF SPECIAL COURTS AND RECORDING OF EVIDENCE

33. Procedure and powers of Special Court.—(1) A Special Court may take cognizance of any offence, without the accused being committed to it for trial, upon receiving a complaint of facts which constitute such offence, or upon a police report of such facts.

(2) The Special Public Prosecutor, or as the case may be, the counsel appearing for the accused shall, while recording the examination-in-chief, cross-examination or re-examination of the child, communicate the questions to be put to the child to the Special Court which shall in turn put those questions to the child.

(3) The Special Court may, if it considers necessary, permit frequent breaks for the child during the trial.

(4) The Special Court shall create a child-friendly atmosphere by allowing a family member, a guardian, a friend or a relative, in whom the child has trust or confidence, to be present in the court.

(5) The Special Court shall ensure that the child is not called repeatedly to testify in the court.

(6) The Special Court shall not permit aggressive questioning or character assassination of the child and ensure that dignity of the child is maintained at all times during the trial.

(7) The Special Court shall ensure that the identity of the child is not disclosed at any time during the course of investigation or trial:

Provided that for reasons to be recorded in writing, the Special Court may permit such disclosure, if in its opinion such disclosure is in the interest of the child.

Explanation.—For the purposes of this sub-section, the identity of the child shall include the identity of the child's family, school, relatives, neighbourhood or any other information by which the identity of the child may be revealed.

(8) In appropriate cases, the Special Court may, in addition to the punishment, direct payment of such compensation as may be prescribed to the child for any physical or mental trauma caused to him or for immediate rehabilitation of such child.

(9) Subject to the provisions of this Act, a Special Court shall, for the purpose of the trial of any offence under this Act, have all the powers of a Court of Session and shall try such offence as if it were a Court of Session, and as far as may be, in accordance with the procedure specified in the Code of Criminal Procedure, 1973 (2 of 1974) for trial before a Court of Session.

34. Procedure in case of commission of offence by child and determination of age by Special Court.—(1) Where any offence under this Act is committed by a child, such child shall be dealt with under the provisions of the Juvenile Justice (Care and Protection of Children) Act, 2000 (56 of 2000).

(2) If any question arises in any proceeding before the Special Court whether a person is a child or not, such question shall be determined by the Special Court after satisfying itself about the age of such person and it shall record in writing its reasons for such determination.

(3) No order made by the Special Court shall be deemed to be invalid merely by any subsequent proof that the age of a person as determined by it under sub-section (2) was not the correct age of that person.

35. Period for recording of evidence of child and disposal of case.—(1) The evidence of the child shall be recorded within a period of thirty days of the Special Court taking cognizance of the offence and reasons for delay, if any, shall be recorded by the Special Court.

(2) The Special Court shall complete the trial, as far as possible, within a period of one year from the date of taking cognizance of the offence.

36. Child not to see accused at the time of testifying.—(1) The Special Court shall ensure that the child is not exposed in any way to the accused at the time of recording of the evidence, while at the same time ensuring that the accused is in a position to hear the statement of the child and communicate with his advocate.

(2) For the purposes of sub-section (1), the Special Court may record the statement of a child through video conferencing or by utilising single visibility mirrors or curtains or any other device.

COMMENTS

(Based on Notes on Clauses of the Bill)

This section makes provision for the child not to see the accused at the time of testifying. It casts upon the Special Court a duty to ensure that the child is not exposed in any way to the accused at the time of recording of the evidence, while at the same time ensuring that the accused is in a position to hear the statement of the child and to communicate with his advocate. It empowers the Special Court to record the statement of a child through video conferencing or by utilizing single visibility mirrors or curtains or any other such device.

37. Trials to be conducted *in camera*.—The Special Court shall try cases *in camera* and in the presence of the parents of the child or any other person in whom the child has trust or confidence:

Provided that where the Special Court is of the opinion that the child needs to be examined at a place other than the court, it shall proceed to issue a commission in accordance with the provisions of section 284 of the Code of Criminal Procedure, 1973 (2 of 1974).

38. Assistance of an interpreter or expert while recording evidence of child.—(1) Wherever necessary, the Court may take the assistance of a translator or interpreter having such qualifications, experience and on payment of such fees as may be prescribed, while recording the evidence of the child.

(2) If a child has a mental or physical disability, the Special Court may take the assistance of a special educator or any person familiar with the manner of communication of the child or an expert in that field, having such qualifications, experience and on payment of such fees as may be prescribed to record the evidence of the child.

CHAPTER IX

MISCELLANEOUS

39. Guidelines for child to take assistance of experts, etc.—Subject to such rules as may be made in this behalf, the State Government shall prepare guidelines for use of non-governmental organisations, professionals and experts or persons having knowledge of psychology, social work, physical health, mental health and child development to be associated with the pre-trial and trial stage to assist the child.

40. Right of child to take assistance of legal practitioner.—Subject to the proviso to section 301 of the Code of Criminal Procedure, 1973 (2 of 1974) the family or the guardian of the child shall be entitled to the assistance of a legal counsel of their choice for any offence under this Act:

Provided that if the family or the guardian of the child are unable to afford a legal counsel, the Legal Services Authority shall provide a lawyer to them.

41. Provisions of sections 3 to 13 not to apply in certain cases.—The provisions of sections 3 to 13 (both inclusive) shall not apply in case of medical examination or medical treatment of a child when such medical examination or medical treatment is undertaken with the consent of his parents or guardian.

[1][**42. Alternate punishment.**—Where an act or omission constitutes an offence punishable under this Act and also under sections 166A, 354A, 354B, 354C, 354D, 370, 370A, 375, 376, 376A, 376C, 376D, 376E or section 509 of the Indian Penal Code (45 of 1860), then, notwithstanding anything contained in any law for the time being in force, the offender found guilty of such offence shall be liable to punishment under this Act or under the Indian Penal Code as provides for punishment which is greater in degree.]

[2][**42A. Act not in derogation of any other law.**—The provisions of this Act shall be in addition to and not in derogation of the provisions of any other law for the time being in force and, in case of any inconsistency, the provisions of this Act shall have overriding effect on the provisions of any such law to the extent of the inconsistency.]

43. Public awareness about Act.—The Central Government and every State Government, shall take all measures to ensure that—

(a) the provisions of this Act are given wide publicity through media including the television, radio and the print media at regular intervals to make the general public, children as well as their parents and guardians aware of the provisions of this Act;

(b) the officers of the Central Government and the State Governments and other concerned persons (including the police officers) are imparted periodic training on the matters relating to the implementation of the provisions of the Act.

44. Monitoring of implementation of Act.—(1) The National Commission for Protection of Child Rights constituted under section 3, or as the case may be, the State Commission for Protection of Child Rights constituted under section 17, of the Commissions for Protection of Child Rights Act, 2005 (4 of 2006), shall, in addition to the functions assigned to them under that Act, also monitor the implementation of the provisions of this Act in such manner as may be prescribed.

(2) The National Commission or, as the case may be, the State Commission, referred to in sub-section (1), shall, while inquiring into any matter relating to any offence under this Act, have the same powers as are vested in it under the Commissions for Protection of Child Rights Act, 2005 (4 of 2006).

---

1. Subs. by Act 13 of 2013, sec. 29, for section 42 (w.r.e.f. 3-2-2013). Section 42, before substitution, stood as under:

   "42. *Alternative punishment.*—Where an act or omission constitute an offence punishable under this Act and also under any other law for the time being in force, then, notwithstanding anything contained in any law for the time being in force, the offender found guilty of such offence shall be liable to punishment only under such law or this Act as provides for punishment which is greater in degree.".

2. Subs. by Act 13 of 2013, sec. 29, for section 42 (w.r.e.f. 3-2-2013).

(3) The National Commission or, as the case may be, the State Commission, referred to in sub-section (1), shall, also include, its activities under this section, in the annual report referred to in section 16 of the Commissions for Protection of Child Rights Act, 2005 (4 of 2006).

45. Power to make rules.—(1) The Central Government may, by notification in the Official Gazette, make rules for carrying out the purposes of this Act.

(2) In particular, and without prejudice to the generality of the foregoing powers, such rules may provide for all or any of the following matters, namely:—

(a) the qualifications and experience of, and the fees payable to, a translator or an interpreter, a special educator or any person familiar with the manner of communication of the child or an expert in that field, under sub-section (4) of section 19; sub-sections (2) and (3) of section 26 and section 38;

(b) care and protection and emergency medical treatment of the child under sub-section (5) of section 19;

(c) the payment of compensation under sub-section (8) of section 33;

(d) the manner of periodic monitoring of the provisions of the Act under sub-section (1) of section 44.

(3) Every rule made under this section shall be laid, as soon as may be after it is made, before each House of Parliament, while it is in session, for a total period of thirty days which may be comprised in one session or in two or more successive sessions, and if, before the expiry of the session immediately following the session or the successive sessions aforesaid, both Houses agree in making any modification in the rule or both Houses agree that the rule should not be made, the rule shall thereafter have effect only in such modified form or be of no effect, as the case may be; so, however, that any such modification or annulment shall be without prejudice to the validity of anything previously done under that rule.

46. Power to remove difficulties.—(1) If any difficulty arises in giving effect to the provisions of this Act, the Central Government may, by order published in the Official Gazette, make such provisions not inconsistent with the provisions of this Act as may appear to it to be necessary or expedient for removal of the difficulty:

Provided that no order shall be made under this section after the expiry of the period of two years from the commencement of this Act.

(2) Every order made under this section shall be laid, as soon as may be after it is made, before each House of Parliament.

THE SCHEDULE

[*See* section 2(c)]

ARMED FORCES AND SECURITY FORCES CONSTITUTED UNDER

(a) The Air Force Act, 1950 (45 of 1950);

(b) The Army Act, 1950 (46 of 1950);

(c) The Assam Rifles Act, 2006 (47 of 2006);

(d) The Bombay Home Guard Act, 1947 (3 of 1947);

(e) The Border Security Force Act, 1968 (47 of 1968);

(f) The Central Industrial Security Force Act, 1968 (50 of 1968);

(g) The Central Reserve Police Force Act, 1949 (66 of 1949);

(h) The Coast Guard Act, 1978 (30 of 1978);

(i) The Delhi Special Police Establishment Act, 1946 (25 of 1946);

(j) The Indo-Tibetan Border Police Force Act, 1992 (35 of 1992);

(k) The Navy Act, 1957 (62 of 1957);

(l) The National Investigation Agency Act, 2008 (34 of 2008);

(m) The National Security Guard Act, 1986 (47 of 1986);

(n) The Railway Protection Force Act, 1957 (23 of 1957);

(o) The Sashastra Seema Bal Act, 2007 (53 of 2007);

(p) The Special Protection Group Act, 1988 (34 of 1988);

(q) The Territorial Army Act, 1948 (56 of 1948);

(r) The State police forces (including armed constabulary) constituted under the State laws to aid the civil powers of the State and empowered to employ force during internal disturbances or otherwise including armed forces as defined in clause (a) of section 2 of the Armed Forces (Special Powers) Act, 1958 (28 of 1958).

THE PROTECTION OF CHILDREN FROM SEXUAL OFFENCES RULES, 2012[1]

In exercise of the powers conferred by sub-section (1), read with clauses (a) to (d) of sub-section (2), of section 45 of the Protection of Children from Sexual Offences Act, 2012 (32 of 2012), the Central Government hereby makes the following rules, namely:—

1. Short title and commencement.—(1) These rules may be called the Protection of Children from Sexual Offences Rules, 2012.

(2) These rules shall come into force on the date[2] of their publication in the Official Gazette.

2. Definitions.—(1) In these rules, unless the context otherwise requires,—

(a) "Act" means the Protection of Children from Sexual Offences Act, 2012 (32 of 2012);

(b) "District Child Protection Unit" (DCPU) means the District Child Protection Unit established by the State Government under section 62A of the Juvenile Justice (Care and Protection of Children) Amendment Act, 2006;

(c) "Expert" means a person trained in mental health, medicine, child development or other related discipline, who may be required to facilitate communication with a child whose ability to communicate has been affected by trauma, disability or any other vulnerability;

(d) "Special educator" means a person trained in communication with children with special needs in a way that addresses the child's individual differences and needs, which include challenges with learning and communication, emotional and behavioural disorders, physical disabilities, and developmental disorders;

(e) "Person familiar with the manner of communication of the child" means a parent or family member of a child or a member of his shared household or any person in whom the child reposes trust and confidence, who is familiar with that child's unique manner of communication, and whose presence may be required for or be conducive to more effective communication with the child;

(f) "Support person" means a person assigned by a Child Welfare Committee, in accordance with sub-rule (8) of rule 4, to render assistance to the child through the process of investigation and trial, or any other person assisting the child in the pre-trial or trial process in respect of an offence under the Act;

(2) Words and expressions used and not defined in these rules but defined in the Act shall have the meanings respectively assigned to them under the Act.

3. Interpreters, translators and Special educators.—(1) In each district, the DCPU shall maintain a register with names, addresses and other contact details

1. *Vide* G.S.R. 823(E), dated 14th November, 2012, published in the Gazette of India, Extra., Pt. II, Sec. 3(i), dated 14th November, 2012.
2. Came into force on 14-11-2012.

of interpreters, translators and special educators for the purposes of the Act, and this register shall be made available to the Special Juvenile Police Unit (hereafter referred to as "SJPU"), local police, magistrate or Special Court, as and when required.

(2) The qualifications and experience of the interpreters, translators, Special educators, and experts, engaged for the purposes of sub-section (4) of section 19, sub-sections (3) and (4) of section 26 and section 38 of the Act, shall be as indicated in these rules.

(3) Where an interpreter, translator, or Special educator is engaged, otherwise than from the list maintained by the DCPU under sub-rule (1), the requirements prescribed under sub-rules (4) and (5) of this rule may be relaxed on evidence of relevant experience or formal education or training or demonstrated proof of fluency in the relevant languages by the interpreter, translator, or special educator, subject to the satisfaction of the DCPU, Special Court or other authority concerned.

(4) Interpreters and translators engaged under sub-rule (1) should have functional familiarity with language spoken by the child as well as the official language of the state, either by virtue of such language being his mother tongue or medium of instruction at school at least up to primary school level, or by the interpreter or translator having acquired knowledge of such language through his vocation, profession, or residence in the area where that language is spoken.

(5) Sign language interpreters, Special educators and experts entered in the register under sub-rule (1) should have relevant qualifications in sign language or special education, or in the case of an expert, in the relevant discipline, from a recognized University or an institution recognized by the Rehabilitation Council of India.

(6) Payment for the services of an interpreter, translator, Special educator or expert whose name is enrolled in the register maintained under sub-rule (1) or otherwise, shall be made by the State Government from the Fund maintained under section 61 of the Juvenile Justice Act, 2000, or from other funds placed at the disposal of the DCPU, at the rates determined by them, and on receipt of the requisition in such format as the State Government may prescribe in this behalf.

(7) Any preference expressed by the child at any stage after information is received under sub-section (1) of section 19 of the Act, as to the gender of the interpreter, translator, Special educator, or expert, may be taken into consideration, and where necessary, more than one such person may be engaged in order to facilitate communication with the child.

(8) The interpreter, translator, Special educator, expert, or person familiar with the manner of communication of the child engaged to provide services for the purposes of the Act shall be unbiased and impartial and shall disclose any real or perceived conflict of interest. He shall render a complete and accurate interpretation or translation without any additions or omissions, in accordance with section 282 of the Code of Criminal Procedure, 1973.

(9) In proceedings under section 38, the Special Court shall ascertain whether the child speaks the language of the court adequately, and that the engagement of

any interpreter, translator, Special educator, expert or other person familiar with the manner of communication of the child, who has been engaged to facilitate communication with the child, does not involve any conflict of interest.

(10) Any interpreter, translator, Special educator or expert appointed under the provisions of the Act or its rules shall be bound by the rules of confidentiality, as described under section 127 read with section 126 of the Indian Evidence Act, 1872.

4. Care and Protection.—(1) Where an SJPU or the local police receives any information under sub-section (1) of section 19 of the Act from any person including the child, the SJPU or local police receiving report of such information shall forthwith disclose to the person making the report, the following details:—

(i) his name and designation;

(ii) the address and telephone number;

(iii) the name, designation and contact details of the officer who supervises the officer receiving the information.

(2) Where an SJPU or the local police, as the case may be, receives information in accordance with the provisions contained under sub-section (1) of section 19 of the Act in respect of an offence that has been committed or attempted or is likely to be committed, the authority concerned shall, where applicable,—

(a) proceed to record and register a First Information Report as per the provisions of section 154 of the Code of Criminal Procedure, 1973, and furnish a copy thereof free of cost to the person making such report, as per sub-section (2) of section 154 of the Code;

(b) where the child needs emergency medical care as described under sub-section (5) of section 19 of the Act or under these rules, arrange for the child to access such care, in accordance with rule 5;

(c) take the child to the hospital for the medical examination in accordance with section 27 of the Act;

(d) ensure that the samples collected for the purposes of the forensic tests are sent to the forensic laboratory at the earliest;

(e) inform the child and his parent or guardian or other person in whom the child has trust and confidence of the availability of support services including counselling, and assist them in contacting the persons who are responsible for providing these services and relief;

(f) inform the child and his parent or guardian or other person in whom the child has trust and confidence as to the right of the child to legal advice and counsel and the right to be represented by a lawyer, in accordance with section 40 of the Act.

(3) Where the SJPU or the local police receives information under sub-section (1) of section 19 of the Act, and has a reasonable apprehension that the offence has been committed or attempted or is likely to be committed by a person living in the same or shared household with the child, or the child is living in a child care institution and is without parental support, or the child is found to be

without any home and parental support, the concerned SJPU, or the local police shall produce the child before the concerned Child Welfare Committee (hereafter referred to as "CWC") within 24 hours of receipt of such report, together with reasons in writing as to whether the child is in need of care and protection under sub-section (5) of section 19 of the Act, and with a request for a detailed assessment by the CWC.

(4) Upon receipt of a report under sub-rule (3), the concerned CWC must proceed, in accordance with its powers under sub-section (1) of section 31 of the Juvenile Justice Act, 2000, to make a determination within three days, either on its own or with the assistance of a social worker, as to whether the child needs to be taken out of the custody of his family or shared household and placed in a children's home or a shelter home.

(5) In making determination under sub-rule (4), the CWC shall take into account any preference or opinion expressed by the child on the matter, together with the best interests of the child, having regard to the following considerations:

- (i) the capacity of the parents, or of either parent, or of any other person in whom the child has trust and confidence, to provide for the immediate care and protection needs of the child, including medical needs and counselling;
- (ii) the need for the child to remain in the care of his parent, family and extended family and to maintain a connection with them;
- (iii) the child's age and level of maturity, gender, and social and economic background;
- (iv) disability of the child, if any;
- (v) any chronic illness from which a child may suffer;
- (vi) any history of family violence involving the child or a family member of the child; and,
- (vii) any other relevant factors that may have a bearing on the best interests of the child:

Provided that prior to making such determination, an inquiry shall be conducted in such a way that the child is not unnecessarily exposed to injury or inconvenience.

(6) The child and his parent or guardian or any other person in whom the child has trust and confidence and with whom the child has been living, who is affected by such determination, shall be informed that such determination is being considered.

(7) The CWC, on receiving a report under sub-section (6) of section 19 of the Act or on the basis of its assessment under sub-rule (5), and with the consent of the child and his parent or guardian or other person in whom the child has trust and confidence, may provide a support person to render assistance to the child through the process of investigation and trial. Such support person may be a person or organisation working in the field of child rights or child protection, or an official of a children's home or shelter home having custody of the child, or a person employed by the DCPU:

Provided that nothing in these rules shall prevent the child and his parents or guardian or other person in whom the child has trust and confidence from seeking the assistance of any person or organisation for proceedings under the Act.

(8) The support person shall at all times maintain the confidentiality of all information pertaining to the child to which he has access. He shall keep the child and his parent or guardian or other person in whom the child has trust and confidence, informed as to the proceedings of the case, including available assistance, judicial procedures, and potential outcomes. He shall also inform the child of the role he may play in the judicial process and ensure that any concerns that the child may have, regarding his safety in relation to the accused and the manner in which he would like to provide his testimony, are conveyed to the relevant authorities.

(9) Where a support person has been provided to the child, the SJPU or the local police shall, within 24 hours of making such assignment, inform the Special Court in writing.

(10) The services of the support person may be terminated by the CWC upon request by the child and his parent or guardian or person in whom the child has trust and confidence, and the child requesting the termination shall not be required to assign any reason for such request. The Special Court shall be given in writing such information.

(11) It shall be the responsibility of the SJPU, or the local police to keep the child and his parent or guardian or other person in whom the child has trust and confidence, and where a support person has been assigned, such person, informed about the developments, including the arrest of the accused, applications filed and other court proceedings.

(12) The information to be provided by the SJPU, local police, or support person, to the child and his parents or guardian or other person in whom the child has trust and confidence, includes but is not limited to the following:—

(i) the availability of public and private emergency and crisis services;

(ii) the procedural steps involved in a criminal prosecution;

(iii) the availability of victims' compensation benefits;

(iv) the status of the investigation of the crime, to the extent it is appropriate to inform the victim and to the extent that it will not interfere with the investigation;

(v) the arrest of a suspected offender;

(vi) the filing of charges against a suspected offender;

(vii) the schedule of court proceedings that the child is either required to attend or is entided to attend;

(viii) the bail, release or detention status of an offender or suspected offender;

(ix) the rendering of a verdict after trial; and

(x) the sentence imposed on an offender.

5. Emergency medical care.—(1) Where an officer of the SJPU, or the local police receives information under section 19 of the Act that an offence under the

Act has been committed, and is satisfied that the child against whom an offence has been committed is in need of urgent medical care and protection, he shall, as soon as possible, but not later than 24 hours of receiving such information, arrange to take such child to the nearest hospital or medical care facility centre for emergency medical care:

Provided that where an offence has been committed under sections 3, 5, 7 or 9 of the Act, the victim shall be referred to emergency medical care.

(2) Emergency medical care shall be rendered in such a manner as to protect the privacy of the child, and in the presence of the parent or guardian or any other person in whom the child has trust and confidence.

(3) No medical practitioner, hospital or other medical facility centre rendering emergency medical care to a child shall demand any legal or magisterial requisition or other documentation as a pre-requisite to rendering such care.

(4) The registered medical practitioner rendering emergency medical care shall attend to the needs of the child, including—

(i) treatment for cuts, bruises, and other injuries including genital injuries, if any;

(ii) treatment for exposure to sexually transmitted diseases (STDs) including prophylaxis for identified STDs;

(iii) treatment for exposure to Human Immunodeficiency Virus (HIV), including prophylaxis for HIV after necessary consultation with infectious disease experts;

(iv) possible pregnancy and emergency contraceptives should be discussed with the pubertal child and her parent or any other person in whom the child has trust and confidence; and,

(v) wherever necessary, a referral or consultation for mental or psychological health or other counselling should be made.

(5) Any forensic evidence collected in the course of rendering emergency medical care must be collected in accordance with section 27 of the Act.

6. Monitoring of implementation of the Act.—(1) The National Commission for the Protection of Child Rights (hereafter referred to as "NCPCR") or the State Commission for the Protection of Child Rights (hereafter referred to as "SCPCR"), as the case may be, shall in addition to the functions assigned to them under the Commissions for Protection of Child Rights Act, 2005, perform the following functions for implementation of the provisions of the Act—

(a) to monitor the designation of Special Courts by State Governments;

(b) to monitor the appointment of Public Prosecutors by State Governments;

(c) to monitor the formulation of the guidelines described in section 39 of the Act by the State Governments, for the use of non-governmental organisations, professionals and experts or persons having knowledge of psychology, social work, physical health, mental health and child development to be associated with the pre-trial and trial stage to assist the child, and to monitor the application of these guidelines;

(d) to monitor the designing and implementation of modules for training police personnel and other concerned persons, including officers of the Central and State Governments, for the effective discharge of their functions under the Act;

(e) to monitor and support the Central Government and State Governments for the dissemination of information relating to the provisions of the Act through media including the television, radio and print media at regular intervals, so as to make the general public, children as well as their parents and guardians aware of the provisions of the Act.

(2) The NCPCR or the SCPCR, as the case may be, may call for a report on any specific case of child sexual abuse falling within the jurisdiction of a CWC.

(3) The NCPCR or the SCPCR, as the case may be, may collect information and data on its own or from the relevant agencies regarding reported cases of sexual abuse and their disposal under the processes established under the Act, including information on the following:—

(i) number and details of offences reported under the Act;

(ii) whether the procedures prescribed under the Act and rules were followed, including those regarding timeframes;

(iii) details of arrangements for care and protection of victims of offences under this Act, including arrangements for emergency medical care and medical examination; and,

(iv) details regarding assessment of the need for care and protection of a child by the concerned CWC in any specific case.

(4) The NCPCR or the SCPCR, as the case may be, may use the information so collected to assess the implementation of the provisions of the Act. The report on monitoring of the Act shall be included in a separate chapter in the Annual Report of the NCPCR or the SCPCR.

7. Compensation.—(1) The Special Court may, in appropriate cases, on its own or on an application filed by or on behalf of the child, pass an order for interim compensation to meet the immediate needs of the child for relief or rehabilitation at any stage after registration of the First Information Report Such interim compensation paid to the child shall be adjusted against the final compensation, if any.

(2) The Special Court may, on its own or on an application filed by or on behalf of the victim, recommend the award of compensation where the accused is convicted, or where the case ends in acquittal or discharge, or the accused is not traced or identified, and in the opinion of the Special Court the child has suffered loss or injury as a result of that offence.

(3) Where the Special Court, under sub-section (8) of section 33 of the Act read with sub-sections (2) and (3) of section 357A of the Code of Criminal Procedure, makes a direction for the award of compensation to the victim, it shall take into account all relevant factors relating to the loss or injury caused to the victim, including the following:—

(i) type of abuse, gravity of the offence and the severity of the mental or physical harm or injury suffered by the child;

(ii) the expenditure incurred or likely to be incurred on his medical treatment for physical and/or mental health;

(iii) loss of educational opportunity as a consequence of the offence, including absence from school due to mental trauma, bodily injury, medical treatment, investigation and trial of the offence, or any other reason;

(iv) loss of employment as a result of the offence, including absence from place of employment due to mental trauma, bodily injury, medical treatment, investigation and trial of the offence, or any other reason;

(v) the relationship of the child to the offender, if any;

(vi) whether the abuse was a single isolated incidence or whether the abuse took place over a period of time;

(vii) whether the child became pregnant as a result of the offence;

(viii) whether the child contracted a sexually transmitted disease (STD) as a result of the offence;

(ix) whether the child contracted human immunodeficiency virus (HIV) as a result of the offence;

(x) any disability suffered by the child as a result of the offence;

(xi) financial condition of the child against whom the offence has been committed so as to determine his need for rehabilitation;

(xii) any other factor that the Special Court may consider to be relevant.

(4) The compensation awarded by the Special Court is to be paid by the State Government from the Victims Compensation Fund or other scheme or fund established by it for the purposes of compensating and rehabilitating victims under section 357A of the Code of Criminal Procedure or any other laws for the time being in force, or, where such fund or scheme does not exist, by the State Government.

(5) The State Government shall pay the compensation ordered by the Special Court within 30 days of receipt of such order.

(6) Nothing in these rules shall prevent a child or his parent or guardian or any other person in whom the child has trust and confidence from submitting an application for seeking relief under any other rules or scheme of the Central Government or State Government.

THE JUVENILE JUSTICE (CARE AND PROTECTION OF CHILDREN) ACT, 2000

INTRODUCTION

To provide for the care, protection, treatment, development and rehabilitation of neglected or delinquent juveniles and for the adjudication of certain matters relating to, and disposition of, delinquent juveniles the Juvenile Justice Act, 1986 (53 of 1986) was enacted by Parliament. Several provisions of the Constitution including clause (3) of article 15, clauses (e) and (f) of article 39, articles 45 and 47 also impose on the State a primary responsibility of ensuring that all the needs of children are met and that their basic human rights are fully protected. On 20th November, 1989 General Assembly of the United Nations adopted the Convention on the Rights of the Child wherein a set of standards to be adhered to by all State parties in securing the best interests of the child has been prescribed. The Convention emphasises social re-integration of child victims, to the extent possible, without resorting to judicial proceedings. The Government of India, having ratified the Convention, has found it expedient to re-enact the existing law relating to juveniles bearing in mind the standards prescribed in the Convention on the Rights of the Child, the United Nations Standard Minimum Rules for the Administration of Juvenile Justice, 1985 (The Beijing Rules), the United Nations Rules for the Protection of Juveniles Deprived of their Liberty (1990), and all other relevant international instruments. To achieve this objective the Juvenile Justice (Care and Protection of Children) Bill was introduced in the Parliament.

STATEMENT OF OBJECTS AND REASONS

A review of the working of the Juvenile Act, 1986 (53 of 1986) would indicate that much greater attention is required to be given to children in conflict with law or those in need of care and protection. The justice system as available for adults is not considered suitable for being applied to a juvenile or the child or any one on their behalf including the police, voluntary organisations, social workers, or parents and guardians, throughout the country. There is also an urgent need for creating adequate infrastructure necessary for the implementation of the proposed legislation with a larger involvement of informal systems specially the family, the voluntary organisations and the community.

2. In this context, the following further proposals have been made—

(i) to lay down the basic principles for administering justice to a juvenile or the child in the Bill;

(ii) to make the juvenile system meant for a juvenile or the child more appreciative of the developmental needs in comparison to criminal justice system as applicable to adults;

(iii) to bring the juvenile law in conformity with the United Convention on the Rights of the Child;

(iv) to prescribe a uniform age of eighteen years for both boys and girls;

(v) to ensure speedy disposal of cases by the authorities envisaged under this Bill regarding juvenile or the child within a time limit of four months;

(vi) to spell out the role of the State as a facilitator rather than doer by involving voluntary organisations and local bodies in the implementation of the proposed legislation;

(vii) to create special juvenile police units with a humane approach through sensitisation and training of police personnel;

(viii) to enable increased accessibility to a juvenile or the child by establishing Juvenile Justice Boards and Child Welfare Committees and Homes in each district or group of districts;

(ix) to minimise the stigma and in keeping with the developmental needs of the juvenile or the child, to separate the Bill into two parts—one for juveniles in conflict with law and the other for the juvenile or the child in need of care and protection;

(x) to provide for effective provisions and various alternatives for rehabilitation and social reintegration such as adoption, foster care, sponsorship and aftercare of abandoned, destitute, neglected and delinquent juvenile and child.

3. The Bill seeks to repeal and re-enact the Juvenile Justice Act, 1986 with a view to achieving the above objects.

ACT 56 OF 2000

The Juvenile Justice (Care and Protection of Children) Bill having been passed by both the Houses of Parliament received the assent of the President on 30th December, 2000. It came on the Statute Book as THE JUVENILE JUSTICE (CARE AND PROTECTION OF CHILDREN) ACT, 2000 (56 of 2000) (*Came into force on 1-4-2001*).

LIST OF AMENDING ACTS

1. The Juvenile Justice (Care and Protection of Children) Amendment Act, 2006 (33 of 2006) (w.e.f. 22-8-2006).
2. The Juvenile Justice (Care and Protection of Children) Amendment Act, 2011 (12 of 2011) (w.e.f. 1-1-2012).

THE JUVENILE JUSTICE (CARE AND PROTECTION OF CHILDREN) ACT, 2000

(56 of 2000)

[*30th December, 2000*]

An Act to consolidate and amend the law relating to juveniles in conflict with law and children in need of care and protection, by providing for proper care, protection and treatment by catering to their development needs, and by adopting a child-friendly approach in the adjudication and disposition of matters in the best interest of children and for their ultimate rehabilitation [1][*and for matters connected therewith or incidental thereto*].

WHEREAS the Constitution has, in several provisions, including clause (3) of article 15, clauses (e) and (f) of article 39, articles 45 and 47, impose on the State a primary responsibility of ensuring that all the needs of children are met and that their basic human rights are fully protected;

AND WHEREAS, the General Assembly of the United Nations has adopted the Convention on the Rights of the Child on the 20th November, 1989;

AND WHEREAS, the Convention on the Rights of the Child has prescribed a set of standards to be adhered to by all State parties in securing the best interests of the child;

AND WHEREAS, the Convention on the Rights of the Child emphasises social reintegration of child victims, to the extent possible, without resorting to judicial proceedings;

AND WHEREAS, the Government of India has ratified the Convention on the 11th December, 1992.

AND WHEREAS, it is expedient to re-enact the existing law relating to juveniles bearing in mind the standards prescribed in the Convention on the Rights of the Child, the United Nations Standard Minimum Rules for the Administration of Juvenile Justice, 1985 (the Beijing Rules), the United Nations Rules for the Protection of Juveniles Deprived of their Liberty (1990), and all other relevant international instruments.

BE it enacted by Parliament in the Fifty-first Year of the Republic of India as follows:—

CHAPTER I

PRELIMINARY

1. Short title, extent [2]**[, commencement and application].**—(1) This Act may be called the Juvenile Justice (Care and Protection of Children) Act, 2000.

(2) It extends to the whole of India except the State of Jammu and Kashmir.

---

1. Subs. by Act 33 of 2006, sec. 2, for "through various institutions established under this enactment" (w.e.f. 22-8-2006).
2. Subs. by Act 33 of 2006, sec. 3, for "and commencement" (w.e.f. 22-8-2006).

(3) It shall come into force on such date[1] as the Central Government may, by notification in the Official Gazette, appoint.

[2][(4) Notwithstanding anything contained in any other law for the time being in force, the provisions of this Act shall apply to all cases involving detention, prosecution, penalty or sentence of imprisonment of juveniles in conflict with law under any such law.]

COMMENTS

Effect

The Juvenile Act is intended to protect the juvenile from the rigours of a trial by a criminal court. It prohibits sentencing of a juvenile and committing him to prison. As its preamble suggests it seeks to adopt a child-friendly approach in the adjudication and disposition of matters in the best interest of children and for their ultimate rehabilitation; *Kallu* v. *State of Haryana*, AIR 2012 SC 3212: (2012) 8 SCC 34: JT 2012 (7) SC 417: (2012) 7 SCALE 404.

2. Definitions.—In this Act, unless the context otherwise requires,—

(a) "advisory board" means a Central or a State advisory board or a district and city level advisory board, as the case may be, constituted under section 62;

[3][(aa) "adoption" means the process through which the adopted child is permanently separated from his biological parents and become the legitimate child of his adoptive parents with all the rights, privileges and responsibilities that are attached to the relationship;]

(b) "begging" means—

(i) soliciting or receiving alms in a public place or entering into any private premises for the purpose of soliciting or receiving alms, whether under any pretence;

(ii) exposing or exhibiting with the object of obtaining or extorting alms, any sore, wound, injury, deformity or disease, whether of himself or of any other person or of an animal;

(c) "Board" means a Juvenile Justice Board constituted under section 4;

(d) "child in need of care and protection" means a child—

(i) who is found without any home or settled place or abode and without any ostensible means of subsistence,

[3][(ia) who is found begging, or who is either a street child or a working child,]

(ii) who resides with a person (whether a guardian of the child or not) and such person—

(a) has threatened to kill or injure the child and there is a reasonable likelihood of the threat being carried out, or

(b) has killed, abused or neglected some other child or children and there is a reasonable likelihood of the child in question being killed, abused or neglected by that person,

(iii) who is mentally or physically challenged or ill children or children suffering from terminal diseases or incurable diseases having no one to support or look after,

(iv) who has a parent or guardian and such parent or guardian is unfit or incapacitated to exercise control over the child,

---

1. Came into force on 1-4-2001, *vide* S.O. 177(E), dated 28th February, 2001, published in the Gazette of India, Extra., Pt. II, Sec. 3(ii), dated 28th February, 2001.
2. Ins. by Act 33 of 2006, sec. 3 (w.e.f. 22-8-2006).
3. Ins. by Act 33 of 2006, sec. 4 (w.e.f. 22-8-2006).

(v) who does not have parent and no one is willing to take care of or whose parents have abandoned [3][or surrendered] him or who is missing and run away child and whose parents cannot be found after reasonable injury,

(vi) who is being or is likely to be grossly abused, tortured or exploited for the purpose of sexual abuse or illegal acts,

(vii) who is found vulnerable and is likely to be inducted into drug abuse or trafficking,

(viii) who is being or is likely to be abused for unconscionable gains,

(ix) who is victim of any armed conflict, civil commotion or natural calamity;

(e) "children's home" means an institution established by a State Government or by voluntary organisation and certified by that Government under section 34;

(f) "Committee" means a Child Welfare Committee constituted under section 29;

(g) "competent authority" means in relation to children in need of care and protection a Committee and in relation to juveniles in conflict with law a Board;

(h) "fit institution" means a governmental or a registered non-governmental organisation or a voluntary organisation prepared to own the responsibility of a child and such organisation is found fit by the [1][State Government on the recommendation of the competent authority;]

(i) "fit person" means a person, being a social worker or any other person, who is prepared to own the responsibility of a child and is found fit by the competent authority to receive and take care of the child;

(j) "guardian", in relation to a child, means his natural guardian or any other person having the actual charge or control over the child and recognised by the competent authority as a guardian in course of proceedings before that authority;

(k) "juvenile" or "child" means a person who has not completed eighteenth year of age;

[2][(l) "juvenile in conflict with law" means a juvenile who is alleged to have committed an offence and has not completed eighteenth year of age as on the date of commission of such offence;]

[3][***]

(n) "narcotic drug" and "psychotropic substance" shall have the meanings respectively assigned to them in the Narcotic Drugs and Psychotropic Substances Act, 1985 (61 of 1985);

---

1. Subs. by Act 33 of 2006, sec. 4, for "competent authority" (w.e.f. 22-8-2006).
2. Subs. by Act 33 of 2006, sec. 4, for clause (l). Clause (l), before substitution, stood as under:

   '(l) "juvenile in conflict with law" means a juvenile who is alleged to have committed an offence;' (w.e.f. 22-8-2006).'.
3. Clause (m) omitted by Act 33 of 2006, sec. 4 (w.e.f. 22-8-2006). Clause (m), before omission stood as under:

   '(m) "local authority" means Panchayats at the village and Zila Parishad at the district level and shall also include a Municipal Committee or Corporation or a Cantonment Board or such other body legally entitled to function as local authority by the Government;'.

(o) "observation home" means a home established by a State Government or by a voluntary organisation and certified by that State Government under section 8 as an observation home for the juvenile in conflict with law;

(p) "offence" means an offence punishable under any law for the time being in force;

(q) "place of safety" means any place or institution (not being a police lock-up or jail), the person incharge of which is willing temporarily to receive and take care of the juvenile and which, in the opinion of the competent authority, may be a place of safety for the juvenile;

(r) "prescribed" means prescribed by rules made under this Act;

(s) "probation officer" means an officer appointed by the State Government as a probation officer under the Probation of Offenders Act, 1958 (20 of 1958);

(t) "public place" shall have the meaning assigned to it in the Immoral Traffic (Prevention) Act, 1956 (104 of 1956);

(u) "shelter home" means a home or a drop-in-centre set up under section 37;

(v) "special home" means an institution established by a State Government or by a voluntary organisation and certified by that Government under section 9;

(w) "special juvenile police unit" means a unit of the police force of a State designated for handling of juveniles or children under section 63;

(x) "State Government", in relation to a Union territory, means the Administrator of that Union territory appointed by the President under article 239 of the Constitution;

(y) all words and expressions used but not defined in this Act and defined in the Code of Criminal Procedure, 1973 (2 of 1974), shall have the meanings respectively assigned to them in that Code.

COMMENTS

Juvenile

(i) The court where the plea of juvenility is raised for the first time should always be guided by the objectives of the Act and be alive to the position that the beneficent and salutary provisions contained in the Act are not defeated by hyper-technical approach and the persons who are entitled to get benefits of the Act get such benefits. The Courts should not be unnecessarily influenced by any general impression that in schools the parents/guardians understate the age of their wards by one or two years for future benefits or that age determination by medical examination is not very precise. The matter should be considered *prima facie* on the touchstone of pre-ponderance of probability; *Abuzar Hossain* v. *State of West Bengal*, (2012) 10 SCC 489: JT 2012 (10) SC 454: (2012) 10 SCALE 101.

(ii) The date relevant for determining the age of the accused, who claims to be a juvenile, would be the date on which the offence had been committed and not the date or which he is produced before the competent authority or in the court; *Bhim* v. *State of West Bengal*, (2010) 12 SCALE 212.

3. Continuation of inquiry in respect of juvenile who has ceased to be a juvenile.—Where an inquiry has been initiated against a juvenile in conflict with law or a child in need of care and protection and during the course of such inquiry the juvenile or the child ceases to be such, then, notwithstanding anything contained in this Act or in any other law for the time being in force, the inquiry may be continued and orders may be made in respect of such person as if such person had continued to be a juvenile or a child.

CHAPTER II

JUVENILE IN CONFLICT WITH LAW

4. Juvenile Justice Board.—(1) Notwithstanding anything contained in the Code of Criminal Procedure, 1973 (2 of 1974), the State Government may, [1][within a period of one year from the date of commencement of the Juvenile Justice (Care and Protection of Children) Amendment Act, 2006, by notification in the Official Gazette, constitute for every district], one or more Juvenile Justice Boards for exercising the powers and discharging the duties conferred or imposed on such Boards in relation to juveniles in conflict with law under this Act.

(2) A Board shall consist of a Metropolitan Magistrate or a Judicial Magistrate of the first class, as the case may be, and two social workers of whom at least one shall be a woman, forming a Bench and every such Bench shall have the powers conferred by the Code of Criminal Procedure, 1973 (2 of 1974), on a Metropolitan Magistrate or, as the case may be, a Judicial Magistrate of the first class and the Magistrate on the Board shall be designated as the principal Magistrate.

(3) No Magistrate shall be appointed as a member of the Board unless he has special knowledge or training in child psychology or child welfare and no social worker shall be appointed as a member of the Board unless he has been actively involved in health, education, or welfare activities pertaining to children for at least seven years.

(4) The term of office of the members of the Board and the manner in which such member may resign shall be such as may be prescribed.

(5) The appointment of any member of the Board may be terminated after holding inquiry, by the Sate Government, if—

(i) he has been found guilty of misuse of power vested under this Act,

(ii) he has been convicted of an offence involving moral turpitude, and such conviction has not been reversed or he has not been granted full pardon in respect of such offence,

(iii) he fails to attend the proceedings of the Board for consecutive three months without any valid reason or he fails to attend less than three-fourth of the sittings in a year.

COMMENTS

The State Government has been authorised to constitute for a district or a group of districts one or more Juvenile Justice Boards for exercising the powers and discharging the duties, conferred or imposed on such Boards in relation to Juveniles in conflict with the law under this Act. The Board shall consist of a Metropolitan Magistrate or a Judicial Magistrate of the first class, as the case may be, and two social workers of whom at least one shall be a woman.

5. Procedure, etc., in relation to Board.—(1) The Board shall meet at such times and shall observe such rules of procedure in regard to the transaction of business at its meetings, as may be prescribed.

(2) A child in conflict with law may be produced before an individual member of the Board, when the Board is not sitting.

(3) A Board may act notwithstanding the absence of any member of the Board, and no order made by the Board shall be invalid by reason only of the absence of any member during any stage of proceedings:

Provided that there shall be at least two members including the principal Magistrate present at the time of final disposal of the case.

1. Subs. by Act 33 of 2006, sec. 6, for "by notification in the Official Gazette, constitute for a district or a group of districts specified in the notification" (w.e.f. 22-8-2006).

(4) In the event of any difference of opinion among the members of the Board in the interim or final disposition, the opinion of the majority shall prevail, but where there is no such majority, the opinion of the principal Magistrate shall prevail.

COMMENTS

A child in conflict with law can be produced before an individual member of the Board, when the Board is not sitting.

6. Powers of Juvenile Justice Board.—(1) Where a Board has been constituted for any district [1][***], such Board shall, notwithstanding anything contained in any other law for the time being in force but save as otherwise expressly provided in this Act, have power to deal exclusively with all proceedings under this Act relating to juvenile in conflict with law.

(2) The powers conferred on the Board by or under this Act may also be exercised by the High Court and the Court of Session, when the proceeding comes before them in appeal, revision or otherwise.

7. Procedure to be followed by a Magistrate not empowered under the Act.—(1) When any Magistrate not empowered to exercise the powers of a Board under this Act is of the opinion that a person brought before him under any of the provisions of this Act (other than for the purpose of giving evidence), is a juvenile or the child, he shall without any delay record such opinion and forward the juvenile or the child and the record of the proceeding to the competent authority having jurisdiction over the proceeding.

(2) The competent authority to which the proceeding is forwarded under sub-section (1) shall hold the inquiry as if the juvenile or the child had originally been brought before it.

[2][**7A. Procedure to be followed when claim of juvenility is raised before any court.**—(1) Whenever a claim of juvenility is raised before any court or a court is of the opinion that an accused person was a juvenile on the date of commission of the offence, the court shall make an inquiry, take such evidence as may be necessary (but not an affidavit) so as to determine the age of such person, and shall record a finding whether the person is a juvenile or a child or not, stating his age as nearly as may be:

Provided that a claim of juvenility may be raised before any court and it shall be recognised at any stage, even after final disposal of the case, and such claim shall be determined in terms of the provisions contained in this Act and the rules made thereunder, even if the juvenile has ceased to be so on or before the date of commencement of this Act.

(2) If the court finds a person to be a juvenile on the date of commission of the offence under sub-section (1), it shall forward the juvenile to the Board for passing appropriate orders and the sentence, if any, passed by a court shall be deemed to have no effect.]

COMMENTS

Claim of Juvenility

In case, exact assessment of the age cannot be done, then the court, for reasons to be recorded, may, if considered necessary, give the benefit to the child or juvenile by considering his or her age on lower side within the margin of one year; *Ashwini Kumar Saxena* v. *State of Madhya Pradesh*, JT 2012 (10) SC 529: (2012) 9 SCALE 90: 2012 Cr LJ 4731.

1. The words "or a group of districts" omitted by Act 33 of 2006, sec. 7 (w.e.f. 22-8-2006).
2. Ins. by Act 33 of 2006, sec. 8 (w.e.f. 22-8-2006).

Scope

Section 7A of the Act gives right to an accused to raise question of juvenility at any point of time and if such an issue is raised, the court is under an obligation to make an inquiry and deal with the question; *Anil Agarwala* v. *State of West Bengal*, (2011) 2 SCALE 429.

8. Observation homes.—(1) Any State Government may establish and maintain either by itself or under an agreement with voluntary organisations, observation homes in every district or a group of districts, as may be required for the temporary reception of any juvenile in conflict with law during the pendency of any inquiry regarding them under this Act.

(2) Where the State Government is of opinion that any institution other than a home established or maintained under sub-section (1), is fit for the temporary reception of juvenile in conflict with law during the pendency of any inquiry regarding them under this Act, it may certify such institution as an observation home for the purposes of this Act.

(3) The State Government may, by rules made under this Act, provide for the management of observation homes, including the standards and various types of services to be provided by them for rehabilitation and social integration of a juvenile, and the circumstances under which, and the manner in which, the certification of an observation home may be granted or withdrawn.

(4) Every juvenile who is not placed under the charge of parent or guardian and is sent to an observation home shall be initially kept in a reception unit of the observation home for preliminary inquiries, care and classification for juveniles according to his age group, such as seven to twelve years, twelve to sixteen years and sixteen to eighteen years, giving due considerations to physical and mental status and degree of the offence committed, for further induction into observation home.

COMMENTS

State Governments have been empowered to establish and maintain either by themselves or under an agreement with voluntary organisations, observation homes in every district or a group of districts, as may be required for the temporary reception of any juvenile in conflict with law during the pendency of any inquiry regarding them. State Governments have also been empowered to certify any institution, other than a home established or maintained by themselves or under an agreement with voluntary organisations, as an observation home for the purposes of this Act.

9. Special homes.—(1) Any State Government may establish and maintain either by itself or under an agreement with voluntary organisations, special homes in every district or a group of districts, as may be required for reception and rehabilitation of juvenile in conflict with law under this Act.

(2) Where the State Government is of opinion that any institution other than a home established or maintained under sub-section (1), is fit for the reception of juvenile in conflict with law to be sent there under this Act, it may certify such institution as a special home for the purposes of this Act.

(3) The State Government may, by rules made under this Act, provide for the management of special homes, including the standards and various types of services to be provided by them which are necessary for re-socialisation of a juvenile, and the circumstances under which, and the manner in which, the certification of a special home may be granted or withdrawn.

(4) The rules made under sub-section (3) may also provide for the classification and separation of juvenile in conflict with law on the basis of age and the nature of offences committed by them and his mental and physical status.

COMMENTS

State Governments have been empowered to establish and maintain, either by themselves or under an agreement with voluntary organisations, special homes in every district or a group of districts for the reception and rehabilitation of juvenile in conflict with law. State Governments have also been empowered to certify any institution, other than a home established or maintained by themselves or under an agreement with voluntary organisations, that it is fit for the reception of juvenile in conflict with law.

10. Apprehension of juvenile in conflict with law.—[1][(1) As soon as a juvenile in conflict with law is apprehended by police, he shall be placed under the charge of the special juvenile police unit or the designated police officer, who shall produce the juvenile before the Board without any loss of time but within a period of twenty-four hours of his apprehension excluding the time necessary for the journey, from the place where the juvenile was apprehended, to the Board:

Provided that in no case, a juvenile in conflict with law shall be placed in a police lockup or lodged in a jail.]

(2) The State Government may make rules consistent with this Act,—

(i) to provide for persons through whom (including registered voluntary organisations) any juvenile in conflict with law may be produced before the Board;

(ii) to provide the manner in which such juvenile may be sent to an observation home.

COMMENTS

When a juvenile in conflict with law is apprehended by police, he has to be placed under the charge of the special juvenile police unit or the designated police officer who shall immediately report the matter to a member of the Board.

11. Control of custodian over juvenile.—Any person in whose charge a juvenile is placed in pursuance of this Act shall, while the order is in force have the control over the juvenile as he would have if he were his parents, and shall be responsible for his maintenance, and the juvenile shall continue in his charge for the period stated by competent authority, notwithstanding that he is claimed by his parents or any other person.

COMMENTS

When any juvenile is placed in the charge of a person he shall have the control over the juvenile as he would have if he were his parents, and shall be responsible for his maintenance and the juvenile shall continue in his charge for the period stated by the competent authority.

12. Bail of juvenile.—(1) When any person accused of a bailable or non-bailable offence, and apparently a juvenile, is arrested or detained or appears or

1. Subs. by Act 33 of 2006, sec. 9, for sub-section (1) (w.e.f. 22-8-2006). Sub-section (1), before substitution, stood as under:

"(1) As soon as a juvenile in conflict with law is apprehended by police, he shall be placed under the charge of the special juvenile police unit or the designated police officer who shall immediately report the matter to a member of the Board.".

is brought before a Board, such person shall, notwithstanding anything contained in the Code of Criminal Procedure, 1973 (2 of 1974) or in any other law for the time being in force, be released on bail with or without surety [1][or placed under the supervision of a Probation Officer or under the care of any fit institution or fit person] but he shall not be so released if there appear reasonable grounds for believing that the release is likely to bring him into association with any known criminal or expose him to moral, physical or psychological danger or that his release would defeat the ends of justice.

(2) When such person having been arrested is not released on bail under sub-section (1) by the officer incharge of the police station, such officer shall cause him to be kept only in an observation home in the prescribed manner until he can be brought before a Board.

(3) When such person is not released on bail under sub-section (1) by the Board it shall, instead of committing him to prison, make an order sending him to an observation home or a place of safety for such period during the pendency of the inquiry regarding him as may be specified in the order.

13. Information to parent, guardian or probation officer.—Where a juvenile is arrested, the officer incharge of the police station or the special juvenile police unit to which the juvenile is brought shall, as soon as may be after the arrest, inform—

(a) the parent or guardian of the juvenile, if he can be found of such arrest and direct him to be present at the Board before which the juvenile will appear; and

(b) the probation officer of such arrest to enable him to obtain information regarding the antecedents and family background of the juvenile and other material circumstances likely to be of assistance to the Board for making the inquiry.

COMMENTS

When any juvenile is arrested, the officer in charge of the police station or the special juvenile police unit to which the juvenile is brought, as soon as may be after the arrest, has to inform the parent or guardian of the juvenile about his arrest and direct him to be present at the Board before which the juvenile will appear and he has also to inform the probation officer of such arrest to enable him to obtain information regarding the antecedents and family background of the juvenile.

14. Inquiry by Board regarding juvenile.—[2][(1)] Where a juvenile having been charged with the offence is produced before a Board, the Board shall hold the inquiry in accordance with the provisions of this Act and may make such order in relation to the juvenile as it deems fit:

Provided that an inquiry under this section shall be completed within a period of four months from the date of its commencement, unless the period is extended by the Board having regard to the circumstances of the case and in special cases after recording the reasons in writing for such extension.

[3][(2) The Chief Judicial Magistrate or the Chief Metropolitan Magistrate shall review the pendency of cases of the Board at every six months, and shall direct

1. Ins. by Act 33 of 2006, sec. 10 (w.e.f. 22-8-2006).
2. Section 14 renumbered as sub-section (1) thereof by Act 33 of 2006, sec. 11 (w.e.f. 22-8-2006).
3. Ins. by Act 33 of 2006, sec. 11 (w.e.f. 22-8-2006).

the Board to increase the frequency of its sittings or may cause the constitution of additional Boards.]

15. Order that may be passed regarding juvenile.—(1) Where a Board is satisfied on inquiry that a juvenile has committed an offence, then, notwithstanding anything to the contrary contained in any other law for the time being in force, the Board may, if it so thinks fit,—

(a) allow the juvenile to go home after advice or admonition following appropriate inquiry against and counselling to the parent or the guardian and the juvenile;

(b) direct the juvenile to participate in group counselling and similar activities;

(c) order the juvenile to perform community service;

(d) order the parent of the juvenile or the juvenile himself to pay a fine, if he is over fourteen years of age and earns money;

(e) direct the juvenile to be released on probation of good conduct and placed under the care of any parent, guardian or other fit person, on such parent, guardian or other fit person executing a bond, with or without surety, as the Board may require, for the good behaviour and well-being of the juvenile for any period not exceeding three years;

(f) direct the juvenile to be released on probation of good conduct and placed under the care of any fit institution for the good behaviour and well-being of the juvenile for any period not exceeding three years;

[1][(g) make an order directing the juvenile to be sent to a special home for a period of three years:

Provided that the Board may, if it is satisfied that having regard to the nature of the offence and the circumstances of the case, it is expedient so to do, for reasons to be recorded, reduce the period of stay to such period as it thinks fit.]

(2) The Board shall obtain the social investigation report on juvenile either through a probation officer or a recognised voluntary organisation or otherwise, and shall take into consideration the findings of such report before passing an order.

(3) Where an order under clause (d), clause (e) or clause (f) of sub-section (1) is made, the Board may, if it is of opinion that in the interests of the juvenile and of the public, it is expedient so to do, in addition make an order that the juvenile in conflict with law shall remain under the supervision of a probation

1. Subs. by Act 33 of 2006, sec. 12, for clause (g) (w.e.f. 22-8-2006). Clause (g), before substitution, stood as under:

"(g) make an order directing the juvenile to be sent to a special home,—

(i) in the case of juvenile, over seventeen years but less than eighteen years of age for a period of not less than two years;

(ii) in case of any other juvenile for the period until he ceases to be a juvenile:

Provided that the Board may, if it is satisfied that having regard to the nature of the offence and the circumstances of the case it is expedient so to do, for reasons to be recorded, reduce the period of stay to such period as it thinks fit.".

officer named in the order during such period, not exceeding three years as may be specified therein, and may in such supervision order impose such conditions as it deems necessary for the due supervision of the juvenile in conflict with law:

Provided that if at any time afterwards it appears to the Board on receiving a report from the probation officer or otherwise, that the juvenile in conflict with law has not been of good behaviour during the period of supervision or that the fit institution under whose care the juvenile was placed is no longer able or willing to ensure the good behaviour and well-being of the juvenile it may, after making such inquiry as it deems fit, order the juvenile in conflict with law to be sent to a special home.

(4) The Board shall while making a supervision order under sub-section (3), explain to the juvenile and the parent, guardian or other fit person or fit institution, as the case may be, under whose care the juvenile has been placed, the terms and conditions of the order and shall forthwith furnish one copy of the supervision order to the juvenile, the parent, guardian or other fit person or fit institution, as the case may be, the sureties, if any, and the probation officer.

16. Order that may not be passed against juvenile.—(1) Notwithstanding anything to the contrary contained in any other law for the time being in force, no juvenile in conflict with law shall be sentenced to death [1][or imprisonment for any term which may extend to imprisonment for life], or committed to prison in default of payment of fine or in default of furnishing security:

Provided that where a juvenile who has attained the age of sixteen years has committed an offence and the Board is satisfied that the offence committed is so serious in nature or that his conduct and behaviour have been such that it would not be in his interest or in the interest of other juvenile in a special home to send him to such special home and that none of the other measures provided under this Act is suitable or sufficient, the Board may order the juvenile in conflict with law to be kept in such place of safety and in such manner as it thinks fit and shall report the case for the order of the State Government.

(2) On receipt of a report from a Board under sub-section (1), the State Government may make such arrangement in respect of the juvenile as it deems proper and may order such juvenile to be kept under protective custody at such place and on such conditions as it thinks fit:

[2][Provided that the period of detention so ordered shall not exceed in any case the maximum period provided under section 15 of this Act.]

17. Proceeding under Chapter VIII of the Code of Criminal Procedure not competent against juvenile.—Notwithstanding anything to the contrary contained in the Code of Criminal Procedure, 1973 (2 of 1974) no proceeding shall be instituted and no order shall be passed against the juvenile under

---

1. Subs. by Act 33 of 2006, sec. 13, for "or life imprisonment" (w.e.f. 22-8-2006).
2. Subs. by Act 33 of 2006, sec. 13, for the proviso (w.e.f. 22-8-2006). The proviso, before substitution, stood as under:

   "Provided that the period of detention so ordered shall not exceed the maximum period of imprisonment to which the juvenile could have been sentenced for the offence committed.".

Chapter VIII of the said Code.

18. No joint proceeding of juvenile and person not a juvenile.—(1) Notwithstanding anything contained in section 223 of the Code of Criminal Procedure, 1973 (2 of 1974) or in any other law for the time being in force, no juvenile shall be charged with or tried for any offence together with a person who is not a juvenile.

(2) If a juvenile is accused of an offence for which under section 223 of the Code of Criminal Procedure, 1973 (2 of 1974) or any other law for the time being in force, such juvenile and any person who is not a juvenile would, but for the prohibition contained in sub-section (1), have been charged and tried together, the Board taking cognizance of that offence shall direct separate trials of the juvenile and the other person.

COMMENTS

No juvenile can be charged with or tried for any offence together with a person who is not a juvenile.

19. Removal of disqualification attaching to conviction.—(1) Notwithstanding anything contained in any other law, a juvenile who has committed an offence and has been dealt with under the provisions of this Act shall not suffer disqualification, if any, attaching to a conviction of an offence under such law.

(2) The Board shall make an order directing that the relevant records of such conviction shall be removed after the expiry of the period of appeal or a reasonable period as prescribed under the rules, as the case may be.

20. Special provision in respect of pending cases.—Notwithstanding anything contained in this Act, all proceedings in respect of a juvenile pending in any court in any area on the date on which this Act comes into force in that area, shall be continued in that court as if this Act had not been passed and if the court finds that the juvenile has committed an offence, it shall record such finding and instead of passing any sentence in respect of the juvenile, forward the juvenile to the Board which shall pass orders in respect of that juvenile in accordance with the provisions of this Act as if it had been satisfied on inquiry under this Act that a juvenile has committed the offence:

[1][Provided that the Board may, for any adequate and special reason to be mentioned in the order, review the case and pass appropriate order in the interest of such juvenile.

Explanation.—In all pending cases including trial, revision, appeal or any other criminal proceedings in respect of a juvenile in conflict with law, in any court, the determination of juvenility of such a juvenile shall be in terms of clause (l) of section 2, even if the juvenile ceases to be so on or before the date of commencement of this Act and the provisions of this Act shall apply as if the said provisions had been in force, for all purposes and at all material times when the alleged offence was committed.]

COMMENTS

By virtue of *Explanation* to section 20, in all pending cases, which would include not only trials but even subsequent proceedings by way of revision or appeal, etc., the determination of juvenility of a juvenile has to be in terms of clause (l) of section 2, even if the juvenile ceases to be a juvenile on or before 1st April, 2001, when the Act of 2000 came into force, and the provisions of the Act would apply as if the said provision had been in force for all purposes and for all material times when the alleged offence was committed; *Dharambir* v. *State (NCT of Delhi)*, AIR 2010 SC 1801: (2010) 5 SCC 344: JT 2010 (6) SC 273.

[2][**21. Prohibition of publication of name, etc., of juvenile in conflict with law or child in need of care and protection involved in any proceeding under**

1. Ins. by Act 33 of 2006, sec. 14 (w.e.f. 22-8-2006).
2. Subs. by Act 33 of 2006, sec. 15, for section 21 (w.e.f. 22-8-2006). Section 21, before substitution, stood as under:

"21. *Prohibition of publication of name, etc., of juvenile involved in any proceeding under the Act.*—(1) No report in any newspaper, magazine, news-sheet or visual media

Contd. on next page

the Act.—(1) No report in any newspaper, magazine, news-sheet or visual media of any inquiry regarding a juvenile in conflict with law or a child in need of care and protection under this Act shall disclose the name, address or school or any other particulars calculated to lead to the identification of the juvenile or child nor shall any picture of any such juvenile or child be published:

Provided that for reasons to be recorded in writing, the authority holding the inquiry may permit such disclosure, if in its opinion such disclosure is in the interest of the juvenile or the child.

(2) Any person who contravenes the provisions of sub-section (1), shall be liable to a penalty which may extend to twenty five thousand rupees.]

COMMENTS

Newspapers, magazines, news-sheet or visual media have been prohibited to disclose the name, address or school or any other particulars calculated to lead to the identification of the juvenile in conflict with law nor they can publish any picture of such juvenile. Any person who contravenes this provision shall be punishable with fine upto one thousand rupees.

22. Provision in respect of escaped juvenile.—Notwithstanding anything to the contrary contained in any other law for the time being in force, any police officer may take charge without warrant of a juvenile in conflict with law who has escaped from a special home or an observation home or from the care of a person under whom he was placed under this Act, and shall be sent back to the special home or the observation home or that person, as the case may be; and no proceeding shall be instituted in respect of the juvenile by reason of such escape, but the special home, or the observation home or the person may, after giving the information to the Board which passed the order in respect of the juvenile, take such steps in respect of the juvenile as may be deemed necessary under the provisions of this Act.

23. Punishment for cruelty to juvenile or child.— Whoever, having the actual charge of, or control over, a juvenile or the child, assaults, abandons, exposes or wilfully neglects the juvenile or causes or procures him to be assaulted, abandoned, exposed or neglected in a manner likely to cause such juvenile or the child unnecessary mental or physical suffering shall be punishable with imprisonment for a term which may extend to six months, or fine, or with both.

COMMENTS

If any person having the actual charge of, or control over, a juvenile or the child, assaults, abandons, exposes or wilfully neglects the juvenile or causes or procures him to be assaulted, abandoned, exposed or neglected in any manner likely to cause such juvenile or the child unnecessary mental or physical suffering, he shall be punishable with imprisonment upto six months, or fine, or with both.

Contd. from previous page

of any inquiry regarding a juvenile in conflict with law under this Act shall disclose the name, address or school or any other particulars calculated to lead to the identification of the juvenile nor shall any picture of any such juvenile be published:

Provided that for reasons to be recorded in writing the authority holding the inquiry may permit such disclosure, if in its opinion such disclosure is in the interest of the juvenile.

(2) Any person contravening the provisions of sub-section (1) shall be punishable with fine, which may extend to one thousand rupees.".

24. Employment of juvenile or child for begging.—(1) Whoever employs or uses any juvenile or the child for the purpose or causes any juvenile to beg shall be punishable with imprisonment for a term which may extend to three years and shall also be liable to fine.

(2) Whoever, having the actual charge of, or control over, a juvenile or the child abets the commission of the offence punishable under sub-section (1), shall be punishable with imprisonment for a term which may extend to one year and shall also be liable to fine.

25. Penalty for giving intoxicating liquor or narcotic drug or psychotropic substance to juvenile or child.—Whoever gives, or causes to be given, to any juvenile or the child any intoxicating liquor in a public place or any narcotic drug or psychotropic substance except upon the order of duly qualified medical practitioner or in case of sickness shall be punishable with imprisonment for a term which may extend to three years and shall also be liable to fine.

26. Exploitation of juvenile or child employee.—Whoever ostensibly procures a juvenile or the child for the purpose of any hazardous employment keeps him in bondage and withholds his earnings or uses such earning for his own purposes shall be punishable with imprisonment for a term which may extend to three years and shall also be liable to fine.

27. Special offences.—The offences punishable under sections 23, 24, 25 and 26 shall be cognizable.

28. Alternative punishment.—Where an act or omission constitute an offence punishable under this Act and also under any other Central or State Act, then, notwithstanding anything contained in any law for the time being in force, the offender found guilty of such offences shall be liable to punishment only under such Act as provides for punishment which is greater in degree.

CHAPTER III

CHILD IN NEED OF CARE AND PROTECTION

29. Child Welfare Committee.—(1) The State Government may, [1][within a period of one year from the date of commencement of the Juvenile Justice (Care and Protection of Children) Amendment Act, 2006, by notification in the Official Gazette, constitute for every district], one or more Child Welfare Committees for exercising the powers and discharge the duties conferred on such Committees in relation to child in need of care and protection under this Act.

(2) The Committee shall consist of a Chairperson and four other members as the State Government may think fit to appoint, of whom at least one shall be a woman and another, an expert on matters concerning children.

(3) The qualifications of the Chairperson and the members, and the tenure for which they may be appointed shall be such as may be prescribed.

(4) The appointment of any member of the Committee may be terminated, after holding inquiry, by the State Government, if—

(i) he has been found guilty of misuse of power vested under this Act;

---

1. Subs. by Act 33 of 2006, sec. 16, for "by notification in Official Gazette, constitute for every district or group of districts specified in the notification" (w.e.f. 22-8-2006).

(ii) he has been convicted of an offence involving moral turpitude, and such conviction has not been reversed or he has not been granted full pardon in respect of such offence;

(iii) he fails to attend the proceedings of the Committee for consecutive three months without any valid reason or he fails to attend less than three-fourth of the sittings in a year.

(5) The Committee shall function as a Bench of Magistrates and shall have the powers conferred by the Code of Criminal Procedure, 1973 (2 of 1974) on a Metropolitan Magistrate or, as the case may be, a Judicial Magistrate of the first class.

COMMENTS

State Governments have been empowered to constitute for every district or group of districts one or more Child Welfare Committees for exercising the powers and discharge the duties in relation to child in need of care and protection under the Act. The Committee shall consist of a Chairperson and four other members, of whom at least one shall be a woman and another an expert on matters concerning children.

30. Procedure, etc., in relation to Committee.—(1) The Committee shall meet at such times and shall observe such rules of procedure in regard to the transaction of business at its meetings, as may be prescribed.

(2) A child in need of care and protection may be produced before an individual member for being placed in safe custody or otherwise when the Committee is not in session.

(3) In the event of any difference of opinion among the members of the Committee at the time of any interim decision, the opinion of the majority shall prevail but where there is no such majority the opinion of the Chairperson shall prevail.

(4) Subject to the provisions of sub-section (1), the Committee may act, notwithstanding the absence of any member of the Committee, and no order made by the Committee shall be invalid by reason only of the absence of any member during any stage of the proceeding.

31. Powers of Committee.—(1) The Committee shall have the final authority to dispose of cases for the care, protection, treatment, development and rehabilitation of the children as well as to provide for their basic needs and protection of human rights.

(2) Where a Committee has been constituted for any area, such Committee shall, notwithstanding anything contained in any other law for the time being in force but save as otherwise expressly provided in this Act, have the power to deal exclusively with all proceedings under this Act relating to children in need of care and protection.

32. Production before Committee.—(1) Any child in need of care and protection may be produced before the Committee by one of the following persons:—

(i) any police officer or special juvenile police unit or a designated police officer;

(ii) any public servant;

(iii) childline, a registered voluntary organisation or by such other voluntary organisation or an agency as may be recognised by the State Government;

(iv) any social worker or a public spirited citizen [1][***]; or

(v) by the child himself:

[2][Provided that the child shall be produced before the Committee without any loss of time but within a period of twenty-four hours excluding the time necessary for the journey.]

(2) The State Government may make rules consistent with this Act to provide for the manner of making the report [3][***] to the Committee and the manner of sending and entrusting the child to children's home pending the inquiry.

33. Inquiry.—(1) On receipt of a report under section 32, the Committee [4][***] shall hold an inquiry in the prescribed manner and the Committee, on its own or on the report from any person or agency as mentioned in sub-section (1) of section 32, may pass an order to send the child to the children's home for speedy inquiry by a social worker or child welfare officer.

(2) The inquiry under this section shall be completed within four months of the receipt of the order or within such shorter period as may be fixed by the Committee:

Provided that the time for the submission of the inquiry report may be extended by such period as the Committee may, having regard to the circumstances and for the reasons recorded in writing, determine.

[5][(3) The State Government shall review the pendency of cases of the Committee at every six months, and shall direct the Committee to increase the frequency of its sittings or may cause the constitution of additional Committees.

(4) After the completion of the inquiry, if, the Committee is of the opinion that the said child has no family or ostensible support or is in continued need of care and protection, it may allow the child to remain in the children's home or shelter home till suitable rehabilitation is found for him or till he attains the age of eighteen years.]

34. Children's homes.—(1) The State Government may establish and maintain either by itself or in association with the voluntary organisations, children's homes, in every district or group of districts, as the case may be,

---

1. The words "authorised by the State Government" omitted by Act 33 of 2006, sec. 17 (w.e.f. 22-8-2006).
2. Ins. by Act 33 of 2006, sec. 17 (w.e.f. 22-8-2006).
3. The words "to the Police and" omitted by Act 33 of 2006, sec. 17 (w.e.f. 22-8-2006).
4. The words "or any police officer or special juvenile police unit or the designated police officer" omitted by Act 33 of 2006, sec. 18 (w.e.f. 22-8-2006).
5. Subs. by Act 33 of 2006, sec. 18, for sub-section (3) (w.e.f. 22-8-2006). Sub-section (3), before substitution, stood as under:

   "(3) After the completion of the inquiry if the Committee is of the opinion that the said child has no family or ostensible support, it may allow the child to remain in the children's home or shelter home till suitable rehabilitation is found for him or till he attains the age of eighteen years.".

for the reception of child in need of care and protection during the pendency of any inquiry and subsequently for their care, treatment, education, training, development and rehabilitation.

(2) The State Government may, by rules made under this Act, provide for the management of children's homes including the standards and the nature of services to be provided by them, and the circumstances under which, and the manner in which, the certification of a children's home or recognition to a voluntary organisation may be granted or withdrawn.

[1][(3) Without prejudice to anything contained in any other law for the time being in force, all institutions, whether State Government run or those run by voluntary organizations for children in need of care and protection shall, within a period of six months from the date of commencement of the Juvenile Justice (Care and Protection of Children) Amendment Act, 2006, be registered under this Act in such manner as may be prescribed.]

COMMENTS

State Governments have been empowered to establish and maintain either by themselves or in association with the voluntary organisations, children's homes in every district or a group of districts for the reception of child in need of care and protection during the pendency of any inquiry and subsequently for their care, treatment, education, training, development and rehabilitation.

35. Inspection.—(1) The State Government may appoint inspection committees for the children's homes (hereinafter referred to as the inspection committees) for the State, a district and city, as the case may be, for such period and for such purposes as may be prescribed.

(2) The inspection committee of a State, district or of a city shall consist of such number of representatives from the State Government, [2][***], Committee, voluntary organisations and such other medical experts and social workers as may be prescribed.

36. Social auditing.—The Central Government or State Government may monitor and evaluate the functioning of the Children's homes at such period and through such persons and institutions as may be specified by that Government.

37. Shelter homes.—(1) The State Government may recognise, reputed and capable voluntary organisations and provide them assistance to set up and administer as many shelter homes for juveniles or children as may be required.

(2) The shelter homes referred in sub-section (1) shall function as drop-in-centres for the children in the need of urgent support who have been brought to such homes through such persons as are referred to in sub-section (1) of section 32.

(3) As far as possible, the shelter homes shall have such facilities as may be prescribed by the rules.

---

1. Ins. by Act 33 of 2006, sec. 19 (w.e.f. 22-8-2006).
2. The words "local authority" omitted by Act 33 of 2006, sec. 5 (w.e.f. 22-8-2006).

COMMENTS

State Governments have been empowered to recognise reputed and capable voluntary organisations and provide them assistance to set up and administer shelter homes for juveniles or children. These shelter homes shall function as drop-in-centres for the children in the need of urgent support.

38. Transfer.—(1) If during the inquiry it is found that the child hails from the place outside the jurisdiction of the Committee, the Committee shall order the transfer of the child to the competent authority having jurisdiction over the place of residence of the child.

(2) Such juvenile or the child shall be escorted by the staff of the home in which he is lodged originally.

(3) The State Government may make rules to provide for the travelling allowance to be paid to the child.

39. Restoration.—(1) Restoration of and protection to a child shall be the prime objective of any children's home or the shelter home.

(2) The children's home or a shelter home, as the case may be, shall take such steps as are considered necessary for the restoration of and protection to a child deprived of his family environment temporarily or permanently where such child is under the care and protection of a children's home or a shelter home, as the case may be.

(3) The Committee shall have the powers to restore any child in need of care and protection to his parent, guardian, fit person or fit institution, as the case may be, and give them suitable directions.

[1][*Explanation.*—For the purposes of this section "restoration of and protection of a child" means restoration to—

(a) parents;

(b) adopted parents;

(c) foster parents;

(d) guardian;

(e) fit person;

(f) fit institution.]

CHAPTER IV

REHABILITATION AND SOCIAL REINTEGRATION

40. Process of rehabilitation and social reintegration.—The rehabilitation and social reintegration of a child shall begin during the stay of the child in a children's home or special home and the rehabilitation and social reintegration of children shall be carried out alternatively by (i) adoption, (ii) foster care, (iii) sponsorship, and (iv) sending the child to an after-care organisation.

---

1. Subs. by Act 33 of 2006, sec. 20, for *Explanation* (w.e.f. 22-8-2006). *Explanation,* before substitution, stood as under:

"*Explanation.*—For the purposes of this section "restoration of child" means restoration to—

(a) parents;

(b) adopted parents;

(c) foster parents.".

41. Adoption.—(1) The primary responsibility for providing care and protection to children shall be that of his family.

[1][(2) Adoption shall be resorted to for the rehabilitation of the children who are orphan, abandoned or surrendered through such mechanism as may be prescribed.

(3) In keeping with the provisions of the various guidelines for adoption issued from time to time, by the State Government, or the Central Adoption Resource Agency and notified by the Central Government, children may be given in adoption by a court after satisfying itself regarding the investigations having been carried out as are required for giving such children in adoption.

(4) The State Government shall recognise one or more of its institutions or voluntary organisations in each district as specialised adoption agencies in such manner as may be prescribed for the placement of orphan, abandoned or surrendered children for adoption in accordance with the guidelines notified under sub-section (3):

Provided that the children's homes and the institutions run by the State Government or a voluntary organisation for children in need of care and protection, who are orphan, abandoned or surrendered, shall ensure that these children are declared free for adoption by the Committee and all such cases shall be referred to the adoption agency in that district for placement of such children in adoption in accordance with the guidelines notified under sub-section (3).]

(5) No child shall be offered for adoption—

(a) until two members of the Committee declare the child legally free for placement in the case of abandoned children,

(b) till the two months period for reconsideration by the parent is over in the case of surrendered children, and

(c) without his consent in the case of a child who can understand and express his consent.

[2][(6) The Court may allow a child to be given in adoption—

(a) to a person irrespective of marital status or;

(b) to parents to adopt a child of same sex irrespective of the number of living biological sons or daughters; or

(c) to childless couples.]

---

1. Subs. by Act 33 of 2006, sec. 21, for sub-sections (2), (3) and (4) (w.e.f. 22-8-2006). Sub-section (2), (3) and (4), before substitution, stood as under:

"(2) Adoption shall be resorted to for the rehabilitation of such children as are orphaned, abandoned, neglected and abused through institutional and non-institutional methods.

(3) In keeping with the provisions of the various guidelines for adoption issued from time to time by the State Government, the Board shall be empowered to give children in adoption and carry out such investigations as are required for giving children in adoption in accordance with the guidelines issued by the State Government from time to time in this regard.

(4) The childern's homes or the State Government run institutions for orphans shall be recognised as an adoption agencies both for scrutiny and placement of such children for adoption in accordance with the guidelines issued under sub-section (3).".

2. Subs. by Act 33 of 2006, sec. 21, for sub-section (6) (w.e.f. 22-8-2006). Sub-section (6), before substitution, stood as under:

"(6) The Board may allow a child to be given in adoption—

(a) to a single parent, and

(b) to parents to adopt a child of same sex irrespective of the number of living biological sons or daughters.".

42. Foster care.—(1) The foster care may be used for temporary placement of those infants who are ultimately to be given for adoption.

(2) In foster care, the child may be placed in another family for a short or extended period of time, depending upon the circumstances where the child's own parent usually visit regularly and eventually after the rehabilitation, where the children may return to their own homes.

(3) The State Government may make rules for the purposes of carrying out the scheme of foster care programme of children.

43. Sponsorship.—(1) The sponsorship programme may provide supplementary support to families, to children's homes and to special homes to meet medical, nutritional, educational and other needs of the children with a view to improving their quality of life.

(2) The State Government may make rules for the purposes of carrying out various schemes of sponsorship of children, such as individual to individual sponsorship, group sponsorship or community sponsorship.

44. After-care organisation.—The Sate Government may, by rules made under this Act, provide—

(a) for the establishment or recognition of after-care organisations and the functions that may be performed by them under this Act;

(b) for a scheme of after-care programme to be followed by such after-care organisations for the purpose of taking care of juveniles or the children after they leave special homes, children homes and for the purpose of enabling them to lead an honest, industrious and useful life;

(c) for the preparation or submission of a report by the probation officer or any other officer appointed by that Government in respect of each juvenile or the child prior to his discharge from a special home, children's home, regarding the necessity and nature of after-care of such juvenile or of a child, the period of such after-care, supervision thereof and for the submission of report by the probation officer or any other officer appointed for the purpose, on the progress of each juvenile or the child;

(d) for the standards and the nature of services to be maintained by such after care organisations;

(e) for such other matters as may be necessary for the purpose of carrying out the scheme of after-care programme for the juvenile or the child:

Provided that any rule made under this section shall not provide for such juvenile or child to stay in the after-care organisation for more than three years:

Provided further that a juvenile or child over seventeen years of age but less than eighteen years of age would stay in the after-care organisation till he attains the age of twenty years.

45. Linkages and co-ordination.—The State Government may make rules to ensure effective linkages between various governmental, non-governmental, corporate and other community agencies for facilitating the rehabilitation and social reintegration of the child.

CHAPTER V
MISCELLANEOUS

46. Attendance of parent or guardian of juvenile or child.—Any competent authority before which a juvenile or the child is brought under any of the provisions of this Act, may, whenever it so thinks fit, require any parent or guardian having the actual charge of or control over the juvenile or the child to be present at any proceeding in respect of the juvenile or the child.

47. Dispensing with attendance of juvenile or child.—If, at any stage during the course of an inquiry, a competent authority is satisfied that the attendance of the juvenile or the child is not essential for the purpose of inquiry, the competent authority may dispense with his attendance and proceed with the inquiry in the absence of the juvenile or the child.

48. Committal to approved place of juvenile or child suffering from dangerous diseases and his future disposal.—(1) When a juvenile or the child who has been brought before a competent authority under this Act, is found to be suffering from a disease requiring prolonged medical treatment or physical or mental complaint that will respond to treatment, the competent authority may send the juvenile or the child to any place recognised to be an approved place in accordance with the rules made under this Act for such period as it may think necessary for the required treatment.

[1][***]

49. Presumption and determination of age.—(1) Where it appears to a competent authority that person brought before it under any of the provisions of this Act (otherwise than for the purpose of giving evidence) is a juvenile or the child, the competent authority shall make due inquiry so as to the age of that person and for that purpose shall take such evidence as may be necessary (but not an affidavit) and shall record a finding whether the person is a juvenile or the child or not, stating his age as nearly as may be.

(2) No order of a competent authority shall be deemed to have become invalid merely by any subsequent proof that the person in respect of whom the order has been made is not a juvenile or the child, and the age recorded by the competent authority to be the age of person so brought before it, shall for the purpose of this Act, be deemed to be the true age of that person.

COMMENTS

The opening words of sub-section (1) of section 49 show that only when a person is "brought before the competent authority" under any of the provisions of the Act, the competent authority is required to make due enquiry as to the age of that person and for that purpose take such evidence as may be necessary and record a finding whether the person is a juvenile or not. Section 49 is, therefore, attracted when a person is brought before the competent authority and not otherwise; *Jabar Singh* v. *Dinesh,* (2010) 3 SCC 757: JT 2010 (2) SC 603: (2010) 2 SCALE 856.

50. Sending a juvenile or child outside jurisdiction.—In the case of a juvenile or the child, whose ordinary place of residence lies outside the jurisdiction of the competent authority before which he is brought, the competent authority may, if satisfied after due inquiry that it is expedient so to do, send the juvenile or the child back to a relative or other person who is fit and willing to receive him at his ordinary place of residence and exercise proper care and control over him, notwithstanding that such place of residence is outside the jurisdiction of the competent authority; and the competent authority exercising jurisdiction over the place to which the juvenile or the child is sent shall in respect of any matter arising subsequently have the same powers in relation to the juvenile or the child as if the original order had been passed by itself.

---

1. Sub-section (2) omitted by Act 12 of 2011, sec. 2 (w.e.f. 1-1-2012). Sub-section (2), before omission, stood as under:

 "(2) Where a juvenile or the child is found to be suffering from leprosy, sexually transmitted disease, Hepatitis B, open cases of Tuberculosis and such other diseases or is of unsound mind, he shall be dealt with separately through various specialised referral services or under the relevant laws as such.".

51. Reports to be treated as confidential.—The report of the probation officer or social worker considered by the competent authority shall be treated as confidential:

Provided that the competent authority may, if it so thinks fit, communicate the substance thereof to the juvenile or the child or his parent or guardian and may give such juvenile or the child, parent or guardian an opportunity of producing such evidence as may be relevant to the matter stated in the report.

52. Appeals.—(1) Subject to the provisions of this section, any person aggrieved by an order made by a competent authority under this Act may, within thirty days from the date of such order, prefer an appeal to the Court of Session:

Provided that the Court of Session may entertain the appeal after the expiry of the said period of thirty days if it is satisfied that the appellant was prevented by sufficient cause from filing the appeal in time.

(2) No appeal shall lie from—

(a) any order of acquittal made by the Board in respect of a juvenile alleged to have committed an offence; or

(b) any order made by a Committee in respect of a finding that a person is not a neglected juvenile.

(3) No second appeal shall lie from any order of the Court of Session passed in appeal under this section.

53. Revision.—The High Court may, at any time, either of its own motion or on an application received in this behalf, call for the record of any proceeding in which any competent authority or Court of Session has passed an order for the purpose of satisfying itself as to the legality or propriety of any such order and may pass such order in relation thereto as it thinks fit:

Provided that the High Court shall not pass an order under this section prejudicial to any person without giving him a reasonable opportunity of being heard.

54. Procedure in inquiries, appeals and revision proceedings.—(1) Save as otherwise expressly provided by this Act, a competent authority while holding any inquiry under any of the provisions of this Act, shall follow such procedure as may be prescribed and subject thereto, shall follow, as far as may be, the procedure laid down in the Code of Criminal Procedure, 1973 (2 of 1974) for trials in summons cases.

(2) Save as otherwise expressly provided by or under this Act, the procedure to be followed in hearing appeals or revision proceedings under this Act shall be, as far as practicable, in accordance with the provisions of the Code of Criminal Procedure, 1973 (2 of 1974) .

55. Power to amend orders.—(1) Without prejudice to the provisions for appeal and revision under this Act, any competent authority may, on an application received in this behalf, amend any order as to the institution to which a juvenile or the child is to be sent or as to the person under whose care or supervision a juvenile or the child is to be placed under this Act:

Provided that there shall be at least two members and the parties or its defence present during the course of hearing for passing an amendment in relation to any of its order.

(2) Clerical mistakes in orders passed by a competent authority or errors arising therein from any accidental slip or omission may, at any time, be corrected by the competent authority either on its own motion or on an application received in this behalf.

56. Power of competent authority to discharge and transfer juvenile or child.—The competent authority [1][***] may, notwithstanding anything contained

1. The words "or the local authority" omitted by Act 33 of 2006, sec. 5 (w.e.f. 22-8-2006).

in this Act, at any time, order a child in need of care and protection or a juvenile in conflict with law to be discharged or transferred from one children's home or special home to another, as the case may be, keeping in view the best interest of the child or the juvenile, and his natural place of stay, either absolutely or on such conditions as it may think fit to impose:

Provided that the total period of stay of the juvenile or the child in a childern's home or a special home or a fit institution or under a fit person shall not be increased by such transfer.

[1][**57. Transfer between children's homes, under the Act, and juvenile homes of like nature in different parts of India.**—The State Government may direct any child or the juvenile to be transferred from any children's home or special home within the State to any other children's home, special home or institution of a like nature or to such institutions outside the state in consultation with the concerned State Government and with the prior intimation to the Committee or the Board, as the case may be, and such order shall be deemed to be operative for the competent authority of the area to which the child or the juvenile is sent.]

[2][**58. Transfer of juvenile or child as are mentally ill or addicted to alcohol or other drugs.**—(1) Where it appears to the competent authority that any juvenile or child kept in a special home or an observation home or a children's home or a shelter home or in an institution in pursuance of this Act, is a mentally ill person or addicted to alcohol or other drugs which lead to behavioural changes in a person, the competent authority may order his removal to a psychiatric hospital or psychiatric nursing home in accordance with the provisions of the Mental Health Act, 1987 (14 of 1987) or the rules made thereunder.

(2) In case the juvenile or child had been removed to a psychiatric hospital or psychiatric nursing home under sub-section (1), the competent authority may, on the basis of the advice given in the certificate of discharge of the psychiatric hospital or psychiatric nursing home, order to remove such juvenile or child to an Integrated Rehabilitation Centre for Addicts or similar centres maintained by the State Government for mentally ill persons (including the persons addicted to any narcotic drug or psychotropic substance) and such removal shall be only for the period required for the in-patient treatment of such juvenile or child.

---

1. Subs. by Act 33 of 2006, sec. 22, for section 57 (w.e.f. 22-8-2006). Section 57, before substitution, stood as under:

   "*57. Transfer between children's homes, under the Act, and juvenile homes, of like nature in different parts of India.*—The State Government or the local authority may direct any child or the juvenile to be transferred from any children's home or special home outside the State to any other children's home, special home or institution of a like nature with the prior intimation to the local Committee or the Board, as the case may be, and such order shall be deemed to be operative for the competent authority of the area to which the child or the juvenile is sent.".

2. Subs. by Act 12 of 2011, sec. 3, for section 58 (w.e.f. 1-1-2012). Section 58, before substitution, stood as under:

   "*58. Transfer of juvenile or child of unsound mind or suffering from leprosy or addicted to drugs.*—Where it appears to the competent authority that any juvenile or the child kept in a special home or a children's home or shelter home or in an institution in pursuance of this Act, is suffering from leprosy or is of unsound mind or is addicted to any narcotic drug or psychotropic substance, the competent authority may order his removal to a leper asylum or mental hospital or treatment centre for drug addicts or to a place of safety for being kept there for such period not exceeding the period for which he is required to be kept under the order of the competent authority or for such further period as may be certified by the medical officer necessary for the proper treatment of the juvenile or the child.".

Explanation.—For the purposes of this sub-section,—

(a) "Integrated Rehabilitation Centre for Addicts" shall have the meaning assigned to it under the scheme called "Central Sector Scheme of Assistance for Prevention of Alcoholism and Substance (Drugs) Abuse and for Social Defence Services" made by the Government of India in the Ministry of Social Justice and Empowerment or any other corresponding scheme for the time being in force;

(b) "mentally ill person" shall have the meaning assigned to it in clause (l) of section 2 of the Mental Health Act, 1987 (14 of 1987);

(c) "psychiatric hospital" or "psychiatric nursing home" shall have the meaning assigned to it in clause (q) of section 2 of the Mental Health Act, 1987 (14 of 1987).]

59. Release and absence of juvenile or child on placement.—(1) When a juvenile or the child is kept in a children's home or special home and on a report of a probation officer or social worker or of Government or a voluntary organisation, as the case may be, the competent authority may consider, the release of such juvenile or the child permitting him to live with his parent or guardian or under the supervision of any authorised person named in the order, willing to receive and take charge of the juvenile or the child to educate and train him for some useful trade or calling or to look after him for rehabilitation.

(2) The competent authority may also permit leave of absence to any juvenile or the child, to allow him, on special occasions like examination, marriage of relatives, death of kith and kin or the accident or serious illness of parent or any emergency of like nature, to go on leave under supervision, [1][for a period generally not exceeding seven days], excluding the time taken in journey.

(3) Where a permission has been revoked or forfeited and the juvenile or the child refuses or fails to return to the home concerned or juvenile to which he was directed so to return, the Board may, if necessary, cause him to be taken charge of and to be taken back to the concerned home.

(4) The time during which a juvenile or the child is absent from a concerned home in pursuance of such permission granted under this section shall be deemed to be part of the time for which he is liable to be kept in the special home:

Provided that when a juvenile has failed to return to the special home on the permission being revoked or forfeited, the time which elapses after his failure so to return shall be excluded in computing the time during which he is liable to be kept in the institution.

60. Contribution by parents.—(1) The competent authority which makes an order for sending a juvenile or the child to a children's home or to a special home or placing the juvenile under the care of a fit person or fit institution may make an order requiring the parent or other person liable to maintain the juvenile or the child to contribute to his maintenance, if able to do so, in the prescribed manner according to income.

(2) The competent authority may direct, if necessary, the payment to be made to poor parent or guardian by the Superintendent or the Project Manager of the home to pay such expenses for the journey of the inmate or parent or guardian or both, from the home to his ordinary place of residence at the time of sending the juvenile as may be prescribed.

61. Fund.—(1) The State Government [2][***] may create a Fund under such name as it thinks fit for the welfare and rehabilitation of the juvenile or the child dealt with under this Act.

---

1. Subs. by Act 33 of 2006, sec. 23, for "for maximum seven days" (w.e.f. 22-8-2006).
2. The words "or local authority" omitted by Act 33 of 2006, sec. 5 (w.e.f. 22-8-2006).

(2) There shall be credited to the Fund such voluntary donations, contributions or subscriptions as may be made by any individual or organisation.

(3) The Fund created under sub-section (1) shall be administered by the State advisory board in such manner and for such purposes as may be prescribed.

COMMENTS

State Governments or local authorities have been empowered to create Funds for the welfare and rehabilitation of the juvenile or the child. Such funds may be created with voluntary donations, contributions or subscriptions as may be made by any individual or organisation. Such funds are to be administered by the State Advisory Boards.

62. Central, State, district and city advisory boards.—(1) The Central Government or a State Government may constitute a Central or a State advisory board, as the case may be, to advise that Government on matter relating to the establishment and maintenance of the homes, mobilisation of resources, provision of facilities for education, training and rehabilitation of child in need of care and protection and juvenile in conflict with law and co-ordination among the various official and non-official agencies concerned.

(2) The Central or State advisory board shall consist of such persons as the Central Government or the State Government, as the case may be, may think fit and shall include eminent social workers, representatives of voluntary organisation in the field of child welfare corporate sector, academicians, medical professionals and the concerned Department of the State Government.

(3) The district or city level inspection committee constituted under section 35 of this Act shall also function as the district or city advisory board.

[1][**62A. Constitution of Child Protection Unit responsible for implementation of the Act.**—Every State Government shall constitute a Child Protection Unit for the State and, such Units for every District, consisting of such officers and other employees as may be appointed by that Government, to take up matters relating to children in need of care and protection and juveniles in conflict with law with a view to ensure the implementation of this Act including the establishment and maintenance of homes, notification of competent authorities in relation to these children and their rehabilitation and co-ordination with various official and non-official agencies concerned.]

63. Special juvenile police unit.—(1) In order to enable the police officers who frequently or exclusively deal with juveniles or are primarily engaged in the prevention of juvenile crime or handling of the juveniles or children under this Act to perform their functions more effectively, they shall be specially instructed and trained.

(2) In every police station at least one officer with aptitude and appropriate training and orientation may be designated as the 'juvenile or the child welfare officer' who will handle the juvenile or the child in co-ordination with the police.

(3) Special juvenile police unit, of which all police officers designated as above, to handle juveniles or children will be members, may be created in every district and city to co-ordinate and to upgrade the police treatment of the juveniles and the children.

1. Ins. by Act 33 of 2006, sec. 24 (w.e.f. 22-8-2006).

64. Juvenile in conflict with law undergoing sentence at commencement of this Act.—In any area in which this Act is brought into force, the State Government [1][***] [2][shall direct] that a juvenile in conflict with law who is undergoing any sentence of imprisonment at the commencement of this Act, shall, in lieu of undergoing such sentence, be sent to a special home or be kept in fit institution in such manner as the State Government [1][***] thinks fit for the remainder of the period of the sentence; and the provisions of this Act shall apply to the juvenile as if he had been ordered by the Board to be sent to such special home or institution or, as the case may be, ordered to be kept under protective care under sub-section (2) of section 16 of this Act:

[3][Provided that the State Government or as the case may be the Board, may, for any adequate and special reason to be recorded in writing, review the case of a juvenile in conflict with law undergoing sentence of imprisonment, who has ceased to be so on or before the commencement of this Act, and pass appropriate order in the interest of such juvenile.

Explanation.—In all cases where a juvenile in conflict with law is undergoing a sentence of imprisonment at any stage on the date of commencement of this Act, his case including the issue of juvenility, shall be deemed to be decided in terms of clause (l) of section 2 and other provisions contained this Act and the rules made thereunder, irrespective of the fact that he ceases to be a juvenile on or before such date and accordingly he shall be sent to the special home or a fit institution, as the case may be, for the remainder of the period of the sentence but such sentence shall not in any case exceed the maximum period provided in section 15 of this Act.]

65. Procedure in respect of bonds.—Provisions of Chapter XXXIII of the Code of Criminal Procedure, 1973 (2 of 1974) shall, as far as may be, apply to bonds taken under this Act.

66. Delegation of powers.—The State Government may, by the general order, direct that any power exercisable by it under this Act shall, in such circumstances and under such conditions, if any, as may be prescribed in the order, be exercisable also by an officer subordinate to that Government [1][***].

67. Protection of action taken in good faith.—No suit or legal proceedings shall lie against the State Government or voluntary organisation running the home or any officer and the staff appointed in pursuance of this Act in respect of anything which is in good faith done or intended to be done in pursuance of this Act or of any rules or order made thereunder.

68. Power to make rules.—(1) The State Government may, by notification in the Official Gazette, make rules to carry out the purposes of this Act:

[4][Provided that the Central Government may, frame model rules in respect of all or any of the matters with respect to which the State Government may make rules under this section, and where any such model rules have been framed in respect of any such matter, they shall apply to the State until the rules in respect

1. The words "or the local authority" omitted by Act 33 of 2006, sec. 5 (w.e.f. 22-8-2006).
2. Subs. by Act 33 of 2006, sec. 25, for "may direct" (w.e.f. 22-8-2006).
3. Ins. by Act 33 of 2006, sec. 25 (w.e.f. 22-8-2006).
4. Ins. by Act 33 of 2006, sec. 26 (w.e.f. 22-8-2006).

of that matter is made by the State Government and while making any such rules, so far as is practicable, they conform to such model rules.]

(2) In particular, and without prejudice to the generality of the foregoing powers, such rules may provide for all or any of the following matters, namely:—

(i) the term of office of the members of the Board and the manner in which such member may resign under sub-section (4) of section 4;

(ii) the time of the meetings of the Board and the rules of procedure in regard to the transaction of business at its meeting under sub-section (1) of section 5;

(iii) the management of observation homes including the standards and various types of services to be provided by them and the circumstances in which and the manner in which, the certification of the observation home may be granted or withdrawn and such other matters as are referred to in section 8;

(iv) the management of special homes including the standards and various types of services to be provided by them and the circumstances in which and the manner in which, the certification of the special home may be granted or withdrawn and such other matters as are referred to in section 9;

(v) persons by whom any juvenile in conflict with law may be produced before the Board and the manner of sending such juvenile, to an observation home under sub-section (2) of section 10;

(vi) matters relating to removal of disqualifications attaching to conviction of a juvenile under section 19;

(vii) the qualifications of the Chairperson and members, and the tenure for which they may be appointed under sub-section (3) of section 29;

(viii) the time of the meetings of the Committee and the rules of procedure in regard to the transaction of business at its meeting under sub-section (1) of section 30;

(ix) the manner of making the report to the police and to the Committee and the manner of sending and entrusting the child to children's home pending the inquiry under sub-section (2) of section 32;

(x) the management of children's homes including the standards and nature of services to be provided by them, and the manner in which certification of a children's home or recognition to a voluntary organisation may be granted or withdrawn under sub-section (2) [1][and the manner of registration of institutions under sub-section (3)] of section 34;

(xi) appointment of inspection committees for children's homes, their tenure and purposes for which inspection committees may be appointed and such other matters as are referred to in section 35;

1. Ins. by Act 33 of 2006, sec. 26 (w.e.f. 22-8-2006).

(xii) facilities to be provided by the shelter homes under sub-section (3) of section 37;

[1][(xiia) rehabilitation mechanism to be resorted to in adoption under sub-section (2), notification of guidelines under sub-section (3) and the manner of recognition of specialised adoption agencies under sub-section (4) of section 41;]

(xiii) for carrying out the scheme of foster care programme of children under sub-section (3) of section 42;

(xiv) for carrying out various schemes of sponsorship of children under sub-section (2) of section 43;

(xv) matters relating to after-care organisation under section 44;

(xvi) for ensuring effective linkages between various agencies for facilitating rehabilitation and social integration of the child under section 45;

(xvii) the purposes and the manner in which the Fund shall be administered under sub-section (3) of section 61;

(xviii) any other matter which is required to be, or may be, prescribed.

[1][(3) Every rule made by the Central Government under this Act shall be laid, as soon as may be after it is made, before each House of Parliament, while it is in session, for a total period of thirty days which may be comprised in one session or in two or more successive sessions, and if, before the expiry of the session immediately following the session or the successive sessions aforesaid, both Houses agree in making any modification in the rule or both Houses agree that the rule should not be made, the rule shall thereafter have effect only in such modified form or be of no effect, as the case may be; so, however, that any such modification or annulment shall be without prejudice to the validity of anything previously done under that rule.]

[2][(4)] Every rule made by a State Government under this Act shall be laid, as soon as may be after it is made, before the Legislature of that State.

69. Repeal and savings.—(1) The Juvenile Justice Act, 1986 (53 of 1986) is hereby repealed.

(2) Notwithstanding such repeal, anything done or any action taken under the said Act shall be deemed to have been done or taken under the corresponding provisions of this Act.

70. Power to remove difficulties.—(1) If any difficulty arises in giving effect to the provisions of this Act, the Central Government may, by order, not inconsistent with the provisions of this Act, remove the difficulty:

Provided that no such order shall be made after the expiry of the period of two years from the commencement of this Act.

(2) However, order made under the section shall be laid, as soon as may be after it is made, before each House of Parliament.

---

1. Ins. by Act 33 of 2006, sec. 26 (w.e.f. 22-8-2006).
2. Sub-section (3) renumbered as sub-section (4) by by Act 33 of 2006, sec. 26 (w.e.f. 22-8-2006).

Part 4

Supreme Court Guidelines on Rape and Allied Issues

EVIDENCE OF PROSECUTRIX

State of Maharashtra v. *Chandraprakash Kewalchand Jain*, AIR 1990 SC 658: (1990) 1 SCC 550

1. It is necessary at the outset to state what the approach of the Court should be while evaluating the prosecution evidence, particularly the evidence of the prosecutrix, in sex-offences. Is it essential that the evidence of the prosecutrix should be corroborated in material particulars before the Court bases a conviction on her testimony? Does the rule of prudence demand that in all cases save the rarest of rare the Court should look for corroboration before acting on the evidence of the prosecutrix? Let us see if the Evidence Act, provides the clue. Under the said statute 'Evidence' means and includes all statements which the Court permits or requires to be made before it by witnesses, in relation to the matters of fact under inquiry. Under section 59 all facts, except the contents of documents, may be proved by oral evidence. Section 118 then tells us who may give oral evidence. According to that section all persons are competent to testify unless the Court considers that they are prevented from understanding the questions put to them, or from giving rational answers to those questions, by tender years, extreme old age, disease, whether of body or mind, or any other cause of the same kind. Even in the case of an accomplice section 133 provides that he shall be a competent witness against an accused person; and a conviction is not illegal merely because it proceeds upon the uncorroborated testimony of an accomplice. However, *Illustration (b)* to section 114, which lays down a rule of practice says that the Court 'may' presurne that an accomplice is unworthy of credit, unless he is corroborated in material particulars. Thus under section 133, which lays down a rule of law, an accomplice is a competent witness and a conviction based solely on his uncorroborated evidence is not illegal although in view of section 114, *Illustration (b)*, Courts do not as a matter of practice do so and look for corroboration in material particulars. This is the conjoint effect of sections 133 and 114, *Illustration (b)*.

2. A prosecutrix of a sex-offence cannot be put on par with an accomplice. She is in fact a victim of the crime. The Evidence Act, nowhere says that her evidence cannot be accepted unless it is corroborated in material particulars. She is undoubtedly a competent witness under section 118 and her evidence must receive the same weight as is attached to an injured in cases of physical violence. The same degree of care and caution must attach in the evaluation of her evidence as in the case of an injured complainant or witness and no more. What is necessary is that the Court must be alive to and conscious of the fact that it is dealing with the evidence of a person who is interested in the outcome of the charge levelled by her. If the Court keeps this in mind and feels satisfied that it can act on the evidence of the prosecutrix, there is no rule

of law or practice incorporated in the Evidence Act similar to *Illustration (b)* to section 114 which requires it to look for corroboration. If for some reason the Court is hesitant to place implicit reliance on the testimony of the prosecutrix it may look for evidence which may lend assurance to her testimony short of corroboration required in the case of an accomplice. The nature of evidence required to lend assurance to the testimony of the prosecutrix must necessarily depend on the facts and circumstances of each case. But if a prosecutrix is an adult and of full understanding the Court is entitled to base a conviction on her evidence unless the same is shown to be infirm and not trustworthy. If the totality of the circumstances appearing on the record of the case disclose that the prosecutrix does not have a strong motive to falsely involve the person charged, the Court should ordinarily have no hesitation in accepting her evidence. We have, therefore, no doubt in our minds that ordinarily the evidence of a prosecutrix who does not lack understanding must be accepted. The degree of proof required must not be higher than is expected of an injured witness.. Ordinarily the evidence of a prosecutrix must carry the same weight as is attached to an injured person who is a victim of violence, unless there are special circumstances which call for greater caution, in which case it would be safe to act on her testimony if there is independent evidence lending assurance to her accusation.

TRIAL OF RAPE CASES

Sakshi v. *Union of India*, AIR 2004 SC 3566: (2004) 5 SCC 518

1. The provisions of sub-section (2) of section 327, Cr. P.C. shall, in addition to the offences mentioned in the sub-section, would also apply in inquiry or trial of offences under sections 354 and 377, I.P.C.

2. In holding trial of child sex abuse or rape:

(i) a screen or some such arrangements may be made where the victim or witnesses (who may be equally vulnerable like the victim) do not see the body or face of the accused;

(ii) the questions put in cross-examination on behalf of the accused, insofar as they relate directly to the incident, should be given in writing to the Presiding Officer of the Court who may put them to the victim or witnesses in a language which is clear and is not embarrassing;

(iii) the victim of child abuse or rape, while giving testimony in Court, should be allowed sufficient breaks as and when required.

The suggestions made by the petitioners will advance the cause of justice and are in the larger interest of society. The cases of child abuse and rape are increasing at alarming speed and appropriate legislation in this regard is, therefore, urgently required. We hope and trust that the Parliament will give serious attention to the points highlighted by the petitioner and make appropriate legislation with all the promptness which it deserves.

ANTICIPATORY BAIL

Gurbaksh Singh Sibbia v. *State of Punjab*, AIR 1980 SC 1632: (1980) 2 SCC 565 as explained in *Savitri Agarwal* v. *State of Maharashtra*, AIR 2009 SC 3173: (2009) 8 SCC 325

1. Though the power conferred under section 438 of the Code can be described as of an extraordinary character, but this does not justify the conclusion that the power must be exercised in exceptional cases only because it is of an extraordinary character. Nonetheless, the discretion under the section has to be exercised with due care and circumspection depending on circumstances justifying its exercise.

2. Before power under sub-section (1) of section 438 of the Code is exercised, the Court must be satisfied that the applicant invoking the provision has reason to believe that he is likely to be arrested for a non-bailable offence and that belief must be founded on reasonable grounds. Mere "fear" is not belief, for which reason, it is not enough for the applicant to show that he has some sort of vague apprehension that someone is going to make an accusation against him, in pursuance of which he may be arrested. The grounds on which the belief of the applicant is based that he may be arrested for a non-bailable offence, must be capable of being examined by the Court objectively. Specific events and facts must be disclosed by the applicant in order to enable the Court to Judge of the reasonableness of his belief, the existence of which is the *sine qua non* of the exercise of power conferred by the section.

3. The observations made in *Balchand Jain* v. *State of Madhya Pradesh*, (1976) 4 SCC 572, regarding the nature of the power conferred by section 438 and regarding the question whether the conditions mentioned in section 437 should be read into section 438 cannot be treated as conclusive on the point. There is no warrant for reading into section 438, the conditions subject to which bail can be granted under section 437(1) of the Code and therefore, anticipatory bail cannot be refused in respect of offences like criminal breach of trust for the mere reason that the punishment provided for is imprisonment for life. Circumstances may broadly justify the grant of bail in such cases too, though of course, the Court is free to refuse anticipatory bail in any case if there is material before it justifying such refusal.

4. No blanket order of bail should be passed and the Court which grants anticipatory bail must take care to specify the offence or the offences in respect of which alone the order will be effective. While granting relief under section 438(1) of the Code, appropriate conditions can be imposed under section 438(2) so as to ensure an uninterrupted investigation. One such condition can even be that in the event of the police making out a case of a likely discovery under

section 27 of the Evidence Act, the person released on bail shall be liable to be taken in police custody for facilitating the recovery. Otherwise, such an order can become a charter of lawlessness and a weapon to stifle prompt investigation into offences which could not possibly be predicated when the order was passed.

5. The filing of First Information Report (FIR) is not a condition precedent to the exercise of power under section 438. The imminence of a likely arrest founded on a reasonable belief can be shown to exist even if an FIR is not yet filed.

6. An anticipatory bail can be granted even after an FIR is filed so long as the applicant has not been arrested.

7. The provisions of section 438 cannot be invoked after the arrest of the accused. After arrest, the accused must seek his remedy under section 437 or section 439 of the Code, if he wants to be released on bail in respect of the offence or offences for which he is arrested.

8. An interim bail order can be passed under section 438 of the Code without notice to the Public Prosecutor but notice should be issued to the Public Prosecutor or to the Government advocate forthwith and the question of bail should be reexamined in the light of respective contentions of the parties. The adinterim order too must conform to the requirements of the section and suitable conditions should be imposed on the applicant even at that stage.

9. Though it is not necessary that the operation of an order passed under section 438(1) of the Code be limited in point of time but the Court may, if there are reasons for doing so, limit the operation of the order to a short period until after the filing of FIR in respect of the matter covered by the order. The applicant may, in such cases, be directed to obtain an order of bail under section 437 or 439 of the Code within a reasonable short period after the filing of the FIR.

At this juncture, it would be appropriate to note that the view expressed by this Court in *Adri Dharan Das* v. *State of West Bengal,* (2005) 4 SCC 303: AIR 2005 SC 1057: to the effect that while dealing with an application under section 438 of the Code, the Court cannot pass an interim order restraining arrest as it will amount to interference in the investigation, does not appear to be in consonance with the opinion of the Constitution Bench in *Gurbaksh Singh Sibbia* v. *State of Punjab,* AIR 1980 SC 1632: (1980) 2 SCC 565. Similarly, the observation that power under section 438 is to be exercised only in exceptional cases seems to be based on the decision in *Balchand's* case (supra), which has not been fully approved by the Constitution Bench.

ANTICIPATORY BAIL – RELEVANT FACTORS

State of Maharashtra v. *Mohd. Sajid Husain Mohd. S. Husain,* AIR 2008 SC 155: (2008) 1 SCC 213

The four factors, which are relevant for considering the application for grant of anticipatory bail, are:

1. the nature and gravity or seriousness of accusation as apprehended by the applicant;
2. the antecedents of the applicant including the fact as to whether he has, on conviction by a Court, previously undergone imprisonment for a term in respect of any cognizable offence;
3. the likely object of the accusation to humiliate or malign the reputation of the applicant by having him so arrested; and
4. the possibility of the appellant, if granted anticipatory bail, fleeing from justice.

ARREST

D.K. Basu v. *State of West Bengal,* (1997) 1 SCC 416: AIR 1997 SC 610

1. The police personnel carrying out the arrest and handling the interrogation of the arrestee should bear accurate, visible and clear identification and name tags with their designations. The particulars of all such police personnel who handle interrogation of the arrestee must be recorded in a register.

2. That the police officer carrying out the arrest of the arrestee shall prepare a memo of arrest at the time of arrest and such memo shall be attested by at least one witness, who may be either a member of the family of the arrestee or a respectable person of the locality from where the arrest is made. It shall also be counter-signed by the arrestee and shall contain the time and date of arrest.

3. A person who has been arrested or detained and is being held in custody in a police station or interrogation centre or other lock-up, shall be entitled to have one friend or relative or other person known to him or having interest in his welfare being informed, as soon as practicable, that he has been arrested and is being detained at the particular place, unless the attesting witness of the memo of arrest is himself such a friend or a relative of the arrestee.

4. The time, place of arrest and venue of custody of an arrestee must be notified by the police where the next friend or relative of the arrestee lives outside the district or and through the Legal Aid Organisation in the District and the police station of the area concerned telegraphically within a period of 8 to 12 hours after the arrest.

5. The person arrested must be made aware of this right to have someone informed of his arrest or detention as soon as he is put under arrest or is detained.

6. An entry must be made in the diary at the place of detention regarding the arrest of the person which shall also disclose the name of the next friend of the person who has been informed of the arrest and the names and particulars of the police officials in whose custody the arrestee is.

7. The arrestee should, where he so requests, be also examined at the time of his arrest and major and minor injuries, if any, present on his/her body, must be recorded at that time. The "Inspection Memo" must be signed both by the arrestee and the police officer effecting the arrest and its copy provided to the arrestee.

8. The arrestee should be subjected to medical examination by a trained doctor every 48 hours during his detention in custody by a doctor on the panel of approved doctors appointed by Director, Health Services of the concerned State or Union Territory, Director, Health Services should prepare such a panel for all Tehsils and Districts as well.

9. Copies of all the documents including the memo of arrest, referred to above, should be sent to the (*sic*) Magistrate for his record.

10. The arrestee may be permitted to meet his lawyer during interrogation, though not throughout the interrogation.

11. A police control room should be provided at all district and State headquarters, where information regarding the arrest and the place of custody of the arrestee shall be communicated by the officer causing the arrest, within 12 hours of effecting the arrest and at the police control room it should be displayed on a conspicuous police board.

ASSISTANCE TO RAPE VICTIMS

Delhi Domestic Working Women's Forum v. *Union of India*, (1995) 1 SCC 14: 1994 (4) SCALE 608: 1995 SCC (Cri) 7

1. The complainants of sexual assault cases should be provided with legal representation. It is important to have someone who is well-acquainted with the criminal justice system. The role of the victim's advocate would not only be to explain to the victim the nature of the proceedings, to prepare her for the case and to assist her in the police station and in court but to provide her with guidance as to how she might obtain help of a different nature from other agencies, *for example*, mind counselling or medical assistance. It is important to secure continuity of assistance by ensuring that the same person who looked after the complainant's interests in the police station represents her till the end of the case.

2. Legal assistance will have to be provided at the police station since the victim of sexual assault might very well be in a distressed state upon arrival at the police station, the guidance and support of a lawyer at this stage and whilst she was being questioned would be of great assistance to her.

3. The police should be under a duty to inform the victim of her right to representation before any questions were asked of her and that the police report should state that the victim was so informed.

4. A list of advocates willing to act in these cases should be kept at the police station for victims who did not have a particular lawyer in mind or whose own lawyer was unavailable.

5. The advocate shall be appointed by the Court, upon application by the police at the earliest convenient moment, but in order to ensure that victims were questioned without undue delay, advocates would be authorised to act at the police station before leave of the court was sought or obtained.

6. In all rape trials anonymity of the victim must be maintained, as far as necessary.

7. It is necessary, having regard to the Directive Principles contained under article 38(1) of the Constitution of India to set up Criminal Injuries Compensation Board. Rape victims frequently incur substantial financial loss. Some, *for example,* are too traumatized to continue in employment.

8. Compensation for victims shall be awarded by the court on conviction of the offender and by the Criminal Injuries Compensation Board whether or not a conviction has taken place. The Board will take into account pain, suffering and shock as well as loss of earnings due to pregnancy and the expenses of child birth if this occurred as a result of the rape.

BAIL

State of U.P. through C.B.I. v. *Amarmani Tripathi,* (2005) 8 SCC 21: AIR 2005 SC 3490

1. The matters to be considered in an application for bail are:

(i) whether there is any *prima facie* or reasonable ground to believe that the accused had committed the offence;

(ii) nature and gravity of the charge;

(iii) severity of the punishment in the event of conviction;

(iv) danger of accused absconding or fleeing if released on bail;

(v) character, behaviour, means, position and standing of the accused;

(vi) likelihood of the offence being repeated;

(vii) reasonable apprehension of the witnesses being tampered with; and

(viii) danger, of course, of justice being thwarted by grant of bail [See *Prahlad Singh Bhati* v. *NCT, Delhi,* (2001) 4 SCC 280 and *Gurcharan Singh* v. *State (Delhi Administration),* AIR 1978 SC 179]. While a vague allegation that accused may tamper with the evidence or witnesses may not be a ground to refuse bail, if the accused is of such character that his mere presence at large would intimidate the witnesses or if there is material to show that he will use his liberty to subvert justice or tamper with the evidence, then bail will be refused.

We may also refer to the following principles relating to grant or refusal of bail stated in *Kalyan Chandra Sarkar* v. *Rajesh Ranjan*, (2004) 7 SCC 528: 2004 SCC (Cri) 1977: "The law in regard to grant or refusal of bail is very well-settled. The Court granting bail should exercise its discretion in a judicious manner and not as a matter of course. Though at the stage of granting bail a detailed examination of evidence and elaborate documentation of the merit of the case need not be undertaken, there is a need to indicate in such orders reasons for *prima facie* concluding why bail was being granted particularly where the accused is charged of having committed a serious offence. Any order devoid of such reasons would suffer from non-application of mind. It is also necessary for the Court granting bail to consider among other circumstances, the following factors also before granting bail; they are:

(a) The nature of accusation and the severity of punishment in case of conviction and the nature of supporting evidence.

(b) Reasonable apprehension of tampering with the witness or apprehension of threat to the complainant.

(c) *Prima facie* satisfaction of the court in support of the charge. [See *Ram Govind Upadhyay* v. *Sudarshan Singh*, (2002) 3 SCC 598: 2002 SCC (Cri) 688 and *Puran* v. *Rambilas*, (2001) 6 SCC 338: 2001 SCC (Cri) 1124]."

BAIL SYSTEMS – NEED FOR REFORMS

Hussainara Khatoon v. *Home Secretary, State of Bihar, Patna,* AIR 1979 SC 1360: (1980) 1 SCC 81

The bail system, as it operates today, is a source of great hardship to the poor and if we really want to eliminate the evil effects of poverty and assure a fair and just treatment to poor in the administration of justice, it is imperative that the bail system should be thoroughly reformed so that it should be possible for the poor, as easily as the rich, to obtain pretrial release without jeopardizing the interest of justice.

It is high time that our Parliament realises that risk of monetary loss is not the only deterrent against fleeing from justice, but there are also other factors which act as equal deterrents against fleeing. Ours is a socialist republic with social justice as the signature tune of our Constitution and Parliament would do well to consider whether it would not be more consonant with the ethos of our Constitution that instead of risk of financial loss, other relevant considerations such as family ties, roots in the community, job security, membership of stable organisations etc., should be the determinative factors in grant of bail and the accused should in appropriate cases be released on his personal bond without monetary obligation. Of course it may be necessary in such a case to provide by an amendment of the penal law that if the accused wilfully fails to appear in compliance with the promise contained in his personal bond, he shall be liable to penal action. But even under the law as it stands today the courts must abandon the antiquated concept under which pretrial release is ordered only against bail with sureties. That concept is outdated and experience has shown that it has done more harm than good. The new insight into the subject of pre-trial release which has been developed in socially advanced countries and particularly the United States should now inform the decisions of our Courts in regard to pre-trial release. If the Court is satisfied, after taking into account, on the basis of information placed before it, that the accused has his roots in the community and is not likely to abscond it can safely release the accused on his personal bond. To determine whether the accused has his roots in the community which would deter him from fleeing, the Court should take into account the following factors concerning the accused:

1. the length of his residence in the community,
2. his employment status, history and his financial condition,
3. his family ties and relationships,
4. his reputation, character and monetary condition,
5. his prior criminal record including any record or prior release on recognizance or on bail,
6. the identity of responsible members of the community who would vouch for his reliability.
7. the nature of the offence charged and the apparent probability of conviction and the likely sentence insofar as these factors are relevant to the risk of non-appearance, and
8. any other factors indicating the ties of the accused to the community or bearing on the risk of wilful failure to appear.

If the court is satisfied on a consideration of the relevant factors that the accused has his ties in the community and there is no substantial risk of non-appearance, the accused may, as far as possible, be released on his personal bond. Of course, if facts are brought to the notice of the Court which go to show that having regard to the condition and background of the accused his previous record and the nature and circumstances of the offence, there may be a substantial risk of his non-appearance at the trial, as *for example,* where the accused is a notorious bad character or a confirmed criminal or the offence is serious (these examples are only by way of illustration), the Court may not release the accused on his personal bond and may insist on bail with sureties. But in the majority of cases, considerations like family ties and relationship, roots in the community, employment status etc. may prevail with the court in releasing the accused on his personal bond had particularly in cases where the offence is not grave and the accused is poor or belongs to a weaker section of the community, release on personal bond could, as far as possible, be preferred. But even while releasing the accused on personal bond it is necessary to caution the Court that the amount of the bond which it fixes should not be based merely on the nature of the charge. The decision as regards the amount of the bond should be an individualised decision depending on the individual financial circumstances of the accused and the probability of his absconding. The amount of the bond should be determined having regard to these relevant factors and should not be fixed mechanically according to a schedule keyed to the nature of the charge. Otherwise, it would be difficult for the accused to secure his release even by executing a personal bond. Moreover, when the accused is released on his personal bond, it would be very harsh and oppressive if he is required to satisfy the Court – and what we have said here in regard to the court must apply equally in relation to the police while granting bail – that he is solvent enough to pay the amount of the bond if he fails to appear at the trial and in consequence the bond is forfeited. The inquiry into the solvency of the accused can become a source of great harassment to him and often result in denial of bail and deprivation of liberty and should not, therefore, be insisted upon as a condition of acceptance of the personal bond. We have no doubt that if the system of bail, even under the existing law, is administered in the manner we have indicated in this judgment; it would go a long way towards relieving hardship of the poor and to help them to secure pre-trial release from incarceration.

CANCELLATION OF BAIL IN BAILABLE OFFENCES

Rasik Lal v. *Kishore*,
AIR 2009 SC 1341: (2009) 4 SCC 446

Bail granted to an accused with reference to bailable offence can be cancelled only if the accused:

(i) misuses his liberty by indulging in similar criminal activity,

(ii) interferes with the course of investigation,

(iii) attempts to tamper with evidence of witnesses,

(iv) threatens witnesses or indulges in similar activities which would hamper smooth investigation,

(v) attempts to flee to another country,

(vi) attempts to make himself scarce by going underground or becoming unavailable to the investigation agency,

(vii) attempts to place himself beyond the reach of his surety, etc. These grounds are illustrative and not exhaustive. However, a bail granted to a person accused of bailable offence cannot be cancelled on the ground that the complainant was not heard. As mandated by section 436 of the Code what is to be ascertained by the officer or the Court is whether the offence alleged to have been committed is a bailable offence and whether he is ready to give bail as may be directed by the officer or the Court. When a police officer releases a person accused of a bailable offence, he is not required to hear the complainant at all. Similarly, a Court while exercising powers under section 436 of the Code is not bound to issue notice to the complainant and hear him.

CANCELLATION OF BAIL GRANTED UNDER SECTION 167(2)

Aslam Babalal Desai v. *State of Maharashtra*, AIR 1993 SC 1: (1992) 4 SCC 272

1. The provisions of the Code, in particular sections 57 and 167, manifest the legislative anxiety that once a person's liberty has been interfered with by the police arresting him without a Court order or a warrant, the investigation must be carried out with utmost urgency and completed within the maximum period allowed by the proviso (a) to section 167(2) of the Code. It must be realised that the said proviso was introduced in the Code by way of enlargement of time for which the arrested accused could be kept in custody. Therefore, the prosecuting agency must realise that if it fails to show a sense of urgency in the investigation of the case and omits or defaults to file a charge-sheet within the time prescribed, the accused would be entitled to be released on.bail and the order passed to that effect under section 167(2) would be an order under section 437(1) or (2) or 439(1) of the Code. Since section 167 does not empower cancellation of the bail, the power to cancel the bail can only be traced to section 437(5) or 439(2) of the Code. The bail can then be cancelled on considerations which are valid for cancellation of bail granted under section 437(1) or (2) or 439(1) of the Code. The fact that the bail was earlier rejected or that it was secured by the thrust of proviso (a) to section 167(2) of the Code then recedes in the background. Once the accused has been released on bail his liberty cannot be interfered with lightly *i.e.*, on the ground that the prosecution has subsequently submitted a charge-sheet. Such a view would introduce a sense of complacency in the investigating agency and would destroy the very purpose of instilling a sense of urgency expected by sections 57 and 167(2) of the Code. We are, therefore, of the view that, once an accused is released on bail under section 167(2) he cannot be taken back in custody merely on the filing of a charge-sheet but there must exist special reasons for so doing besides the fact that the charge-sheet reveals the commission of a non-bailable crime. The ratio of *Rajnikant's* case, AIR 1996 SC 71 to the extent it is inconsistent herewith does not, with respect, state the law correctly.

2. Even where two views are possible, this being a matter belonging to the field of criminal justice involving the liberty of an individual, the provision must be construed strictly in favour of individual liberty since even the law expects early completion of the investigation. The delay in completion of the investigation can be on pain of the accused being released on bail. The prosecution cannot be allowed to trifle with individual liberty if it does not take its task seriously and does not complete it within the time allowed by law. It would also result in avoidable difficulty to the accused if the latter is asked to secure a surety and a few days later be placed behind the bars at the sweet will of the prosecution on production of a charge-sheet. We, are, therefore, of the view that unless there are strong grounds for cancellation of the bail, the bail once granted cannot be cancelled on mere production of the charge-sheet. The view we are taking is

consistent with this Court's view in the case of *Bashir* v. *State of Haryana,* AIR 1978 SC 55 and *Raghubir Singh* v. *State of Bihar,* AIR 1987 SC 149 but if any ambiguity has arisen on account of certain observations in *Rajnikant Jivanlal Patel* v. *Intelligence Officer, Narcotic Control Bureau, New Delhi,* AIR 1990 SC 71 our endeavour is to clear the same and set the controversy at rest.

CATEGORIES OF CASES WHICH SHOULD BE ENTERTAINED UNDER ARTICLE 136 OF CONSTITUTION OF INDIA

Matter Referred to Constitution Bench

Mathai @ Joby* v. *George,

JT 2010 (3) SC 160: 2010 (2) SCALE 172

Recently the two-Judge Bench opined that only **following categories of cases** should be entertained by the Supreme Court under article 136 of the Constitution of India. According to the Bench the time has now come when an authoritative decision by a Constitution Bench should lay down some broad guidelines as to when the discretion under article 136 of the Constitution should be exercised, *i.e.,* in what kind of cases a petition under article 136 should be entertained.

(i) All matters involving substantial questions of law relating to the interpretation of the Constitution of India;

(ii) All matters of national or public importance;

(iii) Validity of laws, Central and State;

(iv) After *Kesavananda Bharati,* (1973) 4 SCC 217, the judicial review of Constitutional Amendments; and

(v) To settle differences of opinion of important issues of law between High Courts.

We are of the opinion that two additional categories of cases can be added to the above list, namely:

(i) where the Court is satisfied that there has been a grave miscarriage of justice and

(ii) where a fundamental right of a person has *prima facie* been violated. However, it is for the Constitution Bench to which we are referring this matter to decide what are the kinds of cases in which discretion under article 136 should be exercised.

In our opinion, the time has now come when an authoritative decision by a **Constitution Bench** should lay down some broad guidelines as to when the discretion under article 136 of the Constitution should be exercised, *i.e.,* in what kind of cases a petition under article 136 should be entertained. If special leave petitions are entertained against all and sundry kinds of orders passed by any court or tribunal, then this Court after some time will collapse under its own burden.

CBI INVESTIGATION

State of West Bengal v. *Sampat Lal,*
AIR 1985 SC 195: (1985) 1 SCC 317

1. The appointment of a Special officer with a direction to enquire into the commission of an offence can only be on the basis that there has not been a proper investigation. There is a well-defined hierarchical administrative set up of the police in the State of West Bengal as in all other States and lo have created 3 new channel of inquiry or investigation is likely to create an impression that everything is not well with the statutory agency and it is likely to cast a stigma on the regular police hierarchy. In the facts and circumstances of the instant case and the nature of the order made in view, the direction to appoint a Special officer with powers to inquire should not have been made until the appellants has been given a hearing and the Court had the papers of investigation laid before it for being *prima facie* satisfied that the investigation had either not been proper or adequate.

2. Under the Code of Criminal Procedure which lays down the procedure to be followed when report of an offence is lodged with the police, the power to investigate is vested in the police. The procedure laid down in the Code is clear and definite. Investigation is a matter for the police under the scheme of the Code. Judicial opinion seems to be settled and there are several authorities of the Supreme Court where interference by the Court into police investigation has not been approved. There is however, residuary jurisdiction left in the Court to give directions to the investigating agency when it is satisfied that the requirements of the law are not being complied with and investigation is not being conducted properly or with due haste and promptitude. The Court has to be alive to the fact that the scheme of the law is that the investigation has been entrusted to the police and it is ordinarily not subject to the normal supervisory power of the Court. But in the instant case, the material placed before the Court did not justify an exception to be made to the rule indicated by the Supreme Court and the appointment of a Special officer was not called for at this stage.

3. 'Inquiry' and 'investigation' are statutory terms defined in the Code. In the instant case whatever name the work entrusted to the Special officer be called, there can be no dispute that he was required to ascertain facts from the witnesses and documents, if any, in regard to the death of the two boys. This process necessarily involved a fact-finding inquiry by ordinarily tapping the same sources as the investigating agency was expected to contact. This, therefore, necessarily involved a duplicate investigation. In view of the fact that there were two separate channels Placed in active charge of investigation to be conducted contemporaneously, confusion was bound to occur and working

of the two channels at a time was likely to prejudice the proper investigation making the exposing of the truth buried under mystery more difficult. Carrying this duplicate process was not likely to serve the cause of justice nor help in achieving the object for which it had been set up. The Special officer was not to exercise the power under section 5 of the Delhi Special Police Establishment Act, 1946, and if be wanted any real assistance in the matter of investigation, it had to be carried through the police officers of the State Administration. This was likely to bring in further confusion inasmuch as the witnesses were likely to be contacted by the same police office on more than one occasion—once in the course of investigation conducted by the police and again to meet the requirements of the Special officer. We are sure that the High Court never intended the cause of justice to be prejudiced and the serious attempt to find out the truth to be aborted.

4. While section 6 of the Delhi Special Police Establishment Act, 1946 would require the consent of the State Government before jurisdiction under section 5 of that Act, is exercised by officer of that establishment, when a direction is given by the court in an appropriate case, consent envisaged under section 6 of the Act, would not be a condition precedent to compliance with the court's direction section 6 of the Act, does not apply when the court gives a direction to the C.B.I. to conduct an investigation. In this view, the impugned order of the learned Single Judge and the appellate decision of the Division Bench appointing DIG, CBI to inquire into the matter would not be open to attack for want of sanction under section 6 of the Act.

5. In the instant case, the Court allowed the appeal and set aside the order of appointment of the Special Officer and observed that the investigation carried out has not been quite satisfactory. However, in the facts and circumstances of the case, there is no necessity to take away the investigation from the hands of the State Police machinery which is the statutory agency. The court pointed out that though there are occasions when death remains a mystery in spite of the best of efforts, it hopes that with an honest attempt and since efforts made, the truth would be found out and the police authorities of the State would be in a position to give a creditable account of themselves. The Court also suggested that the Director General of Police, West Bengal, will appoint a competent supervisory officer from the higher ranks of the State police with expertise in investigation to supervise the investigation in the present case.

CBI INVESTIGATION
Who can Order?

Nirmal Singh Kahlon v. *State of Punjab*,
AIR 2009 SC 984: (2009) 1 SCC 441

Delhi Special Police Establishment Act, 1946 (Central Act 25 of 1946) is a special statute. By reason of the said enactment, the CBI was constituted.

In relation to the matter which was to come within the purview thereof, the CBI could exercise its jurisdiction. The law and order, however, being a State subject, the CBI derives jurisdiction only when a consent therefore is given by the statute. It is, however, now beyond any controversy that the High Court and this Court also direct investigation by the CBI. Our attention has been drawn to the provisions of the CBI Manual, from a perusal whereof it appears that the Director, CBI exercises his power of superintendence in respect of the matters enumerated in Chapter VI of the CBI Manual which includes reference by the State and/or reference by the High Courts and this Court as also the registration thereof. The reference thereof may be received from the following:

"(a) Prime Minister of India;

(b) Cabinet Ministers of Government of India/Chief Ministers of State Governments or their equivalent;

(c) The State Governments;

(d) Supreme Court/High Courts".

The CBI Manual having been framed by the Union of India, evidently, it has accepted that reference for investigation to the CBI may be made either by this Court or by the High Court. Thus, even assuming that reference had been made by the State Government at the instance of the High Court, the same by itself would not render the investigation carried out by it to be wholly illegal and without jurisdiction as assuming that the reference had been made by the High Court in exercise of its powers under article 226 of the Constitution of India in a Public Interest Litigation, the same would also be valid.

CIRCUMSTANTIAL EVIDENCE-I

Sharad Birdhichand Sardar v. *State of Maharashtra*, AIR 1984 SC 1622: (1984) 4 SCC 116

Five golden principles, if we may say so, constitute the panchsheel of the proof of a case based on circumstantial evidence.

1. The circumstances from which the conclusion of guilt is to be drawn should be fully established.

It may be noted here that this Court indicated that the circumstances concerned 'must or should' and not 'may be' established. There is not only a grammatical but a legal distinction between 'may be proved' and 'must be or should be proved' as was held by this Court in *Shivaji Sahebrao Bobade* v. *State of Maharashtra*, (1973) 2 SCC 793 where the following observations were made:

> "Certainly, it is a primary principle that the accused must be and not merely may be guilty before a Court can convict and the mental distance between 'may be' and 'must be' is long and divides vague conjectures from sure conclusions."

2. The facts so established should be consistent only with the hypothesis of the guilt of the accused, that is to say, they should not be explainable on any other hypothesis except that the accused is guilty.

3. The circumstances should be of a conclusive nature and tendency.

4. They should exclude every possible hypothesis except the one to be proved, and

5. There must be a chain of evidence so complete as not to leave any reasonable ground for the conclusion consistent with the innocence of the accused and must show that in all human probability the act must have been done by the accused.

It will be seen that this Court while taking into account the absence of explanation or a false explanation did hold that it will amount to be an additional link to complete the chain but these observations must be read in the light of what this Court said earlier, *viz.*, before a false explanation can be used as additional link, the following essential conditions must be satisfied:

(i) various links in the chain of evidence led by the prosecution have been satisfactorily proved,

(ii) the said circumstance points to the guilt of the accused with reasonable definiteness, and

(iii) the circumstance is in proximity to the time and situation.

If these conditions are fulfilled only then a court can use a false explanation or a false defence as an additional link to lend an assurance to the court and not otherwise. On the facts and circumstances of the present case, this does not appear to be such a case. This aspect of the matter was examined in *Shankarlal Gyarasilal Dixit* v. *State of Maharashtra,* (1981) 2 SCR 384 (390): (1981) 2 SCC 35 (39): 1981 SCC (Cri) 315 (318-19): 1981 Cr LJ 325 where this Court observed thus: [SCC para 30, p. 43: SCC (Cri) p. 322] Besides, falsity of defence cannot take the place of proof of facts which the prosecution has to establish in order to succeed. A false plea can at best be considered as an additional circumstance, if other circumstances point unfailingly to the guilt of the accused.

CIRCUMSTANTIAL EVIDENCE-II

Padala Veera Reddy v. *State of Andhra Pradesh,* AIR 1990 SC 79: (1989) Supp 2 SCC 706

When a case rests upon circumstantial evidence such evidence must satisfy the following tests:—

(i) the circumstances from which an inference of guilt is sought to be drawn, must be cogently and firmly established;

(ii) those circumstances should be of a definite tendency unerringly pointing towards guilt of the accused;

(iii) the circumstances, taken cumulatively, should form a chain so complete that there is no escape from the conclusion that within all human probability the crime was committed by the accused and none else; and

(iv) the circumstantial evidence in order to sustain conviction must be complete and incapable of explanation of any other hypothesis than that of the guilt of the accused and such evidence should not only be consistent with the guilt of the accused but should be inconsistent with his innocence.

[See *Gambhir* v. *State of Maharashtra*, (1982) 2 SCC 351: AIR 1982 SC 1157; *Rama Nand* v. *State of Himachal Pradesh*, (1981) 1 SCC 511: AIR 1981 SC 738; *Prem Thakur* v. *State of Punjab*, (1982) 3 SCC 462: AIR 1983 SC 61; *Earabhadrappa* v. *State of Karnataka*, (1983) 2 SCC 330: AIR 1983 SC 446; *Gian Singh* v. *State of Punjab*, 1986 Supp SCC 676: AIR 1987 SC 1921; *Balvinder Singh* v. *State of Punjab*, (1987) 1 SCC 1: AIR 1987 SC 350].

COMPENSATION UNDER SECTION 357 CR. P.C.

Dilip S. Dahanukar v. *Kotak Mahindra Co. Ltd.*, (2007) 6 SCC 528: JT 2007 (6) SC 204

It is also of some significance to note that whereas under section 357(1) of the Code of Criminal Procedure a fine of Rs. 5000 can be imposed; fine in terms of section 357(2) thereof can be twice the amount of cheque whereas there is no upper limit for award of a compensation. But the same would be subject to other provisions of the Code of Criminal Procedure which mandates that the amount of fine imposed on an accused cannot be more than Rs. 5000. The very fact that the Parliament did not think it fit to put a ceiling limit in regard to the amount of compensation leviable upon an accused, the discretionary jurisdiction thereto must be exercised judiciously.

(i) In a case of this nature, sub-section (2) of section 357 of the Code of Criminal Procedure would be attracted even when appellant was directed to pay compensation;

(ii) The Appellate Court, however, while suspending the sentence, was entitled to put the appellant on terms. However, no such term could be put as a condition precedent for entertaining the appeal which is a constitutional and statutory right;

(iii) The amount of compensation must be a reasonable sum;

(iv) The Court, while fixing such amount, must have regard to all relevant factors including the one referred to in sub-section (5) of section 357 of the Code of Criminal Procedure;

(v) No unreasonable amount of compensation can be directed to be paid.

CONFESSION

Chattar Singh v. *State of Haryana*, AIR 2009 SC 378: (2008) 14 SCC 667

Confessions may be divided into two classes *i.e.*, judicial and extra-judicial. Judicial confessions are those which are made before a Magistrate or a court in the course of judicial proceedings. Extra-judicial confessions are those which are made by the party elsewhere than before a Magistrate or Court. Extra-judicial confessions are generally those that are made by a party to or before a private individual which includes even a judicial officer in his private capacity. It also includes a Magistrate who is not especially empowered to record confessions under section 164 of the Code of Criminal Procedure, 1973 or a Magistrate so empowered but receiving the confession at a stage when section 164 of the Code does not apply. As to extra-judicial confessions, two questions arise:

(i) were they made voluntarily? and

(ii) are they true? As the section enacts, a confession made by an accused person is irrelevant in criminal proceedings, if the making of the confession appears to the Court to have been caused by any inducement, threat or promise,

(1) having reference to the charge against the accused person,

(2) proceeding from a person in authority, and

(3) sufficient, in the opinion of the court to give the accused person grounds which would appear to him reasonable for supposing that by making it he would gain any advantage or avoid any evil of a temporal nature in reference to the proceedings against him. It follows that a confession would be voluntary if it is made by the accused in a fit state of mind, and if it is not caused by any inducement, threat or promise which has reference to the charge against him, proceeding from a person in authority. It would not be involuntary, if the inducement,

(a) does not have reference to the charge against the accused person; or

(b) it does not proceed from a person in authority; or

(c) it is not sufficient, in the opinion of the court to give the accused person grounds which would appear to him reasonable for supposing that, by making it, he would gain any advantage or avoid any evil of a temporal nature in reference to the proceedings against him. Whether or not the confession was voluntary would depend upon the facts and circumstances of each case, judged in the light of section 24 of the Indian Evidence Act, 1872 (in short 'Evidence Act').

The law is clear that a confession cannot be used against an accused person unless the Court is satisfied that it was voluntary and at that stage the question whether it is true or false does not arise. If the facts and circumstances surrounding the making of a confession appear to cast a doubt on the veracity or voluntariness of the confession, the Court may refuse to act upon the confession, even if it is admissible in evidence. One important question, in regard to which the Court has to be satisfied with is, whether when the accused made the confession, he was a free man or his movements were controlled by the police either by themselves or through some other agency employed by them for the purpose of securing such a confession. The question whether a confession is voluntary or not is always a question of fact. All the factors and all the circumstances of the case, including the important factors of the time given for reflection, scope of the accused getting a feeling of threat, inducement or promise, must be considered before deciding whether the Court is satisfied that in its opinion the impression caused by the inducement, threat or promise, if any, has been fully removed. A free and voluntary confession is deserving of the highest credit, because it is presumed to flow from the highest sense of guilt. (See *R.* v. *Warickshall*, (1783) 1 Leach 263) It is not to be conceived that a man would be induced to make a free and voluntary confession of guilt, so contrary to the feelings and principles of human nature, if the facts confessed were not true. Deliberate and voluntary confessions of guilt, if clearly proved, are among the most effectual proofs in law. An involuntary confession is one which is not the result of the free Will of the maker of it. So where the statement is made as a result of harassment and continuous interrogation for several hours after the person is treated as an offender and accused, such statement must be regarded as involuntary. The inducement may take the form of a promise or of a threat, and often the inducement involves both promise and threat, a promise of forgiveness if disclosure is made and threat of prosecution if it is not. (See *Woodroffe's Evidence*, 9th Edn., p. 284.)

A promise is always attached to the confession alternative while a threat is always attached to the silence alternative; thus, in one case the prisoner is measuring the net advantage of the promise, minus the general undesirability of a false confession, as against the present unsatisfactory situation; while in the other case he is measuring the net advantages of the present satisfactory situation, minus the general undesirability of the confession against the threatened harm. It must be borne in mind that every inducement, threat or promise does not vitiate a confession. Since the object of the rule is to exclude only those confessions which are testimonially untrustworthy, the inducement, threat or promise must be such as is calculated to lead to an untrue confession. On the aforesaid analysis the Court is to determine the absence or presence of an inducement, promise etc. or its sufficiency and how or in what measure it worked on the mind of the accused. If the inducement, promise or threat is sufficient in the opinion of the Court, to give the accused person grounds which would appear to him reasonable for supposing that by making it he would gain any advantage or avoid any evil, it is enough to exclude the confession. The words "appear to him" in the last part of the section refer to the mentality of the accused.

An extra-judicial confession, if voluntary and true and made in a fit state of mind, can be relied upon by the court. The confession will have to be proved like any other fact. The value of the evidence as to confession, like any other evidence, depends upon the veracity of the witness to whom it has been made. The value of the evidence as to the confession depends on the reliability of the witness who gives the evidence. It is not open to any Court to start with a presumption that extra-judicial confession is a weak type of evidence. It would depend on the nature of the circumstances, the time when the confession was made and the credibility of the witnesses who speak to such a confession. Such a confession can be relied upon and conviction can be founded thereon if the evidence about the confession comes from the mouth of witnesses who appear to be unbiased, not even remotely inimical to the accused, and in respect of whom nothing is brought out which may tend to indicate that he may have a motive of attributing an untruthful statement to the accused, the words spoken to by the witness are clear, unambiguous and unmistakably convey that the accused is the perpetrator of the crime and nothing is omitted by the witness which may militate against it. After subjecting the evidence of the witness to a rigorous test on the touchstone of credibility, the extra-judicial confession can be accepted and can be the basis of a conviction if it passes the test of credibility.

CRIME AGAINST WOMEN

State of Punjab v. *Gurmit Singh,* AIR 1996 SC 1393: (1996) 2 SCC 384

1. Of late, crime against women in general and rape in particular is on the increase, It is an irony that while we are celebrating women's rights in all spheres, we show little or no concern for her honour. It is a sad reflection on the attitude of indifference of the society towards the violation of human dignity of the victims of sex crimes. We must remember that a rapist not only violates the victim's privacy and personal integrity, but inevitably causes serious psychological as well as physical harm in the process. Rape is not merely a physical assault – it is often destructive of the whole personality of the victim. A murderer destroys the physical body of his victim; a rapist degrades the very soul of the helpless female. The Court, therefore, shoulders a great responsibility while trying an accused on charges of rape. They must deal with such cases with utmost sensitivity. The Courts should examine the broader probabilities of a case and not get swayed by minor contradictions or insignificant discrepancies in the statement of the prosecutrix, which are not of a fatal nature, to throw out an otherwise reliable prosecution case. If evidence of the prosecutrix inspires confidence, it must be relied upon without seeking corroboration of her

statement in material particulars. If for some reason the Court finds it difficult to place implicit reliance on her testimony, it may look for evidence which may lend assurance to her testimony, short of corroboration required in the case of an accomplice. The testimony of the prosecutrix must be appreciated in the background of the entire case and Trial Court must be alive to its responsibility and be sensitive while dealing with cases involving sexual molestations.

2. There has been lately, lot of criticism of the treatment of the victims of sexual assault in the Court during their cross-examination. The provisions of Evidence Act regarding relevancy of facts notwithstanding, some defence counsel adopt the strategy of continual questioning of the prosecutrix as to the details of the rape. The victim is required to repeat again and again the details of the rape incident not so much as to bring out the facts on record or to test her credibility but to test her story for inconsistencies with a view of attempt to twist the interpretation of events given by her so as to make them appear inconsistent with her allegations. The Court, therefore, should not sit as a silent spectator while the victim of crime is being cross-examined by the defence. It must effectively control the recording of evidence in the Court. While every latitude should be given to the accused to test the veracity of the prosecutrix and the credibility of her version through cross-examination, the Court must also ensure that cross-examination is not made a means of harassment or causing humiliation to the victim of crime. A victim of rape, it must be remembered, has already undergone a traumatice experience and if she is made to repeat again and again, in unfamiliar surroundings, what she had been subjected to, she may be too ashamed and even nervous or confused to speak and her silence or a confused stray sentence may be wrongly interpreted as "discrepancies and contradictions" in her evidence.

3. The alarming frequency of crime against women led the Parliament to enact Criminal Law (Amendment) Act, 1983 (Act 43 of 1983) to make the law of rape more realistic. By the Amendment Act, sections 375 and 376 were amended and certain more penal provisions were incorporated for punishing such custodians who molest a woman under their custody or care. Section 114A was also added in the Evidence Act, for drawing a conclusive presumption as to the absence of consent in certain prosecutions for rape, involving such custodians. Section 327 of the Code of Criminal Procedure which deals with the right of an accused to an open trial was also amended by addition of sub-sections (2) and (3) after re-numbering the old section as sub-section (1), sub-sections (2) and (3) of section 327, Cr. P.C. provide as follows:

Section 327, Court to be open—

(2) Notwithstanding anything contained in sub-section (1), the inquiry into and trial of rape or an offence under section 376, section 376A, section 376B, section 376C or section 376D of the Indian Penal Code shall be conducted *in camera*:

Provided that the presiding judge may, if he thinks fit, or on an application made by either of the parties, allow any particular person to have access to, or be or remain in, the room or building used by the Court.

(3) Where any proceedings are held under sub-section (2), it shall not be lawful for any person to print or publish any matter in relation to any such proceedings, except with the previous permission of the Court.

4. These two provisions are in the nature of exception to the general rule of an open trial. In spite of the amendment, however, it is seen that the trial Courts either are not conscious of the amendment or do not realise its importance for hardly does one come across a case where the enquiry and trial of a rape case has been conducted by the Court *in camera*. The expression that the inquiry into and trial of rape "shall be conducted *in camera*" as occurring in sub-section (2) of section 327, Cr. P.C. is not only significant but very important. It casts a duty on the Court to conduct the trial of rape cases etc, invariably "*in camera*". The Courts are obliged to act in furtherance of the intention expressed by the Legislature and not to ignore its mandate and must invariably take recourse to the provisions of section 327(2) and (3), Cr. P.C. and hold the trial of rape cases *in camera*. It would enable the victim of crime to be a little comfortable and answer the questions with greater ease in not too familiar a surroundings. Trial in camera would not only be in keeping with the self-respect of the victim of crime and in tune with the legislative intent but is also likely to improve the quality of the evidence of a prosecutrix because she would not be so hesitant or bashful to depose frankly as she may be in an open Court, under the gaze of public. The improved quality of her evidence would assist the Courts in arriving at the truth and sifting truth from falsehood. The High Courts would therefore be well-advised to draw the attention of the Trial Courts to the amended provisions of section 327, Cr. P.C. and to impress upon the Presiding Officers to invariably hold the trial of rape cases *in camera,* rather than in the open Court as envisaged by section 327(2), Cr. P.C. When trials are held *in camera,* it would not be lawful for any person to print or publish any matter in relation to the proceedings in the case, except with the previous permission of the Court as envisaged by section 327(3), Cr. P.C. This would save any further embarrassment being caused to the victim of sex crime. Wherever possible it may also be worth considering whether it would not be more desirable that the cases of sexual assaults on the females are tried by lady judges, wherever available, so that the prosecutrix can make her statement with greater ease and assist the Courts to properly discharge their duties, without allowing the truth to be sacrificed at the alter of rigid technicalities while appreciating evidence in such cases. The Courts should, as far as possible, avoid disclosing the name of the prosecutrix in their orders to save further embarrassment to the victim of sex crime. The anonymity of the victim of the crime must be maintained as far as possible throughout. In the present case, the Trial Court repeatedly used the name of the victim in its order under appeal, when it could have just referred to her as the prosecutrix. We need say no more on this aspect and hope that the Trial Courts would take recourse to the provisions of section 327(2) and (3), Cr. P.C. Liberally. Trial of rape cases *in camera* should be the rule, and open trial in such cases an exception.

CRIMINAL APPELLATE JURISDICTION OF SUPREME COURT

Chandra Mohan Tiwari v. *State of Madhya Pradesh,* AIR 1992 SC 891: (1992) 2 SCC 105

1. Under sub-clause (a) of article 134(1) an appeal lies as of right to the Supreme Court in a case where the High Court has reversed an order of acquittal of an accused person and sentenced him to death.

2. Under sub-clause (b) of article 134(1) an appeal lies as of right to the Supreme Court in a case where the High Court has withdrawn the case for trial before itself from any Court subordinate to its authority and sentenced him to death.

3. Under section 2(a) of the Act, of 1970 an appeal lies as of right to the Supreme Court in a case where the High Court has reversed an order of acquittal of an accused person and sentenced him to imprisonment for life or imprisonment for a period of not less than 10 years.

4. Under section 2(b) of the Act, of 1970 an appeal lies as of right to the Supreme Court in a case where the High Court has withdrawn for trial before itself any case from any Court subordinate to its authority and has in such trial convicted the accused person and sentenced him to imprisonment for life or imprisonment for a period of not less than 10 years.

5. Under section 379 of the Code, which is now newly introduced in line with the constitutional provisions of article 134(1)(a) and (b) and with section 2 of the Act of 1970, an appeal lies as of right to the Supreme Court in a case where the High Court has on appeal reversed an order of acquittal of an accused person and convicted and sentenced him either to death or to imprisonment for life or imprisonment for a term of 10 years or more.

6. In cases not covered by article 134(1)(a) and (b) or section 2(a) and (b) of the Act of 1970 or by section 379 of the Code of Criminal Procedure an appeal will lie only either on a certificate granted by the High Court under article 134(1)(c) or by grant of special leave to appeal by the Supreme Court under article 136.

DYING DECLARATION-I

Sudhakar v. *State of Maharashtra,* AIR 2000 SC 2602: (2000) 6 SCC 671

1. Section 32 is an exception of the rule of hearsay and makes admissible the statement of a person who dies, whether the death is a homicide or a suicide, provided the statement relates to the cause of death, or exhibits circumstances leading to the death. In this respect, as indicated above, the Indian Evidence

Act, in view of the peculiar conditions of our society and the diverse nature and character of our people, has thought it necessary to widen the sphere of section 32 to avoid injustice.

2. The test of proximity cannot be too literally construed and practically reduced to a cut-and-dried formula of universal application so as to be confined in a straitjacket. Distance of time would depend or vary with the circumstances of each case. For instance, where death is a logical culmination of a continuous drama long in process and is, as it were a finale of the story, the statement regarding each step directly connected with the end of the drama would be admissible because the entire statement would have to be read as an organic whole and not torn from the context. Sometimes statements relevant to or furnishing an immediate motive may also be admissible as being a part of the transaction of death. It is manifest that all these statements come to light only after the death of the deceased who speaks from death. For instance, where the death takes place within a very short time of the marriage or the distance of time is not spread over more than 3-4 months the statement may be admissible under section 32.

3. The second part of clause (1) of section 32 is yet another exception to the rule that in criminal law the evidence of a person who was not being subjected to or given an opportunity of being cross-examined by the accused, would be valueless because the place of cross-examination is taken by the solemnity and sanctity of oath for the simple reason that a person on the verge of death is not likely to make a false statement unless there is strong evidence to show that the statement was secured either by prompting or tutoring.

4. It may be important to note that section 32 does not speak of homicide alone but includes suicide also, hence all the circumstances which may be relevant to prove a case of homicide would be equally relevant to prove a case of suicide.

5. Where the main evidence consists of statements and letters written by the deceased which are directly connected with or related to her death and which reveal a tell-tale story, the said statement would clearly fall within the four corners of section 32 and, therefore, admissible. The distance of time alone in such cases would not make the statement irrelevant."

DYING DECLARATION-II (PRECEDENTS SUMMARIZED)

Paniben v. *State of Gujarat*, AIR 1992 SC 1817: (1992) 2 SCC 474

1. There is neither rule of law nor of prudence that dying declaration cannot be acted upon without corroboration; *Mannu Raja* v. *State of Uttar Pradesh*, (1976) 2 SCR 764: AIR 1976 SC 2199.

2. If the Court is satisfied that the dying declaration is true and voluntary it can base conviction on it, without corroboration; *State of Uttar Pradesh* v. *Ram Sagar Yadav*, AIR 1985 SC 416; *Ramavati Devi* v. *State of Bihar*, AIR 1983 SC 164.

3. This Court has to scrutinise the dying declaration carefully and must ensure that the declaration is not the result of tutoring, prompting or imagination. The deceased had opportunity to observe and identify the assailants and was in a fit state to make the declaration; *Rama Chandra Reddy* v. *Public Prosecutor*, AIR 1976 SC 1994.

4. Where dying declaration is suspicious it should not be acted upon without corroborative evidence; *Rasheed Beg* v. *State of Madhya Pradesh*, (1974) 4 SCC 264: AIR 1974 SC 332.

5. Where the deceased was unconscious and could never make any dying declaration the evidence with regard to it is to be rejected; *Kake Singh* v. *State of Madhya Pradesh*, AIR 1982 SC 1021.

6. A dying declaration which suffers from infirmity cannot form the basis of conviction; *Ram Manorath* v. *State of Uttar Pradesh*, 1981 SCC (Cri) 581.

7. Merely because a dying declaration does not contain the details as to the occurrence, it is not to be rejected; *State of Maharashtra* v. *Krishnamurthi Laxmipati Naidu*, AIR 1981 SC 617.

8. Equally, merely because it is a brief statement it is not be discarded. On the contrary, the shortness of the statement itself guarantees truth; *Surajdeo Oza* v. *State of Bihar*, AIR 1979 SC 1505.

9. Normally the Court in order to satisfy whether deceased was in a fit mental condition to make the dying declaration look up to the medical opinion. But where the eyewitness has said that the deceased was in a fit and conscious state to make this dying declaration, the medical opinion cannot prevail; *Nanahau Ram* v. *State*, AIR 1988 SC 912.

10. Where the prosecution version differs from the version as given in the dying declaration, the said declaration cannot be acted upon; *State of Uttar Pradesh* v. *Madan Mohan*, AIR 1989 SC 1519.

FRAMING OF CHARGES

Union of India v. *Prafulla Kumar Samal*, (1979) 3 SCC 4: AIR 1979 SC 366

"1. That the Judge while considering the question of framing the charges under section 227 of the Code has the undoubted power to sift and weigh the evidence for the limited purpose of finding out whether or not a *prima facie* case against the accused has been made out.

2. Where the materials placed before the Court disclose grave suspicion against the accused which has not been properly explained the Court will be fully justified in framing a charge and proceeding with the trial.

3. The test to determine a *prima facie* case would naturally depend upon the facts of each case and it is difficult to lay down a rule of universal application. By and large however if two views are equally possible and the Judge is satisfied that the evidence adduced before him while giving rise to some suspicion but not grave suspicion against the accused he will be fully within his right to discharge the accused.

4. That in exercising his jurisdiction under section 227 of the Code the Judge which (sic) under the present Code is a senior and experienced Judge cannot act merely as a post office or a mouth-piece of the prosecution, but has to consider the broad probabilities of the case, the total effect of the evidence and the documents produced before the Court, any basic infirmities appearing in the case and so on. This however does not mean that the Judge should make a roving enquiry into the *pros* and *cons* of the matter and weigh the evidence as if he was conducting a trial."

HANDCUFFING-I

Prem Shankar Shukla v. *Delhi Administration,* (1980) 3 SCC 526: AIR 1980 SC 1535

Handcuffing is *prima facie* inhuman and, therefore, unreasonable, is over-harsh and at the first flush, arbitrary. Absent fair procedure and objective monitoring, to inflict 'irons' is to resort to zoological strategies repugnant to article 21. Thus, we must critically examine the justification offered by the State for this mode of restraint. Surely, the competing claims of securing the prisoner from fleeing and protecting his personality from barbarity have to be harmonised. To prevent the escape of an under-trial is in public interest, reasonable, just and cannot, by itself, be castigated. But to bind a man hand and foot, fetter his limbs with hoops of steel, shuffle him along in the streets and stand him for hours in the courts is to torture him, defile his dignity, vulgarise society and foul the soul of our constitutional culture. Where then do we draw the humane line and how far do the rules err in print and praxis?

Insurance against escape does not compulsorily require handcuffing. There are other measures whereby an escort can keep safe custody of a detenu without the indignity and cruelty implicit in handcuffs or other iron contraptions. Indeed, binding together either the hands or the feet or both has not merely a preventive impact, but also a punitive hurtfulness. Manacles are *mayhem* on the human person and inflict humiliation on the bearer. *The Encyclopaedia Britannica*, Vol. II, 1973 Edn., at p. 53, states 'Handcuffs and fetters are instruments for securing the hands or feet of prisoners under arrest, or as a means of punishment'. The three components of 'irons' force on the human person must be distinctly understood. *Firstly,* to handcuff is to hoop harshly. Further, to handcuff is to punish humiliatingly and to vulgarise the viewers also. Iron straps are insult and pain writ large, animalising victim and keeper. Since there are other ways of ensuring security, it can be laid down as a rule that handcuffs or other fetter shall not be forced on the person of an under-trial prisoner ordinarily. The latest police instructions produced before us hearteningly reflect this view. We lay down as necessarily implicit in articles 14 and 19 that when there is no compulsive need to fetter a person's limbs, it is sadistic, capricious, despotic and demoralising to humble a man by manacling him. Such arbitrary conduct surely slaps article 14 on the face. The minimal freedom of movement which even a detainee is entitled to under article 19 (see *Sunil Batra* v. *Delhi Administration*, AIR 1978 SC 1675) (*supra*)) cannot be cut down cruelly by application of handcuffs or other hoops. It will be unreasonable so to do unless the State is able to make out that no other practical way of forbidding escape is available, the prisoner being so dangerous and desperate and the circumstances so hostile to safe-keeping.

Once we make it a constitutional mandate that no prisoner shall be handcuffed or fettered routinely or merely for the convenience of the custodian or escort – and we declare that to be the law – the distinction between classes of prisoners becomes constitutionally obsolete. Apart from the fact that economic and social importance cannot be the basis for classifying prisoners for purposes of handcuffs or otherwise, how can we assume that a rich criminal or under-trial is any different from a poor or pariah convict or under-trial in the matter of security risk? An affluent in custody may be as dangerous or desperate as an indigent, if not more. He may be more prone to be rescued than an ordinary person. We hold that it is arbitrary and irrational to classify prisoners for purposes of handcuffs, into 'B' class and ordinary class. No one shall be fettered in any form based on superior class differential, as the law treats them equally. It is brutalising to handcuff a person in public and so is unreasonable to do so. Of course, the police escort will find it comfortable to fetter their charges and be at ease but that is not a relevant consideration.

The only circumstance which validates incapacitation by irons – an extreme measure – is that otherwise there is no other reasonable way of preventing his escape, in the given circumstances. Securing the prisoner being a necessity of judicial trial, the State must take steps in this behalf. But even here, the policeman's easy assumption or scary apprehension or subjective satisfaction of likely escape if fetters are not fitted on the prisoner is not enough. The heavy deprivation of personal liberty must be justifiable as reasonable restriction in the circumstances. Ignominy, inhumanity and affliction, implicit in chains and shackles are permissible, as not unreasonable, only if every other less cruel means is fraught with risks or beyond availability. So it is that to be consistent with articles 14 and 19 handcuffs must be the last refuge, not the routine regimen. If a few more guards will suffice, then no handcuffs. If a close watch by armed policemen will do, then no handcuffs. If alternative measures may be provided, then no iron bondage. This is the legal norm.

Functional compulsions of security must reach that dismal degree that no alternative will work except manacles. We must realise that our Fundamental Rights are heavily loaded in favour of personal liberty even in prison, and so, the traditional approaches without reverence for the worth of the human person are obsolete, although they die hard. Discipline can be exaggerated by prison keepers;

dangerousness can be physically worked up by escorts and sadistic disposition, where higher awareness of constitutional rights is absent, may overpower the finer values of dignity and humanity. We regret to observe that cruel and unusual treatment has an unhappy appeal to jail keepers and escorting officers, which must be countered by strict directions to keep to the parameters of the Constitution. The conclusion flowing from these considerations is that there must first be well-grounded basis for drawing a strong inference that the prisoner is likely to jump jail or break out of custody or play the vanishing trick. The belief in this behalf must be based on antecedents which must be recorded and proneness to violence must be authentic. Vague surmises or general averments that the under-trial is a crook or desperado, rowdy or maniac, cannot suffice. In short, save in rare cases of concrete proof readily available of the dangerousness of the prisoner in transit-the *onus* of proof which is on him who puts the person under irons – the police escort will be committing personal assault or mayhem if he handcuffs or fetters his charge. It is disgusting to see the mechanical way in which callous policeman, cavalier fashion, handcuff prisoners in their charge, indifferently keeping them company assured by the thought that the detainee is under 'iron' restraint.

Even orders of superiors are no valid justification as constitutional rights cannot be kept in suspense by superior orders, unless there is material, sufficiently stringent, to satisfy a reasonable mind that dangerous and desperate is the prisoner who is being transported and further that by adding to the escort party or other strategy he cannot be kept under control. It is hard to imagine such situations. We must repeat that it is unconscionable, indeed, outrageous, to make the strange classification between better class prisoners and ordinary prisoners in the matter of handcuffing. This elitist concept has no basis except that on the assumption the ordinary Indian is a sub-citizen and freedoms under part III of the Constitution are the privilege of the upper sector of society.

Merely because a person is charged with a grave offence he cannot be handcuffed. He may be very quiet, well-behaved docile or even timid. Merely because the offence is serious, the inference of escape-proneness or desperate character does not follow. Many other conditions mentioned in the Police Manual are totally incongruous with what we have stated above and must fall as unlawful. Tangible testimony, documentary or other, or desperate behaviour, geared to making good his escape, alone will be a valid ground for handcuffing and fettering, and even this may be avoided by increasing the strength of the escorts or taking the prisoners in well-protected vans. It is heartening to note that in some States in this country no handcuffing is done at all, save in rare cases, when taking undertrials to courts and the scary impression that unless the person is confined in irons he will run away is a convenient myth.

Even in cases where, in extreme circumstances, handcuffs have to be put on the prisoner, the escorting authority must record contemporaneously the reasons for doing so. Otherwise, under article 21 the procedure will be unfair and bad in law. Nor will mere recording the reasons do, as that can be a mechanical process mindlessly made. The escorting officer, whenever he handcuffs a prisoner produced in court, must show the reasons so recorded to the Presiding Judge and get his approval. Otherwise, there is no control over possible arbitrariness in applying handcuffs and fetters. The minions of the Police establishment must make good their security recipes by getting judicial approval. And, once the court directs that handcuffs shall be off, no escorting authority can overrule judicial direction. This is implicit in article 21 which insists upon fairness reasonableness and justice in the very procedure which authorises stringent deprivation of life and liberty. The ratio in *Maneka Gandhi* v. *Union of India,* (1978) 2 SCR 621: AIR 1978 SC 597 and *Sunil Batra* v. *Delhi Administration,* AIR 1978 SC 597 and AIR 1978 SC 1675 (*supra*) read in proper light, leads us to this conclusion.

We, therefore, hold that the petition must be allowed and handcuffs on the prisoner dropped, We declare that the Punjab Police Manual, insofar as it puts the ordinary Indian beneath the better class breed (paras 26.21-A and 26.22 of Chapter XXVI) is untenable and arbitrary and direct that Indian humans shall not be dichotomised and the common run discriminated against regarding handcuffs. The provisions in para 26.22 that every under-trial who is accused of a non-bailable offence punishable with more than 3 years' prison term shall be routinely handcuffed is violative of articles 14, 19 and 21, so also para 26.22(b) and (c). The nature of the accusation is not the criterion. The clear and present danger of escape breaking out of the police control is the determinant. And for this there must be clear material, not glib assumption, record of reasons and judicial oversight and summary hearing and direction by the court where the victim is produced. We go further to hold that para 26.22(1) (d), (e) and (f) also hover perilously near unconstitutionality unless read down as we herein direct. 'Desperate character' is who? Handcuffs are not summary punishment vicariously imposed at police level, at once obnoxious and irreversible. Armed escorts, worth the salt, can overpower any unarmed under-trial and extra-guards can make up exceptional needs. In very special situations, we do not rule out the application, of irons. The same reasoning appears to (e) and (f). Why torture the prisoner because others will demonstrate or attempt his rescue? The plain law of under-trial custody is thus contrary to the unedifying escort practice. We remove the handcuffs from the law and humanize the police praxis to harmonize with the satwic values of part III. The law must be firm, not foul, stern, not sadistic, strong, not callous.

We clearly declare – and it shall be obeyed from the Inspector-General of Police and Inspector-General of Prisons to the escort constable and the jail warder – that the rule regarding a prisoner in transit between prison house and court house is freedom from handcuffs and the exception, under conditions of judicial supervision we have indicated earlier, will be restraints with irons, to be justified before or after. We mandate the judicial officer before whom the prisoner is produced to interrogate the prisoner, as a rule, whether he has been subject to handcuffs or other 'irons' treatment and, if he has been, the official concerned shall be asked to explain the action forthwith in the light of this judgment.

HANDCUFFING-II

Citizen for Democracy v. *State of Assam*, AIR 1996 SC 2193: (1995) 3 SCC 743

1. We declare, direct and lay down as a rule that handcuffs or other fetters shall not be forced on a prisoners – convicted or under trial – while lodged in a jail any where in the country or while transporting or in transit from one jail to another or from jail to Court and back. The police and the jail authorities, on their own, shall have no authority to direct the handcuffing of any inmate of a jail in the country or during transport from one jail to another or from jail to Court and back.

2. Where the police or the jail authorities have well grounded basis for drawing a strong inference that a particular prisoner is likely to jump jail or break out of the custody then the said prisoner be produced before the Magistrate concerned and a prayer for permission to handcuff the prisoner be made before the said Magistrate. Save in rare cases of concrete proof regarding proneness of the prisoner to violence, his tendency to escape, he being so dangerous/ desperate and the finding that no other practical way of forbidding escape is available, the Magistrate may grant permission to handcuff the prisoner.

3. In all the cases where a person arrested by police, is produced before the Magistrate and remand – judicial or non-judicial – is given by the Magistrate the person concerned shall not be handcuffed unless special orders in that respect are obtained from the Magistrate at the time of the grant of the remand.

4. When the police arrests a person in execution of a warrant of arrest obtained from a Magistrate, the person arrested shall not be handcuffed unless the police has also obtained orders from the Magistrate for the handcuffing of the person to be so arrested.

5. Where a person is arrested by the police without warrant the police officer concerned may if he is satisfied, on the basis of the guide-lines given by us in para above, that it is necessary to handcuff such a person, he may do so till the time he is taken to the police station and thereafter his production before the Magistrate. Further use of fetters thereafter can only be under the orders of the Magistrate as already indicated by us.

6. We direct all ranks of police and the prison authorities to meticulously obey the above mentioned directions. Any violation of any of the directions issued by us by rank of police in the country or members of the jail establishment shall be summarily punishable under the Contempt of Courts Act apart from other penal consequences under law.

HEARING ON QUESTION OF SENTENCE

Ram Deo Chauhan v. *State of Assam*, AIR 2001 SC 2231: (2001) 5 SCC 714

1. When the conviction is under section 302 IPC (with or without the aid of section 34 or 149 or 120B of IPC) if the Sessions Judge does not propose to impose death penalty on the convicted person it is unnecessary to proceed to hear the accused on the question of sentence. Section 235(2) of the Code will not be violated if the sentence of life imprisonment is awarded for that offence without hearing the accused on the question of sentence.

2. In all other cases the accused must be given sufficient opportunity of hearing on the question of sentence.

3. The normal rule is that after pronouncing the verdict of guilty the hearing should be made on the same day and the sentence shall also be pronounced on the same day.

4. In cases where the Judge feels or if the accused demands more time for hearing on the question of sentence (especially when the Judge propose to impose death penalty) the proviso to section 309(2) is not a bar for affording such time.

5. For any reason the court is inclined to adjourn the case after pronouncing the verdict of guilty in grave offences the convicted person shall be committed to jail till the verdict on the sentence is pronounced. Further detention will depend upon the process of law.

IMMORAL TRAFFIC ACT – PROTECTIVE HOMES FOR VICTIMS

Dr. Upendra Baxi v. *State of Uttar Pradesh*, AIR 1987 SC 191: (1986) 4 SCC 106

Firstly, we would, in the first place call upon the state government to file an affidavit of the Commissioner, Agra Divisional as to why the possession of the old building was handed over to the landlord inspite of the fact that the landlord had lost his suit for eviction and why the protective home was shifted to a place which suffers from various drawbacks setout in the Inspection reports date 17th July 1985 and 2nd September 1985.

Secondly, we would direct the State Government to carry out the following directions:

(1) The approach road to the new building shall be made into a pucca or semipucca road so that it does not get blocked or waterlogged by rain. This shall be done within 3 months from today;

(2) The big hall as also the three rooms used as class-rooms and the kitchen shall be provided with cross ventilation by putting up sufficient number of windows so as to ensure passage of air in and out the rooms. The District Judge or the Additional District Judge nominated by him shall determine how many windows are necessary to be constructed for this purpose;

(3) Exhaust fans shall be provided in the big hall, three class rooms, kitchen and offices;

(4) The State Government shall provide police protection throughout day and night for the inmates of the Protective Home in the new building;

(5) The State Government shall either provide accommodation to the staff of the Protective Home in or near the new building or provide conveyance to the members of the staff for coming to the Protective Home and going back to their respective homes unless public transport is available in the immediate vicinity of the Protective Home;

(6) We are informed that mosquito nets have been provided by the State Government to each and every inmate as also to the members of the staff staying in the Protective Home but if that has not yet been done, the State Government shall immediately take steps to provide mosquito nets to each and every inmate and member of the staff staying in the Protective Home;

(7) The State Government shall provide a conveyance for taking the inmates to the Court and bringing them back to the Protective Home and similarly, conveyance shall also be provided to the District Judge or Additional District Judge inspecting the Protective Home;

(8) The District Manager (Telephones), Agra shall immediately shift the telephone to the new building and whatever steps are necessary for this purpose shall be taken by the State Government without any delay;

(9) The State Government shall immediately provide cooking gas in the kitchen so that it is not necessary to use wood for cooking which may emit a lot of smoke and lead to discomfort and suffocation on account of lack of ventilation;

(10) The State Government shall immediately proceed to carry out rewiring as also to instal the electric meter in a safe place where there is no dampness. We find from the latest Inspection Report of the Additional District Judge dated 30th June, 1986 that the electric meter has been shifted to the chamber of the Superintendent. We hope and trust that the new place to which it is shifted is not damp so as to imperil the safety of the inmates. That is a matter which would have to be looked into by the District Judge or the Additional District Judge when he goes for inspection. But we also think it necessary to direct that since the electric line is of 440 voltage and not 220 voltage and would, therefore, be dangerous for the inmates, the State Government shall without any

undue delay proceed to take the necessary steps to install a generator so that the safety of the inmates is not jeopardised.

Thirdly, we find that despite directions given by this Court on various occasions, the State Government has not yet constituted a Board of Visitors as prescribed in rule 40 of the rules made under the Suppression of Immoral Traffic in Women and Girls Act. We would, therefore, direct the State Government to set up, within a period of two weeks from the receipt of this Order, a Board of Visitors on which there shall be at least three social activists working in the field of welfare of women and particularly suppression of immoral traffic in women and there shall also be included in the Board of Visitors two persons to be nominated by the District Judge, Agra within two weeks from today.

Fourthly, the Superintendent of the Protective Home shall take care to see that no woman or girl is detained in the Protective Home without due authority and process of law. The District Judge, Agra who carries out monthly inspection of the Protective Home shall verify during every visit that no woman or girl is detained except under the authority of law and if he finds that any of them is detained without any authority of law, he shall take steps to see that she is released and repatriated to her parents or husband or other proper authority.

Fifthly, we would direct the District Judge, Agra to nominate two socially committed Advocates who would by turns visit the Protective Home once in a fortnight and enquire from the inmates in regard to their needs and requirements and provide them legal aid and assistance, where required. Each of the Advocates visiting the Protective Home pursuant to this direction shall be paid by the State Government an honorarium of Rs. 50 per visit plus out of pocket expenses.

Lastly, we are pained to point out that though we gave directions from time-to-time for formulating an effective programme of rehabilitation of the inmates in the Protective Home and the State Government also on several occasions promised that they would come forward with a rehabilitation programme, nothing seems to have been done by the State Government so far except engaging a sewing teacher. We have pointed out on more than one occasion that it is absolutely essential that the inmates in the Protective Home should be provided a proper rehabilitation programme so that when they came out of the Protective Home, they are in a position to look after themselves and they do not slide into prostitution on account of economic want. The inmates must be given vocational training and guidance by way of rehabilitation. We would, therefore, once again direct the State Government to produce at the next hearing of the writ petition a detailed rehabilitation programme which they have either set up or they propose to set up within a specified time limit. We would also like the Superintendent of the Protective Home to consider whether it would be possible to arrange for their wedding to proper persons in case they want to get married. The Superintendent of the Protective Home can follow the example of the Nari Niketan in Delhi where a Committee was set up by this Court for the purpose of investigating into the antecedents of the would be bridegrooms in order to ensure that they were genuine persons wishing to marry the inmates and not bogus or sham bridegrooms who were going through the ceremony of marriage merely for the purpose of selling the inmates or pushing them into prostitution. The District Judge will constitute an appropriate Committee for this purpose consisting of himself and at least two social activists. The State Government will also initiate proper follow up action in this behalf with a view to ensuring that the inmates are not taken back to the brothels or/and they do not once again slide into prostitution.

The District Judge, Agra or any other Additional District Judge nominated by him shall visit the Protective Home once every month for the purpose of ensuring that the aforesaid directions given by us are carried out fully and effectively and he shall submit an Inspection Report to this Court on/or before the 15th of every month.

IMPRISONMENT FOR LIFE – REMISSION

State of Madhya Pradesh v. *Ratan Singh,*
AIR 1976 SC 1552: (1976) 3 SCC 470

1. That a sentence of imprisonment for life does not automatically expire at the end of 20 years including the remissions, because the administrative rules framed under the various Jail Manuals or under the Prisons Act cannot supersede the statutory provisions of the Indian Penal Code. A sentence of imprisonment for life means a sentence for the entire life of the prisoner unless the appropriate Government chooses to exercise its discretion to remit either the whole or a part of the sentence under section 401 of the Code of Criminal Procedure.

2. That the appropriate Government has the undoubted discretion to remit or refuse to remit the sentence and where it refuses to remit the sentence no writ can be issued directing the State Government to release the prisoner;

3. That the appropriate Government which is empowered to grant remission under section 401 of the Code of Criminal Procedure is the Government of the State where the prisoner has been convicted and sentenced, that is to say, the transferor State and not the transferee State where the prisoner may have been transferred at his instance under the Transfer of Prisoners Act; and

4. That where the transferee State feels that the accused has completed a period of 20 years it has merely to forward the request of the prisoner to the concerned State Government, that is to say, the Government of the State where the prisoner was convicted and sentenced and even if this request is rejected by the State Government the order of the Government cannot be interfered with by a High Court in its writ jurisdiction.

INTERROGATION OF ACCUSED/WITNESS BY POLICE

Nandini Satpathy v. *P.L. Dani*, AIR 1978 SC 1025: (1978) 2 SCC 424

1. Is a person likely to be accused of crimes *i.e.*, a suspect accused, entitled to the sanctuary of silence as one 'accused of any offence'? Is it sufficient that he is a potential – of course, not distant – candidate for accusation by the police?

2. Does the bar against self-incrimination operate not merely with reference to a particular accusation in regard to which the police investigator interrogates, or does it extend also to other pending or potential accusations outside the specific investigation which has led to the questioning? That is to say, can an accused person who is being questioned by a police officer in a certain case, refuse to answer questions plainly non-criminatory so far as that case is concerned but probably exposes him to the perils of inculpation in other cases *in posse* or *in esse* elsewhere?

3. Does the constitutional shield of silence swing into action only in court or can it barricade the 'accused' against incriminating interrogation at the stages of police investigation?

4. What is the ambit of the cryptic expression 'compelled to be a witness against himself' occurring in article 20(3) of the Constitution? Does 'compulsion' involve physical or like pressure or duress of an unlawful texture or does it cover also the crypto-compulsion or psychic coercion, given a tense situation or officer in authority interrogating an accused person, armed with power to insist on an answer?

5. Does being 'a witness against oneself' include testimonial tendency to incriminate or probative probability of guilt flowing from the answer?

6. What are the parameters of section 161(2) of the Criminal Procedure Code? Does tendency to expose a person to a criminal charge embrace answers which have an inculpatory impact in other criminal cases actually or about to be investigated or tried?

7. Does 'any person' in section 161, Criminal Procedure Code include an accused person or only a witness?

8. When does an answer self-incriminate or tend to expose one to a charge? What distinguishing features mark off nocent and innocent, permissible and impermissible interrogations and answers? Is the setting relevant or should the answer, *in vacuo*, bear a guilty badge on its bosom?

9. Does *mens rea* form a necessary component of section 179, I.P.C., and, if so, what is its precise nature? Can a mere apprehension that any answer has a guilty potential salvage the accused or bring into play the exclusionary rule?

10. Where do we demarcate the boundaries of benefit of doubt in the setting of section 161(2), Criminal Procedure Code and section 179, I.P.C.?

Conclusions

We hold that 'any person supposed to be acquainted with the facts and circumstances of the case' includes an accused person who fills that role because the police suppose him to have committed the crime and must, therefore, be familiar with the facts.

We hold that section 161 enables the police to examine the accused during investigation.

The prohibitive sweep of article 20(3) goes back to the stage of police interrogation – not, as contended, commencing in court only. In our judgment the provisions of article 20(3) and section 161(1) substantially cover the same area, so far as police investigations are concerned. The ban on self-accusation and the right to trial is under way, goes beyond that case and protects the accused in regard to other offences pending or imminent, which may deter him from voluntary disclosure of criminatory matter. So, the legal perils following upon refusal to answer, or answer truthfully cannot be regarded as compulsion within the meaning of article 20(3). The prospect of prosecution may lead to legal tension in the exercise of a constitutional right, but then, a stance of silence is running a calculated risk. On the other hand, if there is any mode of pressure, subtle or crude, mental or physical, direct or indirect, but sufficiently substantial, applied by the policeman for obtaining information from an accused strongly suggestive of guilt, it becomes 'compelled testimony', violative of article 20(3).

A police officer is clearly a person in authority. Insistence on answering is a form of pressure especially in the atmosphere of the police station unless certain safeguards erasing duress are adhered to. Frequent threats of prosecution if there is failure to answer may take on the complexion of undue pressure violating article 20(3). Legal penalty may by itself not amount to duress but the manner of mentioning it to the victim of interrogation may introduce an element of tension and tone of command perilously hovering near compulsion.

We have explained elaborately and summed up, in substance, what is self incrimination or tendency to expose oneself to a criminal charge. It is less than 'relevant' and more than 'confessional'. Irrelevance is impermissible but relevance is licit but when relevant questions are loaded with guilty inference in the event of an answer being supplied, the tendency to incriminate springs into existence. we hold further that the accused person cannot be forced to answer questions merely because the answers thereto are not implicative when viewed in isolation and confined to that particular case. He is entitled to keep his mouth shut if the answer sought has a reasonable prospect of exposing him to guilt in some other accusation actual or imminent, even though the investigation underway is not with reference to that. We have already explained that in determining the incriminatory character of an answer the accused is entitled to consider and the Court while adjudging will take note of the setting, the totality of circumstances, the equation, personal and social, which have a bearing on making an answer substantially innocent but in effect guilty in import. However, fanciful claims, unreasonable apprehensions and vague possibilities cannot be the hiding ground for an accused person. He is bound to answer where there is no clear tendency to criminate.

We have no doubt that section 179, I.P.C. has a component of *mens rea* and where there is no wilful refusal but only unwitting omission or innocent warding off, the offence is not made out. When there is reasonable doubt indicated by the accused's explanation he is entitled to its benefit and cannot be forced to substantiate his ground lest, by this process, be is constrained to surrender the very privilege for which he is fighting. What may apparently be innocent information may really be nocent or noxious viewed in the wider setting.

We hold further that the accused person cannot be forced to answer questions merely because the answers thereto are not implicative when viewed in isolation and confined to that particular case. He is entitled to keep his mouth shut if the answer sought has a reasonable prospect of exposing him to guilt in some other accusation actual or imminent, even though the investigation underway is not with reference to that. However, fanciful claims, unreasonable apprehensions and vague possibilities cannot be the hiding ground for an accused person. He is bound to answer where there is no clear tendency to criminate.

We think that article 20(3) and article 22(1) may, in a way, be telescoped by making it prudent for the Police to permit the advocate of the accused, if there be one, to be present at the time he is examined. Over-reaching article 20(3) and section 161(2) will be obviated by this requirement. We do not lay down that the Police must secure the services of a lawyer. That will lead to 'police station lawyer' system, an abuse which breeds other vices. But all that we mean is that if an accused person expresses the wish to have his lawyer by his side when his examination goes on, this facility shall not be denied, without being exposed to the serious reproof that involuntary self-crimination secured in secrecy and by coercing the will, was the project.

The statement of the accused, if voluntary, is admissible, indeed, invaluable. To erase involuntariness we must erect safeguards which will not 'kill the goose'. To ensure this free will by inbuilt structural changes is the *deside ratum.* Short-run remedies apart, long-run recipes must be innovated whereby fists are replaced by wits, ignorance by awareness, 'third degree' by civilized tools and technology. The factotum policeman who does everything from a guard of honour to traffic patrol to subtle detection is an obsolescent survival. Special training, special legal courses, technological and other detective updating, are important. An aware policeman is the best social asset towards crimelessness. The consciousness of the official as much as of the community is the healing hope for a crime-ridden society. Judge-centred remedies don't work in the absence of community centered rights. All these add up to separation of investigatory personnel from the general mass and in service specialisation of many hues on a scientific basis. This should be done vertically and horizontally. More importantly, the policeman must be released from addiction to coercion and be sensitized to constitutional values.

The symbiotic need to preserve the immunity without stifling legitimate investigation persuades us to indicate that after an examination of the accused, where lawyer of his choice is not available, the police official must take him to a magistrate, doctor or other willing and responsible non-partisan official or non-official and allow a secluded audience where he may unburden himself beyond the view of the police and tell whether he has suffered duress, which should be followed by judicial or some other custody for him where the police cannot teach him. The collector may briefly record the relevant conversation and communicate it – not to the police – but to the nearest Magistrate, Pilot projects on this pattern may yield experience to guide the practical processes of implementing article 20(3). We do not mandate but strongly suggest.

The police officer shall not summon a woman to the police station but examine her in terms of the proviso to section 160(1) of the Criminal Procedure Code.

INVESTIGATION

H.N. Rishbud v. *State of Delhi*, AIR 1955 SC 196: 1955 Cr LJ 526

1. The investigation consists generally of the following steps:

(1) Proceeding to the spot;

(2) Ascertainment of the facts and circumstances of the case;

(3) Discovery and arrest of the suspected offender;

(4) Collection of evidence relating to the commission of the offence which may consist of:

(a) the examination of various persons (including the accused) and the reduction of their statements into writing, if the officer thinks fit;

(b) the search of places or seizure, of things considered necessary for the investigation and to be produced at the trial; and

(5) Formation of the opinion as to whether on the material collected there is a case to place the accused before a Magistrate for trial and if so taking the necessary steps for the same by the filing of a charge-sheet under section 173. The scheme of the Code also shows that while it is permissible for an officer in charge of a police station to depute some subordinate officer to conduct some of these steps in the investigation, the responsibility for every one of these steps is that of the person in the situation of the officer-in-charge of the police station, it having been clearly provided in section 168 that when a subordinate officer makes an investigation he should report the result to the officer-in-charge of the police station. It is also clear that the final step in the investigation, *viz.*, the formation of the opinion as to whether or not there is a case to place the accused on trial is to be that of the officer-in-charge of the police station;

2. A defect or illegality in investigation, however serious, has no direct bearing on the competence or the procedure relating to cognizance or trial. No doubt a police report which results from an investigation is provided in section 190, Criminal Procedure Code as the material on which cognizance is taken. But it cannot be maintained that a valid and legal police report is the foundation of

the jurisdiction of the Court to take cognizance, section 190, Criminal Procedure Code is one out of a group of sections under the heading "Conditions requisite for initiation of proceedings".

JURISDICTION OF HIGH COURTS TO ORDER CBI INVESTIGATION WITHOUT THE CONSENT OF THE STATE

State of West Bengal v. *Committee For Protection of Democratic Rights, West Bengal,* 2010 (2) SCALE 467: AIR 2010 SC 1476

1. The fundamental rights, enshrined in Part III of the Constitution, are inherent and cannot be extinguished by any Constitutional or Statutory provision. Any law that abrogates or abridges such rights would be violative of the basic structure doctrine. The actual effect and impact of the law on the rights guaranteed under Part III has to be taken into account in determining whether or not it destroys the basic structure;

2. Article 21 of the Constitution in its broad perspective seeks to protect the persons of their lives and personal liberties except according to the procedure established by law. The said article in its broad application not only takes within its fold enforcement of the rights of an accused but also the rights of the victim. The State has a duty to enforce the human rights of a citizen providing for fair and impartial investigation against any person accused of commission of a cognizable offence, which may include its own officers. In certain situations even a witness to the crime may seek for and shall be granted protection by the State;

3. In view of the constitutional scheme and the jurisdiction conferred on this Court under article 32 and on the High Courts under article 226 of the Constitution the power of judicial review being an integral part of the basic structure of the Constitution, no Act of Parliament can exclude or curtail the powers of the Constitutional Courts with regard to the enforcement of fundamental rights. As a matter of fact, such a power is essential to give practicable content to the objectives of the Constitution embodied in Part III and other parts of the Constitution. Moreover, in a federal constitution, the distribution of legislative powers between the Parliament and the State Legislature involves limitation on legislative powers and, therefore, this requires an authority other than the Parliament to ascertain whether such limitations are transgressed. Judicial review acts as the final arbiter not only to give effect to the distribution of legislative powers between the Parliament and the State Legislatures, it is also necessary to show any transgression by each entity. Therefore, to borrow the words of Lord Steyn, judicial review is justified by combination of "the principles of separation of powers, rule of law, the principle of constitutionality and the reach of judicial review";

4. If the federal structure is violated by any legislative action, the Constitution takes care to protect the federal structure by ensuring that Courts act as guardians and interpreters of the Constitution and provide remedy under articles 32 and 226, whenever there is an attempted violation. In the circumstances, any direction by the Supreme Court or the High Court in exercise of power under article 32 or 226 to uphold the Constitution and maintain the rule of law cannot be termed as violating the federal structure;

5. Restriction on the Parliament by the Constitution and restriction on the Executive by the Parliament under an enactment, do not amount to restriction on the power of the judiciary under articles 32 and 226 of the Constitution;

6. If in terms of Entry 2 of List II of The Seventh Schedule on the one hand and Entry 2A and Entry 80 of List I on the other, an investigation by another agency is permissible subject to grant of consent by the State concerned, there is no reason as to why, in an exceptional situation, court would be precluded from exercising the same power which the Union could exercise in terms of the provisions of the Statute. In our opinion, exercise of such power by the Constitutional Courts would not violate the doctrine of separation of powers. In fact, if in such a situation the court fails to grant relief, it would be failing in its constitutional duty;

7. When the Special Police Act, itself provides that subject to the consent by the State, the CBI can take up investigation in relation to the crime which was otherwise within the jurisdiction of the State Police, the court can also exercise its constitutional power of judicial review and direct the CBI to take up the investigation within the jurisdiction of the State. The power of the High Court under article 226 of the Constitution cannot be taken away, curtailed or diluted by section 6 of the Special Police Act. Irrespective of there being any statutory provision acting as a restriction on the powers of the Courts, the restriction imposed by section 6 of the Special Police Act, on the powers of the Union, cannot be read as restriction on the powers of the Constitutional Courts. Therefore, exercise of power of judicial review by the High Court, in our opinion, would not amount to infringement of either the doctrine of separation of power or the federal structure;

In the final analysis, our answer to the question referred is that a direction by the High Court, in exercise of its jurisdiction under article 226 of the Constitution, to the CBI to investigate a cognizable offence alleged to have been committed within the territory of a State without the consent of that State will neither impinge upon the federal structure of the Constitution nor violate the doctrine of separation of power and shall be valid in law. Being the protectors of civil liberties of the citizens, this Court and the High Courts have not only the power and jurisdiction but also an obligation to protect the fundamental rights, guaranteed by Part III in general and under article 21 of the Constitution in particular, zealously and vigilantly.

JUVENILE JUSTICE (CARE AND PROTECTION OF CHILDREN) ACT, 2000

Age of Juvenile

Pratap Singh v. *State of Jharkhand*, AIR 2005 SC 2731: (2005) 3 SCC 551

Questions

1. Whether the date of occurrence will be the reckoning date for determining the age of the alleged offender as juvenile offender or the date when he is produced in the court/competent authority;

2. Whether the Act of 2000 will be applicable in the case a proceeding is initiated under the 1986 Act and pending when the Act of 2000 was enforced with effect from 1-4-2001?

Answers

1. The reckoning date for the determination of the age of the juvenile is the date of the offence and not the date when he is produced before the authority or in the court.

2. The 2000 Act, would be applicable in a pending proceeding in any Court/ authority initiated under the 1986 Act and is pending when the 2000 Act came into force and the person had not completed 18 years of age as on 1-4-2001.

LEGAL AID

Centre of Legal Research v. *State of Kerala*, AIR 1986 SC 2195: (1986) 2 SCC 706

We are of the view that the following norms should provide sufficient guidance to the State in this behalf and we would direct that the State Government shall, in compliance with its obligations under article 39A of the Constitution extend its co-operation and support, to the following categories of voluntary organisations and social action groups in running the legal aid programme and organising legal aid camps and lok adalats or niti melas:

1. Voluntary organisations and social action groups which are recognised by the Committee for Implementing Legal Aid Schemes set up by the Government of India or whose programme or programmes are supported by way of grant or otherwise by the Government of India or the State Government or the Committee for Implementing Legal Aid Schemes or the State Legal Aid and Advice Board.
2. Voluntary organisations and social action groups which organise legal aid camps or Lok Adalats or niti melas in conjunction with or with the support of the Committee for Implementing Legal Aid Schemes or the Kerala State Legal Aid and Advice Board.

3. Voluntary organisations and social action groups which are recognised by the State Government or the State Legal Aid and Advice Board on an application being made in that behalf.

Every voluntary organisation or social action group falling within clause (1), (2) or (3) above and to which co-operation and support are directed to be extended by the State Government shall furnish whatever factual information is required by the Central Government or the State Government or the Committee for Implementing Legal Aid Schemes or the State Legal Aid and Advice Board, but we may make it clear that such voluntary organisation or social action group shall not be under the control or direction or supervision of the State Government or the State Legal Aid and Advice Board because we take the view that voluntary organisations and social action groups operating these programmes should be totally free from any Governmental control.

LEGISLATIVE COMPETENCE TO CREATE SPECIAL COURTS

In re *The Special Courts Bill,*
AIR 1979 SC 478: (1979) 2 SCR 476

1. The Parliament has the legislative competence to create Special Courts and to provide that an appeal shall lie as of right from any judgment or order of a Special Court to the Supreme Court. Clauses 2 and 10(1) of the Bill are, therefore, within the Parliament's legislative competence;

2. The classification provided for in clause 4(1) of the Bill is valid to the extent to which the Central Government is empowered to make a declaration in respect of offences alleged to have been committed during the period of Emergency by persons who held high public or political offices in India. Persons who are alleged to have committed offences prior to the declaration of Emergency cannot validly be grouped along with those who are alleged to have committed offences during the period of Emergency. It is, therefore, not competent to the Central Government to make a declaration under clause 4(1) of the Bill in respect of persons who are alleged to have committed offences between February 27, 1975 and June 25, 1975.

3. The procedure prescribed by the Bill for the trial of offences in respect of which a declaration can be validly made by the Central Government under clause 4(1) of the Bill is just and fair except in regard to the following matters:

(a) the provision in clause 7 of the Bill, under which a retired Judge of the High Court can be appointed as a Judge of the Special Court;

(b) the provision in clause 7, under which the appointment of a Judge to the Special Court can be made by the Central Government in consultation with but without the concurrence of the Chief Justice of India; and

(c) the absence of a provision for transfer of a case from one Special Court to another.

4. The Bill is valid and constitutional in all other respects.

MONITORING INVESTIGATION

Sakiri Vasu v. *State of Uttar Pradesh*, (2008) 2 SCC 409: AIR 2008 SC 907

1. Even if an FIR has been registered and even if the police has made the investigation, or is actually making the investigation, which the aggrieved person feels is not proper, such a person can approach the Magistrate under section 156(3), Criminal Procedure Code and if the Magistrate is satisfied he can order a proper investigation and take other suitable steps and pass such order orders as he thinks necessary for ensuring a proper investigation. All these powers a Magistrate enjoys under section 156(3), Criminal Procedure Code.

2. Section 156(3) provides for a check by the Magistrate on the police performing its duties under Chapter XII, Criminal Procedure Code. In cases where the Magistrate finds that the police has not done its duty of investigating the case at all, or has not done it satisfactorily, he can issue a direction to the police to do the investigation properly, and can monitor the same.

3. The power in the Magistrate to order further investigation under section 156(3) is an independent power, and does not affect the power of the investigating officer to further investigate the case even after submission of his report *vide* section 173(8). Hence the Magistrate can order re-opening of the investigation even after the police submits the final report, vide *State of Bihar* v. *J.A.C. Saldanna,* AIR 1980 SC 326.

4. Section 156(3), Criminal Procedure Code is wide enough to include all such powers in a Magistrate which are necessary for ensuring a proper investigation, and it includes the power to order registration of an F.I.R. and of ordering a proper investigation if the Magistrate is satisfied that a proper investigation has not been done, or is not being done by the police. Section 156(3), Criminal Procedure Code though briefly worded, in our opinion, is very wide and it will include all such incidental powers as are necessary for ensuring a proper investigation.

5. Although section 156(3) is very briefly worded, there is an implied power in the Magistrate under section 156(3), Criminal Procedure Code to order registration of a criminal offence and/or to direct the officer-in-charge of the concerned police station to hold a proper investigation and take all such necessary steps that may be necessary for ensuring a proper investigation including monitoring the same. Even though these powers have not been expressly mentioned in section 156(3), Criminal Procedure Code we are of the opinion that they are implied in the above provision.

6. If a person has a grievance that his FIR has not been registered by the police station his first remedy is to approach the Superintendent of Police under section 154(3), Criminal Procedure Code or other police officer referred to in section 36, Criminal Procedure Code. If despite approaching the Superintendent of Police or the officer referred to in section 36 his grievance still persists, then he can approach a Magistrate under section 156(3), Criminal Procedure Code instead of rushing to the High Court by way of a writ petition or a petition under section 482, Criminal Procedure Code. Moreover he has a further remedy of filing a criminal complaint under section 200, Criminal Procedure Code. Why then should writ petitions or section 482 petitions be entertained when there are so many alternative remedies? High Court should not encourage this practice and should ordinarily refuse to interfere in such matters, and relegate the petitioner to his alternating remedy, firstly under section 154(3) and section 36, Criminal Procedure Code before the concerned police officers, and if that is of no avail, by approaching the concerned Magistrate under section 156(3).

7. If the Magistrate on an application under section 156(3), Criminal Procedure Code is satisfied that proper investigation has not been done, or is not being done by the officer-in-charge of the concerned police station, he can certainly direct the officer in charge of the police station to make a proper investigation and can further monitor the same (though he should not himself investigate).

8. No doubt the Magistrate cannot order investigation by the CBI vide *C.B.I.* v. *State of Rajasthan,* (2001) 3 SCC 333 but this Court or the High Court has power under article 136 or article 226 to order investigation by the CBI. That, however should be done only in some rare and exceptional case, otherwise, the CBI would be flooded with a large number of cases and would find it impossible to properly investigate all of them.

NARCO ANALYSIS, BRAIN MAPPING AND POLYGRAPH TESTS

Smt. Selvi v. *State of Karnataka,* JT 2010 (5) SC 11: 2010 (4) SCALE 690

1. In our considered opinion, the compulsory administration of the impugned techniques violates the 'right against self-incrimination'. This is because the underlying rationale of the said right is to ensure the reliability as well as voluntariness of statements that are admitted as evidence. This Court has recognized that the protective scope of article 20(3) extends to the investigative stage in criminal cases and when read with section 161(2) of the Code of Criminal Procedure, 1973 it protects accused persons, suspects as well as witnesses who are examined during an investigation. The test results cannot be admitted in evidence if they have been obtained through the use of compulsion. Article 20(3) protects an individual's choice between speaking and remaining silent, irrespective of whether the subsequent testimony proves to be inculpatory or

exculpatory. Article 20(3) aims to prevent the forcible 'conveyance of personal knowledge that is relevant to the facts in issue'. The results obtained from each of the impugned tests bear a 'testimonial' character and they cannot be categorised as material evidence.

2. We are also of the view that forcing an individual to undergo any of the impugned techniques violates the standard of 'substantive due process' which is required for restraining personal liberty. Such a violation will occur irrespective of whether these techniques are forcibly administered during the course of an investigation or for any other purpose since the test results could also expose a person to adverse consequences of a non-penal nature. The impugned techniques cannot be read into the statutory provisions which enable medical examination during investigation in criminal cases, *i.e.* the *Explanation* to sections 53, 53A and 54 of the Code of Criminal Procedure, 1973. Such an expansive interpretation is not feasible in light of the rule of *'ejusdem generis'* and the considerations which govern the interpretation of statutes in relation to scientific advancements. We have also elaborated how the compulsory administration of any of these techniques is an unjustified intrusion into the mental privacy of an individual. It would also amount to 'cruel, inhuman or degrading treatment' with regard to the language of evolving international human rights norms. Furthermore, placing reliance on the results gathered from these techniques comes into conflict with the 'right to fair trial'. Invocations of a compelling public interest cannot justify the dilution of constitutional rights such as the 'right against self-incrimination'.

3. In light of these conclusions, we hold that no individual should be forcibly subjected to any of the techniques in question, whether in the context of investigation in criminal cases or otherwise. Doing so would amount to an unwarranted intrusion into personal liberty. However, we do leave room for the voluntary administration of the impugned techniques in the context of criminal justice, provided that certain safeguards are in place. Even when the subject has given consent to undergo any of these tests, the test results by themselves cannot be admitted as evidence because the subject does not exercise conscious control over the responses during the administration of the test. However, any information or material that is subsequently discovered with the help of voluntary administered test results can be admitted, in accordance with section 27 of the Evidence Act, 1872.

4. The National Human Rights Commission had published 'Guidelines for the Administration of Polygraph Test (Lie Detector Test) on an Accused' in 2000. These guidelines should be strictly adhered to and similar safeguards should be adopted for conducting the 'Narco analysis technique' and the 'Brain Electrical Activation Profile' test. The text of these guidelines has been reproduced below:

(i) No Lie Detector Tests should be administered except on the basis of consent of the accused. An option should be given to the accused whether he wishes to avail such test.

(ii) If the accused volunteers for a Lie Detector Test, he should be given access to a lawyer and the physical, emotional and legal implication of such a test should be explained to him by the police and his lawyer.

(iii) The consent should be recorded before a Judicial Magistrate.

(iv) During the hearing before the Magistrate, the person alleged to have agreed should be duly represented by a lawyer.

(v) At the hearing, the person in question should also be told in clear terms that the statement that is made shall not be a 'confessional' statement to the Magistrate but will have the status of a statement made to the police.

(vi) The Magistrate shall consider all factors relating to the detention including the length of detention and the nature of the interrogation.

(vii) The actual recording of the Lie Detector Test shall be done by an independent agency (such as a hospital) and conducted in the presence of a lawyer.

(viii) A full medical and factual narration of the manner of the information received must be taken on record.

NON-EXPLANATION OF THE INJURIES SUSTAINED BY THE ACCUSED

Lakshmi Singh v. *State of Bihar,*
AIR 1976 SC 2263: (1976) 4 SCC 394

In a situation like this when the prosecution fails to explain the injuries on the person of an accused depending on the facts of each case, any of the three results may follow:

1. That the accused had inflicted the injuries on the members of the prosecution party in exercise of the right of self-defence.
2. It makes the prosecution version of the occurrence doubtful and the charge against the accused cannot be held to have been proved beyond reasonable doubt.
3. It does not affect the prosecution case at all.

It seems to us that in a murder case, the non-explanation of the injuries sustained by the accused at about the time of the occurrence or in the course of altercation is a very important circumstance from which the Court can draw the following inferences:

1. That the prosecution has suppressed the genesis and the origin of the occurrence and has thus not presented the true version.
2. That the witnesses who have denied the presence of the injuries on the person of the accused are lying on a most material point and therefore their evidence is unreliable;

3. That in case there is a defence version which explains the injuries on the person of the accused it is rendered probable so as to throw doubt on the prosecution case.

The omission on the part of the prosecution to explain the injuries on the person of the accused assumes much greater importance where the evidence consists of interested or inimical witnesses or where the defence gives a version which competes in probability with that of the prosecution one.

PAROLE

Sunil Fulchand Shah v. *Union of India*, AIR 2000 SC 1023: (2000) 3 SCC 409

1. Personal liberty is one of the most cherished freedoms, perhaps more important than the other freedoms guaranteed under the Constitution. It was for this reason that the Founding Fathers enacted the safeguards in article 22 in the Constitution so as to limit the power of the State to detain a person without trial, which may otherwise pass the test of article 21, by humanising the harsh authority over individual liberty. In a democracy governed by the Rule of Law, the drastic power to detain a person without trial for security of the State and/or maintenance of public order, must be strictly construed. However, where individual liberty comes into conflict with an interest of the security of the State or public order, then the liberty of the individual must give way to the larger interest of the nation;

2. That section 10 of COFEPOSA prescribes not only the maximum period of detention but also the method of computation of that period and on a plain reading of the section, the period of detention is to be computed from the date of actual detention and not from the date of the order of detention;

3. That parole, *stricto sensu* may be granted by way of a temporary release as contemplated by section 12(1) or 12(1-A) of COFEPOSA by the Government or its functionaries, in accordance with the Parole Rules or administrative instructions, framed by the Government which are administrative in character. For securing release on parole, a detenu has, therefore, to approach the Government concerned or the jail authorities, who may impose conditions as envisaged by section 12(2) etc. and the grant of parole shall be subject to those terms and conditions;

4. That the Courts cannot, generally speaking, exercise the power to grant temporary release to detenus, on parole, in cases covered by COFEPOSA during the period an order of detention is in force because of the express prohibition contained in clause (6) of section 12. The bar of judicial intervention, to direct temporary release of a detenu would not, however, affect the jurisdiction of the High Courts under article 226 of the Constitution or of this Court under articles 32, 136 or 142 of the Constitution to direct the temporary release of the detenu, where request of the detenu to be released on parole for a specified reason and/or for a specified period, has been, in the opinion of the Court, unjustifiably

refused or where in the interest of justice such an order of temporary release is required to be made. That jurisdiction, however, has to be sparingly exercised by the Court and even when it is exercised, it is appropriate that the Court leaves it to the administrative or jail authorities to prescribe the conditions and terms on which parole is to be availed of by the detenu;

5. That parole does not interrupt the period of detention and, thus, that period needs to be counted towards the total period of detention unless the terms for grant of parole, rules or instructions, prescribe otherwise;

6. The quashing of an order of detention by the High Court brings to an end such an order and if an appeal is allowed against the order of the High Court, the question whether or not the detenu should be made to surrender to undergo the remaining period of detention, would depend upon a variety of factors and in particular on the question of lapse of time between the date of detention, the order of the High Court, and the order of this Court, setting aside the order of the High Court.

A detenu need not be sent back to undergo the remaining period of detention, after a long lapse of time, when even the maximum prescribed period intended in the order of detention has expired, unless there still exists a proximate temporal nexus between the period of detention indicated in the order by which the detenu was required to be detained and the date when the detenu is required to be detained pursuant to the appellate order and the State is able to satisfy the Court about the desirability of 'further' or 'continued' detention;

7. That, where, however, long time has not lapsed or the period of detention initially fixed in the order of detention has not expired, the detenu may be sent back to undergo the balance period of detention. It is open to the Appellate Court, considering the facts and circumstances of each case, to decide whether the period during which the detenu was free on the basis of an erroneous order should be excluded while computing the total period of detention as indicated in the order of detention though normally the period during which the detenu was free on the basis of such an erroneous order may not be given as a 'set off' against the total period of detention. The actual period of incarceration cannot, however, be permitted to exceed the maximum period of detention, as fixed in the order, as per the prescription of the statute.

POWERS OF APPELLATE COURT IN APPEAL AGAINST ACQUITTAL-I

Chandrappa v. *State of Karnataka*, (2007) 4 SCC 415: 2007 Cr LJ 2136

1. An appellate court has full power to review, re-appreciate and reconsider the evidence upon which the order of acquittal is founded.

2. The Code of Criminal Procedure, 1973 puts no limitation, restriction or condition on exercise of such power and an appellate court on the evidence before it may reach its own conclusion, both on questions of fact and of law.

3. Various expressions, such as, "substantial and compelling reasons", "good and sufficient grounds", "very strong circumstances", "distorted conclusions", "glaring mistakes", etc. are not intended to curtail extensive powers of an appellate court in an appeal against acquittal. Such phraseologies are more in the nature of "flourishes of language" to emphasise the reluctance of an appellate Court to interfere with acquittal than to curtail the power of the court to review the evidence and to come to its own conclusion.

4. An Appellate Court, however, must bear in mind that in case of acquittal, there is double presumption in favour of the accused. *Firstly*, the presumption of innocence is available to him under the fundamental principle of criminal jurisprudence that every person shall be presumed to be innocent unless he is proved guilty by a competent court of law. *Secondly*, the accused having secured his acquittal, the presumption of his innocence is further reinforced, reaffirmed and strengthened by the Trial Court.

5. If two reasonable conclusions are possible on the basis of the evidence on record, the Appellate Court should not disturb the finding of acquittal recorded by the Trial Court.

POWERS OF APPELLATE COURT WHILE DEALING AN APPEAL AGAINST ACQUITTAL-II

Sanwat Singh v. *State of Rajasthan,* AIR 1961 SC 715: (1961) 3 SCR 120

The scope of the powers of an Appellate Court in an appeal against acquittal has been elucidated by the Privy Council in *Sheo Swarup* v. *Emperor,* 61 IA 398: AIR 1934 PC 227 (2). There Lord Russell observed:

> "............ the High Court should and will always give proper weight and consideration to such matters as:
>
> (1) the views of the trial Judge as to the credibility of the witnesses,
>
> (2) the presumption of innocence in favour of the accused, a presumption certainly not weakened by the face that he has been acquitted at his trial,
>
> (3) the right of the accused to the benefit of any doubt, and
>
> (4) the slowness of an Appellate Court in disturbing a finding of fact arrived at by a Judge who had the advantage of seeing the witnesses

The foregoing discussion yields the following results:

(1) an Appellate Court has full power to review the evidence upon which the order of acquittal is founded;

(2) the principles laid down in *Sheo Swarup* v. *Emperor,* 61 IA 398: AIR 1934 PC 227 (2) afford a correct guide for the Appellate Court's approach to a case in disposing of such an appeal; and

(3) the different phraseology used in the judgments of this Court, such as,

(i) "substantial and compelling reasons",

(ii) "good and sufficiently cogent reasons", and

(iii) "strong reasons", are not intended to curtail the undoubted power of an appellate court in an appeal against acquittal to review the entire evidence and to come to its own conclusion; but in doing so it should not only consider every matter on record having a bearing on the questions of fact and the reasons given by the court below in support of its order of acquittal is its arriving at a conclusion on those reasons in its judgment, which lead it to hold that the acquittal was not justified.

POWERS OF APPELLATE COURT WHILE DEALING AN APPEAL AGAINST ACQUITTAL-III

Ghurey Lal v. *State of Uttar Pradesh*, (2008) 10 SCC 450: JT 2008 (10) SC 324

1. The Appellate Court may review the evidence in appeals against acquittal under sections 378 and 386 of the Criminal Procedure Code, 1973. Its power of reviewing evidence is wide and the Appellate Court can re-appreciate the entire evidence on record. It can review the Trial Court's conclusion with respect to both facts and law.

2. The accused is presumed innocent until proven guilty. The accused possessed this presumption when he was before the Trial Court. The Trial Court's acquittal bolsters the presumption that he is innocent.

3. Due or proper weight and consideration must be given to the Trial Court's decision. This is especially true when a witness's credibility is at issue. It is not enough for the High Court to take a different view of the evidence. There must also be substantial and compelling reasons for holding that Trial Court was wrong.

In light of the above, the High Court and other appellate courts should follow the well-settled principles crystallized by number of judgments if it is going to overrule or otherwise disturb the Trial Court's acquittal:

1. The appellate court may only overrule or otherwise disturb the Trial Court's acquittal if it has "very substantial and compelling reasons" for doing so. A number of instances arise in which the Appellate Court would have "very substantial and compelling reasons" to discard the Trial Court's decision. "Very substantial and compelling reasons" exist when:

(i) The Trial Court's conclusion with regard to the facts is palpably wrong;

(ii) The Trial Court's decision was based on an erroneous view of law;

(iii) The Trial Court's judgment is likely to result in "grave miscarriage of justice";

(iv) The entire approach of the Trial Court in dealing with the evidence was patently illegal;

(v) The Trial Court's judgment was manifestly unjust and unreasonable;

(vi) The Trial Court has ignored the evidence or misread the material evidence or has ignored material documents like dying declarations/ report of the Ballistic expert, etc.

(vii) This list is intended to be illustrative, not exhaustive.

2. The Appellate Court must always give proper weight and consideration to the findings of the Trial Court.

3. If two reasonable views can be reached – one that leads to acquittal, the other to conviction – the High Courts/Appellate Courts must rule in favour of the accused.

POWERS OF APPELLATE COURT WHILE DEALING AN APPEAL AGAINST ACQUITTAL-IV

Sidhartha Vashisht @ Manu Sharma v. *State (NCT) (Jessica Lal* case), JT 2010 (4) SC 407: 2010 (4) SCALE 1

The following principles have to be kept in mind by the Appellate Court while dealing with appeals, particularly, against the order of acquittal:

(i) There is no limitation on the part of the Appellate Court to review the evidence upon which the order of acquittal is found.

(ii) The Appellate Court in an appeal against acquittal can review the entire evidence and come to its own conclusions.

(iii) The Appellate Court can also review the Trial Court's conclusion with respect to both facts and law.

(iv) While dealing with the appeal preferred by the State, it is the duty of the Appellate Court to marshal the entire evidence on record and by giving cogent and adequate reasons set aside the judgment of acquittal.

(v) An order of acquittal is to be interfered only when there are "compelling and substantial reasons" for doing so. If the order is "clearly unreasonable", it is a compelling reason for interference.

(vi) While sitting in judgment over an acquittal the Appellate Court is first required to seek an answer to the question whether finding of the Trial Court are palpably wrong, manifestly, erroneous or demonstrably unsustainable. If the Appellate Court answers the above question in the negative the order of acquittal is not to be disturbed. Conversely, if the Appellate Court holds, for reasons to be recorded, that the order of acquittal cannot at all be sustained in view of any of the above infirmities, it can reappraise the evidence to arrive at its own conclusion.

(vii) When the Trial Court has ignored the evidence or misread the material evidence or has ignored material documents like dying declaration/ report of Ballistic Experts etc., the Appellate Court is competent to reverse the decision of the Trial Court depending on the materials placed.

POWER OF HIGH COURT TO INTERFERE WITH A FINDING OF FACT

State of Haryana v. *Devi Dutt*, (2006) 13 SCC 32

The High Court ordinarily should not have interfered with the finding of fact. We, although, do not mean to suggest that the findings of fact cannot be interfered with by the Superior Courts in exercise of their jurisdiction under article 226 of the Constitution of India, but the same should be done upon application of the well-known legal principles such as:

(1) when it is perverse;

(2) when wrong legal principles have been applied;

(3) when wrong questions were posed;

(4) when relevant facts have not been taken into consideration; or

(5) the findings have been arrived at on the basis of the irrelevant facts or on extraneous consideration.

The High Court ordinarily also ought not to have entertained an additional affidavit without assigning any sufficient or cogent reason therefor. The parties adduced their evidence before the Industrial Court. Why could they not bring on record any other evidence before the Labour Court, was not explained. The contentions raised before the High Court for the first time in the additional affidavits filed before it, were also not admitted by the appellants herein.

POWERS OF MAGISTRATE ON RECEIPT OF A COMPLAINT

Tula Ram v. *Kishore Singh*, AIR 1977 SC 2401: (1977) 4 SCC 459

1. That a Magistrate can order investigation under section 156(3) only at the pre-cognizance stage, that is to say, before taking cognizance under sections 190, 200 and 204 and where a Magistrate decides to take cognizance under the provisions of Chapter 14 he is not entitled in law to order any investigation under section 156(3) though in cases not falling within the proviso to section 202 he can order an investigation by the police which would be in the nature of an enquiry as contemplated by section 202 of the Code.

2. Where a Magistrate chooses to take cognizance he can adopt any of the following alternatives:

(a) He can peruse the complaint and if satisfied that there are sufficient grounds for proceeding he can straightaway issue process to the accused but before he does so he must comply with the requirements of section 200 and record the evidence of the complainant or his witnesses;

(b) The Magistrate can postpone the issue of process and direct an enquiry by himself;

(c) The Magistrate can postpone the issue of process and direct an enquiry by any other person or an investigation by the police.

3. In case the Magistrate after considering the statement of the complainant and the witnesses or as a result of the investigation and the enquiry ordered is not satisfied that there are sufficient grounds for proceeding he can dismiss the complaint.

4. Where a Magistrate orders investigation by the police before taking cognizance under section 156(3) of the Code and receives the report thereupon he can act on the report and discharge the accused or straightaway issue process against the accused or apply his mind to the complaint filed before him and take action under section 190 as described above.

POWERS UNDER SECTION 482, CRIMINAL PROCEDURE CODE

Inder Mohan Goswami v. *State of Uttaranchal*, AIR 2008 SC 251: (2007) 12 SCC 1

Every High Court has inherent power to act *ex debito justitiae* to do real and substantial justice, for the administration of which alone it exists, or to prevent abuse of the process of the court. Inherent power under section 482, Criminal Procedure Code can be exercised:

(i) to give effect to an order under the Code;

(ii) to prevent abuse of the process of court, and

(iii) to otherwise secure the ends of justice.

Inherent powers under section 482, Criminal Procedure Code though wide have to be exercised sparingly, carefully and with great caution and only when such exercise is justified by the tests specifically laid down in this section itself. Authority of the court exists for the advancement of justice. If any abuse of the process leading to injustice is brought to the notice of the court, then the Court would be justified in preventing injustice by invoking inherent powers in absence of specific provisions in the Statute.

The powers possessed by the High Court under section 482 of the Code are very wide and the very plenitude of the power requires great caution in its exercise. The court must be careful to see that its decision in exercise of this power is based on sound principles. The inherent power should not be exercised to stifle a legitimate prosecution. The High Court should normally refrain from giving a *prima facie* decision in a case where all the facts are incomplete and hazy; more-so, when the evidence has not been collected and produced before the court and the issues involved, whether factual or legal, are of such magnitude that they cannot be seen in their true perspective without sufficient material. Of course, no hard and fast rule can be laid down in regard to cases in which the High Court will exercise its extraordinary jurisdiction of quashing the proceedings at any stage.

PRISON TORTURE AND JURISDICTION OF THE COURT

Rakesh Kaushik v. *B.L. Vig, Superintendent, Central Jail, New Delhi,*
1980 SCC (Cri) 834: AIR 1981 SC 1767

The petition contains specific grievances of physical assault and psychic torture, of tense atmosphere and delinquent pressure for which some 'B' class prisoners and superior officers are responsible. This matter has to be investigated. Furthermore, in the *Sunil Batra's* case (W. P. No. 1009 of 1979): (reported in AIR 1980 SC 1579), precisely to obviate the pernicious potential of prison torture, remedial mechanics had been worked out, formulated and translated into mandates. Whether these have been complied with, and if not, why not, require to be enquired into. When this Court issues a writ recusant parties will have to pay the penalty for non-compliance. This means, the violations and violators will have to be identified after due investigation. Having regard to all these instructions we make the following directions:

(1) The District and Sessions Judge, Delhi, will within three months from today, hold an open enquiry within the jail premises, into the allegations

contained in the petition of the prisoner Kaushik and in the report submitted to this Court by Advocate, Shri Subodh Markandeya.

(2) He will further enquire, with specific reference to the charges of personal assault and compulsion for collaboration in canteen swindle and other vices made by the prisoner against the Superintendent and the Deputy Superintendent.

(3) He will go into the question of the directives issued in the concluding portion of *Sunil Batra's* case (W.P. No. 1009 of 1979): (AIR 1980 SC 1579) with a view to ascertain whether these directions have been substantially complied with and to the extent there is shortfall or default whether there is any reasonable explanation therefor.

(4) Being a visitor of the jail, it is part of his visitatorial functions for the Sessions Judge to acquaint himself with the condition of tension, vice and violence and prisoners' grievances. He will take this opportunity to enquire into these aspects also with a view to suggest remedial action.

The result of this investigation will be crystallised in the shape of findings, followed by specific instructions with a view to see that the petitioner and others like him are not burdened by additional acerbities and harsher pressures than a legal sentence of rigorous imprisonment geared to reformation and intended for deterrence necessarily implied. The Sessions Judge will also give a specific time to the jail authorities for carrying out his directives, and after the period for compliance is over, will make a fresh visit to verify whether those mandates have been fulfilled. In the event of non-fulfilment, a report will be made to this Court before September 30, 1980, whereupon appropriate action to enforce compliance will be taken by this Court in its jurisdiction.

We may make it perfectly clear that the Sessions Judge will allow any person or official who wants to make any representations to him in the course of his enquiry to meet him publicly or in camera, but outsiders and strangers will not be allowed except Shri Subodh Markandeya or Government's counsel of course, it will be open to the Judge if he considers that such a step will advance the interests of justice to allow any other public organisation or legal aid society.

QUASHING OF CRIMINAL PROCEEDINGS-I

State of Haryana v. *Bhajan Lal*, AIR 1992 SC 604: (1992) Supp 1 SCC 335

Categories of cases where inherent power can and should be exercised to quash the proceedings—

1. Where the allegations made in the first information report or the complaint, even if they are taken at their face value and accepted in their entirety do not *prima facie* constitute any offence or make out a case against the accused.

2. Where the allegations in the first information report and other materials, if any, accompanying the FIR do not disclose a cognizable offence, justifying an investigation by police officers under section 156(1) of the Code except under an order of a Magistrate within the purview of section 155(2) of the Code.
3. Where the uncontroverted allegations made in the FIR or complaint and the evidence collected in support of the same do not disclose the commission of any offence and make out a case against the accused.
4. Where, the allegations in the FIR do not constitute a cognizable offence but constitute only a non-cognizable offence, no investigation is permitted by a police officer without an order of a Magistrate as contemplated under section 155(2) of the Code.
5. Where the allegations made in the FIR or complaint are so absurd and inherently improbable on the basis of which no prudent person can ever reach a just conclusion that there is sufficient ground for proceeding against the accused.
6. Where there is an express legal bar engrafted in any of the provisions of the Code or the concerned Act (under which a criminal proceeding is instituted) to the institution and continuance of the proceedings and/or where there is a specific provision in the Code or the concerned Act, providing efficacious redress for the grievance of the aggrieved party.
7. Where a criminal proceeding is manifestly attended with *mala fide* and/or where the proceeding is maliciously instituted with an ulterior motive for wreaking vengeance on the accused and with a view to spite him due to private and personal grudge.

QUASHING OF CRIMINAL PROCEEDINGS-II

M/s. Indian Oil Corporation v. *M/s. NEPC Ltd.*, AIR 2006 SC 2780: (2006) 6 SCC 736

1. A complaint can be quashed where the allegations made in the complaint, even if they are taken at their face value and accepted in their entirety, do not *prima facie* constitute any offence or make out the case alleged against the accused. For this purpose, the complaint has to be examined as a whole, but without examining the merits of the allegations. Neither a detailed inquiry nor a meticulous analysis of the material nor an assessment of the reliability or genuineness of the allegations in the complaint is warranted while examining prayer for quashing of a complaint.

2. A complaint may also be quashed where it is a clear abuse of the process of the court, as when the criminal proceeding is found to have been initiated with *mala fides*/malice for wreaking vengeance or to cause harm, or where the allegations are absurd and inherently improbable.

3. The power to quash shall not, however, be used to stifle or scuttle a legitimate prosecution. The power should be used sparingly and with abundant caution.

4. The complaint is not required to *verbatim* reproduce the legal ingredients of the offence alleged. If the necessary factual foundation is laid in the complaint, merely on the ground that a few ingredients have not been stated in detail, the proceedings should not be quashed. Quashing of the complaint is warranted only where the complaint is so bereft of even the basic facts which are absolutely necessary for making out the offence.

5. A given set of facts may make out: (a) purely a civil wrong; or (b) purely a criminal offence; or (c) a civil wrong as also a criminal offence. A commercial transaction or a contractual dispute, apart from furnishing a cause of action for seeking remedy in civil law, may also involve a criminal offence. As the nature and scope of civil proceedings are different from a criminal proceeding, the mere fact that the complaint relates to a commercial transaction or breach of contract, for which a civil remedy is available or has been availed, is not by itself a ground to quash the criminal proceedings. The test is whether the allegations in the complaint disclose a criminal offence or not.

RAREST OF RARE – GUIDELINES

Machhi Singh v. *State of Punjab*, AIR 1983 SC 957: (1983) 3 SCC 470

1. The extreme penalty of death need not he inflicted except in gravest cases of extreme culpability;

2. Before opting for the death penalty the circumstances of the 'offender' also require to be taken into consideration along with the circumstances of the 'crime';

3. Life imprisonment is the rule and death sentence is an exception. In other words death sentence must he imposed only when life imprisonment appears to be an altogether inadequate punishment having regard to the relevant circumstances of the crime, and provided and only provided, the option to impose sentence of imprisonment for life cannot be conscientiously exercised having regard to the nature and circumstances of the crime and all the relevant circumstances;

4. A balance-sheet of aggravating and mitigating circumstances has to be drawn up and in doing so the mitigating circumstances have to be accorded full weightage and a just balance has to be struck between the aggravating and the mitigating circumstances before the option is exercised.

In order to apply these guidelines inter alia the following questions may be asked and answered:

(a) Is there something uncommon about the crime which renders sentence of imprisonment for life inadequate and calls for a death sentence?

(b) Are the circumstances of the crime such that there is no alterantive but to impose death sentence even after according maximum weightage to the mitigating circumstances which speak in favour of the offender?

If upon taking an overall global view of all the circumstances in the light of the aforesaid proposition and taking into account the answers to the questions posed hereinabove, the circumstances of the case are such that death sentence is warranted, the Court would proceed to do so.

[*'Bachan Singh* v. *State of Punjab'*, (1980) 2 SCC 684: AIR 1980 SC 898]

Factors to be considered (*Machhi Singh's* case)

I. Manner of Commission of Murder

When the murder is committed in an extremely brutal, grotesque, diabolical, revolting, or dastardly manner so as to arouse intense and extreme indignation of the community. For instance:

(i) When the house of the victim is set aflame with the end in view to roast him alive in the house;

(ii) When the victim is subjected to inhuman acts of torture or cruelty in order to bring about his or her death;

(iii) When the body of the victim is cut into pieces or his body is dismembered in a fiendish manner.

II. Motive for commission of murder

When the murder is committed for a motive which evinces total depravity and meanness. For instance when (a) a hired assassin commits murder for the sake of money or reward; (b) a cold-blooded murder is committed with a deliberate design in order to inherit property or to gain control over property of a ward or a person under the control of the murderer or *vis-a-vis* whom the murderer is in a dominating position or in a position of trust; (c) a murder is committed in the course for betrayal of the motherland.

III. Anti-social or socially abhorrent nature of the crime

(a) When murder of a member of a Scheduled Caste or minority community etc., is committed not for personal reasons but in circumstances which arouse social wrath. For instance when such a crime is committed in order to terrorize such persons and frighten them into fleeing from a place or in order to deprive them of, or make them surrender, lands or benefits conferred on them with a view to reverse past injustices and in order to restore the social balance.

(b) In cases of 'bride burning' and what are known as 'dowry-deaths' or when murder is committed in order to remarry for the sake of extracting dowry once again or to marry another woman on account of infatuation.

IV. Magnitude of crime

When the crime is enormous in proportion. For instance when multiple murders say of all or almost all the members of a family or a large number of persons of a particular caste, community, or locality, are committed.

V. Personality of victim of murder

When the victim of murder is (a) an innocent child who could not have or has not provided even an excuse, much less a provocation, for murder; (b) a helpless woman or a person rendered helpless by old age or infirmity; (c) when the victim is a person *vis-a-vis* whom the murderer is in a position of domination or trust; (d) when the victim is a public figure generally loved and respected by the community for the services rendered by him and the murder is committed for political or similar reasons other than personal reasons.

REMAND AND BAIL OF ACCUSED UNDER SECTION 167 OF CR.P.C.

Uday Mohanlal Acharya v. *State of Maharashtra*, AIR 2001 SC 1910: (2001) 5 SCC 453

1. Under sub-section (2) of section 167, a Magistrate before whom an accused is produced while the police is investigating into the offence can authorise detention of the accused in such custody as the Magistrate thinks fit for a term not exceeding 15 days in the whole.

2. Under the proviso to aforesaid sub-section (2) of section 167, the Magistrate may authorise detention of the accused otherwise than the custody of police for a total period not exceeding 90 days where the investigation relates to offence punishable with death, imprisonment for life or imprisonment for a term of not less than 10 years, and 60 days where the investigation relates to any other offence.

3. On the expiry of the said period of 90 days or 60 days, as the case may be, an indefeasible right accrues in favour of the accused for being released on bail on account of default by the Investigating Agency in the completion of the investigation within the period prescribed and the accused is entitled to be released on bail, if he is prepared to and furnish the bail, as directed by the Magistrate.

4. When an application for bail is filed by an accused for enforcement of his indefeasible right alleged to have been accrued in his favour on account of default on the part of the investigating agency in completion of the investigation within the specified period, the Magistrate/Court must dispose it of forthwith, on being satisfied that in fact the accused has been in custody for the period of 90 days or 60 days, as specified and no charge-sheet has been filed by the Investigating Agency. Such prompt action on the part of the Magistrate/Court will not enable the prosecution to frustrate the object of the Act and the legislative mandate of an accused being released on bail on account of the default on the part of the Investigating Agency in completing the investigation within the period stipulated.

5. If the accused is unable to furnish bail, as directed by the Magistrate, then the conjoint reading of *Explanation I* and proviso to sub-section (2) of section 167, the continued custody of the accused even beyond the specified period in paragraph (a) will not be unauthorised, and therefore, if during that period the investigation is complete and charge-sheet is filed then the so-called indefeasible right of the accused would stand extinguished.

6. The expression 'if not already availed of' used by this Court in *Sanjay Dutt* v. *State*, 1994 AIR SCW 3857: 1995 Cr LJ 477 must be understood to mean when the accused files an application and is prepared to offer bail on being directed. In other words, on expiry of the period specified in paragraph (a) of proviso to sub-section (2) of section 167 if the accused files an application for bail and offers also to furnish the bail, on being directed, then it has to be held that the accused has availed of his indefeasible right even though the Court has not considered the said application and has not indicated the terms and conditions of bail, and the accused has not furnished the same.

REMISSION OF SENTENCE

Life Convict Laxman Naskar v. *State of West Bengal*, AIR 2000 SC 2762: (2000) 7 SCC 626

"1. That a sentence of imprisonment for life does not automatically expire at the end of 20 years including the remissions, because the Administrative Rules framed under the various Jail Manuals or under the Prison Act, cannot supersede the statutory provisions of the Indian Penal Code. A sentence of imprisonment for life means a sentence for the entire life of the prisoner unless the appropriate Government chooses to exercise its discretion to remit either the whole or a part of the sentence under section 401 of the Code of Criminal Procedure, 1898;

2. That the appropriate Government has the undoubted discretion to remit or refuse to remit the sentence and where it refuses to remit the sentence no writ can be issued directing the State Government to release the prisoner."

[Vide *State of Madhya Pradesh* v. *Ratan Singh*, (1976) 3 SCC 470: AIR 1976 SC 1552]

3. In *Naib Singh* v. *State of Punjab*, (1983) 2 SCC 454: AIR 1983 SC 855: 1983 Cr LJ 1345, it was noticed that a distinction between 'imprisonment for life' and 'imprisonment for a term' has been maintained in the Indian Penal Code in several of its provisions and, moreover, whenever an offender is punishable with 'imprisonment for life' he is not punishable with 'imprisonment which may be of either description' within the meaning of section 60, I.P.C. and therefore, we cannot come to the conclusion that the Court, by itself, could release the convict automatically before the full life-term is served. This aspect was highlighted in *Gopal Vinayak Godse* v. *State of Maharashtra*, (1961) 3 SCR 440: AIR 1961 SC 600: 1961 (1) Cr LJ 736, wherein it was held that sentence for 'imprisonment for life' ordinarily means imprisonment for the whole of the remaining period of the

convicted person's natural life; that a convict undergoing such sentence may earn remissions of his part of sentence under the Prison Rules but such remissions in the absence of an order of an appropriate Government remitting the entire balance of his sentence under this section does not entitle the convict to be released automatically before the full life-term is served. It was observed that though under the relevant rules a sentence for imprisonment for life is equated with the definite period of 20 years, there is no indefeasible right of such prisoner to be unconditionally released on the expiry of such particular term, including remissions and that is only for the purpose of working out the remissions that the said sentence is equated with definite period and not for any other purpose. In view of this legal position explained by this Court it may not help the petitioner even on the construction placed by the learned counsel for the petitioner on section 61(1) of the West Bengal Correctional Services Act XXXII of 1992 with reference to explanation thereto that for the purpose of calculation of the total period of imprisonment under this section the period of imprisonment for life shall be taken to be equivalent to the period of imprisonment for 20 years. Therefore, solely on the basis of completion of a term in jail serving imprisonment and remissions earned under the relevant rules or law will not entitle an automatic release, but the appropriate Government must pass a separate order remitting the unexpired portion of the sentence.

This Court also issued certain guidelines as to the basis on which a convict can be released prematurely and they are as under:—

"1. Whether the offence is an individual act of crime without affecting the society at large;

2. Whether there is any fruitful purpose of confining of this convict anymore;

3. Whether there is any chance of future reoccurrence of committing crime;

4. Whether the convict has lost his potentiality in committing crime;

5. Socio-Economic condition of the convict's family."

RIGHT OF PRIVATE DEFENCE

Darshan Singh v. *State of Punjab*, JT 2010 (1) SC 306: 2010 (1) SCALE 467

1. Self-preservation is the basic human instinct and is duly recognized by the criminal jurisprudence of all civilized countries. All free, democratic and civilized countries recognize the right of private defence within certain reasonable limits.

2. The right of private defence is available only to one who is suddenly confronted with the necessity of averting an impending danger and not of self-creation.

3. A mere reasonable apprehension is enough to put the right of self-defence into operation. In other words, it is not necessary that there should be an actual commission of the offence in order to give rise to the right of private defence. It is enough if the accused apprehended that such an offence is contemplated and it is likely to be committed if the right of private defence is not exercised.

4. The right of private defence commences as soon as a reasonable apprehension arises and it is co-terminus with the duration of such apprehension.

5. It is unrealistic to expect a person under assault to modulate his defence step by step with any arithmetical exactitude.

6. In private defence the force used by the accused ought not to be wholly disproportionate or much greater than necessary for protection of the person or property.

7. It is well-settled that even if the accused does not plead self-defence, it is open to consider such a plea if the same arises from the material on record.

8. The accused need not prove the existence of the right of private defence beyond reasonable doubt.

9. The Indian Penal Code confers the right of private defence only when that unlawful or wrongful act is an offence.

10. A person who is in imminent and reasonable danger of losing his life or limb may in exercise of self defence inflict any harm even extending to death on his assailant either when the assault is attempted or directly threatened.

RIGHT TO APPEAL

Garikapati Veeraya v. *N. Subbiah Choudhry*, AIR 1957 SC 540: 1957 SCR 488

1. That the legal pursuit of a remedy, suit appeal and second appeal are really but steps in a series of proceedings all connected by an intrinsic unity and are to be regarded as one legal proceeding.

2. The right of appeal is not a mere matter of procedure but is a substantive right.

3. The institution of the suit carries with it the implication that all rights of appeal then in force are preserved to the parties thereto till the rest of the career of the suit.

4. The right of appeal is a vetted right and such a right to enter the superior Court accrues to the litigant and exists as on and from the date the *lis* commences and although it may be actually exercised when the adverse judgment is pronounced such right is to be governed by the law prevailing at the date of the institution of the suit or proceeding and not by the law that prevails at the date of its decision or at the date of the filing of the appeal.

5. This vested right of appeal can be taken away only by a subsequent enactment, if it so provides expressly or by necessary intendment and not otherwise.

RIGHT TO LIFE

Peoples Union for Civil Liberties (PUCL) v. *Union of India*, AIR 2003 SC 2363: (2003) 4 SCC 399

Rights fall within the ambit of article 21 since personal liberty is of widest amplitude and categorised them thus:—

"(1) The right to go abroad; *Satwant Singh Sawhney* v. *D. Ramarathnam, A.P.O., New Delhi,* (1967) 3 SCR 525: AIR 1967 SC 1836.

(2) The right to privacy, *Gobind* v. *State of Madhya Pradesh,* (1975) 2 SCC 148. In this case reliance was placed on the American decision in *Griswold* v. *Connecticut,* 381 US 479 (510); *Govind* v. *State of Madhya Pradesh,* AIR 1975 SC 1378: 1975 Cr LJ 1111.

(3) The right against solitary confinement; *Sunil Batra* v. *Delhi Administration,* (1978) 4 SCC 494 (545): AIR 1978 SC 1675: 1978 Cr LJ 1741.

(4) The right against bar fetters; *Charles Sobraj* v. *Suptd. Central Jail,* (1978) 4 SCC 104: AIR 1978 SC 1514: 1978 Cr LJ 1534.

(5) The right to legal aid; *M.H. Hoskot* v. *State of Maharashtra,* (1978) 3 SCC 544: AIR 1978 SC 1548: 1978 Cr LJ 1678.

(6) The right to speedy trial; *Hussainara Khatoon* v. *Home Secretary, State of Bihar,* (1980) 1 SCC 81: AIR 1979 SC 1360: 1979 Cr LJ 1036.

(7) The right against handcuffing; *Prem Shankar Shukla* v. *Delhi Administration,* (1980) 3 SCC 526: AIR 1980 SC 1535: 1980 Cr LJ 930.

(8) The right against delayed execution; *T.V. Vatheeswaram* v. *State of Tamil Nadu,* (1983) 2 SCC 68: AIR 1983 SC 361 (2): 1983 Cr LJ 481.

(9) The right against custodial violence; *Sheela Barse* v. *State of Maharashtra,* (1983) 2 SCC 96: AIR 1983 SC 378: 1983 Cr LJ 642.

(10) The right against public hanging; *A.G. of India* v. *Lachma Devi,* (1989) Supp 1 SCC 264: AIR 1986 SC 467: 1986 Cr LJ 364.

(11) Doctor's Assistance; *Parmanand Katra* v. *Union of India,* (1989) 4 SCC 286: AIR 1989 SC 2039: 1990 Cr LJ 671: 1989 All LJ 1111.

(12) Shelter, *Shantistar Builders* v. *N.K. Totame,* (1990) 1 SCC 520: AIR 1990 SC 630.

Following decisions of this Court giving meaning to the phrase "freedom of speech and expression":—

"(1) *Romesh Thappar* v. *State of Madras,* AIR 1950 SC 124: 1950 (51) Cr LJ 1514.

Freedom of speech and expression includes freedom of propagation of ideas which is ensured by freedom of circulation.

(2) *Brij Bhushan* v. *State of Delhi,* AIR 1950 SC 129: 1950 (51) Cr LJ 1525.

Pre-censorship of a journal is restriction on the liberty of press.

(3) *Hamdard Dawakhana* v. *Union of India,* AIR 1960 SC 554: 1960 Cr LJ 735.

Advertisements meant for propagation of ideas or furtherance of literature or human thought is a part of Freedom of Speech and Expression.

(4) *Sakal Papers (P) Ltd.* v. *Union of India,* AIR 1962 SC 305.

Freedom of speech and expression carries with it the right to publish and circulate one's ideas, opinions and views.

(5) *Bennett Coleman and Co.* v. *Union of India,* (1972) 2 SCC 788: AIR 1973 SC 106.

Freedom of Press means right of citizens to speak, publish and express their views as well as right of people to read, (Para 45).

(6) *Indian Express Newspapers (Bombay) (P) Ltd.* v. *Union of India,* (1985) 1 SCC 641: AIR 1986 SC 515: 1985 Tax LR 2451 (Para 66).

"Freedom of expression, as learned writers have observed, has four broad social purposes to serve (i) it helps an individual to attain self-fulfilment; (ii) it assists in the discovery of truth; (iii) it strengthens the capacity of an individual in participating in decision making; and (iv) it provides a mechanism by which it would be possible to establish a reasonable balance between stability and social change."

(7) *Odyssey Communication Pvt. Ltd.* v. *Lokvidayan Sanghatana,* (1988) 3 SCC 410: AIR 1988 SC 1642.

Freedom of speech and expression includes right of citizens to exhibit film on doordarshan.

(8) *S. Rangarajan* v. *P. Jagjivan Ram,* (1989) 2 SCC 574.

Freedom of speech and expression means the right to express one's opinion by words of mouth, writing, printing picture or any other manner. It would thus include the freedom of communication and the right to propagate or publish opinions.

(9) *L.I.C.* v. *Mannubhai D. Shah,* (1992) 3 SCC 637: AIR 1993 SC 171: 1992 AIR SCW 3099.

Freedom of speech and expression is a natural right which a human being acquires by birth. It is, therefore, a basic human right (article 19 of Universal Declaration of Human Rights relied on). Every citizen, therefore, has a right to air his or her views through the printing and/or electronic media or through any communication method.

(10) *Secretary, Ministry of Information and Broadcasting, Government of India* v. *Cricket Association of Bengal,* (1995) 2 SCC 161: 1995 AIR SCW 1856: AIR 1995 SC 1236 (Para 17).

"The right to freedom of speech and expression includes the right to receive and impart information. For ensuring the free speech right of the citizens of this country, it is necessary that the citizens have the benefit of plurality of views and a range of opinions on all public issues. A successful democracy posits an 'aware' citizenry. Diversity of opinions, views, ideas and ideologies is essential to enable the citizens to arrive at informed judgment on all issues touching them."

(11) *S.P. Gupta* v. *Union of India,* 1981 Supp SCC 87 (273): AIR 1982 SC 149.

Right to know is implicit in right of free speech and expression. Disclosure of information regarding functioning of the Government must be the rule.

(12) *State of Uttar Pradesh* v. *Raj Narain,* (1974) 4 SCC 428: AIR 1975 SC 865.

Freedom of speech and expression includes the right to know every public act, everything that is done in a public way, by their public functionaries.

(13) *Dinesh Trivedi, Madhya Pradesh* v. *Union of India,* (1997) 4 SCC 306.

Freedom of speech and expression includes right of the citizens to know about the affairs of the Government."

RIGHT TO SPEEDY TRIAL-I

A.R. Antulay v. *R.S. Naik,*
AIR 1992 SC 1701: (1992) 1 SCC 225

Right to speedy trial: Supreme Court guidelines in *A.R. Antulay's (1992)* case:—

1. Fair, just and reasonable procedure implicit in article 21 of the Constitution creates a right in the accused to be tried speedily. Right to speedy trial is the right of the accused. The fact that a speedy trial is also in public interest or that it serves the societal interest also does not make it any-the-less the right of the accused. It is in the interest of all concerned that the guilt or innocence of the accused is determined as quickly as possible in the circumstances.
2. Right to Speedy Trial flowing from article 21 encompasses all the stages, namely the stage of investigation, inquiry, trial, appeal, revision and re-trial. That is how this Court has understood this right and there is no reason to take a restricted view.
3. The concerns underlying the Right to speedy trial from the point of view of the accused are:

(a) the period of remand and pre-conviction detention should be as short as possible. In other words, the accused should not be subjected to unnecessary or unduly long incarceration prior to his conviction;

(b) the worry, anxiety, expense and disturbance to his vocation and peace, resulting from an unduly prolonged investigation, inquiry or trial should be minimal; and

(c) undue delay may well result in impairment of the ability of the accused to defend himself, whether on account of death, disappearance or non-availability of witnesses or otherwise.

4. At the same time, one cannot ignore the fact that it is usually the accused who is interested in delaying the proceedings. As is often pointed out, "delay is a known defence tactic". Since the burden of proving the guilt of the accused lies upon the prosecution, delay ordinarily prejudices the prosecution. Non-availability of witnesses, disappearance of evidence by lapse of time really work against the interest of the prosecution. Of course, there may be cases where the prosecution, for whatever reason, also delays the proceedings. Therefore, in every case, where the right to speedy trial is alleged to have been infringed, the first question to be put and answered is – who is responsible for the delay? Proceedings taken by either party in good faith, to vindicate their rights and interest, as perceived by them, cannot be treated as delaying tactics nor can the time taken in pursuing such proceedings be counted towards delay. It goes without saying that frivolous proceedings or proceedings taken merely for delaying the day of reckoning cannot be treated as proceedings taken in good faith. The mere fact that an application/petition is admitted and an order of stay granted by a superior court is by itself no proof that the proceeding is not a frivolous. Very often these stays obtained on *ex parte* representation.

5. While determining whether undue delay has occurred (resulting in violation of Right to Speedy Trial) one must have regard to all the attendant circumstances, including nature of offence, number of accused and witnesses the work-load of the court concerned, prevailing local conditions and so on – what is called, the systematic delays. It is true that it is the obligation of the State to ensure a speedy trial and State includes judiciary as well, but a realistic and practical approach should be adopted in such matters instead of a pedantic one.

6. Each and every delay does not necessarily prejudice the accused. Some delays may indeed work to his advantage. As has been Observed by Powell, J. in Barker "it cannot be said how long a delay is too long in a system where justice is supposed to be swift but deliberate". The same ideal has been stated by White, J. in *U.S.* v. *Ewell*, (1966) 15 Law Ed 2d 627, in the following words:

> "the sixth amendment right to a speedy trial is necessarily relative, is consistent with delays, and has orderly expedition, rather than mere speed, as its essential ingredients; and whether delay in completing a prosecution amounts to an unconstitutional deprivation of rights depends upon all the circumstances."

However, inordinately long delay may be taken as presumptive proof of prejudice. In this context, the fact of incarceration of accused will also be a relevant fact. The prosecution should not be allowed to become a persecution. But when does the prosecution become persecution, again depends upon the facts of a given case.

7. We cannot recognize or give effect to, what is called the 'demand' rule. An accused cannot try himself; he is tried by the Court at the behest of the prosecution. Hence, an accused's plea of denial of speedy trial cannot be defeated by saying that the accused did at no time demand a speedy trial. If in a given case, he did make such a demand and yet he was not tried speedily, it would be plus point in his favour, but the mere non-asking for a speedy trial cannot be put against the accused. Even in U.S.A., the relevance of demand rule has been substantially watered down in Barker and other succeeding cases.
8. Ultimately, the Court has to balance and weigh the several relevant factors – 'balancing test' or 'balancing process' – and determine in each case whether the right to speedy trial has been denied in a given case.
9. Ordinarily speaking, where the Court comes to the conclusion that Right to speedy trial of an accused has been infringed the charges or the conviction, as the case may be, shall be quashed. But this is not the only course open. The nature of the offence and other circumstances in a given case may be such that quashing of proceedings may not be in the interest of justice. In such a case, it is open to the court to make such other appropriate order – Including an order to conclude the trial within a fixed time where the trial is not concluded or reducing the sentence where the trial has concluded – as may be deemed just and equitable in the circumstances of the case.
10. It is neither advisable nor practicable to fix any time-limit for trial of offences. Any such rule is bound to be qualified one. Such rule cannot also be evolved merely to shift the burden of proving justification on to the shoulders of the prosecution. In every case of complaint of denial of Right to speedy trial, it is primarily for the prosecution to justify and explain the delay. At the same time, it is the duty of the Court to weigh all the circumstances of a given case before pronouncing upon the complaint. The Supreme Court of U.S.A. too has repeatedly refused to fix any such outer time limit in spite of the Sixth Amendment. Nor do we think that not fixing any such outer limit ineffectuates the guarantee of right to speedy trial.
11. An objection based on denial of Right to speedy trial and for relief on that account, should first be addressed to the High Court. Even if the High Court entertains such a plea, ordinarily it should not stay the proceedings, except in a case of grave and exceptional nature. Such proceedings in High Court, must, however, be disposed of on a priority basis.

RIGHT TO SPEEDY TRIAL

Kartar Sing's (1994) case

Kartar Singh v. *State of Punjab*, (1994) 3 SCC 569: 1994 Cr LJ 3139

1. The right to a speedy trial is a derivation from a provision of *Magna Carta*. This principle has also been incorporated into the Virginia Declaration of Rights of 1776 and from there into the Sixth Amendment of the Constitution of United States of America which reads, "In all criminal prosecutions, the accused shall enjoy the right to a speedy and public trial...". It may be pointed out, in this connection, that there is a Federal Act of 1974 called 'Speedy Trial Act' establishing a set of time-limits for carrying out the major events, *e.g.*, information, indictment, arraignment, in the prosecution of criminal cases. See *Black's Law Dictionary*, 6th Edn. p. 1400.

2. The right to a speedy trial is not only an important safeguard to prevent undue and oppressive incarceration, to minimise anxiety and concern accompanying the accusation and to limit the possibility of impairing the ability of an accused to defend himself but also there is a societal interest in providing a speedy trial. This right has been actuated in the recent past and the courts have laid down a series of decisions opening up new vistas of fundamental rights. In fact, lot of cases are coming before the courts for quashing of proceedings on the ground of inordinate and undue delay staling that the invocation of this right even need not await formal indictment or charge.

3. The concept of speedy trial is read into article 21 as an essential part of the fundamental right to life and liberty guaranteed and preserved under our Constitution. The right to speedy trial begins with the actual restraint imposed by arrest and consequent incarceration and continues at all stages, namely, the stage of investigation, inquiry, trial, appeal and revision so that any possible prejudice that may result from impermissible and avoidable delay from the time of the commission of the offence till it consummates into a finality, can be averted. In this context, it may be noted that the constitutional guarantee of speedy trial is properly reflected in section 309 of the Code of Criminal Procedure.

RIGHT TO SPEEDY TRIAL

Common Cause case-I (1996)

Common Cause, a Registered Society v. *Union of India*, AIR 1996 SC 1619: (1996) 4 SCC 33 **Overruled in** *P. Ramachandra Rao* v. *State of Karnataka*, AIR 2002 SC 1856

1. (a) Where the offences under IPC or any other law for the time being in force for which the accused are charged before any Criminal Court are punishable with imprisonment not exceeding three years with or without fine and if trials

for such offences are pending for one year or more and the concerned accused have not been released on bail but are in jail for a period of six months or more, the concerned Criminal Court shall release the accused on bail or on personal bond to be executed by the accused and subject to such conditions, if any, as may be found necessary, in the light of section 437 of the Criminal Procedure Code (Cr. P.C.).

(b) Where the offences under IPC or any other law for the time being in force for which the accused are charged before any Criminal Court are punishable with imprisonment not exceeding five years, with or without fine, and if the trials for such offences are pending for two years or more and the concerned accused have not been released on bail but are in jail for a period of six months or more, the concerned Criminal Court shall release the accused on bail or on personal bond to be executed by the accused and subject to the imposing of suitable conditions, if any, in the light of section 437, Cr. P.C.

(c) Where the offences under IPC or any other law for the time being in force for which the accused are charged before any Criminal Court are punishable with seven years or less, with or without fine, and if the trials for such offences are pending for two years or more and the concerned accused have not been released on bail but are in jail for a period of one year or more, the concerned Criminal Court shall release the accused on bail or on personal bond to be executed by the accused and subject to imposing of suitable conditions, if any, in the light of section 437, Cr. P.C.

2. (a) Where Criminal proceedings are pending regarding traffic offences in any Criminal Court for more than two years on account of non-serving summons to the accused or for any other reason whatsoever, the Court may discharge the accused and close the cases.

(b) Where the cases pending in Criminal Courts for more than two years under IPC or any other law for the time being in force are compoundable with permission of the Court and if in such cases trial have still not commenced, the Criminal Court shall, after hearing the public prosecutor and other parties represented before it or their advocates, discharge or acquit the accused, as the case may be, and close such cases.

(c) Where the cases pending in Criminal Courts under IPC or any other law for the time being in force pertain to offences which are non-cognizable and bailable and if such pendency is for more than two years and if in such cases trials have still not commenced, the Criminal Court shall discharge or acquit the accused, as the case may be, and close such cases.

(d) Where the cases pending in Criminal Courts under IPC or any other law for the time being in force are pending in connection with offences which are punishable with fine only and are not of recurring nature, and if such pendency is for more than one year and if in such cases trial have still not commenced, the Criminal Court shall discharge or acquit the accused, as the case may be, and close such cases.

(e) Where the cases pending in Criminal Courts under IPC or any other law for the time being in force are punishable with imprisonment upto one year, with or without fine, and if such pendency is for more than one year and if in such cases trials have still not commenced, the Criminal Courts shall discharge or acquit the accused, as the case may be, and close such cases.

(f) Where the cases pending in Criminal Courts under IPC or any other law for the time being in force are punishable with imprisonment up to three years, with or without fine, and if such pendency is for more than two years and if in such cases trials have still not commenced, the Criminal Court shall discharge or acquit the accused, as the case may be, and close such cases.

3. For the purpose of directions contained in clauses (1) and (2) above, the period of pendency of criminal cases shall be calculated from the date the accused are summoned to appear in the Court.

4. Directions (1) and (2) made hereinabove shall not apply to cases of offences involving (a) corruption, misappropriation of public funds, cheating, whether under the Indian Penal Code, prevention of Corruption Act or any other statute; (b) smuggling, foreign exchange violation and offences under the Narcotics Drugs and Psychotropic Substances Act; (c) Essential Commodities Act, Food Adulteration Act, Acts dealing with Environment or any other economic offences; (d) offences under Arms Act, Explosive Substances Act, Terrorists and Disruptive Activities Act; (e) offences relating to the Army, Navy and Air Force; (f) offences against public tranquility; (g) offences relating to public servants; (h) offences relating to coins and Government stamp; (i) offences relating to election; (j) offences relating to giving false evidence and offences against public justice; (k) any other type of offences against the State; (l) offences under the Taxing enactments; and (m) offences of defamation as defined in section 499, IPC.

5. The Criminal Courts shall try the offences mentioned in Para (4) above on a priority basis. The High Courts are requested to issue necessary directions in this behalf to all the Criminal Courts under their control and supervision.

6. The Criminal Courts and all Courts trying criminal cases shall take appropriate action in accordance with the above directions. These directions are applicable not only to the cases pending on this day but also to cases which may be instituted hereafter. As and when a particular case gets covered by one or the other direction mentioned in Directions (1) and (2) read with Direction (4) above, appropriate orders shall be passed by the concerned Court without any delay.

RIGHT TO SPEEDY TRIAL

Common Cause case-II (1996)

Common Cause, A Registered Society v. *Union of India*, AIR 1997 SC 1539: (1996) 6 SCC 775 Overruled in *P. Ramachandra Rao* v. *State of Karnataka*, AIR 2002 SC 1856

I. The time limit mentioned regarding the pendency of criminal cases in paragraphs from 2(a) to 2(f) of our judgment shall not apply to cases wherein such pendency of the criminal proceedings is wholly or partly attributable to the dilatory tactics adopted by the concerned accused or on account of any other action of the accused which results in prolonging the trial. In other words it should be shown that the criminal proceedings have remained pending for the requisite period mentioned in the aforesaid clause of paragraph 2 despite full co-operation by the concern accused to get these proceedings disposed of and the delay in the disposal of these cases is not at all attributable to the concerned accused, nor such delay is caused on account of such accused getting stay of criminal proceedings from higher Courts. Accused concerned are not entitled to earn any discharge or acquittal as per paragraphs 2(a) to 2(f) of our judgment if it is demonstrated that the accused concerned seek to take advantage to their own wrong or any other action of their own resulting in protraction of trials against them.

II. The phrase 'pendency of trials' as employed in paragraphs from 1(a) to 1(c) and the phrase 'non-commencement of trial' as employed in paragraphs from 2(b) to 2(f) shall be construed as under:

(i) In case of trials before Sessions Court the trials shall be treated to have commenced when charges are framed under section 228 of the Code of Criminal Procedure, 1973 in the concerned cases.

(ii) In cases of trials of warrant cases by Magistrates if the cases are instituted upon police reports the trials shall be treated to have commenced when charges are framed under section 240 of the Code of Criminal Procedure, 1973 while in trials of warrant cases by Magistrates when cases are instituted otherwise then on police report such trials shall be treated to have commenced when charges are framed against the concerned accused under section 246 of the Code of Criminal Procedure, 1973.

(iii) In cases of trials of summons by Magistrates the trials would be considered to have commenced when the accused who appear or are brought before the Magistrate are asked under section 251 whether they plead guilty or have any defence to make.

III. In paragraph 4 of our judgment in the list of offences to which directions contained in paragraphs 1 and 2 shall not apply, the following additions shall be made:

(n) Matrimonial offences under Indian Penal Code including section 498A or under any other law for the time being in force; (o) offences under the Negotiable Instruments Act including offences under section 138 thereof; (p) offences relating to criminal misappropriation of property of the complainant as well as offences relating to criminal breach of trust under Indian Penal Code or under any other law for the time being in force; (q) offences under section 304A of the Indian Penal Code or any offence pertaining to rash and negligent acts which are made punishable under any other law for the time being in force; (r) offences affecting the public health, safety, convenience, decency and morals as listed in Chapter XIV of the Indian Penal Code or such offences under any other law for the time being in force.

It is further directed that in criminal cases pertaining to offences mentioned under the above additional categories (n) to (r) wherein accused are already discharged or acquitted pursuant to our judgment dated 1st May 1996 and they are liable to be proceeded against for such offences pursuant to be present order and are not entitled to be discharged or acquitted as aforesaid, the concerned Criminal Court shall *suo motu* or on application by the concerned aggrieved parties shall issue within three months of the receipt of this clarificatory order at their end, summons or warrants, as the case may be, to such discharged or acquitted accused and shall restore the criminal cases against them for being proceeded further in accordance with law.

It is, however, made clear that in trials regarding other offences which are covered by the time limit specified in our earlier order dated 1st May, 1996 wherein the concerned accused are already acquitted or discharged pursuant to the said order, such acquitted or discharged accused shall not be liable to be recalled for facing such trials pursuant to the present clarificatory order which *qua* such offences will be treated to be purely prospective and no such cases which are already closed shall be reopened pursuant to the present order.

RIGHT TO SPEEDY TRIAL

Supreme Court Guidelines in *Raj Deo Sharma (I)* case (1998)

Raj Deo Sharma v. *State of Bihar*, AIR 1998 SC 3281: 1998 Cr LJ 4596: Overruled in *P. Ramachandra Rao* v. *State of Karnataka*, AIR 2002 SC 1856

1. In cases where the trial is for an offence punishable with imprisonment for a period not exceeding seven years, whether the accused is in jail or not, the Court shall close the prosecution evidence on completion of a period of two years from the date of recording the plea of the accused on the charges framed whether the prosecution has been examined all the witnesses or not, within the said period and the Court can proceed to the next step provided by law for the trial of the case.

2. In such cases as mentioned above, if the accused has been in jail for a period of not less than one half of the maximum period of punishment prescribed for the offence, the trial Court shall release the accused on bail forthwith on such conditions as it deems fit.

3. If the offence under trial is punishable with imprisonment for a period exceeding 7 years, whether the accused is in jail or not, the Court shall close the prosecution evidence on completion of three years from the date of recording the plea of the accused on the charge framed, whether the prosecution has

examined all the witnesses or not within the said period and the Court can proceed to the next step provided by law for the trial of the case, unless for very exceptional reasons to be recorded and in the interest of justice the Court considers it necessary to grant further time to the prosecution to adduce evidence beyond the aforesaid time limit.

4. But if the inability for completing the prosecution within the aforesaid period is attributable to the conduct of the accused in protracting the trial, no Court is obliged to close the prosecution evidence within the aforesaid period in any of the cases covered by clauses (i) to (iii).

5. Where the trial has been stayed by orders of Court or by operation of law such time during which the stay was in force shall be excluded from the aforesaid period for closing prosecution evidence. The above directions will be in addition to and without prejudice to the directions issued by this Court in *"Common Cause" a Registered Society* v. *Union of India,* (1996) 4 SCC 33: 1996 AIR SCW 2279 as modified by the same Bench through the order reported in *"Common Cause" a Registered Society* v. *Union of India,* (1996) 6 SCC 775: 1997 AIR SCW 290.

RIGHT TO SPEEDY TRIAL

Supreme Court Guidelines in *Rama Chandra Rao's* case (2002)

P. Ramachandra Rao v. *State of Karnataka,* AIR 2002 SC 1856: (2002) 4 SCC 578

In *Common Cause* case (I) (as modified in *Common Cause* (II)) and *Raj Deo Sharma* (I) and (II), the Court could not have prescribed periods of limitation beyond which the trial of a criminal case or a criminal proceeding cannot continue and must mandatorily be closed followed by an order acquitting or discharging the accused. In conclusion we hold:

(1) The dictum in *A.R. Antulay's* case is correct and still holds the field.

(2) The propositions emerging from article 21 of the Constitution and expounding the right to speedy trial laid down as guidelines in *A.R. Antulay's* case, adequately take care of right to speedy trial. We uphold and re-affirm the said propositions.

(3) The guidelines laid down in *A.R. Antulay's* case are not exhaustive but only illustrative. They are not intended to operate as hard and fast rules or to be applied like a *strait-jacket* formula. Their applicability would depend on the fact-situation of each case. It is difficult to foresee all situations and no generalization can be made.

(4) It is neither advisable, nor feasible, nor judicially permissible to draw or prescribe an outer limit for conclusion of all criminal proceedings. The time-limits or bars of limitation prescribed in the several directions

made in *Common Cause (I)*, *Raj Deo Sharma (I)* and *Raj Deo Sharma (II)* could not have been so prescribed or drawn and are not good law. The criminal courts are not obliged to terminate trial or criminal proceedings merely on account of lapse of time, as prescribed by the directions made in *Common Cause* case (I), *Raj Deo Sharma* case (I) and (II). At the most, the periods of time prescribed in those decisions can be taken by the Courts seized of the trial or proceedings to act as reminders when they may be persuaded to apply their judicial mind to the facts and circumstances of the case before them and determine by taking into consideration the several relevant factors as pointed out in *A.R. Antulay's* case and decide whether the trial or proceedings have become so inordinately delayed as to be called oppressive and unwarranted. Such time-limits cannot and will not by themselves be treated by any court as a bar to further continuance of the trial or proceedings and as mandatorily obliging the court to terminate the same and acquit or discharge the accused.

(5) The criminal courts should exercise their available powers such as those under sections 309, 311 and 258 of Code of Criminal Procedure to effectuate the right to speedy trial. A watchful and diligent trial judge can prove to be better protector of such right than any guidelines. In appropriate cases, jurisdiction of High Court under section 482 of Code of Criminal Procedure, 1908 and Articles 226 and 227 of Constitution can be invoked seeking appropriate relief or suitable directions.

(6) This is an appropriate occasion to remind the Union of India and the State Governments of their constitutional obligation to strengthen the judiciary-quantitatively and qualitatively – by providing requisite funds, manpower and infrastructure. We hope and trust that the Government shall act.

RIGHTS OF ARRESTED PERSONS

Joginder Kumar v. *State of Uttar Pradesh*, AIR 1994 SC 1349: (1994) 4 SCC 260

1. An arrested person being held in custody is entitled, if he so requests to have one friend relative or other person who is known to him or likely to take an interest in his welfare told as far as is practicable that he has been arrested and where is being detained.

2. The Police Officer shall inform the arrested person when he is brought to the police station of this right.

3. An entry shall be required to be made in the Diary as to who was informed of the arrest. These protections from power must be held to flow from articles 21 and 22(1) and enforced strictly.

It shall be the duty of the Magistrate, before whom the arrested person is produced, to satisfy himself that these requirements have been complied with.

The above requirements shall be followed in all cases of arrest till legal provisions are made in this behalf. These requirements shall be in addition to the rights of the arrested persons found in the various Police Manuals.

These requirements are not exhaustive. The Directors-General of Police of all the States in India shall issue necessary instructions requiring due observance of these requirements. In addition, departmental instruction shall also be issued that a police officer making an arrest should also record in the case diary, the reasons for making the arrest.

SENTENCING/PUNISHMENTS

Lehna v. *State of Haryana*, (2002) 3 SCC 76: (2002) 1 SCALE 273

In *Machhi Singh* and *Bachan Singh* cases the guidelines which are to be kept in view when considering the question whether the case belongs to the rarest of the rare category were indicated.

In *Machhi Singh* case it was observed: The following questions may be asked and answered as a test to determine the 'rarest of the rare' case in which death sentence can be inflicted:

(a) Is there something uncommon about the crime which renders sentence of imprisonment for life inadequate and calls for a death sentence?

(b) Are the circumstances of the crime such that there is no alternative but to impose death sentence even after according maximum weightage to the mitigating circumstances which speak in favour of the offender?

The following guidelines which emerge from *Bachan Singh* case will have to be applied to the facts of each individual case where the question of imposition of death sentence arises:

(I) The extreme penalty of death need not be inflicted except in gravest cases of extreme culpability.

(II) Before opting for the death penalty the circumstances of the 'offender' also require to be taken into consideration along with the circumstances of the 'crime'.

(III) Life imprisonment is the rule and death sentence is an exception, Death sentence must be imposed only when life imprisonment appears to be an altogether inadequate punishment having regard to the relevant circumstances of the crime, and provided, and only provided, the option to impose sentence of imprisonment for life cannot be conscientiously exercised having regard to the nature and circumstances of the crime and all the relevant circumstances.

(IV) A balance sheet of aggravating and mitigating circumstances has to be drawn up and in doing so the mitigating circumstances has to be accorded full weightage and a just balance has to be struck between the aggravating and the mitigating circumstances before the option is exercised.

In rarest of rare cases when the collective conscience of the community is so shocked, that it will expect the holders of the judicial power centre to inflict death penalty irrespective of their personal opinion as regards desirability or otherwise of retaining death penalty, death sentence can be awarded. The community may entertain such sentiment in the following circumstances:

(1) When the murder is committed in an extremely brutal, grotesque, diabolical, revolting or dastardly manner so as to arouse intense and extreme indignation of the community.

(2) When the murder is committed for a motive which evinces total depravity and meanness; *e.g.*, murder by hired assassin for money or reward; or cold-blooded murder for gains of a person *vis-a-vis* whom the murderer is in a dominating position or in a position of trust; or murder is committed in the course for betrayal of the motherland.

(3) When murder of a member of a Scheduled Caste or minority community etc. is committed not for personal reasons but in circumstances which arouse social wrath, or in cases of 'bride burning' or 'dowry deaths' or when murder is committed in order to remarry for the sake of extracting dowry once again or to marry another woman on account of infatuation.

(4) When the crime is enormous in proportion. For instance when multiple murders, say of all or almost all the members of a family or a large number of persons of a particular caste, community, or locality, are committed.

(5) When the victim of murder is an innocent child, or a helpless woman or old or infirm person or a person *vis-a-vis* whom the murderer is in a dominating position, or a public figure generally loved and respected by the community.

If upon taking an overall global view of all the circumstances in the light of the aforesaid propositions and taking into account the answers to the questions posed by way of the test for the rarest of rare cases, the circumstances of the case are such that death sentence is warranted, the Court would proceed to do so.

A convict hovers between life and death when the question of gravity of the offence and award of adequate sentence comes up for consideration. Mankind has shifted from the state of nature towards a civilized society and it is no longer the physical opinion of the majority that takes away the liberty of a citizen by convicting him and making him suffer a sentence of imprisonment. Award of punishment following conviction at a trial in a system wedded to the rule of law is the outcome of cool deliberation in the court room after adequate hearing is afforded to the parties, accusations are brought against the accused, the prosecuted is given an opportunity of meeting the accusations by establishing his innocence. It is the outcome of cool deliberations and the screening of the material by the informed man *i.e.,* the Judge that leads to determination of the *lis.*

The principle of proportion between crime and punishment is a principle of just desert that serves as the foundation of every criminal sentence that is justifiable. As a principle of criminal justice it is hardly less familiar or less important than the principle that only the guilty ought to be punished. Indeed, the requirement that punishment not be disproportionately great, which is a corollary of just desert, is dictated by the same principle that does not allow punishment of the innocent, for any punishment in excess of what is deserved for the criminal conduct is punishment without guilt.

The criminal law adheres in general to the principle of proportionality in prescribing liability according to the culpability of each kind of criminal conduct. It ordinarily allows some significant discretion to the Judge in arriving at a sentence in each case, presumably to permit sentences that reflect more subtle considerations of culpability that are raised by the special facts of each case. Punishment ought always to fit the crime; yet in practice sentences are determined largely by other considerations. Sometimes it is the correctional needs of the perpetrator that are offered to justify a sentence; sometimes the desirability of keeping him out of circulation, and sometimes even the terrific results of his crime. Inevitably these considerations cause a departure from just desert as the basis of punishment and create cases of apparent injustice that are serious and widespread.

Proportion between crime and punishment is a goal respected in principle, and in spite of errant notions it remains a strong influence in the determination of sentences. The practice of punishing all serious crimes with equal severity is now unknown in civilized societies; but such a radical departure from the principle of proportionality has disappeared from the law only in recent times. Even now a single grave infraction is thought to call for uniformly drastic measures. Anything less than a penalty of greatest severity for any serious crime is thought then to be a measure of toleration that is unwarranted and unwise. But, in fact, quite apart from those considerations that make punishment unjustifiable when it is out of proportion to the crime uniformly disproportionate punishment has some very undesirable practical consequences.

TREATMENT OF PRISONERS

Sunil Batra v. *Delhi Administration,* AIR 1980 SC 1579: (1980) 3 SCC 488

1. The State shall take early steps to prepare a Hindi, a Prisoner's Handbook and circulate copies to bring legal awareness home to the inmates. Periodical jail bulletins stating how improvements and habilitative programmes are brought

into the prison may crease a fellowship which will ease tensions. A prisoner's wall paper, which will freely ventilate grievances will also reduce stress. All these are implementary of section 61 of the Prisons Act.

2. The State shall take steps to keep up to the Standard Minimum Rules for Treatment of Prisoners recommended by the United Nations, especially those relating to work and wages, treatment with dignity, community contact and correctional strategies. In this latter aspect the observations we have made of holistic development of personality shall be kept in view.

3. The Prisons Act, needs rehabilitation and the Prison Manual total overhaul, even the Model Manual being out of focus with healing goals. A correctional-cum-orientation course is necessitous for the prison staff inculcating the constitutional values, therapeutic approaches and tension-free management.

4. The prisoners' rights shall be protected by the court by its writ jurisdiction plus contempt power. To make this jurisdiction viable, free legal services to the prisoner programmes shall be promoted by professional organisations recognised by the Court such as *e.g.*, Free Legal Aid (Supreme Court) Society. The District Bar shall, keep a cell for prisoner relief.

TAPE RECORDED STATEMENT – ADMISSIBILITY

Ziyauddin Burhanuddin Bukhari v. *Brijmohan Ramdass Mehra*, AIR 1975 SC 1788: (1976) 2 SCC 17

The tape records of speeches were "documents", as defined by section 3 of the Evidence Act, which stood on no different footing than photographs, and that they were admissible in evidence on satisfying the following conditions:

(a) The voice of the person alleged to be speaking must be duly identified by the maker of the record or by others who know it.

(b) Accuracy of what was actually recorded had to be proved by the maker of the record and satisfactory evidence, direct or circumstantial had to be there so as to rule out possibilities of tampering with the record.

(c) The subject-matter recorded had to be shown to be relevant according to rules of relevancy found in the Evidence Act. These requirements were deduced by High Court from *R.* v. *Maqsud Ali*, (1965) 2 All ER 464.

TEST IDENTIFICATION PARADE

Dana Yadav v. *State of Bihar*, (2002) 7 SCC 295: AIR 2002 SC 3325

(a) If an accused is well-known to the prosecution witnesses from before, no test identification parade is called for and it would be meaningless and sheer waste of public time to hold the same.

(b) In cases where according to the prosecution the accused is known to the prosecution witnesses from before but the said fact is denied by him and he challenges his identity by the prosecution witnesses by filing a petition for holding test identification parade, a court while dealing with such a prayer, should consider without holding a mini inquiry as to whether the denial is *bona fide* or a mere pretence and/or made with an ulterior motive to delay the investigation. In case court comes to the conclusion that the denial is *bona fide*, it may accede to the prayer, but if, however, it is of the view that the same is a mere pretence and/or made with an ulterior motive to delay the investigation, question for grant of such a prayer would not arise. Unjustified grant or refusal of such a prayer would not necessarily endure to the benefit of either party nor the same would be detrimental to their interest. In case prayer is granted and test identification parade is held in which a witness fails to identify the accused, his so-called claim that the accused was known to him from before and the evidence of identification in court should not be accepted. But in case either prayer is not granted or granted but no test identification parade held, the same *ipso facto* cannot be a ground for throwing out evidence of identification of an accused in court when evidence of the witness, on the question of identity of the accused from before, is found to be credible. The main thrust should be on answer to the question as to whether evidence of a witness in Court to the identity of the accused from before is trustworthy or not. In case the answer is in the affirmative, the fact that prayer for holding test identification parade was rejected or although granted, but no such parade was held, would not in any manner affect the evidence adduced in court in relation to identity of the accused. But if, however, such an evidence is not free from doubt, the same may be a relevant material while appreciating the evidence of identification adduced in Court.

(c) Evidence of identification of an accused in Court by a witness is substantive evidence whereas that of identification in test identification parade is, though a primary evidence but not substantive one, and the same can be used only to corroborate identification of accused by a witness in court.

(d) Identification parades are held during the course of investigation ordinarily at the instance of investigating agencies and should be held with reasonable despatch for the purpose of enabling the witnesses to identify either the properties which are subject-matter of alleged offence or the accused persons involved in the offence so as to provide it with materials to assure itself if the investigation is proceeding on right lines and the persons whom it suspects to have committed the offence were the real culprits.

(e) Failure to hold test identification parade does not make the evidence of identification in Court inadmissible rather the same is very much admissible in law, but ordinarily identification of an accused by a witness for the first time in court should not form basis of conviction, the same being from its very nature inherently of a weak character unless it is corroborated by his previous identification in the test identification parade or any other evidence. The previous identification in the test identification parade is a check valve to the evidence of identification in court of an accused by a witness and the same is a rule of prudence and not law.

(f) In exceptional circumstances only, as discussed above, evidence of identification for the first time in Court, without the same being corroborated by previous identification in the test identification parade or any other evidence, can form the basis of conviction.

(g) Ordinarily, if an accused is not named in the first information report, his identification by witnesses in Court, should not be relied upon, especially when they did not disclose name of the accused before the police, but to this general rule there may be exceptions as enumerated above.

TEST OF OBSCENITY

As summarised in *K.A. Abbas* v. *Union of India*, AIR 1971 SC 481: (1970) 2 SCC 780

In *Ranjit D. Udeshi* v. *State of Maharashtra*, (1965) 1 SCR 65: AIR 1965 SC 881, this Court laid down certain principles on which the obscenity of a book was to be considered with a view to deciding whether the book should be allowed to circulate or withdrawn. Those principles apply *mutatis mutandis* to films and also other areas besides obscenity. The Khosla Committee also adopted them and recommended them for the guidance of the film censors. We may reproduce them here as summarized by the Khosla Committee:

> "The Supreme Court laid down the following principles which must be carefully studied and applied by our censors when they have to deal with a film said to be objectionable on the ground of indecency or immorality:
>
> (1) Treating with sex and nudity in art and literature cannot be regarded as evidence of obscenity without something more.
>
> (2) Comparison of one book with another to find the extent of permissible action is not necessary.
>
> (3) The delicate task of deciding what is artistic and what is obscene has to be performed by Courts and in the last resort, by the Supreme Court and so, oral evidence of men of literature or others on the question of obscenity is not relevant.

(4) An overall view of the obscene matter in the setting of the whole work would of course be necessary but the obscene matter must be considered by itself and separately to find out whether it is so gross and its obscenity is so decided that it is likely to deprave or corrupt those whose minds are open to influence of this sort and into whose hands the book is likely to fall.

(5) The interests of contemporary society and particularly the influence of the book etc. on it must not be overlooked.

(6) Where obscenity and art are mixed, art must be so preponderating as to throw obscenity into shadow or render the obscenity so trivial and insignificant that it can have no effect and can be overlooked.

(7) Treating with sex in a manner offensive to public decency or morality which are the words of our Fundamental Law judged by our national standards and considered likely to pander to lascivious prurient or sexually precocious minds must determine the result.

(8) When there is propagation of ideas, opinions and informations or public interest or profits, the interests of society may tilt the scales in favour of free speech and expression. Thus books on medical science with intimate illustrations and, photographs though in a sense immodest, are not to be considered obscene, but the same *Illustrations* and photographs collected in a book from without the medical text would certainly be considered to be obscene.

(9) Obscenity without a preponderating social purpose or profit cannot have the constitutional protection of free speech or expression. Obscenity is treating with sex in a manner appealing to the carnal side of human nature or having that tendency. Such a treating with sex is offensive to modesty and decency.

(10) Knowledge is not a part of the guilty act. The offender's knowledge of the obscenity of the book is not required under the law and it is a case of strict liability".

TESTIMONIAL COMPULSION/RIGHT AGAINST SELF-INCRIMINATION

State of Bombay v. *Kathi Kalu Oghad*, AIR 1961 SC 1808: (1962) 3 SCR 10

1. An accused person cannot be said to have been compelled to be a witness against himself simply because he made a statement while in police custody, without anything more. In other words, the mere fact of being in police custody at the time when the statement in question was made would not, by itself, as a proposition of law, lend itself to the inference that the accused was compelled to make the statement, though that fact, in conjunction with other circumstances

disclosed in evidence in a particular case, would be a relevant consideration in an enquiry whether or not the accused person had been compelled to make the impugned statement.

2. The mere questioning of an accused person by a police officer, resulting in a voluntary statement, which may ultimately turn out to be incriminatory, is not 'compulsion'.

3. 'To be a witness' is not equivalent to 'furnishing evidence' in its widest significance; that is to say, as including not merely making of oral or written statements but also production of documents or giving materials which may be relevant at a trial to determine the guilt or innocence of the accused.

4. Giving thumb impressions or impressions of foot or palm or fingers or specimen writings or showing parts of the body by way of identification are not included in the expression 'to be a witness'.

5. 'To be a witness' means imparting knowledge in respect of relevant facts by an oral statement or a statement in writing, made or given in Court or otherwise.

6. 'To be a witness' in its ordinary grammatical sense means giving oral testimony in Court. Case law has gone beyond this strict literal interpretation of the expression which may now bear a wider meaning, namely, bearing testimony in Court or out of Court by a person accused of an offence, orally or in writing.

7. To bring the statement in question within the prohibition of article 20(3), the person accused must have stood in the character of an accused person at the time he made the statement. It is not enough that he should become an accused, any time after the statement has been made.

USE OF STATEMENTS MADE BEFORE POLICE

Tahsildar Singh v. *State of Uttar Pradesh*, AIR 1959 SC 1012: 1959 Cr LJ 1213

1. A statement in writing made by a witness before a police officer in the course of investigation can be used only to contradict his statement in the witness box and for no other purpose;

2. Statements not reduced to writing by the police officer cannot be used for contradiction;

3. Though a particular statement is not expressly recorded, a statement that can be deemed to be part of that expressly recorded can be used for contradiction, not because it is an omission strictly so-called but because it is deemed to form part of the recorded statement;

4. Such a fiction is permissible by construction only in the following three cases:

(i) when a recital is necessarily implied from the recital or recitals found in the statement: illustration: in the recorded statement before the police the witness states that he saw *A* stabbing *B* at a particular point of time, but in the witness box he says that he saw *A* and *C* stabbing *B* at the same point of time; in the statement before the police the word "only" can be implied *i.e.*, the witness saw *A* only stabbing *B*;

(ii) a negative aspect of a positive recital in a statement: *Illustration*: in the recorded statement before the police the witness says that a dark man stabbed *B*, but in the witness box he says that a fair man stabbed *B*; the earlier statement must be deemed to contain the recital not only that the culprit was a dark complexioned man but also that he was not of fair complexion; and

(iii) when the statement before the police and that before the Court cannot stand together: *Illustration*: the witness says in the recorded statement before the police that *A* after stabbing *B* ran away by a northern lane, but in the Court he says that immediately after stabbing he ran away towards the southern lane; as he could not have run away immediately after the stabbing *i.e.*, at the same point of time, towards the northern lane as well as towards the southern lane, if one statement is true, the other must necessarily be false.

The aforesaid examples are not intended to be exhaustive but only *Illustrative*. The same instance may fall under one or more heads. It is for the trial Judge to decide in each case, after comparing the part or parts of the statement recorded by the police with that made in the witness box, to give a ruling, having regard to the aforesaid principles, whether the recital intended to be used for contradiction satisfies the requirements of law.

WITNESSES – APPRECIATION OF EVIDENCE

Vadivelu Thevar v. *State of Madras*, AIR 1957 SC 614: 1957 Cr LJ 1000

1. As a general rule, a court can and may act on the testimony of a single witness though uncorroborated. One credible witness outweighs the testimony of a number of other witnesses of indifferent character.

2. Unless corroboration is insisted upon by statute, courts should not insist on corroboration except in cases where the nature of the testimony of the single witness itself requires as a rule of prudence, that corroboration should be insisted upon, for example in the case of a child witness, or of a witness whose evidence is that of an accomplice or of an analogous character.

3. Whether corroboration of the testimony of a single witness is or is not necessary, must depend upon facts and circumstances of each case and no general rule can be laid down in a matter like this and much depends upon the judicial discretion of the Judge before whom the case comes.

4. In view of these considerations, we have no hesitation in holding that the contention that in a murder case, the court should insist upon plurality of witnesses, is much too broadly stated. Section 134 of the Indian Evidence Act, has categorically laid it down that "no particular number of witnesses shall, in any case, be required for the proof of any fact." The legislature determined, as long ago as 1872, presumably after the consideration of the *pros* and *cons*, that it shall not be necessary for proof or disproof of a fact, to call any particular number of witnesses. In England both before and after the passing of the Indian Evidence Act, 1872, there have been a number of statutes as set out in *Sarkar's 'Law of Evidence'* - 9th Edn., at pp. 1100 and 1101, forbidding convictions on the testimony of a single witness. The Indian Legislature has not insisted on laying down any such exceptions to the general rule recognized on section 134 quoted above. The section enshrines the well recognized maxim that "Evidence has to be weighed and not counted." Our Legislature has given statutory recognition to the fact that administration of justice may be hampered if a particular number of witnesses were to be insisted upon. It is not seldom that a crime has been committed in the presence of only one witness, leaving aside those cases which are not of uncommon occurrence where determination of guilt depends entirely on circumstantial evidence. If the Legislature were to insist upon plurality of witnesses, cases where the testimony of a single witness only could be available in proof of the crime, would go unpunished. It is here that the discretion of the presiding judge comes into play. The matter thus must depend upon the circumstances of each case and the quality of the evidence of the single witness whose testimony has to be either accepted or rejected. If such a testimony is found by the court to be entirely reliable, there is no legal impediment to the conviction of the accused person on such proof. Even as the guilt of an accused person may be proved by the testimony of a single witness, the innocence of an accused person may be established on the testimony of a single witness, even though a considerable number of witnesses may be forthcoming to testify to the truth of the case for the prosecution. Hence, in our opinion, it is a sound and well-established rule of law that the court is concerned with the quality and not with the quantity of the evidence necessary for proving or disproving a fact. Generally speaking, oral testimony in this context may be classified into three categories, namely:

(i) Wholly reliable.

(ii) Wholly unreliable.

(iii) Neither wholly reliable nor wholly unreliable.

5. In the first category of proof, the court should have no difficulty in coming to its conclusion either way – it may convict or may acquit on the testimony of a single witness, if it is found to be above reproach or suspicion of interestedness, incompetence or subornation. In the second category, the court equally has no difficulty in coming to its conclusion. It is in the third category of cases, that the court has to be circumspect and has to look for corroboration in material particulars by reliable testimony, direct or circumstantial. There is another danger in insisting on plurality of witnesses. Irrespective of the quality of the

oral evidence of a single witness, if courts were to insist on plurality of witnesses in proof of any fact, they will be indirectly encouraging subornation of witnesses. Situations may arise and do arise where only a single person is available to give evidence in support of a disputed fact. The Court naturally has to weigh carefully such a testimony and if it is satisfied that the evidence is reliable and free from all taints which tend to render oral testimony open to suspicion, it becomes its duty to act upon such testimony. The law reports contain many precedents where the court had to depend and act upon the testimony of a single witness in support of the prosecution. There are exceptions to this rule, for example, in cases of sexual offences or of the testimony of an approver; both these are cases in which the oral testimony is, by its very nature, suspect, being that of a participator in crime. But, where there are no such exceptional reasons operating, it becomes the duty of the Court to convict, if it is satisfied that the testimony of a single witness is entirely reliable.

WITHDRAWAL OF PROSECUTION (SECTION 321 CR. P.C)

Rajendra Kumar Jain v. *State through Special Police Establishment,* AIR 1980 SC 1510: (1980) 3 SCC 435

1. Under the scheme of the Code prosecution of an offender for a serious offence is primarily the responsibility of the Executive.

2. The withdrawal from the prosecution is an executive function of the Public Prosecutor.

3. The discretion to withdraw from the prosecution is that of the Public Prosecutor and none else, and so, he cannot surrender that discretion to someone else.

4. The Government may suggest to the Public Prosecutor that he may withdraw from the prosecution but none can compel him to do so.

5. The Public Prosecutor may withdraw from the prosecution not merely on the ground of paucity of evidence but on other relevant grounds as well in order to further the broad ends of public justice, public order and peace. The broad ends of public justice will certainly include appropriate social, economic and, we add, political purposes sans Tammany Hall enterprises.

6. The Public Prosecutor is an officer of the Court and responsible to the Court.

7. The Court performs a supervisory function in granting its consent to the withdrawal.

8. The Court's duty is not to reappreciate the grounds which led the Public Prosecutor to request withdrawal from the prosecution but to consider whether

the Public Prosecutor applied his mind as a free agent, uninfluenced by irrelevant and extraneous consideration. The Court has a special duty in this regard as it is the ultimate repository of legislative confidence in granting or withholding its consent to withdrawal from the prosecution.

We may add, it shall be the duty of the Public Prosecutor to inform the Court and it shall be the duty of the Court to appraise itself of the reasons which prompt the Public Prosecutor to withdraw from the prosecution. The Court has a responsibility and a stake in the administration of criminal justice and so has the Public Prosecutor, its 'Minister of Justice'. Both have a duty to protect the administration of criminal justice against possible abuse or misuse by the Executive by resort to the provisions of section 321, Criminal Procedure Code. The independence of the judiciary requires that once the case has travelled to the Court, the Court and its officers alone must have control over the case and decide what is to be done in each case.

Part 5

JUSTICE J.S. VERMA COMMITTEE REPORT, 2013 ON ANTI-RAPE LAW (RELEVANT EXTRACTS)

JUSTICE J.S. VERMA COMMITTEE REPORT, 2013 ON ANTI-RAPE LAW

****

CHAPTER THREE

RAPE AND SEXUAL ASSAULT

1. The statutory definition of the offence of "rape" is found under section 375. It reads thus:

> *"375. Rape.—A man is said to commit "rape" who, except in the case hereinafter excepted, has sexual intercourse with a woman under circumstances falling under any of the six following descriptions:.—*
>
> *First.—Against her will.*
>
> *Secondly.—Without her consent.*
>
> *Thirdly.—With her consent, when her consent has been obtained by putting her or any person in whom she is interested in fear of death or of hurt.*
>
> *Fourthly.—With her consent, when the man knows that he is not her husband, and that her consent is given because she believes that he is another man to whom she is or believes herself to be lawfully married.*
>
> *Fifthly.—With her consent, when, at the time of giving such consent, by reason of unsoundness of mind or intoxication or the administration by him personally or through another of any stupefying or unwholesome substance, she is unable to understand the nature and consequences of that to which she gives consent.*
>
> *Sixthly.—With or without her consent, when she is under sixteen years of age.*
>
> *Explanation.—Penetration is sufficient to constitute the sexual intercourse necessary to the offence of rape.*
>
> *Exception.—Sexual intercourse by a man with his own wife, the wife not being under fifteen years of age, is not rape."*

2. Simply put, the offence of rape is "ravishment of a woman" without her consent or against her will by force, fear or fraud and also includes the "carnal knowledge" of a woman.[44]

3. "Carnal Knowledge" means penetration to any slightest degree. This ingredient of rape has been statutory incorporated under the Explanation to section 375.

44. *Bhupendra Sharma* v. *State of Himachal Pradesh*, (2003) 8 SCC 551 [para 10-11].

Ingredients of the offence

Consent

4. In order to bring home the charge of rape against a man, it is necessary to establish that the "sexual intercourse" complained of was either against the will or without her consent. Where the consent is obtained under the circumstances enumerated under clauses firstly to sixthly, the same would also amount to rape.

5. In *Dileep Singh* v. *State of Bihar*[45] the Supreme Court observed that *"though will and consent often interlace and an act done against the will of the person can be said to be an act done without consent, the Indian Penal Code categorizes these two expressions under separate heads in order to as comprehensive as possible."*

6. The difference between the two expressions was brought out by the Supreme Court in *State of UP* v. *Chottey Lal*[46] in the following words:

> *"15. Be that as it may, in our view, clause Sixthly of section 375, IPC is not attracted since the prosecutrix has been found to be above 16 years (although below 18 years). In the facts of the case what is crucial to be considered is whether clause Firstly or clause Secondly of section 375, IPC is attracted. The expressions "against her will" and "without her consent" may overlap sometimes but surely the two expressions in clause Firstly and clause Secondly have different connotation and dimension. The expression "against her will" would ordinarily mean that the intercourse was done by a man with a woman despite her resistance and opposition. On the other hand, the expression "without her consent" would comprehend an act of reason accompanied by deliberation.* (Emphasis supplied)"

7. It must be noted that the Courts have followed the tests laid down under section 90 of the IPC for establishing "consent". Section 90 reads thus:

> *"90. Consent known to be given under fear or misconception.—A consent is not such a consent as is intended by any section of this Code, if the consent is given by a person under fear of injury, or under a misconception of fact, and if the person doing the act knows, or has reason to believe, that the consent was given in consequence of such fear or misconception; or*
>
> ***[Consent of insane person]*** *if the consent is given by a person who, from unsoundness of mind, or intoxication, is unable to understand the nature and consequence of that to which he gives his consent; or*
>
> ***[Consent of child]*** *unless the contrary appears from the context, if the consent is given by a person who is under twelve years of age."*

8. In this context the decision of Supreme Court in *State of H.P* v. *Mango Ram*[47] is noteworthy. The Court observed as follows:

> "13 ....*The evidence as a whole indicates that there was resistance by the prosecutrix and there was no voluntary participation by her for the sexual act. Submission of the body under the fear of terror cannot be construed as a*

45. (2005) 1 SCC 88 (para 14).
46. (2011) 2 SCC 550.
47. (2000) 7 SCC 224.

> *consented sexual act. Consent for the purpose of section 375 requires voluntary participation not only after the exercise of intelligence based on the knowledge of the significance and moral quality of the act but after having fully exercised the choice between resistance and assent. Whether there was consent or not, is to be ascertained only on a careful study of all relevant circumstances. From the evidence on record, it cannot be said that the prosecutrix had given consent and thereafter she turned round and acted against the interest of the accused. There is clear credible evidence that she resisted the onslaught and made all possible efforts to prevent the accused from committing rape on her. Therefore, the finding entered by the learned Sessions Judge that there was consent on the part of the prosecutrix is without any basis."*

9. The United Nations Handbook points out that the definitions of rape and sexual assault have evolved over time, from requiring use of force or violence, to requiring a lack of positive consent.

10. The United Nations recommends that the definition of rape should require the existence of 'unequivocal and voluntary agreement' as well as proof by the accused of steps taken to ascertain whether the complainant was consenting.[48] This has the advantage of shifting the burden to the defence to prove that such steps were taken. This approach was endorsed by the CEDAW committee in its views in *Vertido* v. *The Philippines,*[49] which made it clear that such a definition would assist in minimizing secondary victimization of the complainant/survivor in proceedings.

11. Similarly, under Canadian law, the accused cannot argue that there was belief in consent if the accused did not take reasonable steps to ascertain that there was consent to the specific sexual activity. It is not enough that the accused subjectively believed there was consent. He must also demonstrate that he took reasonable steps to ascertain it.[50]

12. Under the law of England and Wales, a person consents if he or she 'agrees by choice and has the freedom and capacity to make that choice.'[51] There are certain statutory presumptions regarding consent. For example, lack of consent is assumed if violence was used or threatened or the accused had induced a fear of violence; the complainant was unlawfully detained, asleep or unconscious; or the accused had administered a substance capable of causing the complainant to be stupefied or overpowered. Lack of consent is conclusively proved if the defendant intentionally deceived the complainant as to the nature or purpose of the relevant act, or induced consent by impersonating a person known to the complainant.[52] The underlying principle is that consent to sexual activity 'requires a conscious, operating mind, capable of granting, revoking or withholding consent to each and every sexual act.'[53] There are some similar presumptions in the Indian statute. We have defined consent keeping the above in mind.

48. *Ibid.*
49. Above n 96.
50. Canadian Criminal Code, s. 273.2.
51. Sexual Offences Act, 2003 (UK), s. 74.
52. Sexual Offences Act, 2003, ss 75 and 76.
53. *R* v. *J.A.* (n 91).

Penetration

13. The section further clarifies that mere penetration is sufficient to constitute the offence of rape.

14. In *Koppula Venkatrao* v. *State of AP*[54] the Supreme Court held as follows:

> *"12. The sine qua non of the offence of rape is penetration, and not ejaculation. Ejaculation without penetration constitutes an attempt to commit rape and not actual rape. Definition of "rape" as contained in section 375 IPC refers to "sexual intercourse" and the Explanation appended to the section provides that penetration is sufficient to constitute the sexual intercourse necessary to the offence of rape. Intercourse means sexual connection."*

15. Pursuant to the aforesaid observation the offence of 'attempt to commit rape' also need elaboration. Section 376 read with section 511 of IPC penalizes the offence of 'attempt to rape'.

Attempt to commit rape

16. In *Koppula Venkatrao* (supra) the Supreme Court, with respect to the applicability of section 511 to the offence of rape, held the following:

> *"8. The plea relating to applicability of section 376 read with section 511 IPC needs careful consideration. In every crime, there is first, intention to commit, secondly, preparation to commit it, and thirdly, attempt to commit it. If the third stage, that is, attempt is successful, then the crime is complete. If the attempt fails, the crime is not complete, but law punishes the person attempting the act. Section 511 is a general provision dealing with attempts to commit offences not made punishable by other specific sections. It makes punishable all attempts to commit offences punishable with imprisonment and not only those punishable with death. An attempt is made punishable, because every attempt, although it falls short of success, must create alarm, which by itself is an injury, and the moral guilt of the offender is the same as if he had succeeded. Moral guilt must be united to injury in order to justify punishment. As the injury is not as great as if the act had been committed, only half the punishment is awarded.*
>
> *9. A culprit first intends to commit the offence, then makes preparation for committing it and thereafter attempts to commit the offence. If the attempt succeeds, he has committed the offence; if it fails due to reasons beyond his control, he is said to have attempted to commit the offence. Attempt to commit an offence can be said to begin when the preparations are complete and the culprit commences to do something with the intention of committing the offence and which is a step towards the commission of the offence. The moment he commences to do an act with the necessary intention, he commences his attempt to commit the offence. The word "attempt" is not itself defined, and must, therefore, be taken in its ordinary meaning. This is exactly what the provisions of section 511 require. An attempt to commit a crime is to be distinguished from an intention to commit it; and from preparation made for its commission. Mere intention to commit an offence, not followed by any act, cannot constitute an offence. The will is not to be taken for the deed unless there be some external act which*

54. (2004) 3 SCC 602.

shows that progress has been made in the direction of it, or towards maturing and effecting it. Intention is the direction of conduct towards the object chosen upon considering the motives which suggest the choice. Preparation consists in devising or arranging the means or measures necessary for the commission of the offence. It differs widely from attempt which is the direct movement towards the commission after preparations are made. Preparation to commit an offence is punishable only when the preparation is to commit offences under section 122 (waging war against the Government of India) and section 399 (preparation to commit dacoity). The dividing line between a mere preparation and an attempt is sometimes thin and has to be decided on the facts of each case. There is a greater degree of determination in attempt as compared with preparation.

10. An attempt to commit an offence is an act, or a series of acts, which leads inevitably to the commission of the offence, unless something, which the doer of the act neither foresaw nor intended, happens to prevent this. An attempt may be described to be an act done in part-execution of a criminal design, amounting to more than mere preparation, but falling short of actual consummation, and, possessing, except for failure to consummate, all the elements of the substantive crime. In other words, an attempt consists in it the intent to commit a crime, falling short of, its actual commission or consummation/completion. It may consequently be defined as that which if not prevented would have resulted in the full consummation of the act attempted. The illustrations given in section 511 clearly show the legislative intention to make a difference between the cases of a mere preparation and an attempt.

11. In order to find an accused guilty of an attempt with intent to commit a rape, court has to be satisfied that the accused, when he laid hold of the prosecutrix, not only desired to gratify his passions upon her person, but that he intended to do so at all events, and notwithstanding any resistance on her part. Indecent assaults are often magnified into attempts at rape. In order to come to a conclusion that the conduct of the accused was indicative of a determination to gratify his passion at all events, and in spite of all resistance, materials must exist. Surrounding circumstances many times throw beacon light on that aspect."

Evidence and proof

17. It is well settled that the evidence of the victim of rape is on the same footing as the evidence of an injured complainant or witness. Her testimony alone is sufficient for conviction. In prosecutions of rape, the law does not require corroboration. It is only by way of abundant caution that the court may look for some corroboration so as to satisfy its conscience and rule out any false accusation.[55]

18. However, the above principle of presumption while prosecuting rape cases emerged in the aforesaid background.

19. In *Tukaram* v. *State of Maharashtra*[56] the Supreme Court had disbelieved the statement of the victim of rape, on the ground that the circumstantial evidence

55. *Infra* 1 (para 22).

56. (1979) 2 SCC 143.

did not lead to the inference of guilt and "in fact derogates in no uncertain measure from the inference drawn by it."[57]

20. The facts were these – Mathura was a young girl labourer of 14-16. Her bother and she were brought to their local police station to record their statements in respect of a complaint lodged by her brother. While at the police station, Mathura was raped by Head Constable Tukaram and Constable Ganpat, a fact which she reported to a crowd that had gathered outside the police station. Mathura was then examined by a doctor, who advised her to file a police complaint, which complaint was registered by the police after some hesitation and protests from the crowd.

21. Mathura's medical examination revealed no injuries and evidence of prior intercourse. Presence of semen was detected on her clothes and the pyjama of Ganpat. The Trial Court, however, refused to convict the accused. The High Court reversed the finding and sentenced Tukaram to rigorous imprisonment for one year and Ganpat for five years. The High Court held that both these 'gentlemen' were perfect strangers to Mathura and that it was unlikely that *'she would make any overtures and invite the accused to satisfy her sexual desires'*. The High Court came to the conclusion that Mathura did not consent to intercourse. The Supreme Court reversed the High Court verdict and held that as there were no injuries shown by the medical report, the story of 'stiff resistance having been put up by the girl is all false' and the alleged intercourse was a peaceful affair. The Court further held that crimes and alarms were a concoction on her part. The Court further held that under section 375 only the "fear of death or hurt" could vitiate consent for sexual intercourse.

22. Following this verdict a nation-wide protest was launched for inclusion of custodial rape within the legislative provision. The Supreme Court's judgment was criticised by four eminent law teachers – Upendra Baxi, Vasudha Dhagamdar, Raghunath Kelkar, and Lotika Sarkar – who posed the following questions in an open letter to the Supreme Court.—

(a) Was this not a decision which violated human rights of women under the law and the Constitution ?

(b) The judgment provided no cogent analysis as to why the factors which weighed with the High Court were insufficient to justify conviction for rape?

(c) The fact remains that Mathura was asked to remain in the police station even after her statement was recorded and her friends and relations were asked to leave. Why?

(d) Why were the lights put off and the doors shut?

23. The decision of *Tukaram* v. *State of Maharashtra*[58], is a relevant case to show how public opinion and various organisations have espoused the rights of women.

24. Accordingly the Criminal Law Amendment Act, 1983 was passed which included situation of "aggravated rape" under section 376A to E. Further, the Indian Evidence Act, 1872 was also amended by the Criminal Law Amendment Act, 1983 and section 114A was incorporated which imposed the burden of

57. *Ibid* (para 17).

58. (1979) 2 SCC 143.

proving "consent" upon the accused in the aforesaid cases of aggravated rape. This was an exception of the general rule of presumption of innocence of the accused.

25. However, even before the above amendments came in to force in the case of *Bharvada Gohinbhai Hirjibhai* v. *State of Gujarat*[59], the Supreme Court reversed the trend and came to a conclusion that it was open to the Court to rely upon the evidence of a complainant even without seeking corroboration if corroboration by medical evidence is available. We also notice that the said judgment seems to have stereotyped Indian and Western women in a somewhat unorthodox way:

> "9. *In the Indian setting, refusal to act on the testimony of a victim of sexual assault in the absence of corroboration as a rule, is adding insult 'to injury. Why should the evidence of the girl or the woman who complains of rape or sexual molestation be viewed with the aid of spectacles fitted with lenses tinged with doubt, disbelief or suspicion? To do so is to justify the charge of male chauvinism in a male dominated society. We must analyze the argument in support of the need for corroboration and subject it to relentless and remorseless cross-examination. And we must do so with a logical, and not an opiniated, eye in the light of probabilities with our feet firmly planted on the soil of India and with our eyes focussed on the Indian horizon. We must not be swept off the feet by the approach made in the Western World which has its own social milieu, its own social mores, its own permissive values, and its own code of life. Corroboration may be considered essential to establish a sexual offence in the backdrop of the social ecology of the Western World. It is wholly unnecessary to import the said concept on a turn-key basis and to translate it on the Indian soil regardless of the altogether different atmosphere, attitudes, mores, responses of the Indian Society, and its profile. The identities of the two worlds are different. The solution of problems cannot therefore be identical. It is conceivable in the Western Society that a female may level false accusation as regards sexual molestation against a male for several reasons such as:*
>
> (1) *The female may be a 'gold digger' and may well have an economic motive to extract money by holding out the gun of prosecution or public exposure.*
>
> (2) *She may be suffering from psychological neurosis and may seek an escape from the neurotic prison by phantasizing or imagining a situation where she is desired, wanted, and chased by males.*
>
> (3) *She may want to wreak vengeance on the male for real or imaginary wrongs. She may have a grudge against a particular male, or males in general, and may have the design to square the account.*
>
> (4) *She may have been induced to do so in consideration of economic rewards, by a person interested in placing the accused in a compromising or embarrassing position, on account of personal or political vendetta.*
>
> (5) *She may do so to gain notoriety or publicity or to appease her own ego or to satisfy her feeling of self-importance in the context of her inferiority complex.*

59. (1983) 3 SCC 217.

(6) She may do so on account of jealousy.

(7) She may do so to win sympathy of others.

(8) She may do so upon being repulsed.

10. By and large these factors are not relevant to India, and the Indian conditions. Without the fear of making too wide a statement, or of overstating the case, it can be said that rarely will a girl or a woman in India make false allegations of sexual assault on account of any such factor as has been just enlisted. The statement is generally true in the context of the urban as also rural Society. It is also by and large true in the context of the sophisticated, not so sophisticated, and unsophisticated society. Only very rarely can one conceivably come across an exception or two and that too possibly from amongst the urban elites. Because: (1) A girl or a woman in the tradition bound non-permissive Society of India would be extremely reluctant even to admit that any incident which is likely to reflect on her chastity had ever occurred. (2) She would be conscious of the danger of being ostracised by the Society or being looked down by the Society including by her own family members, relatives, friends and neighbours. (3) She would have to brave the whole world. (4) She would face the risk of losing the love and respect of her own husband and near relatives, and of her matrimonial home and happiness being shattered. (5) If she is unmarried, she would apprehend that it would be difficult to secure an alliance. With a suitable match from a respectable or an acceptable family. (6) It would almost inevitably and almost invariably result in mental torture and suffering to herself. (7) The fear of being taunted by others will always haunt her. (8) She would feel extremely embarrassed in relating the incident to others being over powered by a feeling of shame on account of the upbringing in a tradition bound society where by and large sex is taboo. (9) The natural inclination would be to avoid giving publicity to the incident lest the family name and family honour is brought into controversy. (10) The parents of an unmarried girl as also the husband and members of the husband's family of a married woman would also more often than not, want to avoid publicity on account of the fear of social stigma on the family name and family honour. (11) The fear of the victim herself being considered to be promiscuous or in some way responsible for the incident regardless of her innocence. (12 The reluctance to face interrogation by the investigating agency, to face the court, to face the cross examination by Counsel for the culprit, and the risk of being disbelieved, acts as a deterrent".

26. As a listing of these characteristics, we regret that there is a profiling of an Indian girl which has taken place which is an overgeneralisation and it would neither be accurate nor scientific to test the testimony of an Indian women with reference to the criteria which are mentioned in paragraph 10 above. But what is important is that the judgment, in a certain sense, discloses how a woman is viewed in India.

27. We feel that it is the duty of the State as well as civil society to deconstruct the paradigm of shame- honour in connection with a rape victim. Rape is a form of sexual assault just like any other crime against the human body under the IPC. While we agree that it has its distinguishing characteristics, we do not think that there is any basis for society or the State and much less the police/doctors

to treat a rape victim as a victim of any other crime. In other words, we are of the opinion that while the said paragraph quoted illustrates the misplaced juxtaposition of shame and honour with the crime of rape, the juxtaposition is clearly a matter of reality and at the same time we think that it is necessary for this to be deconstructed. It also shows that women have been looped into a vicious cycle of shame and honour as a consequence of which they have been attended with an inherent disability to report crimes of sexual offences against them.

28. In other words, a woman seems to be risking her reputation and honour by reporting a crime of sexual assault against herself. This view must change and while the above passage shows the fundamental misconceptions which are inbuilt in society dealing with women, we are more concerned with the observations in so far as they describe the position of women in Indian society, not in as much as women in the context of rape. In fact, we believe that equality before law, which is guaranteed under the Constitution, invariably means the eschewing of irrelevant considerations and we do believe that many of these considerations must be viewed as irrelevant in a changing society. However, we do notice that the above characteristics are completely inconsistent with fundamental rights which are guaranteed to a woman under the Constitution. We further believe that these cannot be the basis for the purpose of defining the rights of women under the law.

29. At this stage, we notice in *Rafique* v. *State of UP*[60], where Krishna Iyer, J. made the following observations:—

> *"There are several "sacred cows" of the criminal law in Indo-Anglian jurisprudence which are superstitious survivals and need to be re-examined. When rapists are revelling in their promiscuous pursuits and half of humankind-womankind-is protesting against its hapless lot, when no woman of honour will accuse another of rape since she sacrifices thereby what is dearest to her, we cannot cling to a fossil formula and insist on corroborative testimony, even if taken as a whole, the case spoken to by the victim strikes a judicial mind as probable. In this case, the testimony has commanded acceptance from two courts. When a woman is ravished what is inflicted is not merely physical injury, but "the deep sense of some deathless shame".*
>
> *A rape! a rape!...*
>
> *Yes, you have ravish'd justice;*
>
> *Forced her to do your pleasure."*
>
> *"Hardly a sensitized judge who sees the conspectus of circumstances in its totality and rejects the testimony of a rape victim unless there are very strong circumstances militating against is veracity. None we see in his case, and confirmation of the conviction by the courts below must, therefore, be a matter of course. Judicial response to human rights cannot be blunted by legal bigotry."*

30. The effect of the Criminal Law Amendment of 1983 was examined by the Supreme Court[61] and it was observed as follows:

60. (1981) 1 SCR 402.

61. *Shri Bodhisattwa Gautam* v. *Shubra Chakraborty*, (1996) 1 SCC 490.

"15. In spite of the decision of this Court that (depending upon the circumstances of the case) corroboration of the prosecutrix was not necessary, the cases continued to end in acquittal on account of mishandling of the crime by the police and the invocation of the theory of 'consent' by the courts who tried the offence. To overcome this difficulty, the legislature intervened and introduced section 114A in the Evidence Act by Act No. 43 of 1983 reading as under:

> *"114A. Presumption as to absence of consent in certain prosecutions for rape.—In a prosecution for rape under clause (a) or clause (b) or clause (c) or clause (d) or clause (e) or clause (g) of sub-section (2) of section 376 of the Indian Penal Code (45 of I860), where sexual intercourse by the accused is proved and the question is whether it was without the consent of the woman alleged to have been raped and she states in her evidence before the Court that she did not consent, the Court shall presume that she did not consent."*

16. This section enables a court to raise a presumption that the woman who was the victim of rape had not consented and that the offence was committed against her will. The situation, however, has hardly improved. Conviction rates for rape are still lower than any other major crime and the women continue to argue even today that in rape cases the victimised women, rather than the rapists, were put on trial. A large number of women still fail to report rapes to the police because they fear embarrassing and insensitive treatment by the doctors, the law enforcement personnel and/or the cross-examining defence attorneys. The fear has to be allayed from the minds of women so that if and when this crime is committed, the victim may promptly report the matter to the police and on a charge-sheet being submitted, the trial may proceed speedily without causing any embarrassment to the prosecutrix who may come in the witness-box without fear psychosis."

31. Further in *State of Maharashtra* v. *Chandraprakash Kewalchand Jain* the Court observed:[62]

"15. It is necessary at the outset to state what the approach of the court should be while evaluating the prosecution evidence, particularly the evidence of the prosecutrix, in sex offences. Is it essential that the evidence of the prosecutrix should be corroborated in material particulars before the court bases a conviction on her testimony? Does the rule of prudence demand that in all cases save the rarest of rare the court should look for corroboration before acting on the evidence of the prosecutrix? Let us see if the Evidence Act provides the clue. Under the said statute 'Evidence' means and includes all statements which the court permits or requires to be made before it by witnesses, in relation to the matters of fact under inquiry. Under section 59 all facts, except the contents of documents, may be proved by oral evidence. Section 118 then tells us who may give oral evidence. According to that section all persons are competent to testify unless the court considers that they are prevented from understanding the questions put to them, or from giving rational answers to those questions, by tender years, extreme old age, disease, whether of body or mind, or any other cause of the same kind. Even in the case of an accomplice section 133 provides

62. (1990) 1 SCC 550.

that he shall be a competent witness against an accused person; and a conviction is not illegal merely because it proceeds upon the uncorroborated testimony of an accomplice. However, illustration (b) to section 114, which lays down a rule of practice, says that the court 'may' presume that an accomplice is unworthy of credit, unless he is corroborated in material particulars. Thus under section 133, which lays down a rule of law, an accomplice is a competent witness and a conviction based solely on his uncorroborated evidence is not illegal although in view of section 114, illustration (b), courts do not as a matter of practice do so and look for corroboration in material particulars. This is the conjoint effect of sections 133 and 114, illustration (b).

16. A prosecutrix of a sex offence cannot be put on par with an accomplice. She is in fact a victim of the crime. The Evidence Act nowhere says that her evidence cannot be accepted unless it is corroborated in material particulars. She is undoubtedly a competent witness under section 118 and her evidence must receive the same weight as is attached to an injured in cases of physical violence. The same degree of care and caution must attach in the evaluation of her evidence as in the case of an injured complainant or witness and no more. What is necessary is that the court must be alive to and conscious of the fact that it is dealing with the evidence of a person who is interested in the outcome of the charge levelled by her. If the court keeps this in mind and feels satisfied that it can act on the evidence of the prosecutrix, there is no rule of law or practice incorporated in the Evidence Act similar to illustration (b) to section 114 which requires it to look for corroboration. If for some reason the court is hesitant to place implicit reliance on the testimony of the prosecutrix it may look for evidence which may lend assurance to her testimony short of corroboration required in the case of an accomplice. The nature of evidence required to lend assurance to the testimony of the prosecutrix must necessarily depend on the facts and circumstances of each case. But if a prosecutrix is an adult and of full understanding the court is entitled to base a conviction on her evidence unless the same is shown to be infirm and not trustworthy. If the totality of the circumstances appearing on the record of the case disclose that the prosecutrix does not have a strong motive to falsely involve the person charged, the court should ordinarily have no hesitation in accepting her evidence. We have, therefore, no doubt in our minds that ordinarily the evidence of a prosecutrix who does not lack understanding must he accepted. The degree of proof required must not be higher than is expected of an injured witness. For the above reasons we think that exception has rightly been taken to the approach of the High Court as is reflected in the following passage:

"It is only in the rarest of rare cases if the court finds that the testimony of the prosecutrix is so trustworthy, truthful and reliable that other corroboration may not be necessary."

With respect, the law is not correctly stated. If we may say so, it is just the reverse. Ordinarily the evidence of a prosecutrix must carry the same weight as is attached to an injured person who is a victim of violence, unless there are special circumstances which call for greater caution, in which case it would be safe to act on her testimony if there is independent evidence lending assurance to her accusation.

17. We think it proper, having regard to the increase in the number of sex violation cases in the recent past, particularly cases of molestation and rape in custody, to remove the notion, if it persists, that the testimony of a woman who is a victim of sexual violence must ordinarily be corroborated in material particulars except in the rarest of rare cases. To insist on corroboration except in the rarest of rare cases is to equate a woman who is a victim of the lust of another with an accomplice to a crime and therein/ insult womanhood. It would be adding insult to injury to tell a woman that her story of woe will not be believed unless it is corroborated in material particulars as in the case of an accomplice to a crime. Ours is a conservative society where it concerns sexual behaviour. Ours is not a permissive society as in some of the western and European countries. Our standard of decency and morality in public life is not the same as in those countries. It is, however, unfortunate that respect for womanhood in our country is on the decline and cases of molestation and rape are steadily growing. An Indian woman is now required to suffer indignities in different forms, from lewd remarks to eve-teasing, from molestation to rape. Decency and morality in public life can be promoted and protected only if we deal strictly with those who violate the societal norms. The standard of proof to be expected by the court in such cases must take into account the fact that such crimes are generally committed on the sly and very rarely direct evidence of a person other than the prosecutrix is available. Courts must also realise that ordinarily a woman, more so a young girl, will not stake her reputation by levelling a false charge concerning her chastity.

18. But when such a crime is committed by a person in authority, e.g. a police officer, should the court's approach be the same as in any other case involving a private citizen? By our criminal laws wide powers are conferred on police officers investigating cognizable offences. The infrastructure of our criminal investigation system recognises and indeed protects the right of a woman to decent and dignified treatment at the hands of the investigating agency. This is evident from the proviso to sub-section (2) of section 47 of the Code which obliges the police officer desiring to effect entry to give an opportunity to the woman in occupation to withdraw from the building. So also sub-section (2) of section 53 requires that whenever a female accused is to be medically examined such examination must be under the supervision of a female medical practitioner. The proviso to section 160 stipulates that whenever the presence of a woman is required as a witness the investigating officer will record her statement at her own residence. These are just a few provisions which reflect the concern of the legislature to prevent harassment and exploitation of women and preserve their dignity. Notwithstanding this concern, if a police officer misuses his authority and power while dealing with a young helpless girl aged about 19 or 20 years, her conduct and behaviour must be judged in the backdrop of the situation in which she was placed. The purpose and setting, the person and his position, the misuse or abuse of office and the despair of the victim which led to her surrender are all relevant factors which must be present in the mind of the court while evaluating the conduct evidence of the prosecutrix. A person in authority, such as a police officer, carries with him the awe of office which is bound to condition the behaviour of his victim. The court must not be oblivious of the emotional turmoil and the psychological injury that a prosecutrix suffers on being molested or raped. She suffers a tremendous sense of shame and the fear of being shunned by society and her near relatives, including her husband. Instead of treating her with compassion and understanding as one who is an injured victim of a crime, she is, more often then not, treated as a sinner and shunned. It must, therefore, be realised that a woman who is subjected to sex violence would always be slow and hesitant about disclosing her plight. The court must, therefore, evaluate her evidence in the above background.

32. We are of the opinion that these factors are to be kept in mind as we go forward. We do think that the criterion that *'a stigma attaches to the rape victim in Indian society.'* is a counter-productive basis of appraisal. We do not think the victim suffers a stigma. It is a stigma against society. The rights of women in the context of the Constitution are clearly intended to overcome all negative perceptions generated against them. We do think that the reiteration of the theory of stigma and shame has itself led to an 'unintended' diminution of the status of the victim. In other words, the victims can and ought to recover like any other victims from an accident, but that is possible only when there is a due discharge of the functions by the State. Except for this caveat, we think that the formulation by Lodha, J. has substantially aligned itself with modern psychological and scientific understanding of psychosocial trauma.

33. There is some degree of substance in the criticism which we have heard from women's organisations that women do not need sympathy, empathy or charity. They are equal *per se*. In other words, they claim what general human rights and the Constitution guarantees as their natural space to live freely and effect decisions based on individual judgment. We are unable to discountenance this argument. On the contrary this is entirely correct. The fundamental attitude, based on paternalism, must be discarded. We also think that the judgments of courts can sometimes be misconstrued as suggestive of sympathetic consideration in a criminal trial. We also think that the right to justice is a fundamental right under the Constitution and must not be earned out of a sympathy having regard to the social malaise which exists in society. In other words, we advocate an approach that if the juxtaposition between honour and shame on the one hand and the crime of rape is deconstructed, people would be able to step forward and be heard. Such crimes should be registered immediately and investigated impartially and in respect of which we propose to make recommendations in the succeeding paragraphs. If an impartial investigation brings offenders to book, it is going to add to the confidence of not only the individual victim but also to women in society that such crimes can be brought to book. No woman in India must feel a sense of shame or stigma in the event of sexual assault. She is entitled to the redressal of that injury and that offence and she is therefore statutorily and constitutionally capable of access to the rule of law.

34. We believe that there is no danger and no shame or loss of honour in a victim seeking redressal by filing complaints and must in fact exercise, consistent with fundamental rights of women, the right to file complaints and bring offenders to book. We also think that it is the duty of the State to encourage

such a climate and also to make available such resources that enable them to file such complaints.

35. If the depiction of the Indian society is what is depicted by Thakkar, J. in 1983, we must change the situation. We are indeed impressed by the reasoning of Lodha, J. who, although relying upon the decision of Thakkar, J. in *Bharwada Bhoginbai Hirjibai,* has correctly elucidated the psychological factors. We think that the scientific alignment adopted by Lodha, J. is the correct way to fashion the attitude of society towards a rape victim, which is to administer to her not only justice, but also such psychological therapeutic intervention as is necessary for rediscovery of the self and increased self-affirmation.

36. Many people who have faced accidents have overcome the disability caused by those accidents and have proceeded with life in a positive way. We must be able to teach the same rehabilitative methodology to rape victims. But in order to do that, it is necessary that they must be encouraged to report such crimes of sexual violence. In fact, it is the process of reporting such crimes which will be a forward looking step in being able to assert and demand justice. The demand of justice is not a personal aspiration. The demand of justice is a fundamental charter of freedom which is guaranteed under the Constitution to every individual. In the context of a woman, it is all the more necessary that we snap the link between shame and honour, on the one hand, and the crime itself. We urge every victim to have the requisite courage to go forward and we exhort civil society to support all such cases where people who are filing complaints genuinely are given massive support to bring perpetrators to book.

37. We do notice that this concept of shame has somehow led the police to have an upper hand. The police have become arbiters of honour. The police, without registering even a FIR, assume that they have the moral capacity to pronounce upon the rights and wrongs of the rapist as well as the rape victim. This is simply deplorable and it is inconceivable in a modern society, which is governed by republican values. We think that it is necessary for the police officers to be completely sensitised against the honour-shame theory, and to treat every woman complainant as an individual in her own right capable of asserting her grievance. In other words, we feel that an indirect validation of police inaction in rape crimes has taken place as a result of – (a) amorphous attribution of women's position in Indian society; (b) the theory of shame-honour; and (c) the policeman, 'being the male' in a 'patriarchal society, ought to be 'the moral judge'. It not only skews the justice delivery system at the stage of lodging the complaint, but it has a strongly debilitating effect resulting in direct violation of fundamental human freedoms and rights under the Constitution and the various international instruments.

38. We wish to take this point further. When a woman complains of rape, it is not the physical part of the woman which is directly the focus of attention. It is the offence and the offence against the bodily integrity of the woman as a person which is the offence in question. We therefore think that we need a woman to be viewed as a whole and not as a physical centre of sexual congress. At the same time it must not be viewed that a woman, while making a complaint, is

in any way acting less honourably or in any way disturbing what is considered as the repository of honour of the family, community and others.

39. An offence against a person is very different from offence against a community. We think that there has been a completely erroneous connection which is being made between a woman and a community. In other words, we feel very strongly that an assault on a woman is an assault on the person of the woman. In this regard, we would like to quote Sohaila Abdulali, a rape victim, who recounts her experience which took place 32 years ago in Mumbai:

> *"Rape is horrible. But it is not horrible for all the reasons that have been drilled into the heads of Indian women. It is horrible because you are violated, you are scared, someone else takes control of your body and hurts you in the most intimate way. It is not horrible because you lose your "virtue." It is not horrible because your father and your brother are dishonored. I reject the notion that my virtue is located in my vagina, just as I reject the notion that men's brains are in their genitals.*
>
> *If we take honor out of the equation, rape will still be horrible, but it will be a personal, and not a societal, horror. We will be able to give women who have been assaulted what they truly need: not a load of rubbish about how they should feel guilty or ashamed, but empathy for going through a terrible trauma."*[63]

40. We are given to understand that the Government of India had brought out a Criminal Law Amendment Bill, 2012. We notice that a detailed critique of the said Bill was submitted on behalf of women's groups and other stakeholders. We, too, have had the opportunity of examining the said Bill, which is presently pending before Parliament.

41. While we feel that the Criminal Law Amendment Bill, 2012 has provisions that are somewhat protective of the right of safety of women, we feel that the said Bill is far from complete. It needs a series of revisions, many of which we propose to recommend at a later stage in this Report.

42. At this juncture, we would like to revisit the recommendations made by previous Law Commissions on various issues pertaining to crimes against women.

43. We begin with the 84th Law Commission Report[64]. The said report was submitted on 25th April 1980 by the 42nd Law Commission presided over by Mr. Justice P.V. Dixit, former Chief Justice of the Madhya Pradesh High Court. It was pointed out in the said report that:

> *"1.1 During recent years, the impact on the criminal justice system on victims of rape and other sexual offences has received considerable attention both in legal circles and amongst organizations and individuals connected with the welfare of women. In the field of criminology, an increasing interest has been shown in the*

---

63. I Was Wounded; My Honor Wasn't.—Sohaila Abdulali, New York Times, January 7, 2013 http://www.nytrmes.com/2013/01/08/opinion/after-being-raped-i-was-wounded-my-honor-wasnt.html? r=0

64. Law Commission of India, 84th Report on Rape and Allied Offences – Some Questions of Substantive Law, Procedure and Evidence. 1980. http://lawcommissionofindia.nic.in/51-100/Report84.pdf

victim and his or her position with the criminal justice system. In consequence, greater attention has now been paid to female victims of the sexual offence. Psychologists have, for some times past, been studying the effects of rape and other sexual offences upon women or girls and their personality."

44. We agree with the following observations of the 84th Report of the Law Commission:—

"1.2 It is often stated that a woman who is raped undergoes two crisis, the rape and the subsequent trial. While the first seriously moves her dignity, curbs her individual, disturbs her sense of security and may often run her physically, the second is no less potent of mixture, inasmuch as it not only forces her to relive through the traumatic experience, but also does so in the grudge of publicity in a totally alien atmosphere, with the whole apparatus and paraphernalia of the criminal justice system focused upon her."

45. We also agree with the following observation of the 42nd Law Commission regarding the purpose of criminal law:

"Thus, we acknowledge that criminal law is the chief legal instrument to prevent anti-social acts of a serious character. The object is sought to be achieved, in the first instance, by the legislative command embodying that aspect of punishment which is called "general deterrence". Once a crime – whether sexual or any other crime – has been committed, this aspect is, at least for the time being, exhausted in regard to that particular criminal act. The fact that the particular crime has been committed shows that the object of deterrence has failed to prevent the particular criminal act."

46. We must point out that the Law Commission of India in its 42nd Report[65] as well as the 69th Report[66] has also made certain suggestions to the IPC and the Evidence Act. With reference to the IPC, it was suggested that where the circumstances are such that a male may be able to take undue advantage of the situation and seduce the woman to illicit intercourse, the Commission recommended the insertion in the Code of three specific sections, intended respectively to deal with illicit intercourse – (a) by a person having custody of a woman, with that woman; (b) by superintendent of an institution with an inmate of an institution; and (c) by a person in-charge of a hospital, with a mentally disordered patient.

47. We are indeed shocked to note that notwithstanding the fact that these Law Commission Reports were made decades ago, very little attention has been paid to the implementation of these recommendations. We also note that the National Legal Vision Document (drafted by one of us) in fact wanted a separate office of the Attorney General and Solicitor General to be established which would study the implementation of recommendations of the Law Commission. This, unfortunately, has also not been carried out.

---

65. Law Commission of India, 42nd Report on the Indian Penal Code, 1971. http://lawcommissionofindia.nic.in/1-50/Report42.pdf
66. Law Commission of India, 69th Report on the Indian Evidence Act, 1872.1977. http://lawcommissionofindia.nic.in/51-100/Report69.pdf

48. The 42nd Law Commission (in the 84th Report) recommended that sections 375 to 376E be redrafted.

49. While the Law Commission in its 84th Report made recommendations in the context of forcible and fraudulent sexual intercourse as well as illicit sexual intercourse by way of seduction, the 84th Report proceeded further. It examined the issue of 'consent'. According to the Law Commission, the statutory definition of rape in India emphasized the element of absence of consent. In fact, absence of consent is an important aspect. Barring cases where consent is irrelevant and the age of the girl is the only crucial factor (because of the statutory requirement of minimum age), want of consent becomes infructuous as a determining factor in most prosecutions for rape. It is also the factor to which the law has devoted its most detailed attention.

50. We agree with the 84th Report that:—

> *"2.6 Consent is the anti-thesis of rape. Even if some may find any discussion on consent, it is too complicated. The matter cannot consistently with the needs of the subject be put in simple one phrase formulation. When circumstances in life present an infinite variety, the law must be well equipped to deal with them, nuances of consent are therefore unavoidable."*

51. It may also be noted that the 84th Report of the Law Commission therefore dealt with the substantial law relating to the law of consent in the context of rape. Consent must be real. Often, it is vitiated by circumstances which take away the freedom of choice. Section 90 of the IPC runs thus:—

> *"A consent is not such a consent as is intended by any section of this Code, if the consent is given by a person under fear of injury, or under a misconception of fact, and if the person doing the act knows or has reason to believe, that the consent was given in consequence of such fear or conception; or if the consent is given by a person who, from unsoundness of mind, or intoxication, is unable to understand the nature and consequence of that to which he gave his consent; or unless the contrary appears from the context if consent is given by a person who is under 12 years of age."*

52. Thus the 84th Law Commission Report observed as follows:

> *"2.9 The modifications recommended by us in the third clause vitiate consent not only when a woman is put in fear of death or hurt, but also when she is put in fear of any injury being caused to any person (including herself) in body mind, reputation or property and also when her consent is obtained by criminal intimidation, that is to say, by any words or acts intended or calculated to put her in fear of any injury or danger to herself or to any person in whom she is interested or when she is threatened with any injury to her reputation or property or to the reputation of any one in whom she is interested. Thus, if the consent is obtained after giving the woman a threat of spreading false and scandalous rumours about her character or destruction of her property or injury to her children or parents or by holding out other threats of injury to her person, reputation or property, that consent will also not be consent under the third clause as recommended to be amended."*

53. The 84th Law Commission Report correctly said that violence was not mandatory.

> *"2.11. Overt violence, if necessary.—While these are the main amendments on the point of consent, we may also mention a few points that have been raised during the suggestions made to us, concerning the concept of consent. There is a suggestion that the definition of "rape" should make it clear that the crime can take place without overt violence. We have given careful thought to this aspect, hut we do not think that the law needs any clarification in this regard. Overt violence, or, for that matter, violence of any particular category, is not a necessary element of rape as defined in section 375. The cardinal fact is absence of consent on the part of the woman."*

54. There can be cases of consent even when there is no violence. Violence – or, for that matter, marks of resistance – are not conclusive of consent. In any case, after a clarification is made in section 375 on the lines recommended by us, this point would lose much of its practical importance.

55. The 84th Report further recommended that the minimum age should be increased to 18 years and observed as follows:

> *"2.20. Increase in minimum age.—The question to be considered is whether the age should be increased to 18 years. The minimum age of marriage now laid down by law (after 1978) is 18 years in the case of females and the relevant clause of section 375 should reflect this changed attitude. Since marriage with a girl below 18 years is prohibited (though it is not void as a matter of personal law), sexual intercourse with a girl below 18 years should also be prohibited.*

56. On the question of section 354 relating to outraging modesty of women and indecent assaults, the 84th Report suggested that section 354A must be inserted regarding indecent assault on a minor. The 84th Report also opined that eve teasing was amply covered under section 509 of the IPC, and observed as follows:

> *2.31. Recommendation as to section 354A, Indian Penal Code.—Accordingly, we would recommend that, while incorporating section 354A in the Indian Penal Code, after the words "obscene manner", the words "with or without the consent of the minor" should also be added.*

XVI. Indecent gestures

2.32. Section 509, IPC – We may mention here that acts which do not amount to an "assault" – acts such as indecent gestures and acts that have come to be known as "eve teasing" – are amply covered by S. 509 of the Indian Penal Code. The matter strictly does not fall within the purview of rape or assault, but we refer to it because one of the women's organisations with whom we held discussions was anxious that the law should penalise such behaviour in public places or on public transport vehicles particularly."

57. Where there is physical contact or threat of physical contact, the offender can be charged under section 354 of the same Code, punishing a person who *"assaults or uses criminal force to any woman, intending to outrage or knowing it to be likely that he will thereby outrage her modesty"*. The punishment is imprisonment

of either description up to two years or fine or both. Both the offences are, as the law now stands, cognizable.

58. We notice that many other recommendations have been made in respect of female victims of sexual offences. In particular, we have also noticed the suggestion contained in paragraph 3.15 of the 84th Report that a new sub-section be added in section 160 of the CrPC to require the statement of female victims of sexual assault under the age of 12 to be recorded by a woman police officer. It is unfortunate that it is only in 2012, in the Protection of Children from Sexual Offences Act, 2012, that an attempt has been made by Parliament to provide special measures for the recording of statements of children who are victims of sexual offences.

59. We also notice in the 84th Report that the medical report is a document of vital importance and deserves attention.

60. We notice that the medical examination report of the accused in a case of rape or attempt to commit rape is an important document, and we have dealt with this aspect at some length later in this Report. We also think that any delay in reporting rape will result delay in the commencement of the investigation. But at the same time, the police are duty bound to register such cases and must not insult or harass or refuse to hear the victim or the complainant.

61. We notice that the following recommendations were made for the purpose of recording of reasons by inserting sections 53(1A), (IB), (1C) and (1D) in the CrPC:—

> "*4.7. Recommendation as to section 53, CrPC.—It is very important that reasons should he given for the opinion expressed in the report. Accordingly, we recommend the insertion in section 53 of the Code of Criminal Procedure, of the following sub-sections:*
>
> *Sections 53(1A), (1B), (1C) and (1D) Code of Criminal Procedure, 1973 to be inserted.*
>
> *(1A) When a person accused of rape or an attempt to commit rape is arrested and an examination of his person is to be made under this section, he shall be forwarded without delay to the registered medical practitioner by whom he is to be examined.*
>
> *(1B) The registered medical practitioner conducting such examination shall without delay examine such person and prepare a report specifically recording the result of his examination and giving the following particulars:*
>
> *(i) the name and address of the accused and of the person by whom he was brought,*
>
> *(ii) the age of the accused,*
>
> *(iii) marks of injury, if any, on the person of the accused, and*
>
> *(iv) other material particulars in reasonable detail.*
>
> *(1C) The report shall state precisely the reasons for each conclusion arrived at.*
>
> *(1D) The exact time of commencement and completion of the examination shall also be noted in the report, and the registered medical practitioner shall, without*

delay, forward the report to the investigating officer, who shall forward it to the Magistrate referred to in section 1973 as part of the documents referred to in clause (a) of sub-section (5) of that section."

62. We are of the view that section 417A suggested by the 84th Report requires to be enacted, as suggested below:

"When a woman is arrested and there are no suitable arrangements in the locality for keeping her in custody in a place of detention exclusively meant for women she shall be sent to an institution established and maintained for the reception, care, protection and welfare of women or children licensed under the Women's and Children's Institutions (Licensing) Act, 1956 or an institution recognized by the State Government except in cases where any special law requires that she should be sent to a protective home or other place of detention authorized for the purposes of such special law."

63. What is most surprising is that Parliament has ignored the recommendation of the 84th Report, which calls for the punishment of a station-in- charge who fails to register information of a cognizable offence given to him. In this respect the 84th Report recommended as follows:

"X. Non-recording of information relating to cognizable offences

3.29. Section 167A, IPC – Refusal to register case of rape.—We now come to another matter concerning the stage of investigation. During our oral discussions with the representatives of women's organisations, it was stated that in some cases the police fail to register a case of rape reported to them even when the full facts are communicated to them. We have not been able to gather statistics of the number of such cases, as the collection of the relevant figures would take considerable time and the present Report deals with a matter of urgency. We hope that the percentage of such cases would not be high. Nevertheless, we do take the view that in principle, the law should contain a specific provision dealing with refusal (or failure without sufficient cause) to register such cases. The offence of rape is a cognizable offence and if the police fail to register it, it is a clear violation of the provisions of the Code of Criminal Procedure, 1973 in this regard. Cognizable offences reported to the police are "registered".—as the popular usage goes – under section 154(1) of the Code of Criminal Procedure. If the officer in charge of a police station refuses to record the information reported relating to a cognizable offence, there is a remedy already provided in the Code of Criminal Procedure, the relevant provision being in the following terms:

> *"(3) Any person aggrieved by a refusal on the part of an officer in charge of a police station to record the information referred to in sub-section (1) [of section 154] may send the substance of such information, in writing and by post, to the Superintendent of Police concerned who, if satisfied that such information discloses the commission of a cognizable offence, shall either investigate the case himself or direct an investigation to be made by any police officer subordinate to him, in the manner provided by this Code and such officer shall have all the powers of an officer in charge of the police station in relation to that offence."*

3.32. Insertion of section 167A, Indian Penal Code recommended.—Having regard to what we have stated above, we would recommend the insertion of a specific penal provision, say, as section 167A, in the Indian Penal Code on the subject. In view of the general scheme adopted in that Code, the proposed provision would not be confined to refusal to register the offence of rape and would cover other cognizable offences as well. The following is a rough draft of the provision that we recommend:

"167A.—Whoever, being an officer-in-charge of a police station and required by law to record any information relating to the commission of a cognisable offence reported to him, refuses or without reasonable cause fails to record such information shall be punished with imprisonment of either description for a term which may extend to one year, or with fine, or with both."

64. Section 375 of the Indian Penal Code has traditionally defined rape in narrow terms as 'sexual intercourse' or 'penetration' in the circumstances defined in the statute. The Indian Criminal Law Amendment Bill 2012 proposes replacing the offence of 'rape' with that of 'sexual assault'. However, while the new provisions widen the definition of 'penetration' beyond vaginal penetration, the new offence remains limited to that of 'penetration'. Other types of sexual assault are not subject to appropriate legal sanction.

65. Two contrasting positions on this issue have been taken in other jurisdictions examined here.

a. **A wide definition of sexual assault to replace the offence of rape and indecent assault:**

   i. The *UN Handbook* recommends that existing offences of 'rape' and 'indecent assault' be replaced with a broad offence of 'sexual assault' graded according to harm.[67] However, its definition of 'sexual assault' is significantly wider than that of the proposed Indian approach. The *Handbook* recommends that 'sexual assault' be defined as a violation of bodily integrity and sexual autonomy. Moreover, it recommends the removal of any requirement of proof of penetration.

   ii. This follows the approach in Canada, which does not have a separate definition of rape.

   Instead, section 271 of the Criminal Code in Canada prohibits 'sexual assault'. Section 265 defines 'sexual assault' as non-consensual touching in circumstances of a 'sexual nature'.[68] The law does not distinguish between different types of touching from groping to penetration. All are sexual assaults and criminal offences.

   iii. The advantage of this approach is that it does not require complex definitions of 'penetration', which are inevitably unable to capture

---

67. Handbook for Legislation on Violence against Women, 2009, UN http://www.un.org/womenwatch/daw/vaw/handbook/Handboo k% 20f or % 201egislation% 20on% 20violence% 20against% 20women.pdf

68. In certain circumstances- aggravated sexual assault or sexual assault with a weapon- there are increased penalties but this does not change the underlying nature of the offence (sections 272-273 of the Criminal Code).

the full range of violations to which a woman could be subject. Such definitions also considerably increase the evidential burden of the prosecution to prove penetration.

iv. The disadvantage of this approach is that the epithet 'rape' continues to bring with it a high degree of moral and social opprobrium, which is not conveyed by the words 'sexual assault'. By removing the epithet 'rape', there is a risk of diluting the extent of moral condemnation.

b. Retaining an offence of 'rape' within a wider offence of sexual assault.

i. This approach retains the specific offence of rape but includes it in a cluster of offences under the category of sexual assault. This is the approach of the legislation in England and Wales, which specifies offences of 'rape', 'assault by penetration', 'sexual assault' and 'causing a person to engage in sexual activity without consent'.

1. 'Rape' occurs when a person (A) 'intentionally penetrates the vagina, anus or mouth of another person (B) with his penis' without consent. This carries a maximum sentence of life imprisonment.[69]
2. 'Assault by penetration' occurs when (A), without consent, 'intentionally penetrates the vagina or anus of another person (B) with a part of his body or anything else/ and the penetration is sexual. This carries a maximum sentence of life imprisonment.[70]
3. 'Sexual assault' occurs when (A) 'intentionally touches another person (B),' and the touching is sexual. This carries a maximum sentence of 10 years' imprisonment.[71]
4. 'Causing a person to engage in sexual activity without consent' occurs when (A) intentionally causes another person (B) to engage in a sexual activity without consent.[72] Where the activity is equivalent to rape or assault by penetration, the maximum sentence is life imprisonment. In other cases, the maximum sentence is 10 years.

ii. A similar approach is taken by the **South African** legislation, which distinguishes between rape and other forms of sexual assault. Under South African law,[73]

1. 'Rape' is defined as all *penetrative* offences. 'Sexual penetration' is defined in broad and gender-neutral terms which go well

69. Sexual Offences Act, 2003 (UK), s. 1.
70. Sexual Offences Act, 2003 (UK), s. 2.
71. Sexual Offences Act, 2003(UK), s. 3.
72. Sexual Offences Act, 2003 (UK), s. 4.
73. Sexual Offences Act, 2007 (SA), s. 3.

beyond the prior common law restriction to penile-vaginal penetration. [74]

2. 'Sexual assault' replaces the common law offence of 'indecent assault'. Section 5 of the Act provides that sexual assault is committed where a person ('A') unlawfully and intentionally sexually violates a complainant ('B'). 'Sexual violation' has a wide definition.
3. The advantage of this approach is that it retains the moral opprobrium attached to the common understanding of rape. Notably the separation of rape from other forms of sexual assault was supported by the South African Law Reform Commission in its 1999 Discussion Paper on the reform of South African sexual violence laws.[75] The Commission argued that sexual violence involving the penetration of the body using sexual organs is qualitatively different from non-penetrative forms of sexual assault and therefore should be treated as a more severe offence.[76] To combine penetrative acts with non-penetrative acts in a single offence, it argued, would reduce the gravity of the offence. Furthermore, it argued that the division between penetrative and non-penetrative sexual offences would provide a better guide to judicial officers in sentencing.[77]

iii. The disadvantage of this approach is that there will still be disputes as to when an act is penetrative and when it is not, potentially making it more difficult to prove a rape case.

66. **The meaning of 'sexual':** In both cases it is necessary to give some guidance as to when an assault is a sexual as against any ordinary assault.

a. The Canadian Criminal Code is silent as to the definition of 'sexual'. The Supreme Court of Canada in *R* v. *Chase* gave a broad definition: Viewed in the light of all the circumstances, is the sexual or carnal context of the assault visible to a reasonable observer.'[78] Courts will examine the part of the body touched, the nature of the contact, the situation in which it occurred, the words and gestures accompanying the act, threats, intent of the accused and any other relevant circumstances.[79] However, it is not a pre-requisite that the assault be for sexual gratification. The motive of the accused is just 'simply one of many factors to be considered.'[80]

---

74. See *Masiya* v. *Director of Public Prosecutions, Pretoria,* [2007] ZACC 9: 2007 (5) SA 30 (CC) para 26.
75. SALRQ 'Project 105: Sexual Offences, Discussion Paper 85: Sexual Offences – The Substantive Law' (1999) <http://salawreform.justice.gov.za/dpapers/dp85.pdf> accessed 12 January 2013.
76. *Ibid,* p. 80.
77. *Ibid.*
78. *R* v. *Chase,* [1989] 2 SCR 293 para 11, citing *R* v. *Taylor,* (1985) 44 CR (3d) 263 (269).
79. *Ibid.*
80. *Ibid.*

b. The UK legislation has a statutory definition, which like the Canadian, relies on the way in which a 'reasonable observer' might view the activity. Under section 78, an activity is sexual if a reasonable person would consider that it is 'because of its nature sexual' or that 'because of its nature it may be sexual and because of its circumstances or the purpose of any person in relation to it (or both) it is sexual.'

67. We are of the considered opinion that in the Indian context it is important to keep a separate offence of 'rape'. This is a widely understood term which also expresses society's strong moral condemnation. In the current context, there is a risk that a move to a generic crime of 'sexual assault' might signal a dilution of the political and social commitment to respecting, protecting and promoting women's right to integrity, agency and autonomy. However, there should also be a criminal prohibition of other, non-penetrative forms of sexual assault, which currently is not found in the IPC, aside from the inappropriate references to 'outraging the modesty' of women in sections 354 and 509. We recommended the enactment of section 354 in another form while we have recommended the repeal of section 509.

68. We have kept in mind that the offence of *rape* be retained but redefined to include all forms of non-consensual penetration of a sexual nature. Penetration should itself be widely defined as in the South African legislation to go beyond the vagina, mouth or anus.

69. An offence of *sexual assault* should be introduced to include all forms of non-consensual non- penetrative touching of a sexual nature. It is recommended here that the Canadian approach be followed, according to which the 'sexual nature' of an act is established if: Viewed in the light of all the circumstances... the sexual or carnal context of the assault [is] visible to a reasonable observer.'[81] Courts will examine the part of the body touched, the nature of the contact, the situation in which it occurred, the words and gestures accompanying the act, threats, intent of the accused and any other relevant circumstances. It should not be a pre requisite that the assault be for sexual gratification. The motive of the accused is 'simply one of many factors to be considered.'[82]

70. In this background it is necessary to examine the Criminal Law Amendment Bill, 2012. The offence of rape falls under Chapter XVI dealing with "offences affecting human body". Sections 375 to 376D are put under the category of "sexual offences". While Courts have often used the expression "sexual assault" in dealing with not only rape cases but also cases of sexual abuse, the IPC did not define the said expression. The definition of "assault" is found under section 351.

71. By virtue of the Amendment, the legislature has sought to widen the scope of the offence under section 375 to 376D by substituting the expression rape with "sexual assault". While we feel that the proposed Bill (as placed before Parliament) proposes some welcome changes to the law, there is still much

81. *R* v. *Chase* (n 78).

82. *Ibid.*

ground that needs to be covered. Accordingly, this Committee has recommended amendments (appended to this Report) to the Criminal Law Amendment Bill, 2012, which should be considered and enacted by Parliament at the earliest possible, if not immediately. In any event, we feel that the same ought to be promulgated by the Government as an ordinance.

Marital Rape

72. The exemption for marital rape stems from a long out-dated notion of marriage which regarded wives as no more than the property of their husbands. According to the common law of coverture, a wife was deemed to have consented at the time of the marriage to have intercourse with her husband at his whim. Moreover, this consent could not be revoked. As far back as 1736, Sir Matthew Hale declared: '*The husband cannot be guilty of rape committed by himself upon his lawful wife, for by their mutual matrimonial consent and contract the wife hath given herself up in this kind unto her husband which she cannot retract*'.[83]

73. This immunity has now been withdrawn in most major jurisdictions. In England and Wales, the House of Lords held in 1991 that the status of married women had changed beyond all recognition since Hale set out his proposition. Most importantly, Lord Keith, speaking for the Court, declared, '*marriage is in modern times regarded as a partnership of equals*, and no longer one in which the wife must be the subservient chattel of the husband.'[84]

74. Our view is supported by the judgment of the European Commission of Human Rights in *C.R.* v. *UK*, which endorsed the conclusion that a rapist remains a rapist regardless of his relationship with the victim. Importantly, it acknowledged that this change in the common law was in accordance with the fundamental objectives of the Convention on Human Rights, the very essence of which is respect for human rights, dignity and freedom.[85] This was given statutory recognition in the Criminal Justice and Public Order Act, 1994.[86]

75. We find that the same is true in Canada, South Africa and Australia. In Canada, the provisions in the Criminal Code, which denied criminal liability for marital rape, were repealed in 1983.[87] It is now a crime in Canada for a husband to rape his wife. South Africa criminalised marital rape in 1993, reversing the common law principle that a husband could not be found guilty of raping his wife. Section 5 of the Prevention of Family Violence Act, 1993 provides: 'Notwithstanding anything to the contrary contained in any law or in the common law, a husband may be convicted of the rape of his wife.' In Australia, the common law 'marital rape immunity' was legislatively abolished

83. Sir Matthew Hale. History of the Pleas of the Crown, 1 Hale PC (1736) 629. See further S. Fredman Women and the Law (OUP, 1997) pp. 55-57.

84. *R.* v. *R*, [1991] 4 All ER 481 (484).

85. *C.R.* v. *UK Publ.* ECHR, Ser. A, No. 335-C; see Palmer Feminist Legal Studies Vol. V no. 1 [1997] pp. 1-7.

86. Section 142 abolished the marital rape exception by excluding the word 'unlawful' preceding 'sexual intercourse' in section 1 of the Sexual Offences Act, 1956.

87. R.S.C. 1985, c. C-46.

in all jurisdictions from 1976.[88] In 1991, the Australian High Court had no doubt that: 'if it was ever the common law that by marriage a wife gave irrevocable consent to sexual intercourse by her husband, it is no longer the common law.'[89] According to Justice Brennan (as he then was): *'The common law fiction has always been offensive to human dignity and incompatible with the legal status of a spouse.'*[90]

76. These jurisdictions have also gone further and recognised that consent should not be implied by the relationship between the accused and the complainant in any event. In the Canadian 2011 Supreme Court decision in *R* v. *J.A.*, Chief Justice McLachlin emphasised that the relationship between the accused and the complainant 'does not change the nature of the inquiry into whether the complaint consented' to the sexual activity.[91] The defendant cannot argue that the complainant's consent was implied by the relationship between the accused and the complainant.[92] In South Africa, the 2007 Criminal Law (Sexual Offences and Related Matters) Amendment Act ('Sexual Offences Act') provides, at section 56(1), that a marital or other relationship between the perpetrator or victim is not a valid defence against the crimes of rape or sexual violation.

77. Even when marital rape is recognised as a crime, there is a risk that judges might regard marital rape as less serious than other forms of rape, requiring more lenient sentences, as happened in South Africa.[93] In response, the South African Criminal Law (Sentencing) Act of 2007 now provides that the relationship between the victim and the accused may not be regarded as a 'substantial and compelling circumstance' justifying a deviation from legislatively required minimum sentences for rape.

78. It is also important that the legal prohibition on marital rape is accompanied by changes in the attitudes of prosecutors, police officers and those in society more generally. For example, in South Africa, despite these legal developments, rates of marital rape remain shockingly high. A 2010

88. Criminal Law Consolidation Act, 1935, s. 73(3). See also s. 73(4) which provides that 'No person shall, by reason only of the fact that he is married to some other person, be presumed to have consented to an indecent assault by that other person.' The Crimes (Sexual Assault) Amendment Act, 1981 (NSW) inserted s. 61A(4) into the Crimes Act 1900 (NSW), which provided that the fact that a person is married to a person on whom an offence of sexual assault is alleged to have been committed is no bar to conviction for that offence. The Crimes (Amendment) Ordinance (No 5), 1985 (ACT) inserted s. 92R into the Crimes Act, 1900 (NSW), as it applied to the ACT, which provided that the fact that a person is married to a person upon whom an offence of sexual intercourse without consent contrary to s. 92D is alleged to have been committed shall be no bar to the conviction of the first-mentioned person for the offence. In Victoria, the Crimes (Amendment) Act, 1985 (Vic) substituted for s. 62(2) of the Crimes Act, 1958 (Vic) a new sub-section providing that the existence of a marriage does not constitute, or raise any presumption of, consent by a person to a sexual penetration or indecent assault by another person.

89. *R* v. *L*, [1991] HCA 48: (1991) 174 CLR 379 (390) *per* Mason CJ, Deane and Toohey JJ.

90. *R* v. *L*, [1991] HCA 48: (1991) 174 CLR 379 (402).

91. [2011] 2 SCR 40, para 64.

92. *Ibid.*, para 47.

93. *See*, for example, *S* v. *Moipolai*, [2004] ZANWHC 19 (Mogoeng J) and *S* v. *Modise*, [2007] ZANWHC 73.

study suggests that 18.8% of women are raped by their partners on one or more occasion.[94] Rates of reporting and conviction also remain low, aggravated by the prevalent beliefs that marital rape is acceptable or is less serious than other types of rape.[95] Changes in the law therefore need to be accompanied by widespread measures raising awareness of women's rights to autonomy and physical integrity, regardless of marriage or other intimate relationship. This was underlined in *Vertido* v. *The Philippines,* a recent Communication under the Optional Protocol of the Convention on the Elimination of Discrimination Against Women (CEDAW), where the CEDAW Committee emphasised the importance of appropriate training for judges, lawyers, law enforcement officers and medical personnel in understanding crimes of rape and other sexual offences in a gender-sensitive manner.[96]

79. We, therefore, recommend that:

i. The exception for marital rape be removed,

ii. The law ought to specify that:

a. A marital or other relationship between the perpetrator or victim is not a valid defence against the crimes of rape or sexual violation;

b. The relationship between the accused and the complainant is not relevant to the inquiry into whether the complainant consented to the sexual activity;

c. The fact that the accused and victim are married or in another intimate relationship may not be regarded as a mitigating factor justifying lower sentences for rape.

80. We must, at this stage, rely upon Prof. Sandra Fredman of the University of Oxford, who has submitted to the Committee that *"training and awareness programmes should be provided to ensure that all levels of the criminal justice system and ordinary people are aware that marriage should not be regarded as extinguishing the legal or sexual autonomy of the wife"*.

---

94. Gender Links and the South African Medical Research Council, "The War at Home' (2010) <http://www.mrc.ac.za/gender/gbvthewar.pdf>accessed 12 January, 2013.

95. *See* further Gemma Hancox, 'Marital Rape in South Africa: Enough is Enough' (2012) BUWA Journal on African Women's Experiences 70 <http: / / www.osisa.org/buwa/south-africa/marital-rape-south- africa> accessed 12 January, 2013.

96. *Vertido* v. *The Philippines Communication* No. 18/2008, Committee on the Elimination of Discrimination against Women July 2010.

Part 6

LAW COMMISSION OF INDIA REPORTS ON RAPE LAWS (RELEVANT EXTRACTS)

INTRODUCTION TO 172nd REPORT, 2000 ON RAPE LAWS

The One Hundred and Seventy-second Report of the Law Commission focussed on the Rape laws.

With what the present Report was precisely concerned, was the need to review the rape laws in the light of increasing incidents of custodial rape and crime of sexual abuse against youngsters. As noted by the Commission, the crime of sexual assault on a child causes lasting psychic damage to the child and, as such, it becomes essential to prevent sexual abuse of children through stringent deterrent provisions.

The genesis of the present Report was in a Writ Petition filed in the Supreme Court, in 1997, by an organisation known as "Sakshi", which had interest in issues concerning women. The petitioner had urged the court for directions concerning the definition of the expression "sexual intercourse" as contained in section 375 of the Indian Penal Code.

Although the Commission was not made a party to the proceedings, the Supreme Court, however, directed it by an Order to indicate its response with respect to the issues raised in the said Writ Petition. Thus, the subject was taken up by the Commission for study and examination.

The Law Commission presented its Report on March 25, 2000.

REVIEW OF RAPE LAWS

CHAPTER I

INTRODUCTORY

1.1. Under an order dated August 9, 1999 made in Writ Petition (Crl.) No. 33 of 1997, the Supreme Court of India requested the Law Commission "to examine the issues raised by the petitioners and examine the feasibility of making recommendations for amendment of the Indian Penal Code or deal with the same in any other manner so as to plug the loopholes".

1.1.1. The petitioner 'Sakshi', an organisation interested in the issues concerning women, had approached the Supreme Court of India with the aforesaid Writ Petition praying for—(a) issuance of a writ in the nature of a declaration or any other appropriate writ or direction declaring *inter alia* that 'sexual intercourse' as contained in section 375 of the Indian Penal Code shall include all forms of penetration such as penile/vaginal penetration, penile/oral penetration, penile/anal penetration, finger/vaginal and finger/anal penetration and object/vaginal penetration, and (b) to issue a consequential writ, order or direction to the respondents in the Writ Petition and to their servants and agents to register all such cases found to be true on investigation.

1.1.2. The Law Commission was not made a party to the Writ Petition. The Supreme Court however directed the Law Commission, by its Order dated 13th January, 1998, to indicate its response with respect to the issues raised in the said Writ Petition. The Law Commission in its affidavit dated 25-3-1998 brought to the notice of the Hon'ble Court that the 156th Report of the Law Commission on the Indian Penal Code had dealt, *inter alia,* with the issues raised in the Writ Petition, but since the said Report was not yet placed on the table of the Houses of Parliament, the matter may be adjourned by a few months. The matter was adjourned by three months. Meanwhile, the aforesaid Report of the Law Commission was placed on the table of both the Houses of Parliament. Thereafter, the Law Commission filed its affidavit dated 28.7.98 setting out in extenso the portions of the said Report dealing with the issues in question. Suffice it to say that by and large the then Law Commission (14th Law Commission) did not agree with the viewpoint of the writ petitioners except in certain minor respects which would be indicated at the appropriate stage later. It is after considering the said affidavit and the affidavit filed by the Ministry of Law, Justice and Company Affairs, that the Hon'ble Court passed the aforesaid order dated 9th August, 1999.

1.1.3. The order of the Hon'ble Court records the statement of the learned counsel for the writ petitioners that the contents of the 156th Report of the Law Commission were known to the petitioners, but since according to them the Report did not deal with the precise issues raised in the writ petition, a request was made by the counsel for the petitioner to seek further consideration of the issues by the Law Commission and the Government of India. The Court was inclined to agree with the said submissions. The Court also noted that the 156th Report was submitted by the Law Commission prior to these issues being referred to the Commission and further that the said Report of the Law Commission did not in terms deal with various aspects of the issues raised in the Writ Petition. The order further recorded that at the suggestion of the Hon'ble Court, the petitioner did draw up a note containing the precise issues involved in the Writ Petition as well as other connected issues. After perusing the same, the Court asked the Law Commission to examine the said issues afresh. A copy of the 'precise issues' with the appendix and affidavit were sent to the Secretary, Law Commission with a request to place the same before the Chairman of the Law Commission for consideration. It was also observed that the Law Commission may, if so advised, call upon the petitioner to assist it in such manner as the Commission thought appropriate. The issues, the Court observed, "need a thorough examination". The matter was accordingly adjourned for three months within which period the Law Commission was expected to submit its response to the Hon'ble Court.

1.1.4. The order of the Hon'ble Court was received by the Secretary to the Law Commission on 19-8-99 and placed before the Chairman.

1.2. "Precise issues".—The `precise issues' submitted by the petitioner before the Court and which have been sent to the Law Commission for consideration are divided into three parts (*Annexure A*). Part I carries the title "Precise issues submitted for consideration of the Law Commission and the Government of India". Part II carries the heading "Existing inadequacies" and Part III is titled "Suggestions for amendment to the Indian Penal Code". We shall set out in brief the substance of the submissions made in all the three parts.

1.2.1. Part I: Precise issues submitted for consideration of the Law Commission and the Government of India.—(1) Having regard to the widespread prevalence of child sexual abuse, would it not be appropriate to include all forms of penetration such as penile/vaginal penetration, penile/oral penetration, penile/anal penetration, finger/vagina and finger/anal penetration and object/vaginal penetration within the meaning of the expression "penetration" in the Explanation to section 375 of the I.P.C.. The restrictive interpretation of 'penetration' in the Explanation to section 375 defeats the very purpose and object underlying section 376(2)(f);

(2) Is it not wrong to classify the penetrative abuse of a child below the age of 12 as unnatural offence under section 377, I.P.C. or as outraging the modesty of a woman under section 354, depending upon the 'type' of penetration ignoring the 'impact' on such child;

(3) Is it not wrong to continue to treat non-consensual penetration upon such a child as offence under section 377, I.P.C. on par with certain forms of consensual penetration (*e.g.* consensual homosexual sex) where consenting party can be held liable as an abettor or otherwise?

1.2.2. 'Appendix A' appended to Part I contains three notes, which we shall refer to in seriatum:

Note 1.—The Explanation to sections 375 and 376 says that "penetration is sufficient to constitute the sexual intercourse necessary to the offence of rape". By the Criminal Law (Amendment) Act 1983, raping of a woman under twelve years of age was made punishable with rigorous imprisonment for a term which shall not be less than ten years but which may be for life in addition to fine. In such a situation, it would be appropriate to broaden the meaning of penetration to include not only vaginal penetration but also anal and oral penetration as well as penetration by any part of the body or by any object.

Note 2.—In a vast majority of child sexual abuse cases the penetration is other than penile-vaginal. Such penetration causes lasting psychic damage to the child. In such a situation, a restrictive meaning attached to penetration is likely to prove inadequate.

Note 3(a).—The 156th Report of the Law Commission has recommended that penile/oral penetration and penile/anal penetration be covered by section 377, I.P.C. and that finger penetration and object penetration into vagina or anus can be adequately covered under section 354, with a more severe punishment. This recommendation requires reconsideration Such a restrictive view fails to take into consideration several forms of child abuse and the further fact that very often the sexual abuse of children is by persons known to them. As a matter of fact, rape is really intended to humiliate, violate or degrade a woman sexually. It adversely affects the sexual integrity and autonomy of women and children. The aforesaid recommendation of the Law Commission therefore defeats the very object underlying the Criminal Law (Amendment) Act, 1983 which inserted sub-section (2) and in particular clause (f) thereof in section 376. The above recommendation also does not take into account the fact that a child of tender years can not discern the degree of difference in terms of which orifice of hers is penetrated. Certain instances are then set out to illustrate the aforesaid point.

Note 3(b).—Under this note, the petitioner has sought to argue in the light of the instances mentioned under Note 3(a) that the 156th Report of the Law Commission requires reconsideration.

1.3. Part II: Existing Inadequacies.—Various instances set out in Appendix B to Annexure-A (a copy of the submissions of Sakshi including Appendix B is enclosed herewith) to this part, the petitioner argues, would not amount to rape and perhaps not even to natural offence under section 377 or to outraging the modesty of a woman under section 354, in view of the existing law. They might just be a limited form of assault or criminal force, if at all, though all the said instances are of a grave nature and extremely disturbing. It is therefore necessary that there should be a rethinking on this issue and the offence of 'sexual assault' should be more precisely defined and its parameters indicated.

1.4. Part III: Suggestions for amendment to Indian Penal Code.—This part sets out the several amendments proposed by the petitioner. Suffice it to say that they seek to substitute the definition of 'rape' with the definition of 'sexual assault' and make it gender neutral. The object is to widen the scope of the offence. The expression 'consent' is also sought to be defined. A new section, section 375A with the heading 'Aggravated sexual assault' is sought to be created. This new offence seeks to synthesise the offences now categorised under sub-section (2) of section 376 as well as sections 376B to 376D.

CHAPTER II

VIEWS INVITED ON PROPOSED PROVISIONS

2.1. UN Convention and Constitutional provisions. Several cases of child abuse have all over the world have caused grave concern to the humanity. Article 34 of the Convention on Rights of the Child (20 November, 1989) ordains the Member States to protect the child from all forms of sexual exploitation and sexual abuse. For these purposes, State Parties are required to take all appropriate national, bilateral and multilateral measures to prevent:

(a) The inducement or coercion of a child to engage in any unlawful sexual activity;

(b) The exploitative use of children in prostitution or other unlawful sexual practices;

(c) The exploitative use of children in pornographic performances and materials.

2.1.1. Article 39(f) of the Constitution of India, one of the Directive Principles of State Policy requires the State to direct its policy, *inter alia,* towards securing that childhood and youth are protected against exploitation and against moral and material abandonment. There is, therefore, great need for tightening the existing provisions relating to child sexual abuse or assault.

2.2. Draft of the Law Commission's proposals.—On a consideration of the 'precise issues' submitted by the petitioner and in the light of the order of the Hon'ble Court and also taking into account the laws in force in certain western countries on this subject, the Law Commission prepared a draft (Annexure B) containing the proposed new sections, namely, sections 375, 376, 376A, 376B, 376C, 376D in substitution of the existing sections 375 to 376D and also suggested a new section, section 376E. The purport of these new sections is to substitute the offence of 'rape' under section 375 with the offence of 'sexual assault' by including all kinds of penetration in the vagina, anus or urethra of another, whether by a part of the human body or by an object. Section 376 is, accordingly, modified in the light of the change in section 375. Sections 376A, 376B, 376C and 376D are retained substantially except adapting them to the changes made in the offence under section 375 and a few changes in the matter of punishment. A new offence, namely, section 376E with the title 'unlawful sexual contact' is sought to be created. Besides the above, section 377 is proposed to be deleted as unnecessary in the light of the preceding provisions. Section 509 of I.P.C. is also sought to be amended providing higher punishment where the offence set out in the said section is committed with sexual intent.

2.2.1. Views invited.—A copy of the said draft was forwarded to Sakshi on 27-8-99 and they were invited for a discussion on 13-9-99. It was indicated that the discussion would not only be with respect to the draft prepared by the Law Commission but that they shall be free to put forward their other suggestions and ideas, if any, and further they could also bring representations of other women's organisations, along with them, for discussion. Accordingly, three persons, namely, Ms. Naina Kapur (Director, Sakshi), Ms. Jasjit Purewal (Director, Interventions for Support, Healing and Awareness - IFSHA) and Ms.

Kirti Singh (All India Democratic Women's Association–AIDWA) participated in the discussion, on behalf of their respective organisations. All the three organisations have also put forward their suggestions in writing apart from what Sakshi had filed before the Supreme Court

We may mention that hereafter whenever we speak of or refer to Sakshi, it means not only the Sakshi, but also the two other women's organisations, namely IFSHA (Interventions for Support, Healing and Awareness) and AIDWA (All India Democratic Women's Association) as well as the National Commission for Women (NCW), who were also heard on the proposals contained herein.

2.3. Views of the "Sakshi" on the I.P.C. provisions.—On the first day of hearing (13-9-99), the said three persons expressed their appreciation of the draft prepared by the Law Commission stating that it was a substantial advance on the subject and met many of their ideas. Even so, after a good amount of discussion, they came forward with the following changes in the said draft:

(a) The age of the person assaulted – referred to in clause "sixthly" in section 375 and in Explanation (2) to section 375 and in section 376(1) (where the age of the wife is referred to) – should be raised to sixteen. Raising the said age to eighteen may not be appropriate.

(b) A provision must be inserted to the effect that if the person assaulted gives his/her age, the court shall presume it to be so. A provision on the lines of section 114A of the Evidence Act be suggested.

(c) In the definition of sexual assault in section 375, there should be an explanation saying that penetration shall mean penetration to any extent whatsoever, inasmuch the penetration is never complete in the case of children.

(d) Explanation (2) to draft section 375 (which says that sexual intercourse by a man with his own wife, the wife not being under 15 years of age, does not amount to sexual assault) should be deleted. Forced sexual intercourse by a husband with his wife should equally be treated as an offence just as any physical violence by a husband against the wife is treated as an offence. Following the same logic, they submitted that the words "unless the person subjected to sexual assault is his own wife and is not under 15 years of age in which case he shall be punished with imprisonment of either description for a term which may extend to two years or with fine or with both" in section 376(1) of the Law Commission's draft [adaptation of the existing section 376(1)] should also be deleted. Section 376A should also be deleted, they said, on the same reasoning.

(e) In the first proviso to draft section 376(1) (in the draft of the Commission), the words "the father, grandfather or brother" should be substituted with the words "a person holding position of trust *vis-a-vis* the other person" and further to add an explanation saying that the said expression shall include father/step father, brother/step brother, teacher, instructor, guardian and the like.

(f) Consent should be defined to mean "unequivocal voluntary agreement".

2.3.1. A copy of the handout given by the persons mentioned in paragraph 2.2.1, *supra,* of this chapter, on the first date of meeting is placed at Annexure C.

2.4. Views of the "Sakshi" on the relevant provisions of the Code of Criminal Procedure and the Indian Evidence Act.—At the end of the discussion on the first day, it was indicated to the persons mentioned in para above that if they wished to suggest any changes of a procedural nature, whether in the Criminal Procedure Code or in the Evidence Act, they could send the same by the next date, which was specified as 17th September, 1999. Though the "precise issues" did not speak of any changes in the procedural laws (and was confined to amendments to Indian Penal Code only), we were of the opinion that unless certain changes are effected simultaneously in the relevant provisions of the Cr. PC. and Evidence Act, the purpose underlying the changes in the substantive law I.P.C. – may not be fully served. It is for this reason that we suggested to Sakshi to come forward with their suggestions, if any, for amendment of procedural laws to achieve the purpose underlying changes in substantive laws. Accordingly, they came forward with as many as 14 suggestions proposing amendments not only in the Criminal Procedure Code and Evidence Act but also in the Indian Penal Code (Annexure D). The procedural amendments suggested by them are to the following effect:

(1) The 84th Report of the Law Commission had suggested that where the statement of a girl-victim below twelve years of age is recorded, it should be done by a woman police officer or by a woman belonging to an organisation interested in the cause of women or children. The said recommendation should be accepted with certain changes set out in their note.

(2) The present proviso to sub-section (1) of section 160 of the Code of Criminal Procedure should be substituted by the following proviso:

> "Provided that no male person under the age of sixteen years or a woman shall be required to attend at any place other than his or her home or place of his or her choice."

(3) A new sub-section, namely, sub-section (6) should be inserted in section 160, Cr. PC. to the effect that the statement of a male person under the age of sixteen years or a female, during the course of investigation, should be recorded only in the presence of a relative, a friend or a social worker of the person's choice.

(4) A new section, namely, section 164A should be inserted in the Code of Criminal Procedure stating that as soon as a case of sexual assault is reported to a Police person, he shall have the person (allegedly assaulted sexually) examined medically by a registered medical practitioner and that such medical practitioner shall after due examination, prepare a report setting out the various specified particulars. This proposal is a slight modification of the recommendation contained in the 84th Report of the Law Commission.

(5) Sub-sections (1A), (1B), (1C) and (1D) should be inserted in section 53 of the Criminal Procedure Code as recommended by the 84th Report of the Law Commission, with necessary adaptations.

(6) While granting bail to a person accused of sexual assault, one of the conditions which should be imposed by the court shall be that such person shall not be in the proximity of the person assaulted.

(7) In the case of sexual assault, there shall be no interference with or disturbance of the natural habitat of the person sexually assaulted by or through the criminal justice process.

(8) The investigation and trial of sexual offences should be time-bound and should be concluded within six months.

(9) The expression 'social worker' shall be defined to mean a woman interested in or working for the cause of women and/or children and who is familiar with issues of violence against women and children.

(10)(a) A new section 114B should be introduced in the Evidence Act stating that where in a prosecution for aggravated sexual assault under sections 376A to 376D of the I.P.C., the question is whether the person so assaulted consented to it and where such person states before the court that he/she did not so consent, the court shall presume it to be so.

(b) Clause (4) in section 155 to the Evidence Act (which permits the person accused of rape or attempt to ravish to prove that the prosecutrix was of generally immoral character) should be deleted.

(c) In section 146 of the Evidence Act, another clause, namely, clause (4) should be added stating expressly that in a prosecution for sexual assault, it shall not be permissible to adduce evidence or to put questions in cross-examination of the person assaulted with respect to his/her previous sexual history, character or conduct whether to establish consent or otherwise.

(d) The absence of a medical report in the case of a sexual assault shall not be a factor against the complainant/person assaulted.

(11) There should be a provision either in the Cr. PC. or in the Evidence Act to the effect that a minor who has been assaulted sexually, should not be required to give his/her evidence in the presence of the accused as it will certainly traumatise the minor. Steps should also be taken to provide an appropriate and safe environment in which the child can recover.

(12) The testimony of a child who is subjected to sexual assault should be recorded at the earliest opportunity by a judge/magistrate in the presence of a friend, relative or social worker whom the minor trusts. For a proper implementation of the above suggestion, videotape/circuit television should be provided. Further, where the child is to be cross-examined, the questions shall be handed over to the judge who shall in turn put those questions to the minor. While recording the evidence of the minor, appropriate breaks should also be given to make the minor feel comfortable.

(13) All cases of sexual assault should be tried by special courts which shall be manned by judges, prosecutors and counsellors, 'specially trained/ sensitised to issues of sexual assault'.

(14) A new offence should be created by appropriately amending section 166, I.P.C. making it an offence for a public servant to disobey the direction of law prohibiting the summoning of a minor/woman at any place other than her place of choice and also a public servant who disobeys any direction of law with respect to the manner in which the investigation concerning a minor shall be conducted.

2.4.1. Discussion on the suggestions of "Sakshi".—Each of the above suggestions were discussed in the Commission in the presence of the three persons representing organisations mentioned in para 2.2.1 above, in the light of the 84th Report of the Law Commission as well as the 154th Report of the Law Commission. While we agree with some of the aforesaid suggestions (as would be evident from the recommendations set out in the succeeding chapters), we find ourselves unable to agree with all of them.

2.5. Views of the National Commission for Women (NCW) invited.—The Law Commission would also wish to put on record that before finalising their recommendations, the Law Commission had also sent a letter to the National Commission for Women (NCW) enclosing the aforementioned draft (prepared by the Law Commission) (Annexure B) and inviting them to come and have a discussion with the Law Commission on 16-9-99. The National Commission for Women deputed their Joint Secretary, Ms Leena Mehendale. One of the Members of the Law Commission, Mrs Justice Leila Seth, heard the Joint Secretary and also asked her to put her ideas/suggestions in writing. Accordingly, the NCW sent a set of suggestions in writing signed by the Joint Secretary. A copy of the said proposals is appended herewith (Annexure E).

CHAPTER III

CHANGES RECOMMENDED IN THE INDIAN PENAL CODE, 1860

3.1. Substitution of definition of 'rape' by definition of 'sexual assault'.—Not only women but young boys, are being increasingly subjected to forced sexual assaults. Forced sexual assault causes no less trauma and psychological damage to a boy than to a girl subjected to such offence. Boys and girls both are being subjected to oral sexual intercourse too. According to some social activists like Ms. Sheela Barse, both young girls and boys are being regularly used for all kinds of sexual acts and sexual perversions in certain tourist centres like Goa - mainly for edification of the foreign tourists. Sakshi have also recommended for widening the scope of the offence in section 375 and to make it gender neutral. Some of the Western countries have already done this. It is also necessary to include under this new definition (sexual assault) not only penile penetration but also penetration by any other part of the body (like finger or toe) or by any other object. Explanation to section 375 has also been substituted by us to say that penetration to any extent whatsoever shall be deemed to be penetration for the purpose of this section. This is so provided for the reason that in the case of children, penetration is rarely complete—for physical reasons. So far as the Exception is concerned, we have retained the existing Exception the only change made being in the matter of age; we have raised the age of the 'wife' from fifteen to sixteen. The age of the person assaulted sexually referred to in the clause "sixthly" has also been raised to sixteen from fifteen.

3.1.1. We may also mention that in redrafting the section, we have stuck to the existing provision as far as possible. This is for the reason that since these provisions have already been interpreted and elucidated by the decisions of the courts, it is better to stick to them rather than use new expressions and new wording. In drafting clauses (a) to (e) in section 375, we have drawn inspiration from the Criminal Law Western Australia.

3.1.2. Substitution of existing section 375 of the I.P.C. recommended.—We accordingly recommend that the existing section 375 be substituted by the following:

"375. *Sexual Assault.*—Sexual assault means—

(a) penetrating the vagina (which term shall include the labia majora), the anus or urethra of any person with—

(i) any part of the body of another person; or

(ii) an object manipulated by another person,

except where such penetration is carried out for proper hygienic or medical purposes;

(b) manipulating any part of the body of another person so as to cause penetration of the vagina (which term shall include the labia majora), the anus or the urethra of the offender by any part of the other person's body;

(c) introducing any part of the penis of a person into the mouth of another person;

(d) engaging in cunnilingus or fellatio; or

(e) continuing sexual assault as defined in clauses (a) to (d) above in circumstances falling under any of the six following descriptions:

First—Against the other person's will.

Secondly—Without the other person's consent.

Thirdly—With the other person's consent when such consent has been obtained by putting such other person or any person in whom such other person is interested, in fear of death or hurt.

Fourthly—Where the other person is a female, with her consent, when the man knows that he is not the husband of such other person and that her consent is given because she believes that the offender is another man to whom she is or believes herself to be lawfully married.

Fifthly—With the consent of the other person, when, at the time of giving such consent, by reason of unsoundness of mind or intoxication or the administration by the offender personally or through another of any stupefying or unwholesome substance, the other person is unable to understand the nature and consequences of that to which such other person gives consent.

Sixthly—With or without the other person's consent, when such other person is under sixteen years of age Explanation: Penetration to any extent is penetration for the purposes of this section Exception: Sexual intercourse by a man with his own wife, the wife not being under sixteen years of age, is not sexual assault."

3.1.2.1. Representatives of Sakshi wanted us to recommend the deletion of the Exception, with which we are unable to agree. Their reasoning runs thus: where a husband causes some physical injury to his wife, he is punishable under the appropriate offence and the fact that he is the husband of the victim is not an extenuating circumstance recognized by law; if so, there is no reason why concession should be made in the matter of offence of rape/sexual assault where the wife happens to be above 15/16 years. We are not satisfied that this Exception should be recommended to be deleted since that may amount to excessive interference with the marital relationship

3.2. Modification of section 376.—So far as the proposed section 376 is concerned, we are not suggesting any substantial changes except two and adapting the language of the section to accord with the change in section 375. In the light of instances coming before the courts and the instances mentioned in the Note prepared by Sakshi, we have proposed addition of a proviso to sub-section (1) (while treating the existing proviso as the second proviso) providing that where the sexual assault is committed by the father, grandfather or brother, the punishment should be severe. On the basis of suggestions made by Sakshi, we have also added the words "or any other person being in a position of trust or authority towards the other person" after the words "father, grandfather or brother". The second change suggested by us is in the matter of the age of wife referred to in proposed sub-section (1) as also of the person assaulted in clause (f) of sub-section (2). The age "fifteen" is raised to "sixteen".

3.2.1. The reasons for these changes are: (1) to visit with a severe penalty the near relations and persons in position of trust and authority who more often than not commit the offence of sexual assault on the members of the family or on unsuspecting and trusting young persons. We have in this connection taken note of the extremely odious and debased conduct of the father of the minor girl in the facts highlighted in *Sudesh Jakhoo* v. *K.C.J.*, 1996 (3) AD Del 653: (1996) 62 DLT 563 and (2) to maintain uniformity in the matter of age of wife or any other young person who needs special protection – as sixteen.

3.2.2. Views of "Sakshi" considered.—Though the representatives of Sakshi have suggested that we should delete the second proviso to section 376(1) and the proviso to section 376(2) (which confer a discretion upon the court to award a sentence lesser than the minimum punishment prescribed by the sub-sections), we are not satisfied that there are any good reasons for doing so.

Any number of situations may arise, which it is not possible to foresee, and which may necessitate the awarding of lesser punishment than the minimum punishment prescribed. Safeguard against abuse is provided by requiring that adequate and special reasons be mentioned in the judgment, for awarding such lesser punishment. Nor is there justification in the criticism that such discretion once conferred is liable to be abused or that it will always be misused to help the accused.

3.2.3. Re-casting of section 376 of the I.P.C. recommended.—Accordingly, we recommend that section 376 shall be re-cast as follows:—

"376. *Punishment for sexual assault.*—(1) Whoever, except in the cases provided for by sub-section (2), commits sexual assault shall be punished with imprisonment of either description for a term which shall not be less than seven years but which may be for life or for a term which may extend to ten years and shall also be liable to fine unless the person subjected to sexual assault is his own wife and is not under sixteen years of age, in which case, he shall be punished with imprisonment of either description for a term which may extend to three years and shall also be liable to fine.

If the sexual assault is committed by a person in a position of trust or authority towards the person assaulted or by a near relative of the person assaulted, he/she shall be punished with rigorous imprisonment for a term which shall not be less than ten years but which may extend to life imprisonment and shall also be liable to fine:

Provided that the court may, for adequate and special reasons to be mentioned in the judgment, impose a sentence of imprisonment for a term of less than minimum punishment prescribed in this sub-section.

(2) Whoever,—(a) being a police officer commits sexual assault—

(i) within the limits of the police station to which he is appointed; or

(ii) in the premises of any station house whether or not situated in the police station to which he is appointed; or

(iii) on a person in his custody or in the custody of a police officer subordinate to him; or

(b) being a public servant, takes advantage of his official position and commits sexual assault on a person in his custody as such public servant or in the custody of a public servant subordinate to him; or

(c) being on the management or on the staff of a jail, remand home or other place of custody established by or under any law for the time being in force or of a women's or children's institution takes advantage of his official position and commits sexual assault on any inmate of such jail, remand home, place or institution; or

(d) being on the management or on the staff of a hospital, takes advantage of his official position and commits sexual assault on a person in that hospital; or

(e) commits sexual assault on a woman knowing her to be pregnant; or

(f) commits sexual assault on a person when such person is under sixteen years of age; or

(g) commits gang sexual assault,

shall be punished with rigorous imprisonment for a term which shall not be less than ten years but which may be for life and shall also be liable to fine:

Provided that the court may, for adequate and special reasons to be mentioned in the judgment, impose a sentence of imprisonment of either description for a term of less than ten years.

Explanation 1.—Where a person is subjected to sexual assault by one or more in a group of persons acting in furtherance of their common intention, each of the persons shall be deemed to have committed gang sexual assault within the meaning of this sub-section.

Explanation 2.—"Women's or children's institution" means an institution, whether called an orphanage or a home for neglected women or children or a widows' home or an institution called by any other name, which is established and maintained for the reception and care of women or children.

Explanation 3.—"Hospital" means the precincts of the hospital and includes the precincts of any institution for the reception and treatment of persons during convalescence or of persons requiring medical attention or rehabilitation."

3.3. Amendment of section 376A.—Representatives of Sakshi wanted us to recommend the deletion of section 376A (as well as Exception to section 375). Their logic was this: when a man who causes hurt or any other physical injury to his own wife is liable to be punished for such offence like any other person causing such hurt or physical injury, why should a husband who sexually assaults his wife, who is living separately under a decree of separation or under any custom or usage, be not punished like any other person. Section 376A, which provides a lesser punishment to a husband who sexually assaults his own wife living separately in the aforesaid circumstances, they argued, is arbitrary and discriminatory. They say that once section 376A is deleted, the husband in such a case would be punished under section 376(1) which carries higher punishment than section 376A. While we appreciate the force of said argument in the context of the wife who is living separately under a decree of separation or under any custom or usage, we can not at the same time ignore the fact that even in such a case the bond of marriage remains unsevered. In the circumstances, while recommending that this section should be retained on the statute book, we recommend enhancement of punishment under the section.

3.3.1. Modification in section 376A of the I.P.C. recommended.—Accordingly, section 376A shall read as follows:—

"376A. *Sexual assault by the husband upon his wife during separation.*—Whoever commits sexual assault upon his wife, who is living separately from him under a decree of separation or under any custom or usage, without her consent, shall be punished with imprisonment of either description for a term which shall not be less than two years and which may extend to seven years and shall also be liable to fine."

3.4. Amendment of sections 376B, 376C and 376D.—Having regard to the gravity of these offences, we recommend enhancement of punishment - with a minimum punishment of not less than five years. We have also added an Explanation which will govern all these three sections. The Explanation defines "sexual intercourse" to mean any of the acts mentioned in clauses (a) to (e) of section 375. Explanation to section 375 will however apply even in the case of sexual intercourse as defined by the Explanation to this section.

3.4.1. Modifications in sections 376B, 376C and 376D of the I.P.C. recommended.—Accordingly, section 376B with necessary adaptations and changes, shall read as follows:—

"376B. *Sexual intercourse by public servant with person in his custody.*—Whoever, being a public servant, takes advantage of his/her official position and induces or seduces any person, who is in his/her custody as such public servant or in the custody of a public servant subordinate to him, to have sexual intercourse with him/her, such sexual intercourse not amounting to the offence of sexual assault, shall be punished with imprisonment of either description for a term which shall not be less than five years and which may extend to ten years and shall also be liable to fine:

Provided that the court may, for adequate and special reasons to be mentioned in the judgment, impose a sentence of imprisonment for a term of less than five years.

Explanation.—"Sexual intercourse" in this section and sections 376C and 376D shall mean any of the acts mentioned in clauses (a) to (e) of section 375. Explanation to section 375 shall also be applicable."

"376C. *Sexual intercourse by superintendent of jail, remand home, etc.*—Whoever, being the superintendent or manager of a jail, remand home or other place of custody established by or under any law for the time being in force or of a women's or children's institution takes advantage of his/her official position and induces or seduces any inmate of such jail, remand home, place or institution to have sexual intercourse with him/her, such sexual intercourse not amounting to the offence of sexual assault, shall be punished with imprisonment of either description for a term which shall not be less than five years and which may extend to ten years and shall also be liable to fine:

Provided that the court may, for adequate and special reasons to be mentioned in the judgment, impose a sentence of imprisonment for a term of less than five years.

Explanation 1.—"Superintendent" in relation to a jail, remand home or other place of custody or a women's or children's institution includes a person holding any other office in such jail, remand home, place or institution by virtue of which he/she can exercise any authority or control over its inmates.

Explanation 2.—The expression "women's or children's institution" shall have the same meaning as in Explanation 2 to sub-section (2) of section 376.

376D. Sexual intercourse by any member of the management or staff of a hospital with any woman in that hospital.—Whoever, being on the management of a hospital or being on the staff of a hospital takes advantage of his/her position and has sexual intercourse with any person in that hospital, such sexual intercourse not amounting to the offence of sexual assault, shall be punished with imprisonment of either description for a term which shall not be less than five years and which may extend to ten years and shall also be liable to fine:

Provided that the court may, for adequate and special reasons to be mentioned in the judgment, impose a sentence of imprisonment for a term of less than five years.

Explanation.—The expression "hospital" shall have the same meaning as in Explanation 3 to sub-section (2) of section 376."

3.5. Insertion of section 376E.—This is a wholly new section recommended by us. We have called it the offence of 'unlawful sexual contact'. This section is intended to cover a wide variety of offences including sexual harassment at work place and sexual perversions of the kind mentioned in the note submitted by Sakshi. Sub-section (1) of this new section covers touching, directly or indirectly, with a part of the body or with an object, any part of the body of another person (not being the spouse of such person), with sexual intent and without the consent of such other person. In case the other person is below sixteen years of age, we have recommended higher punishment. Sub-section (2) is an extension or elaboration of the offence mentioned in sub-section (1), while sub-section (3) deals with a case where such offence is committed on a young person – young person being defined by the Explanation to mean a person below the age of sixteen years. If the offence of unlawful sexual contact is committed on a young person by a person with whom such young person is in a relationship of dependency, the punishment is rigorous imprisonment which may extend to seven years or with fine or with both and in case the offender happens to be the father, grandfather or brother, a still higher punishment is provided for. In the case of a 'young person', consent is treated as irrelevant. (Sections 151, 152 and 153 of the Canadian Criminal Code also contain similar provisions).

3.5.1. Insertion of new section 376E recommended.—We therefore recommend that a new section, namely, section 376E be inserted in the I.P.C. in the following terms:

"376E. *Unlawful sexual contact.*—(1) Whoever, with sexual intent, touches, directly or indirectly, with a part of the body or with an object, any part of the body of another person, not being the spouse of such person, without the consent of such other person, shall be punished with simple imprisonment for a term which may extend to two years or with fine or with both.

(2) Whoever, with sexual intent, invites, counsels or incites a young person to touch, directly or indirectly, with a part of the body or with an object, the body of any person, including the body of the person who so invites, counsels or incites, or touches, with sexual intent, directly or indirectly, with a part of the body or with an object any part of the body of a young person, shall be punished with imprisonment of either description which may extend to three years and shall also be liable to fine.

(3) Whoever being in a position of trust or authority towards a young person or is a person with whom the young person is in a relationship of dependency, touches, directly or indirectly, with sexual intent, with a part of the body or with an object, any part of the body of such young person, shall be punished with imprisonment of either description which may extend to seven years and shall also be liable to fine.

Explanation.—"Young person" in this sub-section and sub-section (2) means a person below the age of sixteen years."

3.6. Deletion of section 377.—In the light of the change effected by us in section 375, we are of the opinion that section 377 deserves to be deleted. After the changes effected by us in the preceding provisions (sections 375 to 376E), the only content left in section 377 is having voluntary carnal intercourse with any animal. We may leave such persons to their just deserts.

3.7. Amendment of section 509.—So far as this section is concerned, the only change we are suggesting is enhancement of punishment. We recommend that the existing section 509 be amended as follows:

"509. *Word, gesture or act intended to insult the modesty of a woman.*—Whoever, intending to insult the modesty of any woman, utters any word, makes any sound or gesture, or exhibits any object intending that such word or sound shall be heard, or that such gesture or object shall be seen, by such woman, or intrudes upon the privacy of such woman, shall be punished with simple imprisonment for a term which may extend to three years and shall also be liable to fine."

3.8. New section 166A, I.P.C..—The 84th Report of the Law Commission had recommended (para 3.20) that a new section, namely, section 166A, be inserted in the Indian Penal Code. The object behind this new section was to punish a public servant who knowingly disobeys any direction of law prohibiting him from requiring the attendance at any place of any person for the purpose of investigation into an offence or other matter or knowingly disobeys any other direction of law regulating the manner in which he shall conduct such investigation and which act of his causes prejudice to any person. The representatives of Sakshi with whom we had a discussion, requested that a new section as recommended by 84th Report of the Law Commission be recommended to be inserted in the I.P.C.. This provision must be understood in the light of the fact that in the next chapter, we are recommending several measures with respect to the manner in which the statement of women and children (below 16 years) should be recorded, the place where it should be recorded and so on.

3.8.1. New section 166A of the I.P.C. recommended.—Accordingly, we recommend that a new section be introduced in the I.P.C. in the following terms:

"166A. *Whoever, being a public servant*—(a) knowingly disobeys any direction of the law prohibiting him from requiring the attendance at any place of any person for the purpose of investigation into an offence or other matter, or

(b) knowingly disobeys any other direction of the law regulating the manner in which he shall conduct such investigation, to the prejudice of any person, shall be punished with imprisonment for a term which may extend to one year or with fine or with both."

3.9. Views of "Sakshi" for defining `consent' considered.—Lastly, we may refer to a request of Sakshi to insert the definition of "consent" for the purpose of the aforesaid sections. We are however of the opinion that no such definition is called for at this stage, for the reason that the said expression has already been interpreted and pronounced upon by the courts in India in a good number of cases. Reference in this behalf may be made to page 700 of the Commentary on Indian Penal Code by Justice Jaspal Singh (1st Edn., 1998) where it is stated, on the basis of the decisions of the Madras, Punjab and Nagpur High Courts, that "consent implies the exercise of a free and untrammelled right to forbid or withhold what is being consented to; it always is a voluntary and conscious acceptance of what is proposed to be done by another and concurred in by the former".

CHAPTER IV

CHANGES RECOMMENDED IN THE CODE OF CRIMINAL PROCEDURE, 1973

4.1. Proposals of "Sakshi" relating to the Code of Criminal Procedure.—As stated in chapter two, the representatives of Sakshi have come forward with as many as 14 recommendations proposing amendments to the Code of Criminal Procedure and the Evidence Act. We had mentioned them in the said chapter. We shall now proceed to discuss them.

4.2. Addition of sub-sections (3) to (5) in section 160, Cr. P.C.—The 84th Report of the Law Commission had recommended (paragraphs 3.1 to 3.15) that sub-sections (3) to (7) be added in section 160. Instead of paraphrasing the reasons given in the 84th Report in our own words, it would be appropriate to set out paragraphs 3.11 to 3.15 of that Report hereinbelow:

"IV. Interrogation of female victims of sexual offences

3.11 *Reporting and Investigation.*—These matters concern the arrest and detention of women in general. We now deal with certain matters peculiar to women who are victims of sexual offences. Women who have been raped are reluctant to report it, partly because of the embarrassment of discussing the details with male policemen, and partly because of the very fear of even more painful humiliation of being a witness in Court.

They get scared and become confused when, in the strange environment of the Court room, they have to conduct themselves in a manner foreign to their custom and under a restraint not conducive to clear and coherent thought or free expression.

3.12 *Investigation by female police – No statutory change recommended.*—A woman is often discouraged from pressing a charge of rape or other sexual offence by the fact that she usually encounters only male police and prosecution officers. It is presumably for this reason that it has been suggested that the investigation of such offences should be done by women police officers only.

We would be happy if the questioning of female victims of sexual offences would be done by women police officers only. We are not, however, inclined to recommend a statutory provision in this regard. A mandatory provision to that effect may prove to be unworkable. The number of women police officers in rural areas is very small.

Even in urban areas, unless a centralised cell (with the status of a police station) is created for investigation into sexual offences against women, such a provision may not be practicable.

We regard this difficulty as a transient one. An all-out effort for the recruitment of sufficient number of women police officers, who could be drafted for the police duties of interrogation and investigation, should be made.

3.13 *Practice to be adopted in metropolitan cities.*—Till then, in metropolitan cities or big cities where there are sufficient number of women police officers, a practice should be established that women police officers alone investigate sexual offences and interrogate the victim.

We are, therefore, not in favour of any statutory provision being made in this respect, subject to what we are recommending in the next paragraph.

3.14 *Interrogation of child victim of rape—Statutory provision recommended.*—The practice as suggested above could be adopted in metropolitan areas and big cities. But there is one matter which is of importance for the whole country. It is necessary that in the case of girls below a certain age – say, below twelve years who are victims of rape, there should be a statutory provision to ensure that the girl must be interrogated only by a woman. A woman police officer would be preferable. But, if a woman police officer is not available, an alternate procedure as detailed below should be followed.

The alternate procedure that we contemplate is this. Where a woman police officer is not available, the officer in charge of the police station should forward a list of questions to a qualified female (we shall suggest details later) who would, after recording the information as ascertained from the child victim, return the papers to the officer in charge of the police station. If necessary, further questions to be put to the child may be sent by the police to the interrogator.

For the present, this procedure may be applied to female victims below 12 years. It could later be utilised for child witnesses in general, if found practicable.

The "qualified female" whom we have in mind should be one who is a social worker belonging to a recognised social organisation. If she possesses some knowledge of law and procedure, it would be all the more useful, but that need not be a statutory requirement.

3.15. *Amendment of section 160 recommended by insertion of sub-sections (3) to (7).*—In view of what is stated above, we would recommend the addition of the following provision – say, as new sub-sections – in section 160 of the Code of Criminal Procedure, 1973:

"(3) Where, under this chapter, the statement of a girl under the age of twelve years is to be recorded, either as first information of an offence or in the course of an investigation into an offence, and the girl is a person against whom an offence under sections 354, 354A or 375 of the Indian Penal Code is alleged to have been committed or attempted, the statement shall be recorded either by a female police officer or by a person authorised by such organisation interested in the welfare of women or children as is recognised in this behalf by the State Government by notification in the official gazette.

(4) Where the case is one to which the provisions of sub-section (3) apply, and a female police officer is not available, the officer in charge of the police station shall, in order to facilitate the recording of the statement, forward to the person referred to in that sub-section a written request setting out the points on which information is required to be elicited from the girl.

(5) The person to whom such a written request is forwarded shall, after recording the statement of the girl, transmit the record to the officer in charge of the police station.

(6) Where the statement recorded by such person as forwarded under sub-section (5) appears in any respect to require clarification or amplification, the officer in charge of the police station shall return the papers to the person by whom it was forwarded, with a request for clarification or amplification on specified matters; and such person shall thereupon record the further statement of the girl in conformity with the request and return the papers to the officer in charge of the police station.

(7) The statement of the girl recorded and forwarded under sub-sections (3) to (6) shall, for the purpose of the law relating to the admissibility in evidence of statements made by any person, be deemed to be a statement recorded by a police officer."

4.2.1. The representatives of Sakshi supported the said recommendation and wanted us to reiterate the same.

4.2.2. The 154th Report of the Law Commission dealt with the above recommendation in paragraphs 6.5 to 6.9. After setting out the aforesaid sub-sections in para 6.5, the 154th Report makes the following comments and recommendation in paragraphs 6.6 to 6.9 of chapter XVIII:

"6.6. The origin of this suggestion in its embryonic form can be traced to the Law Commission's Reports on "Rape and Allied Offences" and "Women in Custody".

6.7. The Bill (NCW) has gone beyond the Law Commission's earlier recommendations in that, insisting on the presence of a female police officer. Though the presence of such female officer is useful and necessary, their absence should not lead to delay in the investigation of the offences. Sub-sections (4), (5), (6) and (7) referred to above obligates the officer incharge of the police station to forward the person to a representative of a government, recognised women's organisation and the statement recorded by such person shall be deemed to be a statement recorded by the police officer.

6.8. It may be pointed out that the 1994 Bill does not incorporate the above amendment.

6.9. We are of the opinion that section 160 be amended on the lines suggested above subject to certain modifications. The recommendation made in sub-section (4) of NCW Bill is not practicable having regard to the present condition and dearth of female police officers. It may also not be practicable for the victim or any person interested in her to approach the person mentioned in sub-section (3). Instead, we suggest that sub-section (4) may be amended to the effect that where a female police officer is not available and to contact the person mentioned in sub-section (3) is difficult, the officer in charge of the police station, for reasons to be recorded in writing, shall proceed with the recording of the statement of the victim in the presence of a relative of the victim Further, the age of "twelve years" be raised to "eighteen years" in conformity with the Convention on the Rights of the Child."

4.2.3. Reiteration of the recommendations made in the 154th Report.—On a consideration of all the relevant facts and the realities of life, we too are of the opinion that the procedure indicated in the sub-sections (4), (5) and (6) is too involved besides being impracticable. Implementation of the several steps mentioned in the said sub-sections (4) to (6) would indeed result in unnecessary harassment to the victim of the offence or to the complainant, as the case may be. We are inclined to agree with the opinion expressed in para. 6.9 of the 154th Report of the Law Commission in this behalf. We have however changed the language of sub-section (3) by including a woman government officer. Changes are also called for in the light of the amendments effected by Act 43 of 1983 and also in the light of the recommendations made by us in paras. 3.2 and 3.5 (substitution of the offence in section 375 and the addition of section 376E).

4.2.3.1. Insertion of sub-sections (3) & (4) in section 160 of the Code of Criminal Procedure, 1973. Accordingly, we recommend that the following two sub-sections be inserted in section 160 of the Code of Criminal Procedure:

"(3) Where under this chapter, the statement of a female is to be recorded either as first information of an offence or in the course of an investigation into an offence and she is a person against whom an offence under sections 354, 375, 376, 376A, 376B, 376C, 376D, 376E or 509 of the Indian Penal Code is alleged to have been committed or attempted, the statement shall be recorded by a female police officer and in case a female police officer is not available, by a female government servant available in the vicinity and in case a female government servant is also not available, by a female authorised by an organisation interested in the welfare of women or children.

(4) Where in any case none of the alternatives mentioned in sub-section (3) can be followed for the reason that no female police officer or female government servant or a female authorised by an organisation interested in the welfare of women and children is available, the officer in charge of the police station shall, after recording the reasons in writing, proceed with the recording of the statement of such female victim in the presence of a relative of the victim."

4.3. Substitution of the proviso to sub-section (1) of section 160.—Sub-section (1) of section 160 deals with the power of a police officer to require the attendance of witnesses who appear to be acquainted with the facts and circumstances of the case being investigated by him. It also casts an obligation upon the person so required to attend. The proviso as it now stands, however, says that "no male person under the age of 15 years or woman shall be required to attend at any place other than the place in which such male person or woman resides". We recommend raising the age from 15 years mentioned in the said proviso to 16 years.

4.3.1. Consideration of the view of "Sakshi" regarding presence of a relative or a friend or a social worker during the investigation.—At this stage, we may deal with another suggestion put forward by Sakshi to provide that even where the statement of a male person under the age of 16 years or of a female is recorded by a police officer during the course of investigation, a relative or a friend or a social worker of the choice of such male person below 16 years or the woman, as the case may be, shall be allowed to be present throughout the period during which the statement is recorded. We are inclined to agree with this suggestion, particularly in the light of the decision of the Supreme Court in *Nandini Satpathy* v. *P.L. Dani,* AIR 1978 SC 1025.

4.3.2. Substitution of the proviso to sub-section (1) of section 160 recommended.—Accordingly, we recommend that the proviso to sub-section (1) of section 160 be substituted to read as below:

"Provided that no male person under the age of 16 years or woman shall be required to attend at any place other than the place in which such male person or woman resides. While recording the statement, a relative or a friend or a social worker of the choice of the person whose statement is being recorded shall be allowed to remain present. The relative, friend or social worker so allowed to be present shall not interfere with the recording of statement in any manner whatsoever."

4.4. *Insertion of a new section, namely section 164A in the Code of Criminal Procedure.*—The 84th Report of the Law Commission had recommended insertion of such a provision in paragraphs 4.8 to 4.11 of chapter 4. The reasons for such a provision and the provision suggested are the following:

"III. *Examination of the victim*

4.8. *Section 164A, Cr. PC. (To be added).*—We next deal with the victim. In many cases, the report of the medical examiner as to the examination of the female victim is also found to be somewhat cursory and does not give adequate information about the material particulars which are necessary for an adjudication as to the various ingredients of section 375. Further, it is sometimes noticed that the medical examination report is not sent promptly to the investigating officer. As a result, the possibility of tampering with the report remains.

In our opinion, the report of the examination of the victim in a case of rape should (besides containing the usual formal particulars) deal specifically with—

(i) the age of the victim,

(ii) the question whether the victim was previously used to sexual intercourse,

(iii) injuries to the body of the victim,

(iv) general mental condition of the victim, and

(v) other material particulars in reasonable detail.

It is also necessary that the report should note the time of examination and be sent without delay to the investigating officer. It is very important that the report should state reasons for the conclusions recorded.

4.9. *Need for legislative provisions.*—Ordinarily, such matters are left to be dealt with by executive instructions. However, having regard to the importance of the subject, it would be proper to insert in the Code of Criminal Procedure, at an appropriate place, a provision incorporating the guidelines that we have suggested above. In the light of the practical working of the provision, further improvements could be made in the relevant provisions.

4.10. *Section 164A, Cr. P.C., recommended.*—Accordingly, we recommend that the following new section should be inserted in the Code of Criminal Procedure, 1973:

"164A. (1) Where, during the stage when an offence of rape or attempt to commit rape is under investigation, it is proposed to get the person of the woman with whom rape is alleged to have been committed or attempted, examined by a medical expert, such examination shall be conducted by a registered medical practitioner, with the consent of the woman or of some person competent to give such consent on her behalf and the woman shall be forwarded to the registered medical practitioner without delay.

(2) The registered medical practitioner to whom such woman is forwarded shall without delay examine her person and prepare a report specifically recording the result of his examination and giving the following details:

(i) the name and address of the woman and of the person by whom she was brought,

(ii) the age of the woman,

(iii) whether the victim was previously used to sexual intercourse,

(iv) marks of injuries, if any, on the person of the woman,

(v) general mental condition of the woman, and

(vi) other material particulars, in reasonable detail.

(3) The report shall state precisely the reasons for each conclusion arrived at.

(4) The report shall specifically record that the consent of the woman or of some person competent to give such consent on her behalf to such examination had been obtained.

(5) The exact time of commencement and completion of the examination shall also be noted in the report, and the registered medical practitioner shall without delay, forward the report to the investigating officer, who shall forward it to the Magistrate referred to in section 173 as part of the documents referred to in clause (a) of sub-section (5) of that section.

(6) Nothing in this section shall be construed as rendering lawful any examination without the consent of the victim or of any person competent to give such consent on her behalf."

4.11 *Medical examination of the victim of rape.*—In regard to the examination of the person of the accused, section 53(2) of the Code of Criminal Procedure provides that whenever the person of a female is to be examined under that section, the examination shall be made only by, or under the supervision of, a female registered medical practitioner.

The question whether a provision should be inserted to the effect that where a female victim of a sexual offence is to be examined, the medical examination shall be conducted only by a female medical practitioner has been carefully considered by us. We think that a statutory provision is not necessary, for two reasons. In the first place, this is almost the invariable practice in India and a statutory mandate is not needed. In the second place, if a female victim does not wish to submit to examination by a male doctor, there is no legal obligation on her part to do so. For that reason also, a statutory provision is not necessary. It may be mentioned that such medical examination cannot be lawfully made without the consent of the woman or of some person competent to give consent."

4.5. Reiteration of the above proposal in the 154th Report.—The 154th Report of the Law Commission has reiterated the said proposal in paras 7.1 to 7.3 of Chapter XVIII. The Commission expressed the opinion that such a provision is eminently desirable subject to the modification that medical examination be made preferably by a female medical practitioner. The Report also emphasises the importance and significance of a speedy and detailed medical examination of rape victims and speedy despatch of such report to the investigating officer.

4.5.1. *Acceptance of the proposal with consequential changes.*—We affirm and reiterate the aforesaid recommendations contained in the 84th and 154th Reports. However, in the light of the changes proposed by us in section 375, necessary changes by way of adaptation have to be made.

4.5.2. *Insertion of section 164A in the Code of Criminal Procedure recommended.*—Accordingly, we recommend that the following section 164A be inserted in the Code of Criminal Procedure:

"*164A.* (1) Where, during the stage when any offence under section 376, section 376A, section 376B, section 376C, section 376D or section 376E is under investigation and it is proposed to get the victim examined by a medical expert, such examination shall be conducted by a registered medical practitioner, with the consent of the victim or of some person competent to give such consent on his/her behalf. In all cases, the victim should be sent for such examination without any delay:

Provided that if the victim happens to be a female, the medical examination shall be conducted by a female medical officer, as far as possible.

(2) The registered medical practitioner to whom the victim is forwarded shall without delay examine the person and prepare a report specifically recording the result of his examination and giving the following details:

(i) the name and address of the victim and the person by whom he/she was brought,

(ii) the age of the victim,

(iii) marks of injuries, if any, on the person of the victim,

(iv) general mental condition of the victim, and

(v) other material particulars, in reasonable detail.

(3) The report shall state precisely the reasons for each conclusion arrived at.

(4) The report shall specifically record that the consent of the victim or of some person competent to give such consent on his/her behalf to such examination had been obtained.

(5) The exact time of commencement and completion of the examination shall also be noted in the report, and the registered medical practitioner shall without delay, forward the report to the investigating officer, who shall forward it to the Magistrate referred to in section 173 as part of the documents referred to in clause (a) of sub-section (5) of that section.

(6) Nothing in this section shall be construed as rendering lawful any examination without the consent of the victim or any person competent to give such consent on his/her behalf."

4.6. Insertion of a new section 53A in the Code of Criminal Procedure.—The 84th Report of the Law Commission had recommended the insertion of new section 53A in paras 4.5 to 4.7 of chapter 4, which reads as follows:

"II. Examination of the accused

4.5. *Provision in the Code – Need for timely examination.*—The Code of Criminal Procedure has, in section 53, a general provision on the subject of medical examination of the accused in all cases where such examination would afford evidence of commission of offence.

It is, however, seen that the report of the medical examination is often cursory, or is not sent in time, in cases of rape or attempt to commit rape.

In a recent Calcutta case (*Narayan Dutta* v. *State*, 1980 Cr LJ 264, paras. 1-2), the High Court was constrained to observe—

"It is also striking that the appellant, though arrested on that very night (9th May) was not produced before Dr. Pal (P.W. 11) who examined P.Ws. 1 and 10 on 10-5-1970."

4.6. *Particulars to be entered and reasons to be given.*—It is also desirable that the report should (besides containing the usual formal particulars) deal specifically with – (i) the age of the accused, (ii) injuries to the body of the accused, and (iii) other material particulars in reasonable detail. It should also note the precise time of examination. It should be sent without delay by the registered medical practitioner to the investigating officer and the latter should file it before the Magistrate empowered to take cognisance along with the documents sent with the challan under section 173(5) of the Code

4.7. *Recommendation as to section 53, Cr. P.C.*—It is very important that reasons should be given for the opinion expressed in the report. Accordingly, we recommend the insertion in section 53 of the Code of Criminal Procedure, of the following sub-sections:

"Section 53(1A), (1B), (1C) and (1D), Code of Criminal Procedure, 1973 to be inserted—

(1A) When a person accused of rape or an attempt to commit rape is arrested and an examination of his person is to be made under this section, he shall be forwarded without delay to the registered medical practitioner by whom he is to be examined.

(1B) The registered medical practitioner conducting such examination shall without delay examine such person and prepare a report specifically recording the result of his examination and giving the following particulars:

(i) the name and address of the accused and of the person by whom he was brought,

(ii) the age of the accused,

(iii) marks of injury, if any, on the person of the accused, and

(iv) other material particulars in reasonable detail.

(1C) The report shall state precisely the reasons for each conclusion arrived at.

(1D) The exact time of commencement and completion of the examination shall also be noted in the report, and the registered medical practitioner shall, without delay, forward the report to the investigating officer, who shall forward it to the Magistrate referred to in section 173 as part of the documents referred to in clause (a) of sub-section (5) of that section."

4.6.1. Views of "Sakshi" considered.—The representatives of Sakshi supported the said proposal with a few additions. By means of these additions it was sought to be provided that the registered medical practitioner shall also state in his report with respect to "any traces of blood, semen and evidence of any recent sexual activity in reasonable detail". We are, however, of the opinion that the said addition suggested by Sakshi is unnecessary since the provision as suggested by the 84th Report is comprehensive enough to take in the said particulars as well. Accordingly, we affirm and reiterate the recommendation of the 84th Report, subject, however, to changes and adaptations in the light of our recommendation for substitution of section 375 of the I.P.C..

4.6.2. New section 53A in the Code of Criminal Procedure, 1973 recommended.—Thus the proposed section 53A shall read as follows:

"*53A*. (1) When a person accused of any of the offences under sections 376, 376A, 376B, 376C, 376D or 376E or of an attempt to commit any of the said offences, is arrested and an examination of his/her person is to be made under this section, he/she shall be sent without delay to the registered medical practitioner by whom he/she is to be examined.

(2) The registered medical practitioner conducting such examination shall without delay examine such person and prepare a report specifically recording the result of his examination and giving the following particulars:

(i) the name and address of the accused and the person by whom he was brought,

(ii) the age of the accused,

(iii) marks of injury, if any, on the person of the accused, and

(iv) other material particulars in reasonable detail.

(3) The report shall state precisely the reasons for each conclusion arrived at.

(4) The exact time of commencement and completion of the examination shall also be noted in the report, and the registered medical practitioner shall, without delay, forward the report to the investigating officer, who shall forward it to the Magistrate referred to in section 173 as part of the documents referred to in clause (a) of sub-section (5) of that section."

4.7. *Consequential amendments in the First Schedule to the Code of Criminal Procedure, 1973 recommended.*—Consequent upon the proposed amendments in sections 376 to 376D, 377 and 509 and the insertion of new section 376E in

I.P.C., the First Schedule to the Code of Criminal Procedure, 1973 will need to be amended and the existing entries in respect of sections 376 to 376D, 377 and 509 of the I.P.C. will have to be substituted and entry in respect of new section 376E will have to be inserted as under:

376	Sexual assault	Imprisonment for life or imprisonment for 10 years and fine	Ditto	Non-bailable	Court of Session
	Sexual assault by a man on his own wife being under 16 years of age.	Imprisonment for 3 years and fine	Non-cognizable	Ditto	Ditto
	Sexual assault committed by a person in a position of trust or authority towards the person assaulted or by a near relative of the person assaulted.	Imprisonment for life and fine	Cognizable	Non-bailable	Ditto
	Sexual assault by a police officer or by a public servant or by a person being on the management or on the staff of a jail, remand home or other place of custody or women's or children's institution or by a person on the management or on the staff of a hospital, taking advantage of his official position.	Imprisonment for life and fine	Cognizable	Non-bailable	Ditto
376A	Sexual assault by the husband upon his wife during separation.	Imprisonment for 7 years and fine	Cognizable (but only on the complaint of the victim)	Non-bailable	Ditto

376B	Sexual intercourse by public servant with person in his custody.	Imprisonment for 10 years and fine	Cognizable (but no arrest shall be made without a warrant or without an order of a Magistrate)	Non-bailable	Ditto
376C	Sexual intercourse by Superintendent of jail, remand home etc.	Ditto	Ditto	Ditto	Ditto
376D	Sexual intercourse by any member of the management or staff of a hospital with any woman in that hospital.	Ditto	Ditto	Ditto	Ditto
376E	Unlawful sexual contact.	Imprisonment for 2 years, or fine or both	Non-cognizable	Bailable	Magistrate of the First Class
	Unlawful sexual contact with a young person.	Imprisonment for 3 years	Cognizable if information relating to the commission of the offence is given to an Officer-in-charge of a Police Station by the person aggrieved by the offence or by any person related to her/him by blood, or adoption or if there is no such relative, by any public servant belonging to such class or	Non-bailable	Ditto

			category as may be notified by the State Government in this behalf		
	Unlawful sexual contact by a person in a position of trust or authority towards a young person.	Imprisonment for 7 years and fine	Ditto	Non-bailable	Court of Session
377	Delete	Delete	Delete	Delete	Delete
509	Uttering any word or making any gesture intended to insult the modesty of a woman etc.	Simple imprisonment for 3 years and fine	Cogni-zable	Non-bailable	Magis-trate of the First Class

4.8. Amendment of sub-section (6) of section 198 of the Code of Criminal Procedure, 1973.—Consequent upon proposed amendment of section 376 of I.P.C., sub-section (6) of section 198, Cr. P.C. shall be amended in the following manner:

> The words "sexual intercourse" shall be substituted by the words "sexual assault" and the word "fifteen" shall be substituted by the word "sixteen".

4.9. Insertion of new section 198B of the Code of Criminal Procedure, 1973.—After section 198A of the Code of Criminal Procedure, 1973, the following new section 198B shall be inserted:

> "*Prosecution of offences under sub-sections (2) and (3) of section 376E of the Indian Penal Code.*—No court shall take cognizance of an offence punishable under sub-sections (2) and (3) of section 376E of the Indian Penal Code (45 of 1860) except upon a police report of facts which constitute such offence or upon a complaint made by the person aggrieved by the offence or by his/her father, mother, brother, sister or by his/her father's or mother's brother or sister or, by any other person related to him/her by blood or adoption, if so permitted by the court."

4.10. Proposals for amending Cr. P.C. put forward by Sakshi with which we do not agree.—Sakshi have put forward certain other suggestions which we have set out under items 6, 7, 8 and 9 in chapter two of this report. In our opinion, the said proposals are unnecessary in view of the existing provisions and the recommendations made by us herein. It is better to leave these matters to the discretion of the court.

CHAPTER V

CHANGES RECOMMENDED IN THE EVIDENCE ACT, 1872

5.1. Suggestions of "Sakshi" considered.—The representatives of Sakshi have suggested three amendments to the Evidence Act, *viz.* (a) amendment of section 114A saying that in a prosecution for aggravated sexual assault and where sexual intercourse is proved and the question is whether it was without the consent of the complainant and the complainant states in her evidence before the court that she did not consent, the court shall presume that she did not consent; (b) clause (4) in section 155, which permits a man prosecuted for rape or an attempt to ravish, to show that the prosecutrix was of generally immoral character should be deleted, and (c) in section 146, a new clause, clause (4), shall be added stating that in a prosecution for sexual assault or an attempt to commit sexual assault and where the question of consent is in issue, it shall not be permissible to put any questions in the cross-examination of the complainant with respect to his/her previous sexual history, character or conduct for proving consent or the quality of consent.

5.1.1. Suggestion No. 1.—So far as the first suggestion is concerned, it has evidently been made without taking note of Act 43 of 1983 which had introduced section 114A in the Evidence Act. The section reads as follows:

> "*114A. Presumption as to absence of consent in certain prosecutions for rape.*—In a prosecution for rape under clause (a) or clause (b) or clause (c) or clause (d) or clause (e) or clause (g) of sub-section (2) of section 376 of the Indian Penal Code (45 of 1860), where sexual intercourse by the accused is proved and the question is whether it was without the consent of the woman alleged to have been raped and she states in her evidence before the court that she did not consent, the court shall presume that she did not consent."

5.1.2. A reading of the above section shows that it does provide for the matter which the representatives of Sakshi wanted.

5.1.3. Recommendations on section 114A of the Evidence Act.—It is however necessary to point out that section 114A is confined only to the aggravated forms of rape mentioned under clauses (a) to (e) and (g) of sub-section (2) of section 376. It does not apply to sub-section (1) of section 376 or for that matter to sections 376A to 376D. But the representatives of Sakshi also wanted such a presumption to be raised only in respect of "aggravated sexual assault" and that is exactly what section 114A provides. No amendment is therefore called for in section 114A except some modifications – by way of adaptation – in the light of amendment proposed by us to section 375, I.P.C..

5.1.4. Modification of section 114A of the Evidence Act recommended.—Accordingly, we recommended that section 114A be modified to read as follows:

> "114A. *Presumption as to absence of consent in certain prosecutions for sexual assault.*—In a prosecution for sexual assault under (a) or clause (b) or clause (c) or clause (d) or clause (e) or clause (g) of sub-section (2) of

section 376 of the Indian Penal Code (45 of 1860) where sexual intercourse by the accused is proved and the question is whether it was without the consent of the other person alleged to have been sexually assaulted and such other person states in his/her evidence before the court that he/she did not consent, the court shall presume that he/she did not consent.

Explanation.—"Sexual intercourse" in this section and sections 376C and 376D shall mean any of the acts mentioned in clauses (a) to (e) of section 375. Explanation to section 375 shall also be applicable."

5.1.4.1. It goes without saying that the aforesaid presumption is a rebuttable presumption of law ('shall presume') within the meaning of section 4 of the Evidence Act

5.1.5. Consideration of the suggestion of "Sakshi" to create presumption in respect of the age of the victim.—We may in this connection refer to another suggestion of Sakshi that a similar presumption be created in respect of the age of the victim. We however do not see any necessity for such a provision since the question of age is really and ultimately a matter of evidence and be better left to the judgment of the court.

5.2.1. Suggestion No. 2.—For a proper appreciation of the suggestion for amendment of section 155, it would be appropriate to set out section 155 in full (omitting the illustrations). It reads as follows:

"155. *Impeaching credit of witness.*—The credit of a witness may be impeached in the following ways by the adverse party, or with the consent of the court, by the party who calls him:—

(1) by the evidence of persons who testify that they, from their knowledge of the witness, believe him to be unworthy of credit;

(2) by proof that the witness has been bribed, or has accepted the offer of a bribe, or has received any other corrupt inducement to give his evidence;

(3) by proof of former statements inconsistent with any part of his evidence which is liable to be contradicted;

(4) when a man is prosecuted for rape or an attempt to ravish, it may be shown that the prosecutrix was of generally immoral character.

Explanation.—A witness declaring another witness to be unworthy of credit may not, upon his examination-in-chief, give reasons for his belief, but he may be asked his reasons in cross-examination, and the answers which he gives cannot be contradicted, though if they are false, he may afterwards be charged with giving false evidence."

5.2.2. Section 155 sets out the manner in which the credit of a witness may be impeached. Clause (4) specifically deals with prosecution for rape. In such a prosecution, the Act permits the man prosecuted for rape (or an attempt to ravish) to show that the prosecutrix was of generally immoral character. We are of the opinion that this clause ought to be deleted. We see no relevance or reasonable connection between offence of sexual assault (mentioned under sections 375 to 376E) and the general immoral character of the victim. No one can claim to have a right to have forced sexual intercourse with a woman even if she is generally of an immoral character. In this context, we may refer to the pertinent observations of the Supreme Court in *State of Punjab* v. *Gurmit Singh*, AIR 1996 SC 1393 which are to the following effect:

"15. We must express our strong disapproval of the approach of the trial Court and its casting a stigma on the character of the prosecutrix. The observations lack sobriety expected of a Judge. Such like stigmas have the potential of not only discouraging an even otherwise reluctant victim of sexual assault to bring forth complaint for trial of criminals, thereby making the society to suffer by letting the criminal escape even a trial. The Courts are expected to use self-restraint while recording such findings which have larger repercussions so far as the future of the victim of the sex crime is concerned and even wider implications on the society as a whole – where the victim of crime is discouraged – the criminal encouraged, and in turn crime gets rewarded. Even in cases, unlike the present case, where there is some acceptable material on the record to show that the victim was habituated to sexual intercourse, no such inference like the victim being a girl of "loose moral character" is permissible to be drawn from that circumstance alone. Even if the prosecutrix, in a given case, has been promiscuous in her sexual behaviour earlier, she has a right to refuse to submit herself to sexual intercourse to anyone and everyone because she is not a vulnerable object or prey for being sexually assaulted by anyone and everyone. No stigma, like the one as cast in the present case should be cast against such a witness by the Courts, for after all it is the accused and not the victim of sex crime who is on trial in the Court."

5.2.3. Deletion of clause (4) of section 155 of the Evidence Act recommended.—Reference may also be made in this context to the 84th Report of the Law Commission which, inter alia, deals with this aspect. In Chapter 7 of the Report under item "V. Past Sexual History", the Commission had emphasised the desirability of amending clause (4) in section 155 (to make such questions permissible only to the extent of her previous sexual relationship with the accused but otherwise to bar any questions regarding the prosecutrix's general immoral character or previous sexual experience) as well as addition of a new clause, clause (4) in section 146. Indeed the Commission had recommended insertion of a new section, section 53A in the Act. It is not necessary to set out the entire reasoning given in the 84th Report in support of amendment of clause (4) in section 155 inasmuch as the purport of such amendment is now incorporated by us in section 146. In that view, clause (4) in section 155 becomes untenable. We, therefore, recommend deletion of clause (4) of section 155.

5.3.1. Suggestion No. 3.—So far as the addition of a new clause, namely, clause (4) in section 146 is concerned, the 84th Report of the Law Commission had suggested the following addition:

"(4) In a prosecution for rape or attempt to commit rape, where the question of consent to sexual intercourse or attempted sexual intercourse is at issue, it shall not be permissible to adduce evidence or to put questions in the cross-examination of the prosecutrix as to her general immoral character, or as to her previous sexual experience with any person other than the accused for proving such consent or the quality of consent."

5.3.2. The 84th Report of the Law Commission had further recommended the addition of a new section, section 53A, to the following effect:

"53A. In a prosecution for rape or attempt to commit rape, where the question of consent to sexual intercourse or attempted sexual intercourse is at issue, evidence of the character of the prosecutrix or of her previous sexual experience with any person other than the accused shall not be relevant on the issue of such consent or the quality of consent."

5.3.3. Obviously, section 53A was recommended to be inserted for the reason that section 146 is confined to questions that may be put in cross-examination and is therefore of a limited operation, whereas section 53A is much wider and bars such evidence to be adduced in any manner whatsoever.

5.3.4. Reiteration of the recommendations made in the 84th Report and reference to the New South Wales Law Reform Commission's recommendations.—We are in agreement with the above recommendations contained in the 84th Report of the Law Commission and do herewith reiterate them. In this context, however, we may refer to a set of recommendations proposed by the New South Wales Law Reform Commission to amend section 409B of the Crimes Act, 1900 (New South Wales). Sub-section (2) of section 409B of the New South Wales Act provides that "in prescribed sexual offence proceedings, evidence relating to the sexual reputation of the complainant is inadmissible". Sub-section (3) makes evidence of any sexual experience or lack of sexual experience of the complainant equally inadmissible except in certain specified situations. The New South Wales Law Commission has proposed retaining the existing sub-section (2) as clause (a) of sub-section (2) and to add a new clause, clause (b) in sub-section (2). It has also proposed addition of sub-sections (3) to (11). We do not, however, propose to set out all the said proposed sub-sections, except sub-section (2), which reads as follows:

"(2)(a) In proceedings to which this section applies, evidence relating to the sexual reputation of the complainant is inadmissible (b) Notwithstanding sub-section (2)(a), evidence about any sexual experience or sexual activity, or lack of experience or activity, of the complainant shall not be inadmissible merely because it also relates to the sexual reputation of the complainant."

5.3.5. For ready reference, we are enclosing both section 409B as it now stands as well as the recommendation for its amendment as suggested by the New South Wales Law Reform Commission. (The recommendation was made in November 1998.) (Annexure F).

5.3.6. We do not think that we need to draw any inspiration from the highly involved and intricate provisions suggested by the New South Wales Law Reform Commission by way of clause (b) of sub-section (2) or by way of sub-sections (3) to (7) of section 209B. The provision as suggested herein are sufficient. It is, of course, for the government to decide whether any provisions on the lines of the suggestions made by the New South Wales Law Commission should be made.

5.3.7. In the light of changes proposed by us in section 375, the language of section 53A and of clause (4) in section 146, recommended in the 84th Report of the Law Commission, have to be modified and adapted.

5.3.8. Consequential amendments recommended in proposed section 53A and proposed clause (4) of section 146 of the Evidence Act.—Accordingly, we recommend that the following amendments be made in the Evidence Act:

5.3.8.1. After section 53, the following section be inserted:

"*53A.* In a prosecution for an offence under sections 376, 376A, 376B, 376C, 376D or 376E or for attempt to commit any such offence, where the question of consent is in issue, evidence of the character of the victim or of his/her previous sexual experience with any person shall not be relevant on the issue of such consent or the quality of consent."

5.3.8.2. In section 146 of the Evidence Act, the following clause shall be added after clause (3):

"(4) In a prosecution for an offence under sections 376, 376A, 376B, 376C, 376D or 376E or for attempt to commit any such offence, where the question of consent is in issue, it shall not be permissible to adduce evidence or to put questions in the cross-examination of the victim as to his/her general immoral character, or as to his/her previous sexual experience with any person for proving such consent or the quality of consent."

CHAPTER VI

MISCELLANEOUS SUGGESTIONS OF SAKSHI

6.1. The representatives of Sakshi have made three other suggestions which we have set out under items 11, 12 and 13 in chapter two of this Report. So far as suggestion under item 11 is concerned, we may refer to section 273 of the Criminal Procedure Code, which requires that "except as otherwise expressly provided, all evidence taken in the course of the trial or other proceeding, shall be taken in the presence of the accused or when his personal attendance is dispensed with, in the presence of his pleader". We do not think that this general principle, founded upon natural justice, should be done away with altogether in trials and enquiries concerning sexual offences. In an appropriate case, it may be open to the prosecution to request the court to provide a screen in such a manner that the victim does not see the accused, while at the same time providing an opportunity to the accused to listen to the testimony of the victim and give appropriate instructions to his advocate for an effective cross-examination. However, with a view to allay any apprehensions on this score, a proviso can be added to section 273 of the Criminal Procedure Code to the following effect:

"Provided that where the evidence of a person below sixteen years who is alleged to have been subjected to sexual assault or any other sexual offence, is to be recorded, the court may, take appropriate measures to ensure that such person is not confronted by the accused while at the same time ensuring the right of cross-examination of the accused".

The proviso can be placed above the Explanation to the section.

6.2. The suggestion mentioned under item 12 is, in our opinion, impractical; it is not possible to accede to the said request. The same comment holds good with respect to the proposal under item 13. We are therefore unable to make any recommendation for the present in terms of or on the basis of the aforesaid requests of Sakshi.

CHAPTER VII

CONCLUSION

7.1. On the basis of the discussions contained in the preceding chapters, the Commission is of the considered opinion that the following amendments need to be carried out in the Indian Penal Code, 1860; the Code of Criminal Procedure, 1973 and the Indian Evidence Act, 1872.

7.2. Changes recommended in the Indian Penal Code, 1860:

7.2.1. Substitution of existing section 375 of the I.P.C. recommended.—The existing section 375 be substituted by the following:

"375. *Sexual Assault:* Sexual assault means—

(a) penetrating the vagina (which term shall include the labia majora), the anus or urethra of any person with—

(i) any part of the body of another person; or

(ii) an object manipulated by another person;

except where such penetration is carried out for proper hygienic or medical purposes;

(b) manipulating any part of the body of another person so as to cause penetration of the vagina (which term shall include the labia majora), the anus or the urethra of the offender by any part of the other person's body;

(c) introducing any part of the penis of a person into the mouth of another person;

(d) engaging in cunnilingus or fellatio; or

(e) continuing sexual assault as defined in clauses (a) to (d) above,

in circumstances falling under any of the six following descriptions:

First—Against the other person's will.

Secondly—Without the other person's consent.

Thirdly—With the other person's consent when such consent has been obtained by putting such other person or any person in whom such other person is interested, in fear of death or hurt.

Fourthly—Where the other person is a female, with her consent, when the man knows that he is not the husband of such other person and that her consent is given because she believes that the offender is another man to whom she is or believes herself to be lawfully married.

Fifthly—With the consent of the other person, when, at the time of giving such consent, by reason of unsoundness of mind or intoxication or the administration by the offender personally or through another of any stupefying or unwholesome substance, the other person is unable to understand the nature and consequences of that to which such other person gives consent.

Sixthly—With or without the other person's consent, when such other person is under sixteen years of age.

Explanation—Penetration to any extent is penetration for the purposes of this section.

Exception—Sexual intercourse by a man with his own wife, the wife not being under sixteen years of age, is not sexual assault."

Further we are not satisfied that the Exception should be deleted.

(Paras. 3.1.2 and 3.1.2.1, *supra*)

7.2.2. Re-casting of section 376 of the I.P.C. recommended.—Section 376 shall be re-cast as follows:

"*376. Punishment for sexual assault.*—(1) Whoever, except in the cases provided for by sub-section (2), commits sexual assault shall be punished with imprisonment of either description for a term which shall not be less than seven years but which may be for life or for a term which may extend to ten years and shall also be liable to fine unless the person subjected to sexual assault is his own wife and is not under sixteen years of age, in which case, he shall be punished with imprisonment of either description for a term which may extend to three years and shall also be liable to fine.

If the sexual assault is committed by a person in a position of trust or authority towards the person assaulted or by a near relative of the person assaulted, he/she shall be punished with rigorous imprisonment for a term which shall not be less than ten years but which may extend to life imprisonment and shall also be liable to fine:

Provided that the court may, for adequate and special reasons to be mentioned in the judgment, impose a sentence of imprisonment for a term of less than minimum punishment prescribed in this sub-section.

(2) Whoever,—

(a) being a police officer commits sexual assault—

(i) within the limits of the police station to which he is appointed; or

(ii) in the premises of any station house whether or not situated in the police station to which he is appointed; or

(iii) on a person in his custody or in the custody of a police officer subordinate to him; or

(b) being a public servant, takes advantage of his official position and commits sexual assault on a person in his custody as such public servant or in the custody of a public servant subordinate to him; or

(c) being on the management or on the staff of a jail, remand home or other place of custody established by or under any law for the time being in force or of a women's or children's institution takes advantage of his official position and commits sexual assault on any inmate of such jail, remand home, place or institution; or

(d) being on the management or on the staff of a hospital, takes advantage of his official position and commits sexual assault on a person in that hospital; or

(e) commits sexual assault on a woman knowing her to be pregnant; or

(f) commits sexual assault on a person when such person is under sixteen years of age; or

(g) commits gang sexual assault,

shall be punished with rigorous imprisonment for a term which shall not be less than ten years but which may be for life and shall also be liable to fine:

Provided that the court may, for adequate and special reasons to be mentioned in the judgment, impose a sentence of imprisonment of either description for a term of less than ten years.

Explanation 1.—Where a person is subjected to sexual assault by one or more in a group of persons acting in furtherance of their common intention, each of the persons shall be deemed to have committed gang sexual assault within the meaning of this sub-section.

Explanation 2.—"Women's or children's institution" means an institution, whether called an orphanage or a home for neglected women or children or a widows' home or an institution called by any other name, which is established and maintained for the reception and care of women or children.

Explanation 3.—"Hospital" means the precincts of the hospital and includes the precincts of any institution for the reception and treatment of persons during convalescence or of persons requiring medical attention or rehabilitation."

(Para. 3.2.3, *supra*)

7.2.3. Modification in section 376A of the I.P.C. recommended.—Section 376A shall read as follows:

"376A. *Sexual assault by the husband upon his wife during separation.*—Whoever commits sexual assault upon his wife, who is living separately from him under a decree of separation or under any custom or usage, without her consent, shall be punished with imprisonment of either description for a term which shall not be less than two years and which may extend to seven years and shall also be liable to fine."

(Para. 3.3.1, *supra*)

7.2.4. *Amendment of sections 376B, 376C and 376D.*—We recommend enhancement of punishment – with a minimum punishment of not less than five years. We have also added an Explanation which will govern all these three sections. The Explanation defines "sexual intercourse" to mean any of the acts mentioned in clauses (a) to (e) of section 375. Explanation to section 375 will however apply even in the case of sexual intercourse as defined by the Explanation to this section.

Accordingly, the modified sections 376B, 376C and 376D of the I.P.C. shall read as follows:

"376B. *Sexual intercourse by public servant with person in his custody.*—Whoever, being a public servant, takes advantage of his/her official position and induces or seduces any person, who is in his/her custody as such public servant or in the custody of a public servant subordinate to him, to have sexual intercourse with him/her, such sexual intercourse not amounting to the offence of sexual assault, shall be punished with imprisonment of either description for a term which shall not be less than five years and which may extend to ten years and shall also be liable to fine:

Provided that the court may, for adequate and special reasons to be mentioned in the judgment, impose a sentence of imprisonment for a term of less than five years.

Explanation.—"Sexual intercourse" in this section and sections 376C and 376D shall mean any of the acts mentioned in clauses (a) to (e) of section 375. Explanation to section 375 shall also be applicable."

"376C. *Sexual intercourse by superintendent of jail, remand home, etc.*—Whoever, being the superintendent or manager of a jail, remand home or other place of custody established by or under any law for the time being in force or of a women's or children's institution takes advantage of his/her official position and induces or seduces any inmate of such jail, remand home, place or institution to have sexual intercourse with him/her, such sexual intercourse not amounting to the offence of sexual assault, shall be punished with imprisonment of either description for a term which shall not be less than five years and which may extend to ten years and shall also be liable to fine:

Provided that the court may, for adequate and special reasons to be mentioned in the judgment, impose a sentence of imprisonment for a term of less than five years.

Explanation 1.—"Superintendent" in relation to a jail, remand home or other place of custody or a women's or children's institution includes a person holding any other office in such jail, remand home, place or institution by virtue of which he/she can exercise any authority or control over its inmates.

Explanation 2.—The expression "women's or children's institution" shall have the same meaning as in Explanation 2 to sub-section (2) of section 376.

376D. *Sexual intercourse by any member of the management or staff of a hospital with any woman in that hospital.*—Whoever, being on the management of a hospital or being on the staff of a hospital takes advantage of his/her position and has sexual intercourse with any person in that hospital, such sexual intercourse not amounting to the offence of sexual assault, shall be punished with imprisonment of either description for a term which shall not be less than five years and which may extend to ten years and shall also be liable to fine:

Provided that the court may, for adequate and special reasons to be mentioned in the judgment, impose a sentence of imprisonment for a term of less than five years.

Explanation.—The expression "hospital" shall have the same meaning as in Explanation 3 to sub-section (2) of section 376."

(Paras. 3.4 & 3.4.1, *supra*)

7.2.5. Insertion of new section 376E recommended.—A new section, namely, section 376E be inserted in the I.P.C. in the following terms:

"376E. *Unlawful sexual contact.*—(1) Whoever, with sexual intent, touches, directly or indirectly, with a part of the body or with an object, any part of the body of another person, not being the spouse of such person, without the consent of such other person, shall be punished with simple imprisonment for a term which may extend to two years or with fine or with both.

(2) Whoever, with sexual intent, invites, counsels or incites a young person to touch, directly or indirectly, with a part of the body or with an object, the body of any person, including the body of the person who so invites, counsels or incites, or touches, with sexual intent, directly or indirectly, with a part of the body or with an object any part of the body of a young person, shall be punished with imprisonment of either description which may extend to three years and shall also be liable to fine.

(3) Whoever being in a position of trust or authority towards a young person or is a person with whom the young person is in a relationship of dependency, touches, directly or indirectly, with sexual intent, with a part of the body or with an object, any part of the body of such young person, shall be punished with imprisonment of either description which may extend to seven years and shall also be liable to fine.

Explanation.—"Young person" in this sub-section and sub-section (2) means a person below the age of sixteen years."

(Paras. 3.5 & 3.5.1, *supra*)

7.2.6. Deletion of section 377.—Section 377, I.P.C. deserves to be deleted in the light of the changes effected by us in sections 375 to 376E. We leave persons having carnal intercourse with any animal, to their just deserts.

(Para. 3.6, *supra*)

7.2.7. Amendment of section 509, I.P.C.—We recommend that the existing section 509 be amended as follows:

"509. *Word, gesture or act intended to insult the modesty of a woman.*—Whoever, intending to insult the modesty of any woman, utters any word, makes any sound or gesture, or exhibits any object intending that such word or sound shall be heard, or that such gesture or object shall be seen, by such woman, or intrudes upon the privacy of such woman, shall be punished with simple imprisonment for a term which may extend to three years and shall also be liable to fine."

(Para. 3.7, *supra*)

7.2.8. New section 166A, I.P.C. recommended.—We recommend that a new section 166A be introduced in the I.P.C. in the following terms:

"166A. Whoever, being a public servant—

(a) knowingly disobeys any direction of the law prohibiting him from requiring the attendance at any place of any person for the purpose of investigation into an offence or other matter, or

(b) knowingly disobeys any other direction of the law regulating the manner in which he shall conduct such investigation, to the prejudice of any person, shall be punished with imprisonment for a term which may extend to one year or with fine or with both."

(Paras. 3.8 & 3.8.1, *supra*)

7.2.9. No definition of the expression "consent" is called for at this stage.

(Para. 3.9, *supra*)

7.3. Changes recommended in the Code of Criminal Procedure, 1973:

7.3.1. Insertion of sub-sections (3) and (4) in section 160 of the Code of Criminal Procedure, 1973.—We recommend that the following two sub-sections be inserted in section 160 of the Code of Criminal Procedure:

"(3) Where under this chapter, the statement of a female is to be recorded either as first information of an offence or in the course of an investigation into an offence and she is a person against whom an offence under sections 354, 375, 376, 376A, 376B, 376C, 376D, 376E or 509 of the Indian Penal Code is alleged to have been committed or attempted, the statement shall be recorded by a female police officer and in case a female police officer is not available, by a female government servant available in the vicinity and in case a female government servant is also not available, by a female authorised by an organisation interested in the welfare of women or children.

(4) Where in any case none of the alternatives mentioned in sub-section (3) can be followed for the reason that no female police officer or female

government servant or a female authorised by an organisation interested in the welfare of women and children is available, the officer in charge of the police station shall, after recording the reasons in writing, proceed with the recording of the statement of such female victim in the presence of a relative of the victim."

(Paras. 4.2.3 & 4.2.3.1, *supra*)

7.3.2. Modification of the proviso to sub-section (1) of section 160.—We recommend raising the age mentioned in the proviso to sub-section (1) of section 160 from fifteen years to sixteen years.

(Para. 4.3, *supra*)

7.3.3. Substitution of the proviso to sub-section (1) of section 160 recommended.—We recommend that in addition to the above modification, the proviso to sub-section (1) of section 160 be substituted to read as follows:

"Provided that no male person under the age of 16 years or woman shall be required to attend at any place other than the place in which such male person or woman resides. While recording the statement, a relative or a friend or a social worker of the choice of the person whose statement is being recorded shall be allowed to remain present. The relative, friend or social worker so allowed to be present shall not interfere with the recording of statement in any manner whatsoever."

(Paras. 4.3.1 & 4.3.2, *supra*)

7.3.4. Insertion of a new section, namely, section 164A in the Code of Criminal Procedure, 1973.— We recommend that the following section 164A be inserted in the Code of Criminal Procedure:

"164A. (1) Where, during the stage when any offence under section 376, section 376A, section 376B, section 376C, section 376D or section 376E is under investigation and it is proposed to get the victim examined by a medical expert, such examination shall be conducted by a registered medical practitioner, with the consent of the victim or of some person competent to give such consent on his/her behalf. In all cases, the victim should be sent for such examination without any delay:

Provided that if the victim happens to be a female, the medical examination shall be conducted by a female medical officer, as far as possible.

(2) The registered medical practitioner to whom the victim is forwarded shall without delay examine the person and prepare a report specifically recording the result of his examination and giving the following details:

(i) the name and address of the victim and the person by whom he/she was brought,

(ii) the age of the victim,

(iii) marks of injuries, if any, on the person of the victim,

(iv) general mental condition of the victim, and

(v) other material particulars, in reasonable detail.

(3) The report shall state precisely the reasons for each conclusion arrived at.

(4) The report shall specifically record that the consent of the victim or of some person competent to give such consent on his/her behalf to such examination had been obtained.

(5) The exact time of commencement and completion of the examination shall also be noted in the report, and the registered medical practitioner shall without delay, forward the report to the investigating officer, who shall forward it to the Magistrate referred to in section 173 as part of the documents referred to in clause (a) of sub-section (5) of that section.

(6) Nothing in this section shall be construed as rendering lawful any examination without the consent of the victim or any person competent to give such consent on his/her behalf."

(Paras. 4.5.1 and 4.5.2, *supra*)

7.3.5. Insertion of new section 53A in the Code of Criminal Procedure recommended.—The proposed section 53A shall read as follows:

"53A. (1) When a person accused of any of the offences under sections 376, 376A, 376B, 376C, 376D or 376E or of an attempt to commit any of the said offences, is arrested and an examination of his/her person is to be made under this section, he/she shall be sent without delay to the registered medical practitioner by whom he/she is to be examined.

(2) The registered medical practitioner conducting such examination shall without delay examine such person and prepare a report specifically recording the result of his examination and giving the following particulars:

(i) the name and address of the accused and the person by whom he was brought,

(ii) the age of the accused,

(iii) marks of injury, if any, on the person of the accused, and

(iv) other material particulars in reasonable detail.

(3) The report shall state precisely the reasons for each conclusion arrived at.

(4) The exact time of commencement and completion of the examination shall also be noted in the report, and the registered medical practitioner shall, without delay, forward the report to the investigating officer, who shall forward it to the Magistrate referred to in section 173 as part of the documents referred to in clause (a) of sub-section (5) of that section."

(Para. 4.6.2, *supra*)

7.3.6. Consequential amendments in the First Schedule to the Code of Criminal Procedure, 1973 recommended.—Consequent upon the proposed amendments in the I.P.C., the existing entries in respect of sections 376 to 376D, 377 and 509 will have to be substituted and entry in respect of new section 376E, I.P.C. will have to be inserted as under:

376	Sexual assault.	Imprisonment for life or imprisonment for 10 years and fine	Ditto	Non-bailable	Court of Session
	Sexual assault by a man on his own wife being under 16 years of age.	Imprisonment for 3 years and fine	Non-cognizable	Ditto	Ditto
	Sexual assault committed by a person in a position of trust or authority towards the person assaulted or by a near relative of the person assaulted.	Imprisonment for life and fine	Cognizable	Non-bailable	Ditto
	Sexual assault by a police officer or by a public servant or by a person being on the management or on the staff of a jail, remand home or other place of custody or women's or children's institution or by a person on the management or on the staff of a hospital, taking advantage of his official position.	Imprisonment for life and fine	Cognizable	Non-bailable	Ditto
376A	Sexual assault by the husband upon his wife during separation.	Imprisonment for 7 years and fine	Cognizable (but only on the complaint of the victim)	Non-bailable	Ditto
376B	Sexual intercourse by public servant with person in his custody.	Imprisonment for 10 years and fine	Cognizable (but no arrest	Non-bailable	Ditto

			shall be made without a warrant or without an order of a Magistrate)		
376C	Sexual intercourse by Superintendent of jail, remand home etc.	Ditto	Ditto	Ditto	Ditto
376D	Sexual intercourse by any member of the management or staff of a hospital with any woman in that hospital.	Ditto	Ditto	Ditto	Ditto
376E	Unlawful sexual contact.	Imprisonment for 2 years, or fine or both	Non-cognizable	Bailable	Magistrate of the First Class
	Unlawful sexual contact with a young person.	Imprisonment for 3 years	Cognizable if information relating to the commission of the offence is given to an Officer-in-charge of a Police Station by the person aggrieved by the offence or by any person related to her/him by blood, or adoption or if there is no such relative, by any public servant belonging to such class or category as may be notified by the State Government in this behalf	Non-bailable	Ditto

	Unlawful sexual contact by a person in a position of trust or authority towards a young person.	Imprisonment for 7 years and fine	Ditto	Non-bailable	Court of Session
377	Delete	Delete	Delete	Delete	Delete
509	Uttering any word or making any gesture intended to insult the modesty of a woman etc.	Simple imprisonment for 3 years and fine	Cognizable	Non-bailable	Magistrate of the First Class

(Para. 4.7, *supra*)

7.3.7. Amendment of sub-section (6) of section 198 of the Code of Criminal Procedure, 1973.—Consequent upon proposed amendment of section 376 of I.P.C., sub-section (6) of section 198 Cr. PC. shall be amended in the following manner:

> The words "sexual intercourse" shall be substituted by the words "sexual assault" and the word "fifteen" shall be substituted by the word "sixteen".

(Para. 4.8, *supra*)

7.3.8. Insertion of new section 198B of the Code of Criminal Procedure, 1973.—After section 198A of the Code of Criminal Procedure, 1973, the following new section 198B shall be inserted:

> "Prosecution of offences under sub-sections (2) and (3) of section 376E of the Indian Penal Code.
>
> No court shall take cognizance of an offence punishable under sub-sections (2) and (3) of section 376E of the Indian Penal Code (45 of 1860) except upon a police report of facts which constitute such offence or upon a complaint made by the person aggrieved by the offence or by his/her father, mother, brother, sister or by his/her father's or mother's brother or sister or, by any other person related to him/her by blood or adoption, if so permitted by the court."

(Para. 4.9, *supra*)

7.3.9. Amendment of section 273, Code of Criminal Procedure, 1973.—A proviso to the following effect be added under section 273 above the Explanation clause therein:

> "Provided that where the evidence of a person below sixteen years who is alleged to have been subjected to sexual assault or any other sexual offence, is to be recorded, the court may, take appropriate measures to

ensure that such person is not confronted by the accused while at the same time ensuring the right of cross-examination of the accused."

(Para. 6.1, *supra*)

7.4. Changes recommended in the Indian Evidence Act, 1872:

7.4.1. Modification of section 114A of the Evidence Act recommended.—We recommend that section 114A be modified to read as follows:

"*114A. Presumption as to absence of consent in certain prosecutions for sexual assault.*—In a prosecution for sexual assault under (a) or clause (b) or clause (c) or clause (d) or clause (e) or clause (g) of sub-section (2) of section 376 of the Indian Penal Code (45 of 1860) where sexual intercourse by the accused is proved and the question is whether it was without the consent of the other person alleged to have been sexually assaulted and such other person states in his/her evidence before the court that he/she did not consent, the court shall presume that he/she did not consent.

Explanation.—"Sexual intercourse" in this section and sections 376C and 376D shall mean any of the acts mentioned in clauses (a) to (e) of section 375. Explanation to section 375 shall also be applicable."

(Para. 5.1.4, *supra*)

It goes without saying that the aforesaid presumption is a rebuttable presumption of law ("shall presume") within the meaning of section 4 of the Evidence Act.

(Para. 5.1.4.1, *supra*)

7.4.2. Deletion of clause (4) of section 155 of the Evidence Act.—We recommend deletion of clause (4) of section 155 of the Evidence Act.

(Paras. 5.2.2 and 5.2.3, *supra*)

7.4.3. Amendments recommended in proposed section 53A, Evidence Act.—We recommend that after section 53, the following section be inserted:

"53A. In a prosecution for an offence under section 376, 376A, 376B, 376C, 376D or 376E or for attempt to commit any such offence, where the question of consent is in issue, evidence of the character of the victim or of his/her previous sexual experience with any person shall not be relevant on the issue of such consent or the quality of consent."

(Para. 5.3.8.1, *supra*)

7.4.4. Insertion of clause (4) in section 146 of the Evidence Act recommended.—In section 146 of the Evidence Act, the following clause shall be added after clause (3):

"(4) In a prosecution for an offence under section 376, 376A, 376B, 376C, 376D or 376E or for attempt to commit any such offence, where the question of consent is in issue, it shall not be permissible to adduce evidence or to put questions in the cross-examination of the victim as to his/her general immoral character, or as to his/her previous sexual experience with any person for proving such consent or the quality of consent."

(Para. 5.3.8.2, *supra*)

We recommend accordingly and urge the Government to initiate steps to amend all the three Acts, namely, the Indian Penal Code, the Code of Criminal Procedure and the Indian Evidence Act on the lines suggested by us.

Mr. Justice B.P. Jeevan Reddy (Retd.),	*Chairman.*
Ms. Justice Leila Seth (Retd.),	*Members.*
Dr. N.M. Ghatate	
Dr. Subhash C. Jain,	*Member-Secretary.*

Dated: 13th March, 2000.

42nd REPORT, 1971 ON FOCUS ON INDIAN PENAL CODE

SEXUAL OFFENCES

16.113. Section 375—Applicability of section 90 to 'consent' of woman.—The definition of rape in section 375, which refers to the woman's consent in four of its five clauses, raises the question as to how far, if at all, the general exception in section 90 is applicable in relation to the consent "intended" by the second clause of the definition. Concretely, if the consent is given by a woman, who from unsoundness of mind or intoxication, is unable to understand the nature and consequence of the act to which she has in fact submitted, has the man committed rape? If the second paragraph of section 90 is applicable, such consent must be ignored and the man must be regarded as having had sexual intercourse with the woman without her consent. While there are quite a few English cases leading to this conclusion under the common law of England, the question does not appear to have arisen in any Indian case.[1]

The special exceptions in the second and third clauses of section 375 obviously do not cover the same ground as the general exception formulated in the first paragraph of section 90. Under section 375 read by itself, it is only when the woman's consent to the act has been obtained by putting *her* in fear of death or physical hurt, the consent does not count; whereas, under section 90, if she has given her consent under fear of 'injury'—a wider term than physical hurt—to herself or any one else *and* the man knows that the consent was given in consequence of such fear, the consent does not count. In a Nagpur case,[2] the High Court held that, where the woman had consented or submitted to sexual intercourse with the accused who pretended to have a warrant to arrest and take her to Bombay, and, by that deceit, abducted her to a circuit house for the purpose, the consent was not vitiated by its being given in fear of some 'injury' to herself other than bodily hurt. The applicability of section 90 to the charge of rape in those circumstances was neither raised nor considered in the judgment.

Similarly, under the fourth clause of section 375, only one misconception of fact, *viz.*, the induced belief that the man is her husband, vitiates the consent of the woman; whereas, under section 90, any misconception of fact vitiates, provided the man knows or has reason to believe that the consent was given in consequence of such misconception. Here again, we have no Indian decisions on the applicability or otherwise of the general exceptions to a charge of rape when the particular exception in the fourth clause of section 375 is not applicable.

The third paragraph of section 90 raises no such problem. The minimum age of 'consent' for the offence of rape being specified as 16 in the fifth clause, the 12 year age limit in the general exception does not apply.

---

1. V.B. Raju cites *Bhonri*, 1953 RLW 254, for the view that "sexual intercourse with a woman under the influence of drink cannot be said to be with consent. (Raju *Commentaries on the Indian Penal Code*, 3rd Edn., Vol. II, p. 1321). A full report of the decision was not available.
2. *Motiram* v. *State*, AIR 1955 Nag 121.

It seems possible to take the view that the third and fourth clauses of section 375 relating to fear of hurt and misconception are special provisions and hence exclude the application of the corresponding general provision in the first paragraph of section 90; but the general exception in the second para is *not* excluded by any thing specified in section 375. We do not, however, consider it necessary to clarify this point by an amendment of that section since no difficulty has been felt in practice.

16.114. Consent obtained by threatening death or hurt to another person present on the spot.—Under the third clause of section 375, the consent of the woman is vitiated only when she has been put in fear of death or body hurt to herself. The clause does not extend to a case where death or grievous hurt is threatened to some one else present on the spot, *e.g.*, the woman's child, parent or husband, and she is thereby compelled to submit to sexual intercourse. Though such cases would be very rare there is no reason in principle why such consent should not be held to be vitiated.

We notice that the definition of rape proposed in the American Draft Penal Code includes the case where the man "compels (the woman) to submit by force or threat of imminent death, serious bodily injury, extreme pain or kidnapping, *to be inflicted on any one.*"[1] We propose to amplify the third clause to cover the cases envisaged above.

16.115. Exception—"rape" by husband.—The exception in section 375 provides that sexual intercourse by a man with his own wife, the wife not being under fifteen years of age, is not rape. The punishment for statutory rape by the husband is the same when the wife is under twelve years of age, but when she is between 12 and 15 years of age, the punishment is mild, being imprisonment upto two years, or fine, or both. Naturally, the prosecutions for this offence are very rare. We think it would be desirable to take this offence altogether out of the ambit of section 375 and not to call[2] it rape even in a technical sense. The punishment for the offence also may be provided in a separate section.

Under the exception, a husband cannot be guilty of raping his wife, if she is above 15 years of age. This exception fails to take note of one special situation, namely, when the husband and wife are living apart under a decree of judicial separation or by mutual agreement. In such a case, the marriage technically subsists, and if the husband has sexual intercourse with her against her will or without her consent, he cannot be charged with the offence of rape. This does not appear to be right. We consider that, in such circumstances, sexual intercourse by a man with his wife without her consent should be punishable as rape.

16.116. Sexual intercourse with consenting minor girl to be a separate offence.—Under the fifth clause of section 375, it is rape for a man to have sexual intercourse with a girl, not being his wife, who is over twelve years but under sixteen years of age, even when she has consented. We are of the opinion that this offence need not be equated to, and punishable as severely as, rape. It sometimes happens in such cases that the man has been led to believe, and in

1. Section 213.1, clause (1)(a), Model Penal Code.
2. The marginal heading of section 198A, Criminal Procedure Code, refers to the offence as 'marital misbehaviour'.

good faith believes, that the girl is over sixteen. A *bona fide* mistake as to age should be a defence to a charge of rape of this type. We propose, therefore, to deal with this offence in a separate section.

16.117. Section 375—revision recommended.—In the light of the above discussion, section 375 may be revised as follows:—

"375. *Rape.*—A man is said to commit rape who has sexual intercourse with a woman, other than his wife,—

(a) against her will; or

(b) without her consent; or

(c) with her consent when it has been obtained by putting her in fear of death or of hurt, either to herself or to anyone else present at the place; or

(d) with her consent, knowing that it is given in the belief that he is her husband.

Explanation I.—Penetration is sufficient to constitute the sexual intercourse necessary to the offence of rape.

Explanation II.—A woman living separately from her husband under a decree of judicial separation or by mutual agreement shall be deemed not to be his wife for the purpose of this section."

16.118. Section 376 to be amended.—In view of the proposed changes in the definition of rape, the latter part of section 376 has to be omitted. Further, in place of the punishment now provided in the section, *viz.*, imprisonment for life or imprisonment of either description for ten years, we propose to substitute rigorous imprisonment for fourteen years. We considered the question whether a minimum sentence of say, three years imprisonment, should be provided for this offence, but decided against it. Adequate punishments are imposed by Sessions Courts by which this offence is ordinarily triable. The section will accordingly read as follows:

"376. *Punishment for rape.*—Whoever commits rape shall be punished with rigorous imprisonment for a term which may extend to fourteen years, and shall also be liable to fine."

16.119. Prohibition of intercourse by husband with child wife.—The separate section penalising sexual intercourse by a man with his child wife may run as follows:—

"376A. *Sexual intercourse with child wife.*—Whoever has sexual intercourse with his wife, the wife being under fifteen years of age, shall be punished—

(a) if she is under twelve years of age with rigorous imprisonment for a term which may extend to seven years, and shall also be liable to fine; and

(b) in any other case, with imprisonment of either description for a term which may extend to two years or with fine, or with both.

16.120. Illicit intercourse with a girl under sixteen.—The provision against illicit intercourse by a man with a girl under sixteen years of age, with her consent, may be as follows:—

"376B. *Illicit intercourse with a girl between twelve and sixteen.*—Whoever has illicit intercourse with a girl under sixteen years, but not under twelve years of age, with her consent, shall be punished with imprisonment of either description for a term which may extend to seven years, and shall also be liable to fine.

It shall be a defence to a charge under this section for the accused to prove that he, in good faith, believed the girl to be above sixteen years of age."

16.121. Compelling or seducing a boy to illicit intercourse.—It was suggested that a mature woman, who compels or seduces a boy under sixteen years of age to sexual intercourse, should be just as severely punishable as a man in the converse case. Apart from the physiological fact that forcing a boy, in the strict sense, to perform the act is impossible, complaints of either forcing or seducing minor boys to such illicit intercourse are unheard of. Such lascivious acts on the part of the woman are socially not so evil as to merit a penal provision.

16.122. Knowingly infecting another with venereal disease.—We considered the need for a new section punishing a person who knowingly exposes another to infection of venereal disease by sexual intercourse. We are of the view that such an act need not be made an offence. It may be that if the act causes the disease, then it might amount to causing hurt which, as defined in section 319, perhaps includes disease; this is, however, doubtful, the notion of hurt and the notion of disease being basically different from each other. If at all such an act is to be made an offence, then it has to be by means of a specific provision, but it is fairly obvious that any such provision is unlikely to be enforced in practice. It is, therefore, not recommended.

16.123. Compelling a woman to illicit intercourse in certain special situations.—There are certain situations in which, although force or fraud cannot be established, the compulsion of the situation is such that the woman's will is dominated by the will of the man, and taking an undue advantage of the situation, the man takes liberties with the woman. The woman's submission to sexual intercourse in such a situation is really not a willing consent, and we think that provisions punishing this reprehensible conduct on the part of the man should be included in the Penal Code. We do not, however, wish to make the provisions very wide because they may furnish a weapon for blackmail in the hands of unscrupulous women or their relations. We would confine it to those situations where the need for throwing a cloak around the woman for protecting her chastity outweighs the opportunity for blackmail. On this principle, we recommend the insertion of three new sections as follows:—

"376C. *Illicit intercourse of public servant with woman in his custody.*—Whoever, being a public servant, compels or seduces to illicit intercourse any woman who is in his custody as such public servant shall be punished with imprisonment of either description for a term which may extend to two years, or with fine, or with both.

376D. *Illicit intercourse of superintendent etc. with inmate of women's or children's institution.*—Whoever, being the superintendent or manager of a woman's or children's institution or holding any other office in such institution by virtue of which he can exercise any authority or control over its inmates, compels or seduces to illicit sexual intercourse any female inmate of the institution shall be punished with imprisonment of either description for a term which may extend to two years, or with fine, or with both.

Explanation.—In this section, "women's or children's institution" means an institution, whether called an orphanage, home for neglected women or children, widow's home or by any other name, which is established and maintained for the reception and care of women or children,[1] but does not include—

(a) any hostel or boarding house attached to, or controlled or recognised by, an educational institution,[2] or

(b) any reformatory, certified or other school, or any home or workhouse, governed by any enactment for the time being in force.[3]

376E. *Illicit intercourse of manager etc. of a hospital with mentally disordered patient.*—Whoever, being concerned with the management of a hospital or being on the staff of a hospital, has illicit sexual intercourse with a woman who is receiving treatment for a mental disorder in that hospital, shall be punished with imprisonment of either description for a term which may extend to two years, or with fine, or with both.

Explanation.—It shall be a defence to a charge under this section for the accused to prove that he did not know, and had no reason to believe, that the woman was a mentally disordered patient."

16.124. Section 377—questions put.—Section 377, which is the last section in this Chapter, deals with unnatural offences, including buggery and bestiality, and provides for these a punishment as severe as that provided for rape in section 376. In order to elicit informed public opinion on the subject, we had included in our Questionnaire the following two questions:—

(a) Should unnatural offences be punishable at all, or with heavy sentences as provided in section 377?

(b) Should exception be made for cases where the offence consists of acts done in private between consenting adults?

The replies received by us are conflicting, but a larger number of those who have cared to express an opinion are in favour of retaining the section more or less as it stands. Some were of the view that homo-sexual acts done in private between consenting adults need not be treated as offences, but other thought that such acts are "abominable and loathsome which tend to make men and women depraved" and should be punishable in all circumstances. There was, however, a general feeling that the punishment provided in section 377 is unduly harsh and quite unrealistic. No court is likely to sentence a man to imprisonment for life for committing such acts.

1. *Cf.* section 2, Women's and Children's Institutions (Licensing) Act, 1956.
2. *Cf.* section 10, Women's and Children's Institutions (Licensing) Act, 1956.
3. *Cf.* section 21, Suppression of Immoral Traffic in Women and Girls Act, 1956.

16.125. Arguments against punishing homo-sexual acts.—The question has in recent times received much attention in the West. The Wolfenden Committee in England set out the main arguments against punishing homo-sexual acts, *viz.*, that the act harms no body, that it falls within a sphere of private immorality which is not the law's business and that it could be tackled by other measures. Referring to the punishment of imprisonment usually awarded for the offence, one American psychiatrist has pertinently observed that "segregating a male homo-sexual for months or years in a prison, where he will see only other men and where he will often be isolated with a group of other homo-sexual, can hardly result in anything but reinforcement of the homo-sexual tendencies."[1]

16.126. Arguments for retaining present law.—There are, however, a few sound reasons for retaining the existing law in India. First, it cannot be disputed that homo sexual acts and tendencies on the part of one spouse may affect the married life and happiness of the other spouse, and from this point of view, making the acts punishable by law has a social justification. Secondly, even assuming that acts done in private with consent do not in themselves constitute a serious evil, there is a risk involved in repealing legislation which has been in force for a long time. The position might be different if we were merely refraining from legislating about a type of private conduct whose suitability for punishment is in dispute, but we are not legislating on a blank slate. Ultimately, the answer to the question whether homo-sexual acts ought to be punished depends on the view one takes of the relationship of criminal law to morals. The debate on the subject, sparked off by the Report of the Wolfenden Committee, has not yet come to an end. There will always be two views on the question how far it is the business of criminal law to enforce notions of private morality. If one shares the reasoning of the Committee, namely, that there *is* a sphere of private morality in which criminal law has no business, then the answer is clear, but it is well known that there are distinguished thinkers who take a different view, emphasising the need for preserving the society's cherished beliefs.

It appears to us that, in this highly controversial field, the only safe guide is what would be acceptable to the community. We are inclined to think that Indian society, by and large, disapproves of homo-sexuality and this disapproval is strong enough to justify it being treated as a criminal offence even where adults indulge in it in private.

16.127. Amendments recommended.—We think, however, that cases of bestiality should be regarded as pathological manifestations ignored by the criminal law. Buggery may continue to be an offence, punishable much less severely than at present, but where it is committed by an adult on a minor boy or girl, the punishment should be higher.

We propose that section 377 may be revised as follows:—

> "377. *Buggery.*—Whoever voluntarily has carnal intercourse against the order of nature with any man or woman shall be punished with

---

1. Prof. Karl M. Bowman *Review of Sex Legislation and Control of Sex Offenders in the U.S.A.*, cited in Donnelly Criminal Law, (1962), p. 163.

imprisonment of either description for a term which may extend to two years, or with fine, or with both;

and where such offence is committed by a person over eighteen years of age with a person under that age, the imprisonment may extend to seven years."

"*Explanation.*—Penetration is sufficient to constitute the carnal intercourse necessary to the offence described in this section."

156th REPORT, 1997 ON REVIEW OF INDIAN PENAL CODE

CHAPTER IX

OFFENCES AGAINST WOMEN AND CHILDREN

I. Rape

9.01. The Law Commission in its Eighty-fourth Report *on Rape and Allied offences: Some Questions of Substantive Law, Procedure and Evidence* has defined rape as "the ultimate violation of the self. It is a humiliating event in a woman's life which leads to fear for existence and a sense of powerlessness".[1] Other scholars have described rape as an internal assault or sexual invasion which is characterised by violent taking away of control over the sexual autonomy of the woman. Rape is an act of violence affecting the physical and emotional integrity and dignity of the victim.[2]

9.02. The Law Commission in its Forty-second Report had recommended certain changes in section 375 which deals with the offence of rape. The following were the changes recommended by the Commission to section 375.

Clause 'Thirdly' of section 375 defines sexual intercourse as rape with the woman's consent when it has been obtained by putting her in fear of death or of hurt. The Commission had recommended that the words "either to herself or to anyone else present at the place" be added after the word "hurt".

On the question of consent, the Commission had pointed out that section 90 of I.P.C. includes the term "injury" which is of wider import. Injury includes any injury to mind, body, reputation or property. The Commission, however, did not recommend any amendment on this count.

9.03. The Commission also recommended that marital rape should be removed from the scope of section 375 and placed as a separate offence. The Commission observed:[3]

> "The exception in section 375 provides that sexual intercourse by a man with his own wife, the wife not being under 15 years of age is not rape. The punishment for statutory rape by the husband is the same when the wife is under 12 years of age but when she is between 12 and 15 years of age the punishment is mild, being imprisonment upto two years, or fine or both. Naturally, the prosecutions for this offence are very rare. We think, it would be desirable to take this offence altogether out of the ambit of section

1. Law Commission, Eighty-fourth Report, para. 1.2 (1980).
2. *See* Susan Brownmiller *Against Our Will: Men, Women and Rape,* (1990); Lotika Sarkar *Rape: A Human Rights versus a Patriarchal Interpretation,* (I) Indian Journal of Gender Studies 69 (1994); Flavia Agnes *Protecting Women against Violences,* 27 Economic and Political Weekly (EPW) 19 (1992); also by the same author *State Gender and the Rhetoric of Law Reform* (1995), Lorenne Clark and Debra Lewis *Rape – The Price of Coercive Sexuality* (1977).
3. Law Commission, Forty-second Report, para. 16.115.

375 and not to call it rape even in a technical sense. The punishment for the offence also may be provided in a separate section."

9.04. The Commission considered the position of legally separated wife *vis-a-vis* the offence of rape. It was observed:

"Under the exception, a husband cannot be guilty of raping his wife if she is above fifteen years of age. This exception is to take note of one special situation, namely when the husband and wife are living apart under a decree of judicial separation or by mutual agreement. In such a case, the marriage technically subsists and if the husband has sexual intercourse with her against her will or without her consent, he cannot be charged with the offence of rape. This does not appear to be right. We consider that, in such circumstances, sexual intercourse by a man with his wife without her consent will be punishable as rape."[1]

9.05. *Explanation II* as recommended by the Commission is as follows:

"A woman living separately from her husband under a decree of judicial separation or by mutual consent shall be deemed not to be his wife for the purpose of this section."

9.06. The Forty-second Report had recommended amendment in section 375 on the following lines:

"*375. Rape.*—A man is said to commit rape who has sexual intercourse with a woman other than his wife—

(a) against her will; or

(b) without her consent; or

(c) with her consent when it has been obtained by putting her in fear of death or of hurt, either to herself or to anyone else present at the place; or

(d) with her consent, knowing that it is given in the belief that he is the husband.

Explanation I.—Penetration is sufficient to constitute the sexual intercourse necessary to the offence of rape.

Explanation II.—A woman living separately from her husband under a decree of judicial separation or by mutual agreement shall be deemed not to be his wife for the purpose of this section."[2]

9.07. The existing section 375 stipulated a maximum sentence of life or imprisonment of either description for 10 years for rape. The Commission suggested that it should be rigorous imprisonment for a term upto 14 years.

9.08. The Commission recommended the incorporation of sections 376A and 376B. Section 376A distinguished sexual intercourse between a wife of 12 to 15 years of age and a wife of less than 12 years of age, sexual intercourse with the wife over 15 years of age without her consent not being an offence. The Commission recommended rigorous imprisonment upto 7 years if the wife was under 12 years and in any other case, imprisonment upto 2 years of either description.

---

1. Law Commission, Forty-second Report, para. 16.115.
2. *Ibid.*, para. 16.117.

9.09. Section 376B made illicit intercourse with a girl under 16 years but not under 12 years of age even with her consent punishable with imprisonment of either description upto 7 years.

9.10. The Commission added that it shall be a defence to a charge under this section for the accused to prove that he, in good faith, believed the girl to be above sixteen years of age.[1]

9.11. The Forty-second Report's signal contribution to the reform of rape laws was the introduction of the concept of custodial rape. The Commission recommended the addition of sections 376C, 376D and 376E dealing with custodial rape by a public servant or by a superintendent etc. of a women's or children's institution, and by a manager of a hospital with a woman patient suffering from mental disorder respectively.

9.12. The provisions on rape law remained unamended, as the Indian Penal Code Amendment Bill could not be passed due to the dissolution of the Lok Sabha in 1979.

9.13. In the interregnum the Supreme Court of India decided some cases which took a restricted view of the scope of the offence of rape and acquitted the accused. The relevant decisions are *Pratap Misra* v. *State of Orissa*[2] and *Tuka Ram* v. *State of Maharashtra*.[3] The latter case popularly known as the *Mathura Rape* case involved the rape of a young girl aged between 14-16 years of age by two police constable in the police station. The Bombay High Court reversed the order of acquittal of the accused by the Session Court and sentenced them to rigorous imprisonment of varying terms. The High Court came to the conclusion that the policemen had "taken advantage of the fact that Mathura was involved in a complaint filed by her brother, and she was alone in the dead hour of the night" in a police station. This proved that she could not, in any probability, have consented to intercourse. The Supreme Court after assessing the evidence on record concluded that the circumstantial evidence was such that it did not lead to "reasonable evidence of guilt" and reversed the Bombay High Court decision and acquitted the accused. This led to four law teachers writing an Open Letter to the Chief Justice of India criticising the judgment. The Open Letter generated nationwide protests from women's organisations and different sections of the Indian society.[4] Their collective demand was for reform of the law on rape. The Union Government responded to the public campaign and referred the matter of reforming rape laws to the Law Commission.

9.14. The Law Commission sent its 84th Report on "Rape and Allied Offences; Some Questions of Substantive Law, procedure and Evidence" to the Government in 1980.

9.15. The Commission gave particular attention to the definition of consent and to rape of girls below the minimum age. It also took into account some of the

1. Law Commission, Forty-second Report, paras. 16.115, 16.120.
2. AIR 1977 SC 1307.
3. AIR 1979 SC 185.
4. *See* Vasudha Dhagamwar *Law, Power and Justice*, 237-287 (2nd Edn., 1992).

recommendations incorporated in the Forty-second Report. The Commission had dispensed with the suggestions in the earlier Report which had characterized rape as—

1. rape proper;
2. rape with child-wife; and
3. rape *i.e.* sexual intercourse with the girl between 12-16 years of age, with her consent.

The reasons given by the Commission for discarding the above categorisation were:[1]

> "....the Commission now feels that such a restructuring would be out of tune with the current thinking on the question of trial of offenders for rape and, therefore, structure of section 375 should not be altered. Since the making of the recommendation by the Commission in its earlier Report, there has been a radical and revolutionary change in the approach to the offence of rape; its enormity is frequently brought into prominence and heightened by the revolting and gruesome circumstances in which the crime is committed; the case law has blurred the essential ingredients of the offence and introduced instability into the previously well established law bearing on the offence of rape. The Commission feels that restructuring will produce uncertainty and distortion in section 375, which should in its opinion, retain its present logical and coherent structure."

Consequently, the Commission recommended the omission of section 375A and section 375B. Instead, the Commission recommended leaving rape of child-wife (section 375A) in the general section 375 instead of placing it in a separate section. Section 375B which dealt with rape on a girl between 12-16 years of age with her consent was omitted altogether. Further, the Commission retained sections 376C, 376D and 376E which dealt with custodial rape; but renumbered them as sections 376A, 376B and 376C.

9.16. On the question of consent, the Commission observed that they would not only include the suggestions made in the earlier Report but suggested further amendments which would strengthen the concept of "free consent" for the purposes of section 375. The Commission felt that the term "consent" was inadequate and should be substituted by the phrase "free and voluntary consent". The Commission observed:[2]

> "The substitution of the expression "free and voluntary consent" for the word "consent" in the second clause makes it clear that the consent should be active consent as distinguished from that consent which is said to be implied by silence."

The Commission proceeded to say:

> "Under the amendment as recommended, it would not be open to the Court to draw an inference of consent on the part of the woman from her silence

1. Law Commission, Eighty-fourth Report, para. 1.2 (1980), para. 2.21.
2. *Ibid.*, para 2.8.

due to timidity or meekness or from such circumstances without any more – as that the girl meekly followed the offender when he pulled her, catching hold of her hand, or that the woman kept silent and did not shout or protest or cry out for help."

The Commission further stated:[1]

"The modifications recommended by us in the third clause vitiated consent not only when a woman is put in fear of death or hurt, but also when she is put in fear of any "injury" being caused to any person (including herself) in body, mind, reputation or property and also when her consent is obtained by criminal intimidation, that is to say by any words or acts intended or calculated to put her in fear of any injury or danger to herself or to any person in whom she is interested or when she is threatened with any injury to her reputation or property or to a reputation of any one in whom she is interested. Thus, if the consent is obtained after giving the woman a threat of spreading false and scandalous rumours about her character or destruction of her property or injury to her children or parents or by holding out other threats of injury to her person, reputation or property, that consent will also not be consent under the third clause as recommended to be amended."

9.17. The Commission made significant recommendations on age of consent. The age of consent as applicable to the offence under section 375 has been amended several times since the framing of I.P.C.. The 84th Report has graphically presented in the form of a chart which is given below:[2]

CHART

Year	Age of consent under section 375, 5th clause, I.P.C.	Age mentioned in the Exception to section 375, I.P.C.	Minimum age of marriage under the Child Marriage Restraint Act, 1929
1860	10 yrs.	10 yrs.	—
1891 (Act 10 of 1891) (after the amendment of I.P.C.)	12 yrs	12 yrs.	—
1925 (after the amendment of I.P.C.)	14 yrs.	13 yrs.	—
1929 (after the passing of the Child Marriage Act)	14 yrs.	13 yrs.	14 yrs.

1. Law Commission, Eighty-fourth Report, (1980), paras. 2.9, 2.21.
2. *Ibid.*, para 2.19.

1	2	3	4
1940 (after the amendment of the Penal Code and the Child Marriage Act)	16 yrs.	15 yrs.	15 yrs.
1978	16 yrs.	15 yrs.	18 yrs.

9.18. As may be seen from the chart, the minimum age of marriage for girls has been increased to 18 years after the amendment of the Child Marriage Restraint Act, 1929 in 1978. The Commission recommended that "since marriage with a girl below eighteen years is prohibited ... sexual intercourse with a girl below eighteen years should also be prohibited".

9.19. The 84th Report did not recommend any changes in section 376 which provides punishment for the offence of rape. The Commission was of the view that judicial discretion be not fettered by prescribing a minimum sentence.

9.20. The 84th report by introducing a broader concept of "misconception of fact" has eliminated any examination of morality or the sexual antecedents of the victim of rape. Section 375, fourthly allows this under a broader misconception of fact which includes the narrower mistake of identity.

9.21. Consequent on the recommendations of the Law Commission in its 84th Report, the Government introduced in the Lok Sabha the Criminal Law (Amendment) Bill, 1980 to amend, *inter alia*, the Indian Penal Code. The Government accepted the following recommendations of the Law Commission:

1. accepting the concept of consent as free and voluntary consent;
2. making a distinction between judicially separated wife and wife; and
3. accepting the three concepts of custodial rape as recommended in the Commission's 42nd Report.

9.22. The Bill made a significant addition by introducing the separate offence of gang rape by two or more persons.

9.23. The Bill was sent to the Joint Committee of the Parliament. The changes made by the Committee were:

1. It reduced the age of marital rape. The exception to section 375 stated that sexual intercourse by a man with his own wife, the wife not being under 15 years of age, is not rape. The Committee reduced this age to 12 years.
2. A new section, section 376A was incorporated, which deals with sexual intercourse with judicially separated wife without her consent. The Committee provided a lower punishment for rape of a judicially separated wife.
3. The Committee did not accept the expanded concept of free and voluntary consent in section 375.

9.24. In the Draft Bill reported by the Joint Committee, one change was made in its final reading stage. The age above which sexual intercourse with the wife is not rape was retained at 15.

9.25. The Parliament enacted the Criminal Law (Amendment) Act, 1983. The chief features of which, so far as the offence of rape in I.P.C. was concerned, were:

1. increase in the punishment of rape;
2. distinction between gang rape and custodial rape and stiffer penalties for the same;
3. separate category of rape on pregnant woman;
4. distinguishing rape on a judicially separated wife and provision for a lower punishment for it than in other instances of rape;
5. reduction in the punishment of rape on wife between 12 and 15 years of age;
6. distinguishing rape on woman of unsoundmind or one who is intoxicated.

9.26. Accordingly sections 375 and 376 were amended and new sections 376A, 376B and 376C were inserted. All the important recommendations of the Law Commission have been incorporated.

The provisions read as follows:

"*375. Rape.*—A man is said to commit "rape" who, except in the case hereinafter excepted, has sexual intercourse with a woman under circumstances falling under any of the six following descriptions:—

First.—Against her will.

Secondly.—Without her consent.

Thirdly:—With her consent, when her consent has been obtained by putting her or any person in whom she is interested in fear of death or of hurt.

Fourthly.—With her consent, when the man knows that he is not her husband, and that her consent is given because she believes that he is another man to whom she is or believes herself to be lawfully married.

Fifthly.—With her consent, when at the time of giving such consent, by reason of unsoundness of mind or intoxication or the administration by him personally or through another of any stupefying or unwholesome substance she is unable to understand the nature and consequences of that to which she gives consent.

Sixthly.—With or without her consent, when she is under sixteen years of age.

Explanation.—Penetration is sufficient to constitute the sexual intercourse necessary to the offence of rape.

Exception.—Sexual intercourse by a man with his own wife, the wife not being under fifteen years of age, is not rape."

"376. *Punishment for rape.*—(1) Whoever, except in the cases provided for by sub-section (2), commits rape shall be punished with imprisonment of either description for a term which shall not be less than seven years but which may be for life or for a term which may extend to ten years and shall also be liable to fine unless the woman raped is his own wife and is not under twelve years of age, in which case, he shall be punished with imprisonment of either description for a term which may extend to two years or with fine or with both:

Provided that the court may, for adequate and special reasons to be mentioned in the judgment, impose a sentence of imprisonment for a term of less than seven years.

(2) Whoever,—

- (a) being a police officer commits rape—
  - (i) within the limits of the police station to which he is appointed; or
  - (ii) in the premises of any station house whether or not situated in the police station to which he is appointed; or
  - (iii) on a woman in his custody or in the custody of a police officer subordinate to him; or
- (b) being a public servant, takes advantage of his official position and commits rape on a woman in his custody as such public servant or in the custody of a public servant subordinate to him; or
- (c) being on the management or on the staff of a jail, remand home or other place of custody established by or under any law for the time being in force or of a women's or children's institution takes advantage of his official position and commits rape on any inmate of such jail, remand home, place or institution; or
- (d) being on the management or on the staff of a hospital, takes advantage of his official position and commits rape on a woman in the hospital; or
- (e) commits rape on a woman knowing her to be pregnant; or
- (f) commits rape on a woman when she is under twelve years of age; or
- (g) commits gang-rape,

shall be punished with rigorous imprisonment for a term which shall not be leas than ten years but which may be for life and shall also be liable to fine:

Provided that the court may, for adequate and special reasons to be mentioned in the judgment, impose a sentence of imprisonment of either description for a term of less than ten years.

Explanation 1.—Where a woman is raped by one or more in a group of persons acting in furtherance of their common intention, each of the persons shall be deemed to have committed gang-rape within the meaning of this sub-section.

Explanation 2.—"Women's or children's institution" means an institution, whether called an orphanage or a home for neglected women or children or a widows' home or by any other name, which is established and maintained for the reception and care of women or children.

Explanation 3.—"Hospital" means the precincts of the hospital and includes the precincts of any institution for the reception and treatment of persons during convalescence or of persons requiring medical attention or rehabilitation."

"*376A. Intercourse by a man with his wife during separation.*—Whoever has sexual intercourse with his own wife, who is living separately from him under a decree of separation or under any custom or usage without her consent shall be punished with imprisonment of either description for a term which may extend to two years and shall also be liable to fine."

"*376B. Intercourse by public servant with woman in his custody.*—Whoever, being a public servant, takes advantage of his official position and induces or seduces, any woman, who is in his custody as such public servant or in the custody of a public servant subordinate to him, to have sexual intercourse with him, such sexual intercourse not amounting to the offence of rape, shall be punished with imprisonment of either description for a term which may extend to five years and shall also be liable to fine."

"*376C. Intercourse by Superintendent of jail, remand home, etc.*—Whoever, being the Superintendent or Manager of a jail, remand home or other place of custody established by or under any law for the time being in force or of a women's or children's institution takes advantage of his official position and induces or seduces any female inmate of such jail, remand home, place or institution to have sexual intercourse with him, such sexual intercourse not amounting to the offence of rape, shall be punished with imprisonment of either description for a term which may extend to five years and shall also be liable to fine.

Explanation 1.—"Superintendent" in relation to a jail, remand home or other place of custody or a women's or children's institution includes a person holding any other office in such jail, remand home, place or institution by virtue of which he can exercise any authority or control over its inmates.

Explanation 2.—The expression "women's or children's institution" shall have the same meaning as in Explanation 2 to sub-section (2) of section 376."

"376D. *Intercourse by any member of the management or staff of a hospital with any woman in that hospital.*—Whoever, being on the management of a hospital or being on the staff of a hospital takes advantage of his position and has sexual intercourse with any woman in that hospital, such sexual intercourse not amounting to the offence of rape, shall be punished with imprisonment of either description for a term which may extend to five years and shall also be liable to fine.

Explanation.—The expression 'hospital' shall have the same meaning as in Explanation 3 to sub-section (2) of section 376."

9.27. Now we shall examine the recommendations of the National Commission for Women (NCW) and other suggestions made in response to the Questionnaire. Following are the recommendations of the National Commission for Women:

1. Section 375 be amended to change the reference to 16 years in paragraph, sixthly, to 18 years to provide for the increase in the age of majority of girls to 18 years.
2. Also a consequential amendment to change the reference to 15 years to 18 years, has also been made in the Exception which deals with "sexual intercourse by a man with his own wife not being under 15 years of age".
3. Section 376 providing for punishment of rape be amended thus:
   (a) The reference of sentence of punishment to 2 years for rape by the husband with his own wife who is more than 12 years of age is proposed to be increased to 5 years [section 376 sub-clause (1)].
   (b) The punishment provided in sub-section (2) is proposed to be increased from a minimum punishment of 10 years to punishment of rigorous imprisonment for life. At the same time, the punishment for rape when a woman who is less than 12 years, of age is proposed to be taken out of this section and dealt with in a separate section providing for higher punishment. This is sought to be done by incorporating a new section, namely sub-section (3) to section 376 which would read as:

      Whoever commits rape on a woman when she is under twelve years of age shall be punished with rigorous imprisonment for a term which shall not be less than ten years and shall also be liable to fine.

It is also recommended that three new sections, section 376E, section 376F and section 376G be incorporated in the Indian Penal Code.

> "*Section 376E: Offence under section 378A to section 376D against children.*—Whoever commits an offence under section 378A to section 376D (both inclusive) shall, if the woman is under eighteen years of age, be punished with imprisonment of either description for a term which may extend to ten years and shall also be liable to fine.
>
> *Section 376F: Offence of eve-teasing.*—Whoever intending to annoy any woman utters any word or makes any sound or gesture or exhibits any object or does any other act in any public place intending that such word or sound shall be heard or that such gesture or object shall be seen or that such act shall be noticed or felt by such woman, commits the offence of eve-teasing.
>
> *Section 376G: Punishment for eve-teasing.*—Whoever commits the offence of eve-teasing shall be punished with imprisonment of either description for a term which may extend to 5 years and shall also be liable to fine."

9.28. According to the latest report of the National Crime Records Bureau entitled *Crime in India*, 98,948 cases of crime against women were registered in

1994 compared to 83,954 cases in 1993 and 79,037 cases in 1992. This amounts to an increase of 17.9 per cent. in crime against women at the national level in 1994 with considerable increase in cases registered under rape, kidnapping and abduction. The Report points out that Delhi, Rajasthan, Tamil Nadu, Madhya Pradesh, Himachal Pradesh, Karnataka and Pondicherry have been categorised as "high crime prone" States. In 1994 Madhya Pradesh reported the highest incidence of rape (2,929) accounting for 22.2 per cent. of the national ratio. This was followed by Uttar Pradesh (2,078), Maharashtra (1,304), Bihar (1,130), Rajasthan (1,002). Other States which recorded more than 500 cases of rape during the year were Andhra Pradesh, West Bengal and Assam. Delhi reported 309 incidents contributing 2.3 per cent. towards national average.

Among the cities, Delhi and Mumbai continued to record more cases of rape. At the national level, victims of rape were the highest in the age group of 16-30 years accounting for 56.3 per cent. of the total victims. But in the metropolitan cities, the situation was altogether different as 50 per cent. of the total victims were girls below 16 years of age.[1]

The Delhi State Commission for Women in its Report *Situation of Girls and Women in Delhi* (1997) has pointed that the "rate of rape" in Delhi is twice as high as in the whole country. During 1993 as many as 233 rape cases were reported which rose to 321 in 1994, to 362 in 1995 and to 470 in 1996. An analysis of 1996 crime data showed that in 88 per cent. of the rape cases relatives and acquaintances were involved and in 89 per cent. of the cases the crime was committed at home. The Report also points out that 60 per cent. of the reported cases in Delhi are of girls below 18 years. Further in 1913 as many as 18 per cent. of rape victims were below 10 years of age as against 5 per cent. in the whole country. About 42 per cent. of the rape victims were in the 10 to 16 age groups compared to 23 per cent. in the country.[2]

9.29. The UN Commission on the Status of Women in its Draft Declaration of Violence Against Women declares that "violence nullifies women's enjoyment of human rights of freedom". The Convention for the Elimination of All Forms of Discrimination Against Women (CEDAW 1979), ratified by India recently, also does not speak of gender-based violence. It is generally agreed that violence against women is an infringement of their fundamental rights to life, liberty and dignity

9.30. There is a school of thought that the existing definition of rape in I.P.C. is narrow and does not cover different forms of sexual violence experienced by women.[3] The present definition requires proof of penetration by penis and lack of consent by the complainant. Consent plays a crucial part in a rape trial.

1. See *Upsurge in Crime against Women,* Report, Hindu (Delhi Ed.), 9-12-1996.
2. See *Delhi's Shame: Women Most unsafe,* incorporating an analysis of the Report of the Delhi State Commission for Women, Hindustan Times (Delhi Ed.), 5-2-1997.
3. *See* provisions of the Sexual Assault Draft Bill, 1993 prepared by the *Ad hoc* Committee of the National Commission for Women; also see the Memorandum on Reform of Laws relating to Sexual Offences prepared by Shomona Khanna and Ratna Kapur, Centre for Feminist Legal Research, New Delhi.

9.31. Further, section 354 (assault or criminal force on a woman with intent to outrage her modesty) and section 509 (word, gesture or act intended to insult the modesty of a woman) as interpreted by the courts do not cover virulent forms of sexual assault on women.

9.32. The proponents of this view advocate that the sections of I.P.C. dealing with rape (sections 375 and 376) and sections 354 and 509 be repealed and be substituted by provisions on "Sexual Assault" – to be defined broadly to include all forms of sexual violence on women including rape.

9.33. After giving considerable thought to the point of view referred to above, the Law Commission is of the opinion that the offence of rape including custodial rape and its punishment be retained in I.P.C. subject to the modifications stated below in para. 9.34.

9.34. The Law Commission recommends that clause 'Thirdly' in section 375 be amended on the following lines:

"*Section 375*: A man is said to commit rape—

Firstly.— ....

Secondly.— ....

Thirdly.—With her consent, when her consent has been obtained by putting her or any person in whom she is interested, in fear of death or of hurt, *or of any other injury.*"

The words "or of any other injury" expand the scope of this clause to provide for situations of rape by persons in position of trust, authority, guardianship or of economic or social dominance. These cases will include incestuous rape and other instances where a victim of rape is totally dependent on the offender who is in a dominant position.

The National Commission for Women has recommended that section 375 be amended to change the reference of age to 16 years in clause 'Sixthly' (rape with or without her consent) to 18 years. The Law Commission approves that the charge proposed by NCW is necessary particularly in view of raising the age in section 361 (Kidnapping from lawful guardianship – age changed from 16 to 18 years).

The Law Commission, however, does not endorse the change proposed by NCW in the Exception to section 375 (sexual intercourse by a man with his wife) increasing age from 15 years to 18 years. Consequently, there need not be any amendment to section 198(6), Cr. P.C. as suggested by the National Commission for Women.

The Law Commission is of the opinion that the offence of child rape and its punishment is provided for under the existing section 376(2)(f). Consequently, the incorporation of a new sub-section (3) to section 378, as recommended by the National Commission for Women, is not called for.

9.35. To deal with the issue of increasing sexual violence on women and female children, the Law Commission recommends that the offence of sexual assault be added to the existing offence of outraging the modesty of women in section 354 and punishment be increased from two years to five years. Accordingly, section 354 be amended on the following lines:

"354. *Assault or criminal force to woman with intent to outrage her modesty.*—Whoever assaults or uses criminal force to any woman, intending to outrage her modesty or to commit sexual assault to her or knowing it to be likely that he will thereby outrage her modesty or commit sexual assault to her, shall be punished with imprisonment of either description for a term which may extend to five years and shall also be liable to fine."

Expanding the scope of section 354 in the above manner, would in our view, cover the varied forms of sexual violence other than rape on women and female children.

The Law Commission is further of the view that the offence of eve teasing falls within the scope of section 509 and there is no need for a new section 376F as recommended by the National Commission for Women. However, the Law Commission feels that the quantum of punishment be increased from 1 year to 3 years and fine. Accordingly, we recommend that section 509 be amended in the following manner:

"509. *Word, gesture or act intended to insult the modesty of a woman.*—Whoever, intending to insult the modesty of any woman, utters any word, makes any sound or gesture, or exhibits any object, intending, that such word or sound shall be heard, or that such gesture or object shall be seen, by such woman, or intrudes upon the privacy of such woman, shall be punished with imprisonment of either description for a term which may extend to three years and shall also be liable to fine."

II. Bigamy

9.36. Section 494 defines bigamy as the act of a person who, having a husband or wife living, marries but only in a case where such subsequent marriage is void under his or her personal law.

9.37. Till the enactment of the Hindu Marriage Act, 1955, the impact of this section fell only on Christians and Parsis. But after the coming into force of that Act, Hindus also have come within the purview of this provision. Muslims and some tribes, who are permitted by their family law and customs to practice polygamy, are excluded.

9.38. The Law Commission in its 42nd Report had revised the section as follows:

"494. *Bigamy.*—Whoever, being married, contracts another marriage in any case in which such marriage is void by reason of its taking place during the subsistence of the earlier marriage, commits bigamy.

Explanation.—Where a marriage has been dissolved by the decree of a competent court under an enactment but the parties are, by virtue of a provision of the enactment under which their marriage is dissolved prohibited from re-marrying within a specified period, then, for the purpose of this section, the marriage shall, notwithstanding its dissolution, be deemed to subsist during that period.

Exception.—The offence is not committed by any person who contracts the later marriage during the life of the spouse by earlier marriage, if, at the time of the later marriage, such spouse shall have been continually absent from such person for seven years and shall not, within that period, have heard of by such person as being alive, provided the person contracting the later marriage inform the person with whom it is contracted of the real state of facts so far as the same are within his or her knowledge."

The Commission felt that the punishment for bigamy was "unnecessarily high" and so be reduced from seven years to three years.[1]

9.39. The Commission also recommended the reduction of punishment for the aggravated form of bigamy, under section 495 namely where bigamy is accompanied by the concealment of the fact of former marriage from the person with whom the subsequent marriage is contracted, from ten years to seven years.[2]

9.40. But the I.P.C. Bill (clause 198) has not accepted the recommendation of reduction of punishment for bigamy under section 494.

9.41. The Bill significantly has added *Explanation I* which stipulates that a person shall be deemed to marry again whatever legal defect there may be in contracting, celebrating or performing such marriage.

For prosecution for bigamy to succeed, prosecution must show first of all that at the time of second marriage, there was a valid subsisting marriage. Where proof of either marriage is unsatisfactory, there would be no conviction. *Explanation I* to section 494 in the Bill has introduced a deeming fiction. It deems the second marriage valid despite legal defects in contracting, celebrating or performing such marriage. By this, the accused cannot take the defence of non-performance of ceremonies in the second marriage to save himself from the clutches of the offence of bigamy.

The incorporation of this deeming provision in Explanation was in consequence of the judicial decisions on the scope of section 17 of the Hindu Marriage Act, 1955. The Supreme Court in *Bhaurao* v. *State of Maharashtra*[3] held that the offence of bigamy was not proved unless it was established that the second marriage was celebrated with proper ceremonies and due form. This conclusion was reached on the ground that section 17 of the Hindu Marriage Act, had used the word "solemnized". Accordingly the court held that it was essential for the purpose of section 17, that the marriage to which section 494 applies on account of the provisions of the Act, should have been celebrated with proper ceremonies and due form. As the law requires no specific ceremonies but recognises ceremonies of marriage according to custom, it becomes extremely difficult to determine which ceremony or ceremonies were really essential. *Bhaurao* decision was reiterated in two subsequent decisions of the Supreme Court in *Keval Ram* v. *H.P.*

1. Report, para. 20.10.
2. *Ibid.*, para. 20.10.
3. AIR 1965 SC 1964.

Administration[1] and *Priya Bala* v. *Suresh Chandra*.[2] Consequently a great burden is cast on the prosecution to show that the second marriage is performed with all due formalities. This burden in many cases cannot be discharged satisfactorily to prove the offence of bigamy. Therefore, it was felt necessary to add the Explanation. The Committee on the Status of Women in its Report *"Towards Equality"* (1975) had recommended the incorporation of Explanation to section 17 of the Hindu Marriage Act that an omission to perform some essential ceremonies by parties shall not be construed to mean that the offence of bigamy was not committed. This recommendation has also found a place in *Explanation (1)* to section 494 in the Bill.

Explanation 2 has been added to section 494 by which it is made clear that where the relevant divorce law prohibits re-marriage of the parties within a specified period after the decree of dissolution, such re-marriage amounts to bigamy. *Explanation 2* is as follows:

> "Where a marriage has been dissolved by a decree of a competent court but the parties are, by virtue of a provision of the enactment under which their marriage is dissolved, prohibited from re-marrying within a specified period, then for the purposes of this section, the marriage shall, notwithstanding its dissolution, be deemed to subsist during that period."

The Supreme Court in *Sarla Mudgal's*[3] case held that conversion from a monogamous religion (Hinduism) to a polygamous religion (Islam) for the purpose of second marriage, during the subsistence of first marriage, would make the second marriage violative of justice, equity and good conscience etc. The Court also held that the apostate husband would be guilty of the offence of bigamy. The Court has thus removed the uncertainty as regards the effect of conversion on marriage.

9.42. We recommend that another *Explanation*, *Explanation 3* be added to section 494 incorporating the principle laid down by the Supreme Court in the *Sarla Mudgal's* case on the following lines to put the matter beyond doubt:

> "*Explanation 3.*—The offence of bigamy is committed when any person converts himself or herself to another religion for the purpose of marrying again during the subsistence of the earlier marriage."

III. Adultery

9.43. In the First Report on the Draft Indian Penal Code, adultery was not made an offence. However, the First Law Commission in its Second Report on the Draft Indian Penal Code, after giving due consideration to the subject, came to the conclusion that it was not advisable to exclude this offence from the Code.[4]

9.44. The offence of adultery under section 497 is very limited in scope in comparison to the misconduct of adultery in divorce (civil) proceedings. The

1. AIR 1966 SC 1564.
2. AIR 1971 SC 1153.
3. *Sarla Mudaal* v. *Union of India*, AIR 1995 SC 1531.
4. Second Report on the Draft Indian Penal Code (1847), Law Commission.

offence is committed only by a man who has sexual intercourse with the wife of another man without the letter's consent or connivance. The wife is not punishable for being an adulteress or even as an abettor. Punishment is imprisonment of either description for a term up to five years or with fine or with both.

9.45. The Law Commission in its 42nd Report recommended the retention of section 497 in its present form with the modification that, even the wife, who has sexual relations with a person other than her husband, should be made punishable for adultery. The Commission also recommended that five years' imprisonment is "unreal and not called for in any circumstances and should be reduced to two years".[1] The Commission recommended that the section may be revised as follows:—

> "*497. Adultery.*—If a man has sexual intercourse with a woman who is, and whom he knows or has reason to believe to be the wife of another man, without the consent or connivance of that man, such sexual intercourse not amounting to the offence of rape, the man and the woman are guilty of the offence of adultery, and shall be punished with imprisonment of either description for a term which may extend to two years, or with fine, or with both."[2]

9.46. The constitutionality of section 497 was challenged under Article 32 as violative of the right to equality in Article 14 in *Sowmithri Vishnu* v. *Union of India*[3]. The basis of challenge was that the section makes an irrational classification between men and women and it unjustifiably denies to women the right given to men. This section confers upon the husband the right to prosecute the adulterer but does not confer any right upon the wife of the adulterer to do so. The Supreme Court negatived the contention and upheld the constitutionality of section 497.

Clause 199 of the Indian Penal Code Amendment Bill, 1976 reads as section 497:

> "Whoever has sexual intercourse with a person who is, and whom he or she knows, or has reason to believe, to be the wife or husband as the case may be, of another person, without the consent or connivance of that other person, such sexual intercourse by the man not amounting to the offence of rape, commits adultery, and shall be punished with imprisonment of either description for a term which may extend to five years, or with fine, or with both."

The I.P.C. (Amendment) Bill has brought in the concept of equality between sexes in marriage *vis-a-vis* the offence of adultery in the substituted section 497. However, the Law Commission recommends that the phraseology of clause 199 has to be modified on the following lines to reflect the concept of equality between sexes. Accordingly clause 199 shall read as:

---

1. Forty-second Report on the *Indian Penal Code,* (1971), para. 20.18.
2. *Ibid.*
3. AIR 1985 SC 1618: 1985 Supp SCC 137.

> "*Section 497.*—Whoever has sexual intercourse with a person who is, and whom he or she knows, or has reason to believe, to be the wife or husband, as the case may be, of another person, without the consent or connivance of that other person, such sexual intercourse not amounting to the offence of rape, commits adultery, and shall be punished with imprisonment of either description for a term which may extend to five years, or with fine or with both."

The Supreme Court in *Sowmithri Vishnu* case had observed that "it is for the Legislature to consider whether section 497 should be amended appropriately so as to take note of the 'transformation' which the society has undergone". The proposed change reflects the transformation of women's status in the Indian society. The punishment of five years remains the same.

9.47. If section 497 is amended on the lines indicated above, sub-section (2) of section 198 of the Code of Criminal Procedure, 1973 needs to be suitably amended.

IV. Unnatural Offences

9.48. Section 377 deals with unnatural offences like sodomy, buggery and bestiality. This section was amended in 1955 making the punishment more stringent to one of imprisonment for life or with imprisonment of either description for a term up to ten years and fine. Section 377 reads as:

> "Whoever voluntarily has carnal intercourse against the order of nature with any man, woman or animal, shall be punished with imprisonment for life, or with imprisonment of either description for a term which may extend to ten years."

9.49. The Law Commission in its 42nd Report had recommended that cases of bestiality should be regarded as pathological manifestations to be ignored by the criminal law.

9.50. The Commission, however, felt that "Indian society, by and large, disapproves of homo-sexuality and this disapproval is strong enough to justify it being treated as a criminal offence even where adults indulge in it in private", and observed that "Buggery" may continue as an offence punishable less severely than at present but, where it is committed by an adult on a minor boy or girl, the punishment be higher. So the Commission had recommended that section 377 be revised as follows:—

> "*377. Buggery.*—Whoever voluntarily has carnal intercourse against the order of nature with any man or woman shall be punished with imprisonment of either description for a term which may extend to two years, or with fine or with both,

and where such offence is committed by a person over eighteen years of age with a person under that age, the imprisonment may extend to seven years.

> *Explanation.*—Penetration is sufficient to constitute the carnal intercourse necessary to the offence described in this section."

The Indian Penal Code (Amendment) Bill (clause 160) has adopted the above recommendation of the Law Commission.

9.51. We recommend that in view of the growing incidence of child sexual abuse in the country, where unnatural offence is committed on a person under the age of eighteen years, here should be a minimum mandatory sentence of imprisonment of either description for a term not less than two years, but which may extend to seven years. The court shall, however, have discretion to reduce the sentence for adequate and special reasons to be recorded in the judgment. Consequently section 377 be amended on the following lines:—

> "377. *Unnatural offences.*—Whoever voluntarily has carnal intercourse against the order of nature with any man or woman shall be punished with imprisonment of either description for a term which may extend to two years, or with fine, or with both; and where such offence is committed by a person over eighteen years of age with a person under that age, he shall be punished with imprisonment of either description for a term which shall not be less than two years but may extend to seven years and fine:
>
> Provided that the court may for adequate and special reasons to be recorded in the judgment, impose a sentence of imprisonment of either description for a term of less than two years.
>
> *Explanation.*—Penetration is sufficient to constitute the carnal intercourse necessary to the offence described in this section."

V. Child Sexual Abuse

9.52. Child sexual abuse (CSA) is considered one of the 'new' epidemics of the last decade. CSA could be any kind of "physical or mental violation of the child with sexual intent usually by an elder person who is in possession of trust or power *vis-a-vis* the child".[1] The experience may vary from an adult exposure of genitals to the child or to persuade the child to do the same, the adult touching the child's genital or making the child to touch his own, involving the child in pornography – both printed and visual, having oral, vaginal or anal intercourse with the child, making verbal or other sexual suggestions or indecent overtures. In addition, fondling or fingering, touching or voyeurism or any such attempt could also be CSA.[2]

9.53. According to the statistics reported in *Crime in India*, of the total victims of rape cases, children accounted for more than 25 per cent. There is an increasing trend since 1990 as regards child rape.

While 3,393 cases of child rape were reported in 1993, it increased to 3,986 in 1994. Giving the state-wise incidence of child rape, the Report says Madhya Pradesh led in reporting the highest number of 809 child rape cases, followed by Uttar Pradesh (538), Rajasthan (205) and Delhi (206) in 1994. Among the cities, Delhi and Mumbai reported more victims of child rape in the age group below 10 years and also in the age group of 10-16 years.[3]

---

1. Child Sexual Abuse, literature by 'Sakshi', New Delhi.
2. Schwartz, Horovitz and Cardarelli *Child Sexual Abuse*, pp. 58-59 (Sage Publications, 1990).
3. Amod Kanth *"CSA": Legal and Investigative Perspective*, in Sheela Barse (Ed.) *Child Victims' Right*, Report of International Conference on Child Sex Abuse: *Victim Protective Investigation and Trial Procedure*, 11 at 13 (1996).

While conducting the study of CSA in Delhi, the Delhi Police found that information regarding the offences of molestation or outraging of modesty (section 354, I.P.C.) and unnatural sex offences (section 377, I.P.C.) committed on children below 16 years was not readily available. Information was collected for 1994 wherein a total number of 291 cases was recorded out of which 69 girls were below 16 years. (31%). In respect of unnatural offences, out of 24 cases, there were 22 boys and 2 girls indicating that 95.9% of the victims were children below 16 years.[1]

It is difficult to get hard data on the extent of CSA in the country. But there is a silver lining in the horizon. Some NGOs have undertaken studies on CSA and preliminary findings are none too happy. Samvada, a Bangalore based NGO found, in a study of 348 college girls, that 47 per cent. of students had been subjected to sexual abuse. About 45 per cent. had experienced such abuse before the age of 14. The most common offender was a known male family member. Similar are the findings of Sakshi, a Delhi based NGO in a study made of 357 girls of government and private schools. It was found that 63 per cent. of the children had suffered some form of sexual abuse, about 22 per cent. suffered serious sexual abuse and in 29 per cent. of the cases, the abuse was by a person whom they trusted fully. In their analysis of 19 cases of CSA in 1995 it was found that in majority of the cases, the victims were children between one and twelve years.

9.54. The Constitution of India provides special protection to children. Article 15(3) confers powers on the State to make special provisions for women and children. Article 39(f) provides that children are given opportunities and facilities to develop in a healthy manner and in conditions of freedom and dignity and that childhood and youth are protected against exploitation and against moral and material abandonment. This provision was added to the Constitution by the Constitution (Forty-fourth Amendment) Act, 1978. Article 45 mandates the State to provide for free and compulsory education for all children until they complete the age of 14 years.

9.55. Since 1945 the welfare and rights of children have been a matter of great concern for the United Nations. One of the first acts of the General Assembly was to establish the United Nations Children Fund (UNICEF). In 1959, the Declaration on The Rights of the Child was drafted which has been serving as a guide post to private and public action in the interest of children on the basis "that mankind owes to the child the best it has to give". This Declaration ultimately led to the drafting of the Convention on The Rights of the Child which was adopted unanimously by the General Assembly on 20th November, 1989. 187 States have ratified this Convention. The Convention came into force in India on 11th January, 1993. Some of the provisions of the Convention specifically deal with the protection of children from sexual offences and violation, in particular Articles 34, 35 and 36. Article 34 of the Convention imposes an obligation on the State parties to protect the child from all forms of sexual exploitation and

1. *See* Pioneer (Delhi Edn.) dated 7-11-1996, p. 3. *See* also *Incestuous Father Poisons Pregnant Daughter to Death,* Indian Express – Express News Line (Delhi Edn.) 3-12-1996.

sexual abuse. For these purposes the States are mandated to take appropriate measures to prevent: (i) the inducement or coercion of children to engage in any unlawful sexual activity; (ii) the exploitative use of children in prostitution or other unlawful sexual practices, and (iii) the exploitative use of children in pornographic performances and materials. Article 35 requires States to take all measures to prevent the abduction of the sale of or traffic in children for any purpose or in any form. Article 36 mandates states to protect the children against all other forms of exploitation prejudicial to any aspects of the child's welfare.

9.56. So far as rape of children under 12 years is concerned, the existing section 376(2)(f) provides a minimum mandatory sentence of 10 years rigorous imprisonment which may extend to life and fine.

9.57. To counter the evil of all other forms of sexual abuse of female children, the Law Commission's recommendations for amendment of section 354 as stated in para. 9.35. in Part IV should be adequate. In addition, the Law Commission's recommendation in para. 9.52 of Part IV for aggravated punishment for the commission of unnatural offences under section 377, I.P.C., on both male and female persons under eighteen years of age by adults would cover child sexual abuse on children, both male and female.

9.58. In the opinion of the Law Commission, the existing section 376(2)(f), and the Law Commission's recommendations for amendment of sections 354 and 377 are adequate to deal with child sexual abuse. Consequently, the Law Commission does not recommend the incorporation of new section 364A as suggested in clause 146 of the Indian Penal Code (Amendment) Bill.

9.59. Sexual-child abuse may be committed in various forms such as sexual intercourse, carnal intercourse and sexual assaults. The cases involving penile penetration into vagina are covered under section 375 of the I.P.C.. If there is any case of penile oral penetration and penile penetration into anus, section 377, I.P.C. dealing with unnatural offences, *i.e.*, carnal intercourse against the order of nature with any man, woman or animal, adequately takes care of them. If acts such as penetration of finger or any inanimate object into vagina or anus are committed against a woman or a female child, the provisions of the proposed section 354, I.P.C. where under a more severe punishment is also prescribed can be invoked and as regards the male child, the penal provisions of the I.P.C. concerning 'hurt', 'criminal force' or 'assault' as the case may be, would be attracted. A distinction has to be naturally maintained between sexual assault/use of criminal force falling under section 354, sexual offences falling under section 375 and unnatural offences falling under section 377 of the Indian Penal Code. It may not be appropriate to bring unnatural offences punishable under section 377, I.P.C. or mere sexual assault or mere sexual use of criminal force which may attract section 354 I.P.C. within the ambit of 'rape' which is a distinct and graver offence with a definite connotation. It is needless to mention that any attempt to commit any of these offences is also punishable by virtue of section 511, I.P.C.. Therefore, any other or more changes regarding this law may not be necessary.

84th REPORT, 1980 ON RAPE AND ALLIED OFFENCES - SOME QUESTIONS OF SUBSTANTIVE LAW, PROCEDURE AND EVIDENCE

CHAPTER 1

INTRODUCTORY

1.1. The criminal justice system and the offence of rape.—During recent years, the impact of the criminal justice system on victims of rape and other sexual offences has received considerable attention, both in legal circles and amongst organisations and individuals connected with the welfare of women. In the field of criminology, an increasing interest is being shown in the victim and his or her position in the criminal justice system. In consequence, greater attention is now being paid to the female victim of a sexual offence. Psychologists have, for some time past, been studying the effects of rape and other sexual offences upon women or girls and their personality.

1.2. The crisis of rape.—It is often stated that a woman who is raped undergoes two crisis—the rape and the subsequent trial. While the first seriously wounds her dignity, curbs her individual, destroys her sense of security and may often ruin her physically, the second is no less potent of mischief, inasmuch as it not only forces her to re-live through the traumatic experience, but also does so in the glare of publicity in a totally alien atmosphere, with the whole apparatus and paraphernalia of the criminal justice system focused upon her.

In particular, it is now well established that sexual activities with young girls of immature age have a traumatic effect which often persists through life, leading subsequently to disorders, unless there are counter-balancing factors in family life and in social attitudes which could act as a cushion against such traumatic effects.

Rape is the 'ultimate violation of the self'.[1] It is a humiliating event in a woman's life which leads to fear for existence and a sense of powerlessness. The victim needs empathy and safety and a sense of re-assurance. In the absence of public sensitivity to these needs, the experience of figuring in a report of the offense may itself become another assault.

Forcible rape is unique among crimes, in the manner in which its victims are dealt with by the criminal justice system. Raped women have to undergo certain tribulations. These begin with their treatment by the police and continue through a male-dominated criminal justice system. Acquittal of many *de facto* guilty rapists adds to the sense of injustice.

In effect, the focus of the law upon corroboration, consent and character of the prosecutrix and a standard of proof of guilt going beyond reasonable doubt

1. Hilbermen *Rape: The Ultimate Violation of the Self,* (1976), Vol. 133, No. 4, Am. J. Psychiatry, pp. 436-437.

have resulted in an increasing alienation of the general public from the legal system, who find the law and legal language difficult to understand and who think that the courts are not run so well as one would expect.

1.3. Reference by Government.—In view of the recent discussions that have taken place in the press and in other forums regarding the inadequacy of the law to protect women who have been victims of rape or assaults on their modesty, Government has asked the Law Commission[1] to make a special study of the law relating to rape. Government has also requested the Commission to consider certain material[2] relevant to the subject, which was referred to in the letter of reference, and forwarded to the Commission by a supplementary letter. The material so forwarded includes a letter addressed by a lady Member of Parliament, a newspaper cutting containing report of a meeting at which some suggestions for reform were made, extract from the I.P.C. Amendment Bill, as also certain administrative instructions issued by the Government of India in the Ministry of Home Affairs on the subject of arrest and interrogation of women.

It has been suggested in the letter of reference that the study should cover not only the substantive law relating to rape, but also the rules of evidence and procedure and other related matters. The Commission has been requested to forward its Report within as short a period as possible.

Later, on 15th April, 1980, certain other materials,[3] namely, copy of a petition addressed to the Lok Sabha by Smt. Lata Mani and a copy of the uncorrected record of the discussion in the Lok Sabha on the 27th and 28th March, 1980 on a motion (relating to rape on women) moved in the Lok Sabha by Smt. Geeta Mukherjee were forwarded to us. We have carefully considered the points made in the petition and in the Lok Sabha Debates.

1.4. Suggestions for amendment.—Besides the reference made by the Government, the Commission has also received a suggestion[4] for considering certain changes in the law of rape. The points made in the suggestion have been duly considered by the Commission.

The Commission has also made an attempt to ascertain the views of organisations interested in the subject, as also of one of the Members of Parliament who had in a letter addressed to the Government suggested, reforms on certain points which we have carefully considered. The Commission is grateful to them for their co-operation.

---

1. D.O. letter No. PS/LS/LA/80, dated 27th March, 1980, from the Secretary, Department of Legal Affairs, Ministry of Law to the Member-Secretary, Law Commission of India (Letter of reference).
2. D.O. letter No. 1482/80A, dated 31st March, 1980 from Joint Secretary & Legal Adviser, Department of Legal Affairs to the Member-Secretary, Law Commission of India (Supplementary letter).
3. D.O. letter dated 14/15 April, 1980 addressed by Shri P.K. Kartha, Joint Secretary and Legal Adviser to Member-Secretary, Law Commission of India.
4. Suggestion made by the Lawyers Collective, Bombay, Letter No. IJ/ES/22/80, dated 18th March, 1980.

While our consideration of the question was in full progress, we also received from the Ministry of Law[1] a copy of a letter addressed by the Bhagini Samaj, Bombay to the Minister for Law, stating that women in villages and Harijan women were molested and that cases of rape of women were increasing in the country. The Samaj had, in the letter, also made suggestions for amendment of the law on certain points, including a suggestion that women police should interview and interrogate women who were molested, that the trial should be held *in camera* and that well-known women's associations should be selected to "examine and deal with" such cases. The various points made in the letter of the Samaj have been duly taken by us into consideration.

The Ministry of Law has also forwarded to us a letter[2] of the Maharashtra State Women's Council, enclosing copy of a resolution passed by that body as to the increasing incidence of rape, and making certain suggestions in brief for amendment of the law. The suggestions in the main are that the law should be radically altered, that the burden of proving innocence should be on the accused, and so on.

Certain recent judicial decisions[3] in India have also provoked a debate as to the deficiencies—real or supposed—of the law relating to rape and allied offences.

1.5. Role of the criminal law.—It is elementary that the criminal law is the chief legal instrument for preventing anti-social acts of a serious character. This object is sought to be achieved, in the first instance, by the legislative command embodying that aspect of punishment which is called "general deterrence". Once a crime—whether sexual or of any other category—has been committed, this aspect is, at least for the lime being, exhausted in regard to that particular criminal act. The fact that the particular crime has been committed shows that the object of deterrence has failed to prevent the particular criminal act.

However, one can still expect of the legal system that it should make reasonable provisions to ensure that the criminal act already committed is dealt with adequately—consistently, of course, with the general norms of the judicial process, so that the legislative command is enforced, the object of deterrence is realised and (if the accused is found guilty) the punishment to be imposed is such as to deter others also—thus bringing the aspect of "general deterrence" again in play.

In this field, thus, the main objective of legal reform would be to promote justice after the offence is committed.

It is in this background that reforms in the law have been considered in this Report.

1.6. Earlier reports of the Law commission.—At this stage, it is proper to mention that some of the matters that now fall for consideration have been dealt

1. Endorsement No. 1807/80-Adv. A, dated 16th April, 1980 from Shri P.K. Kartha, Joint Secretary & Legal Adviser, Department of Legal Affairs forwarding a copy of letter dated 7th April, 1980 addressed by the Bhagini Samaj, Bombay to the Minister for Law.
2. Letter No. 233/80, dated 8th April, 1980 from Maharashtra State Women's Council to the Minister for Law.
3. *Tukaram* v. *State of Maharashtra*, AIR 1979 SC 185 (January).

with by the Law Commission in its Report on the Penal Code[1] and in its Report on the Indian Evidence Act,[2] wherein certain recommendations were made for reform of the law. We shall, at the proper place, make a reference in detail to those recommendations, and also indicate our views as to whether any further changes in the law are needed.

However, it would be appropriate to mention here a very important recommendation made by the Commission in regard to the Penal Code. In order to deal with cases where the circumstances are such that a male may be able to take undue advantage of the situation and seduce the woman to illicit intercourse, the Commission recommended the insertion in the Code of three specific sections, intended respectively to deal with illicit intercourse—

(i) by a person having custody of a woman, with that woman,

(ii) by superintendent of an institution, with an inmate of the institution, and

(iii) by a person in charge of a hospital, with a mentally disordered patient.

These recommendations,[3] made after careful consideration and intended to deal with social problems of some seriousness that were anticipated by the Law Commission, have assumed still greater importance during the period of nine years that has, elapsed since the Commission forwarded its recommendations. The substantive law relating to the offence of rape and sexual exploitation of women would, to a large extent, be fortified and improved by implementing these recommendations.

1.7. Method adopted.—Reverting to the matters that fall to be considered in the present Report, we may state that the reference made by the Government to the Law Commission—and also the suggestions that the Commission has received—raise a variety of questions. It will be convenient to deal with the various questions separately under appropriate headings, so that aspects of the substantive law, of procedure and of the law of evidence, may all be dealt with.

1.8. Desultory implementation.—It should, however, be pointed out that on several matters the present statutory law is adequate, in so far as the matter could be dealt with by legislation and the need is for effective implementation. Hardship and injustice arise because implementation of the law is desultory.

1.9. Steps to be taken to avoid suspicion of harassment.—In the views expressed by the representatives of several women's organisations with whom we were able to hold discussions, great emphasis has been placed on the need to take adequate precautions for the protection of women who, being the victims of rape, are required to make their statements to the police for the purposes of investigation. There seems to be a strong feeling that the present arrangements are not adequate and do not ensure that no opportunities arise for complaints against male police officers of harassment or molestation of such women. This

1. Law Commission of India, 42nd Report (Indian Penal Code).
2. Law Commission of India, 69th Report (Indian Evidence Act, 1872).
3. Law Commission of India, 42nd Report (Indian Penal Code), paras. 16.113 to 16.123.

feeling is universal and intense. We are aware that the matter is primarily one which should be, and can effectively be, dealt with by appropriate executive steps, and it may not be practicable to hedge in the functioning of the police with too many restrictions. Nevertheless, we consider it proper to make certain recommendations for an amendment of the law in order to safeguard the legitimate interests of such women—being amendments which, we hope, will not unduly hamper the efficient functioning of the police force.

CHAPTER 2

RAPE AND INDECENT ASSAULT: THE SUBSTANTIVE LAW

I. Present Law as to Rape

2.1. Scope.—We propose to consider in this Chapter the substantive law relating to rape and indecent assault.

2.2. Section 375, Indian Penal Code.—Section 375 of the Indian Penal Code defines rape as under:

"375. A man is said to commit 'rape' who except in the case hereinafter excepted, has sexual intercourse with a woman under circumstances falling under any of the five following descriptions:

First.—Against her will.

Secondly.—Without her consent.

Thirdly.—With her consent, when her consent has been obtained by putting her in fear of death, or of hurt.

Fourthly.—With her consent, when the man knows that he is not her husband, and that her consent is given because she believes that he is another man to whom she is or believes herself to be lawfully married.

Fifthly.—With or without her consent, when she is under sixteen years of age.

Explanation.—Penetration is sufficient to constitute the sexual intercourse necessary to the offence of rape.

Exception.—Sexual intercourse by a man with his own wife, the wife not being under fifteen years of age, is not rape."

II. Recommendation in 42nd Report

2.3. Earlier Report.—Here, it would be appropriate to reproduce the re-draft of the relevant sections as recommended in the 42nd Report of the Commission:

Re-draft of sections 375 *to* 376E *as recommended in 42nd Report:*

"375. *Rape.*—A man is said to commit rape who has sexual intercourse with a woman, other than his wife—

(a) against her will; or

(b) without her consent; or

(c) with her consent when it has been obtained by putting her in fear of death or of hurt, *either to herself or to anyone else present at the place;* or

(d) with her consent, knowing that it is given in the belief that he is her husband.

Explanation I.—Penetration is sufficient to constitute the sexual intercourse necessary to the offence of rape.

Explanation II.—A woman living separately from her husband under a decree of judicial separation or by mutual agreement shall be deemed not to be his wife for the purpose of this section."

"376. *Punishment for rape.*—Whoever commits rape shall be punished with rigorous imprisonment for a term which may extend to *fourteen years,* and shall also be liable to fine."

"376A. *Sexual intercourse with child wife.*—Whoever has sexual intercourse with his wife, the wife being under fifteen years of age, shall be punished—

(a) if she is under twelve years of age, with rigorous imprisonment for a term which may extend to seven years, and shall also be liable to fine; and

(b) in any other case, with imprisonment of either description for a term which may extend to two years or with fine, or with both."

"376B. *Illicit intercourse with a girl between twelve and sixteen.*—Whoever has illicit intercourse with a girl under sixteen years, but not under twelve years of age, with her consent, shall be punished with imprisonment of either description for a term which may extend to seven years, and shall also be liable to fine.

It shall be a defence to a charge under this section for the accused to prove that he, in good faith, believed the girl to be above sixteen years of age."

"376C. *Illicit intercourse of public servant with woman in his custody.*—Whoever, being a public servant, compels or seduces to illicit intercourse any woman who is in his custody as such public servant shall be punished with imprisonment of either description for a term which may extend to two years, or with fine, or with both."

"376D. *Illicit intercourse of superintendent etc. with inmate of women's or children's institution.*—Whoever, being the superintendent or manager of a women's or children's institution or holding any other office in such institution by virtue of which he can exercise any authority or control over its inmates, compels or seduces to illicit sexual intercourse any female inmate of the institution shall be punished with imprisonment of either description for a term which may extend to two years, or with fine, or with both.

Explanation.—In this section 'women's or children's institution' means an institution whether called an orphanage, home for neglected women or children, widow's home or by any other name, which is established and maintained for the reception and care of women or children, but does not include—

(a) any hostel or boarding house attached to, or controlled or recognised by, an educational institution, or

(b) any reformatory, certified or other school, or any home or workhouse, governed by any enactment for the time being in force."

"376E. *Illicit intercourse of manager etc. of a hospital with mentally disordered patient.*—Whoever, being concerned with the management of a hospital or being on the staff of a hospital, has illicit sexual intercourse with a woman who is receiving treatment for a mental disorder in that hospital, shall be punished with imprisonment of either description for a term which may extend to two years, or with fine, or with both.

Explanation.—It shall be a defence to a charge under this section for the accused to prove that he did not know, and had no reason to believe, that the woman was a mentally disordered patient."

2.4. Recommendation in earlier Report as dealing with force and fraud.—It would be noted that these recommendations of the Law Commission in the earlier Report deal with forcible and fraudulent sexual intercourse as well as with illicit sexual intercourse by way of seduction, in all their ramifications. We are, however, for reasons to be stated later,[1] adopting a different and wider scheme.[2]

III. CONSENT: ITS SIGNIFICANCE

2.5. Absence of consent.—The statutory definition[3] of rape in India emphasises the element of absence of consent. In fact, absence of consent is an important aspect of the *actus reus* of the offence. Barring cases where consent is irrelevant and the age of the girl is the only crucial factor (because of the statutory requirement of minimum age), want of consent becomes, in practice, a determining factor in most prosecutions for rape. It is also the factor to which the law has devoted the most detailed attention—as is manifest from the elaborate rules and refinements that are to be met with in various clauses of the statutory definition of rape, and from the richness of material to be found in case law and lengthy discussion on the subject to be found in academic writings.

2.6. Consent is the antithesis of rape. Even if some may find any discussion on consent as too complicated, the matter cannot, consistently with the needs of the subject, be put in simple one-phrase formulation. When circumstances in life present an infinite variety, the law must be well-equipped to deal with them. Nuances of consent are therefore, unavoidable.

IV. REALITY OF CONSENT: SECTION 90

2.7. The concept of free consent—section 375, 3rd clause and section 90.—The most important question of substantive law relates, then, to the concept of consent in the context of the offence of rape. Consent must be real. Often, it is vitiated by circumstances that take away the freedom of choice. Taking note of this aspect, the third clause of section 375 (definition of "rape") provides that sexual intercourse with a woman amounts to rape if it is "with her consent, when her consent has been obtained by putting her in fear of death or of hurt". The vitiating factor here is duress or coercion, but only one specific aspect of it is dealt with. In contrast, the matter is dealt with more comprehensively in section 90, which is too often overlooked by courts. The section reads as under:—

1. *See* paras. 2.17 to 2.20, *infra*.
2. *See* para. 2.21, *infra*.
3. Para. 2.2, *supra*.

"*90. Consent known to be given under fear or misconception.*—A consent is not such a consent as is intended by any section of this Code, if the consent is given by a person under fear of injury, or under a misconception of fact, and if the person doing the act knows or has reason to believe, that the consent was given in consequence of such fear or misconception; or

Consent of insane person.—If the consent is given by a person who, from unsoundness of mind, or intoxication, is unable to understand the nature and consequence of that to which he gives his consent; or

Consent of child.—Unless the contrary appears from the context, if the consent is given by a person who is under twelve years of age."[1]

V. Free and Voluntary Consent

2.8. Effect of recommended amendment.—We shall indicate later the changes that we are recommending to section 375, particularly those on the issue of consent. It will be seen that the amendments recommended by us in the second and third circumstances enumerated in section 375 considerably widen their scope. The substitution of the expression "free and voluntary consent" for the word "consent" in the second clause makes it clear that the consent should be active consent, as distinguished from that consent which is said to be implied by silence.

Under the amendment as recommended, it would not be open to the Court to draw an inference of consent on the part of the woman from her silence due to timidity or meekness or from such circumstances without any more—as that the girl meekly followed the offender when he pulled her, catching hold of her hand, or that the woman kept silent and did not shout or protest or cry out for help.

2.9. Effect of modifications recommended as to fear of injury and criminal intimidation.—The modifications recommended by us in the third clause vitiate consent not only when a woman is put in fear of death or hurt, but also when she is put in fear of any "injury" being caused to any person (including herself) in body, mind, reputation or property and also when her consent is obtained by criminal intimidation,[2] that is to say, by any words or acts intended or calculated to put her in fear of any injury or danger to herself or to any person in whom she is interested or when she is threatened with any injury to her reputation or property or to the reputation of any one in whom she is interested. Thus, if the consent is obtained after giving the woman a threat of spreading false and scandalous rumours about her character or destruction of her property or injury to her children or parents or by holding out other threats of injury to her person, reputation or property, that consent will also not be consent under the third clause as recommended to be amended.

VI. Use of Intoxicants and Stupefying Substances

2.10. Drugs, intoxicants and anesthetics.—We may now mention one situation which should also, in our view, be dealt with in section 375. Medico-legal literature furnishes cases of intercourse being attempted or consummated not only with

1. *See* also section 7, Indian Penal Code.
2. *Cf.* section 503, Indian Penal Code.

the help of intoxicants—a situation covered by section 90, though not expressly by section 375, Indian Penal Code—but also by the use of stupefying substances. It is obvious that consent to intercourse given in such cases is not real consent. Such intercourse would possibly constitute rape if the requirement of "free and voluntary" consent is introduced—as is going to be our recommendation. However, it may be desirable to cover it specifically in section 375.

VII. Violence Not Necessary

2.11. Overt violence, if necessary.—While these are the main amendments on the point of consent, we may also mention a few points that have been raised during the suggestions made to us, concerning the concept of consent. There is a suggestion that the definition of "rape" should make it clear that the crime can take place without overt violence. We have given careful thought to this aspect, but we do not think that the law needs any clarification in this regard. Overt violence, or, for that matter, *violence* of any particular category, is not a necessary element of rape as defined in section 375. The cardinal fact is absence of consent on the part of the woman.[1]

There can be cases of consent even when there is no violence. Violence—or, for that matter, marks of resistance—are not conclusive of consent. In any case, after a clarification is made in section 375 on the lines recommended by us, this point would lose much of its practical importance.[2]

2.12. The proof of violence.—It would, of course, be realistic to state that most women in our society are not equipped to repel an attempt at rape, even in, self-defence. When attached, they might submit in terror and are unable to muster enough physical strength for offering effective resistance. We have no doubt that courts will continue to attach due weight to this consideration and we hope that the amendment recommended by us in section 375 will be a reminder to all concerned of the true position.

VIII. Submission Not Amounting to Consent

2.13. Submission and consent.—It has been represented to us during our oral discussions with women's organisations that the law should enact that submission does not amount to consent, in the context of offence of rape. We are recommending changes in section 375, particularly in relation to the requirement of "free and voluntary" consent.[3] In view of these changes which define the legal quantity of consent, we do not propose to make any such clarification as has been suggested.

2.14. Cases of helpless resignation.—In the course of the oral discussions which we held with the representatives of the women's organisations, it has been suggested that in order to cover cases of submission to intercourse, there should be added below section 375 of the Indian Penal Code a suitable Explanation on the following lines:—

> "A mere act of helpless resignation in the face of inevitable compulsion, acquiescence, non-resistance and passive giving in when volitional faculty is either clouded by fear or vitiated by duress cannot be deemed to be consent."

1. *See* also para. 7.8, *infra*.
2. *See* discussion as to "free and voluntary" consent, *supra*.
3. *See* discussion as to "free and voluntary" consent, *supra*.

One can have no objection to the principle underlying the suggestion. However, two observations may be made on the subject. In the first place, the requirement of "free and voluntary" consent which we are going to add in section 375 implies an active mental participation of the woman in the transaction and a qualification of the nature suggested would not be required. In the second place, it would not be correct to deal with only *certain aspects of submission* or certain varieties thereof, because then there is the risk that other situations to which the qualifying epithets do not apply would be left out. It is better to have a simpler but more comprehensive provision. Our recommendation to cover fear of "injury" or use of criminal intimidation meets the point.

IX. Recklessness

2.15. Recklessness.—It has further been suggested that it should be provided in section 375 that rape can take place when the man does not care whether the woman consented or not. It is difficult to see how the incorporation of this suggestion in section 375 will improve the present legal position. It must be remembered that a person out to commit rape is motivated by a strong uncontrollable passion or the lust of a savage. He will have his desire satisfied at any cost, no matter whether the woman consents or not, or whether or not he is being reckless in committing the act or in assuming consent. His approach to the act of rape is mechanical, non-emotional one. A rapist cannot be likened to a person wooing a lady with boastful phrases like "I came, I saw and I conquered" or by saying "you may strive, you may struggle for a while, but you too will ultimately fall like the lady in Don Juan". The crucial question is of consent; and on this question, the feelings of recklessness of a person about to commit rape have no bearing whatsoever.

X. Other Suggestions Relevant to Consent

2.16. Suggestion to add cases of reprisal by person in authority.—It has been suggested[1] that the following amendment should be made to clause thirdly of section 375 of the Indian Penal Code:—

> Add after "or of hurt", the words "or of any reprisal by any authority or person who may have authority over her".

A second Explanation to section 375, which would read thus, has also been suggested—

> " 'authority' here would mean and include any police official, village kotwal, village panch, or landlord or employer."

In view of the wider amendment that we are recommending in section 375—in particular, the amendment covering fear of any "injury"—this point is substantially met.

2.17. Fear of agony.—With reference to section 375, third clause of the Indian Penal Code, a suggestion has been made to add the following words:—

> "or of physical or mental agony to herself or to her nearest blood relations, including her husband if she is married."

We are of the view that the expansion of the third clause which we contemplate, namely, its extension to cover any "injury", amply takes care of the type of cases

1. Mrs. Sushila Adivarekar, M.P. (Rajya Sabha).

for which this suggestion is intended. "Injury" as defined in section 44 includes, *inter alia,* harm illegally cause in body or mind.

XI. Rape of Girls Below Minimum Age

2.18. Section 375, fifth clause.—The discussion in the few preceding paragraphs was concerned with rape constituted by sexual intercourse *without consent.* The fifth clause of section 375 may now be considered. It is concerned with sexual intercourse with a woman under 16 years of age. Such sexual intercourse is an offence irrespective of the consent of the woman.

2.19. History.—The age of consent has been subjected to increase more than once in India. The historical development may, for convenience, be indicated in the form of a chart as follows[1]:—

CHART

Year	Age of consent under sec. 375, 5th clause, I.P.C.	Age mentioned in the Exception to sec. 375, I.P.C.	Minimum age of marriage under the Child Marriage Restraint Act, 1929
1860	10 years	10 years	—
1891 (Act 10 of 1891) (after the amendment of I.P.C.[2])	12 years	12 years	—
1925 (after the amendment of I.P.C.)	14 years	13 years	—
1929 (after the passing to the Child Marriage Act)	14 years	13 years	14 years
1940 (after the amendment of the Penal Code and the Child Marriage Act)	16 years	15 years	15 years
1978	16 years	15 years	18 years

2.20. Increase in minimum age.—The question to be considered is whether the age should be increased to 18 years. The minimum age of marriage now laid down by law (after 1978) is 18 years in the case of females and the relevant clause of section 375 should reflect this changed attitude. Since marriage with a girl below 18 years is prohibited (though it is not void as a matter of personal law), sexual intercourse with a girl below 18 years should also be prohibited.

XII. Comments on Earlier Report

2.21. Earlier Report.—Here it would be pertinent to refer to the recommendation that the Commission, in its 42nd Report on the Indian Penal Code, had made

1. Position as on 31st March, 1980.
2. Amendment Act 10 of 1891 amending the I.P.C. was the result of the Calcutta case of *Queen Empress* v. *Hurree Mohan Mythee,* 1890 ILR Cal 49, in which the accused caused the death of his child wife, aged about 11 years and 3 months, by having sexual intercourse with her. The accused was convicted under section 338, I.P.C. (causing grievous hurt by act endangering life etc.), since the law of rape as it stood then was inapplicable to intercourse with a girl above the age of 10 years.

for re-structuring section 375, I.P.C. by splitting it up into three categories, namely,[1]—

(a) rape proper,

(b) rape with a child wife, and

(c) statutory rape.

It is not necessary to repeat here the reasons which the Commission, gave to support this recommendation. Suffice to say that the Commission now feels that such a re-structuring would be out of tune with the current thinking on the question of trial of offenders for rape and, therefore, the structure of section 375 should not be altered. Since the making of the recommendation by the Commission in its earlier Report, there has been a radical and revolutionary change in the approach to the offence of rape; its enormity is frequently brought into prominence and heightened by the revolting and gruesome circumstances in which the crime is committed; the case law has blurred the essential ingredients of the offence and introduced instability into the previously well established law bearing on the offence of rape. The Commission feels that re-structuring will produce uncertainty and distortion in section 375, which should, in its opinion, retain its present logical and coherent structure.

2.22. Freedom of consent as dealt with in earlier Report.—As to the relationship between section 90 of the Code (which lays down what is not consent for the purposes of the code) and the specific factors vitiating consent in relation to the offence of rape which are to be considered as relevant under section 375, the Commission, in its earlier Report, as already stated,[2] considered the position at some length and also made recommendations for specifically adding certain situations in section 375. Since this aspect of the matter has, during the last few years, assumed even greater importance, we are not only incorporating whatever was recommended in the earlier Report, but, pursuing the same approach, we are suggesting amendments which[3] would fortify the concept of "free consent" for the purposes of section 375 and spell it out more clearly in its application to several conceivable situations that represent the variety of flaws in consent.

2.23. Sexual offences besides rape.—In its earlier Report, the Commission also recommended the inclusion (in the Chapter on "Offences against the body") of three other sexual offences—(i) A public servant compelling or seducing to illicit intercourse any woman who is in his custody as such public servant, (ii) a superintendent or manager of a women's or children's institution compelling or seducing to illicit intercourse any female inmate of the institution, and (iii) a person on the management or staff of a mental hospital having illicit intercourse with a woman who is receiving treatment for a mental disorder in that hospital, should be punishable.[4-5]

We endorse[6] and adopt those recommendations.

1. Law Commission of India, 42nd Report (Indian Penal Code), paras. 16.113 to 16.123.
2. *See* para. 2.3, *supra.*
3. Para. 2.24, *infra.*
4. Law Commission of India, 42nd Report (Indian Penal Code), proposed sections 376C, 376D, 376E.
5. Para. 2.3, *supra.*
6. The numbering of sections, however, differs.

XIII. Recommendation

2.24. Recommendation as to section 375.—In the light of the above discussion, we recommend that section 375 of the Penal Code should be revised as under:—

Revised section 375, Indian Penal Code

"375. *Rape.*—A man is said to commit 'rape' who, except in the case hereinafter excepted, has sexual intercourse with a woman under circumstances falling under any of the *six* following descriptions:—

First.—Against her will.

[Ex. section 375, first clause]

Secondly.—Without her *free and voluntary* consent.

[Ex. section 375, second clause amplified]

Thirdly.—With her consent, when her consent has been obtained by putting her in fear of death *or of hurt or of any injury either to herself or to any other person or by criminal intimidation as defined in section 503.*

[Ex. section 375, third clause amplified]

Fourthly.—With her consent,

(a) when the man knows that he is not her husband, and that her consent is given because she believes that he is another man to whom she is or believes herself to be lawfully married, or

(b) *when her consent is given under a misconception of fact, when the man knows or has reason to believe that the consent was given in consequence of such misconception.*

[Ex. section 375, fourth clause amplified]

Fifthly.—With her consent, if the consent is given by a woman who, from unsoundness of mind or intoxication or by reason of the consumption or administration of any stupefying[1] *or unwholesome substance, in unable to understand the nature and consequences of that to which she gives consent, or is unable to offer effective resistance.*

[New]

Sixthly.—With or without her consent, when she is under *eighteen* years of age.

[Ex. section 375, fifth clause modified]

Exception.—Sexual intercourse by a man with his own wife, the wife not being under *eighteen* years of age, is not rape.

[Ex. section 375, exception modified]

Explanation 1.—Penetration is sufficient to constitute the sexual intercourse necessary to the offence of rape.

[Ex. section 375, Explanation]

1. *Cf.* section 328, Indian Penal Code.

Explanation 2.—A woman living separately from her husband under a decree of judicial separation or by mutual agreement shall be deemed not to be his wife for the purposes of this section."

[New]

[As to the second Explanation, *see* the earlier Report[1]].

XIV. Punishment for Rape

2.25. Section 376—Minimum punishment for rape by more than one person—Suggestion not accepted.—It has been suggested that in section 376 of the Penal Code, which deals with the punishment for rape, the situation where more than one person join in the act should be dealt with by stringent provisions, by providing, say, a minimum punishment of 10 years' rigorous imprisonment.

2.26. Aspect of group liability considered.—The offence of rape is, in law, a single act of sexual intercourse. That being so, if more than one person rape a woman one after another, each one of them would be punishable under section 376, I.P.C. When one person commits rape and others abet the Act by instigation or aid, the principal would be guilty of rape, and others would be punishable for abetment under section 109, Indian Penal Code. It is, however, doubtful whether, when the members of an unlawful assembly[2] attacking a village or a section of people rape several women during the course of the raid or attack, they can be punished under section 376 with the aid of section 149, Indian Penal Code.

2.27. Minimum punishment not favoured.—Be that as it may, it should be noted that a rule prescribing a certain minimum punishment would not be in consonance with the "modern penology" which has been of late expounded in many cases by the Supreme Court. The circumstances in which the offence of rape is committed differ from case to case. Section 376, Indian Penal Code permits the Court to award life imprisonment or imprisonment upto ten years. The discretion of the Court in the matter of punishment should not be fettered by prescribing a certain minimum sentence. If the sentence awarded is heavy or light, it can always be corrected by the appellate or revisional court.

XV. Assaults, Outraging Modesty of Women and Indecent Assaults

2.28. Section 354 and proposed section 354A.—We have so far discussed the offence of rape. We now deal with a few allied but less heinous offences. What is generally known as the offence of indecent assault is dealt with in section 354 of the Penal Code. This section punishes a person who assaults or uses criminal force to a woman with intent to outrage her "modesty". The Law Commission,[3] in its Report on the Penal Code, had occasion to refer to a judgment of the Supreme Court[4] in which it was held that even a baby of seven and a half months old has "modesty" that can be "outraged" by the use of criminal force within the meaning of this section.

1. Law Commission of India, 42nd Report (Indian Penal Code).
2. Section 141, Indian Penal Code.
3. Law Commission of India, 42nd Report (Indian Penal Code), paras. 16.85 to 16.87.
4. *State of Punjab* v. *Major Singh,* AIR 1967 SC 63 (65, 67): 1967 Cr LJ 1: 1966 (Suppl) SCR 286.

The Commission was of the opinion that (apart from assault to outrage "modesty"), acts of indecency with children should be made specifically punishable by a new section, reading as follows:—

> "354A. *Indecent assault on a minor.*—Whoever assaults any minor under sixteen years of age in an indecent, lascivious or obscene manner, shall be punished with imprisonment of either description for a term which may extend to three years, or with fine, or with both."

We agree with the recommendation quoted above from the earlier Report, in so far as it goes.

2.29. Consent not to be a defence.—However, we would like to make one addition. An indecent assault otherwise punishable under section 354 would presumably escape punishment if the assault is committed on the girl with her consent. The reason is, that if a girl consents, her "modesty"' cannot be outraged, and one of the essential requirements of the section would not then be satisfied. This, at least, has been the judicial construction[1] of the section.

Moreover, an act done with consent may not fall within "assault", unless the law, in a particular case, provides expressly to the contrary.

2.30. Need for change.—We are of the opinion that the law should expressly so provide in the case of indecent conduct with girls below 16 years. Having regard to the current thinking on the subject, it appears to be desirable to deal specifically with such indecency (with girls below 16, even with their consent).

In our opinion, besides incorporating section 354A in the Indian Penal Code, it is also necessary to further ensure by an express provision that the section will apply even where there is consent. In other words, consent of the woman should not prevent an act from being an assault for the purposes of this section and should not be a defence to a charge under this section.

2.31. Recommendation as to section 354A, Indian Penal Code.—Accordingly, we would recommend that, while incorporating section 354A in the Indian Penal Code, after the words "obscene manner", the words "*with or without the consent of the minor*" should also be added.

XVI. Indecent Gestures

2.32. Section 509, I.P.C.—We may mention here that acts which do not amount to an "assault"—acts such as indecent gestures and acts that have come to be known as "eve teasing"—are amply covered by section 509 of the Indian Penal Code.[2] The matter strictly does not Fall within the purview of rape or assault, but we refer to it because one of the women's organisations with whom we held discussions was anxious that the law should penalise such behaviour in public places or on public transport vehicles particularly.

Where there is physical contact or threat of physical contact, the offender can be charged under section 354 of the same Code, punishing a person who "assaults or uses criminal force to any woman, intending to outrage or knowing

1. *Sadananda Borgohin* v. *State,* 1972 Cr LJ 658 (Assam).
2. Section 509, Indian Penal Code.

it to be likely that he will thereby outrage her modesty". The punishment is imprisonment of either description upto two years or fine or both. Both the offences are, as the law now stands, cognizable.

2.33. Eve teasing in Delhi and charges under the Police Act.—We should now deal with one point concerning the mischief of what has popularly come to be known as "eve teasing". We have been given to understand[1] that practice of the Delhi Police is to take or suggest action under sections 91 and 92, read with section 97 of the Delhi Police Act[2] for such mischief. These provisions, so far as they are material to the point under discussion, punish indecent exposure, indecent and obscene conduct and the like in a public place.

2.34. Recommendation as to police practice..—Unfortunately, the provisions, of section 509, Indian Penal Code have been lost sight of by the police in almost all the States. The attention of the police should be drawn[3] to that section and they should be asked to proceed under section 509 or section 354, Indian Penal Code, as the case may be, whenever an incident of "eve teasing" is reported or takes place.

The offences under sections 509 and 354, Indian Penal Code an cognizable, as already stated above.

XVII. Obscene Telephone Calls

2.35. Section 294, I.P.C.—Obscene telephone calls.—In the context of offences against the modesty of women, a suggestion has been made that the making of obscene telephone calls should be made an offence. We have examined the relevant statutory provisions (including the Indian Penal Code and the Indian Telegraphs Act) in this connection.

Although section 509 may cover it, it is desirable to make an express provision. We find that section 20 of the Indian Post-office Act, 1898 punishes the sending of postal communications bearing on the cover indecent, obscene, seditious scurrilous, threatening or offensive matter.[4] There is no corresponding provision in the Indian Telegraphs Act with reference to the sending of such messages on telephone. It is for this reason that a specific provision on the subject appears to be needed.

2.36. Recommendation to amend section 294.—We would, therefore, recommend the insertion of the following clause in the Indian Penal Code under section 294 to deal with the mischief of obscene telephone calls:—

> "(c) *sings, recites or utters on the telephone any obscene song, ballad or words or any abusive words.*"

---

1. Discussions with the representatives of the National Federation of Women Lawyers (15th April, 1980).
2. Delhi Police Act, 1978 (34 of 1978).
3. Matter may kindly be looked into by Government of India, Ministry of Home Affairs.
4. Section 20, Post-office Act, 1898.

CHAPTER 3

ARREST AND INVESTIGATION

I. Introductory

3.1. Scope.—We propose to deal in this Chapter with the provisions as to arrest of women and certain aspects of investigation into offences. We also propose to consider the question how far workers of social organisations should be associated with the process of investigation.[1]

As to arrest, our discussion will cover certain matters concerning the arrest of women and their detention—these would apply to arrest and detention for any offence.[2]

As regards investigation, some of the matters to be discussed in this Chapter are confined to rape and allied offences.[3]

Some of them would, however, be applicable to the interrogation of women in general.[4]

Some[5] have a still wider application, concerned as they are with the duties of police officers concerning the recording of information relating to offences in general or charges against police officers.

3.2. Instructions issued by Ministry of Home Affairs.—The letter of reference[6] requests us to go through the instructions issued by the Government of India in the Ministry of Home Affairs on the subject of arrest and interrogation of women and to consider the question whether any of them could be placed on a statutory footing.

We have carefully gone through all the instructions, and we feel that while some of them can appropriately and conveniently be in the form of executive and administrative directions, the others should be placed on a statutory footing as rules and regulations under the Police Act.

3.3. Feeling of insecurity.—It has been strongly impressed upon us by all the women's organisations, and also by those who sent us suggestions in writing, that whenever a woman is called to a police station for interrogation or when she is arrested or detained in a police station, she feels insecure and always apprehends that the police will subject her to bodily pain, suffering and harassment and may even rape her. The feeling is held too strongly not to have some basis of fact. In any case, the very fact that such a feeling exists is, in itself, a sad commentary on the uprightness and credit of the police. It is not one born of the events in the comparatively recent past, but is one which has grown up over the years on account of the conduct and attitude of the police towards the women with whom they come in contact during the course or investigation of offences.

---

1. Paras. 3.33 and 3.34, *infra*.
2. *E.g.* paras. 3.5 to 3.10, *infra*.
3. *E.g.* paras. 3.11 to 3.15, *infra* and paras. 3.26 and 3.27, *infra*.
4. *E.g.* paras. 3.16 to 3.25, *infra* and paras. 3.34 and 3.35, *infra*.
5. *E.g.* paras. 3.28 to 3.32, *infra*.
6. Chapter 1, *supra*.

In our view, as criminal activities involving women grow, the need for an elimination of this feeling of apprehension and of giving adequate protection against police misdeeds to women, whenever they are called to police stations, becomes far more insistent.

3.4. Need for change in attitudes of the police.—Elimination, of this apprehension, so far as possible, may be achieved by remedies both administrative and legal. Under the former, we recommend that it should be strongly impressed on the police that their attitude and outlook towards women at the time of interrogation and investigation is entirely wrong and contrary to the traditions of the service. It should be impressed upon them that their behaviour towards women should be one of civility and courtesy and not one of harassment; with every desire to help in the detection of crime. The necessity for cultivating such an attitude should form part of their training.

So far as the law and legal processes are concerned, certain amendments, to be stated presently,[1] should be carried out in the Code of Criminal Procedure.

II. Arrest of Women

3.5. Arrest—Section 40, Code of Criminal Procedure.—Taking, first, the subject of arrest, the material provision of the Code of Criminal Procedure is contained in section 46, which reads as under:—

> "46. (1) In making an arrest the police officer or other person making the same shall actually touch or confine the body of the person to be arrested, unless there be a submission to the custody by word or action.
>
> (2) If such person forcibly resists the endeavour to arrest him, or attempts to evade the arrest, such police officer or other person may use all means necessary to effect the arrest.
>
> (3) Nothing in this section gives a right to cause the death of a person who is not accused of an offence punishable with death or with imprisonment for life."

The section requires a police officer making an arrest to actually touch or confine the body of the person to be arrested, unless there be a submission to custody by word or action. We are of the view that a provision should be added to the effect that in the case of women, their submission to custody shall be presumed unless proved otherwise, and that unless the circumstances otherwise require or unless the officer arresting is a female, the police officer should not actually touch the person of the woman for making an arrest.

3.6. Recommendation as to section 46(1), Cr. P.C., 1973.—Accordingly, we recommend that the following proviso should be added to section 46(1) of the Code of Criminal Procedure, 1973:—

> *"Provided that where a woman is to be arrested, then, unless the circumstances indicate to the contrary, her submission to custody on an oral intimation of arrest shall be presumed, and unless the circumstances otherwise require or unless the police officer arresting is a female, the police officer shall not actually touch the person of the woman for making her arrest."*

---

1. Para. 3.5, *et seq*, infra.

3.7. Section 46—Time of arrest.—With reference to this provision [section 46(1)] of the Code of Criminal Procedure, 1973, we are further of the view that a provision should be inserted to the effect that, except in unavoidable circumstances, no woman should be arrested after sunset and before sunrise. Where such unavoidable circumstances exist, the police officer must, by making a written report, obtain the prior permission of his superior officer, or, if the case is one of urgency, he must, after making the arrest, report the matter in writing to his immediate superior officer without delay with the reasons for arrest and reasons for not taking prior permission.

3.8. Recommendation to amend section 46.—Accordingly, we recommend that the following new sub-section should be inserted in section 46 of the Code of Criminal Procedure, 1973:—

> "(4) *Except in unavoidable circumstances, no woman shall be arrested after sunset and before sunrise, and where such unavoidable circumstances exist, the police officer shall, by making a written report, obtain the prior permission of his immediate superior officer for effecting such arrest or, if the case is one of extreme urgency, he shall, after making the arrest, forthwith report the matter in writing to his immediate superior officer with the reasons for arrest and the reasons for not taking prior permission as aforesaid.*"

III. Detention of Women

3.9. Section 417A, Cr. P.C. (Proposed)—Detention in women's institutions.—There are certain matters concerned with detention of women which require discussion. Where a woman is arrested and there are no suitable arrangements in the locality for keeping her in custody in a place of detention exclusively meant for women, it is, in our view desirable to send her to an institution established and maintained for the reception, care, protection and welfare of women or children, licensed under the Women's and Children's Institutions (Licensing) Act, 1956 or an institution recognised by the State Government. In cases where any special Act (such as the Suppression of Immoral Traffic in Women and Girls Act, 1956) requires that she should be sent to a protective home or other place of detention authorised for the purposes of such special Act, this will not apply. It is desirable that the law should be amended for the purpose by inserting a new section—say, section 417A—in the Code of Criminal Procedure. The following is a very rough draft:—

> "417A. *Where a woman is arrested and there are no suitable arrangements in the locality for keeping her in custody in a place of detention exclusively meant for women, she shall be sent to an institution established and maintained for the reception, care, protection and welfare of women or children, licensed under the Women's and Children's Institutions (Licensing) Act, 1956 or an institution recognised by the State Government, except in cases where any special law requires that she should he sent to a protective home or other place of detention authorised for the purposes of such special law.*"

3.10. Suggestions regarding presence of male relative near the lock up.—During our oral discussions with various women's organisations,[1] it has been suggested that when women are detained in police custody or in judicial lock up, a male relative of the woman should be allowed to remain at a place close to the lock up, so that he may be able to keep vigilance over what is happening in the lock up to the female inmate.

While we do not consider it practicable to make it a mandatory statutory requirement, we do recommend that it should be included in the executive instructions on the subject. The reason why we do not, at the moment, feel inclined to suggest a statutory provision is that we are not sure if such arrangements can be made at every police station. The shape and size of a police station and its precincts would vary from area to area; so would the facilities that could be provided for the purpose.

IV. Interrogation of Female Victims of Sexual Offences

3.11. Reporting and investigation.—These matters concern the arrest and detention of women in general. We now deal with certain matters peculiar to women who are victims of sexual offences. Women who have been raped are reluctant to report it partly because of the embarrassment of discussing the details with male policemen, and partly because of the very fear of the even more painful humiliation of being a witness in Court.

They get scared and become confused when, in the strange environment of the Courtroom, they have to conduct themselves in a manner foreign to their custom and under a restraint not conducive to clear coherent thought or to free expression.

3.12. Investigation by female police—No statutory change recommended.—A woman is often discouraged from pressing a charge of rape or other sexual offence by the fact that she usually encounters only male police and prosecution officers. It is presumably for this reason that it has been suggested that the investigation of such offences should be done by women police officers only.

We would be happy if the questioning of female victims of sexual offences would be done by women police officers only. We are not, however, inclined to recommend a statutory provision in this regard. A mandatory provision to that effect may prove to be unworkable. The number of women police officers in rural areas is very small. Even in urban areas, unless a centralised cell (with the status of a police station) is created for investigation into sexual offences against women, such a provision may not be practicable.

We regard this difficulty as a transient one. An all-on effort for the recruitment of sufficient number of women police officers, who could be drafted for the police duties of interrogation and investigation, should be made.

3.13. Practice to be adopted in metropolitan cities.—Till then, in metropolitan cities or big cities where there are sufficient number of women police officers, a practice should be established that women police officers alone investigate sexual offences and interrogate the victim.

---

1. Discussions held on the 15th April, 1980.

We are, therefore, not in favour of any statutory provision being made in this respect, subject to what we are recommending in the next paragraph.

3.14. Interrogation of child victim of rape—Statutory provision recommended.—The practice as suggested above[1] could be adopted in metropolitan areas and big cities. But there is one matter which is of importance for the whole country. It is necessary that in the case of *girls below a certain age*—say, below twelve years who are victims of rape, there should be a *statutory provision* to ensure that the girl must be interrogated only by a woman. A woman police officer would be preferable. But, if a woman police officer is not available, an alternate procedure as detailed below should be followed.

The alternate procedure that we contemplate is this. Where a woman police officer is not available, the officer in charge of the police station should forward a list of questions to a qualified female (we shall suggest details later) who would, after recording the information as ascertained from the child victim, return the papers to the officer in charge of the police station. If necessary, further questions to be put to the child may be sent by the police to the interrogator.

For the present, this procedure may be applied to female victims of offences below 12 years. It could later be utilised for child witnesses in general, if found practicable.

The "qualified female" whom we have in mind should be one who is a social worker belonging to a recognised social organisation. If she possesses some knowledge of law and procedure, it would be all the more useful, but that need not be a statutory requirement.

3.15. Amendment of section 160 recommended by insertion of sub-sections (3) to (7).—In view of what is stated above, we would recommend the addition of the following provision—say, as new sub-sections—in section 160 of the Code of Criminal Procedure, 1973:—

> "(3) *Where, under this Chapter, the statement of a girl under the age of twelve years is to be recorded, either as first information of an offence or in the course of an investigation into an offence, and the girl is a person against whom an offence under sections* 354, 354A *or* 375 *of the Indian Penal Code*[2] *is alleged to have been committed or attempted, the statement shall be recorded either by a female police officer or by a person authorised by such organisation interested in the welfare of women or children as is recognised in this behalf by the State Government by notification in the official gazette.*
>
> (4) *Where the case is one to which the provisions of sub-section* (3) *apply, and a female police officer is not available, the officer in charge of the police station shall, in order to facilitate the recording of the statement, forward to the person referred to in that sub-section a written request setting out the points on which information is required to be elicited from the girl.*
>
> (5) *The person to whom such a written request is forwarded shall, after recording the statement of the girl, transmit the record to the officer in charge of the police station.*

---

1. Para. 3.13, *supra.*
2. Proposed sections 376A, 373B and 376C, Indian Penal Code could also be added.

(6) *Where the statement recorded by such person as forwarded under sub-section* (5) *appears in any respect to require clarification or amplification, the officer in charge of the police station shall return the papers to the person by whom it was forwarded, with a request for clarification or amplification on specified matters; and such person shall thereupon record the further statement of the girl in conformity with the request end return the papers to the officer in charge of the police station.*

(7) *The statement of the girl recorded and forwarded under sub-sections* (3) *to* (6) *shall, for the purpose of the law relating to the admissibility in evidence of statements made by any person, be deemed to be a statement recorded by a police officer.*"[1]

V. Interrogation of Women at The Place of Residence

3.16. Section 160(1), Proviso, Cr. P.C.—There is another aspect of investigation which is in need of reform. Under section 160(1) of the Code of Criminal Procedure, 1973 a police officer making an investigation under Chapter 14 of the Code may, by order in writing, require, the attendance before himself of any person "being within the limits of his own or any adjoining station" (for the purposes of investigation). The proviso to this sub-section provides that "no male person under the age of fifteen or woman shall be required to attend *at any place other than the place in which such male person or woman resides*".

The proviso has been taken over by the present Code from the earlier Code of 1898. In that Code, it was inserted by an amending Act of 1955 in response to the observations made in a number of earlier judicial decisions, suggesting that women should not ordinarily be called to the police station.[2]

3.17. Defect in drafting.—Though it is clearly the policy of the law to ensure that the interrogation of the persons in question (women and young boys) should be done at *their residence,* the object is not, at present, fully reflected in the words employed for the purpose in section 160(1), proviso. The expression "place" is a wide one. Its definition[3] in the Code is also an inclusive one, and in any case, does not indicate very clearly that in the context of section 160(1), proviso, "place" means a place *where the person resides.*

It is a mistake to think that section 160(1), proviso enjoins the police officer to interrogate a woman at the place where the woman *resides.* This is not so. "Place" means the locality in which the woman resides and ever which the police officer has jurisdiction.

In order to reflect the legislative policy more fully and to fortify the protection sought to be enacted in the proviso, the phraseology, in our opinion, requires a slight alteration.

3.18. Recommendation to revise section 160(1), proviso, Cr. P.C.—Accordingly, we recommend that section 160(1), proviso of the Code of Criminal Procedure, should be revised as under:—

To be substituted for section 160(1), *proviso, Code of Criminal Procedure:*

---

1. *See* further, *infra.*
2. Compare the observations made in *Haldar* v. *Sub-Inspector of Police,* 9 CWN 199 (201), 1st Column. *See* also (1905) 2 Cr LJ 51 (53).
3. Section 2(p), Code of Criminal Procedure, 1973.

"Provided that no male person under the age of fifteen years or woman shall be required to attend at any place *other than his or her dwelling place.*"

3.19. Punishment for violation of section 160(1) not adequate.—Another point arising out of section 160(1), proviso of the Code of Criminal Procedure may now be discussed, namely, penalty for violation thereof. The position in this regard is not satisfactory. At present, the mere summoning of a person in violation of the statutory mandate[1] would presumably be punishable as wrongful restraint under section 341, Indian Penal Code[2] (imprisonment upto one month or fine upto five hundred rupees).

In our view, the punishment under section 341, I.P.C. is, inadequate for an offence of this nature. Perhaps, a charge of an offence under section 166, Indian Penal Code (public servant disobeying direction of law with intent to cause injury to any person) could be made for the violation of the prohibition in question. But, in our opinion, it would be better to have a specific provision—say, as section 166A—in the Indian Penal Code to cover such violations. The provision could be appropriately placed in the Chapter on "Offences by or against public servants". The proposed offence should be cognisable, bailable and triable by any Magistrate.

3.20. Section 166A, I.P.C. recommended.—The following is a rough draft of the provision that we would recommend to be inserted in the Indian Penal Code on the subject mentioned above:—

(To be inserted in the Indian Penal Code)

"166A. *Whoever, being a public servant*—

(*a*) *knowingly disobeys any direction of the law prohibiting him from requiring the attendance at any place of any person for the purpose of investigation into an offence or other matter, or*

(*b*) *knowingly disobeys any other direction*[3] *of the law regulating the manner in which he shall conduct such investigation, to the prejudice of any person, shall be punished with imprisonment for a term which may extend to one year or with fine or with both.*"[4]

VI. Interrogation of Women—Time of

3.21. Interrogation of women after sunset and before sunrise.—The last few paragraphs were concerned with the *place* of interrogation of women. We should now deal with the *time* of interrogation. In the views expressed before us by a representative of one of the women's organisations, it was suggested that women, even when they are not the persons accused or victims of the offence

1. Section 160(1), Proviso, Code of Criminal Procedure, 1973.
2. *Raja Ram* v. *State of Haryana,* (1971) 3 SCC 945 (949).
3. *Cf.* sections 162(1), 163, 171, Code of Criminal Procedure, 1973.
4. Consequential amendment to be made in the Schedule to the Code of Criminal Procedure, 1973, so as to provide that the proposed offence shall be cognisable, bailable and triable by any Magistrate.

and are merely witnesses to the crime, should not be interrogated by the police after sunset and before sunrise. It seems to us that if the statutory provision for interrogating women at their residence,[1] as proposed to be clarified by us,[2] is properly and adequately implemented, there should be no need for a further and additional provision totally barring the interrogation of women after sunset and before sunrise.

After all, the principal object sought to be achieved by such restrictions is to ensure that no opportunity arises for the molestation of women. That object is, in a large measure, achieved by the statutory provision referred to above.

VII. Social Workers

3.22. Association of women social workers with investigation.—Another aspect of investigation on which emphasis has been placed by one of the women's organisations during our oral discussions with them is the need to associate women social workers with investigation into cases relating to rape and allied offences. After giving the matter deep thought, we find it difficult to accede to the suggestion.

Under our system of procedure, investigation is primarily in the hands of the police officer. Cognisance of offences can, no doubt, be taken by the competent Magistrate directly on a complaint[3] made by any person (generally speaking, that person need not even be the victim of the offence). But even the Magistrate to whom such a complaint is made would not have adequate investigative machinery at his disposal. He will also have to depend generally[4] on the police for the purpose, the only difference being that an investigation so directed by the Magistrate who has taken cognisance on a complaint remains—in certain respects—subject to the orders of that Magistrate.

3.23. Investigation an arduous task.—That apart, investigation of an offence is not a light duty. We have the highest opinion and respect for women's intelligence, ability and competence, yet we feel that they may not be able to cope with the arduous duties which an investigating police officer is required to discharge. There is also the danger of a male police officer completely abdicating his duties if a social worker is associated on an equal footing with him for investigation of an offence. If the investigation is successful and fruitful, then the male police officer will take all the credit for it, but if it fails, he will try to escape the liability for the failure by throwing the entire blame on the female associate.

This being the position, it may not he practicable to confer on women social workers any specific legal status.[5]

3.24. Recommendation to amend section 160, Cr. P.C.—However, in our view, it would be useful to provide that a female social worker should be allowed to be present whenever the victim of rape is interrogated by the police.

1. Section 160(1), Proviso, Cr. P.C., 1973.
2. Para. 3.18, *supra*.
3. Section 190(1), Code of Criminal Procedure, 1973.
4. Section 202(1), Code of Criminal Procedure, 1973.
5. *See* also para. 3.34, *infra*.

We recommend that in section 160 of the Code of Criminal Procedure, 1973, a suitable amendment should be made for the purpose. The social worker must belong to an organisation recognised by the State Government.

3.25. Amendment of section 160 recommended by insertion of sub-section (8).—In view of what is stated above, we would recommend the insertion of the following provision—say as a new sub-section—in section 160 of the Code of Criminal Procedure, 1973:—

"(8) *Where, under this Chapter, the statement of a male person under the age of fifteen years or of a woman is recorded by a male police officer, either as first information of an offence or in the course of an investigation into an offence, a relative or friend of such male person or woman, and also a person authorised by such organisation interested in the welfare of women or children as is recognised in this behalf by the State Government by notification in the official gazette, shall be allowed to remain present throughout the period during which the statement is being recorded.*"[1]

VIII. Police Report to be Accompanied by Medical Reports

3.26. Section 173(5), Cr. P.C.—Report of a police officer to be accompanied with certain documents.—The process of investigation generally culminates in the report of a police officer. The report of a police officer on which a Magistrate usually takes cognisance is the subject-matter of section 173 of the Code of Criminal Procedure. Alongwith such report, certain documents are to be forwarded as provided in sub-section (5) of that section, quoted below:—

"173. (5) When such report is in respect of a case to which section 170 applies, the police officer shall forward to the Magistrate along with the report—

(a) all documents or relevant extracts thereof on which the prosecution proposes to rely other than those already sent to the Magistrate during investigation;

(b) the statements recorded under section 161 of all the persons whom the prosecution proposes to examine as its witnesses."[2]

3.27. Section 173(5), Cr. P.C.—Amendment recommended as to medical reports.—Our recommendations relating to medical reports to be made in a later Chapter[3] contemplate the forwarding of the medical reports to the police officer investigating the offence. As a consequence of those amendments, it is necessary to amplify sub-section (5) of section 173.

Accordingly, we recommend that in section 173(5) of the Code of Criminal Procedure, 1973, after the words "on which the prosecution proposes to rely", the following words, figures and marks should be inserted:—

"*including the report of medical examination of the arrested person accused of rape or attempt to commit rape forwarded to the police officer under section* 53,

---

1. For sub-sections (3) to (7) to be inserted in section 160, *see* para. 3.15, *supra*.
2. For other points concerned with medical reports, *see* Chapter 4, *infra*.
3. Chapter 4, *infra*, paras. 4.7 and 4.10.

and the report of medical examination of the victim of such an offence forwarded to the police officer under section 164A."

IX. Investigation where Police Officer is The Accused

3.28. Investigation into cases where a police officer is an accused.—We may note that during the debates on a motion in the Lok Sabha on the subject of rape of women,[1] it was suggested that where a police officer is the accused, the investigation into the offence alleged to have been committed by the police officer should be by some other agency, as otherwise it would be well-nigh impossible to convict the accused.

It is not clear what is meant by 'some other agency'. Perhaps the idea is that where a police officer is involved in rape, then the investigation should be by a police officer of the district or area other than the district or area where the culprit officer was posted at the time of the crime. We commend the suggestion for the consideration of Government.

X. Non-recording of Information Relating to Cognisable Offences

3.29. Section 167A, I.P.C.—Refusal to register case of rape.—We now come to another matter concerning the stage of investigation. During our oral discussions with the representatives of women's organisations, it was stated that in some cases the police fail to register a case of rape reported to them even when the full facts are communicated to them. We have not been able to gather statistics of the number of such cases, as the collection of the relevant figures would take considerable time and the present Report[2] deals with a matter of urgency. We hope that the percentage of such cases would not be high. Nevertheless, we do take the view that in principle, the law should contain a specific provision dealing with refusal (or failure without sufficient cause) to register such cases. The offence of rape is a cognisable offence and if the police fail to register it, it is a clear violation of the provisions of the Code of Criminal Procedure, 1973 in this regard.[3] Cognisable offences reported to the police are "registered"—as the popular usage goes—under section 154(1) of the Code of Criminal Procedure. If the officer in charge of a police station refuses to record the information reported relating to a cognisable offence, there is a remedy already provided[4] in the Code of Criminal Procedure, the relevant provision being in the following terms:—

> "(3) Any person aggrieved by a refusal on the part of an officer in charge of a police station to record the information referred to in sub-section (1) [of section 154] may send the substance of such information, in writing and by post, to the Superintendent of Police concerned who, if satisfied that such information discloses the commission of a cognisable offence, shall either investigate the case himself or direct an investigation to be made by any police officer subordinate to him, in the manner provided by this Code, and such officer shall have all the powers of an officer in charge of the police station in relation to that offence."

---

1. Lok Sabha Debaters, 27th March, 1980, Column 8349.
2. *See* Chapter 1, *supra.*
3. Cf. *Kurukshetra University* v. *State of Haryana,* AIR 1977 SC 2220.
4. Section 154(3), Code of Criminal Procedure, 1973.

3.30. Penal sanctions needed.—The provision of the Code of Criminal Procedure quoted above, however, is not of a penal character, though, no doubt, when the matter is reported to the Superintendent of Police thereunder, a departmental action can be taken. We have, therefore, examined the question whether there is need for any penal sanction and, if so, whether the present law is adequate in this regard. In our opinion, and having particular regard to the fact that we have been given to understand during our oral discussions that administrative action does not prove very effective, *prima facie* there is need for a suitable penalty.

3.31. Present law.—As to the present law on the subject, it would appear that the matter is not very specifically covered by the substantive criminal law. No doubt, there are provisions in the Indian Penal Code punishing public servants for the malicious exercise of their powers in certain cases, which it is unnecessary to discuss for the present purpose. Many Police Acts also contain provisions punishing a police officer for "violation of his duty"[1] or provisions similarly worded. The punishment laid down is, however, usually mild; for example, in the Delhi Police Act it is imprisonment upto three months or fine upto Rs. 100. The punishment is mild presumably because such provisions are of a general character, embracing "violations of duty" of various degrees and shades.

3.32. Insertion of section 167A, Indian Penal Code recommended.—Having regard to what we have stated above, we would recommend the insertion of a specific penal provision, say, as section 167A, in the Indian Penal Code on the subject. In view of the general scheme adopted in that Code, the proposed provision would not be confined to refusal to register the offence of rape and would cover other cognisable offences as well. The following is a rough draft of the provision that we recommend:—

> "167A.—*Whoever, being an officer-in-charge of a police station and required by law to record any information relating to the commission of a cognisable offence reported to him, refuses or without reasonable cause fails to record such information shall be punished with imprisonment of either description for a term which may extend to one year, or with fine, or with both.*"[2]

XI. Other Points Concerning Investigation

3.33. Other points made in suggestions.—At this stage, we may also note a few other points concerned with investigation on which improvements have been suggested in the views expressed orally before us or in written points handed over to us. These may be enumerated briefly—

First, offences of rape etc. should be promptly registered.

Secondly, in such cases the officer-in-charge of a Police Station must proceed to investigate the offence in person and shall not depute any subordinate of his to make the investigation.

---

1. Compare section 122(f)(iv), Delhi Police Act, 1978.
2. The proposed offence should be cognisable, bailable and triable by any Magistrate. Complaint of any particular police officer should not be required for taking cognisance.

Thirdly, a copy of the information lodged must forthwith be forwarded to the nearest Magistrate whether such Magistrate is empowered to take cognisance or not.

Fourthly, such Magistrate on receiving the information should be empowered to issue directions regarding investigation of the case until cognisance is taken by a Magistrate who is empowered to take cognisance of the offence.

Fifthly, in Presidency towns and district towns or Sub-Divisions, investigation should be made by an officer not below the rank of a Deputy Superintendent of Police.

Some of these points have been already dealt with.[1] The rest seem to be concerned with matters proper for administrative action, rather than for legal amendment.

3.34. Conferment of Magisterial and Police powers on women.—It has also been suggested that certain Magisterial powers and limited police powers may be conferred on educated and respected ladies in villages nearby, like social workers or school teachers. It has been suggested[2] that suitable amendments may be made in the Code of Criminal Procedure in this behalf.

We would leave this matter for appropriate action by the authorities competent to appoint Magistrates. Conferment of police powers on ladies, however, does not appear to be practicable.

The question of associating social workers with investigation has already been dealt with.[3]

3.35. Questions relating to medical examination.—An important part of investigation into cases of rape is in the shape of physical examination of the accused and the victim by medical experts. This topic deserves separate treatment, and will accordingly be discussed later.[4] We may, however, mention that one of the amendments that we have recommended in the present Chapter (documents to be forwarded with a police report) is concerned with medical reports.[5]

CHAPTER 4

MEDICAL EXAMINATION OF THE ACCUSED AND THE VICTIM

I. Importance of Medical Examination

4.1. Scope.—We propose to deal in this Chapter with the medical examination (of the accused and the victim) in cases relating to rape. The medical report in such cases is a document of vital importance. The matter has both medical and legal aspects, deserving of attention.

---

1. *E.g.* para. 3.28, *supra.*
2. *See* also paras. 3.22 and 3.23, *supra.*
3. Para. 3.25, *supra.*
4. *See* Chapter 4, *infra.*
5. Para. 3.26, *supra.*

4.2. Position of examining doctor.—An eminent writer on legal medicine[1] has observed that the situations in which the practising clinician may find himself involved in the examination of either the alleged victim or the alleged assailant in sexual offences are unique in regard to the degree of emotional tension that may be generated in all the persons involved in the situation. "Here, possibly more than in any other medico-legal situation, it behaves a clinician to remember the general principles of *detail, suspicion, impartiality and observation*".

He has pointed out that many of the examinations required in such cases will take place late at night, or in the early hours of the morning when the doctor himself is likely to be tired, and the value and importance of a set routine becomes very important indeed.

4.3. Importance from the legal point of view.—From the legal point of view also, it is well recognised that the medical examination report of the accused in a case of rape or attempt to commit rape is a very important document. Of that part of the *actus reus* of the offence which consists of sexual intercourse by the accused, there cannot ordinarily be a better evidence than the medical report, so far as the male party is concerned.

4.4. Proper examination—conditions for.—It has been pointed out that the proper and thorough investigation of an alleged rape depends on:[2]

Early notification to the police;

Full co-operation between the victim and the various investigating agencies;

An experienced and understanding police officer in charge.

Any delay in reporting an alleged rape will result in delay in the commencement of the investigation, with the loss of trace evidence on the victim, the accused and the scene. It is for these reasons that the victim must be interviewed at some length as soon after the offence has taken place as is possible, and before she has had a chance to wash, clean or repair her clothing, or change her clothing.

The medical examination must be a complete one, and must include the complete medical history of the victim, a detailed history of the alleged assault, a complete body examination and the taking of all relevant biological samples.

II Examination of The Accused

4.5. Provision in the Code—Need for timely examination.—The Code of Criminal Procedure has, in section 53, a general provision on the subject of medical examination of the accused in all cases where such examination would afford evidence of commission of offence.[3]

---

1. David M. Paul, Department of Forensic Medicine, Guy's Hospital, London, *The Medical Examination in Sexual Offences*, (1978 July), Vol. 15, No. 3, *Medicine, Science and the Law*, pp. 154-162.
2. British Academy of Forensic Sciences *Memorandum on rape*, (July 1976), Vol. 16, *Medicine, Science and the Law*, pp. 154, 156, 157.
3. Section 53, Cr. P.C., 1973.

It is, however, seen that the report of the medical examination is often cursory, or is not sent in time, in cases of rape or attempt to commit rape.

In a recent Calcutta case,[1] the High Court was constrained to observe—

"It is also striking that the appellant, though arrested on that very night (9th *May) was not produced before Dr. Pal (P.W.* 11) *who examined P.Ws.* 1 *and* 10 *on* 10-5-1970."

4.6. Particulars to be entered and reasons to be given.—It is also desirable that the report should (besides containing the usual formal particulars) deal specifically with—(i) the age of the accused, (ii) injuries to the body of the accused, and (iii) other material particulars in reasonable detail. It should also note the precise time of examination. It should be sent without delay by the registered medical practitioner to the investigating officer and the latter should file it before the Magistrate empowered to take cognisance along with the documents sent with the challan under section 173(5) of the Code.[2]

4.7. Recommendation as to section 53, Cr. P.C.—It is very important that reasons should be given for the opinion expressed in the report. Accordingly, we recommend the insertion in section 53 of the Code of Criminal Procedure, of the following sub-sections:—

"Sections 53(1A), (1B), (1C) *and* (1D), *Code of Criminal Procedure,* 1973 *to be inserted.*

(1A) When a person accused of rape or an attempt to commit rape is arrested and an examination of his person is to be made under this section, he shall be forwarded without delay to the registered medical practitioner by whom he is to be examined.

(1B) The registered medical practitioner conducting such examination shall without delay examine such person and prepare a report specifically recording the result of his examination and giving the following particulars:

(i) *the name and address of the accused and of the person by whom he was brought,*

(ii) *the age of the accused,*

(iii) *marks of injury, if any, on the person of the accused, and*

(iv) *other material particulars in reasonable detail.*

(1C) The report shall state precisely the reasons for each conclusion arrived at.

(1D) The exact time of commencement and completion of the examination shall also be noted in the report, and the registered medical practitioner shall, without delay, forward the report to the investigating officer, who shall forward it to the Magistrate referred to in section 1973 *as part of the documents referred to in clause (a) of sub-section* (5) *of that section."*

III. Examination of The Victim

4.8. Section 164A, Cr. P.C. (To be added).—We next deal with the victim. In many cases, the report of the medical examiner as to the examination of the

1. *Narayan Dutta* v. *State,* 1980 Cr LJ 264, paras. 1-2 (March 1980) (Cal).
2. *See* Chapter 3, *supra.*

female victim is also found to be somewhat cursory and does not give adequate information about the material particulars which are necessary for an adjudication as to the various ingredients of section 375. Further, it is sometimes noticed that the medical examination report is not sent promptly, to the investigating officer. As a result, the possibility of tampering with the report remains.

In our opinion, the report of the examination of the victim in a case of rape should (besides containing the usual formal particulars) deal specifically with—

(i) the age of the victim,

(ii) the question whether the victim was previously used to sexual intercourse,

(iii) injuries to the body of the victim,

(iv) general mental condition of the victim, and

(v) other material particulars in reasonable detail.

It is also necessary that the report should note the time of examination and be sent without delay to the investigating officer. It is very important that the report should state reasons for the conclusions recorded.

4.9. Need for legislative provisions.—Ordinarily, such matters are left to be dealt with by executive instructions. However, having regard to the importance of the subject, it would be proper to insert in the Code of Criminal Procedure, at an appropriate place, a provision incorporating the guidelines that we have suggested above. In the light of practical working of the provision, further improvements could be made in the relevant provisions.

4.10. Section 164A, Cr. P.C. recommended.—Accordingly, we recommend that the following new section should be inserted in the Code of Criminal Procedure, 1973:

"164A. (1) *Where, during the stage when an offence of rape or attempt to commit rape is under investigation, it is proposed to get the person of the woman with whom rape is alleged to have been committed or attempted, examined by a medical expert, such examination shall be conducted by a registered medical practitioner, with the consent of the woman or of some person competent to give such consent on her behalf and the woman shall he forwarded to the registered medical practitioner without delay.*

(2) *The registered medical practitioner to whom such woman is forwarded shall without delay examine her person and prepare a report specifically recording the result of his examination and giving the following detail:*

(i) *the name and address of the woman and of the person by whom she was brought,*

(ii) *the age of the woman,*

(iii) *whether the victim was previously used to sexual intercourse,*

(iv) *marks of injuries, if any, on the person of the woman,*

(v) *general mental condition of the woman, and*

(vi) *other material particulars, in reasonable detail.*

(3) *The report shall state precisely the reasons for each conclusion arrived at.*

(4) *The report shall specifically record that the consent of the woman or of some person competent to give such consent on her behalf to such examination had been obtained.*

(5) *The exact time of commencement and completion of the examination shall also be noted in the report, and the registered medical practitioner shall without delay, forward the report to the investigating officer, who shall forward it to the Magistrate referred to in section* 173 *as part of the documents referred to In clause* (a) *of sub-section* (5) *of that section.*

(6) *Nothing in this section shall be construed as rendering lawful any examination without the consent of the victim or of any person competent to give such consent on her behalf."*

4.11. Medical examination of the victim of rape.—In regard to the examination of the person of the accused, section 53(2) of the Code of Criminal Procedure provides that whenever the person of a female is to be examined under that section, the examination shall be made only by, or under the supervision of, a female registered medical practitioner.

The question whether a provision should be inserted to the effect that *where a female victim* of a sexual offence is to be examined, the medical examination shall be conducted only by a female medical practitioner has been carefully considered by us. We think that a statutory provision is not necessary, for two reasons. In the first place, this is almost the invariable practice in India and a statutory mandate is not needed. In the second place, if a female victim does not wish to submit to examination by a male doctor, there is no legal obligation on her part to do so. For that reason also, a statutory provision is not necessary. It may be mentioned that such medical examination cannot be lawfully made without the consent of the woman or of some person competent to give consent.[1]

IV. Chronology and Modes

4.12. Chronology and modes of examination.—We have so far dealt with matters on which legislative provisions have been suggested by others or recommended by us, on the subject of medical examination. It would be useful now to refer to certain other aspects.

As to the chronological stages of the examination and the mode of conducting it, there is interesting material available.

A distinguished writer suggests[2] that date, time and place of examination should be noted at the commencement of the examination and the time at which the examination terminated should also be noted.

Further, he adds, history of the person examined is important. Full general history must be taken and this must include all previous illness, operation and accident. It should also include the time and nature of the last meal eaten, the amount and nature of the alcoholic drink consumed and the time it was consumed and the amount, nature and time of any medication taken.

1. Para. 4.10, *supra.*
2. David M. Paul *The Medical Examination in Sexual Offences,* (1975 July), Vol. 15, No. 3, *Medicine, Science & Law,* pp. 154, 162.

Specific history should be taken, preferably from the complainant and before any account is heard from the police authority, instructing solicitor or parent. This history is an essential part of the clinical examination and full notes must be made of it because one of the essentials of physical examination is to decide it the physical findings are compatible with the history taken.

4.13. Examination of various body sheets.—Each system of body should be examined and "all the examination findings should be noted even if they are normal findings". Skeletal deformity or injury, he points out, may reduce the effectiveness of any resistance; intoxication may reduce the power to resist or the ability to form an intention. Natural disease may affect the behaviour. The general examination must, therefore, include the skin, teeth, finger, nails, cardio-vascular system, respiratory system, abdomen, skeletal system and central nervous system, for only in this way can the examining doctor be sure that he has not missed any relevant feature.

4.14. Injuries.—As to injuries, the description must include an accurate description of the site of the injury with special reference to fixed body points, a measurement of the size of the injury; a general description of the type of the injury; a detailed description of its shape; and a description of the colour of any bruising or exudate present.

V. Rapid Reference Sheets

4.15. Rapid reference sheets.—The distinguished expert in legal medicine[1] (to whose writing we have already referred) has prepared the following "rapid reference sheet" for the examination, of the person accused and the victim of rape:

Accused

(1) Consent to examination.[2]

(2) Detailed general history: past illness, surgery, accident, food, drink and drugs.

(3) Observe: manner, clothing.

(4) Examine all clothing: remove in presence of doctor; inspect each item separately; retain each item in a clean bag; ultra-violet light on trouser-shirt, vest, under pants.

(5) Full general clinical examination: examine the whole body; record all findings; record all injuries, old, new, location, size and description.

(6) Examine the affected portions: injury to various parts (details are given).

(7) Specimens of substances from the body: Blood; urine; saliva; avulsed hair; loose hairs, avulsed pubic hair; matted pubic hair; finger nail

1. David M. Paul *The Medical Examination in Sexual Offences* (1975 July), Vol. 15, No. 3, *Medicine Science and the Law*, pp. 154, 158, 159.

2. In India, this is governed by a statutory provision in section 53, Code of Criminal Procedure, 1973.

scrappings; clippings; areas of soiling; pubic hair combings; swabs from urethral orifice; prepuce etc.

(8) Equipment: sterile swabs; sellotape; glass slides; syringe; large bore needles, tape measures; clean paper bags; labels.

Victim

(1) Consent to examination.

(2) Detailed general history: past illness, accident, operation, food, drink and drugs.

(3) Detailed specific history: obstetric; menstrual etc.; past sexual experience; details of present incident.

(4) Observe: manner, dress; make-up.

(5) Examination of clothing: remove in presence of doctor; inspect each item separately; retain each item in a clean bag; damage, staining, soiling; ultra-violet light on pants, tights, pantragirdle.

(6) Full general clinical examination: examine the whole body; record all findings; record all injuries old, new, location, size, description.

(7) Examine the affected parts (details given).

(8) Specimens (details given).

(9) Equipment: sterile swabs; hypodermic syringe; needles, gloves, slides; labels, speculum; tape measure, cello tape; clean paper bags.

VI. Conditions in which Examination is Conducted

4.16. Conditions for physical examination.—We have so far discussed the contents of medical reports. Certain matters concerning the conditions for physical examination are also of interest. Justice cannot be done to either parties (the prosecution or the defence) or to the doctor, if adequate conditions for examination of the victim are not available. It is, therefore, necessary that the equipment and environment of the examination should be adequate; in particular, the premises should be well-lit.

In order to put the victim at ease, it would be desirable (unless the victim is an adult woman of mature years), to examine orally first the mother or other older relative by whom she is accompanied. The circumstances in which the offence is alleged to have been committed should be first ascertained from such relative.

4.17. Order of examination.—As regards the actual examination of the victim, the general physical examination should be first commenced, in order to induce a feeling of relaxation in the victim. The parts of the body more directly affected could be examined later on.

4.18. Conditions and equipment.—There have been many learned discussions as to the conditions in which such examination should be made and as to the equipment that may be used. For example, one expert in legal medicine has stated his experience thus[1]—

1. K.F.M. Pole, Letter in (January 1970) *Medicine, Science and the Law*, p. 73.

"Examination with an ultra-violet lamp I consider to be very useful and the police put a mains' model at my disposal whenever I need it—that is, in every reasonably recent case. Details depend on the history of baths and ablutions since the incident, but I would rather err on the side of using it too often than too rarely."

VII. Colour Photographs

4.19. Colour photographs.—It is also desirable to take colour photographs of injuries, for these are the only photographs that give a true picture of the age and extent of many significant injuries, such as bruises and abrasions. It is these comparatively minor injuries that are often of the greatest importance in reaching a medical diagnosis in a case of alleged rape.[1]

CHAPTER 5

PROCEDURE FOR TRIAL, TRIAL *IN CAMERA* AND PUBLICATION OF PROCEEDINGS

I. Cognisance of Offences

5.1. Scope of Chapter.—We propose to deal in this Chapter with certain aspects of procedure relating to the trial of rape and allied offences.

5.2. Section 198(6), Cr. P.C., 1973—Amendment recommended.—We first deal with the cognisance of offences. Section 198(6) of the Code of Criminal Procedure, 1973 requires a complaint to be filed within one year in case of rape constituted by sexual intercourse by husband with a wife under 15 years. The portion referring to "wife under 15 years" should be deleted from this sub-section. The reason is that under the amendments recommended in the 42nd Report[1] to the Indian Penal Code, the scope of section 375, I.P.C. would be expanded, so as to cover not only intercourse with a child wife, but also, in certain circumstances, intercourse with the wife (irrespective of her age) if the wife is living separately.

Accordingly, we recommend that section 198(6) of the Code of Criminal Procedure, 1973 should be revised as under[2]—

Revised section 198(6), Code of Criminal Procedure, 1973

"(6) No Court shall take cognisance of an offence under section 376 of the Indian Penal Code, where such offence consists of sexual intercourse by a man with his own wife, ... if more than one year has elapsed from the date of the commission of the offence."

5.3. Court competent to try.—The offence of rape can be tried only by the Court of Session. The position in this regard needs no change.

II. Stages of Trial

5.4. Procedure for trial—the chronology.—Under the Code of Criminal Procedure, 1973, the procedure for trial in Courts of Session is governed by

1. British Academy of Forensic Sciences *Memorandum on Law Regarding Rape,* (July 1976), *Medicine, Science and the Law,* pp. 154, 158.
2. *See* para. 2.24, *supra.*

provisions contained in a separate Chapter devoted to such trials, which does not seem to need any change so far as the various stages of trial in regard to the offences dealt with in this Report are concerned.

III. TRIAL *IN CAMERA*

5.5. Trial *in camera*—Section 327, Cr. P.C.—There is, however, one matter of procedure in regard to which there is scope for reform. A trial for rape, like other criminal trials, is, in general, conducted in public. This is in accordance with the statutory provision in the Code of Criminal Procedure on the subject.[1]

The reasons why trials are held in public (subject to specific statutory exceptions) have been discussed judicially[2] and otherwise, more than once, and we need not set them out. However, in the case of sexual offences, there is an overriding consideration which justifies an exception being made to the general rule of public trial. Certain details of an intimate character may have to be narrated in court in such trials. It is not only embarrassing for the victim to narrate them in the full glare of publicity. Often, by reason of such embarrassment, she may not be able to give all the factual details, and the cause of justice may ultimately suffer. It is, therefore, on the wider ground of interests of justice, that we would recommend that in the absence of special reasons to be recorded by the Court, a trial for rape or allied offences must be held *in camera*.

5.6. Need to modify general rule.—We may state that the broad principle of publicity can be modified where the Court thinks that justice could not be done at all if it had to be done in public.[3]

The proposition that 'where secrecy begins justice ends' is one held by most lawyers as sacred. However, in the area of rape, and indeed of all the serious sexual offences, there is a particular burden on the complainant and on the accused with the real risk of courtroom defamation repeated in the press, which may subsequently be found by the Court to be totally unjustifiable.[4]

It is for this reason that in England, the National Council for Civil Liberties[5] in their pamphlet on *The Rape Controversy*, said—

> *"The law should recognise the fact that there is still a stigma attached to rape from which the victims may suffer for years afterwards."*

We would wish to extend this view to include the stigma that may attach itself to the accused for years afterwards even following an acquittal. In this context, it should be remembered that the making of an allegation of rape against any man imposes upon him an equally unpleasant, humiliating and embarrassing experience in respect of which he should be entitled to the same protection as may be accorded to the alleged victim.

---

1. Section 327, Cr. P.C., 1973.
2. *Naresh* v. *State of Maharashtra,* AIR 1967 SC 1.
3. *Scott* v. *Scott,* 1913 AC 417 (437).
4. British Academy of Forensic Sciences *Memorandum on Rape,* (July 1976) *Medicine, Science and the Law,* 154, 155.
5. National Council for Civil Liberties *The Rape Controversy,* (1975).

5.7. Recommendation to amend section 327, Cr. P.C.—In the light of the above discussion, a specific proviso should be added to section 327 of the Code of Criminal Procedure, as under:—

Proviso to be added to section 327 of the Code of Criminal Procedure, 1973:[1]

"Provided further that unless the presiding judge or magistrate, for reasons to be recorded, directs otherwise, the inquiry into and trial of rape or allied offence shall be conducted in camera.

Explanation.—In this sub-section, the expression 'rape or allied offence' applies to—

(a) *an offence punishable under section* 354 *or section* 354A *of the Indian Penal Code;*[2]

(b) *an offence punishable under section* 376, *section* 376A, *section* 376B *or section* 376C *of that Code;*[3]

(c) *an attempt to commit, abetment of or conspiracy to commit any such offence as is mentioned in clause (a) or (b) of this Explanation."*

Further, the following sub-section should be added to section 327:—

Sub-section to be added to section 327, Code of Criminal Procedure, 1973 after re-numbering present section as sub-section (1).

"(2) *Where any proceedings are held in camera, it shall not be lawful for any person to print or publish any matter in relation to any such proceeding except with the previous permission of the Court."*[4-5]

IV. Publication of Proceedings

5.8. Publication of names of parties.—Connected with the question of holding the proceedings *in camera* is that of publication of the names of the victim and the accused in cases of charges of rape.

As the law stands at present, the names and details of the victim as well as the accused as disclosed at a trial for a sexual offence can be legally published in the press, unless the proceedings were held *in camera.*[6] This is in view of the general rule about the reporting of judicial proceedings. What takes place in the Court is public, and the publication of proceedings merely enlarges the area of the Court and gives to the trial that added publicity which is favoured by the rule that the trial should be open and public. It is only when the public is excluded from audience that the privilege of publication also goes, "because

1. Section 327, Code of Criminal Procedure, 1973.
2. Section 354A was recommended to be inserted by the Law Commission in the 42nd Report (Indian Penal Code).
3. The section references are according to the proposals made in this Report.
4. For violation, penalty may be introduced as section 228A, I.P.C. (fine upto Rs. 1000), para. 5.13, *infra.*
5. Jurisdiction of the High Court under contempt of court is already saved by the Code.
6. *Naresh* v. *State of Maharashtra,* AIR 1967 SC 1.

then the public would have no right to obtain at the second hand what it cannot obtain at first hand".[1]

5.9. Special provisions.—This general rule, however, sometimes causes embarrassment. Realising the need for modification of the general position, the legislature has enacted, in regard to proceedings of a special nature, special rules on the subject. We need not enumerate here Central Acts and a few State Acts that contain such provisions.

5.10. Preserving anonymity of complainant and accused in sexual offences.—On a careful consideration, we are of the opinion that there is need for legislation to preserve the anonymity of the complainant and the accused in the case of rape and allied offences (subject to exceptions in regard to certain specified cases).

The principal object of the amendment would be to save avoidable embarrassment to the victim and to the accused. The justification for such a provision need not be spelt out. Restrictions on the reporting of judicial proceedings are not unknown to our law,[2] though such restrictions should be imposed only for the weightiest reasons. The present seems to be such a case.

5.11. Anonymity at the stage of investigation.—We have considered the question of anonymity under two heads—

(i) anonymity of the victim and the accused at the stage of investigation and before the trial commences;

(ii) anonymity of the victim and the accused as regards proceedings in Court at the trial stage.

As regards the stage of investigation, we do not propose to make any recommendations for statutory amendment or for the enactment of separate legislation. Though we do appreciate that the victim and the members of her family find it embarrassing that the name of the victim is given publicity, we would leave the matter to the good sense of the journalistic profession—and to such provisions of the existing law as may be applicable.

5.12. Publicity at the stage of trial—Trial *in camera* and penalty for illegal publicity to court proceedings.—As regards anonymity at the stage of trial, some special provisions are, in our view, called for. Here again, we do not propose the enactment of separate legislation. We have recommended[3] that the trial of cases relating to rape (and allied offences) should be held *in camera.* On the enactment of such a provision, the publication (without permission of the Court) of proceedings so held *in camera* would be a contempt of Court,[4] for which the High Court can take appropriate action.

5.13. Section 228A, I.P.C. (New)—Recommended.—However, to fortify the present law, we recommend that there should be inserted, in the Indian Penal Code, a new section[5]—say, as section 228A—in the following terms:—

---

1. *Naresh* v. *State of Maharashtra,* AIR 1967 SC 1 (27), para. 97: (1966) 3 SCR 744.
2. *See* para. 5.9, *supra.*
3. *See* para. 5.27, *supra.*
4. *Naresh* v. *State of Maharashtra,* AIR 1967 SC 1.
5. Section 228A, Indian Penal Code (proposed).

Section 228A, I.P.C.
(To be inserted)

"228A. Where, by any enactment for the time being in force, the printing or publication of any matter in relation to a proceeding held in a Court *in camera* is declared to be unlawful, any person who prints or publishes any matter in violation of such prohibition shall be punished with fine which may extend to rupees one thousand."[1]

5.14. Consequential amendment of other laws.—The proposed provision will cover every case of violation of any statutory provision which declares unlawful the printing or publication of such matter. If our recommendation is accepted, it will be possible to delete, at a convenient time, similar provisions in special enactments[2] so as to prevent duplication.

5.15. Publication after conviction.—We may make it clear that publication of the name of the convict *as a punishment* is a matter which will be dealt with later.[3]

V. Examination on Commission

5.16. Examination on commission.—A suggestion was made by some of the representatives of women's organisations (during our oral discussions with them) that women should be examined on commission and should not be made to come to Court (in criminal cases). We have carefully considered the matter, but we do not consider any such statutory provision to be practicable.

In important cases, so many persons (and not merely the Judge) have to take part in the trial. Moreover, the accused may have to be identified, or the property in dispute may have to be shown to the witness. All these arrangements cannot, in many cases, be made when the examination is on commission.

5.17. The issue of a commission is generally a time-consuming process. Save in exceptional cases of hardship and the like, the procedure of examination on commission may, if made mandatory by law, be productive of injustice in most cases.

If the object is to save embarrassment, that object would amply be secured by holding the trial *in camera*, as recommended by us.[4]

We are not, therefore, in a position to accept the suggestion.

VI. Participation in Trial

5.18. Participation by organisations & suggestion considered.—It has been suggested by one of the women's organisations with whom we had oral discussions that there should be a provision entitling an organisation interested in criminal matters to intervene in a criminal trial, so as to enable it to put forth its point of view. The suggestion was made without elaborating the value, object and purpose of the intervention of 'interested parties' in the trial of the person

1. Proposed offence to be non-cognisable, bailable and triable by any magistrate. Complaint of the Court holding the proceeding or its superior Court to be required.
2. *E.g.* section 23, Hindu Marriage Act, 1955.
3. *See* Chapter 6, *infra.*
4. *See* para. 5.7, *supra.*

alleged to be the offender. On the face of it, the suggestion appears to us as one having dangerous potentialities and implications.

5.19. Risks attendant on acceptance of the suggestion.—It may be that the idea behind the suggestion is to keep a watch on the working of the courts, the judges and the lawyers and to prevent them from straying away from the path of justice. If that be so, the suggestion is one down-grading the present judicial system, the judges and lawyers and expressing a lack of faith and confidence in them. It is not known whether the suggestion has been made with the ideology of a judiciary under 'popular control'. It is all right to say that the intervention of third parties is necessary in the public interest. This sounds good so far as the words go.

The interests of the prosecution and the accused in a criminal case are well protected by their relations, lawyers and the court. But an utter stranger seeking intervention in a criminal trial cannot have any joint or common interest with the accused or the person aggrieved in a criminal case. A body of persons cannot claim to have this joint or common interest merely because it is an organised body interested in criminal matters.

5.20. Peculiar features of a case relating to rape.—It must be remembered that in cases relating to rape, where the raped woman belongs to one caste or community or group and the accused belongs to any other caste or community, the feelings between the two parties run high. It is easy to see that if, in such cases third parties claiming to be interested in the woman raped or in the accused are allowed to intervene, the proceedings in the Court will be reduced to a trial of the accused by the public and the Court will be turned into a forum for a class or caste or communal warfare. The trial will thus become a farcical one, prejudicing one party or the other. We have, therefore, no hesitation in refusing to accept the suggestion.

CHAPTER 6

PUBLICITY ON CONVICTION

6.1. Suggestion to give publicity.—In the course of our oral discussions, a suggestion has been made that in cases of conviction of murder and other serious offences, suitable publicity in newspapers and other media should be given, so that the public may come to know of the state of crime in the country and it might also act as a deterrent. While we appreciate the object underlying the suggestion, we should point out that there are certain other countervailing considerations that might require to be taken note of. It is true that the object of deterrence may, to some extent, be achieved by such publicity; but, as against that, it should not be overlooked that modern penological theory places emphasis on the rehabilitation of the criminal as well. Where there is no possibility of a repetition of the offence by the convicted person, such publicity might have no utility from the point of view of deterrence of *that particular individual*, and might come in the way of full rehabilitation being achieved.

6.2. Discussion in earlier Report.—In this context, we may also note that the question of giving publicity to convictions was considered at some length when the Law Commission dealt with the Indian Penal Code.[1] After an examination of the pros and cons of the matter the Commission recommended the introduction of publicity as a type of punishment in certain cases—mainly those were cases of anti-social offences which are indulged in persistently by "white-collar criminals" and in regard to which publicity might act as a real deterrent. Likelihood of repetition of such offences is very high, having regard to the nature of the activity. The same may not necessarily be true of rape.

6.3. Suggestion not accepted.—We are not, therefore, inclined to accept the suggestion which, in any care, is concerned with serious offences in general and is not confined to sexual offences.

CHAPTER 7
EVIDENCE

I. INTRODUCTORY

7.1. Scope.—We propose to consider in this Chapter certain matters pertaining to the law of evidence in so far as its provisions or rules are relevant to the offences with which this Report is concerned. Although, in general, rules of evidence occupy a subordinate position in legal literature, in this particular case, they seem to have a very important bearing on the subject of this Report.

7.2. Disadvantageous position of the victim.—When one views the matter exclusively from the point of view of the victim, the difficulties which confront a woman who alleges she has been raped, become apparent. First, she must convince the police, then be subjected to a medical examination and finally undergo an embarrassing and humiliating cross-examination in Court. In rape cases, evidence about the victim's past sexual or gynaecological experiences is presumed to have a bearing on the outcome of the trial.

7.3. Issues in the field of evidence.—In the field of evidence as relevant to the offence of rape, the main issues that are usually discussed are complaint,[2] proof of want of consent,[3] the need for corroboration of the testimony of the victim,[4] and evidence of character of the victim,[5] and other improper questions.[6] Besides these, we shall also deal with one suggestion as to evidence of character of the accused.[7]

7.4. Earlier Report on Evidence Act.—The Law Commission, when it examined the Indian Evidence Act some time ago, had occasion to consider the difficulties faced by a witness who has to undergo cross-examination as to character, and made certain recommendations on the subject.[8]

1. Law Commission of India, 42nd Report (Indian Penal Code), paras. 3.21 to 3.25.
2. Paras. 7.5 and 7.6, *infra*.
3. Paras. 7.7 to 7.13, *infra*.
4. Para. 7.14, *infra*.
5. Paras. 7.15 to 7.28, *infra*.
6. Para. 7.29, *infra*.
7. Para. 7.30, *infra*.
8. Law Commission of India, 69th Report (Indian Evidence Act, 1872) (May 1977), Chapter 87.

However, these recommendations were concerned with witnesses in general. As regards a woman who is a victim of a sexual offence, no change of substance was considered. In section 155(4) of the Evidence Act—which permits evidence of 'general immoral character' of the prosecutrix—a verbal change was recommended.

This being the position, a few aspects relevant to evidence of character of the victim which did not then come up before the Commission[1] will have to be gone into, in the present Report.

II. Complaints

7.5. Complaint (section 8) and the doctrine of "hue and cry".—On the subject of evidence, we may first mention a rule which is of special relevance to the offence of rape—the rule governing the admissibility of a complaint made by the female soon after an alleged sexual offence. This is based on the principle that the complaint is a part of the same transaction, and also on the reasoning that the law considers a complaint as a natural expression of the feelings of the victim, thereby lending credibility. While, on the one hand, long delay or failure in making the complaint is regarded as a suspicious circumstance, on the other hand, a prompt complaint is regarded as evidence confirming or corroborating the allegation of the victim, and repels any possible doubt that the story was a mere fabrication.

It may be that the rule permitting evidence of complaint is a survival of the ancient requirement that the injured woman should make a "hue and cry"[2] as a preliminary to her "appeal of felony".[3] But the rule, in its present form, does not operate to the detriment of the female. The rule enables evidence to be given to confirm her credibility, and operates as an exception to the rule against hearsay as incorporated in section 60 of the Evidence Act.

7.6. Matter needing change.—There are, however, certain other matters in regard to which there is need for change in the law of evidence. We shall address ourselves, in particular, to certain questions concerning the past character of the woman. The law on the subject is unduly harsh against women who are victims of sexual offences.

III. Want of Consent—how Proved

7.7. Burden of proof of want of consent.—Want of consent being a cardinal element of rape under section 375, second clause of the Indian Penal Code, it is for the prosecution to prove it. Now, it is common experience that many prosecutions for rape tail for want of such proof. There often arise situations where the probability is that the woman did not consent, but sufficient legal proof of want of consent is not forthcoming.

For example, the woman may be physically too weak or mentally too dazed to resist (so that no marks of violence could come into existence). Or, the venue

1. Law Commission of India, 69th Report (Indian Evidence Act, 1872), paras. 87.18 to 87.24.
2. *See* Black *Law Dictionary,* (1979), p. 667, Left-hand column and stroud *Judicial Dictionary,* (1972), Vol. 2, p. 1270.
3. As to "appeal of felony", *see* Stephen *History of Criminal Law,* Vol. 1, p. 244.

of the offence—*e.g.* the secluded place in which rape is committed—may totally take away the inclination to resist, even if there is a physical capacity to do so, because resistance in such circumstances would be futile, same would be the case where the woman about to be attacked knows that the offender is well armed, or where what has come to be known as "gang rape" is committed. In such cases also, resistance would be futile, and may even cause more harm than passive submission. In such situations, marks of resistance or other visible signs of "no consent" cannot be insisted upon.

In our opinion, it should be obligatory for the Court to draw *prima facie* inference of want of consent, once the woman who is alleged to be the victim states in the witness box before the Court in her evidence that she did not consent.[1]

7.8. Section 114, Evidence Act.—Even now, if due regard be had to the provisions of section 114 of the Indian Evidence Act, the Court is competent to presume want of consent in such special circumstances as are mentioned above[2]—provided, of course, the other circumstances are consistent with want of consent.

The extent to which the victim may resist is for her to determine, and there are naturally no minima or maxima in this regard. The woman is required to go no further than is necessary to make manifest her unwillingness to yield to the attack. The amount of visible resistance, if any, must depend on the facts. Resistance is important only as evidence of non-consent. The crime does not hinge upon the woman's exertion.[3]

7.9. Signs of violence.—It is a peculiarity of the offence of rape that usually there are no witnesses excepting the victim herself. Proof of the offence, therefore, primarily depends on the credibility of the allegations of the victim. It is mainly for this reason that a statement of the woman that there was intercourse *without her consent* is often not accepted unless there is some overt evidence of want of consent. Bruises, scratches or other marks of struggle may constitute such evidence, but that would, at best, be a feeble evidence of want of consent.

Unfortunately, such marks of struggle are sometimes regarded as constituting the only evidence of want of consent. Such an attitude, though deeply regrettable, has no basis in the statutory provisions constituting the law of evidence in India. In fact, the Indian law of evidence does not, in general, lay down that a particular species of evidence should be insisted upon in proof or disproof of a particular fact. The Evidence Act lays down certain general rules which indicate the nature of facts that can be proved. If a fact to be proved is a fact in issue, its consequences (effects) are, no doubt, relevant. But proof of those consequences or effects is not limited to particular species of evidence. Thus, if want of consent is the fact in issue, its consequence—the physical resistance or struggle—is, no doubt, relevant; and so is the consequence of that physical struggle, namely, marks on the body. But the law does not lay down that only that piece of evidence can be given.

The point, in fact, need not be laboured further.

1. For draft *see* para. 7.11, *infra*.
2. Para. 7.7, *supra*.
3. *See* also para. 2.11, *supra*.

7.10. Need to change the law.—We would have left the matter at that. However, having regard to the *modus operandi* of committing rape that has become more frequent during recent years, it would be useful if, by a specific statutory provision, the statement made in evidence by the prosecutrix is regarded as raising a presumption of want of consent. As life becomes more complex and the ways of criminals more sophisticated, situations of the nature that we have mentioned above might become more frequent, and the necessity of invoking some such presumption as is suggested above may become more apparent. We are, therefore, of the view that where rape is alleged to have been constituted by sexual intercourse without the consent of the woman—*i.e.*, in the case contemplated by section 375, second clause—the court shall presume that there was want of consent, provided the prosecutrix has stated so in her evidence.

It may be mentioned that under the Evidence Act, the use of the expression "shall presume" does not bar rebutting evidence in regard to the fact about which a presumption is made.

7.11. Recommendation to add section 111A in the Evidence Act.—In the light of the above discussion, we recommend the insertion of the following new section in the Indian Evidence Act, 1872:—

> "111A. *In a prosecution for rape or attempt to commit rape, where sexual intercourse is proved and the question is whether if was without the consent of the woman and the woman with whom rape is alleged to have been committed or attempted states in her evidence before the Court that she did not consent, the Court shall presume that she did not consent.*"

7.12. Presumption of want of consent.—One of the points made in the Debates on the motion in the Lok Sabha[1] on the subject of rape of women was that if intercourse is proved, it should be presumed that it was an act of rape against the consent of the girl.

7.13. Burden of proof in case of a person in authority.—In the course of our oral discussions[2] with women's organisations, it was stated that in the case of a person *in authority* who has sexual intercourse with a woman under his authority, the burden of proof of consent should be placed on the accused.

The amendment just now recommended by us[3] would, in substance, achieve the object underlying these suggestions.

IV. Corroboration

7.14. Corroboration.—During the debates[4] on the motion in the Lok Sabha on the subject of rape, it was also pointed out that for a crime committed some time in the dark hours of night or in the dark corner of a house, it was impossible to get corroboration. It was also suggested that it was time to change the practice in this regard. We have taken note of this aspect, and hope that the

1. Lok Sabha Debates, 28th March, 1980, column 8975.
2. Oral discussions held on 15th April, 1980.
3. Para. 7.11, *supra*.
4. Lok Sabha Debates, 28th March, 1980, column 8972.

amendments recommended by us in the law of evidence, together with the law as expounded by the Supreme Court on the subject of corroboration in two important judgments,[1-2] will serve the purpose and advance the cause of justice. The judgments were pronounced in 1952 and 1958, and were followed in later judgments[3-4] of 1972 and 1973.

V. Past Sexual History

7.15. Past character as a relevant fact—Sections 8, 9, 11 and 14, Evidence Act.—We now deal with a very vital question of evidence related to prosecutions for rape. The question is this—how far should the past sexual history of the victim of rape be allowed to be given in evidence in Court on behalf of the accused? More than any other point of evidence, this has been the source of the very grave dissatisfaction with the legal system and of the feeling of alienation of the general public from the law and its processes, to which we have made a reference in the introductory[5] Chapter.

In the first place, where the issue is one of consent, evidence of past intercourse with the accused may become relevant under the omnibus provision in section 11 of the Evidence Act, under which a fact is relevant if it renders highly probable or improbable the existence of another fact in issue or relevant fact.

Secondly, evidence of past acts of intercourse with the accused may become admissible as showing passion (a "state of mind"—section 14).

Thirdly, sections 8 and 9 of the Evidence Act could arguably be invoked to render past acts of sexual intercourse relevant as showing conduct influenced by a fact in issue or a relevant fact.

7.16. Of course, the sections[6] of the Evidence Act referred to above[7] would be material only on the issue of consent, and the evidence that can be permitted thereunder must also relate to specific acts of sexual intercourse with the accused (or undue sexual familiarity with the accused).

7.17. Section 155(4), Evidence Act.—Besides these sections, however, there is a more specific provision in section 155(4) of the Evidence Act, under which, in a prosecution for rape or attempt to lavish, evidence can be given of the "general immoral character" of the "prosecutrix". This provision, it will be noticed, is not confined to past sexual familiarity *only with the accused*. It is wide enough to cover sexual immorality in relation to others. We need not, at the moment, concern ourselves with the question whether *particular sexual episodes* can be given in evidence under this provision. What needs to be emphasised is that matters in which the accused is not at all concerned can also be brought on the record

1. *Rameshwar* v. *State of Rajasthan*, AIR 1952 SC 54: 1952 SCR 377: 1952 Cr LJ 547.
2. *Sidheswar Ganguly* v. *State of West Bengal*, AIR 1958 SC 143: 1958 SCR 749: 1958 Cr LJ 273.
3. *Gurcharan Singh* v. *State of Haryana*, AIR 1972 SC 2661.
4. *Madho Ram* v. *State of Uttar Pradesh*, AIR 1973 SC 469.
5. Chapter 1, *supra*.
6. Sections 8, 9, 11 and 14, Evidence Act.
7. Para. 7.15, *supra*.

under the head of "general immoral character" by virtue of section 155(4). This means that even if the charge is one of sexual intercourse with a girl below the age of sixteen years—section 375, clause fifthly, Indian Penal Code—which is punishable irrespective of the girl's consent, evidence can be given of her "general immoral" character.

7.18. Section 146, Evidence Act.—Finally, there is the general provision as to impeaching the credit of witnesses by "injuring their character", and other modes of impeaching credit mentioned in section 146 of the Evidence Act. Of course, this section is not confined to sexual offences or to the "prosecutrix". It is a general provision applicable to all trials. But, since this Report is concerned with sexual offences and since the present discussion is concerned with the position of women who are the victims of such offences, it is proper to mention that under this section, questions are, in practice, often put relating to the past character of the prosecutrix in sexual offences.

7.19. General approach adopted.—We shall indicate, in due course,[1] our precise recommendations on the relevant provisions mentioned above.

But it would be appropriate to mention at this stage that these recommendations are all connected by a common thread. The connecting guideline is this—in a case of rape or attempted rape, even if past immoral character of the "prosecutrix" is technically permissible as substantive evidence or in cross-examination under the present law, that position needs to be modified and such evidence or cross-examination should be prohibited except as regards sexual relations with the accused.

The reasons for such an approach may be thus stated:

(a) in so far as such evidence relates to the *issue of consent*, there are social evils resulting from the tendering of such evidence and those evils counter-balance the possible probative value of the evidence,

(b) in so far as such evidence does not relate to the issue of consent and is offered merely to injure the character or shake the credit of the woman, it is not proper for the law to countenance it—when such evidence cannot be given against men who are victims of sexual offences.

We are happy to mention here that the general approach that we have adopted in regard to the purposes for which, and the extent to which, the past sexual history of the "prosecutrix" may be permitted to be raised as substantive evidence (or in cross-examination) is in broad and substantial harmony with the views expressed during our oral discussions by some social organisations, including an organisation of women lawyers.[2]

7.20. Sections 155(4), 146 and 53A (proposed), Evidence Act—Recommendation.—Having indicated the connecting guideline that constitutes the common thread underlying our approach to various provisions under which the question of the sexual history of the prosecutrix may be raised, we now proceed

1. See *infra*.
2. Discussions from 9th to 15th April, 1980.

to indicate more concretely, and in regard to each section of the Evidence Act, the amendment that we have in mind so as to carry out the general approach mentioned above.

With reference to section 155(4) of the Evidence Act, it is pertinent to point out that the rule which permits evidence of previous sexual history of the complainant should be considered under two headings, namely, (i) previous sexual relations with the accused, and (ii) such relations with other persons.

So far as sexual relations with the accused are concerned, the assumption underlying the admissibility of such evidence would appear to be that once a woman has consented to a sexual relationship with a *particular* man, she is unlikely to dissent at a later stage. Though such an assumption may not be necessarily realistic in every case, it could occasionally be true. There is, therefore, justification for retaining it.

7.21. Section 155(4) and sexual relations with other persons.—So far as previous sexual relations with other persons are concerned, there is, in our opinion, strong justification for change in section 155(4). The case for admitting such evidence is totally weak, if not completely without foundation. Such an evidence is not permissible as regards male victims,[1] or even in the generality of cases not involving sexual offences. It seems, therefore, hardly defensible, at least at the present day, to continue a legal provision whereunder the character of a female witness can be impeached merely because she happens to be a "prosecutrix" in an offence of rape or attempt to commit rape.

Evidence of acts of intercourse with persons other than the accused indicates a remote or faint likelihood of the woman having consented to the particular act. Even when a harlot or a prostitute is raped, her consent at the time of the commission of the crime must be proved by evidence *aliunde.*

For all these reasons, section 155(4) requires modification so as to *exclude evidence of sexual relations with persons other than the accused.*

7.22. Section 155(4)—another point for amendment.—We find that another aspect of section 155(4) also requires to be looked into. Section 155(4) is, at present, applicable even where consent is not material. The section is wide enough to apply not only where rape is charged under the category of "want of consent", but also where it is charged under some other head—for example—where the offence is committed in respect of a girl below the statutory age. The fact that the prosecutrix is a person of "general immoral character" cannot have significance whatsoever where the prosecution is not based on the want of consent. As regards the credibility of the girl as a witness, that is to say, leaving aside the issue of consent, there does not seem to be any reason why the law should contain a rule discriminating against women. If "general immoral character" is regarded as shaking the credit of the female, it can as well be regarded as shaking the character of a male witness. But there is no corresponding provision applicable to a male "prosecutor".

1. See *supra.*

It is wrong to assume that a *female witness* is less likely to tell the truth when she has a generally immoral character. Evidence of sexual immorality cannot be admitted in other cases as substantive evidence.

7.23. Difficulties caused by section 155(4).—These are not merely theoretical arguments. The provision in section 155(4) sometimes causes serious hardship. The victim of rape, questioned at length, very often feels humiliated, particularly at home or amongst neighbours or at work or at school. Self-consciousness and shame, resulting from queries and adverse comments, might even result in a permanent scar on her peace of mind and psychic well-being. In this respect, the provision in section 155(4) may be regarded as deserving of serious reconsideration.

7.24. Harm to reputation—danger of.—There can hardly be any doubt that an unrestrained questioning on such matters can amount to a destruction of the reputation and self-respect of the woman. There must be struck a balance between the demands of fair trial and the dignity of the woman. The law should reflect an approach which protects her interests, without compromising those of fair trial.

7.25. Amendment of section 155(4)—recommendation.—On a careful consideration of the matter, we have come to the conclusion that section 155(4) of the Evidence Act should be amended as suggested above.[1] In brief, it should be confined to sexual relations with the accused and that too only where consent is in issue.

7.26. Section 146, Evidence Act.—But this amendment of section 155(4) of the Evidence Act would not be an adequate measure for reforming the law. Theoretically, it would still continue to be permissible to give evidence about the "character" of the female prosecutrix under the general provision in section 146 of the Evidence Act. The possibility of such an alternative being open to the accused in cross-examination of the female prosecutrix in a prosecution of rape or attempt to commit rape ought, in our view, to be totally eliminated, for the reasons stated above.

One effective method of doing so would be to insert a provision in the Act by way of addition to section 146, to the effect that in a prosecution for rape or attempt to commit rape, where the question at issue is the consent of the woman, it shall not be permissible to adduce evidence or to put questions in the cross-examination of the prosecutrix as to her general immoral character, or as to her prior sexual experience with any person other than the accused.

7.27. Amendment of section 146.—Accordingly, we recommend that the following sub-section should be added to section 146 of the Evidence Act:—

"(4) *In a prosecution for rape or attempt to commit rape, where the question of consent to sexual intercourse or attempted sexual intercourse is at issue, it shall not be permissible to adduce evidence or to put questions in the cross-examination of the prosecutrixes to her general immoral character, or as to her previous sexual*

1. Paras. 7.21 and 7.22, *supra*.

experience with any person other than the accused for proving such consent or the quality of consent."

7.28. Section 53A (proposed) to exclude evidence as to character.—Even this amendment of the law, however, would not be enough. In our opinion, it is also necessary to exclude the possibility of evidence of general immoral character being tendered under the sections[1] of the Act which relate to substantive evidence.[2]

Accordingly, we recommend that the following new section should be inserted, in the Evidence Act, say—as section 53A:—

> "53A. *In a prosecution for rape or attempt to commit rape, where the question of consent to sexual intercourse or attempted sexual intercourse is at issue, evidence of the character of the prosecutrix or of her previous sexual experience with any person other than the accused shall not be relevant on the issue of such consent or the quality of content."*

VI. Improper Questions

7.29. Section 150, Evidence Act—Amendment recommended.—So much as regards evidence of sexual history. We now deal with the position as to improper questions in general. The Evidence Act has a catena of provisions whose object is to ensure that questions intended to shake the credit of witnesses by injuring their character are kept within legitimate bounds. Nevertheless, it is sometimes seen that such questions are put indiscriminately in the lower courts. It then becomes the duty, though unpleasant, of the presiding officer of the court to report the matter to the appropriate authority for action, if the question is put by a legal practitioner. The Evidence Act has a specific provision in this regard, to be found in section 150. The object of the provision is that the authority to which the matter is reported may take suitable action. With this end in view, the section provides that "if the court is of opinion that any such question was asked without reasonable grounds, it may, if it was asked by any barrister, pleader, vakil or attorney, report the circumstances of the case to the High Court or other authority to which such barrister, pleader, vakil or attorney is subject in the exercise of his profession".

7.30. Various amendments suggested in section 150.—So far as the words referring to the various categories of "legal practitioners" are concerned, they should now be replaced by the word "advocate", and such a recommendation was, in fact, made by the Law Commission, in its Report on the Evidence Act.[3]

The Law Commission, in its Report on the Act, also recommended deletion of the words "or other authority" from this section. This would mean that the matter would be reported to the High Court. We would, however, recommend that instead of the matter being reported to the High Court, it should be

1. Sections 8, 9, 11 and 14, Evidence Act.
2. *See* para. 7.15, *supra*.
3. Law Commission of India, 69th Report (Indian Evidence Act, 1872), para. 84.33.

reported to the State Bar Council, which (under the present statutory set up) is empowered to take appropriate disciplinary action in such cases. We, therefore, recommend that section 150 of the Evidence Act should be revised so as to read as under:—

Revised section 150, Evidence Act

"150. If the Court is of opinion that any such question was asked without reasonable grounds, it may, if it was asked by any *advocate*, report the circumstances of the case to the *State Bar Council.*"

VII. Character of The Accused

7.31. Character of the accused.—One of the women's organisations with whom we have held oral discussions has suggested that the Evidence Act should be amended suitably by providing that evidence of character of the accused shall be relevant in all cases of rape and molestation of women. Since we are recommending[1] amendment of the provision in section 155(4) of the Evidence Act which at present permits evidence of the "general immoral character" of the prosecutrix, we do not propose to recommend the change contemplated in the suggestion.

CHAPTER 8

CONCLUSION

8.1. Effect of our proposals.—We have come to the end of the task committed to us. We believe that we have made proposals to secure that no person who has committed rape escapes punishment, that women who become victims of rape are not harassed during the course of investigation and trial in the Court and that the trial of persons charged with rape is speeded up, to ensure that the police discharge efficiently and promptly the manifold and complex problems that confront them in rape cases, and to assure the free movement of women by giving them protection when they move cut, as also to the inmates of women's lodgings and hostels.

8.2. Changes whether going for enough or too far.—There may be some who feel that the changes recommended by us are likely to be for the worse. Such persons are too complacent for our taste. There may be still others, who may regard our recommendations as nothing more than an attempt to patch-up the system of criminal justice, which, according to them, is so defective as to be beyond redemption. We do not delude ourselves into thinking that our proposals will bring into the investigation and trial of cases of rape a state of perfection. Sometimes one's best endeavours go away. What we have attempted is to strike a balance between the interests of the accused and those of the victim in a case relating to rape, and thus to protect the interests of the society.

8.3. Effect of films and the real challenge.—During the course of discussion with us, a lady Member of Parliament[2] pointed out the pernicious influence of

1. *See* recommendation as to section 155(4), Evidence Act, para. 7.25, *supra.*
2. Mrs. Sushila Adivarekar, M.P. (Rajya Sabha).

Indian films highlighting rape and its attendant violence. The real challenge, therefore, in dealing with the problems of rape and its horrors lies in rousing public consciousness against it, and in preventing the publication and exhibition in any form of that trash material, which only corrupts the minds of the youth and of the depraved. To this problem we commend Governments earnest and immediate attention.

P.V. Dixit, *Chairman.*

S.N. Shankar,
Gangeshwar Prasad, } *Members.*

P.M. Bakshi, Member-Secretary.

New Delhi,
Dated: 25th April, 1980.

226th REPORT, 2009 ON INCLUSION OF ACID ATTACKS AS SPECIFIC OFFENCES IN THE INDIAN PENAL CODE AND A LAW FOR COMPENSATION FOR VICTIMS OF CRIME

CHAPTER I

INTRODUCTION

The victim of a gruesome acid attack, Laxmi, has filed a writ petition in the Supreme Court of India in May, 2006 in which the Law Commission of India has been arrayed as the Respondent No. 2. Though the Law Commission had pointed out to the Court that the reliefs in the petition cannot be prayed for from the Law Commission, it has decided to take up the matter *suo moto* in view of the gravity of the offence of acid attacks.

Acid attacks are becoming a growing phenomenon in India. *Laxmi's* case is an example of what normally occurs in such cases. The petition states that Laxmi, a young girl, was subject to an acid attack following her refusal to marry the accused. As a result of the attack the victim's arms, face and other body parts were severely disfigured and deformed. Though the victim and her parents were/are poor they were fortunately helped by a benefactor who bore the medical expenses approximating to Rs. 2.5 lakhs. However, even after 4 plastic surgeries the victim's physical appearance remains horrific and many more surgeries would be required to make her physical appearance a semblance of what it was. The victim can of course never look as she did before the attack.

Though acid attack is a crime which can be committed against any man or woman, it has a specific gender dimension in India. Most of the reported acid attacks have been committed on women, particularly young women for spurning suitors, for rejecting proposals of marriage, for denying dowry etc. The attacker cannot bear the fact that he has been rejected and seeks to destroy the body of the woman who has dared to stand up to him.

Thus, acid throwing is an extremely violent crime by which the perpetrator of the crime seeks to inflict severe physical and mental suffering on his victim. As stated above this kind of violence is often motivated by deep-seated jealousy or feelings of revenge against a woman. For instance, in Bangladesh 78 per cent. of the reported acid violence is inflicted on women with the most common reasons for attack being the refusal of marriage, the denial of sex, and the rejection of romance.[1] The acid is usually thrown at the victim's face. The perpetrator wants to disfigure the victims and turn them into a monster. Aside from the reasons

1. Acid Survivors Foundation. *Acid Throwing Fact Sheet.* Dhaka, Bangladesh, 2001.

stated above the other reasons for acid attacks include robbery, land disputes etc.

Perpetrators of the crime act cruelly and deliberately. Acid violence is a premeditated act of violence as the perpetrator of the crime carries out the attack by first obtaining the acid, carrying it on him and then stalking the victim before executing the act.

Furthermore, an acid attack has long-lasting consequences on the life of the victim who faces perpetual torture, permanent damage and other problems for the rest of her life. Victims normally feel worthless, afraid and mortified and become social outcasts because of their appearance. They may become too traumatized and embarrassed to walk out of their house and carry out simple tasks let alone get married, have children, get a job, go to school, etc. Even if they are willing to pursue a normal life, there is no guarantee that society itself will treat them as normal human beings given their appearance and disabilities after an attack. They may not be able to work, or be able to find a job, and thus perpetually struggle to survive.[1]

It has been contended by those working for these victims that the Criminal law relating to grievous hurts in sections 320, 322, 325 and 326 of the Indian Penal Code (I.P.C.) is insufficient to deal with the phenomenon of acid attacks. Section 320 deals with grievous hurt and reads as under—

Section 320. Grievous hurt.—The following kinds of hurt only are designated as "grievous":—

First.—Emasculation.

Secondly.—Permanent privation of the sight of either eye.

Thirdly.—Permanent privation of the hearing of either ear,

Fourthly.—Privation of any member or joint.

Fifthly.—Destruction or permanent impairing of the powers of any member or joint.

Sixthly.— Permanent disfiguration of the head or face.

Seventhly.—Fracture or dislocation of a bone or tooth.

Eighthly.—Any hurt which endangers life or which causes the sufferer to be during the space of twenty days in severe bodily pain, or unable to follow his ordinary pursuits.

This definition of grievous hurt has been criticized as the definition does not take within its purview the various kinds of deliberate hurts that are inflicted on important parts of a female's body nor does this definition apply to offences like acid attack in which multiple types of grievous hurts occur.

---

1. *Baseline Survey with International Comparative Analysis of the Legal Aspects of Acid Violence in Uganda,* Commissioned by: Acid Survivors Foundation Uganda with funding support from the US Democracy & Human Rights Fund, Legal Consultant: Rachel Forster, November, 2004.

Section 322[1] IPC defines voluntarily causing grievous hurt and section 325[2] IPC provides for punishment for grievous hurt. The offence is punishable by imprisonment upto seven years and is cognizable, bailable, and compoundable as well as being triable by a first class Magistrate. The offence of grievous hurt is not caused unless the offender both causes grievous hurt and intends, or knows himself to be likely, to cause grievous hurt.

Section 326 of the Indian Penal Code which applies in cases of voluntarily causing grievous hurt by means of any corrosive substance is punishable with imprisonment for life or with imprisonment of either description for a term which may extend to 10 years and fine. Thus, punishment for voluntarily causing grievous hurt even by corrosive substances like Acid can be imprisonment lasting from extremely short periods of time till 10 years. It has been argued that this period of punishment does not match the gravity of the offence.

The petition argues that though in some cases like the petitioner's case section 307 of the I.P.C. has been applied, even this is not enough as courts tend to grant bail easily in cases of section 307 I.P.C. and *mens rea* is extremely difficult to prove.

The Laxmi Writ Petition further states that compensation to victims of acid attacks is of vital importance as huge medical costs are often involved. The victims of acid attack need both short term as well as long term specialized medical treatments and plastic surgeries. The provisions in the Indian law for giving compensation to the victims are insufficient. The writ petition therefore prays that:

- An amendment be made in the Indian Penal Code, Evidence Act and the Criminal Procedure Code for dealing with acid attack as a special offence;
- Guidelines be framed and an act be passed to attend to the needs of all the acid attack victims in India;
- A committee be constituted and appointed for adopting measures for the proper treatment, aftercare and rehabilitation of the victims of acid attacks;
- That acid in all forms be made a scheduled banned chemical which is not readily available over the counter.

It is therefore important to examine and analyse the various provisions of the Indian Penal Code to see whether the law as it exists in India is sufficient

1. **Section 322. Voluntarily causing grievous hurt.**—Whoever voluntarily causes hurt, if the hurt which the intends to cause or knows himself to be likely to cause is grievous hurt, and if the hurt which he causes is grievous hurt, is said to "voluntarily to cause grievous hurt."

   Explanation.—A person is not said voluntarily to cause grievous hurt except when he both causes grievous hurt and intends or knows himself to be likely to cause grievous hurt. But he is said voluntarily to cause grievous hurt, if intending or knowing himself to be likely to cause grievous hurt of one kind; he actually causes grievous hurt of another kind.

2. **Section 325. Punishment for voluntarily causing grievous hurt.**—Whoever, except in the case provided for by section 335 (Voluntarily causing grievous hurt on provocation), voluntarily causes grievous hurt, shall be punished with imprisonment of either description for a term which may extend to seven years, and shall also be liable to fine.

to deal with the phenomenon of acid attacks. The Law Commission has also examined the laws relating to acid attacks in different countries before giving its recommendations, both for punishing the perpetrators of these attacks and for monetary and economic rehabilitation of the victim of the attack.

CHAPTER II

A BRIEF OVERVIEW

A Statistical Overview

While very little data is available on acid attacks in India some studies have reported an increasing trend in cases relating to acid attack. According to a study 174 cases of acid attack were reported in India in 2000. This was a per capita incidence of about 1/15 of that of Bangladesh, which has the highest incidence rate as well as the highest number of acid attack cases in the world. However, the absolute number of cases was approaching those of Bangladesh.[1]

35 cases of acid attacks were reported in Karnataka between 1999 and 2004.[2] This figure does not include victims that do not report their case because they fear further violence or being socially stigmatized. In this regard, the Campaign and Struggle Against Acid Attacks on Women (CSAAAW) noted one incidence in Bangalore in July 2004 that was not included as part of the reported cases partly because the victim and her family have opted not to go public with their trauma.[3] The number of cases added up to 53 by 2006 in Karnataka and, as reported by the CSAAAW, verdicts were given in only 9 of these 53 cases[4]. A newspaper report[5] put the total number of acid attacks as 60 by 2007 in Karnataka alone adding 8 more cases till February 2007.

In most of these cases Hydrochloric and Sulphuric acid were used and all the victims were women. The victims in Karnataka were very young women between 16 and 25 years of age, and were attacked by men known to them. Most attacks took place in public places or at home.[6]

These cases showed the kind of injuries that victims of acid attack suffered. The injuries range from burns to permanent disfigurement to death. In many acid attacks the victim suffers a slow and painful death. On the other hand, some victims who do survive the attack like Hasina[7] (in April 1999) and Shruti (in October 2001) are permanently disfigured, maimed and confined to homes for life.[8] Acid attack survivors are physically, psychologically and socially

1. Acid Attacks: Bangladesh's Efforts to Stop the Violence, Jordan Swanson, Harvard Health Policy Review Archives, Spring 2002; Vol. 3, No. 1.
2. Burnt Not Defeated, Report by CSAAAW, April 2007, CSAAAW Bangalore publication.
3. The Hindu, Another Face of Violence, 15-08-2004.
4. The Hindu, PIL filed for steps to curb acid attacks, 20-09-2006.
5. The Hindu, The 'acid test': will Government regulate sale of deadly chemicals?, Bageshree S. and M.V. Chandrashekhar, 5 February, 2007.
6. Deccan Herald News Service, Bangalore, Acid test of Humanity, Bala Chauhan.
7. *State of Karnataka* v. *Joseph Rodrigues,* decided by the Hon'ble Karnataka High Court on 22-8-2006.
8. The Hindu, The 'acid test': will Government regulate sale of deadly chemicals?, Bageshree S. and M.V. Chandrashekhar, 5 February, 2007.

traumatized. The physical extents of their injuries are deep, permanent and have a direct impact on their psychological well-being and social functionality.

Hydrochloric, Sulphuric and other acids all have a catastrophic effect on human flesh. These corrosive substances cause the skin tissue to melt. The bones of victims become exposed and sometimes the acid dissolves the bones too. Permanent scars as can be seen in *Hasina's*[1] case disfigure a human being's body for life. Furthermore, if acid enters the eyes of the victim during an attack, as is common in acid attack cases, it damages these vital organs permanently. Many acid attack survivors have lost the use of one or both eyes.

As a result of disfigurement and disability victims are permanently debilitated and are forced to give up their lives, their work, their education. In this regard, compensation to cover vital surgeries for victims who can no longer support themselves becomes imperative.

However aside from compensation there are other points as well that the law should be sensitized to when it comes to dealing with acid attack victims. In an interview with the Hindu newspaper CSAAAW's lawyer, Sheela Ramanathan, pointed out that acid attack victims had to be handled separately as their situation entails a series of "medical complications, social stigma, psychological trauma, gender bias and a complete loss of livelihood".[1] Ms. Ramanathan particularly drew attention to the medical negligence of these victims: "Medical awareness on the mode of treatment is also abysmal," "(t)here have been cases where coconut oil has been applied on the affected area and the victim wrapped in blankets. Such mishandling can cause irreparable damage.[2]

Acid attacks and their Consequences

As stated earlier acid attacks are a form of violence against women, where the perpetrator splashes a person or object with acid in order to deface or kill them.[3] Although acid throwing, also known as vitriol age, has been a form of violence known to be committed throughout history, there has been a steep rise in the cases documented in recent years, particularly in certain South Asian countries. Some of this increase has been attributed to better documentation of cases and also to the fact that victims of attacks have begun to report an attack more often. However, there appears to be a substantive increase in the number of acid attacks that are being committed in recent times due to various factors.

Acid attacks are seen as one of the most vicious crimes as it causes perpetual suffering to the victim. As acid melts flesh and even the bones of a person, it causes an unparalleled degree of pain to the victim and leaves her mutilated and scarred as well as giving permanent disabilities at times such as blindness. Victims face lifetime physical, social, psychological and economic consequences.

Some of the well known effects of acid are as under:

---

1. *State of Karnataka* v. *Joseph Rodrigues,* decided by the Hon'ble Karnataka High Court on 22-8-2006.
2. The Hindu, PIL filed for steps to curb acid attacks, 20-09-2006.
3. Wikipedia Encyclopedia.

- Acids are corrosive substances that will cause visible necrosis (death) of human skin tissue and will even corrode a metal in higher concentration.
- They can cause serious poisoning, burning and serious injury can result from exposure to strong acids.
- Commonly available acids include Sulphuric acid, Hydrochloric acid Hydrofluoric acid, Phospaic acid etc. Acids are used in laboratories and factories/industries.
- In an acid attack the skin is the main organ of contact. The effects of acid on the skin may include redness, and burns. In severe cases, it could lead to shock and death. Some other effects include permanent hair loss and scaring. If inhaled in large quantity it can also lead to pulmonary disorders.

The consequences of acid attack have been well documented and include the following:[1]

Injuries and Physical Consequences

Acid eats through two layers of the skin, *i.e.* the fat and muscle underneath, and sometimes not only eats through to the bone but it may even dissolve the bone. The deepness of injury depends on the strength of the acid and the duration of contact with the skin. Burning continues until the acid is thoroughly washed off with water.

Thrown on a person's face, acid rapidly eats into eyes, ears, nose and mouth. Eyelids and lips may burn off completely. The nose may melt, closing the nostrils, and ears shrivel up.

Acid can quickly destroy the eyes, blinding the victim. Skin and bone on the skull, forehead, cheeks and chin may dissolve. When the acid splashes or drips over the neck, chest, back, arms or legs, it burns everywhere it touches.

The biggest immediate danger for victims is breathing failure. Inhalation of acid vapors can create breathing problems in two ways: *i.e.* by causing a poisonous reaction in the lungs or by swelling the neck, which constricts the airway and strangles the victim.

When the burns from an acid attack heal, they form thick scars which pull the skin very tight and can cause disfigurements. For instance, eyelids may no longer close, the mouth may no longer open; and the chin becomes welded to the chest.

The following information on physical consequences has been described by an NGO:[2]

Skull: May be partly destroyed or deformed. Hair is often lost.

Forehead: Skin may shrink, as though stretched tightly, and be scarred.

1. These consequences are listed in; Living in the Shadows: Acid Attacks in Cambodia, 2003 LICADHO Report.
2. Medecins Du Monde and doctors at Calmette hospital in Phnom Penh.

Ears: Shriveled up and deformed. Deafness may occur immediately or later.

Cartilage in the ear is usually partly or totally destroyed, exposing the victim to future infection and hearing loss.

Eyes: Direct acid contact or acid vapors can damage eyes, causing blindness.

Even if the eyes survive the acid attack, they remain vulnerable to other threats which can cause blindness during the victim's recovery. Eyelids may have been burned off, or may be deformed by scarring, leaving the eyes to dry up and go blind. This is very difficult to prevent.

Nose: Shrunken and deformed. Nostrils may close completely because the cartilage is destroyed.

Cheeks: Scarred and deformed.

Mouth: Shrunken and narrowed, and may lose its shape. Lips may be partly or totally destroyed. Lips may be permanently flared, exposing the teeth. Movement of the lips, mouth and face may be impaired. Eating can be difficult.

Chin: Scarred and deformed. The scars may run downward, welding the chin to the neck or chest.

Neck: Often badly damaged. It may have a thick cord of scarred flesh running down from the chin to the upper chest, or a wide, heavily-scarred area on one side of the neck. Victim may be unable to extend the neck, or the head may constantly lean to one side.

Chest: Often badly scarred. The chest may have narrow lines of scars or wide patches of scars from acid splashes or drips. In girls and young women, the development of their breasts may be stopped, or their breasts may be destroyed completely.

Shoulder: May be badly scarred, especially around the underarm, which may limit the victim's arm movement. In some cases, one or both of the victim's upper arms may be stuck like glue to the sides of their body.

Treatment

The first thing that should be done when the acid gets in contact with the skin is to flush the burned flesh with water for at least 60 minutes and to wash off the acid with water for as long as possible.

Emergency treatment at hospitals should include cleaning and bandaging the burns, and relieving any breathing problems caused by acid fumes.

Infection is a major danger because the dead tissue around deep burns becomes easily infected and prevents the burns from healing. Infection may spread to the healthy part of the skin, and may even kill the victim and it can attack the victim at any stage during the weeks and months right after the attack. Thus the wounds need to be kept clean and antibiotics need to be given to fight infection.

The eyes are very vulnerable to infection and can cause blindness. Most important is to ensure that victims can close their eyes, preventing them from becoming dry and infected. Surgery may be needed to rebuild the eyelids, if they were destroyed by acid, or remove thick scars around the eyes as burns heal.

Eating enough food is vital because victims' bodies require a lot of energy to fight infection and heal the wounds. This may be difficult if the victim has burns around the mouth and has difficulty swallowing, or cannot afford the necessary diet.

It can take 3 to 12 months for burn wounds to heal. Thick scars, which are painful and itchy, grow over the healed burns. The scars grow and change over 1 to 2 years. As the scars thicken and contract, they can cause permanent disability by stiffening joints and restricting movement. For example, the scarring on the neck and shoulders, can prevent a patient from moving his head or arms. Doctors may need to perform many operations to release the scars and graft new skin over them. Scars may also grow over the nostrils or ear canals, and surgery is required to remove them.

Long periods of physical therapy are needed to minimize victims' lack of movement from scarring, and special elastic bandages can dramatically reduce the thickness and stiffness of scars.

The final stage of treatment is to try to restore the appearance of the victim as much as possible. By now, the wounds must have healed completely and the full extent of scarring and deformities of the body must be visible. The victim may require many operations over a period of two to three years.

Psychological Consequences

Victims of attacks do not only undergo severe physical trauma but also undergo traumatic changes in the way they feel and think. Psychological trauma is caused by both the terror victims suffer during the attack, as they feel their skin burning away, and after the attack by the disfigurement or disabilities that they have to live with for the rest of their lives. Victims suffer psychological symptoms such as depression, insomnia, nightmares, fear about another attack and/or fear about facing the outside world, headaches, weakness and tiredness, difficulty in concentrating and remembering things, etc. They feel perpetually depressed, ashamed, worried, and lonely.

Victims suffer severe psychological symptoms for years, if not forever, because they are reminded every day of their physical scars. The feeling of lack of hope and worth may never leave them.

Social and Economic Consequences

Victims face a lifetime of discrimination from society and they become lonely. They are embarrassed that people may stare or laugh at them and may hesitate to leave their homes fearing an adverse reaction from the outside world. Victims who are not married are not likely to get married and those victims who have got serious disabilities because of an attack, like blindness, will not find jobs and earn a living. Discrimination from other people, or disabilities such as blindness, makes it very difficult for victims to fend for themselves and they become dependent on others for food and money.

It has therefore been argued that acid attacks need to be classified as a separate offence and harsher punishment needs to be prescribed. It has been further stated that the law must include guidelines for handling/supporting victims economically, socially, and psychologically as well as compensation. It is relevant to mention that in 2006 CSAAAW filed a Public Interest Litigation in the Karnataka High Court seeking a court order to the State Government to ensure speedy and gender-sensitive trials for victims of acid attacks as well as better medical treatment and rehabilitation. The CSAAAW also demanded the production, distribution and storage of toxic acids be strictly monitored by the State.[1]

Infact since acid is so readily available across the counter in medical and other stores, acid attacks become a relatively cheap and effective way of committing acts of violence against women. In a random check carried out by The Hindu newspaper in Karnataka in 2007, the researchers found that buying "Hydrochloric acid is as easy as cheap as buying a bar of soap." A litre of acid costs anywhere between Rs. 16 and Rs. 25 and can be bought at various locations including Nagaratpet, Ragipet and Raja Market.[1]

There is however no law to regulate acid sales except for the Manufacture, Storage and Import of Hazardous Chemicals Rules, 1989 (amended in 2000) and this only applies to industrial situations.[1] Furthermore there are no regular inspections and stock checking for acid sales as there are for explosives.[1]

It has been argued by some that controlling or regulating acid sales is an impossible task, as acid is used for many things including car batteries etc. Thus, the deterrence should come in the form of stringent laws that punish the perpetrators. However, Bangladesh, a country with the highest incident rate of acid attacks, has passed a law in 2002 to control acid sales. Thus, Acid violence can be tackled on both fronts simultaneously with a harsher punishment on the perpetrator as well controlling the sale of acid to stop it from getting into the hands of the criminal. Besides as a member of CSAAAW perhaps rightly said, it is unconscionable "how any responsible democracy can cite difficulty in regulation as an excuse for not framing laws."[1]

International commerce of sulphuric acid is controlled under the *United Nations Convention Against Illicit Traffic in Narcotic Drugs and Psychotropic Substances, 1988,* which lists sulfuric acid under Table II of the convention as a chemical frequently used in the illicit manufacture of narcotic drugs or psychotropic substances.

The next Chapter therefore discusses how the courts in India have dealt with the issue of acid attacks and what the cases show.

CHAPTER III

CASES RELATING TO ACID ATTACK IN INDIA

As India does not have a separate law governing the crime of acid attack, cases have been registered under different sections of the Indian Penal Code (IPC) particularly the sections relating to hurt, grievous hurt, grievous hurt by corrosive substances and attempt to murder and murder. However, as discussed

1. The Hindu, Acid Attack victims yet to get assistance, 27-04-2007.

earlier, the after effects of an acid attack, even if the victim survives, are distinct and scar the victim; who is usually a woman throughout her life both physically and mentally.

In some of the positive cases the accused have been charged with murder, as the intention of the attacker has been construed as an intention to kill the victim. Even in these positive cases however the amount of fine which has been levied has often been an insignificant amount. The victim has also often not been given this fine by the court.

In a 1998 Maharashtra case[1] acid was thrown on a woman, while she was holding her two and a half year old baby, by her brother-in-law for refusing to give money to maintain her husband's second wife. She sustained acid burns on the left side of her face, left hand and left breast and both she and her infant daughter lost their eyesight. The woman finally died due to burn injuries. In this case, the brother-in-law was sentenced by the Court under section 302 of IPC, to undergo imprisonment for life and pay a fine of Rs. 1000 and also sentenced to rigorous imprisonment for a month. Under section 326 of the IPC he was awarded 5 years of imprisonment apart from a fine of Rs. 2000 and 3 months of rigorous imprisonment. Though the accused was found guilty the learned Judge failed to appreciate that he should levy an adequate amount as fine and give this fine to the victim's child, who suffered from the attack in multiple ways.

In a 2002 case,[2] the accused was suspicious about the character of his wife and inserted mercuric chloride into her vagina. The victim died due to renal failure. The accused was charged and convicted under sections 302 and 307 IPC.

In another case[3] before the Hon'ble Supreme Court in 1975, acid was poured on a woman by her husband for refusing to grant him divorce. The husband was involved in an extra-marital affair. Due to the attack, the victim suffered multiple acid burns on her face and other parts of her body, leading to her death. The accused was charged and convicted under section 302 of the IPC. However, life imprisonment was not imposed even though the victim had died.

In a case before the Madras High Court,[4] a person suspected his wife had developed an illicit relationship with one of his acquaintances. In that fit of anger he threw acid on her resulting in severe burns and death of the victim. The husband was convicted under sections 302 IPC and 313 IPC (causing miscarriage of a woman without her consent) with life imprisonment and a fine of Rs. 2000. The fine was thus again a meager amount.

In *Devanand* v. *The State*[5] a man threw acid on his estranged wife because she refused to cohabit with him. The wife suffered permanent disfigurement and loss of one eye. The accused was convicted under section 307 and was imprisoned for 7 years.[6]

1. *Gulab Sahiblal Shaikh* v. *The State of Maharashtra,* 1998 Bom CR (Cri).
2. *Marepally Venkata Sree Nagesh* v. *State of A.P.,* 2002 Cr LJ 3625.
3. *Revinder Singh* v. *State of Haryana,* AIR 1975 SC 856.
4. *Balu* v. *State Represented Inspector of Police,* decided on 26-10-2006.
5. 1987 (1) Crimes 314.
6. *See* also *Veerla Stayanarayna* v. *State of Andhra Pradesh,* 2002 (Supp) 1 SC 489.

In a case before the Calcutta High Court[1] the accused had made a previous abortive attempt to throw acid on the victim and succeeded on a second attempt. The motive for the crime was revenge as the victim had rebuffed the overtures of the accused, Ramesh. The accused along with two others went to the victim's house and threw a bottle of acid on the victim outside her house where she, her mother, her aunt and her little son were sitting. The victim, her mother, her aunt and her son sustained injuries. The victim Padma died due to extensive acid burns on the neck, chest, right alna, breasts, legs, knees and scalp. Her aunt received 25% burns and her aunt's son received 11% burns. The additional sessions Judge awarded imprisonment for life and a fine for Rs. 5000 under sections 302 and 34 of the IPC. The appellants were also convicted under section 324/34 IPC and sentenced to R.I. for one year and to pay a fine of Rs. 1,000 each or in default to suffer S.I. for two months. Both sentences were to run concurrently. The High Court on appeal however, set aside the conviction and sentence against the other two accused by stating that there was no evidence to show they had a common intention and their presence with the accused on the scene of the crime was not enough.[2]

In *Srimanthula Chinna Sathaiah* v. *State of Andhra Pradesh*[3] enmity developed between two men. The accused was suspicious that the other person had falsely implicated him in a case. He also suspected that his wife was having an affair with the victim's elder son. As a revenge the accused threw acid on the victim, which resulted in severe acid burns on the face and body. The accused was charged under section 302 and 34 of the IPC and was awarded rigorous imprisonment for life.

In some cases which are targeted against women dowry and property can be the reasons for acid attacks. Property and land disputes and sometimes revenge[4] can prove to be a motive for acid attacks against men. It appears that the idea that acid is an easy effective method of harming and killing enemies can spread to general attacks against both women and men.

In case before the Supreme Court of India[5] the accused was the husband of the deceased, Sushila and wanted to kill her and their daughters, Bindu and Nandini to grab property as he was the immediate beneficiary to her estate. He poured acid over her to kill her. She received extensive burn injuries on large parts of their bodies including the face, chest, neck, etc. According to the Doctor the death was due to the corrosive acid burns and shock. The High Court convicted the appellants Ram Charittar and Kishori Lal under section 302/34 IPC, and sentenced them to life imprisonment. The appeal for their acquittal was dismissed by the Hon'ble Supreme Court. No compensation was awarded to the victims.

In another case[6] before the Madras High Court a nurse and a compounder conspired and poured a mixture of acid and kerosene over a doctor as revenge

1. *Ramesh Dev* v. *State of West Bengal,* Decided on 16-5-2007.
2. *See* also *Smt. Bhagwan Kuar* v. *Krishna Maharaja,* AIR 1973 SC 1346.
3. 1998 (4) ALD 18.
4. See *State of Madhya Pradesh* v. *Jhaddu,* 1991 Supp (1) 545.
5. *Ram Charittar* v. *State of Uttar Pradesh,* (04-04-2007 - SC).
6. *Mahesh and Parimaladevi* v. *State,* decided on 10-4-2003 by the Madras High Court.

for an alleged rape by him of the nurse. The doctor sustained 100% burn injuries and later expired due to them. The accused were charged under sections 302 and 109 of the IPC but were acquitted for the lack of evidence.

In a case before the Supreme Court[1] in a dispute between the deceased and accused regarding encroachment, the accused poured acid on the deceased and this caused severe acid burns resulting in death. The main accused was charged under section 302 of the IPC and awarded rigorous imprisonment for life.

Many cases in which death doesn't occur get registered under the sections related to hurt and grievous hurt and not attempt to murder as no intention of killing or knowledge that the offence is likely to cause death is attributed to the accused.

In a case before the Jharkhand High Court[2] the victim was standing with her friend at a Bus Stop in Dhanbad. The Appellant came and poured acid over her head and face. The appellant had a photograph of the victim and was blackmailing her but she refused to accede to his demands. The victim suffered burn injuries over the left side of her eye, neck and chest and had to be hospitalized. A case was registered under sections 324, 326, 307 IPC. The police investigated the case and finally submitted a chargesheet against the appellant under the aforesaid sections. The learned 2nd Additional Sessions Judge, Dhanbad held the appellant guilty under section 324 IPC and convicted and sentenced him to undergo RI for three years. The appellant's conviction was upheld by the Hon'ble High Court. No compensation whatsoever was awarded to the victim. In this case the court seems to have been guided by the nature of injuries which in its opinion did not amount to grievous hurt.[3]

In one of the most famous cases involving acid attack[4] the accused threw acid on a girl, Hasina, for refusing his job offer. This deeply scarred her physical appearance, changed the colour and appearance of her face and left her blind. The accused was convicted under section 307 of IPC and sentenced to imprisonment for life. A compensation of Rs. 2,00,000 in addition to the Trial Court fine of Rs. 3,00,000 was to be paid by the accused to Hasina's parents.

This was a landmark case as it was the first time that a compensation which was quite a large sum was given to the victim to meet the medical expenses including that of plastic surgeries. However, no compensation was awarded for the after effects of the attack such as loss of income etc.

In a case from Delhi[5] the accused threw acid on the victim's face. The liquid splashed on her face & produced some redness (erythema) on the skin over a part of her face involving her upper eye-lids. There was no corrosion of the skin or other deformity. The accused was convicted for causing hurt under section

1. *Barati* v. *State of Uttar Pradesh,* AIR 1974 SC 839.
2. *Awadhesh Roy* v. *State of Jharkhand* (Decided on 12-6-2006).
3. *See* also *Students of A.P.A.U and Miss Anuradha, Student* v. *Registrar, A.P.A.U, N. Sreeniwasa Reddy, Student,* 1997 (1) ALT 547.
4. *State of Karnataka by Jalahalli Police Station* v. *Joseph Rodrigues S/o V.Z. Rodrigues,* (Decided in the Hon'ble High Court of Kerala on 22-8-2006).
5. *State (Delhi Administration)* v. *Mewa Singh,* 5 (1969) DLT 506.

323 of the IPC and a meager fine of Rs. 300 along with 15 days imprisonment was awarded. This sort of punishment for acid attack is in itself a mockery of sorts and does not take into consideration the gravity of the crime and its after effects like trauma which affects the victim throughout her life.

In *Syed Shafique Ahmed* v. *State of Maharashtra*[1] personal enemity with his wife was the reason behind a gruesome acid attack by the husband on his wife as well as another person. This caused disfiguration of the face of both the wife as well as that of the other person and loss of vision of right eye of wife. The accused was charged under sections 326 and 324 of the IPC and was awarded Rs. 5000 as fine and 3 years imprisonment. This case again shows that the punishment that is often awarded does not take into account the deliberate and gruesome nature of the attack and rests only on technicalities of injuries.

In another case[2] due to enmity, acid was poured by a mother and son duo over the victims. One of the victims suffered from multiple acid burns on the whole back extending from scapular spine to iliac crest. The other victim suffered Chemical burns on the right side of forehead just above medial end of right eye brow and the skin was blackened. He also suffered from multiple acid burns on the lateral aspect of left upper arm and the skin was blackened apart from other burns. The accused were convicted under section 304 (punishment for culpable homicide not amounting to murder) and 323/34 IPC (punishment for voluntarily causing hurt with common intention), with imprisonment of a year and rigorous imprisonment for one year.

Thus over the years various kinds of acid attacks have been registered under the sections related to hurt, grievous hurt, murder etc. However, the nature and effect of the crime of acid attack is very distinct and complex and the sections relating to hurt and grievous hurt do not provide an adequate relief and punishment. Apart from this the police often use their discretion to decide what sections should be registered in the case of acid attacks and this discretion is at times influenced by gender bias and corruption or is a wrong assessment.

In most of the cases no compensation has been awarded. In those in which compensation has been awarded the sum is minimal and is totally inadequate to meet even the medical expenses. Normally courts just levy fines without even giving these to the victims. The section on Compensation in the CrPC should therefore clearly spell out that the fines levied should be given to the victim or their dependents.

The victims suffer a great deal due to a slow judicial process, inadequate compensation and obviously from the after affects of the acid attack itself.

Thus, there is an urgent need to legislate distinct sections in the IPC to deal with "acid attacks and to setup a Criminal Injuries Compensation Board in India to deal with such cases in an effective and efficient manner, to help the victims of acid attack to get compensation for medical expenses and rehabilitation apart from making section 357 CrPC mandatory in certain respects.

1. 2002 Cr LJ 1403.
2. *State of Uttar Pradesh* v. *Smt. Aqueela*, 1999 Cr LJ 2754.

CHAPTER IV

LAW IN OTHER COUNTRIES

Acid Violence in Other Countries: A Situational Analysis

Acid attacks have been documented in various different parts of the world including Australia, Bangladesh, Cambodia, China, El Salvador, Ethiopia, Italy, Laos, Malaysia, Nepal, Pakistan, Sri Lanka, Thailand, Uganda, UK, USA, and Vietnam. However, the number of incidences in Bangladesh, India, Pakistan, Cambodia and Uganda are much higher and are on the rise. Certain social and cultural issues responsible for these attacks have been "refusals of a relationship or marriage proposal, failures of a girl to bring a dowry to her husband, marital disputes, family disputes, political rivalries, land disputes and the accidental presence of the victims at the scene."[1] Most of the reasons are specifically related to gender and are common reasons in countries like Bangladesh, India, Pakistan, Cambodia, and Uganda; where other crimes against women like dowry related crimes, domestic violence and honor crimes exist. Infact in India, it has been said that "acid attacks on women are a systemic form of gendered sexual violence. Unlike acid attacks on men, these attacks are used as a weapon to silence and control women by destroying what is constructed as the primary constituent of her identity, i.e., her body. It is important then for any campaign against acid attacks to mobilize public opinion towards recognizing acid attacks as a form of gendered sexual violence and more importantly to recognize the patriarchal notions underlying these attacks".[2]

Furthermore, depicting country specific trends is useful while drawing up an appropriate legislation to address the problem. For instance, as many of cases of acid violence in Cambodia occur in the household, the crime has been proposed to be addressed in their Domestic Violence Act. A similar approach was taken in Bangladesh in 1995 when the government initially thought acid attacks to be a gender specific crime and passed the Cruelty to Women and Children Act. In 2000 the Prevention of Oppression against Women and Children Act again dealt with acid attacks on women and children. However the rise in trends of acid violence against men that ensued in the late 1900s made it necessary for the Bangladeshi government to pass a law that dealt with the crime against both women and men in specific terms. Hence, in 2002 two new laws, the Acid Offences Prevention Act, 2002 and Acid Control Act were enacted in 2002 to address the growing problem.

Bangladesh

There has been a steady increase in acid attacks in Bangladesh from approximately 12 per year to 50 per year in the mid-1990s. An even more significant jump was observed in the late 1990s when NGOs in Bangladesh reported up to 250 cases per annum. The sudden increase in cases has been partly attributed to better reporting and making the cases more visible by NGOs like Naripokkho, a women's advocacy organization, in 1995 and the Acid Survivors

---

1. Internet Edition Holiday, The acid violence against women, Shadnaz Khan, May 27, 2005.
2. Burnt not Destroyed-Report by CSAAAW.

Foundation in Dhaka in 1999. These NGOs made sure that as many cases as possible were reported and recorded and that the victims received help and compensation.[1] However, only part of this increase can be explained by this progress that was made in the documentation of cases[2]. In 2001, 340 cases were reported, in 2002, 336 cases were reported and in 2003, 335 cases were reported.[3] Earlier attacks were almost always committed against young women and girls by men who were angered by their victims rejecting their sexual advances or marriage proposals. However, as the crime became more common the motives for attacks grew more varied and presently more than 30% of victims are men, and land disputes are one of the biggest reasons for attacks.[4]

Between 1999 and 2002, acid attacks in Bangladesh increased at a rate of 50% per year, culminating in 485 attacks in 2002. In 2003 there was a 15% decrease in cases to 410 per year.[4]

The experience in Bangladesh was that acid violence cases took up to 10 years to be prosecuted in court and as many as 1 in 10 cases did not go to trial.[5] By 1999 only 10 men had been imprisoned as a result of an acid crime. Between 1999 and 2001 of the 750 acid attack cases reported and only 25 were convicted.[6]

The Acid Offences Prevention Act, 2002[7] reads as follows—

Section 4: Punishment for killing of a person by acid: Whoever kills anyone by acid shall be punished with, death or rigorous imprisonment for life and also with fine no exceeding One Lac Taka.

Section 5: Punishment for hurt by acid: Whoever causes such bodily injury to a person, by acid, that—

(a) His/Her sight or ear is damaged fully or partly or face or breast or sexual organ is disfigured or damaged, he shall be punished with, death or rigorous imprisonment for life and also a fine not exceeding One Lac Taka.

(b) Any member or joint of his/her body is disfigured or damaged or injured in any part thereof, he shall be punished with, imprisonment of either description which may extend to 14 years but not less than 7 years of rigorous imprisonment.

Section 6: Punishment for acid throwing or attempt to throwing: Whosoever throws or attempts to throw acid on any other person even if such an act causes no damage or injury to that other person whether physically, mentally or otherwise, he shall be punished with, imprisonment of either description

1. Acid Attacks: Bangladesh's Efforts to Stop the Violence, Jordan Swanson, Harvard Health Policy Review Archives, Spring 2002; Vol. 3, No. 1.
2. Baseline Survey with International Comparative Analysis of the Legal Aspects of Acid Violence in Uganda, Commissioned by: Acid Survivors Foundation Uganda, Legal Consultant: Rachel Forster, November, 2004.
3. Acid Violence Against Women, Quoting ASF statistics.
4. Acid Survivors Foundation Bangladesh.
5. Monira Rahman, Executive Director, Acid Survivors Foundation, Bangladesh.
6. The Hindu, Acid Attack victims yet to get assistance, 27-04-2007.
7. Unofficial translation of Act 2 of 2002, The Parliament of Bangladesh.

which may extend to 7 years but not less than 3 years of rigorous imprisonment also with a fine not exceeding Fifty Thousand Taka.

It is relevant to mention that prior to 1983, all acid crimes in Bangladesh were prosecuted using the penal code. In 1983, the word "acid" was included in the penal code to try to provide some clarity, but there were still gaps in the law when considering the very specific nature of acid crimes.[1] In 1995 the government enacted the Cruelty to Women and Children Act and this Act addressed acid attacks specifically. At that point in time, acid violence was thought to be a gender specific issue and all acid crimes against women and children were prosecuted through this Act. However any attack committed against a man had to be prosecuted through the old penal code. From 1995 onwards there was an increased trend in the use of acid against men and so a new law was needed to prosecute cases inflicted on men. When the law was revised and in 2002, the maximum punishment was increased from 7 years under the penal code to death.

1. The law addresses the problem of delay in prosecuting cases by providing a fixed time for investigations:

    o The investigating police officer must complete the investigation within 30 days following the reported attack or the Magistrate's order for an investigation.

    o Two extensions of 15 days each can be granted on application to the court.

    o If after 60 days, the officer is unable to complete the investigation, a new officer must be assigned and action will be taken against the first officer.

    o The new officer has 15 days to complete the investigation.

2. Trial Procedures:

    o The total time allowed for investigations is 90 days. The trial then has to be completed and a conviction secured within 90 days of the end of the investigation period.

3. The court is very proactive in ensuring that the police investigate acid cases. Section 13 in the Act states that legal action will be taken against any officers who are negligent or corrupt in investigating the crime.

4. Medical Examination of the Victim: This section is to ensure that the acid attack victim gets proper medical examination immediately and receive a certificate regarding the examination. The Section also lays down that action will be taken against a negligent doctor.

5. All offences under the Act are cognizable, non-compoundable and non-bailable.

6. Although the crime is regarded as non-bailable in section 13 of the Act, section 14 of the Act is a specific provision that gives the Court some discretion as to when it can grant bail. This section states that a bail petition cannot be filed

1. The Hindu, Acid Attack victims yet to get assistance, 27-04-2007.

if the Court is convinced that the complainant is not given the chance for hearing on the bail petition, or there are reasonable ground for conviction or He/she is not woman or child, or not physically impaired and the tribunal is not satisfied that ends of justice will not be hampered if he is enlarged on bail. If the Court is satisfied that the person is not involved in the offence, it can grant bail.

7. Acid-offences Prevention Tribunals have been set up solely to try acid cases, headed by district or session judges. These topic-specific Tribunals are to ensure that members on the Tribunals are properly sensitized to acid attack cases.

The Acid Control Act, deals with restricting and controlling the sale and supply of acid in Bangladesh. This Act attempts to control the sale and supply of acid in Bangladesh. 15-member National Acid Control Councils have been established across the country. Each council is headed by a District Commissioner. Members of the Councils are selected from the government and also lawyers, commerce people, medical professionals, specialists in women's issues and members of the media. The councils make proposals to take action to enforce and monitor the laws regarding acid sale in their respective area as well as to assist in the proper reporting, treatment and rehabilitation of victims.

The councils raise public awareness about the consequences of acid crime. In spite of the enactment of the new law the experience in Bangladesh has been that it is still very hard to restrict the sale of acid. It is first difficult to find the source of the acid used during the attack and thus to prosecute the supplier. It is also easy disguising the reason for requiring acid by proposing legitimate excuses. Furthermore, covering up the real supply of acid in their records is an effortless task for suppliers and as bribery is common in Bangladesh, acid is easy to obtain.

Cambodia

In a 2003 report on acid attacks in Cambodia,[1] collected from newspapers it was reported that between December 1999 and November 2002, 63 people were subject to acid attack. Out of these, 30 victims were female and 31 male. However, 29% of the victims were not targets of the attack and 12 males and 4 females, plus two others whose sex had not been reported were injured by accidents and included friends and family members of the victims or their drivers and other nearby passers. Thus, most the intended victims were women. Thereafter it has been reported[2] that atleast 60 known cases of acid attack violence occurred in 2005. However, others[3] suspect that the annual incidence rate could be as high as 100. A newspaper report[4] states that from October 1999 to December 2006 there have been 111 cases of acid attacks with a total of 181 victims. Most of these attacks were perpetrated on women[5] and involved husbands throwing acid

1. 2003 report by licadho, living in the shadows; acid attacks in Cambodia.published by project against torture Cambodian league for the promotion of human rights (licadho).
2. Data provided by Cambodian Acid Survivors Charity (CASC).
3. suspect Acid Survivors Trust International (ASTI).
4. The Cambodia Daily, 5 December, 2006.
5. 2003 report by LICADHO, Living in the Shadows: Acid Attacks in Cambodia.

on their wives or former wives, wives throwing acid on the second wives or mistresses and in some cases women throwing acids at their husband because of husband's violence (beating and abusing) towards them.

The Law

Acid Violence is not specifically addressed in Cambodian criminal law. Perpetrators can be charged with battery with injury, which carries a sentence of up to 10 years imprisonment.

Article 41: assault and battery[1]

1. Anyone who voluntarily strikes another resulting in injury leading to permanent disability or temporary disability lasting more than six months, is guilty of battery and shall be liable to a punishment of one to five years in prison.

2. If the disability lasts less than six months, the offence shall be punished by a term of imprisonment of six months to two years.

3. If there is no disability, the punishment shall be a term of imprisonment of two months to one year.

4. If any weapon is used to strike the blows, the period of imprisonment shall be doubled.

If the victims dies or receives life-threatening injuries, more serious charges such as murder, attempted murder or manslaughter should be laid. They carry sentences of 10 years to life imprisonment.

Article 31: murder

1. Anyone who kills or attempts to kill another person after premeditating the crime, or by preparing an ambush, or who kills or attempts to kill another person in the course of theft or rape, is guilty of the murder, and shall be liable to a punishment of imprisonment for a term of ten to twenty years.

2. Premeditation is the process of conceiving and preparing an attack on another person before the actual execution of the attack. An ambush consists of lying in wait with the intention of committing an act of violence against another person.

Article 32: Voluntary manslaughter

Anyone who voluntarily kills or attempts to kill another person without any of the aggravating circumstances mentioned in Article 31, whether or not a weapon is used, is guilty of the crime of voluntary manslaughter, and shall be liable to imprisonment for a term of eight to fifteen years.

However, convictions have been reported in only 6 cases and women have normally received more severe punishments than men.[2]

A draft provision in Cambodia's domestic violence law is being approved by the National Assembly and Senate. It proposes a punishment for acid throwers

1. Provisions dated September 10, 1992 relating to the judiciary and criminal law and procedure applicable in Cambodia during the transitional period, www.licadho.org.
2. 2003 LICADHO report.

of between 5-10 years imprisonment. Activists are still campaigning for the wording to be changed to apply to any person who throws acid, rather than just the current application only to family members who throw acid on other family members. This would exclude people who throw acid at victims who are not related to them. Also, activists argue that the maximum penalty for acid throwing should be increased, especially if permanent disfigurement or disability, like blindness, has been caused. This would be the first time that Cambodian law specifically refers to acid attacks.

However till date the Domestic Violence Law, which was approved in 2005 does not deal with acid attacks in specific terms.

Uganda

In Uganda according to Acid Survivor's Foundation (ASFU) Acid violence in affects both men (48%) and women (52%) in almost equal numbers.[1] The motives behind the attacks are domestic arguments, land disputes, business rivalry etc. There are also cases of victims that have been injured by mistake for being there at the time of the acid throwing as there were in Cambodia. These are often children who were being carried by the mother victims at the time of the attack. ASFU is also aware of many cases where victims have no idea why they were the target of an attack. Acid violence crosses the social strata of society in Uganda — from the very poorest to some very influential and wealthy people. ASFU has found that attacks are not only carried out by the person with the grievance but in 15 % of cases, the acid is thrown by an assassin; who can be hired at a very low cost.

ASFU suspects under-reporting of acid violence cases due to public stigma attached to victims, poor access to justice, police inefficiency and the victim's lack of finances to fight the case through the police system and then the courts.

The relevant section to arrest, prosecute, convict and sentence perpetrators of acid violence under the Ugandan Penal Code is section 216(g) (formerly S209) and it carries life imprisonment and reads as under:—

> "Any person who, with intent to maim, disfigure or disable any person, or to do some grievous *harm to any person or to resist or prevent the lawful arrest or detention of any person—*
>
> *(f) puts any corrosive fluid or any destructive or explosive substance in any place; or*
>
> *(g) unlawfully casts or throws any such fluid or substance at or upon any person, or otherwise applies any such fluid or substance to the person of any person, commits a felony and is liable to imprisonment for life.* "

However, it has been reported that the above section is not applied consistently by the police or the courts. Many attackers have been charged under other sections of the Penal Code, for example, under section 219 for "grievous harm" which carries a sentence of upto seven years only. Another problem that arises

1. Baseline Survey with International Comparative Analysis of the Legal Aspects of Acid Violence in Uganda, 2004.

is that police officers have too much discretion in terms of the degree of charges that they are able to bring on. Moreover, the police are not consistent in bringing charges, as charges that are filed often seem to be dependent on the individual decision of the police officer rather than one of policy.

A charge is also often levied according to the level of injury rather than by investigating the intent and motive behind the attack. Therefore if the victim manages to avoid major injuries, the perpetrator is released or only charged with a minor assault, despite the fact that the perpetrator had intended to disfigure or kill the victim. ASFU has recorded cases where there had not been physical injury and therefore no prosecution of the perpetrator or only a light sentence, resulting in the victim living in fear of a later attack. In Uganda only a few acid attacks have been charged under attempted murder which seems unfair given the premeditated nature of acid attacks.[1] Apart from this in Uganda the police are often corrupt, the prosecutors inefficient and sometimes cases are dropped because the victims are either silenced by threats or paid off.

As eluded to above, there is no consistency in sentencing, a fact confirmed generally in the sentencing system of Uganda. Sentences vary from a few months (most of which is spent on remand) to life imprisonment. Police and judiciary discretion apply and since many do not understand the severity of acid cases, often light charges and lenient sentences result. Generally sentences are too lenient given the permanent damage caused to the victim in terms of health, job, family and social status. Prior to ASFU intervention, in 62% of known acid cases in Uganda, perpetrators received custodial sentences of less than 10 years. Since the intervention of ASFU, the figure has dropped to 46%.

There is currently no form of compensation available to victims of acid attacks, despite the significant costs incurred by victims and their families as a result of the attacks. No government fund exists to provide any form of compensation, fines are not imposed on perpetrators and ASFU has no records of any civil actions being brought against perpetrators.

Concentrated sulphuric acid, commonly used in Uganda for re-charging batteries is readily available at petrol stations, street sides and from outlets in the industrial areas of cities for purchase by any individual without any questions being asked.

Currently there is no adequate legislation to control and regulate the sale and supply of acid and there are no laws to control businesses that use acid in their manufacturing process, nor for those who transport, import and export such chemicals. There are no licensing laws controlling the sale and supply of acid by vendors and no records are kept of those who buy acid and the reasons for their purchase.

However, though it is hardly used section 230 of the Ugandan Penal Code punishes a person with imprisonment for 6 months and a fine of two thousand shillings "who does with any poisonous substance any act in a manner so rash or negligent as to endanger human life or to be likely to cause hurt or injury to

1. ASFU Report 2004.

any other person or knowingly or negligently omits to take such care with any poisonous substance in his or her possession as is sufficient to guard against probable danger to human life from such poisonous substance."

Nigeria

Acid violence first reported in the city of Port Harcourt in the early 1990's.[1] The reported cases of acid attacks on women between 2001 and 2004 was 21 and another 14 cases between 1990 and 2000.[1] Although acid violence is a gender-based crime in Nigeria, there have also been reported cases of attacks against men more recently. Between 2003 and 2004 reported 7 attacks that were committed against men by women.[1]

There is no law currently in Nigeria that specifically deals with acid attacks. Offenders are prosecuted under the penal code for battery or for causing grievous harm.[2] The relevant sections of the Penal Code in Nigeria reads as under—

Chapter 28

Offences Endangering Life or Health

332. Any person who, with intent to maim, disfigure or disable, any person, or to do some grievous harm to any person, or to resist or prevent the lawful arrest or detention of any person—

(1) unlawfully wounds or does any grievous harm to any person by any means whatever; or

(2) unlawfully attempts in any manner to strike any person with any kind of projectile or with a spear, sword, knife, or other dangerous or offensive weapon; or

(3) unlawfully causes any explosive substance to explode; or

(4) sends or delivers any explosive substance or other dangerous or noxious thing to any person; or

(5) causes any such substance or thing to be taken or received by any person; or

(6) puts any corrosive fluid or any destructive or explosive substance in any place; or

(7) unlawfully casts or throws any such fluid or substance at or upon any person, or otherwise applies any such fluid or substance to the person of any person;

is guilty of a felony, and is liable to imprisonment for life.

335. Any person who unlawfully does grievous harm to another is guilty of a felony, and is liable to imprisonment for seven years.

Thus in Nigeria a person can be punished with imprisonment upto life for putting a corrosive fluid in any place or for unlawfully casting or throwing any such fluid at or upon any person even if no injury is caused.

---

1. Project Alert on Violence Against Women, 2004.
2. Acid Survivors Foundation Uganda, *Mahesh and Parimaladevi* v. *State,* decided on 10-4-2003 by the Madras High Court.

Jamaica

In Jamaica the Offences Against Persons Act (OAPA) provides for a life imprisonment for causing grievous bodily harm. There is no specific law dealing with acid attack even though Jamaica is said to have the largest number of absolute acid attack victims. The relevant sections of the OAPA read as follows—

Offences Against the Persons Act

Penalty for Murder: Death or life imprisonment, not being less than 15 years.

Attempts to Murder:

13. Whosoever shall administer to, or cause to be administered to, or to be taken by any person, any poison or other destructive thing, or shall, by any means whatsoever, wound, or cause any grievous bodily harm to any person, with intent, in any of the cases aforesaid, to commit murder, shall be guilty of felony, and, being convicted thereof, shall be liable to be imprisoned for life, with or without hard labour.

Acts Causing or Tending* to *Cause Danger to Life, or Bodily *Harm:*

20. Whosoever shall unlawfully and maliciously, by any means whatsoever, wound, or cause any grievous bodily harm to any person, or shoot **at** any person, or, by drawing a trigger, or in any other manner attempt to discharge any kind of loaded arms at any person, with intent in any of the cases aforesaid, to maim, disfigure or disable any person, or to do some other grievous bodily harm to any person, or with intent to resist or prevent the lawful apprehension or detainer **of** any person, shall be guilty **of** felony, and, being convicted thereof, shall be liable, to be imprisoned for life with or without hard labour.

22. Whosoever shall unlawfully and maliciously wound or inflict any grievous bodily harm **upon** any other person, either with or without any weapon or instrument, shall be guilty of a misdemeanour, and, being convicted thereof, shall be liable to be imprisoned for a term not exceeding three years, with or without hard labour.

29. Whosoever shall unlawfully and maliciously by the explosion of gunpowder or other explosive substance, burn, maim, disfigure, disable, or do any grievous bodily harm to any person, shall be guilty of felony and, being convicted thereof, shall be liable to be imprisoned **for** life, with or without hard labour.

United Kingdom[1]

Although acid violence is not common in the UK, the courts have punished the perpetrators harshly, when there have been such attacks. Attacks are charged under section 29 of the Offences Against the Person Act, 1861 (OAPA). This section of the Act specifically refers to *"casting or applying any corrosive fluid with intent to burn maim disfigure or disable any person."* If not charged under this provision, they are dealt with as murder or attempted murder.

1. The facts in this chapter have been taken from The Baseline Survey with International Comparative Analysis of the Legal Aspects of Acid Violence in Uganda.

Offences against the Person Act, 1861

20. Inflicting bodily injury, with or without weapon.

Whosoever shall unlawfully and maliciously wound or inflict any grievous bodily harm upon any other person, either with or without any weapon or instrument, shall be guilty of a misdemeanor, and being convicted thereof shall be liable [...][34] to be kept in penal servitude [...][35]

29. Causing gunpowder to explode, or sending to any person an explosive substance, or throwing corrosive fluid on a person, with intent to do grievous bodily harm. Whosoever shall unlawfully and maliciously cause any gunpowder or other explosive substance to explode, or send or deliver to or cause to be taken or received by any person any explosive substance or any other dangerous or noxious thing, or put or lay at any place, or cast or throw at or upon or otherwise apply to any person, any corrosive fluid or any destructive or explosive substance, with intent in any of the cases aforesaid to burn, maim, disfigure, or disable any person, or to do some grievous bodily harm to any person, shall, whether any bodily injury be effected or not, be guilty of felony, and being convicted thereof shall be liable, at the discretion of the court, to be kept in penal servitude for life or to be imprisoned.

The sentencing guidelines under section 29 of OAPA, 1861, state that there should always be a custodial sentence for this offence and the maximum sentence is life imprisonment. Lengthy sentences have mostly been given by the courts in tune with the premeditated nature of the crime. Sentences of 5-6 years imprisonment have been upheld in cases where there was no or minimal injury to the victim. For cases of severe disfigurement, sentences of 14-16 years imprisonment are awarded. The case of Radford upheld in 1986 where the victim substantially lost vision in one eye and the perpetrator was given only a 5 year sentence, now seems to be out of line with the lengthier sentences imposed in the 1990's and 2000's.

Below are some cases taken from judgments of the UK courts are as under:

- ***Radford* (1986) 8 CR App R (S) 60: 5** ***years imprisonment*** was upheld when a corrosive substance was squirted into the victim's face causing substantial loss of vision in one eye. The appellant had pleaded guilty at the trial and claimed that he had not intended to blind the victim only to disable. However the Appeal judge held that because the attack was premeditated and deliberate, the conviction and sentence would be upheld.
- ***Ismail* (1992) 13 CR App R (S) 395:** ***14 years imprisonment*** was upheld for throwing nitric acid into the face of an estranged partner, causing gross disfigurement and blindness.
- In the case ***Boumphrey* (1994) 15 Cr App.R.(S.) 733**, a sentence of ***13 years imprisonment*** was upheld for the total blinding of an innocent young man. There was a plea of guilty and the appellant was a 47-year-old man with a serious heart condition. And although there were indications of

previous violence, he had no previous convictions for violence. These facts reduced the length of the sentence slightly.

- *Carrington* **(1999) 2CR App R (S) 206:** ***6 years imprisonment*** was upheld when sulphuric acid was thrown into the face of the offender's former girlfriend. No long term damage was sustained due to prompt first aid but because the attack was premeditated and no remorse was shown, the sentence was upheld. The judge stated that the fact that the victim did not sustain any serious permanent injury was not something that could go to the credit of the appellant. It was due solely to assistance given by others.
- In the case of ***Newton*** **[1999] 1 Cr.App.R.(S.) 438** a planned acid attack occurred on an estranged wife by her husband at her place of work, leaving her with 10 per cent. burns to her body and with the aggravating feature that he robbed her till at the same time. ***A 15- year sentence was reduced by the Court of Appeal to 12 years.*** However, it is important to note that in that case there was no permanent scarring and no element of conspiracy, which serve to increase the length of a sentence.
- In the case of ***Jones*** **[1999] 1 Cr.App.R.(S.) 473** a man was held in a car for 45 minutes and acid poured over him following a dispute between him and the attacker over money, which was said to be owed as the proceeds of a fraudulent enterprise on their mutual behalves. Extensive burns to the face and the possible loss of one eye was incurred. ***Sixteen years was upheld as a proper sentence*** on the tariff basis for that offence, although a four-year sentence then being served was ordered to run concurrently on the basis of the totality principle.
- In ***Krishan Raja Rai & Earl Robinson*** **(2000) 2 CR App R (S) 120:*****15 years imprisonment*** was upheld for both offenders — one who had the intent and the other who actually threw the acid. Rai had issued threats to his former girlfriend that "you think you're so pretty, you won't be for long" and to the girlfriend's father he had said "If I don't get her I'll spoil her face or I will kill her." Robinson, who was unknown to the girlfriend ran up one evening on the street and poured concentrated nitric acid over her head from a lucozade bottle. As a result of the attack the girlfriend lost her right ear, significant scarring to her face, neck, scalp and chest. She required several surgical procedures. She also needed regular counselling from a clinical psychologist.

  The judge in the first instance held that the penalty for an offence of this nature must be longer than a normal sentence. Also he felt that the public needed to be protected from such offenders.
- The English courts have been equally severe against those behind an attack who have hired someone else to commit the crime. In the unreported case of **Humphries (1996),** Mr Peter Humphries, hired a stranger to throw acid on his former wife. Miss Hammett was babysitting for the former wife and was injured in a case of mistaken identity as the

attacker did not know that she was not the intended victim. Although the attacker was never caught, Humphries received a ***12 year sentence.***

The table below shows the kind of sentences that have been awarded in cases of acid attack in different countries where such data was available till...

6.8 Summary table of laws and sentences in other countries.

Country	Specific Law mentioning acid	Maximum Sentence	Usual sentence
Bangladesh	Acid Crime Suppression Act	Life/Death	7 years - death
Cambodia	Draft resolution being presented	10 years	9 months-10 years
India	No specific law	Not known	Not known
Nigeria	No specific law	Not known	Not known
Pakistan	No specific law	Not known	Not known
Uganda	Section 216(g) Penal Code	Life	2 years – 15 years
UK	Section 29 Offences Against the Person Act, 1861	Life	10-15 years

6.9 Summary Table of Incidence Rates where yearly figures available.

Country	Population	Number of attacks per year	Incidence
Jamaica	2.6 million	56	1:46,428
Pakistan	148.4 million	1,030	1:144,077
Bangladesh	138.1 million	410	1:336,829
Uganda	25.3 million	25	1:1,012,000
Cambodia	13.4 million	10	1:1,340,000

Source *Tables taken from the Baseline Survey with International Comparative Analysis of the Legal Aspects of Acid Violence in Uganda.*

CHAPTER V

COMPENSATION FOR THE VICTIM

In the *Delhi Domestic Working Women's Forum* case[1] the Supreme Court of India had pronounced upon the need by the government to setup a Criminal Injuries Compensation Board for rape victims within 6 months. The Supreme Court had suggested that this board should give compensation whether or not a conviction takes place. The Supreme Court explained the justification for this proposal as under—

> "It is necessary, having regard to the Directive Principles contained under Article 38(1) of the Constitution of India to setup Criminal Injuries Compensation Board. Rape victims frequently incur substantial financial loss. Some, for example are too traumatised to continue in employment.
>
> Compensation for victims should be awarded by the court on conviction of the offender and by the Criminal Injuries Compensation Board whether or not a conviction takes place. The board will take into account pain, suffering

1. *Delhi Domestic Working Women's Forum* v. *Union of India,* (1995) I SCC 14.

and shocks as well as loss of earnings due to pregnancy and the expenses of the child but if this occurred as a result of the rape.

In the present situation, the third respondent will have to evolve such scheme as to wipe out the fears of such unfortunate victims..."

In *Bodhisattwa Gautam's* case,[1] The Supreme Court again reiterated the above decision and further laid down that courts had arrived to award interim compensation which should also be provided for in the scheme.

An examination of acid attack cases again underlines the urgent need for a scheme of compensation for the victims. Acid attack victims often have to, as stated earlier, undergo multiple surgeries costing Lakhs of Rupees. They are also in urgent need of rehabilitation as they often need financial help to exist. They may not be able to seek employment.

The National commission for Women has suggested a separate legislation to deal with the offence of acid attack and as part of the proposed legislation has suggested that the Central government should establish a National Acid Attack Victims Assistance Board which will provide assistance to the acid attack victims by way of ensuring medical treatment and other services such as psychological counseling. The board has also been given the task to recommend to the Government strategies to regulate and control *inter-alia* the production and sale of acids. It has been suggested that the board administers a fund to be called. The National Acid Attack Victims Assistance Fund to which the Central and State government can give grants apart from others. It has been provided that the board can give interim financial relief upto Rs. 1 lakh within a period of 30 days directly to the hospital. Apart from other issues the main problem with the suggestions of the N.C.W is that it is restricting the function of the board to only acid attack cases.

The Law Commission has also examined the Canadian legislation for payment of compensation under the "Compensation for Victims of Crime Act". This Act applies to compensation claims arising from an injury or death resulting from certain offences. Thus, the Act provides for compensation *inter-alia* to victims of offences like sexual assault, aggravated sexual assault, murder, manslaughter, sexual exploitation, assault, kidnapping etc. The act sets up a Criminal Injuries Compensation Board, which can pay compensation to the victim or a person who is responsible for maintenance of the victim or where death has occurred, the dependants or any of them of the victim or the person who was responsible for the victim's maintenance. The compensation can be awarded under the following heads—

(a) Expenses actually and reasonably incurred or to be incurred as a result of the victims injury or death;

(b) Pecuniary loss or damages incurred by the victim as a result of total or partial disability affecting the victims capacity for work;

(c) Pecuniary loss or damages incurred by the dependants as a result of the victim's death;

---

1. *Bodhisattwa Gautam* v. *Shubhra Chakraborty*, AIR 1996 SCC 922.

(d) Pain and suffering;

(e) Maintenance of a child born as a result of sexual assault;

(f) Other pecuniary loss or damages resulting from the victims injury and any expense that in the opinion of the board it is reasonable to incur.

Interim payments to the applicant preceding the award can also be made. The total compensation ordered to be paid cannot exceed $100,000 in lump sum payments for one occurrence. The payment of the compensation has to be paid out of the consolidated fund.

The U.K. Criminal Injuries Compensation Act, 1995[1] makes the government responsible for setting up a scheme and states as under—

"(1) The Secretary of State shall make arrangements for the payment of compensation to, or in respect of, persons who have sustained one or more criminal injuries.

(2) Any such arrangements shall include the making of a scheme providing, in particular, for—

(a) the circumstances in which awards may be made; and

(b) the categories of person to whom awards may be made.

(3) The scheme shall be known as the Criminal Injuries Compensation Scheme."[2]

It states that a standard amount of compensation will be determined by reference to the nature of the injury and additional amounts with respect to special expenses and fatal injuries can be provided for. The Act states that the government should prepare a table showing the amount which should be paid in different cases or for different injuries. A claim officer to award the claim and adjudicators to hear an appeal have also been specified under the Act.

It has been pointed out that Financial Compensation for the victim can be very generous in the UK. The UK Criminal Injuries Compensation Board provided a victim GBP £86,250 (approximately US $140,000). The Assessment of general damages read as under:—

"The women was aged 44 at the date of the assault and 50 when she was injured in an acid attack. 31 She had 8% thickness burns to her face, right arm, dorsum of both hands and the left upper chest plus damage to both eyes. She had to have several skin grafts 10 months, two years eight months and two years 11 months after the assault. She was left with extensive scarring to her whole face, loss of hair above the left forehead, severe scarring to the right arm and left forearm and scarring to both hands. All scarring was permanent. Her left earlobe was destroyed, she suffered a perforated left eardrum, likely to have been caused by chemical burns and suffered permanent hearing loss, tinnitus and a persistent and foul smelling variable discharge from the left ear. She also experienced pain in the throat, on the left side of the face and ear, particularly when in the cold, soreness in her eyes with extensive watering on a permanent basis. There was some visual impairment. She also suffered from headaches, dizziness and a loss

1. http://www.opsi.gov.uk/acts/acts 1995/ukpga_l9950053_en_l #11 gl
2. Section 1 of Criminal Injuries Compensation Act, 1995.

of balance. Prior to the attack she had worked full time in a supermarket that she ran with her husband and was outgoing and sociable. Following the attack she developed agoraphobic tendencies and suffered from sleep disturbance, anxiety, frequent flashbacks, excessive sensitivity to heat and became socially withdrawn and more distant in her relationships. There was a diagnosis of severe post traumatic stress disorder and a moderately severe depressive reaction. The prognosis for the psychiatric injuries was poor although there had been some small improvement by the hearing. Due to the severity of her injuries, S was unable to work again."

After looking at the various legislations we feel that a separate act should be proposed for dealing with compensation to victims of acid attacks, rape, sexual assault, kidnapping etc. We are suggesting a broader legislation so that it can deal with the problems of victims of different crimes who need rehabilitation and compensation for survival.

CHAPTER VI
CONCLUSION AND RECOMMENDATIONS

The preceding Chapters highlight that acid attacks are an increasing phenomenon in India. However, since no special section in the Indian Penal Code deals with acid attacks, the incidents are not even recorded separately. Section 326 of the I.P.C., which deals with causing grievous hurt by throwing of a corrosive substance etc. is insufficient & inadequate to deal with the issue. *Firstly*, the definition of grievous hurt is not broad enough to cover the various kinds of injuries which are inflicted during acid attacks. *Secondly*, the section does not cover the act of administering acid. *Thirdly*, the section gives a wide discretion to the courts as far as punishment is concerned. The cases on acid attacks in India show that normally inadequate punishment is awarded in these cases. *Fourthly*, the section in the I.P.C. does not punish the intentional act of throwing of acid if no injuries occur. *Lastly*, the section also does not specify who the fine should be awarded to.

We also feel that if a person has thrown acid on or administered acid to another person a presumption should be raised against the person, who has thrown or administered the acid, that he has done so deliberately.

Apart from the above we feel that the distribution and sale of Acid should be banned except for commercial and scientific purposes. Acid should be made a scheduled banned chemical which should not be available over the counter. The particulars of purchasers of acid should be recorded.

We have also examined the various laws in different countries relating to compensation for criminal injuries. While the U.K. Act provides for the setting up of a scheme, the Canadian statute sets up a Criminal Injuries Compensation Board to dispense compensation to victims of violence. The suggestion of the National Commission for Women for setting up a board specifically for acid victims has also been examined by us. We however feel that since not only victims of acid attacks but other victims of different crimes also need compensation for rehabilitation, like victims of rape, a law should be enacted to set in place Criminal Injuries Compensation Boards at the Centre, State and District levels in our country.

1. We therefore propose that a new section 326A be added to the Indian Penal Code. The proposed section 326A will read as follows—

   326A. (i) Hurt by acid attack.—Whoever burns or maims or disfigures or disables any part or parts of the body of a person or causes grievous hurt by throwing acid on or administering acid to that person, with the intention of causing or with the knowledge that he is likely to cause such injury or hurt, shall be punishable with imprisonment of either description which shall not be less than 10 years but which may extend to life and with fine which may extend to Rs. 10 lakhs:

   Provided that any fine levied under this section shall be given to the person on whom acid has been thrown or administered.

   CLASSIFICATION OF OFFENCE

   Minimum Imprisonment of 10 years extendable upto imprisonment for life and fine—cognizable—non-bailable—triable by court of session—non-compoundable.

   (ii) Intentionally throwing or administering acid.—Whoever throws acid on, or administers acid to, any person with the intention of causing burns or maiming or disfiguring or disabling or causing grievous hurt to that person shall be liable to imprisonment of either description for a term not less than 5 years but which may extend to 10 years and with fine which may extend to Rs. 5 lakh even if no burn etc. occurs.

   CLASSIFICATION OF OFFENCE

   Minimum Imprisonment of 5 years extendable upto 10 years and fine—cognizable— non-bailable—triable by court of session—non-compoundable.

2. We further propose, for the reasons stated above, that in cases of acid attack a presumption be incorporated in the Indian Evidence Act as section 114B. The proposed section 114B of the Indian Evidence Act shall read as under:

   Section 114B: Presumption as to acid attack.—If a person has thrown acid on, or administered acid to, another person, the court shall presume that such an act has been done with the intention of causing, or with the knowledge that such an act is likely to cause such hurt or injury as is mentioned in section 326A of the Indian Penal Code.

3. We propose that a law known as "Criminal Injuries Compensation Act" be enacted as a separate Law by the government. This law should provide both interim and final monetary compensation to victims of certain acts of violence like Rape, Sexual Assault, Acid Attacks etc., and should provide for their medical and other expenses relating to rehabilitation, loss of earnings etc. Any compensation already received by the victim can be taken into account while computing compensation under this Act.

4. We further recommend that the distribution and sale of acid be strictly regulated and the sale of Acid across shop counters be banned.

(Justice AR. Lakhmanan)

Chairman, Law Commission of India

198th REPORT, 2006 ON WITNESS IDENTITY PROTECTION AND WITNESS PROTECTION PROGRAMMES

CHAPTER V

NEED FOR EXTENSION OF VICTIM IDENTITY PROTECTION GENERALLY TO CASES OF SERIOUS OFFENCES TRIABLE BY COURT OF SESSION

Having referred to the responses to the Questionnaire, we shall now deal with some of the important issues.

The subject of this chapter is important and is part of Question No. 3 of the Questionnaire.

In Chapters II and III, we have traced the development of the procedure in criminal law in relation to inquiries and trials in Courts. We have seen that while there are some general provisions with regard to open public trial and the right of the accused to have the witnesses against him or her examined in his or her presence, these rights of the accused are not treated as absolute. There are indeed specific types of special cases of protection to (a) victims in sexual offences against publicity, (b) victims and witnesses in cases of terrorist acts, in respect of their identity during inquiries and trials. In the case of sexual offences, the Supreme Court in *Sakshi* agreed that using video-screens cannot be treated as diluting the right of the accused for examination of witnesses in the presence of the accused.

But barring these special provisions, the legislature has not so far actively considered the problems of victim protection and witness identity protection during inquiries and trial in the case of witnesses deposing in *'serious offences'* such as murder, dowry deaths, rape, offences against the State, kidnapping, abduction, mischief by fire or explosives, dacoity, etc., falling within the Indian Penal Code, 1860 which are triable by Courts of Session where their lives or property may be equally in danger.

It appears to be accepted today that such protection to victims and witnesses can no longer be confined to special cases of terrorists or sexual offences against women and juveniles because even in the case of grave offences like murder, dowry-deaths, rape, dacoity, kidnapping and abduction, etc., there can be serious problems for victims and witnesses who give evidence in inquiries or trials.

Serious offences: Need for protection of victims and identity of witnesses

Such a need for protection of identity of victims and identity of witnesses in the case of *serious offences* has been felt in several countries and the protection has been extended to inquiries and trials of serious offences under the ordinary penal codes. Witnesses turning hostile on account of threats having increased in the cases of such crimes, protection appears to have become necessary.

(i) Consultation Paper

In para 3.7 of the Consultation Paper, it was stated by us as follows:

"In recent times, the cases where witnesses are turning hostile at trial due to threats, is no longer confined to cases of terrorism. Even in other types of offences falling under the Indian Penal Code or other statutes, this phenomenon has reached alarming proportions. There is, therefore, need, as in other countries, to generally empower the Court in such cases – where muscle power, political power, money power or other methods employed against witnesses and victims – for the purposes of protecting witnesses so that witnesses could give evidence without any fear of reprisals and witnesses do not turn hostile on account of threats of witnesses. That indeed is the purpose of this Consultation Paper."

(ii) Several judgments of Courts have applied protection principle to witnesses in serious offences who suffer from fear or threats:

There are several judgments of Courts visualizing the need for protection of victims and witnesses generally in the case of serious offences which do not belong to the above special categories referred to in the earlier chapters.

The Supreme Court of India stated, as long back as 1952 in *Gurbachan Singh* v. *State of Bombay,* AIR 1952 SC 221, while ordering externment of the accused and directing him to be shifted to a different place (*viz.*) Amritsar (later modified for being shifted to Kalyan), observed that such an order was permissible under section 27 of the Bombay Police Act, 1902. In respect of offences in Chapters XII, XVI or XVII of the Indian Penal Code, 1860, or abetment of such offences, where *'witnesses are not willing to come forward to give evidence in public* on account of apprehension for *'safety of their person or property'*, it was permissible to pass such orders under that Act. The Court said: "Such orders could be passed in the interest of the general public and to protect them against *dangerous* and *bad characters* whose presence in a particular locality may jeopardize the peace and safety of the citizens". This was a general case and not a case relating to terrorists or sexual offences.

In *Talab Haji Hussain* v. *Madhukar Purushottam Mondka,* AIR 1958 SC 374, the Supreme Court observed that 'witnesses should be able to give evidence without inducement or threat either from the prosecutor or the defence'. If 'any conduct on the part of an accused person is likely to obstruct a fair trial, there is occasion for the exercise of the *inherent power of the High Court* to secure ends of justice' to prevent suborning or intimidation of witnesses or obstruction of a fair trial'. The Court based the principle on the 'inherent powers' of the High Court. This too was a general case not concerned with terrorism or sexual offences.

Even though *Kartar Singh* v. *State of Punjab,* 1994 (3) SCC 569 related to trial of terrorists (TADA), there are general observations of the Supreme Court in regard to 'fear of harassment' of witnesses which needs to be prevented.

In *Swaran Singh* v. *State of Punjab,* AIR 2000 SC 2017, the Supreme Court described the plight of witnesses who were not only threatened but are maimed, or are done away with or even bribed. This was again a general case.

Likewise, though *PUCL* v. *Union of India,* 2003 (10) SCALE 967 was dealing with the terrorist (POTA), there are general observations as to the protection of victims and witnesses so that they can give evidence without fear.

The concept of a fair trial was explained in *NHRC* v. *State of Gujarat*, 2003 (9) SCALE 329 to mean that the trial must be fair not only to the accused but also to the victims. Protection of victims and witnesses becomes necessary in several cases. (The above case was a case of a serious offence under the Indian Penal Code).

The Delhi High Court in *Ms Neelam Katara* v. *Union of India*, (Crl. WP 247 of 2002) (dated 14-10-2003) issued guidelines for witness protection in a case relating to alleged murder. In the guidelines framed, the word 'accused' was defined as follows:

> "Accused means a person charged with or suspected with the commission of crime punishable *with death or life imprisonment*".

We have referred to the detailed guidelines laid down by the Delhi High Court to the above case in para 5.14 of the Consultation Paper and do not propose to repeat them.

It is clear that the Delhi High Court felt that if the offences were such that they attracted a maximum punishment of death or life sentence, witness protection may become necessary.

A recent case relating to serious offences under the Indian Penal Code, 1860 where the Supreme Court emphasised the need for protection of witnesses is the one in *Zahira's* case, 2004 (4) SCALE 373.

(iii) Provisions in other jurisdictions which generally deal with witness protection

(a) To start with, Article 14(1) of the ICCPR and Article 6(1) of the European Convention permit restrictions in case there is 'prejudice' to administration of justice. Impliedly, they permit witness protection as an exception. In our view, the scope for the said protection applies both to special offences as well as general ones provided there is proof of 'prejudice' to the administration of justice.

The reason is not far to seek. In the case of victims of terrorism and sexual offences against women and juveniles, we are dealing with a section of society consisting of very vulnerable people, be they victims or witnesses. The victims and witnesses are under fear of or danger to their lives or lives of their relations or to their property. It is obvious that in the case of serious offences under the Indian Penal Code, 1860 and other special enactments, some of which we have referred to above, there are bound to be absolutely similar situations for victims and witnesses. While in the case of certain offences under special statutes such fear or danger to victims and witnesses may be more common and pronounced, in the case of victims and witnesses involved or concerned with some serious offences, fear may be no less important. Obviously, if the trial in the case of special offences is to be fair both to the accused as well as to the victims/ witnesses, then there is no reason as to why it should not be equally fair in the case of other general offences of serious nature falling under the Indian Penal Code, 1860. It is the fear or danger or rather the likelihood thereof that is common to both cases. That is why several general statutes in other countries provide for victim and witness protection.

(b) The best example of general protection is the New Zealand Evidence Act, 1908 as amended by the Evidence (Witness Anonymity) Amendment Act, 1997.

The protection that sections 13B to 13J visualise, is applicable to all indictable offences and is, therefore, not offence specific but is witness specific (see section 13B and section 13C). Section 13C(4) of the above Act states that the Judge may, make an anonymity order, if he is satisfied that:

> "(a) the safety of the *witness or of any other person* is likely to be endangered, or there is *likely* to be serious damage to the property, if the witness's identity is disclosed; and
>
> (b) either
>
> (i) there is no reason to believe that the witness has a motive to be untruthful having regard (where applicable) to the witness's previous convictions or the witness's relationship with the accused or any associates of the accused; or
>
> (ii) the witness's credibility can be tested properly without the disclosure of the witness's identity; and
>
> (c) the making of the order would not deprive the accused of a fair trial."

(c) On the same lines, the Portuguese Act No. 93 of 1999 speaks of 'witness protection' and section 16 thereof requires that identity of witnesses may not be disclosed if the witnesses or their relatives or other persons in close contact with them 'face serious danger of attempt to their lives, physical integrity, freedom or property of considerable high value' where the offences attract a *sentence of imprisonment of 8 years or more,* or under sections 169, 299, 300, 301 of the Criminal Code and section 28 of the Cabinet Order No. 15/93 dated 22nd January. The section requires that the witness' credibility is beyond reasonable doubt and has probative value.

(d) The provisions of section 2A(1)(b) of the Australian Evidence Act, 1989 deals with 'special witnesses' who are described as persons suffering from trauma or are likely to be intimidated or to be disadvantaged as witnesses. Special arrangements can be made by the court in their favour including exclusion of public or the accused from the Court. Video-taped evidence can also be allowed.

(e) We shall refer to a few cases decided in other countries dealing with victim protection and witness identity protection generally.

In England, such a general principle of administration of justice was laid down in *Marks* v. *Beysus,* (1890) 25 QBD 494.

In *Cain* v. *Glass,* (NUL) (1985) NSWLQ 230 McHugh JA said that the principle of anonymity was applicable not only to police informers but that the said principle applied even to persons other than registered informers.

The Supreme Court of Victoria (Australia), in *Jarvie* v. *The Magistrate's Court of Victoria at Brunswick,* 1995 (1) VR 84 held that the Magistrate had the 'jurisdiction' to pass anonymity order in favour of all witnesses and that the power was not confined to undercover police officers. It applied

> "to other witnesses whose personal safety may be endangered by the disclosure of their identity."

The Court laid down four propositions of which proposition (2) reads as follows:

> "(2) the same policies which justify the protection of informers as an aspect of public immunity also justify the protection of undercover police officers. However, the claim to anonymity *can also extend to other witnesses* whose personal safety is endangered by disclosure of their identity."

Summary and conclusion

Thus, while it is the common law rule that the accused has a right to know the names and addresses of prosecution witnesses so that he may inquire whether the witnesses were competent to give evidence in regard to the offence and so that he may exercise his right of cross-examination, the said right is not absolute. It has to be balanced against the rights of the victim and other prosecution witnesses so that they can depose without any fear or danger to their lives or property or to the lives or property of their close relatives. In such cases, the victim can be permitted to depose with an intervening screen or through video-link so that he need not face the accused; and the prosecution witnesses may depose by an arrangement under which the accused will not be able to see them and their identity will not be disclosed to the accused or his lawyer. In either case, the Judge will be enabled to see the victim or the prosecution witness while they are deposing.

We may reiterate that today it is accepted that the need for protection of victims and witnesses is not necessarily confined to cases of terrorism, or sexual offences against women or children in respect of whom special statutes exist so that they may give evidence without fear and the prosecution witnesses may also depose without fear. The principle has been extended *generally to cases of serious offences* where the Court is satisfied that there is evidence about the *likelihood of danger* to the lives or property of the victim or to their relatives or to the lives or property of the witnesses or of their relatives. No doubt, it is also accepted that this procedure must be resorted only in exceptional circumstances and provided further the Court is satisfied that the victim or witness's evidence is credible. It must be further assured that the Judge while deciding about the guilt of the accused must not be weighed against the accused merely because an anonymity order is passed or a victim is given protection.

The Judge must be satisfied, as held in *Accused* (CA 60/97) (1997) 15 CRNZ 148 (156) (NZ) (CA) that:

(1) a substantial risk of serious harm to a witness exists;

(2) the risk should not be undertaken; and

(3) there is no reasonably practicable alternative means of avoiding the risk or lessening it to an acceptable level.

Factors (2) and (3) require "assessment bearing in mind any possible detrimental effect which may result to an accused ... by the particular order envisaged". The right to a fair trial to the accused must be treated as relevant when the Judge exercises his jurisdiction to pass such orders in a criminal case. It is also necessary to bear in mind that the fears or dangers to the victims or witnesses or to their relatives or property must be proved in the individual facts of each case.

We have stated that victim and witness protection must be available to all cases where offences are 'serious'. What is the meaning of the words 'serious offences'. We propose to describe them as offences triable by Court of Sessions. The criterion obviously is the nature of the offence and the procedure for the trial.

The Code of Criminal Procedure provides for four types of procedures. They are:

(a) Trial before a Court of Session (Ch XVIII);

(b) Trial of warrant cases by a Magistrate (Ch XIX);

(c) Trial of summon cases by a Magistrate (Ch XX);

(d) Summary trials (Ch XXI).

Schedule 1 of the Code classifies cases according to the Court by which they are triable. The Court of Session is the highest Court on the criminal side. Obviously, cases relating to offences which are serious are classified as triable by Courts of Sessions.

There may also be Courts equivalent in rank as Sessions Courts and also Special Courts dealing with serious offences.

Therefore, in our view, all criminal cases relating to offences under the Indian Penal Code, 1860 or under special laws, if they are exclusively triable by a Courts of Session, or by Courts equivalent in rank to Courts of Session or by Special Courts trying serious offences, then they must be treated as 'serious' cases for purposes of victim and witness protection.

CHAPTER VIII

STAGE AT WHICH IDENTITY OF WITNESS HAS TO BE PROTECTED – INVESTIGATION, PRE-TRIAL OR TRIAL AND POST-TRIAL

The next important question that has to be considered is as to the stage at which the witness identity protection is to be granted in our country. We must make it clear that our proposals in this Report deal only with 'serious offences', namely, those triable by a Sessions Court or equivalent designated/ Special Court.

There is some distinction between protection to victims on the one hand and witnesses on the other.

(a) In several cases, the *victims* may be known to the accused but this is not an absolute rule. There may be cases where the victim may not be known to the accused such as a case in which there is an indiscriminate firing by the accused. There may be several such situations. There may also be cases where the victim and the accused are known to each other.

(b) So far as *witnesses* other than victims are concerned, it is possible in most cases, that the accused does not know the witness. Barring close associates or eye-witnesses to the offence who may sometimes be known to the accused, most of the prosecution witnesses may generally be not known to the accused. It can also happen that in the matter of serious offences, not only the life but the property of the witnesses or their relatives may be in grave danger if the witness identity becomes known to the accused during investigation or during the inquiry or before the commencement of trial.

It is, therefore, necessary to deal separately with the stages of (A) *investigation;* (B) *inquiry;* (C) *trial;* and (D) *post-trial.*

(A) Investigation

This is the first stage. We are of the view that witness identity protection is necessary at the stage of investigation also. In fact, in the responses to the Questionnaire issued alongwith the Consultation Paper, it was stated in 36 responses out of 43 that such protection is necessary even at the stage of investigation.

There are certain stages of the investigation at which point the witness identity may get revealed to the accused and it is there that witness identity protection is necessary. We shall refer to the relevant steps in the investigation where such anonymity is necessary.

(1) Chapter XII of the Code of 1973 deals with 'Information to Police and their power to investigate'. (sections 154 to 176) Section 173 deals with the 'Report of Police Officer on Completion of Investigation'.

Section 173(1) states that the Report must contain—

(a) name of the parties;

(b) nature of the information;

(c) the names of the persons who appear to be acquainted with the circumstances of the case.

....

and section 173(5) states that—

(e) all documents or relevant extracts thereof on which the prosecution proposes to rely other than those already sent to the Magistrate during investigation;

(f) the statement recorded under section 161 of all the persons whom the prosecution proposes to examine as its witnesses;

be filed along with the Report.

Further sub-section (6) states as follows:—

"*Section 173(6)*: If the police officer is of opinion that any part of any such statement is not relevant to the subject-matter of the proceedings or that its disclosure to the accused is *not essential in the interests of justice and is inexpedient in the public interest,* he shall indicate that part of the statement and append a note requesting the Magistrate to exclude that part from the copies to be granted to the accused and stating the reasons for making such request."

(2) Again, under section 164(6), the Magistrate recording a confession of the accused or statement of a witness shall forward the same to the Magistrate who inquires or tries the case.

Therefore, these provisions relating to certain stages of investigation show that the identity of witnesses may, unless protected, become known to the accused *i.e.*, at the stage of recording statements under section 161 or section 164 or at the stage of filing of the charge-sheet under section 173 into the Magistrate's Court. At these stages of investigation, protection of identity may become necessary in some cases.

The copies of the charge-sheet, FIR, section 161 and 164 statements of the persons and other documents, as stated above, have to be given to the accused under section 207 except where the Police under section 173(6) may request that those portions of the statements which disclose the identity of the witnesses be not granted. There may be a large number of cases where the police officer has not made a request under section 173(6).

As we propose to grant protection to witnesses in the cases of serious offences, namely, offences triable by the Sessions Court, it is obvious that even at the above stages of investigation adequate safeguards as to the non-disclosure of identity of the witnesses has to be considered and granted by the Magistrate. We have to devise a procedure and confer statutory power on these courts.

Procedure for 'Preliminary inquiry' for granting anonymity during Investigation:

(i) Where a police officer, before recording statements of witnesses under section 161, feels that witness identity has to be protected, he must have the liberty to apply before the Magistrate concerned seeking permission to record the statement under a pseudonym subject to making the identity known only to the Magistrate.

(ii) However, where the identity is *not* kept confidential at the stage of recording the statement of witnesses as stated in (i) above but where the prosecution feels later during investigation, that it has to be kept confidential when copies of charge-sheet and section 161 statements, etc., will be granted under section 207, the police must be at liberty to apply to the Magistrate for such protection before the Magistrate takes cognizance of the offence.

(iii) There should be a preliminary inquiry, *in camera,* and at the stage of investigation, there is no need to hear the accused or giving him an opportunity.

We are proposing to provide such a procedure for seeking witness identity protection at the stage of *investigation,* by way of an application to be presented to the Magistrate under sections 4, 5 and 6 of the Draft Bill attached to this Report. This is so far as investigation is concerned.

(B) Preliminary inquiry during Inquiry as provided in Chapter 14 to Chapter 16 before the Magistrate

(a) Chapter XVI of the Code of Criminal Procedure, 1973 is titled 'Commencement of Proceedings before Magistrates'. There are some sections in this chapter which are relevant on the question of identity of witnesses. Section 207, as stated above, deals with 'Supply of police report by the police and other documents'. The documents referred to in section 207 are:

(i) the police report;

(ii) the first information report recorded under section 154;

(iii) the statement recorded under sub-section (3) of section 161 *of all persons* whom the *prosecution proposes to examine as its witnesses, excluding* therefrom any part in regard to which a request for such exclusion has been made by the police officer *under sub-section (6) of section 173;*

(iv) confessions and statements, if any, recorded under section 164;

(v) any other documents or relevant extract thereof forwarded to the Magistrate with the police report under sub-section (5) of section 173.

Section 208 likewise refers to supply of copies of statements and documents to accused in other cases triable by a Court of Session.

(b) A preliminary hearing has to be conducted by the Magistrate or the Session Judge, *in camera*, but it will be necessary to hear the accused. We are proposing that the accused may be heard separately and not in the presence of the victim or witness who are not known to the accused.

(c) In as much as, during the course of *investigation,* when the Police applies through the public prosecutor before the Magistrate for a preliminary order granting anonymity, the accused is not given a hearing, it is necessary, in our opinion, that at the stage of *inquiry,* there should be a fresh preliminary hearing, even in respect of the same witness, for the purpose of granting anonymity at the stage the witness gives evidence at the regular trial. This is because, in the preliminary inquiry now conducted (*i.e.*, the preliminary inquiry after investigation), the accused will have to be heard on the question of granting anonymity to the witness.

Whenever such an application is made after commencement of inquiry, the Magistrate has to conduct a preliminary or *voir dire* inquiry as to whether the witness's life or property or that of his relatives is in danger. An *in camera* hearing is necessary. As to how this will be conducted will be explained in the next chapter.

Where during Inquiry, the Magistrate grants an anonymity order, it will ensure for the subsequent stages including trial and thereafter.

We are providing the procedure in sections 8 to 11 which covers the preliminary inquiry procedure at the stage of Inquiry and before commencement of recording evidence at the trial.

(C) Preliminary inquiry before the Sessions Judge before commencement of recording statement of witnesses in Sessions Court

In respect of other witnesses whose identity protection has not been sought at the stage of sections 161, 164 or 207, *i.e.*, during investigation or inquiry but where it is still considered necessary and in the case of fresh witnesses to be examined at the trial, there must again be an opportunity to the prosecution to apply for maintaining anonymity during the trial and, if need be, thereafter. Such power has again to be conferred on the Sessions Court.

In this connection, we may refer to the judgment of the Supreme Court in *Kartar Singh's* case, 1994 (3) SCC 569 under the TADA where in relation to section 16 of that Act, the Supreme Court stated (at p. 290) that the "*identity, names and addresses of the witnesses* may be *disclosed before the trial commences*" as was held by the Full Bench of the Punjab and Haryana High Court in *Bimal Kaur's* case, AIR 1988 P&H 95 (FB).

We may also refer in this connection to the judgment of the Canadian Supreme Court in *R* v. *Khela*, 1995 (4) SCR 201 where the said Court too stated that if there was danger to the witness's life, the name and address need not be disclosed till *'just before the trial'*.

But in our opinion, the view expressed in these judgments for grant of identity protection to witness at a stage just before the starting of the trial, would in most cases frustrate the very object for protection. There are today not many cases coming before the Sessions Court in which the trial is completed in respect of all witnesses nor even of a single prosecution witness in a single day . Hence, in our view, the protection granted by the Magistrate or by the Sessions Court must last till the completion of the trial in the Sessions Court and cannot be confined to a stage just before the trial.

(D) Procedure for recording statement of such witnesses at the Regular trial in Sessions Court and beyond

(i) So far as the identity protection at the trial is concerned, if indeed the witnesses have been given a pseudonym during the investigation or inquiry or before commencement of trial, there can be no difficulty in allowing the further proceedings at the trial to be held on the basis of the same pseudonym. Here, we are proposing (see Chapter IX) a two-way television or video link and two-way audio link for recording evidence of victims and witnesses not known to the accused and for whom anonymity is considered necessary.

(ii) After the trial, in appeals and even after the conviction or acquittal the said pseudonym will continue. We do not see any advantage to the accused in the Court proceedings if the identity is not disclosed after trial. If the disclosure of the identity of the witnesses is not going to be of any advantage to the accused then, in our view, in the further proceedings like appeal etc., or after the conviction has become final, or even if he is acquitted, the anonymity may still be continued. If that is done, the life and property of the witness or relatives can remain out of any danger during the further proceedings also.

The procedure at the trial is proposed in section 12 and Schedule 1 of the proposed Bill.

(iii) So far as victims who are known to the accused and who have not sought anonymity and victims who have been refused a protection order, but whose trauma has to be taken care of, the evidence at the trial will be by use of a two-way close-circuit television or video-link and two-way audio system so that the victim need not depose in the immediate presence of the accused for otherwise he may face trauma.

This procedure is proposed in section 13 read with Schedule 2 of the proposed Bill.

CHAPTER IX

TWO-WAY CLOSED-CIRCUIT TELEVISION FOR EXAMINING THE VICTIM AND WITNESSES DURING TRIAL IN THE SESSIONS COURT

We shall now refer to the procedure of closed circuit television or video link, to which we have referred to earlier. That procedure can be followed at the trial by the Sessions Court in respect of witnesses or victims who have earlier obtained witness protection orders during investigation or inquiry or before commencement of recording of evidence at the trial.

So far 'screening or closed-circuit television' is not part of the Code of Criminal Procedure, 1973 or Special Acts

Screening or closed-circuit television methods are not contained in the Code of Criminal Procedure, 1973 nor in the special Acts referred to in the earlier chapters.

We have noticed in Chapter III that the TADA 1987 did deal with procedure for witness protection in section 16. Neither 'screening' nor 'closed circuit television' were mentioned in section 16. Section 16 mentioned *in camera* proceedings. Section 16(3)(c) merely stated that the Court may issue 'any directions for securing that the identity and addresses of the witnesses are not disclosed'.

In the POTA 2002, section 30(1) referred to 'in camera' proceedings and section 30(2)(c) was in the same language as section 16(3)(c).

In *Kartar Singh's* case, (1994) 3 SCC 569 which dealt with section 16 of the TADA, there is no reference to 'screening' or 'closed-circuit television'.

In *PUCL* v. *Union of India*, 2003 (10) SCALE 967, which dealt with section 30 of the POTA, the Supreme Court observed (para 62) (at p. 994):

> "It is not feasible for us to suggest the procedure that has to be adopted by the Special Courts for keeping the identity of the witness secret."

For the first time, before the Law Commission when it was preparing the 172nd Report (2000) (as stated earlier) in the case of child abuse or sexual offences there was a *request* for incorporating provisions such as:

(i) video taped interview of the child;

(ii) *via* closed-circuit television testimony or giving evidence from behind a *screen*.

But the Law Commission *accepted* the *'screening'* method. In the draft amendment, it however, did not use the word 'screening' but proposed insertion of a general proviso in section 273 which stated:

> "Provided that where the evidence of a person below sixteen years who is alleged to have been subjected to sexual assault or any other sexual offence, is to be recorded, the Court may take *appropriate measures* to ensure that such

person is not confronted by the accused at the same time ensuring the right of cross-examination of the accused."

When the 172nd Report came up before the Supreme Court in *Sakshi* v. *Union of India,* 2004 (6) SCALE 15, the Supreme Court referred to the argument of the NGO, *(Sakshi)* before the Law Commission as stated earlier. The Supreme Court accepted as admissible video-conferencing method for purpose of hearing the victim or witnesses. Recording by way of *video-conferencing* was accepted in view of the earlier judgment of the Supreme Court in *State of Maharashtra* v. *Dr. Praful B. Desai,* (2003) 4 SCC 601 (see para 31). It was stated that this was consistent with section 273 of the Code. However, in the final directions, the Supreme Court suggested the method of using a *'screen' or 'some such arrangement'* (see para 32). The Court also referred to the need for *in camera* proceedings as stated in section 327 of the Code.

Praful B. Desai's case was not a criminal case but was a civil case in which one party wanted to examine a foreign medical expert. While permitting *video-conferencing,* the Supreme Court relied upon *Maryland* v. *Craig,* (1990) 497 US 836 (which was a criminal case) to say that video-conferencing evidence is admissible in evidence.

In a case arising under the Consumer (Protection) Act, 1986 the Supreme Court in *J.J. Merchant* v. *Shrinath Chaturvedi,* AIR 2002 SC 2931 stated that under that Act, the Commission could examine witnesses on commission under section 13(4)(v) and that cross-examination could take place by video-conferencing. The Supreme Court stated that affidavits could be initially filed and,

> "if the cross-examination is sought for by the other side and the Commission finds it proper, it can easily evolve a procedure permitting the party who intends to cross-examine by putting certain questions in writing and those questions also could be replied by experts including doctors on affidavits. In case where stakes are very high and still party intends to cross-examine such doctors or experts, there can be *video-conferences* or asking questions by arranging telephone conference and at the initial stage, this cost should be borne by the person who claims the video-conference. Further cross-examination can be taken by the Commissioner appointed by it at the working place of such experts at a fixed time."

In sum, so far as the criminal jurisdiction is concerned, there is, at the moment, no provision in the Code of Criminal Procedure, 1973 which permits 'screening' or 'closed-circuit television'. In *Sakshi,* the Supreme Court referred to screening and video-conferencing as acceptable procedures but in the ultimate directions given by it, it used the words 'screening' or 'some other arrangement' and followed *Praful B. Desai* case. *Praful B. Desai* followed *Maryland* v. *Craig.*

The Maryland Rules on closed-circuit television:

As the Supreme Court in *Praful Desai's* case referred to *Maryland* v. *Craig,* (1990) 497 US 836, we shall refer to the Rules applicable to Maryland Courts which were interpreted in *Maryland* v. *Craig.* There, under the procedure contained in the Maryland Courts & Judicial Procedure Code, 1989 (sections 9-102(a)(i)(ii)) the child aged six years, who was allegedly sexually abused would be at a distant place and would be examined in chief and also cross-examined while the Judge, Jury and the accused would remain in the Courtroom, where the testimony would be displayed on a video-screen by using a closed-circuit television. In *Maryland* v. *Craig,* the Supreme Court rejected Craig's objection that the use of *one-way closed-circuit* procedure violated the confrontation clause contained in the Sixth Amendment. The Court held that if there was direct confrontation between them in the Courtroom, the *child victim and other witnesses* would suffer serious emotional distress which they would not be able to express.

The Supreme Court held that the purpose of the Sixth Amendment was to ensure the reliability of the evidence against an accused by subjecting the witness to rigorous testing in an adversarial proceeding before the trial Court and that purpose is served by the combined effects of confrontation, physical presence, oath, cross-examination and observation of demeanour by the trial Court. Although face to face confrontation formed the core of the Sixth Amendment, it was not an indispensable element of the confrontation right. If it were, the Sixth Amendment would abrogate virtually every hearsay exception, a result rejected as unintended and too extreme (*Ohio* v. *Roberts,* 448 US 50). The Amendment must be interpreted in a manner sensitive to its purpose and to the necessities of trial and adversary process (*Kirby* v. *US,* 174 US 47). Nonetheless, the right to confront accusatory witnesses may be satisfied absent a physical, face to face confrontation or trial only where denial of such *confrontation is necessary to further an important public policy* and only where the testimony's reliability is otherwise answered (*Coy* v. *Iowa*). A State's interest in the physical and psychological well-being of child-abuse victims may be sufficiently important to outweigh, at least in some cases, an accused's right to face his or her accusers in Court. The Court will use the *video-procedure* only if it is satisfied that the child would otherwise be traumatized. *Maryland* v. *Craig* has been approved by our Supreme Court in *Praful B. Desai's* case, 2003 (4) SCC 601.

The same reasoning applies to cases of witnesses who, in the case of serious offences, are likely to suffer danger to their lives or properties, or where victims suffer emotional distress and the need to allow them to give evidence fearlessly outweighs the rights of the accused for face to face cross-examination.

Victim's evidence procedure under Maryland Rules

Maryland's rule deals with child abuse cases and procedure at trial and Title 11, dealing with 'Victims and Witnesses' and section 11.303, is in 4 clauses:

(a) scope of section;

(b) in general;

(c) preliminary determination by Court (whether to allow the child victim to testify by closed circuit television);

(d) procedure during testimony.

It contemplates a preliminary hearing before regular trial.

As to (a), scope of section, it is said that the section applies to a case of child-abuse under Title 5, Sub-title 7 of the Family Law Article or section 3.601 or section 3.602 of the Criminal Law Code.

As to (b), 'in general', it refers (i) to the preliminary hearing *i.e.,* when a Court decides if evidence in Court can result in the victim suffering such emotional distress which will make the victim not reasonably communicate, and (ii) to the evidence taken during the proceedings *i.e.,* regular proceeding.

Clause (c) is important. It refers to 'determination by Court' *i.e.,* the *preliminary hearing* procedure. It contains sub-clause (1)(i) and (ii) and sub-clause (2)(i) and (ii) Under sub-clause (1)(i), the Court may observe and question the child victim inside or outside Courtroom *and* under sub-clause (1)(ii), the Court may hear testimony of a parent or guardian and the person who has dealt with the child in a therapeutic setting. Under sub-clause (2), it is stated that when the Court decides the issue *'whether* to allow a child victim to testify by *closed-circuit television,* (i) each accused can have one attorney in the Court alongwith the victims' attorney and the prosecuting agency *(i.e., neither victim nor the accused),* and (ii) if the Court decides to observe or question the child victim, the Court may not allow the accused but the counsel for accused and the prosecuting agency and one attorney for the victim will be present.

Hence, under those Rules, at the preliminary hearing, the accused will not be physically present though the counsel for accused will be present, wherever the Court wants to observe or question the child victim. If the Court decides in the preliminary hearing to use of closed-circuit television, then *under (d)* the following procedure had to be followed:

(1) *Where the victim is present, the prosecutor, the attorney for accused and attorney for victim and the operators of the closed-circuit equipment, and any other person whose presence, according to the Court, contributes to the well-being of the child, including the person who dealt with the child in therapeutic sitting shall be present.*

(2) *In the Courtroom, the Judge, the accused shall be present.*

In addition, there would be *a two-way audio connection* between the room where the victim and lawyers are stationed and the Courtroom where the Judge and accused are present.

INDIA

Closed circuit television procedure at the trial in the Sessions Court

We have already referred to the *in camera* examination of the witness before the Magistrate at the stage of investigation for purpose of deciding anonymity during investigation. Here the accused is not heard.

We have also referred to the preliminary inquiry procedure before the Magistrate during inquiry or before the Sessions Judge before the commencement of recording of evidence at the regular trial. In these preliminary inquiries, the accused is separately heard. Therefore, there is no need to go in for a two-way television or video link procedure.

Such a need, as stated below, arises only at the stage of recording evidence at the regular trial before the Sessions Judge.

At the trial, if a witness or victim has not sought for anonymity earlier or had sought and the request was rejected, there is no need for a closed-circuit television or video link procedure. But where the witness or victim had applied at the stage of inquiry before the Magistrate or before the stage of recording evidence at trial before the Sessions Court and where those Courts have granted anonymity, there is need for closed circuit television procedure to be followed at the trial. The following situations may arise:

(i) There may be a case in which a *victim's* identity *is known* to the accused and *vice-versa;*

(ii) There may also be cases where the *victim is not known* to the accused such as where an accused fires with his pistol at random. In such cases, a victim may need anonymity;

(iii) There are cases where the *witness's* identity *is not known* to the accused and the witness may need identity protection.

It is obvious that a common procedure can be evolved for (ii) and (iii) where victims as well as witnesses are not known to the accused and a separate procedure can be prescribed for (i) where victim is known to the accused.

(i) Victim known to the accused

So far as cases under (i) are concerned, where a victim is known to the accused, there is no need to prevent the accused from seeing the victim. But the witness has to be permitted to give evidence without facing the accused if he claims trauma. Here, the only need is to prevent trauma for the victim-witness which he or she will suffer if there is face to face confrontation with accused and there is no need for victim identity protection. As we shall discuss presently, even here two-way television or video link is necessary but is limited to victim deposing without seeing the accused physically or on the video screen, so as to prevent trauma.

(ii) Victim and witness not known to the accused

(a) So far as (ii) victims whose identity is not known to the accused are concerned and so far as (iii) other witnesses whose identity is not known to the accused, prosecution may seek and that the Court may grant identity protection after conducting a preliminary hearing. Here the victim or witness cannot be allowed to be seen by the accused. A two-way television or video link is necessary for achieving that object.

(b) In the Draft Bill, we propose to define 'witness' as including a victim also, so that the same procedure for securing a 'identity' protection order may be applicable (a) both at the stage of investigation, and (b) also at subsequent stages *i.e.,* inquiry and trial.

(c) It is obvious that a *victim* who is not known to the accused – such as where the accused has indiscriminately fired at several persons, and who fears danger to his life or property or to those of his close relatives is in the same position of a witness not known to the accused who has similar apprehensions.

(d) It is equally obvious that where the prosecution or a victim feels that his or her identity is known to the accused, the prosecution or the victim will not apply for identity protection and such victims may apply only for an order that they may not be required to depose in the immediate physical presence of the accused or they may not even like to see the accused on the video screen while deposing.

We propose two separate sections in the Draft Bill to deal with (1) victims and witnesses not known to the accused, who have obtained a protection order before trial, and (2) victims known to the accused who found no need to obtain any such protection order before trial.

Procedure: (Trial stage)

(i) Victim-witnesses who have not sought identity protection as they are known to the accused (protection from trauma)

Where the victim-witness is known to the accused, though the victim had not sought identity protection earlier, he may, as already stated, not like, during trial, to suffer from any trauma by deposing to the details of the crime while physically facing the accused. The mechanism by which this can be achieved is not difficult to prescribe.

We can have an arrangement where the victim-witness does not, while deposing, see the accused but the accused is able to see the victim-witness. This is, however, subject to one exception. The victim must face the accused at least once for the purpose of identifying the accused as the person who is guilty of the crime and for that purpose also, the arrangement can provide a mechanism.

The Supreme Court has, no doubt, made an observation in *Sakshi* case that a screen may be erected to preclude the victim seeing the accused. But, in our view, psychologically, a victim is not free if the accused is in the same room and they are merely separated by a screen.

In our view, if the victim is in a different room, he or she will be more free to depose without any trauma. We, therefore, propose a two-way television or video link coupled with a two-way audio system connecting two rooms.

We can have a two-way closed-circuit television with a video screen in each of two different rooms. The victim-witness will be present in a room and in that room, the prosecutor, the defence lawyer and the technical personnel who operate the close-circuit television will also be present. The Judge and the accused, the technical personnel, the courtmaster and stenographer, will be in the Courtroom.

There will be a video screen in the Courtroom so that the Judge and the accused can watch the victim-witness, the prosecutor and the defence lawyer examining the victim-witness. In the other room where the victim and the two lawyers are present, there can be another screen which will be used only at the initial stage when the victim has to identify the accused. After that is done, that video camera in the room where the accused is stationed, will not be focussed on the accused. While the victim deposes thereafter in chief or cross-examination, he will not be seeing the accused in the screen in his room any longer. The defence lawyer sees the victim directly in his room and can examine his or her demeanour. The Judge and the accused can see the victim on the screen in their room and watch his or her demeanour. The courtmaster and the stenographer can also be in the room where the Judge is sitting.

There will be a two-way audio mechanism by which the persons in each room can talk to the others in another room.

(ii) & (iii) Victim and witnesses who have sought identity protection

Where the victim-witness or other witnesses seek identity protection at the trial, it is necessary to protect their identity at the stage of investigation, inquiry and before trial – as per the procedure already indicated, provided danger to the life or property of such victim or witness or of their relatives is proved. (We have already stated that there may be victims – such as those injured in an indiscriminate firing by an accused – who may not be known to the accused.)

Question is as to the mechanism by which this can be achieved in cases where identity protection has been granted to witnesses, including victims who have to finally depose at the trial.

Where victim/witness has been granted identity protection earlier and he is giving evidence at the trial, it is essential that the accused as well as the counsel for accused must be precluded from identifying the victim/witness concerned. But, here too, – in the case of both the victim-witness or the witness, – who are, in both cases, not known to the accused – they may have to first identify the accused as the person guilty of the crime. Therefore, there must be a two-way closed-circuit television with screens in the room where such victim-witnesses are present and give evidence. Both the accused and defence lawyer must be in a separate room, in as much as both of them should not see the victim-witness or witness concerned, who will be in another room. If such victim-witness or witnesses seeking protection is in another room and the public prosecutor also is in that room, there can be allegations of the victim/witness for prosecution being prompted invisibly by the prosecutor. Therefore, it is advisable that the Judge also must be in that room wherefrom the victim-witness or witness deposes.

Thus, the arrangement must be that the victim/witness who seeks protection of identity, the public prosecutor and the Judge, his courtmaster and stenographer and the technical personnel will be in the Courtroom while the accused and the defence lawyer will be in another room. There will be a video-screen in each room. The camera in the room of the victim/witness, Prosecutor and Judge will not be focussed on the victim/witness whose identity is to be kept confidential. It will be focussed on the Judge and the prosecutor who are in the Courtroom. The Judge and the prosecutor over whom the camera is focussed will be seen on the screen which is kept in the room of the accused and the defence lawyer.

There will have to be a two-way audio system also connecting both rooms.

We are providing these procedures in Schedule 1 and Schedule 2 of the proposed Bill.

The courtmaster, the stenographer and the technical personnel must take an oath that they will not disclose the identity of the witness-victim (who has earlier obtained protection order) who is giving evidence at the trial. Breach of the oath can be visited by proceedings for Contempt of Court, in accordance with law.

Part 7

Rape and Murder – Judicial Activism

RAPE AND MURDER – JUDICIAL ACTIVISM

RAPE AND MURDER OF BROTHER'S DAUGHTER

Laxman Naik

v.

State of Orissa,

AIR 1995 SC 1387

JUDGE(S): DR. A.S. ANAND AND FAIZAN UDDIN

(Criminal Appeal No. 407 of 1992, dated 22-2-1994)

FACTS

The case reveals a sordid story which took place sometime in the afternoon of February 17, 1990, in which the alleged sexual assault followed by brutal and merciless murder by the dastardly and monstrous act of abhorrent nature was said to have been committed by the appellant, who was none else but an agnate and paternal uncle of the deceased victim Nitma, a girl of the tender age of 7 years who fell a prey to his lust which sends shocking waves not only to the judicial conscience but to everyone having slightest sense of human values and particularly to the blood relations and the society at large.

The appellant Laxman Naik was charged and tried under sections 376 and 302 of the Penal Code for committing rape and soon after murder of the victim inside the forest known as Chhotsima jungle, situated on the way between the Villages Patkadihi and Tangarjoda.

Briefly stated, the prosecution case as it turns out from the evidence on record was that Rema Naik, PW 2 resident of Village Patkadihi had performed funeral rites at his house on February 16, 1990 in which he had invited his relatives and other villagers. Smt. Nitma Naik, PW 3, the mother of the present appellant was the sister of the father of Rema Naik, PW 2. Smt Nitma Naik, PW 3, her son the appellant Laxman and the deceased Nitma daughter of elder brother of the appellant, being close relatives of Rema Naik, also went from their Village Tangarjoda to the house of Rama Naik at Village Patkadihi to attend the said ceremony. It was said that in the afternoon of February 17, 1990 when all the relatives assembled in the ceremony including Rema Naik, PW 2 were busy in the observance of the ceremony, the appellant commanded the deceased to accompany him back to their village and the deceased followed him in obedience of his command. Around 4 p.m. the appellant and the deceased were found to be absent from function. Shortly thereafter Genada *alias* Ganga Ram, PW 1, resident of Village Patkadihi saw the appellant and the deceased near Chhotsima jungle, going towards their Village Tangarjoda. Sometime later, the appellant alone reached his house in Village Tangarjoda where on being asked about the deceased by his elder brother Hindu Naik, PW 4, the father of the deceased, the appellant was said to have told him that the mother and the deceased Nitma were at the house of Rema Naik in Village Patkadihi. In the same evening the appellant returned back to Village Patkadihi and on being questioned by his mother Nitma Naik, PW 3 as to the whereabouts of the deceased, the appellant told her that she had safely reached her Village Tangarjoda. The next morning when the appellant's mother Nitma Naik was heading towards her Village Tangarjoda, she noticed the appellant roaming about near Chhotsima jungle. On being asked again as to the whereabouts of the deceased, the appellant told his mother that she was there in Village Tangarjoda. But to her utter surprise when Nitma Naik, PW 3, the mother of the appellant reached her Village Tangarjoda she did not find the deceased there and, therefore, she rushed back to Village Patkadihi where she told Rema Naik, PW 2 and other villagers that the deceased was missing. They therefore, including Hindu Naik, PW 4, the father of the deceased proceeded towards Chhotsima jungle in search of the deceased. The searching party found the deceased lying in a lonely place in Chhotsima jungle in revealing circumstances. The said party found the torn wearing apparel (underwear) of the appellant near the dead body of the victim. There were marks of violence over the dead body of the victim and bleeding injury in her private part. A ribbon belonging to the deceased and some tamarinds were also found lying near her dead body.

A ward member of Village Patkadihi, Bhagala Majhi, PW 5 who had also gone to the jungle with the search party, dictated a report Exh. 1 to his son Apna Majhi, PW 7 which was handed over to Rasananda Rout, PW 9, Sub-Inspector of Police, Jharadihi Outpost under Tirang Police Station. He entered the said report in the station diary and sent the report to the Officer-in-charge of the Police Station with his endorsement and took up the investigation. The ASI reached the spot at about 1.30 p.m. same day and prepared inquest report - Exh. 3. He seized the frock, underwear and ribbon belonging to the deceased and some tamarinds under Exh. 2. He also seized a sample of blood-smeared earth from the place of occurrence, Exh. 6. He also recorded the statement of some of the witnesses.

DECISION OF THE TRIAL COURT AND THE HIGH COURT

Learned Sessions Judge, Mayurbhanj, Baripade, relying on the circumstantial evidence found to be established against the appellant, convicted him for an offence under section 376 as well as under section 302 of the Penal Code and having regard to the peculiar facts and circumstances of the present case found it to be rarest of the rare cases and, therefore, sentenced him to death. However, no separate sentence for the offence under section 376 of the Penal Code was awarded. The learned Sessions Judge made a reference to the High Court of Orissa for confirmation of the death sentence. The appellant Laxman Naik also preferred an appeal in the High Court of Orissa challenging his conviction and sentence as aforesaid. After a careful and close scrutiny of the evidence on record the High Court dismissed the appellant's appeal and confirmed the death sentence awarded to him. An appeal, therefore, was filed before the Supreme Court on being granted special leave.

ADVOCATE'S PLEA IN THE SUPREME COURT

Learned counsel for the appellant, urged that mother and brother of the appellant (PW 3 and PW 4) were not happy with the appellant because most often he used to disappear from his house for days together and it was for this reason that they made the statement against the appellant and as such no weight should be attached to their testimony. Be that as it may, the Court opined that, it was beyond comprehension to think that a real mother and real brother would ever think of falsely implicating the appellant in a heinous crime like this only because the appellant was in habit of disappearing from the town very frequently. The argument simply deserved to be rejected as without any merit.

JUDGMENT OF THE SUPREME COURT

The Court observed that the aforementioned circumstances found to be established against the appellant form a complete chain of evidence as not to leave any reasonable ground for a conclusion consistent with the hypothesis of the innocence of the appellant but on the contrary the same were of exclusive nature consistent only with the hypothesis of the guilt of the appellant and conclusively lead to the irresistable conclusion that it was the appellant and he alone who had committed murder of the girl Nitma after subjecting her to forcible sexual intercourse.

Regarding the question of sentence to be imposed upon the appellant, it may be pointed out that the Supreme Court in the case of *Bachan Singh* v. *State of Punjab,* [(1980) 2 SCC 684: 1980 SCC (Cri) 580] while discussing the sentencing policy, also laid down norms indicating the area of imposition of death penalty taking into consideration the aggravating and mitigating circumstances of the case and affirmed the view that the sentencing discretion is to be exercised judicially on well-recognised principles, after balancing all the aggravating and mitigating circumstances of the crime guided by the legislative policy discernible from the provisions contained in sections 253(2) and 354(3) of the Code of Criminal Procedure. In other words, the extreme penalty can be inflicted only in gravest cases of the extreme culpability and in making choice of the sentence, in addition to the circumstances of the offender also. Having regard to these principles with regard to the imposition of the extreme penalty it may be noticed that there were absolutely no mitigating circumstances in the present case. On the contrary the facts of the case disclosed only aggravating circumstances against the appellant.

The hard facts of the present case were that the appellant Laxman was the uncle of the deceased and almost occupied the status and position that of a guardian. Consequently the victim who was aged about 7 years must have reposed complete confidence in the appellant and while reposing such faith and confidence in the appellant must have believed in his *bona fides* and it was on account of such a faith and belief that she acted upon the command of the appellant in accompanying him under the impression that she was being taken to her village unmindful of the preplanned unholy designs of the appellant. The victim was a totally helpless child there being no one to protect her in the place where she was taken by the appellant misusing her confidence to fulfil his lust. It appears that the appellant had preplanned to commit the crime by resorting to diabolical methods and it was with that object that he took the girl to a lonely place to execute his dastardly act.

The evidence of Dr. Pushp Lata, PW 12, who conducted the post-mortem over the dead body of the victim went to show that she had several external and internal injuries on her person including a serious injury in her private parts showing the brutality which she was subjected to while committing rape on her. The victim of the age of Nitma could not have even ever resisted the act with which she was subjected to. The appellant seemed to have acted in a beastly manner as after satisfying his lust he thought that the victim might expose him for the commission of the offence of forcible rape on her to the family members and others, the appellant with a view to screen the evidence of his crime also put an end to the life of innocent girl who had seen only seven summers. The evidence on record was indicative of the fact as to how diabolically the appellant had conceived of his plan and brutally executed it and such a calculated, cold-blooded and brutal murder of a girl of a very tender age after committing rape on her would undoubtedly fall in the category of rarest of the rare cases attracting no punishment other than the capital punishment and consequently the Court confirmed the sentence of death imposed upon the appellant for the offence under section 302 of the Penal Code. As regards the punishment under section 376, neither the learned trial Judge nor the High Court awarded any separate and additional substantive sentence and in view of the fact that the sentence of death awarded to the appellant was confirmed and did not impose any sentence on the appellant under section 376.

In the result the appeal preferred by the appellant failed and was dismissed.

RAPE AND MURDER BY SECURITY GUARD (DHANANJOY CHATTERJEE CASE)

Dhananjoy Chatterjee **alias** *Dhana*

v.

State of West Bengal,

(1994) 2 SCC 220

JUDGE(S): A.S. ANAND AND N.P. SINGH

Criminal Appeal No. 584 of 1992 (From the Judgment and Order dated August 7, 1992 of the Calcutta High Court in Death Reference No. 3 of 1991), decided on January 11, 1994.

ADVOCATES

Appellant – A.K. Ganguli.

Respondent – D.N. Mukherjee.

FACTS

According to the prosecution case, the appellant Dhananjoy was one of the security guards deputed to guard the building 'Anand Apartment' by Security and Investigating Bureau of which Mr. Shyam Karmakar PW 21 was the proprietor. On March 2, 1990, Hetal, the deceased complained to her mother Yashmoti Parekh PW 3 that the appellant had been teasing her on her way to and back from the school and had proposed to her on that day to accompany him to cinema hall to watch a movie. She had made complaints about the teasing by the appellant to her mother previously also. Yashmoti PW 3 told her husband Nagardas Parekh PW 4 on March 3, 1990 about the behaviour of the appellant towards their daughter, who in turn complained to Shyam Karmakar PW 21 and requested him to replace the appellant. At the asking of Shyam Karmakar PW 21, who came to meet Nagardas PW 4 in his flat in that connection, PW 4 gave a written complaint also and the appellant was transferred and a transfer order posting the appellant at 'Paras Apartment' was issued by PW 21. Bijoy Thapa, a security guard at Paras Apartment was posted in his place, at Anand Apartment. The transfer was to take effect from March 5, 1990.

As per their normal routine, Nagardas Parekh PW 4 and his son Bhawesh Parekh PW 5, father and brother of the deceased respectively, left for their place of business and college in the morning on March 5, 1990. Bhawesh PW 5 returned to the flat at about 11.30 a.m. and after taking his meals, left for his father's place of business as was his routine. The deceased returned to her flat after taking her examination at about 1 p.m. Yashmoti PW 3, the mother of the deceased used to visit Laxmi Narayan Mandir between 5 and 5.30 p.m. daily. As usual, on the date of the occurrence also she left for the Temple at about 5.20 p.m. Hetal was all alone in the flat at that time. The appellant, in spite of the order of transfer, did not report at Paras Apartment and instead performed his duties, as a security guard, at Anand Apartment between 6 a.m. and 2 p.m. on March 5, 1990. Shortly after Yashmoti PW 3, the mother of the deceased left for the Temple, the appellant met Dasarath Murmu PW 7, another security guard who was at that time on duty at the building and told him that he was going to Flat No. 3-A for contacting his office over the telephone. The appellant used the lift to go to the said flat. At about 5.45 p.m., Pratap Chandra Pali PW 6, Supervisor of the Security and Investigating Bureau, visited Anand Apartment and enquired from PW 7 whether Bijoy Thapa had performed his duty in place of the appellant in the morning but was told by Dasarath PW 7, that Bijoy Thapa had not come to that building and that the duties had been performed by the appellant between 6 a.m. and 2 p.m. on that day. On inquiry by the supervisor as to where the appellant was, PW 7 told the Supervisor that at that particular time, the appellant had gone to Flat No. 3-A with a view to contact his office over the telephone. The Supervisor Pratap Chandra PW 6 asked Dasarath PW 7 to call the appellant and since, he was not able to contact him through the intercom, there being no response from Flat No. 3-A, he called out the name of the appellant, who appeared at the balcony of Flat No. 3-A and on being told that PW 6, the supervisor had come and wanted to see him, told him that he would come down. The appellant after a little while came down by the stairs and even though the supervisor PW 6 and Dasarath PW 7 were waiting for him, he hurriedly went past them and on being asked by PW 6 that he wanted to talk to him, told him to come outside the gate and speak to him. The appellant on inquiry by PW 6 as to why he had not obeyed the transfer order told him that due to some personal difficulty he could not report for duty at Paras Apartment. He was advised to take charge at Paras Apartment without fail the next day. The appellant thereafter left.

At about 6.05 p.m. Yashmoti PW 3 returned from the Temple. While going to her flat in the lift, she was told by Ramdhan Yadav PW 8, the lift operator, that the appellant had gone to her flat in her absence to make a telephone call to his office. She was annoyed on getting this information because of the complaint which the deceased had made to her earlier. On reaching her flat, she rang the bell repeatedly but there was no response and nobody opened the door. She raised alarm which attracted several of her neighbours. They also rang the bell and knocked at the door but there was no response. Eventually, the lock of the door was broken open by the neighbours, their servant and the liftman, and as she entered the flat along with some of her neighbours, she found the door of her bedroom open. Hetal deceased was lying on the floor. Her skirt and blouse had been pulled up and her private parts and breasts were visible. There were patches of blood near her head as well as on the floor. There were bloodstains on her hands and vagina also. Her wearing apparel was bloodstained. There were some marks of violence and blood was found on her face as well. There were blood marks on the 'Jhoola' lying in the room. Her torn panty was found lying near the entrance of the door and the deceased appeared to be unconscious at that time. Her mother, PW 3, lifted the deceased in her arms and rushed down through the lift with a view to take her to the doctor. In the meantime, a doctor had been summoned by the neighbours who arrived and on examining the deceased in the lift itself, where she was lying in the lap of her mother, pronounced her dead. Information of the occurrence was sent to the father of the deceased and at about 7 p.m. Bhawesh PW 5, returned. In the meantime, another doctor, who had also been called, arrived and after examining the deceased certified her as dead. The dead body of Hetal was taken back to the flat and laid on her bed in her room and was covered by a sheet. At about 8.30 p.m. father of the deceased, Nagardas PW 4, returned to the flat and on being told of the murder of Hetal, he informed Bhawanipore Police Station at about 9.15 p.m. on the telephone. On receipt of the telephonic message, Sub-Inspector Gurupad Som PW 28, the acting duty officer, rushed to the place of occurrence along with some other police personnel and recorded the FIR on the statement of Yashmoti Parekh PW 3, the mother of the deceased and commenced investigation. During the search of the room where the deceased was allegedly raped and murdered, bloodstained earth, a broken chain, a cream colour button, the torn panty of the deceased and some other articles were seized and sealed into a parcel after preparing seizure memos. Statements of some witnesses were also recorded.

Search was made for the appellant by the police at different places during the night intervening 5th and 6th March, 1990 but in vain. The appellant did not even visit his employers to collect his wages for the past 5 days. He did not report at 'Paras Apartment' either. Though he was also doing night duty at another places, he did not report for duty there and did not collect his wages for four days service rendered with the other employer either. He was not traceable. Some raids were conducted in the village of the appellant at Kuludihi, within the jurisdiction of Chatna Police Station on different dates but ultimately it was only on May 12, 1990 that the appellant came to be arrested. Pursuant to a disclosure statement made by him under section 27 of the Evidence Act, a 'Richo' wrist-watch was recovered. Appellant also led to the recovery of his shirt and trousers wrapped in a newspaper from his house pursuant to a disclosure statement. At the trial the appellant pleaded innocence and alleged false implication "due to quarrel with PW 4 over his transfer". In his statement made at the trial under section 313 Cr PC, the appellant stated that after his duty hours as the security guard at Anand Apartment on the date of the occurrence he had gone to a cinema and then purchased some fruits in connection with the sacred thread ceremony of his younger brother and left for his native place with the fruits to participate in the said ceremony. He denied the recoveries allegedly made from him. He, however, led no defence evidence.

There was no eye-witness of this occurrence. The entire case rests on circumstantial evidence. Hetal Parekh, the unfortunate young school-going girl of about 18 years of age, had been subjected to rape before her death and that the death was homicidal in nature stood amply established by the testimony of Dr. Dipankar Guha PW 20, who conducted the post-mortem examination on the dead body. As many as 21 injuries were noticed by Dr. Dipankar Guha on the deceased. The medical witness found that the hymen of the deceased showed fresh tears at 4, 5 and 7 O' clock positions with evidence of fresh blood in the margins. He also found presence of bloodstains on the vagina and matted pubic hair of the deceased. Blood was also noticed at nostril and face of the deceased. The hair from the scalp were also found matted with blood. There was "fracture and dislocation of hyoid bone on its greater cornu of left side" (Injury No. 21). In the opinion of the doctor, the deceased had been subjected to rape before murder and that the death was due to the fact of smothering with strangulation and injuries were anti-mortem and homicidal. Injury No. 21, as noticed above, was found sufficient to cause the death of the victim in the ordinary course of nature. According to the report of the Senior Scientific Officer-cum-Assistant Chemical Examiner, Forensic Science Laboratory, Government of West Bengal, Ex. 36, semen was detected on the panty (undergarment) and the pubic hair of the deceased. The presence of bloodstains, marks of violence on the face of the deceased and the state of her clothes indicated that the victim had offered resistance but was helpless. Thus there remains no doubt that the deceased was subjected to rape before her murder. Medical evidence was clear and cogent and Mr. Ganguli, the learned Senior Advocate, appearing for the appellant, did not question the same either. The Supreme Court, in appeal, addressed itself to determine whether or not the appellant was the assailant who raped and murdered the defenceless young girl.

DECISION OF THE TRIAL COURT AND THE HIGH COURT

The High Court found that after the telephonic message was sent to the police station, the investigating officer after making an entry in the GD rushed to the scene of occurrence to record the statement of Yashmoti PW 3, that statement of PW 3 could not be treated as a First Information Report and that the "telephonic message as recorded in the GD" was the First Information Report and the statement of PW 3 was only a statement recorded during the investigation of the case and not the FIR. In the words of the High Court:

> "We are, therefore, of the opinion that the statement of PW 3 recorded by the Police after the investigation had already commenced could not be treated as the First Information Report."

As against this observation of the High Court, the Supreme Court said:—

> "We are unable to agree with the opinion of the High Court. The cryptic telephonic message received at the police station from Nagardas PW 4 had only made the police agency to rush to the place of occurrence and record the statement of Yashmoti PW 3 and thereafter commence the investigation as was admitted by the investigating officer in his testimony which testimony was not challenged during the cross-examination of the investigating officer. The High Court failed to notice that the vague and indefinite information given on the telephone which made the investigating agency only to rush to the scene of occurrence could not be treated as a First Information Report under section 154 of the Cr PC. The unchallenged statement of the investigating officer that he commenced the investigation only after recording the statement of PW 3 Yashmoti unmistakably shows that it was that statement which alone could be treated as the first information report. The High Court fell in error in observing that the statement of PW 3 Yashmoti was recorded "after the investigation had already commenced". There is no material on the record for the above opinion of the High Court. The cryptic telephonic message given to the police by Nagardas PW 4 was only with the object of informing the police so that it could reach the spot. The investigation in the case only started after the statement of PW 3 Yashmoti was recorded. Though initially Mr. Ganguli did try to support the finding of the High Court but in the face of the evidence on the record and more particularly in the absence of any challenge to the testimony of the investigating officer, in fairness to Mr. Ganguli, we must record that he rightly did not pursue that argument any further. We, therefore, find ourselves unable to agree with the opinion of the High Court and hold that the statement of Yashmoti PW 3, recorded by the investigating officer PW 28, was rightly treated as FIR in this case by the prosecution and the Trial Court."

The following circumstances were relied upon by the prosecution which was accepted as conclusively established both by the Trial Court and the High Court to connect the appellant with the crime:

(1) **Motive:** In a case based on circumstantial evidence, the existence of motive assumes significance though the absence of motive does not necessarily discredit the prosecution case, if the case stands otherwise

established by other conclusive circumstances and the chain of circumstantial evidence is so complete and is consistent only with the hypothesis of the guilt of the accused and inconsistent with the hypothesis of his innocence. In this case, there is ample evidence on the record to show that the appellant had a motive to commit the alleged crime.

The deceased was being teased by the appellant when she used to go to or came back from the school. She brought it to the notice of her mother PW 3 on a number of occasions, the latest in the series being on March 2, 1990. Yashmoti PW 3 informed her husband Nagardas PW 4 about the complaints. From the testimony of Nagardas PW 4, it transpires that after he came to know about the misbehaviour of the appellant from his wife PW 3 on March 2, 1990, he called some other dwellers of the apartment to appraise them of the same. Mahendra Chauhatia PW 13 and Harish Vakharia PW 14 have deposed that they had been called by Nagardas PW 4 who reported to them that the appellant had been teasing his daughter and that PW 4 had suggested that the appellant should be replaced by another security guard. They (PW 13 and PW 14) both agreed. The testimony of PW 13 and PW 14 has remained totally unchallenged in cross-examination. After consulting PW 13 and PW 14, Nagardas PW 4 asked Shyam Karmakar PW 21, the employer of the appellant, to meet him and according to the statement of PW 21 Karmakar he came to the flat of Nagardas PW 4 on March 3, 1990, where he was informed about the teasing of the daughter of PW 4 by the appellant. PW 21 deposed that Nagardas PW 4 told him to replace the appellant by another security guard and even handed over a written complaint Ex. 4 to him. The defence has not challenged this part of the testimony of PW 21 during his cross-examination at all. PW 21 after receiving the complaint Ex. 4 against the appellant from PW 4, made an order of transfer of the appellant from 'Anand Apartment' to 'Paras Apartment' and deputed Bijoy Thapa another security guard in place of the appellant with effect from March 5, 1990. The order of transfer was handed over to Riazul Haq PW 9, who delivered it to the appellant. The copy of the transfer order Ex. 23 was handed over by Riazul Haq PW 9 to the appellant on March 4, 1990 while the appellant was on duty at the 'Anand Apartment'. This part of the testimony of PW 9 has not been assailed during his cross-examination. From the prosecution evidence, the teasing of the deceased by the appellant, his invitation to her to accompany him to watch a movie on March 2, 1990 and the order of his transfer from 'Anand Apartment' made by PW 21 on the complaint of the deceased, through her father PW 4, stand amply established on the record. It is pertinent to note that there has been no challenge worth the name to this part of the case of the prosecution during the cross-examination of various witnesses produced by the prosecution in its support. Mr. Ganguli, however, submitted that the delay in the seizure of complaint Ex. 4 and the transfer order, on June

29, 1990 were indicative of the fact that both the documents had come into existence subsequently as an afterthought. We do not find any force in this submission. PW 4 who gave a written complaint to PW 21 and PW 9 who delivered the transfer order issued by PW 21 to the appellant were not challenged in the cross-examination about the same. Even the investigating officer was not asked for an explanation as to why the documents had been seized so late. In any event the seizure of the documents on June 29, 1990 after the appellant had been arrested only a couple of weeks earlier, would not go to show that the documents were either fabricated or were an afterthought. In this connection, it is also relevant to notice that a positive suggestion was made by the defence to PW 4 during his cross-examination that the appellant had quarrelled with him "over his transfer from Anand Apartment" and on account of that quarrel the appellant had been "falsely implicated". Of course, PW 4 denied the suggestion but defence suggestion does not militate against the prosecution case regarding the annoyance of the appellant on that score. Corroboration is available from the statement of Pratap Chandra Pali PW 6, the supervisor of Security and Investigating Bureau, who had visited 'Anand Apartment' at about 5.45 p.m. on March 5, 1990 and inquired from the guard on duty as to how the appellant had reported for duty at Anand Apartment when he stood transferred to Paras Apartment. Moreover, when PW 6 demanded an explanation from the appellant on March 5, 1990 as to why he had not reported for duty at Paras Apartment, the appellant is alleged to have told him that it was on account of "certain personal inconvenience" that he could not so join on that date. PW 6 was not challenged with regard to his testimony as regards the transfer of the appellant. The Court found no substance in the submission of Mr. Ganguli that in a private organisation, written transfer orders are not given and that the written transfer order in this case is a created piece of evidence. There is no hard and fast rule regarding giving of oral or written transfer orders in private organisations and in any event neither PW 21 nor PW 9 nor PW 6 were questioned on this aspect. Once service of the transfer order by PW 9 is not assailed during the cross-examination of the witness, the above argument of Mr. Ganguli hardly deserves any serious consideration. The evidence on the record has, thus, clearly and cogently established the improper attitude of the appellant towards the young girl, Hetal, and appellant teasing her often and seeking her company to go to a movie. The appellant, therefore, had certainly improper designs so far as the deceased is concerned. His transfer from 'Anand Apartment' on the allegation that he had teased the deceased, therefore, provided sufficient motive for him not only to satisfy his lust and teach a lesson to the deceased girl for spurning his offer but also as a measure of retaliation for being reported to his employer and being transferred from Anand Apartment to Paras Apartment on the basis of the said complaint. The transfer of the appellant on grounds of his improper behaviour with the deceased was an aspersion on his character and that appears to have provided him the immediate motive for committing the crime in retaliation and even may be to remove the evidence of committing rape on the deceased. The Court therefore was of the opinion that the prosecution has successfully established the existence of motive on the part of the appellant to commit the crime.

JUDGMENT OF THE SUPREME COURT

The Court observed that in recent years, the rising crime rate – particularly violent crime against women has made the criminal sentencing by the Courts a subject of concern. Today there are admitted disparities. Some criminals get very harsh sentences while many receive grossly different sentence for an essentially equivalent crime and a shockingly large number even go unpunished thereby encouraging the criminal and in the ultimate making justice suffer by weakening the system's credibility. Of course, it is not possible to lay down any cut and dry formula relating to imposition of sentence but the object of sentencing should be to see that the crime does not go unpunished and the victim of crime as also the society has the satisfaction that justice has been done to it. In imposing sentences in the absence of specific legislation, Judge must consider variety of factors and after considering all those factors and taking an overall view of situation, impose sentence which they consider to be an appropriate one. Aggravating factors cannot be ignored and similarly mitigating circumstances have also to be taken into consideration.

The Court opined that the measure of punishment in a given case must depend upon the atrocity of the crime; the conduct of the criminal and the defenceless and unprotected state of the victim. Imposition of appropriate punishment is the manner in which the Courts respond to the society's cry for justice against the criminals. Justice demands that Courts should impose punishment befitting the crime so that the Courts reflect public abhorrence of the crime. The Courts must not only keep in view the rights of the criminal but also the rights of the victim of crime and the society at large while considering imposition of appropriate punishment.

The sordid episode of the security guard, whose sacred duty was to ensure the protection and welfare of the inhabitants of the flats in the apartment, should not have subjected the deceased, a resident of one of the flats, to gratify his lust and murdered her in retaliation for his transfer on her complaint, makes the crime even more heinous. Keeping in view the medical evidence and the state in which the body of the deceased was found, it is obvious that a most heinous type of barbaric rape and murder was committed on a helpless and defenceless school-going girl of 18 years. If the security guards behave in this manner who will guard the security? The faith of the society by such a barbaric act of the guard, get totally shaken and its cry for justice becomes loud and clear. The offence was not only inhuman and barbaric but it was a totally ruthless crime of rape followed by cold blooded murder and an affront to the human dignity of the society. The savage nature of the crime has shocked the Court's judicial conscience. There were no extenuating or mitigating circumstances whatsoever in the case. The Court agreed that a real and abiding concern for the dignity of human life is required to be kept in mind by the Courts while considering the confirmation of the sentence of death but a cold blooded preplanned brutal murder, without any provocation, after committing rape on an innocent and defenceless young girl of 18 years, by the security guard certainly made this case a "rarest of the rare" cases which calls for no punishment other than the capital punishment and the Court accordingly confirmed the sentence of death imposed upon the appellant for the offence under section 302 IPC. The order of sentence imposed on the appellant by the Courts below for offences under sections 376 and 380 of IPC were also confirmed along with the directions relating thereto as in the event of the execution of the appellant, those sentence would only remain of academic interest. The appeal was thus dismissed.

RAPE AND MURDER

Jaharlal Das

v.

State of Orissa,

AIR 1991 SC 1388

JUDGE(S): K. JAYACHANDRA REDDY AND S. RATNAVEL PANDIAN

Criminal Appeal No. 276 of 1991 (arising out of Special Leave Petn. (Crl.) No. 1370 of 1990), dated 12-4-1991.

ADVOCATES

Appellant – Mr. H.K. Puri (*Amicus Curiae*)

Respondent – Mr. A.D. Giri, Solicitor General and Mr. A.K. Panda

FACTS

The deceased Disco *alias* Sukumari, a girl aged 5 years was the daughter of PWs. 1 and 6, the father and the mother who were drummers by caste. They belonged to village Badachatra, an interior part of Mayurbhanj District. They had three children and the deceased was the eldest. In the year 1988 during Kalipuja time the accused who was the resident of Tulsibani village about one kilometre away, came to the house of PWs. 1 and 6. He named their newly born daughter. He took his meals in their house and went away saying that he would come with the new dresses for the newly born daughter. Next day *i.e.* on November 9, 1988 he came to their house in the morning with new dresses. He told the parents that he would take the deceased with him to Bombay Chhak to get new dresses for the other two children. He took his lunch and went with the deceased towards Bombay Chhak. Some time after his departure PW 6 told her husband PW 1 to proceed to Bombay Chhak as the deceased might be crying. Accordingly PW 1 accompanied by one Sambhu proceeded towards that Chhak. On way they met one Babuli and asked him whether he had seen the accused and the deceased to which he replied in the negative. PW 1 came back to the village and sat in the shop of PW 2 who informed that he had seen the accused going towards village Tulsibani along with the deceased. PW 1 and Sambhu then went to that village but could not find them there. Thereafter they went to Jharpokharia police station and gave a report to the officer-in-charge PW 11, stating that the deceased and the accused have not returned. He made an entry in the station diary. From there PW 1 again went to the Tulsibani village where a person informed him that he has seen the accused going towards his house. PW 1 went there and enquired of the accused. He told PW 1 that the deceased had gone back home but PW 1 caught hold of him but the accused squirmed away from his grip. PW 1, however, again caught him and took him to his village and according to PW 1 on being questioned the accused confessed to have raped and committed murder of the deceased. The accused was alleged to have pointed the place where he had thrown the dead body, whereafter PW 1 and others proceeded in that direction. PW 11 the police officer also came in a jeep and took the accused into custody, drew up an FIR and sent the same to the police station for registration of a case. The accused was alleged to have led the police party to the spot where the dead body was lying. PW 11 found the deceased lying with injuries on her vagina and other parts. He held the inquest in the presence of PW 4 and others and sent the dead body for post-mortem. PW 7 conducted the post-mortem. He noticed abrasions all over the body. He also found one bruise on the left side of the forehead and a lacerated wound of 2.5 cm x 1 cm x muscle deep starting from the posterior angle of vagina along the perineum up to the anus. On internal examination he found the following injuries:

"(1) Soft tissues and muscles below the external injuries to the neck were contused with extra-vassation of blood into the soft tissues.

(2) Haematoma under the scalp corresponding to external injury No. 11.

(3) The hymen was torn and the floor of the vagina *i.e.*, vaginal channel was lacerated. This injury corresponds to external injury No. 15."

DECISION OF THE TRIAL COURT AND THE HIGH COURT

The trial Court did not accept PW 1's evidence regarding the extra-judicial confession alleged to have been made by the accused. It held that nobody else has mentioned about this extra-judicial confession and at any rate it was supposed to have been made in the presence of the police. After examining the evidence of PW 1 as well as the evidence of the other witnesses the trial Court rejected this part of the prosecution case regarding the alleged extra-judicial confession. As a matter of fact it was not found anywhere mentioned that such a confession was made by the accused to PW 1 neither in the FIR nor in the evidence of other witnesses who were also said to have been present when the accused was brought to the village by PW 1. PW 6, who was no other than the wife of PW 1, did not even mention about it.

The trial Court relied on the following circumstances:

"(a) 'Last seen' theory – that the accused and the deceased were last seen together;

(b) Conduct of the accused – that the accused attempted to flee away when he could be seen at his village by PW 1;

(c) False explanation – the accused when questioned gave false explanation regarding the whereabouts of the deceased;

(d) Recovery of the dead body of the deceased on the showing of the accused – That the accused pointed out the place where the dead body of the deceased was lying inside a paddy field;

(e) Presence of injury on the genital as well as stains of blood on the wearing apparel and nail clippings of the accused."

Relying on the above circumstances the trial Court convicted the accused under sections 302 and 376 IPC and sentenced him to death subject to confirmation by the High Court and for seven years rigorous imprisonment for the offence of rape. The sentences were directed to run concurrently. The High Court confirmed the conviction and sentence awarded by the trial Court.

JUDGMENT OF THE SUPREME COURT

The Supreme Court held that it was conscious that a grave and heinous crime has been committed but when there was no satisfactory proof of the guilt, it had no other option but to give the benefit of doubt to the accused and was constrained to do so in this case. Accordingly, the appeal was allowed. The conviction and sentence of the accused was set aside. The Court ordered that he should be set at liberty forthwith if not required in any other case.

Kamta Tiwari
v.
State of Madhya Pradesh,
AIR 1996 SC 2800

JUDGE(S): M K MUKHERJEE AND S P KURDUKAR

Criminal Appeal No. 267 of 1996, dated 4-9-1996.

FACTS

Briefly stated the case of the prosecution was as follows:

(a) Parmeshwar Lal Sharma (PW 1) along with his wife and three children used to reside at Bhutari Tolla in the township of Budhar. Of the three children, Pinky (the deceased) was the youngest and her age at the time of her death was about seven years. The appellant who was also a resident of the same locality used to occasionally visit the family of Parmeshwar and his children used to address him as 'Tiwari Uncle'.

(b) On April 30, 1995 at or about 6 p.m. Parmeshwar had gone to a hair-cutting saloon in the local market along with his son Santosh (PW 4) and daughter Pinky. After Santosh and Pinky had their hair cut they went out of the saloon to play outside while Parmeshwar stayed back for his turn. After sometime Pinky went to the television repairing shop of the appellant which was by the side of the saloon. The appellant was then playing ludo with Suresh Gupta (PW 8) in his shop. Pinky requested the appellant to give her some toffees and biscuits whereupon he took her to the nearby grocery shop of Budhsen Gupta (PW 3), purchased a packet of biscuits and gave it to her. Thereafter both of them left the shop of Budhsen.

(c) After his hair-cut when Parmeshwar came out of the saloon and enquired of his daughter, Santosh told him that Pinky had gone to the shop of the appellant and that he had given biscuits to her. On getting that information Parmeshwar along with Santosh went to the shop of the appellant but found it closed. They then went back to their house only to find that Pinky had not returned. Parmeshwar then went to the house of the appellant but he was not available there. Accompanied by his wife and other two children Parmeshwar then went in search of Pinky and in the course of the search they met Hari Krishna Soni (PW 10) and Subhash Chander Soni (PW 2) at or about 10.30 p.m. on a crossroad near the shop of the appellant. As advised by them he sent back his wife and children home and again went to the house of the appellant accompanied by them. While they were waiting there they saw the appellant coming towards his house completely drenched. He was then wearing only an underwear with some clothes pressed under his armpit. When they enquired about Pinky he told them that after he had given the packet of biscuits to her she left. All three of them then went to Budhar Police Station at or about 1 a.m. and reported that Pinky was missing.

(d) After recording the report in the station diary book (Ext. P-15/C) H.C. Munna Prasad went in search of Pinky but could not trace her out. However, on the basis of the enquiry conducted by him Station House Officer Shri V.D. Tripathi (PW 11) registered a case under sections 363, 364 and 366 IPC (Ext. P-16) and took up investigation. On the following day, *i.e.*, 2-5-1995 in the afternoon the appellant was arrested by Shri Tripathi and then interrogated in the presence of Hari Krishna and Din Dayal. On such interrogation the appellant disclosed that he had thrown the dead body of Pinky in a well and concealed her frock near a mahua tree. Shri Tripathi recorded the disclosure statement of the appellant (Ext. P-8) and then, led by the appellant and accompanied by the above two witnesses went to the well of one Ramjiyawan Lodhi and found the dead body of Pinky floating in the water. After Shri Tripathi took the photograph of the floating dead body (Ext. P-3) it was brought out of the well. He then prepared a recovery memo of the dead body (Ext. P-9) which was signed by the appellant as also the witnesses present there. Shri Tripathi held inquest thereupon, prepared a report in respect thereof (Ext. P-14), and then sent it for post-mortem examination. Pursuant to the statement made by the appellant, Shri Tripathi recovered a bloodstained frock (Article A) and seized it under a seizure memo (Ext. P-10).

(e) On the same day Dr. K.K. Gautam (PW 13) held autopsy on the dead body of Pinky and found a lacerated wound on the right side of the mouth, abrasions on both arms, contusion on the left knee, laceration on the labia majora with clotted blood, laceration on the posterior vaginal wall, hymen ruptured, labia majora and labia minora swollen and blood around the orifice of the vagina. Dr. Gautam also found three contusions on the left side of the neck below the level of the thyroid with abrasions all around, brain and its membrane congested, hyoid bone and thyroid cartilage fractured with hemorrhage on the tissue around the fractures, the fourth rib on both the sides fractured and uterus deeply congested and swollen. He opined that the deceased was raped and that the cause of her death was asphyxia owing to throttling. According to him all the injuries were ante-mortem in nature. Dr. Gautam prepared a slide from the vaginal discharge of the deceased and arranged to send it for chemical analysis by the Forensic Science Laboratory (FSL) through the investigating officer.

(f) On the following day (May 3, 1995) the appellant was sent to the Primary Health Center for his medical examination. Dr. B.N. Sharma (PW 7), who examined him found one abrasion on his right knee and another on the glans penis out there was no smegma. In his opinion the appellant was competent to commit sexual intercourse and that the injury found on the glans penis could have been caused while committing rape on the girl of tender age. According to him the injury found on the knee of the appellant could have been caused while committing sexual intercourse with the victim lying on the bare floor of a room. Dr. Sharma prepared a slide of semen of the appellant and along with his underwear sent the same for chemical analysis through Constable Kamla Prasad. The frock which was recovered in pursuance of the statement of the appellant and was identified by Parmeshwar as that of Pinky was also sent for such examination. On receipt of the reports of the FSL and completion of investigation Shri Tripathi submitted a charge-sheet against the appellant.

DECISION OF THE TRIAL COURT AND THE HIGH COURT

The trial Court convicted the accused, Kamta Tiwari under sections 363, 376, 302 and 201, IPC. For his conviction under section 302, IPC, he was sentenced to death and for the other convictions to different terms of rigorous imprisonment.

He preferred an appeal to the High Court, which was dismissed.

Thereafter he preferred an appeal to the Supreme Court by special leave.

JUDGMENT OF THE SUPREME COURT

The Supreme Court held that the concurrent findings entered by the learned Courts below were unexceptionable. The Court observed that although the entire case was based on circumstantial evidence but the tell-tale circumstances, all of which stood firmly established were not compatible with any other reasonable hypothesis except that the appellant kidnapped Pinky, committed rape on her, then strangulated her to death and to cause disappearance of evidence of the murder threw her dead body in a well. The conviction of the appellant for the offences under sections 363, 376, 302 and 201 IPC must, therefore, be upheld.

The Court then considered the question whether the sentence of death imposed upon the appellant by the trial Court for his conviction under section 302 IPC and confirmed by the High Court should be maintained or not and said that in *Bachan Singh* v. *State of Punjab,* [(1980) 2 SCC 684: 1980 SCC (Cri) 580: AIR 1980 SC 898] the Supreme Court indicated, while discussing the sentencing policy, the guidelines to be followed for imposing the extreme penalty of death. From the guidelines so indicated, this Court in its later judgment in *Machhi Singh* v. *State of Punjab,* [(1983) 3 SCC 470: 1983 SCC (Cri) 681: AIR 1983 SC 957] formulated the following propositions, which are to be applied when the question of awarding death sentence arises:

"(i) The extreme penalty of death need not be inflicted except in gravest cases of extreme culpability.

(ii) Before opting for the death penalty the circumstances of the 'offender' also require to be taken into consideration along with the circumstances of the 'crimes'.

(iii) Life imprisonment is the rule and death sentence is an exception. In other words death sentence must be imposed only when life imprisonment appears to be an altogether inadequate punishment having regard to the relevant circumstances of the crime, and provided, and only provided, the option to impose sentence of imprisonment for life cannot be conscientiously exercised having regard to the nature and circumstances of the crime and all the relevant circumstances.

(iv) A balance-sheet of aggravating and mitigating circumstances has to be drawn up and in doing so the mitigating circumstances have to be accorded full weightage and a just balance has to be struck between the aggravating and the mitigating circumstances before the option is exercised."

Taking an overall view of all the facts and circumstances of the instant case in the light of the above propositions the Court was of the opinion that the sentence of death should be maintained. The Court said that it searched for mitigating circumstances in vain, but found aggravating circumstances aplenty. The evidence on record clearly established that the appellant was close to the family of Parmeshwar and the deceased and her siblings used to call him 'Tiwari Uncle'. Obviously her closeness with the appellant encouraged her to go to his shop, which was near the saloon where she had gone for a haircut with her father and brother, and asked for some biscuits. The appellant readily responded to the request by taking her to the nearby grocery shop of Budhsen and handing over a packet of biscuits apparently as a prelude to his sinister design which unfolded in her kidnapping, brutal rape and gruesome murder – as the numerous injuries on her person testify; and the finale was the dumping of her dead body in a well. The Court held that when an innocent helpless girl of 7 years was subjected to such barbaric treatment by a person who was in a position of her trust, his culpability assumes the proportion of extreme depravity and arouses a sense of revulsion in the mind of the common man. The Court, in view of the motivation of the perpetrator, the vulnerability of the victim, the enormity of the crime, the execution thereof opined that this was a "rarest of rare" case where the sentence of death was eminently desirable not only to deter others from committing such atrocious crimes but also to give emphatic expression to society's abhorrence of such crimes.

The appeal was therefore dismissed by the Court.

Raju
v.
State of Haryana,
AIR 2001 SC 2043

JUDGE(S): BRIJESH KUMAR AND M.B. SHAH

Criminal Appeal No. 581 of 2000, dated 2-5-2001.

FACTS

It was the prosecution case that Rinku aged about 11 years was missing from the evening of January 5, 1997. Her body was found on the next day at about 6.30 a.m. The prosecution story as revealed by PW 1 Ram Kewal was that he lodged the FIR at 7.30 a.m. on finding the dead body of Rinku near the bushes at Medical College ground. It was his say that on January 5, 1997, she had gone out of the house at about 6.00 p.m. to bring milk. After she brought milk, he saw Raju (accused) offering toffees to Rinku and other children. PW 2 Makhan Lal, a neighbour had also seen Rinku and Raju going towards Chandan Nagar. As Rinku had not returned till 9.00 p.m., they looked for her as well as Raju throughout the night. In the morning they found the dead body of Rinku. Blood stained brick and blood was also found lying on the spot. Immediately, after asking PW 2 to wait at the scene of offence, PW 1 Ram Kewal reached at the Gurgaon Police Station and lodged the FIR at about 7.30 a.m. Further, the prosecution version was that on January 6, 1997 accused contacted PW 3 Subhash Sharma and made confessional statement to him that he committed rape and murder of Rinku near the boundary wall of college building. He stated that he caused injury to the deceased by the brick on her head and mouth as the deceased stated that she would report at the house with regard to the rape committed by him. Accused sought his help to save him. It was the say of the witness that when he was taking the accused towards the police station, the uncle of the girl and the police met him and he handed over the accused to the police.

DECISION OF THE TRIAL COURT AND THE HIGH COURT

The Sessions Judge convicted the appellant for the offence punishable under sections 302, 363 and 376, IPC and sentenced him to death under section 302 to 7 years rigorous imprisonment under section 376 and to 3 years rigorous imprisonment under section 363, IPC.

The High Court of Punjab and Haryana in appeal and in the death reference confirmed the conviction and sentence.

He then preferred an appeal to the Supreme Court challenging the decision of the High Court.

ADVOCATES PLEA IN THE SUPREME COURT

Mr. Tara Chand Sharma, learned counsel for the appellant submitted that the High Court committed error in convicting the appellant as there was no evidence on record to connect the accused with the crime. The circumstantial evidence upon which reliance was placed by the High Court was not sufficient so as to convict the appellant for the offence for which he was charged and in any case, it was not a case for imposing the punishment of death. It was his contention that if Ram Kewal PW 1 and Makhan Lal PW 2 were knowing that the deceased child had accompanied the accused by evening time, and she did not return till midnight, they would have immediately lodged the FIR for kidnapping. As they did not do, it would mean that they were not knowing that the deceased had gone in the company of the accused who was the tenant of PW 1 for few months and thereafter residing in neighbourhood.

As against this, learned counsel for the State submitted that the crime committed by the accused was heinous. There was sufficient circumstantial evidence on record to connect the accused with the crime and the Courts below have rightly convicted the accused and imposed the death sentence.

JUDGMENT OF THE SUPREME COURT

The Supreme Court held that the High Court after appreciating the entire evidence had rightly confirmed the conviction order passed by the Sessions Court. Regarding the question that whether this was a rarest of rare cases where extreme punishment of death was required to be imposed, the Court held that in the present case, from the confessional statement made by the accused, it would appear that there was no intention on the part of the accused to commit the murder of the deceased child. He caused injury to the deceased by giving two brick blows as she stated that she would disclose the incident at her house. The learned Sessions Judge committed error in recording the evidence of S.I. Shakuntala, PW 15 with regard to the confessional statement made to her, but in any set of circumstances, evidence, on record discloses that accused was not having intention to commit the murder of the girl who accompanied him. On the spur of the moment without there being any premeditation, he gave two brick blows which caused her death. The Court further observed that there was nothing on record to indicate that the appellant was having any criminal record nor he can be said to be a grave danger to the society at large. Basing on these circumstances, the Court said that it would be difficult to hold that the case of the appellant would be rarest of rare case justifying imposition of death penalty.

Thus the Court upheld the conviction of the appellant under section 302, but commuted the sentence of death to imprisonment of life. Subject to the aforesaid modification of sentence, the appeal was dismissed.

Amit alias Ammu
v.
State of Maharashtra,
AIR 2003 SC 3131

JUDGES: Y.K. SABHARWAL AND BRIJESH KUMAR

Criminal Appeal No. 376 of 2003, dated 6-8-2003.

ADVOCATES

Appellant – M.R. Daga, C.R. Thakur and R.S. Lambat.

Respondent – Ravindra Keshavrao Adsure.

FACTS

The dead body of deceased, a young child aged about 11-12 years and student of VI standard, was first sighted by PW-1 on 29th March, 2001 at about 3.45 p.m. Immediately, he reported the matter to the concerned police station. His oral report was recorded into writing, *i.e.* FIR Ex. No. 28.

On Ex. 28, it has been recorded that on March 29, 2001, PW-1 accompanied by Ajay PW-11, had gone to the rear portion of a place known as Gaimukh for grazing she-buffaloes. One of the buffaloes went in a dilapidated building close-by. In order to drive out that animal on going inside, he noticed the dead body of a school girl in school uniform lying in supine condition. He informed the police. The two police officials came to the site along with him. The said unidentified girl was seen by him the previous day as well in the forest in the area where he usually goes for grazing of the animals. At that time she was in the company of a boy aged about 20 years. She was carrying school bag. At that time too, PW-11 was with PW-1. The description of the boy has also been given. The said boy was having with him bicycle like that of Ranger type. The boy on being asked gave his name as 'Gandhi' and stated that the name of the accompanying girl is Vidya who was his sister and as her family members were going to Devi Temple, he had brought her directly from her school. Both were brought up to the road and went away by sitting on the bicycle. The girl seen by PW-1 and PW-11 was the same whose body had been found. The investigation led to the arrest of the appellant at 11.00 p.m. on March 29, 2001. The father of the deceased and the appellant work in same office. Deceased and the appellant knew each other.

DECISION OF THE TRIAL COURT AND THE HIGH COURT

The appellant was charged and found guilty of offence under section 302, IPC for the murder of the deceased as also for her rape under section 376, IPC. The Sessions Court, for offence under section 302 awarded death penalty and for offence under section 376, rigorous imprisonment for 10 years. Compensation of Rs. 25,000 in terms of the judgment of the Sessions Court was awarded under section 357, Cr PC for being paid to the parents of the victim for mental torture, agony and the loss sustained of their only female child.

The High Court by impugned judgment confirmed the award of death penalty to the appellant as also other sentences and compensation awarded. The appellant, aggrieved therefrom, approached the Supreme Court on grant of leave.

ADVOCATE'S PLEA IN THE SUPREME COURT

The main submission of learned counsel for the appellant was that unless time of death is established it is not permissible to rely upon circumstance of last seen so as to convict the appellant. The main circumstance against the appellant was of last seen with the deceased as deposed by PW-1 and PW-11.

JUDGMENT OF THE SUPREME COURT

The Supreme Court after examining the testimony of PW-1 and PW-11 found that their evidence was trustworthy and reliable. It had ring of truth. The Court said that it stands fully established that they had seen the deceased and the appellant on 28th March. Apparently, both left as deposed by PW-1 but as the circumstances showed that, in fact, they did not leave. When the next day PW-1 again came to the same area for grazing of buffaloes, he found the body of the deceased whereupon the matter was reported to the police and FIR recorded and investigation conducted. It also came in evidence that usually PW-1 used to go to the same area for grazing of the animals which was a secluded area and also had a dilapidated building. It was apparent from the site plan as well. The appellant knew the deceased. His father and that of deceased were colleagues. The appellant at about 11.30 a.m. had gone to the house of the deceased on March 28, 2001 and had enquired about the deceased as deposed to by PW-6, the elder brother of the deceased. PW-6 told the appellant that the deceased had not come back from the school. In his statement under section 313, Cr PC the appellant admitted to have so gone to the house of the deceased. The father of the deceased PW-5 used to drop her daughter at the school and as usual on March 28, 2001 at about 7.30 a.m. he dropped her at the school. She used to return home from school around 12.00 noon. Since on that date, she did not return, mother of the deceased informed her husband on telephone. He rushed back home from the office and they searched for their daughter and ultimately not finding her, a missing report was lodged by PW-5. Regarding the contention that the time of the accident had not been established and, therefore, the circumstance of last seen was not sufficient to convict the appellant, the High Court on examination of the evidence reached the following conclusion:—

> "In the instant case, the region being temperate, *rigor mortis* lasts for about two to three days. If we apply this analogy, then at the time of post-mortem examination, which was conducted on March 3, 2001 and begun at 11.40 a.m., the doctor did not find *rigor mortis*. That means the time of death must have been on March 28, 2001 between 3.00 p.m. and 4.00 p.m., since the *rigor mortis* in a temperate region lasts for two days. This is not the case, therefore, where time of death cannot be ascertained on the basis of these recognised guidelines, merely because the same is not given in the post-mortem report. In our considered view, this is not the circumstance which affects the material particulars of the prosecution case in the crime in question."

The Court said that it was in complete agreement with the conclusion of the High Court on the aspect of the time of death.

Learned counsel for the appellant has placed reliance on the decision of the Supreme Court by a Bench (of which Justice Brijesh Kumar was a member) in *Mohibur Rahman* v. *State of Assam*, [(2002) 6 SCC 715: 2002 AIR SCW 3523: AIR 2002 SC 3064] for the proposition that the circumstance of last seen does not by itself necessarily lead to the inference that it was the accused who committed the crime. But the Court said that it depends upon the facts of each case. In the decision relied upon it was observed that there may be cases where, on account of close proximity of place and time between the event of the accused having been last seen with the deceased and the *factum* of death, a rational mind may be persuaded to reach an irresistible conclusion that either the accused should explain how and in what circumstances the victim suffered the death or should own the liability for the homicide. The Court was of the view that in this case the observation as aforesaid and principle laid squarely applies and the circumstances of the case cast a heavy responsibility on the appellant to explain and in absence thereof suffer the conviction. Those circumstances have already been noticed. In which case such an irresistible conclusion can be reached will depend on the facts of each case. Here it has been established that the death took place on 28th March between 3 and 4 p.m. It was just about that much time that the appellant and deceased were last seen by PW-1 and PW-11. No explanation has been offered in statement by the appellant recorded under section 313, Cr PC. His defence was of complete denial. The Court thus held that the conviction for offence under sections 302 and 376 was rightly recorded by Court of Session and affirmed by the High Court.

Regarding the question of sentence, the Court was of the view that the appellant was a young man and at the time of the incident his age was about 20 years; he was a student; there was no record of any previous heinous crime and also there was no evidence that he will be a danger to the society, if the death penalty was not awarded. Though the offence committed by the appellant deserves severe condemnation and was a most heinous crime, but on cumulative facts and circumstances of the case, the Court was of the opinion that the case did not fall in the category of rarest of the rare case and the appellant will learn a lesson and have opportunity to ponder over what he did during the period he undergoes the life sentence. Thus the Court modified the impugned judgment and instead of death penalty, awarded life imprisonment to the appellant for offence under section 302, IPC. In all other respects, the impugned judgment was maintained. The appeal was allowed to this limited extent.

State of Uttar Pradesh
v.
Satish,
(2005) 3 SCC 114

JUDGE(S): ARIJIT PASAYAT AND S.H. KAPADIA

Criminal Appeal Nos. 256-257 of 2005, decided on February 8, 2005.

ADVOCATES

Pramod Swarup, Prashant Chaudhary, Praveen Swarup, Vijay Hansaria, Sunita Bhardwaj, Draupad Kashyap Das, Satyendra Kumar, Ranbir Singh Yadav, H.M. Singh.

FACTS

On August 16, 2001 the victim who was studying in Sarvodya Public School had gone to school and did not return at the usual time. On the next day morning her dead body was found in the sugarcane field of one Moolchand around 6.00 a.m. She was lying in a dead condition and blood was oozing from her private parts and there were marks of pressing on her neck. Report was lodged at the nearby Police Station and the dead body was sent for post-mortem examination. Dr. R.K. Gupta (PW-7) conducted the post-mortem around 2.00 p.m. on August 17, 2001 and opined that death was within the preceding 24 hours.

Three persons claimed to have seen the accused nearby the place of occurrence between 1.00 p.m. and 2.00 p.m. on the date of occurrence. Two of them, namely, Sanjeev Kumar Tyagi (PW-3) and Kulbhushan (PW-5) claimed to have seen the deceased being carried on a bicycle by the accused who was taking the bicycle with the deceased sitting on the handle thereof. Anil (PW-2) stated that he had seen the accused in perplexed state around 2.00 p.m. near the place from where the dead body of deceased was found. Investigation was undertaken. During such investigation, there was recovery of accused's underwear and also the undergarment which the deceased was wearing. This recovery was treated to be under section 27 of the Indian Evidence Act, 1872.

DECISION OF THE TRIAL COURT AND THE HIGH COURT

The Trial Court found that the circumstances highlighted by the prosecution were sufficient to fasten guilt on the accused. It, therefore, convicted him under sections 363, 366, 376(2), 302 and 201 of the Indian Penal Code, 1860 (in short the 'IPC'). The crime was held to be one falling under rarest of rare category. Death sentence was imposed for the offence under section 302 IPC. Various custodial sentences and fines were also imposed for other offences. Since a death sentence was awarded, the matter was referred to the High Court for confirmation in terms of section 366 of the Code of Criminal Procedure, 1973 (in short "the Code"). The accused preferred an appeal before the High Court. Both the capital sentence reference and the criminal appeal were heard together. By the impugned judgment the High Court set aside the judgment of conviction. It was held that the case rested on circumstantial evidence and the circumstances highlighted by the prosecution did not inspire confidence. Three circumstances were highlighted by the High Court to arrive at the aforesaid conclusions. Firstly, it was held that examination of PWs. 3 and 5 after long passage of time rendered their version unacceptable and improbable. The prosecution did not offer any explanation for such delayed examination. Secondly, in the FIR name of the accused was not indicated. Thirdly, presence of the accused nearby the place from where the dead body was recovered, as deposed by PW-2, may be a suspicious circumstance but was not determinative. Accordingly, it was held that the prosecution had failed to prove its accusations.

ADVOCATE'S PLEA IN THE SUPREME COURT

In support of the appeals, learned counsel for the State submitted that the approach of the High Court was clearly erroneous both on legal and factual aspects. No question was put to the Investigating Officer (PW-8) regarding alleged delayed examination. Further the evidence of PWs. 2, 3 and 5 clearly established the circumstances which unerringly point the accusing finger at the accused. Additionally, explanation was given for non-inclusion of the name of the accused in the FIR by PW-1 and without indicating any reason the High Court had treated the same to be unacceptable.

During trial no question was raised about the delayed examination and not even a plea was raised before the trial Court that the delayed examination of PWs. 3 and 5 affected credibility of the prosecution version.

In response, learned counsel for the accused-respondent submitted that the High Court by a well-reasoned judgment has found the prosecution version to be unreliable. That being so, the Supreme Court should not interfere with the order of acquittal. Further, the evidence tendered by the prosecution was not sufficient to prove unerringly that the accused was responsible for the crime. The case being one which rests on circumstantial evidence, the view taken by the High Court was a possible view and, therefore, the Supreme Court should not interfere.

JUDGMENT OF THE SUPREME COURT

The Court expressed that the following questions may be asked and answered as a test to determine the 'rarest of the rare' case in which death sentence can be inflicted:—

(a) Is there something uncommon about the crime which renders sentence of imprisonment for life inadequate and calls for a death sentence?

(b) Are the circumstances of the crime such that there is no alternative but to impose death sentence even after according maximum weightage to the mitigating circumstances which speak in favour of the offender?

The Court observed that the following guidelines which emerge from *Bachan Singh case* (*supra*) will have to be applied to the facts of each individual case where the question of imposition of death sentence arises:

(i) The extreme penalty of death need not be inflicted except in gravest cases of extreme culpability.

(ii) Before opting for the death penalty the circumstances of the 'offender' also require to be taken into consideration along with the circumstances of the 'crime'.

(iii) Life imprisonment is the rule and death sentence is an exception. Death sentence must be imposed only when life imprisonment appears to be an altogether inadequate punishment having regard to the relevant circumstances of the crime, and provided and only provided, the option to impose sentence of imprisonment for life cannot be conscientiously exercised having regard to the nature and circumstances of the crime and all the relevant circumstances.

(iv) A balance sheet of aggravating and mitigating circumstances has to be drawn up and in doing so the mitigating circumstances have to be accorded full weightage and a just balance has to be struck between the aggravating and the mitigating circumstances before the option is exercised.

The Court held that in rarest of rare cases when collective conscience of the community is so shocked, that it will expect the holders of the judicial power centre to inflict death penalty irrespective of their personal opinion as regards desirability or otherwise of retaining death penalty, death sentence can be awarded. The community may entertain such sentiment in the following circumstances:

(1) When the murder is committed in an extremely brutal, grotesque, diabolical, revolting or dastardly manner so as to arouse intense and extreme indignation of the community.

(2) When the murder is committed for a motive which evinces total depravity and meanness; *e.g.* murder by hired assassin for money or reward or a cold-blooded murder for gains of a person *vis-a-vis* whom the murderer is in a dominating position or in a position of trust, or murder is committed in the course for betrayal of the motherland.

(3) When murder of a member of a Scheduled Caste or minority community etc., is committed not for personal reasons but in circumstances which arouse social wrath; or in cases of 'bride burning' or 'dowry deaths' or when murder is committed in order to remarry for the sake of extracting dowry once again or to marry another woman on account of infatuation.

(4) When the crime is enormous in proportion. For instance when multiple murders, say of all or almost all the members of a family or a large number of persons of a particular caste, community, or locality, are committed.

(5) When the victim of murder is an innocent child, or a helpless woman or old or infirm person or a person *vis-a-vis* whom the murderer is in a dominating position or a public figure generally loved and respected by the community.

If upon taking an overall global view of all the circumstances in the light of the aforesaid propositions and taking into account the answers to the questions posed by way of the test for the rarest of rare case, the circumstances of the case are such that death sentence is warranted, the Court would proceed to do so.

The Court said that a convict hovers between life and death when the question of gravity of the offence and award of adequate sentence comes up for consideration. Mankind has shifted from the state of nature towards civilized society and it is no longer the physical power of a litigating individual or the might of the ruler nor even the opinion of the majority that takes away the liberty of a citizen by convicting him and making him suffer a sentence of imprisonment. Award of punishment following conviction at a trial in a system wedded to the rule of law is the outcome of cool deliberation in the Courtroom after adequate hearing is afforded to the parties, accusations are brought against the accused, the prosecutor is given an opportunity of supporting the charge and the prosecuted is given an opportunity of meeting the accusations by establishing his innocence. It is the outcome of cool deliberations and the screening of the material by the informed man *i.e.* the Judge, that leads to determination of the *lis*.

The Court held that the principle of proportion between crime and punishment is a principle of just deserts that serves as the foundation of every criminal sentence that is justifiable. As a principle of criminal justice it is hardly less familiar or less important than the principle that only the guilty ought to be punished. Indeed, the requirement that punishment not be disproportionately great, which is a corollary of just deserts, is dictated by the same principle that does not allow punishment of the innocent, for any punishment in excess of what is deserved for the criminal conduct is punishment without guilt.

The Court observed that the Criminal law adheres in general to the principle of proportionality in prescribing liability according to the culpability of each kind of criminal conduct. It ordinarily allows some significant discretion to the judge in arriving at a sentence in each case, presumably to permit sentences that reflect more subtle considerations of culpability that are raised by the special facts of each case. Judges in essence affirm that punishment ought always to fit the crime; yet in practice sentences are determined largely by other considerations. Sometimes it is the correctional needs of the perpetrator that are offered to justify a sentence. Sometimes the desirability of keeping him out of circulation, and sometimes even the tragic results of his crime. Inevitably these considerations cause a departure from just desert as the basis of punishment and create cases of apparent injustice that are serious and widespread.

Proportion between crime and punishment is a goal respected in principle, and in spite of errant notions, it remains a strong influence in the determination of sentences. Anything less than a penalty of greatest severity for any serious crime is thought to be a measure of toleration that is unwarranted and unwise. But in fact quite apart from those considerations that make punishment unjustifiable when it is out of proportion to the crime, uniformly disproportionate punishment has some very undesirable practical consequences.

Considering the view expressed by it in *Bachan Singh's* case (*supra*) and *Machhi Singh's* case (*supra*) the Court held that the case at hand falls in rarest of rare category and death sentence awarded by the Trial Court was appropriate. The acquittal of the respondent-accused was clearly unsustainable and was set aside. In the ultimate result, the judgment of the High Court was set aside and that of the Trial Court was restored. The appeals were thus allowed.

Part 8

Rape and Murder – Death Sentence – Rarest of Rare Cases

RAPE AND MURDER – DEATH SENTENCE – RAREST OF RARE CASES

KIDNAPPING, RAPE AND MURDER OF 10 YEAR OLDGIRL AND 7 YEAR BOY: DEATH SENTENCE: RAREST OF RARE CASE

Manohoran

v.

State,

2014 (2) MLJ (Cri) 1: 2015 Cr. LJ 1215

Two children were kidnapped, one of them was gang raped and then both of them were given poison and pushed into canal alive. Nothing was brought on record to suggest that accused suffered from emotional or mental imbalance while committing offence. Death sentence was confirmed by High Court.

RAPE AND MURDER OF TWO YEAR OLD GIRL: RAREST OF RARE CASE: DEATH SENTENCE

State of Maharashtra

v.

Ravi Ashok Ghumare,

2016 (1) AIR Bom R (Cri) 876: 2016 (2) Bom CR (Cri) 346

The victim was found in the house. She was lying under the bed in a naked and unconscious condition. Blood was oozing from her private part with multiple injuries in the body. She was taken to the hospital was declared brought dead. The clothes of accused were stained with blood. The motive of accused was proved. The accused failed his defence. The death sentence was confirmed.

TWO ACCUSED PERSONS COMMITTED RAPE ON A YOUNG GIRL AND SMASHED HER HEAD

Purushottam Dashrata Borate
v.
State of Maharashtra,
(2015) 6 SCC 652: 2015 (3) Crimes 114: 2015 (2) Andh LD 218: 2015 (3) RLW 2586: 2015 (4) JLJR 1: 2015 (2) RAJ (SC) 572: 2015 All MR 2421: 2015 (4) PLJR 162

Two accused persons committed rape on a young girl and thereafter smashed her head. The death sentence was awarded to them.

RAREST OF RARE CASE: RAPE AND MURDER OF 4 YEAR OLD CHILD: DEATH PENALTY

Vasanta Sampata Dupare
v.
State of Maharashtra,
2014 (13) SCALE 199: 2015 Cr LJ 774: 2015 (1) AIR Jhar R 567: (2015) 1 SCC 253

The offence of rape and murder was committed on a four year old child by an accused of 47 years. The offence was proved by cogent evidence. The accused was sentenced to death. It was held as rarest of rare cases.

RAPE AND MURDER: DEATH SENTENCE: RAREST OF RARE CASE

Jawed Khan
v.
State,
2016 (1) AIR Bom R (Cri) 932: 2016 (2) Bom CR (Cri) 19;
State
v.
Shatrughan,
2015 (4) Bom CR (Cri) 744;
State
v.
Kheraj,
(2003) 8 CCC 224

The victim was alone in the house at night of incidence. The mobile of victim was recovered from co-accused. The co-accused admitted that the accused had given it to him. The accused after incident of rape had changed his blood-stained clothes and worn clothes of brother of victim which were available in the house. The blood-stained clothes were recovered. Medical report was corroborated with live reports DNA report, injuries of victim and blood group of victim. On these grounds the accused was awarded death sentence on account of of rarest of rare case.

RAPE AND MURDER: DEATH SENTENCE: RAREST OF RARE CASE

Prakash Nichad

v.

State of Maharashtra,

2016 (2) AIR Bom R (Cri) 49

Motive of accused, vulnerability of victim girl, barbaric and inhuman nature of crime and execution thereof persuaded that this was the "rarest of rare case" and sentence of death was eminently desirable. Hence the death sentence has upheld by the Court.

RAPE AND MURDER OF MINOR GIRL: DEATH SENTENCE: RAREST OF RARE CASE

State of Maharashtra

v.

Viran Gyanlal Rajput,

2015 (2) Bom CR (Cri) 102: 2015 (2) Crimes 472: 2015 (1) AIR Bom R (Cri) 903

The *modus operandi* to commit the crime by resorting the diabolical method exhibited depravity, degration and uncommonality of the crime. It shocked collective conscience of communists and villagers who were required to send their minor girls to another village for education. Only two mitigating circumstances that accused was 22 years old at relevant time and had family responsibilities of his wife, children and parent was pleaded. But the Court held the case as rarest of rare cases, hence awarded death sentence.

RAPE AND MURDER OF TWO YEAR OLD GIRL: DEATH SENTENCE: RAREST OF RARE CASE

State of Maharashtra

v.

Shatrughan Baban Meshram,

2015 (4) Bom CR (Cri) 744

The medical evidence showed that the death of prosecutrix was caused due to the forceful intercourse. The prosecution was able to establish that the child was subjected to a forceful sexual violence. The death of victim was homicidal was proved. On considering all circumstances that the accused acted in absolute pervert, inhumane and beastly manner, the death sentence awarded by the lower court was upheld by the High Court.

RAPE ON 8 YEAR OLD GIRL: MURDER OF HER: DEATH SENTENCE TO ACCUSED: RAREST OF RARE CASE

State of Rajasthan

v.

Manoj Pratap Singh,

2015 (3) Cri LR 1076: 2015 (4) Cr CC 633: 2015 (6) RCR (Cri) 237: 2013 (3) WLN 377

The victim was 8 year old child. She was having 70% permanent disability. The accused abducted her and gave her a chocolate. The accused not only committed rape but also murdered her. It was held that such cases fell as rarest of rare case. The death sentence was confirmed by High Court.

RAPE AND MURDER OF 5 YEARS OLD GIRL: DEATH SENTENCE: RAREST OF RARE CASE

State of Maharashtra

v.

Dattatraya,

2014 (18) RCR (Cri) 920: 2014 All MR (Cri) 2078

The accused who was of 53 year old committed rape, sodomy and murder of a 5 year old girl. The accused had known that out of past experience that if he tried to rape a full grown woman, she would resist and he would land into trouble. Hence he chose young, innocent, defenceless, minor girl as his victim knowing that such young child of tender age would not be able to put up a resistance. Looking to the evidences of such witnesses it was held that the case of accused, fell under rarest of rare cases. Death sentence was awarded.

RAPE AND MURDER OF SEVEN YEARS OLD GIRL

Kamta Tiwari
v.
State of Madhya Pradesh,
AIR 1996 SC 2800: 1996 Cr LJ 4158: 1996 AIR SCW 3567: JT 1996 (8) SC 198: (1996) 6 SCC 250

FACT: Parmeshwar Lal Sharma along with his wife and three children used to reside at Bhutari Tolla in the township of Budhar. Of the three children, Pinky (deceased) was the youngest and her age at the time of her death was about seven years. The appellant who was also a resident of the same locality used to occasionally visit the family of Parmeshwar and his children used to address him as 'Tiwari uncle."

On April 30, 1995, at or about 6 p.m. Parmeshwar had gone to hair cutting saloon in the local market along with his son Santosh (Prosecution Witness No. 4) and daughter Pinky. After Santosh and Pinky had their hair cut they went out of the saloon to play outside while Parmeshwar stayed back for his turn. After sometime Pinky went to the television repairing shop of the appellant which was by the side of the saloon. The appellant was then playing ludo with Suresh Gupta in his shop. Pinky requested the appellant to give her some toffees and biscuits whereupon he took her to the nearby grocery shop of Budhsen Gupta, purchased a packet of biscuit and gave it to her. Thereafter both of them left the shop of Budhsen.

After his hair-cut when Parmeshwar came out of the saloon and enquired of his daughter, Santosh told him that Pinky had gone to the shop of the appellant and that he had given biscuits to her. On getting that information Parmeshwar along with Santosh went to the shop of the appellant but found it closed. They then went back to their house only to find that Pinky had not returned. Parmeshwar then went to the house of the appellant but he was not available there. Accompanied by his wife and other two children Parmeshwar then went in search of Pinky and in course of the search they met Hari Krishna Soni, and Subhash Chander Soni at or about 10.30 p.m. on a cross road near the shop of the appellant. As advised by them he sent back his wife and children home and again went to the house of the appellant accompanied by them. While they were waiting there they saw the appellant coming towards his house completely drenched. He was then wearing only an underwear with some clothes pressed under his armpit. When they enquired about Pinky he told them that after he had given the packet of biscuits to her she left. All three of them then went to Budhar Police Station at or about 1 a.m. and reported that Pinky was missing.

After recording the report in the Station diary book H.C. Munna Prasad went in search of Pinky but could not trace here out. However, on the basis of the enquiry conducted by him Station House Officer Shri V.D. Tripathi registered a case under sections 363, 364 and 366 I.P.C. and took up investigation. On the following day, *i.e.,* May 2, 1995, in the afternoon the appellant was arrested by Shri Tripathi and then interrogated in presence of Hari Krishna and Din Dayal. On such interrogation the appellant disclosed that he had thrown the dead body of Pinky in a well and concealed her frock near a mahua tree. Shri Tripathi recorded the disclosure statement of the appellant and then, led by the appellant and accompanied by the above two witnesses went to the well of one Ramjiyawan Lodhi and found the dead body of Pinky floating in the water. After Shri Tripathi took photograph of the floating dead body it was brought out of the well. He then prepared a recovery memo of the dead body which was signed by the accused as also the witnesses present there. Shri Tripathi held inquest thereupon, prepared a report in respect thereof, and then sent if for post-mortem examination. Pursuant to the statement made by the accused, Shri Tripathi recovered a blood stained frock and seized it under a seizure memo.

On the same day Dr. K.K. Gautam held autopsy on the dead body of Pinky and found a lacerated wound on the right side of the mouth, abrasions on both arms, contusion on the left knee, laceration on the labia majora with clotted blood, laceration on the posterior vaginal wall, hymen ruptured, labia majora and labia minora swollen and blood around the orifice of the vagina. Dr. Gautam also found three contusions on the left side of the neck below the level of the thyroid with abrasions all around, brain and its membrane congested, hyoid bone and thyroid cartilage fractured with haemorrhage on the tissues around the fractures, the fourth rib on both the sides fractured and uterus deeply congested and swollen. He opined that the deceased was raped and that the cause of her death was asphyxia owing to throttling. According to him all the injuries were ante mortem in nature. Dr. Gautam prepared a slide from the vaginal discharge of the deceased and arranged to send it for chemical analysis by the Forensic Science laboratory (F. S.L.) through the Investigating Officer.

On the following day (May 3, 1995), the appellant was sent to the Primary Health Centre for his medical examination. Dr. B.N. Sharma, who examined him found one abrasion on his right knee and another on the glans penis but there was no smegma. In his opinion the appellant was competent to commit sexual intercourse and that the injury found on the glans penis could have been caused while committing rape on the girl of tender age. According to him the injury found on the knee of the appellant could have been caused while committing sexual intercourse with the victim lying on the bare floor of a room. Dr. Sharma prepared a slide of semen of the appellant and along with his underwear sent the same for chemical analysis through Const. Kamla Prasad. The frock which was recovered in pursuance of the statement of the appellant and was identified by Parmeshwar as that of Pinky was also sent for such examination. On receipt of the reports of the F.S.L. and completion of investigation Shri Tripathi submitted a charge-sheet against the accused.

The accused pleaded not guilty to the charges levelled against him and his defence was that he had been falsely implicated.

In the absence of any eye witness the prosecution relied upon the following circumstances to establish the charges levelled against the accused:

(i) In the evening of April 30, 1995, the deceased went to the T.V. repairing shop of the appellant when he was playing ludo with Suresh Gupta and asked him to give him some biscuits;

(ii) Accompanied by the deceased the appellant went to the grocery shop of Budhsen, purchased a packet of biscuits and gave it to her;

(iii) At or about 8.30 p.m. Purshottam Lal saw the appellant along with a girl aged about 6/7 years going towards the bus stand;

(iv) Around mid night the accused was found by Parmeshwar Lal, Subhas Chander Soni and Hari Krishna Soni returning to his house completely drenched (which indicated that he had taken a bath) and wearing only an underwear with some clothes under his armpit;

(v) Pursuant to the statement made by the appellant on May 2, 1995, to Inspector V.D. Tripathi in the presence of Hari Krishna Soni and others, the dead body of Pinky was recovered from a well and her frock from a place which was not accessible to all;

(vi) While conducting autopsy Dr. Gautam found a large number of injuries on the person of the deceased, nature of which indicated that she had been raped and strangulated to death;

(vii) On examining the appellant on May 3, 1995, Dr. Sharma found some injuries on his person which were about 72 hours old and likely to have been caused while having sexual intercourse with a girl of tender age; and

(viii) Blood was found on the frock of the deceased and her vaginal smear on the underwear of the appellant.

Trial Court's View

Both the Trial Court and the High Court detailed and discussed at length the evidence of all the witnesses who were examined by the prosecution to prove the above circumstances and held that each of the above circumstances stood conclusively proved and that those circumstances unerringly pointed to the guilt of the accused.

Supreme Court's View

The Supreme Court also closely scrutinised the evidence and our such exercise persuades us to unhasitatingly hold that the concurrent findings entered by the learned lower Courts were unexceptionable. It is unnecessary therefore for us to burden this judgment with a repetition of the details of the evidence. It is of course true that the entire case is based on circumstantial evidence but the tell-tale circumstances all of which stand firmly established are not compatible with any other reasonable hypothesis except that the appellant kidnapped Pinky, committed rape on her, then strangulated her to death and to cause disappearance of evidence of the murder threw her dead body in a well. The convictions of the appellant for the offences under sections 363, 376, 302 and 201, of Indian Penal Code must, therefore, be upheld.

That brought to Supreme Court to the question whether the sentence of death imposed upon the appellant by the Trial Court for his conviction under section 302, of I.P.C and confirmed by the High Court should be maintained or not. In *Bachan Singh* v. *State of Punjab,* AIR 1980 SC 898: (1980) 2 SCC 684: 1980 Cr LJ 636: 1980 SCC (Cri) 580, the Supreme Court indicated, while discussing the sentencing policy, the guidelines to be followed for imposing the extreme penalty of death. From the guidelines so indicated, the Court in its later judgment in *Machhi Singh* v. *State of Punjab,* (1983) 3 SCC 470: AIR 1983 SC 957: 1983 Cr LJ 1457: 1983 SCC (Cri) 681: (1983) 3 SCR 413, formulated the following propositions, which were to be applied when the question of awarding death sentence arises:

(i) The extreme penalty of death need not be inflicted except in gravest cases of extreme culpability;

(ii) Before opting for the death penalty the circumstances of the 'offender' also require to be taken into consideration along with the circumstances of the crime;

(iii) Life imprisonment is the rule and death sentence is an exception. In other words death sentence must be imposed only when life imprisonment appears to be an altogether inadequate punishment having regard to the relevant circumstances of the crime, and provided, and only provided, the option to impose sentence of imprisonment of life cannot be conscientiously exercised having regard to the nature and circumstances of the crime and all the relevant circumstances;

(iv) A balance sheet of aggravating an mitigating circumstances has to be drawn up and in doing so the mitigating circumstances has to be accorded full weightage and a just balance has to struck between the aggravating and mitigating circumstances before the option is exercised."

Taking an overall view of the all facts and circumstances of the instant case in the light of the above propositions the Supreme Court was of the firm opinion that the sentence of death should be maintained. In vain the Supreme Court searched for mitigating circumstances – but found aggravating circumstances aplenty. The evidence on record clearly established that the appellant was close to the family of Parmeshwar and the deceased and her siblings used to call her Tiwari uncle. Obviously her closeness with the accused encouraged her to go to his shop, which was near the saloon where she had gone for a haircut with her father and brother, and asked for some biscuits. The accused readily responded to the request by taking her to the nearby grocery shop of Budhsen and handing over a packet of biscuits apparently as a preclude to his sinister design which unfolded in her kidnapping, brutal rape and gruesome murder – as the numerous injuries on her person testify; and the finale was the dumping of her dead body in a well. When an innocent hapless girl of 7 years was subjected to such barbaric treatment by a person who was in a position of her trust his culpability assumes the proportion of extreme depravity and arouses a sense of revulsion in the mind of the common man. In fine, the motivation of the perpetrator, the vulnerability of the victim, the enormity of the crime, the execution thereof persuade us to hold that this is a "rarest of rare" cases where the sentence of death is eminently desirable not only to deter others from committing such atrocious crimes but also to give emphatic expression to society's abhorrence of such crimes.

RAPE AND BRUTAL KILLING OF A GIRL BELOW SIX YEARS

State of Uttar Pradesh

v.

Satish,

(2005) 3 SCC 114: AIR 2005 SC 1000: 2005 Cr LJ 1428: 2005 AIR SCW 905

FACT: One Vishakha *alias* Akansha victim who had not even seen six summers in her life lost her life on account of bestial acts of the respondent Satish (hereinafter referred to as the 'accused') who allegedly raped her and thereafter murdered her. When the victim went out to school on 16-3-2001, her parents would have never thought in their widest dreams that she would not come back home and would fall victim to the barbaric and inhuman acts of the respondent. Rape was one of the most depraved acts. The iniquitous flagitious act becomes abominable when the victim is a child. The diabolic act reaches the lowest level of humanity when the rape is followed by brutal murder.

In a nutshell the accused faced trial in the following backdrop:

On 16th August, 2001 the victim who was studying in Sarvodya Public School had gone to school and did not return at the usual time. On the next morning her dead body was found in the sugarcane field of one Moolchand around 6.00 a.m. She was lying in a dead condition and blood was oozing from her private parts and there were marks of pressing on her neck. Report was lodged at the nearby Police Station and the dead body was sent for post-mortem examination. Dr. R.K. Gupta conducted the post-mortem around 2.00 p.m. on 17th August, 2001 and opined that death was within the preceding 24 hours.

Three persons claimed to have seen the accused nearby the place of occurrence between 1.00 p.m. and 2.00 p.m. on the date of occurrence. Two of them, namely, Sanjeev Kumar Tyagi and Kulbhushan claimed to have seen the deceased being carried on a bicycle by the accused who was taking the bicycle with the deceased sitting on the handle-bar thereof. Anil stated that he had seen the accused in perplexed state around 2.00 p.m. near the place from where the dead body of deceased was found. Investigation was undertaken. During such investigation, there was recovery of the accused's underwear as also the undergarment the deceased was wearing. This recovery was treated to be under section 27 of the Indian Evidence Act, 1872.

Trial Court's View

The Trial Court found that the circumstances highlighted by the prosecution were sufficient to fasten guilt on the accused. it, therefore, convicted him under sections 363, 366, 376(2), 302 and 201 of the Indian Penal Code, 1860. The crime was held to be one falling under the rarest of rare category. Death sentence was imposed for the offence under section 302 of the Indian Penal Code. Various custodial sentences and fines were imposed for other offences. Since a death sentence was awarded the matter was referred to the High Court for confirmation in terms of section 366 of the Code of Criminal Procedure, 1973. The accused preferred an appeal before the High Court. Both the capital sentence reference and the criminal appeal were heard together. By the impugned judgment the High Court set aside the judgment of conviction. It was held that the case rested on circumstantial evidence and the circumstances highlighted by the prosecution did not inspire confidence. Three circumstances were highlighted by the High Court to arrive at the aforesaid conclusions. *Firstly*, it was held that examination of Sanjeev Kumar Tyagi and Kulbhushan after long passage of time rendered their version unacceptable and improbable. The prosecution did not offer any explanation for such delayed examination. *Secondly*, in the FIR name of the accused was not indicated. *Thirdly*, presence of the accused nearby the place from where the dead body was recovered, as deposed by Anil, may be a suspicious circumstance but was not determinative. Accordingly, it was held that the prosecution had failed to prove its accusations.

The learned counsel for the State submitted that the approach of the High Court was clearly erroneous both on legal and factual aspects. No question was put to the Investigating Officer regarding alleged delayed examination. Further the evidence of prosecution witnesses 2, Sanjeev Kumar Tyagi and Kulbhushan clearly established the circumstances which unerringly point the accusing finger at the accused. Additionally, explanation was given for non-inclusion of the name of the accused in the FIR by prosecution witness No.1 and without indicating any reason the High Court had treated the same to be unacceptable.

It is relevant to point out that during trial no question was raised about the delayed examination and not even a plea was raised before the Trial Court that the delayed examination of Sanjeev Kumar Tyagi and Kulbhushan affected credibility of the provision version.

In response, learned counsel for the accused-respondent submitted that the High Court by a well-reasoned judgment has found the prosecution version to be unreliable. That being so, this Court should not interfere with the order of acquittal. Further, the evidence tendered by the prosecution is not sufficient to prove unerringly that the accused was responsible for the crime. The case being one which rests on circumstantial evidence, the view taken by the High Court is a possible view and, therefore, this Court should not interfere.

The High Court has placed reliance on a decision of this Court in *Ganesh Bhavan Patel* v. *State of Maharashtra*, (1978) 4 SCC 371: AIR 1979 SC 135: 1979 Cr

LJ 51: (1979) 2 SCR 94. A bare reading of the fact situation of that case shows that the delayed examination by I.O. was not the only factor which was considered to be determinative. On the contrary it was held that there were catena of factors which when taken together with the delayed examination provided basis for acquittal.

It is to be noted that the explanation when offered by I.O. on being questioned on the aspect of delayed examination, by the accused has to be tested by the Court on the touchstone of credibility. If the explanation is plausible then no adverse inference can be drawn. On the other hand, if the explanation is found to be implausible, certainly the Court can consider it to be one of the factors to effect credibility of the witnesses who were examined belatedly. It may not have any effect on the credibility of prosecution's evidence tendered by the other witnesses.

One significant factor which seems to have been missed by the High Court was that there was no suggestion to either Sanjeev Kumar Tyagi and Kulbhushan that in fact they had not seen the accused and deceased together. Even no question was asked about that aspect in cross-examination. On the contrary, an irrelevant suggestion was given that though the witness had seen them together, the witness had not asked the accused as to why he was walking while carrying the deceased on the bicycle. That being so, the High Court could not have come to the conclusion that there was no credible evidence of the accused and the deceased being seen together by Sanjeev Kumar Tyagi and Kulbhushan. As noted above, the I.O. was never asked the reason for delayed examination of Sanjeev Kumar Tyagi and Kulbhushan. The cross-examination was only on the aspect of the recovery of the underwear and undergarment of the accused and the deceased respectively.

The last-seen theory comes into play where the time-gap between the point of time when the accused and the deceased were seen last alive and when the deceased is found dead is so small that possibility of any person other than the accused being the author of the crime becomes impossible. It would be difficult in some cases to positively establish that the deceased was last seen with the accused when there is a long gap and possibility of other persons coming in between exists. In the absence of any other positive evidence to conclude that the accused and the deceased were last seen together, it would be hazardous to come to a conclusion of guilt in those cases. In this case there is positive evidence that the deceased and the accused were seen together by witnesses Sanjeev Kumar Tyagi and Kulbhushan, in addition to the evidence of prosecution witness No. 2.

The reason as to why accused's name did not find place in the FIR was explained by the informant when he was recalled. The High Court drew an adverse inference without indicating any reason therefor. Looked at from above angle, the High Court's order is clearly untenable and unsustainable and deserves to be set aside.

There was no embargo on the appellate Court reviewing the evidence upon which an order of acquittal is based. Generally, the order of acquittal shall not be interfered with because the presumption of innocence of the accused is further strengthened by acquittal. The golden thread which runs through the web of administration of justice in criminal cases is that if two views are possible on the evidence adduced in the case, one pointing to the guilt of the accused and the other to his innocence, the view which is favourable to the accused should be adopted. The paramount consideration of the Court is to ensure that miscarriage of justice is prevented. A miscarriage of justice which may arise from acquittal of the guilty is no less than from the conviction of an innocent. In a case where admissible evidence is ignored, a duty is cast upon the appellate Court to re-appreciate the evidence where the accused has been acquitted, for the purpose of ascertaining as to whether any of the accused really committed any offence or not. *Bhagwan Singh* v. *State of Madhya Pradesh,* 2002 (2) Supreme 567: AIR 2002 SC 1621: 2002 AIR SCW 1532: (2002) 4 SCC 85. The principle to be followed by appellate Court considering the appeal against the judgment of acquittal is to interfere only when there are compelling and substantial reasons for doing so. If the impugned judgment is clearly unreasonable and relevant and convincing materials have been unjustifiably eliminated in the process, it is a compelling reason for interference. These aspects were highlighted by this Court in *Shivaji Sahabrao Bobade* v. *State of Maharashtra,* AIR 1973 SC 2622: 1973 2 SCWR 426: 1973 Cr LJ 1783: (1973) 2 SCC 793; *Ramesh Babulal Doshi* v. *State of Gujarat,* 1996 (4) Supreme 167; *Jaswant Singh* v. *State of Haryana,* 2000 (3) Supreme 320: AIR 2000 SC 1833: 2000 Cr LJ 2212: 2000 AIR SCW 1430; *Raj Kishore Jha* v. *State of Bihar,* 2003 (7) Supreme 152: AIR 2003 SC 4664: 2003 Cr LJ 5040: 2003 AIR SCW 5095; *State of Punjab* v. *Karnail Singh,* 2003 (5) Supreme 508: AIR 2003 SC 3609: 2003 Cr LJ 3892: 2003 AIR SCW 4065 and *State of Punjab* v. *Phola Singh,* 2003 (7) Supreme 17: AIR 2003 SC 4407: 2003 Cr LJ 5010: 2003 AIR SCW 5044.

In *Bachan Singh* v. *State of Punjab,* AIR 1980 SC 898: (1980) 2 SCC 684: 1980 Cr LJ 636: 1980 SCC (Cri) 580 and *Machhi Singh* v. *State of Punjab,* (1983) 3 SCC 470: AIR 1983 SC 957: 1983 Cr LJ 1457: 1983 SCC (Cri) 681: (1983) 3 SCR 413 the guidelines which are to be kept in view when considering the question whether the case belongs to the rarest of the rare category for awarding death sentence were indicated.

A convict hovers between life and death when the question of gravity of the offence and award of adequate sentence comes up for consideration. Mankind has shifted from the state of nature towards a civilized society and it is no longer the physical opinion of the majority that takes away the liberty of a citizen by convicting him and making him suffer a sentence of imprisonment. Award of punishment following conviction at a trial in a system wedded to the rule of law is the outcome of cool deliberation in the court room after adequate hearing is afforded to the parties, accusations are brought against the accused, the prosecuted is given an opportunity of meeting the accusations by establishing his innocence. It is the outcome of cool deliberations and the screening of the material by the informed man *i.e.,* the Judge that leads to determination of the *lis.*

The principle of proportion between crime and punishment was a principle of just desert that serves as the foundation of every criminal sentence that is justifiable. As a principle of criminal justice it was hardly less familiar or less important than the principle that only the guilty ought to be punished. Indeed, the requirement that punishment not be disproportionately great, which was a corollary of just desert, was dictated by the same principle that does not allow punishment of the innocent, for any punishment in excess of what was deserved for the criminal conduct was punishment without guilt.

The criminal law adheres in general to the principle of proportionality in prescribing liability according to the culpability of each kind of criminal conduct. It ordinarily allows some significant discretion to the Judge in arriving at a sentence in each case, presumably to permit sentences that reflect more subtle considerations of culpability that are raised by the special facts of each case. Judges in essence affirm that punishment ought always to fit the crime; yet in practice sentences are determined largely by other considerations. Sometimes it is the correctional needs of the perpetrator that are offered to justify a sentence. Sometimes the desirability of keeping him out of circulation, and sometimes even the tragic results of his crime. Inevitably these considerations cause a departure from just desert as the basis of punishment and create cases of apparent injustice that are serious and widespread.

Proportion between crime and punishment is a goal respected in principle, and in spite of errant notions, it remains a strong influence in the determination of sentences. Anything less than a penalty of greatest severity for any serious crime is thought to be a measure of toleration that is unwarranted and unwise. But in fact quite apart from those considerations that make punishment unjustifiable when it is out of proportion to the crime, uniformly disproportionate punishment has some very undesirable practical consequences.

Court's View

Considering the view expressed by Supreme Court in *Bachan Singh's* case (supra) and *Machhi Singh's* case (supra) we have no hesitation in holding that the case at hand fell in rarest of rare category and death sentence awarded by the Trial Court was appropriate. The acquittal of the respondent-accused was clearly unsustainable and was set aside. In the ultimate result, the judgment of the High Court was set aside and that of the Trial Court was restored.

RAPE BY SECURITY GUARD

Dhananjay Chatterjee @ Dhana
v.
State of West Bengal,
(1994) 2 SCC 220

The Sorbid episode of security guard, whose sacred duty was to ensure protection and welfare of inhabitants of the flats in the apartment, should not have subjected the deceased, a resident of one of the flats to gratify his lust and murdered her in retaliation for his transfer on her complaint, makes the crime even more heinous. Keeping in view the medical evidence and the state in which the body of deceased was found, it is obvious that a most heinous type of barbaric rape and murder was committed on a helpless and defenceless school going girl of 18 years. If the security guards behave in this manner who will guard the security? The faith of the society by such a barbaric act of the guard, get totally shaken and its cry for justice becomes loud and clear. The offence was not only inhuman and barbaric but it was a totally outhless crime of rape followed by cold-blooded murder and an affront to the human dignity of the society. Hence the court held it as rarest of rare cases and the accused was hanged.

GANG RAPE AND MURDER: DEATH SENTENCE: RAREST OF RARE CASE

State

v.

Ram Singh,

2014 (4) CCR 174: 2014 (18) RCR (Cri) 254: 2014 (212) DLT 99

The victim was a young girl was on the verge of completing her physiotherapy course and provided healing touch to many patients in need of physiotherapy. After being gang raped and insertion of rod in her private parts, she was further tortured in a most inhuman and barbaric manner by inserting hand in her vagina and putting out her internal organ. All these evidences were proved. Death sentence was awarded on the ground of rarest of rare case test.

GANG RAPE AND MURDER: DEATH SENTENCE: RAREST OF RARE CASE

Rahul

v.

State of Delhi,

2014 (3) JCC 2195: 2014 (2014) DLJ 179

The accused persons had brutally extinguished the life of victim after raping her. The testimony of witnesses were wholly reliable and trustworthy. The acts revealed that the intention to carry out a crime for satisfying their lust was present. The dead body was recovered at the point of accused persons. The prosecution story fully corroborated with medical evidence. Hence the death sentence was confirmed.

Part 9

Supreme Court on Rape Cases

SUPREME COURT ON RAPE CASES

RAPE AND MURDER OF 11 YEAR OLD GIRL

State of Uttar Pradesh

v.

Munesh,

AIR 2013 SC 147

Accused committed rape and then strangulated the victim girl of 11 year old to death. The First Information Report was not delayed. Two passer-by witness gave evidence and their evidence was corroborated with the medical evidence and also with the evidence of victim's father. The eye-witnesses were independent witnesses. Both these witnesses identified the accused before trial court. Though there was contradiction of statements of witnesses given to police and given in court the Supreme Court held that those contractions were not trivial and rejection of their evidence and acquittal of accused was improper. The Supreme Court awarded rigorous life imprisonment to accused and refused the death sentence.

DEATH SENTENCE SHOULD BE GIVEN IN CASE OF RAPE AND MURDER OF MINOR GIRL

Gurvail Singh

v.

State of Punjab,

(2013) 2 SCC 713

The rarest of rare cases test depends on the perception of the society and is not judge-centric, that is, whether the society will approve the awarding of death sentence to certain types of crime or not. While applying this test, the court has to look into a variety of factors like society's abhorrence, extreme indignation and antipathy to certain types of crimes like *rape and murder of minor girls*, especially intellectually challenged minor girls, minor girls with physical disability, old and infirm women with those disabilities, etc., these examples are only illustrative and not exhaustive. Courts award death sentence, because the situation demands, due to constitutional compulsion reflected by the will of the people, and is not judge-centric.

RAPE ON A FOREIGN GIRL: VIDEO CONFERENCE

Sujoy Mitra

v.

State of West Bengal,

2016 (1) RCR (Cri) 594: 2016 (1) RAJ 82: 2016 All SCR (Cri) 146: 2016 (158) AIC 106: 2016 (1) JBCJ 245: (2016) 1 Crimes 105: 2016 (1) Cal LT 53: 2016 (1) Cal LJ 100: 2016 (1) AIC LR 192: 2016 (2) Cal Cr LR 337: 2016 RAJ Cr C 281

It was held that the State is to install equipment for video conference for which the embassy shall nominate a responsible officer, in whose presence the statement of prosecutrix is to be recorded and the officer who shall be deputed to record statement shall be present and there will be no other person besides the witness, in the room, and the statement shall be recorded by trial court.

RAPE AND MURDER: DEATH SENTENCE COMMUTED TO LIFE IMPRISONMENT

Sandeep

v.

State of Uttar Pradesh,

2012 (6) SCC 107: 2012 (3) MLJ (Cri) 56: 2012 (3) RCR (Cri) 839: 2012 (78) A Cr C 178: 2012 (4) RAJ 145: 2012 (5) SCR 952: 2012 (5) SCALE 444

Awarding of death sentence is the rule, death is an exception. The application of the "rarest of rare case" principle is dependent upon and differs from case to case. In a deliberately planned crime executed meticulously in a diabetic manner touching the conscience of everyone and thereby disturb the moral fibre of the society, would call for imposition of capital punishment in order to ensure that it acts as a deterrent.

RAPE ON 8 YEAR OLD GIRL

Shyam Narain

v.

State of NCT of Delhi,

2013 (3) Er C 147: 2013 (3) RAC 563: 2014 (1) AIR Jhar R 318: 2013 (3) SCC 1: 2013 (3) CCR 73: JT 2013 (9) SC 42: 2013 AIR SCW 3026: 2013 (2) Crimes 342

The Court must hear the loud cry for justice by the society in cases of the heinous crime of rape on innocent helpless girls of tender age and response by imposition of proper sentence. The public abhorrence of the crime needs reflection through imposition of appropriate sentence by Court.

RAPE ON MENTALLY CHALLENGED GIRL OF 11 YEAR OF OLD

Shankar Kisanrao Khade

v.

State of Maharashtra,

JT 2013 (6) SC 315: 2013 (3) Cal Cr LR 481: 2013 (2) ALT 240: (2013) 5 SCC 546: (2013) 4 RAJ 166: 2013 AIR SCW 2668

The sodomy, rape and murder of 11 year old mentally challenged girl was committed by the accused. The accused was awarded death sentence by High Court, *inter alia*. On the ground that some criminal cases were pending against him. The death sentence was commuted to life imprisonment. The mere pendency of few criminal cases against accused cannot be taken note of to award death sentence. The death sentence commuted to life imprisonment.

GANG RAPE WITH MURDER

Ramaresh

v.

State of Chhattisgarh,

2012 (2) RCR (Cri) 169: 2012 (1) RAJ 391: 2012 AIR SCW 1917: 2012 (2) MLJ (Cri) 683: 2012 (2) PLJR 338: AIR 2012 SC 1357

The accused who was brother-in-law of victim committed gang rape along with his friends. The High Court awarded death sentence. The Supreme Court though held that the accused committed heinous crime for satisfaction of their lust, but it cannot be held as "rarest of rare cases" but commuted the sentence to life imprisonment.

RAPE AND MURDER OF 5 YEARS CHILD

State of Rajasthan

v.

Jamil Khan,

2014 (1) E Cr C 209: 2014 (1) Mh LJ 42: 2013 (4) CCR 209: 2013 (4) MLJ (Cri) 324: 2013 AIR SCW 5705: 2013 (131) AIC 45: 2013 (6) AIR Bom R 982: (2013) 10 SCC 721

Though it was a rarest of rare case, but the Court found it too hard to impose death sentence as well delay of 11 years in trial and final order. At the same time awarding of life imprisonment was too inadequate. In such a case if death sentence is altered to life imprisonment then the life imprisonment should be without commutation or remission.

GANG RAPE AND MURDER BY 3 ACCUSED PERSONS

State of Rajasthan

v.

Balveer,

2013 (6) RAJ 368: 2014 Cr LJ 314: (2013) 16 SCC 321: (2013) 4 CCR 460: (2013) 13 SCALE 429: 2013 AIR SCW 6471

Three accused persons committed rape on a girl and thereafter strangulated her to death. One of the accused was tender aged and made and approver. The two other accused persons were convicted on the basis of evidence of approver. The order of acquittal by High Court was set aside. They were awarded with the punishment of life imprisonment.

RAPE WITH A 11 YEAR OLD VICTIM

Radhakrisha Nagesh

v.

State of Andhra Pradesh,

2013 (1) RCR (Cri) 659: 2012 (6) RAJ 582: 2013 (1) AIC LR 537: 2013 (1) Crime 325

Accused was convicted on basis of sole statement of victim because the Court found that statement of victim was reliable, trustworthy and by itself sufficient to convict the accused, by virtual of it being the statement of the victim herself.

OFFENCE OF RAPE

Bhupendra Sharma

v.

State of Himachal Pradesh,

(2003) 8 SCC 551

The offence of rape is "ravishment of a woman" without her consent or against her will by force, fear or fraud and also includes the "carnal knowledge" of a woman.

WILL AND CONSENT FOR RAPE

Dillip Singh
v.
State of Bihar,
(2005) 1 SCC 88

Though will and consent often intertace and an act done against the will of the person can be said to be an act done without consent, the Indian Penal Code categories these two expressions under separate heads in order to be as comprehensive as possible.

SUBSTANTIAL EQUALITY AND WOMEN'S RIGHTS

Ashok Kumar Thakur
v.
Union of India,
(2008) 6 SCC 1

The substantive equality and women's rights as human rights have been established both in domestic and international legal regimes. The Constitution of India embraces the substantive equality approach as provided in Article 15(1) and 15(3).

AGE OF PROSECUTRIX

State of Uttar Pradesh
v.
Chottey Lal,
(2011) 2 SCC 550

Where the prosecutrix has been found to be above 16 years (although below 18 years), the clause *Sixthly* of section 375 of Indian Penal Code is not attracted. The expression "against her will" and "without her consent" may overlap. The expression "against her will" would ordinarily mean that the intercourse was done by a man with a woman despite her resistance and opposition. On the other hand, the expression "without her consent" would comprehend an act of reason accompanied by deliberation.

RESISTANCE OF PROSECUTRIX AND HER CONSENT

State of Himachal Pradesh

v.

Mango Ram,

(2000) 7 SCC 224

The evidence indicated that there was resistance by prosecutrix and there was no voluntary participation by her for the sexual act. Submission of the body under fear of teror cannot be construed as a consented sexual act. The consent for the purpose of section 375 of Indian Penal Code requires voluntary participation not only after the exercise of intelligence based on the knowledge of the significance and moral quality of the act but after having fully exercised the choice between resistance and assent. Whether there was consent or not, is to be ascertained only on a careful study of all relevant circumstances.

There was clear evidence that the prosecutrix resisted the onslaught and made all possible efforts to prevent the accused from committing rape on her. Hence, Trial Court's finding that there was consent of rape was rejected.

PENETRATION IN OFFENCE OF RAPE

Koppula Venkatrao

v.

State of Andhra Pradesh,

(2004) 3 SCC 602

The *sine qua non* of the offence of rape is penetration. Ejaculation without penetration constitutes an attempt to commit rape and not actual rape. The definition of "rape" as contained in section 375 of Indian Penal Code refers to "sexual intercourse" and the Explanation appended to the section provides that penetration is sufficient to constitute the sexual intercourse necessary to the offence of rape. Intercourse means sexual connection.

DISBELIEVE OF STATEMENT OF VICTIM OF RAPE

Tukaram

v.

State of Maharashtra,

(1979) 2 SCC 143

The statement of victim of rape is not believable on the ground that the circumstantial evidence did not lead to inference of guilt and in fact derogates in no uncertain measure from the inference drawn by it.

CORROBORATION AND EVIDENCE OF COMPLAINANT OF RAPE

Bharvada Gohinbhai Hirjibhai

v.

State of Gujarat,

(1983) 3 SCC 217

It is open to the court to rely upon the evidence of a complainant even without seeking corroboration if corroboration by medical evidence is available.

PHYSICAL INJURY AND DEATHLESS SHAME TO VICTIM OF RAPE

Rafique

v.

State of Uttar Pradesh,

(1981) SCR 1 402

There are several "Sacred Cows" of the Criminal Law in Indo-Anglian jurisprudence which are superstitions survivals and need to be re-examined. When rapists are revelling in their promiscuous pursuits and half of humankind-womankind is proposing against to its hapless lot, when no woman of honour will accuse another of rape since she sacrifice thereby what is dearest to her, the court cannot cling to a fossil formula and insist on corroborative testimony, even if taken as a whole, the case spoken to by the victim strikes a judicial mind as probable. In this instant case the testimony had commanded acceptance from two court. When a woman is ravished what is inflicted was not merely physical injury, but "the deep sense of some death less shame".

EFFECT OF CRIMINAL LAW (AMENDMENT) ACT, 1983 RELATING TO RAPE

Bodhishattwa Gautam

v.

Shubra Chakraborty,

1996 SCC (1) 490

The corroboration of the prosecutrix is not necessary, the cases continued to end in acquittal on account of mishandling of the crime by the police and the invocation of the theory of "consent" by the courts who tried the offence. To overcome this difficulty, the legislature intervened and introduced 114A in Evidence Act.

EVIDENCE OF PROSECUTRIX

State of Maharashtra
v.
Chandraprakash Kewalchand Jain,
(1990) 1 SCC 550

It is necessary at the outset to state what the approach of the court should be while evaluating the prosecution evidence, particularly the evidence of the prosecutrix, in sex offences. Is it essential that the evidence of the prosecutrix should be corroborated in material particular before the court bases a conviction on her testimony? Does the rule of prudence demand that in all cases save the rarest of rare, the court should look for corroboration before acting on the evidence of the prosecutrix?

A prosecutrix of a sex offence cannot be put on par with an accomplice. She is in fact a victim of the crime. In case of physical violence with the prosecutrix, the evidence of her must receive same weight as is attached to an injured.

Further it is only in the rarest of rare cases if the court finds that the testimony of the prosecutrix is so trustworthy, truthful and reliable that other corroboration may not be necessary.

ACID ATTACK ON VICTIM

Sachin Jana
v.
State of West Bengal,
(2008) 3 SCC 390.

The acid caused disfigurement of victim. The Supreme Court applied section 307, (attempt to murder) because under section 307 it is not necessary that "bodily injury capable of causing death is to be inflicted". It is sufficient if there is intent coupled with an overt act in execution thereof.

EVE TEASING

DIG
v.
S. Samudiram,
(2012) 11 SCALE 420

The eve-teasing as a euphemism, which attracts penal action.

TRAFFICKING OF WOMEN AND CHILDREN

Bachpan Bachao Andolan
v.
Union of India,
(2011) 5 SCC 1

The offences were committed initially on women and children never come to light. Over time the sexual abuse becomes part of their life. It then gets termed as prostitution and then the abuse borders on being consensual. It is this vicious circle of missing children and women-trafficking abuse prostitution needs to be curbed with urgent measures.

KHAP PANCHAYAT AND HONOUR KILLING

Arumugam Servai
v.
State of Tamil Nadu,
(2011) 6 SCC 405

The Khap Panchayat or Katta Panchayat in Tamil Nadu offen decrees or encourage honour killings or other atrocities in an institutionalised way on boys and girls of different castes and religion, who wish to get married or have been married or interfere with the personal lives of people.

This is wholly illegal and has to be ruthlessly stamped out. There is nothing honourable in honour killing or other atrocities and, in fact, it is nothing but barbaric and shameful murder.

Lata Singh
v.
State of Uttar Pradesh,
(2006) 5 SCC 475

The caste system is a curse on the nation and the sooner it is destroyed the better. In fact, it is dividing the nation at a time.

Bhagwandas
v.
State (NCT of Delhi),
(2011) 6 SCC 396

The honour killing for whatever reason would come within the category of rarest of rare case deserving death penalty.

RAPE OR AN ATTEMPT TO RAPE NOT A CRIME AGAINST AN INDIVIDUAL BUT DESTROYS BASIC EQUILIBRIUM OF LOCAL ATMOSPHERE

Jugendra Singh

v.

State of Uttar Pradesh,

(2012) 6 SCC 297

It is to be kept in mind that an offence against the body of a woman lowers her dignity and mars reputation. It is said that one's physical frame is his/ her temple. No one has any right of encroachment. An attempt for momentary pleasure of the accused has caused the death of a child and had a devastating effect on her family and, in the ultimate eventuate on collective at large.

GANG RAPE ON A GIRL STUDENT BY TEACHERS: LIFE IMPRISONMENT

Mohan Lal

v.

State of Punjab,

2013 (2) RAJ 746: 2013 (3) AIC LR 192: JT 2013 (10) SC 384: 2013 Cr LJ 3265: 2013 (12) SCC 519: 2013 (2) CCR 538

The teachers gang raped their girl student. The trial court imposed 10 years rigorous imprisonment to them. It was held by the Supreme Court that considering the relationship of the parties. The life imprisonment should be imposed.

RAPE ON A MARRIED WOMAN

Mukesh

v.

State of Chhattisgarh,

2014 (4) E Cr C 284: 2015 (145) AIC 143: 2014 (4) CCR 208: 2014 (4) Crimes 299

The evidence on record proved that the accused committed rape on a married lady. The award was punished with 10 years rigorous imprisonment. It was also held that the contention of the accused that he had been falsely implicated in the case because he had seen the prosecutrix in a compromising position with her brother-in-law was baseless and could not be accepted.

RAPE ON 14 YEAR OLD GIRL: MINIMUM SENTENCE: NO REDUCTION

***Parminder* v.**
State of Delhi,

2014 (2) E CR C 279: 2014 (3) Mh LJ (Cri) 265:
(2014) 2 SCC 592: 2014 AIR (SCW) 709: 2014 (1118) Cal LJ 40

The accused, the brother trained caught held of prosecutrix and committed rape on her. Parents of prosecutrix stopped her from going to school and asked her privately. Considering the age of prosecutrix, conduct of accused and the consequences of the rape it cannot be said to be adequate and special reasons in the case in question to reduce the sentence to less than the minimum sentence under section 376 (1) of Indian Penal Code.

PROSECUTRIX OF EASY VIRTUE

Narender Kumar
v.
State (NCJ of Delhi),

2012 (3) RAJ 138: 2012 (3) RCR (Cri) 66: 2012 (2) Ker LJ 698:
2012 (190) DLT 1: 2012 (78) A Cr C 137: 2012 (115) AIC 80:
2012 (7) SCC 171: 2012 AIR SCW 3391

Once the statement of prosecutrix inspires confidence and is accepted by the Court as such, the conviction can be based only on the solitary evidence of the prosecutrix and no corroboration would be required under these. They can be treated as compelling reasons which necessitate the court for corroboration of the statement.

RAPE AND MURDER ON 3 YEAR OLD GIRL: DEATH SENTENCE

Rajendra Prachaadrao Wasnik
v. *State of Maharashtra,*

2012 (2) SCC (Cri) 30: 2012 (2) RCR (Cri) 696: 2012 (2) RAJ 385:
2012 (2) Cri CC 318: 2012 AIR SCW 1939: (2012) 2 SCR 205

The accused convicted and sentenced to death on basis of last seen evidence which was successfully proved by the prosecution. The accused failed to explain circumstances. The death sentence was upheld by Supreme Court.

Part 10

HIGH COURTS ON RAPE CASES

HIGH COURTS ON RAPE CASES

RAPE ON MINOR GIRL: REDUCTION OF SENTENCE

Dashrath Aba More

v.

State of Maharashtra,

2016 All MR (Cri) 2016: 2016 (2) AIR Bom R (Cri) 581

The evidence of Medical Officer showed that though in injury on body parts of victim was found, her hymen was ruptured. No iota of material showed that accused was falsely implicated. The prosecution failed to prove that the victim was below 16 years old. Hence the conviction under section 376(2)(f) of IPC set aside and the offence was made out under section 376(1) of IPC. As the accused was poor labourer the imprisonment of 7 years rigorous imprisonment was held proper.

RAPE ON MINOR GIRL WITH CONSENT: REDUCTION OF SENTENCE

Ajay Kumar Smar

v.

State,

2016 (2) RCR (Cri) 1050: 2016 (1) JCC 719

The rape was committed on a minor girl aged 15 years with consent. The accused convicted and sentenced to 7 years rigorous imprisonment. As the accused was not a previous convict and not involved in any other criminal activity, and his conduct in jail was not bad and as he has a widowed mother and two unmarried brothers, his sentence was reduced to 5 years rather than 7 years.

RAPE : BASE OF PUNISHMENT

Kingkong Das

v.

State of Assam,

2016 (2) Gau LR 461

If the statement of victim is found to be worthy of credence and inspires confidence, then the punishment for rape is permissible on such evidence. The victim categorically stated that the accused committed rape. Hence the conviction and sentence was held proper.

OFFENCE OF RAPE: IDENTIFICATION PARADE

Sham Vitthal Nimbale

v.

State of Maharashtra,

2016 All MR (Cri) 1765

The prosecutrix identified all the accused in identification parade. It was held that since prosecutrix identified the accused before the Court by attributing specific role was sufficient to hold positive involvement of accused. Hence the accused was convicted and sentenced.

RAPE AND DIABOLIC GRUESOME MURDER OF TWO MINOR GIRLS: CONCURRENT TWO TERMS OF LIFE IMPRISONMENT

R.P. Raj

v.

State,

2015 (3) Cal Cr LR 297

The gruesome and diabolic murder of two defenceless minor girls were committed not only by appellant only, but also by three juveniles. The appellant was of 24 years old at the time of commission of the crime and he was continuing his study through correspondence course in the correctional home. It was held that the sentence of term of life imprisonment in both the trials would run concurrently but the sentence of life imprisonment in each of the trials will run consecutively.

RAPE OF 18 YEAR UNMARRIED GIRL: CONVICTION WAS HELD PROPER

Ravinder

v.

State of Himachal Pradesh,

2016 (1) Sim LC 417

The accused committed rape upon prosecutrix at that time when the accused was a married person aged 32 years and the prosecutrix was an unmarried girl of 18 years. It was held that the murder destroyed the body of victim but rapist degrades soul of an unmarried girl. The anarchy will prevail in society, as was held, if a married man aged 32 years is allowed to commit rape upon an unmarried girl of 18 years. In order to maintain the majesty of law and in order to maintain honour of unmarried girl, it is expedient for Court to meet end of justice maintain sentence passed by trial court.

RAPE: VIDEO CONFERENCE OF EVIDENCE AND STATEMENT

Sujay Mitra

v.

State of West Bengal,

2015 (153) AIC 438: 2015 (3) Cal LJ 462: 2016 (1) Cal Cri LR 510

The petitioner pleaded that the trial court did not follow the guidelines of the Supreme Court for recording evidence through video conference and summons were not issued to the victim. The plea was rejected. It was also held that there was no illegality or irregularity in the order of trial court in convicting to accused.

INGREDIENTS OF OFFENCE OF RAPE: CONVICTION

State of Himachal Pradesh

v.

Vipan Kumar,

2015 (8) RCR (Cri) 192: 2015 (2) Him LR 668: 2015 Cr LJ 1812

The accused forcibly entered to house of prosecutrix and dragged her to the spot of occurrence. He attempted to rape there. In view of Chemical Analysis Report the human semen found on clothes of prosecutrix and human blood and semen was found in vaginal swab of prosecutrix. Hence the offence of rape was made out by the Court and the accused was convicted.

KIDNAPPING AND GANG RAPE: COMPENSATION OF 5,00,000 TO VICTIM

Mojib Ansari

v.

State of Jharkhand,

2015 (3) Crimes 569: 2015 (4) AIR Jhar R 121: 2015 (4) E Cr C 366: 2015 (4) JCR 322: 2015 Cr LJ 4702: 2015 (3) JBCJ 633

The Court cannot lose sight towards loud cry for justice by society in such heinous crimes of gang rape by large number of accused persons of different age groups on an innocent helpless teen age girl. Hence, on such grounds, the sentence recorded by the trial court was maintained by the High Court. Hence the Court imposed compensation of 5,00,000 upon accused to be paid to the family of deceased.

RAPE ON MINOR GIRL: CONVICTION ON TESTIMONY OF PROSECUTRIX

Sunil Kumar

v.

State of Himachal Pradesh,

2015 (2) Sim LC 1056: 2015 (9) RCR (Cri) 577

The testimony of prosecutrix was found by Court as trustworthy, reliable and inspired confidence. It was minor prosecutrix to eliminate her in case she would disclose the incident to anyone. The oral and documentary evidence on record was rightly appreciated by the Court. Hence the accused was convicted and sentenced.

RAPE ON MINOR GIRL OF SEVEN YEARS OLD GIRL BY 58 YEARS OLD MAN: REDUCTION OF SENTENCE

Narinder Kumar Sharma

v.

State of Punjab,

2015 (4) RCR (Cri) 669

The private parts of victim had been badly affected. The conviction of 10 years rigorous imprisonment was awarded on the bag's of testimony of prosecutrix which was trustworthy and credential.

RAPE OF MINOR GIRL: CONVICTION

Subhash

v.

State of Himachal Pradesh,

2015 (3) Sim LC 1745

The mother of the prosecutrix came to know of incident immediately after rape. The testimony of victim was consistent and corroborated with medical evidence. The oral evidence corroborated with the link of evidence. Hence the conviction and sentence of High Court was upheld.

RAPE BY EIGHTY THREE YEAR OLD MAN ON FOUR YEAR OLD GIRL: SENTENCE WAS REDUCED

Bakshi Ram

v.

State Himachal Pradesh,

2015 Latest HLJ (HP) 1517

The accused of 83 year old age committed sexual assault upon the victim of four year of age girl. Considering the age of accused and he was not having criminal background his sentence of 10 years rigorous imprisonment was reduced to 4 years imprisonment.

GANG RAPE AND MURDER: CONVICTION OF LIFE IMPRISONMENT

Santosh Rai

v.

State of Uttar Pradesh,

2016 (93) A Cr C 362: 2016 (3) ADJ 646

The deceased visited the house of the accused persons and thereafter all the four accused persons and deceased were found missing and then the accused persons were seen with dead body of victim. They threw the dead body and tried to escape when seen by the witness. The evidence and the circumstances showed the common intention which led them to be punished with life imprisonment.

RAPE ON 16 YEARS OLD GIRL: CONVICTION

Surendra Nath

v.

State of Uttar Pradesh,

2011 (93) A Cr C 765: 2016 (4) ADJ 14

The victim successfully undergone the test of cross-examination and her statement was supported by the forensic report. The factum of rape with the girl of 16 years by accused was proved beyond reasonable doubt. Hence the conviction of accused was confirmed by the Supreme Court.

OFFENCE OF RAPE: FIR NOT TO BE QUASHED

Arjinder Singh

v.

State of Punjab,

2016 (3) RCR (Cri) 246: 2016 (3) Law Herald 2107

Accused developed physical relations with victim with a promise to marry but booked out subsequently. FIR was lodged. Later on, the compromise was arrived at between the parties and then FIR was sought to be quashed on the ground that FIR was lodged due to some misunderstanding. Hence it was held that in an offence of serious nature like rape case, quash the FIR on the basis of compromise is not justified as offence of rape is such an offence which not only castes stigma on the reputation of a girl but spoils the future prospectus of victim also.

RAPE: ORDER OF CONVICTION AND SENTENCE UPHELD BY SUPREME COURT

Akash

v.

State of Uttar Pradesh,

2016 (93) A Cr C 335: 2014 (4) ADJ 11

The plea of appellant was that the victim was not enticed by him but victim had gone on her own accord with him, no consequence. The victim was recovered with the appellant. The victim further stated that in her evidence when police recovered her she was four months pregnant and accused was the father of child. She admitted her relation with accused. The prosecution fully proved the guilt of accused. The conviction of accused was confirmed as per evidence and circumstances of the case in hand.

RAPE ON MINOR: CONVICTION CONFIRMED

Tikina

v.

State of Orissa,

2016 (162) AIC 418

The victim was raped twice in April 2007. No improbability in prosecution story was found. The inconsistencies and omissions had occurred due to several reasons. While narrating the incident in the complaints petition, dates of each of the specific incidents had been given. The long delay in FIR stood explained in the manner the victim's parents claim to have tackled with the situation. The victim did not get corroboration even from medical evidence. The Court from other evidences also, inspirited the conviction and modified the sentence to 8 years of rigorous imprisonment.

RAPE OF AN OLD LADY: CONVICTION OF ACCUSED

Islam

v.

State of Uttar Pradesh,

2016 (4) ADJ 19

The injuries inflicted on victim revealed that the indication of struggle and force was used by the accused. The victim was an old lady. She was forcibly and sexually assaulted by the accused. The medical evidence fully corroborated with the oral evidence of victim. Hence the order of conviction and sentence was confirmed.

OFFENCE OF RAPE: ACQUITTAL SET ASIDE

State of Gujarat

v.

Shailesh Javerchand Malde Mahajan,

2016 (2) GCD 1069: 2016 (2) GLR 1591

The complainant turned hostiled. The mother and brother of complainant also turned hostiled. The material witness was not examined. The prosecutor even dropped all other witness and closed the Parsley's. The trial court acquitted the accused. It was held that, the trial court erred in not examining the material witness. And it was held that the pious duty of the Court is to appreciate evidence for search of truth. The acquittal was quashed. It was remanded to trial court for retrial.

RAPE: MAINTAINABILITY OF SENTENCE

Akbar

v.

State of Uttar Pradesh,

2016 (13) A Cr C 838: 2016 (4) ADJ 18

There was no dispute about that the accused was 67 years old and in jail continuously and did not appear to be any complaint regarding his conduct as inmate of jail. Further in evidence of informant that the victim solemnised her second marriage. Therefore it was held that, the ends of justice was to be served in case the sentence of accused is reduced. But the conviction was confirmed and the sentence was modified.

ESSENTIAL INGREDIENTS OF RAPE

Davshi Keshav Vara

v.

State of Gujarat,

2016 (2) GLR 1080: 2016 (163) AIC 460

While considering the offence under section 375 of IPC, inserting of some object or figure into private parts of woman is covered under the definition of rape under section 375. It is not necessary that there has to be penetration of penis. The absence of injury is not sufficient to disregard the testimony of victim regarding the offence under section 376 of IPC. Hence the order of conviction and sentence was confirmed.

PHYSICAL RELATIONSHIP OF ACCUSED WITH VICTIM: RAPE

Ashok

v.

State of Haryana,

2016 (3) RCR (Cri) 763

The rape victim was having physical relationship with the accused under the impression that she was legally wedded wife. The other party was aware about the earlier marriage. It was held that, offence of rape in such circumstances was made out.

RAPE: CONVICTION AND CONFIRMED

Suresh Pal

v.

State of Uttar Pradesh,

2016 (4) ADJ 8: 2016 (94) AIC 947

The Court will be entitled to draw the presumption under section 114A of the Evidence Act, against the accused holding that he committed the act of sexual intercourse on the prosecutrix against her will and without her consent. It was held that the prosecution has fully proved the charges levelled against the accused and conviction if the accused is based on sufficient evidence on record. Hence, it was held that the sentence on accused was proper.

KIDNAPPING AND RAPE: MODIFICATION REDUCTION OF SENTENCE

Thakur Bharatji Jevanji Sataji
v.
State of Gujarat,
2016 (162) AIC 718

When the victim is minor in case of of rape, consent is not relevant. For the offence under section 363 and 366 of the IPC, the age of the girl child is 18 years. Therefore, the offence under sections 363 and 366 of IPC requires the consent of guardian and not of the victim. As such, conviction of accused held proper in the light of undisputed and churching evidence with regard to age of victim. However, considering background, coupled with facts and circumstances, it was held that the modification and reduction of sentence was justified.

RAPE AND MURDER OF MINOR GIRL

Raju Singh* v. *State of Jharkhand,
2016 (2) JBCJ 375: 2016 (2) AIR Jhar R 704:
2016 (2) E Cr C 689: 2016 (2) JLJR 284;
Rajendra Prasad Rao Wasnik* v. *State of Maharashtra,
(2012) 4 SCC 37;
Ramesh Bhan* v. *State,
(2009) 5 SCC 740;
Amit* v. *State,
(2003) 8 SCC 93;
Bantu* v. *State,
(2001) 9 SCC 615

There was proof of medical evidence. The testimonies of witnesses corroborated with last seen theory. The post-mortem report and DNA report were proved. The High Court confirmed death sentence. But the Supreme Court considering the other aspects of accused like absence of criminal history of accused which commuted the death sentence to life imprisonment.

RAPE ON MINOR GIRL: COUNSELLING OF RAPE VICTIMS: NO PERMISSION TO MEDICAL TERMINATION OF PREGNANCY

R.

v.

State of Haryana,

2016 (3) RCR (Cri) 1: 2016 (3) RCR (Civil) 428: (2016) 3 Law Herald 1900

The Court observed that the perpetuators of rape as heinous crimes roam in streets like wolves in forests and threaten victims and their families of dire consequences as a result. The rape of minors and young girls, at to hands of unconscientions criminals increasing the various parts of the country, is itself a matter to be ashamed of as a society and needs deliberations to curb the menace. The counselling is necessary to help her overcome such trauma. The Indians are perceived to have faith in religions and God. God is a wonderful Counsellor. And on other grounds termination of pregnancy was not permitted by the Court.

RAPE ON MENTALLY CHALLENGED GIRL: UNNATURAL OFFENCE

State of Maharashtra* v. *Ramchandra Sambhaji Karanjule,

2016 (2) Bom CR 615;

Gangabhawani* v. *Ranapatti Venkat Reddi,

AIR 2013 SC 3681;

Mritunjay* v. *Pranab,

AIR 2013 SC 3334;

Phink Singh* v. *State,

(2016) 4 SCC 9;

Ritesh* v. *State,

(2010) 10 SCC 677;

Shyam* v. *State,

(2012) 7 SCC 45

The accused was director of orphanage of mentally challenged girls and other accused, alleged rape with mentally challenged orphan children and committed carnal sex against order of nature. The medical examination of all inmates showed that all were subject to sexual abuse and many of them habituated to the same. Deposition of victim girls also supported prosecution case. The accused failed to assail prosecution evidence. Hence the conviction of accused was confirmed by the Supreme Court.

RAPE ON MINOR GIRL: RELIABILITY OF TESTIMONY OF VICTIM

***Anju* v. *State of Uttar Pradesh*,**
2016 (5) ADJ 611: 2016 (194) A Cr C 618;
***Mohd. Ali* v. *State*,**
(2015) 7 SCC 272;
***Musauddin* v. *State*,**
AIR 2010 SC 3813;
***Rajesh* v. *State of Jharkhand*,**
(2013) 3 SCC 791

In case of rape, the statement of prosecutrix is to be given due consideration and importance. The statement of prosecutrix is to be kept on high pedestal than that of injured witness. At the same time broad principle requiring prosecution to prove case beyond reasonable doubt also applies equally to case of rape. No presumption to be drawn that prosecutrix always tell entire story truthful.

RAPE ON 7 YEAR OLD MINOR GIRL: DEATH SENTENCE COMMUTED TO LIFE IMPRISONMENT

***State of Maharashtra* v. *Vittlesh Tukaram Atugade*,**
(2016) 2 Crimes 340;
***Duryodhan Rout* v. *State of Orissa*,**
(2014) SC 5308;
***Rajendra* v. *State*,**
(2012) 4 SCC 37;
***Rajesh Kuar* v. *State*,**
(2011) 13 SCC 706;
***Rohtash* v. *State*,**
2013 All MR (Cri) 2620;
***Shankarrao* v. *State*,**
(2013) 5 SCC 546

The accused raped a 7 year old minor girl and murdered her. The accused showed the spot where he raped and killed the victim. Dead body recovered from the spot. All the evidences were proved. The lower court convicted the accused by awarding death sentence. But the Supreme Court commuted to life imprisonment.

GANG RAPE: SOLE TESTIMONY OF VICTIM

Biswamohan Debbarma

v.

State of Tripura,

2016 (2) Gau LT 905

Both the accused trespassed in the house of victim at mid night. One accused entered into room and pulled out victim from the house and both accused took her to the cowshed, raped her there and again took her to jungle and raped her there. The statement of victim inspired confidence which were supported to the evidence of her parent and medical report. Hence both the accused persons were sentenced to 13 years rigorous imprisonment and with fine.

RAPE ON GIRL OF 5 YEAR OLD

Raj Kumar* v. *State of Uttar Pradesh,

2016 (94) A Cr C 372: 2016 (5) ADJ 252;

Guru Bagavaraj* v. *State,

2012 (8) SCC 734;

Jameel* v. *State,

(2010) 12 SCC 532

The accused brutally raped 5 year old girl after sun set. Apart from mother and independent witness, the statement of the victim proved the offence. The medical report and forensic laboratory were corroborated to prove the case. Hence the Court held the conviction of accused as proper.

RAPE ON GIRL OF 4 YEAR OLD: CONVICTION

Haneef

v.

State of Uttar Pradesh,

2016 5 ADJ 584: 2016 (94) A Cr C 646

The testimony of child witness is to form basis of conviction if the same is credible and corroborated by other evidence. The corroboration however is not must but only rule of prudence. The evidence of victim was clear and consistent with facts. Hence the conviction of accused was held proper by Supreme Court.

RAPE ON MINOR GIRL: REDUCTION OF SENTENCE

Gyarsi Lal

v.

State of Rajasthan,

2016 (1) Cr LR 415: 2016 (2) Raj Cr C 547

The prosecutrix stated that accused had put figure in her private part, and later raped her. As per evidence of prosecution witnesses, the prosecutrix was last seen with the accused. The medical evidence proved the fact of rape. The conviction was upheld. But the conviction of life imprisonment was reduced to 10 years rigorous imprisonment.

RAPE ON 16 YEAR OLD GIRL: CONVICTION

Sunny

v.

State of Himachal Pradesh,

2015 (3) Sim LC 1676

The accused brought the prosecutrix in a room and committed sexual intercourse. Next day she was brought back to home. The medical evidence proved the offence of sexual intercourse. The accused was convicted and sentenced.

RAPE ON MINOR GIRL: CONSENT NOT ACCEPTED BY COURT

Arvindbhai Karshanbhai Godavariya

v.

State of Gujarat,

2015 Cr LJ 3931

The evidence showed that the victim was aged 15 years and moved from placed to place with accused. Yet to victim being minor, her consent cannot be taken into consideration. Hence the order of conviction and was confirmed by High Court.

RAPE ON MINOR GIRL BY HER TEACHER IN HIS CAR: CONVICTION AND SENTENCE

Ram Singh

v.

State of Himachal Pradesh,

2016 (2) Crimes 264: 2015 (3) Sim LC 1765

The physical education teacher of minor girl victim took her in his car and sexually assaulted her. The testimony of prosecutrix was that the accused put his private part into her private part. The case was proved on merits. The accused was convicted and sentenced to 10 years imprisonment.

RAPE ON A GIRL WITH FALSE PROMISE TO MARRY

Dinesh Kmar

v.

State of Himachal Pradesh,

2016 (157) AIC 574: 2016 (2) Crimes 38:
2015 (3) Sim LC 1494: 2016 (2) Cr CC 850

The accused used to rape on the prosecutrix under the false promise to marry her. The prosecutrix was removed from the lawful guardianship of her parents, without their consent. Even thereafter she was subjected to rape on false promise. But he did not marry to prosecutrix. Hence the conviction of accused was upheld, by the High Court.

OFFENCE OF RAPE PROVED: NO REDUCTION OF SENTENCE

Vipulbhai Gandabhai Senma

v.

State of Gujarat,

2016 Cr LJ 324: 2016 (2) GLR 1327

The accused dragged the minor girl to bushes and forcibly raped her and ran away after the commission of rape. It was proved beyond reasonable doubt. The accused appealed in High Court. But it was held by the High Court that for commission of such serious crime, the sentence of 10 years rigorous imprisonment cannot be disproportionate.

SIXTEEN YEARS OLD GIRL WAS RAPED BY HER OWN FATHER: CONVICTION

Balbir Chand

v.

State (NCT of Delhi),

2015 (6) AD (Del) 539: 2015 (9) RCR (Cri) 309: 2015 (220) DLJ 479

The version of victim daughter was consistent throughout the case. It was held that, unless such an offence has really been committed, an unmarried little girl would be extremely reluctant to make such allegations which are likely to reflect on her chastity against her own father. Hence the accused-father was properly convicted and sentenced.

RAPE ON A GIRL OF 6 YEAR OLD: CONVICTION

Devan Das

v.

State of Rajasthan,

2015 (2) Cr LR 539: 2015 (4) WLC 16: 2015 (4) RLW 3054: 2015 (155) AIC 613: 2015 (9) RCR (Cri) 841: 2015 Cr LJ 1996

The evidence of prosecution witness was relied. The allegation of rape was corroborated with medical evidence. It was held as heinous crime against society. Hence it was held by the Court that the order of conviction and sentence by lower court was proper.

RAPE ON A GIRL OF 16 YEAR OLD: CONSENTING PARTY: REDUCTION OF SENTENCE

Satish

v.

State (Government of Delhi),

2015 (4) JCC 2760

The prosecutrix and the accused, both were in love and prosecutrix was consenting party. Hence the sentence of 7 years was reduced to 5 years.

RAPE ON 15 YEAR OLD GIRL WITH CONSENT: PARTIES SEPARATELY MARRIED: IMPRISONMENT AND COMPENSATION

State of Maharashtra

v.

Vinod Damarkmar Shahi,

2015 (4) RCR (Cri) 267

At the time of rape, the prosecutrix was 15 years old girl. The offence was proved and hence the accused was convicted under section 376(1) of Indian Penal Code. The parties thereafter married separately and had children. The parties entered into compromise. The accused was released after 15 months imprisonment already undergone. It was order that 100,000 compensation will be paid by accused to prosecutrix.

RAPE ON WIDOW OF 50 YEAR OLD: CONVICTION

Mahendra Singh

v.

State of Haryana,

2015 (3) RCR (Cri) 317

The accused was convicted on sole testimony of prosecutrix. No infirmity was pointed out in the statement of prosecutrix. It was held that if the statement of prosecutrix was found to be worthy of credence, then it requires no corroboration. The Court can record the conviction of an accused on the sole testimony of prosecutrix. The accused was convicted.

RAPE ON DEAF AND DUMB VICTIM OF 17 YEAR OLD: CONVICTION

Lachmi

v.

State of West Bengal,

2016 (1) Cal LT 443

There is no escape from irresistible conclusion that accused utilised his acquaintance to take the prosecutrix to abandoned shack and took advantage of her helpless and disability and raped her. Then after to avoid consequences of his wrongful act, made false promise of marriage to her which later was gullible enough to accept. Hence the prosecution case was proved beyond reasonable doubt. Hence conviction was held proper by High Court.

TESTIMONY OF WITNESS IN RAPE CASE

Jagdish Balaram Narangikar

v.

State of Maharashtra,

(2012) 116 AIC 441 (Bom)

Conviction in offence of rape can be based on sole testimony of a witness, provided such testimony is found to be cogent, reliable and trustworthy. Otherwise conviction is to be set aside.

NO PENETRATION, STILL PROSECUTION

Simal @ Maru Datta

v.

State of Tripura,

(2012) 116 AIC 559 (Gau)

The case was based on sole testimony of prosecutrix. The prosecutrix was subjected to sexual assault established without any doubt. The medical examination report overshadowed the testimony of prosecutrix as to her statement that appellant inserted his penis into her vagina and retained the same upto 3 minutes. Such minute details of sexual act as depicted by prosecutrix of an age of 7 ½ years acquired serious doubt about her testimony. But attempt of rape could not be excluded even if, the act of penetration was disbelieved. The appellant convicted under section 376 read with 511 of Indian Penal Code.

SEXUAL ASSAULT ON MINOR GIRL AND PUNISHMENT

State of Himachal Pradesh

v.

Narain Singh,

(2012) 116 AIC 944 (HP)

There was allegation of sexual assault on prosecutrix. There was also no injury on person of prosecutrix noticed by doctors. Even no injury noticed on private part of victim. There was no injury on body of accused. No birth certificate produced in support of date of birth of victim. The prosecutrix victim was about 16 years old. The alleged sexual assault against wishes of victim was not proved. The prosecution failed to prove its case beyond reasonable doubt. Hence, prosecution by lower courts was sustained.

CONVICTION ON STATEMENT OF PROSECUTRIX

Pushkar Singh

v.

State of Uttarakhand,

(2012) 118 AIC 343 (Uttr)

The conviction can be based on statement of prosecutrix in a case of rape if it is trustworthy and no corroboration is required in such type of rape cases.

RAPE ON MINOR GIRL

Sukhchand Sheikh @ Mondal

v.

State of West Bengal,

(2012) 118 AIC 490 (Cal)

Where fact of rape on a particular date and time on prosecutrix by appellant was established, the evidence of prosecutrix cannot be discarded simply because her mother and brother made statement regarding Salish which had not tallied with her statement. The commission of rape on minor girl was established. She became pregnant and gave birth to a child. Appellant refused to marry. The Trial Court by applying its judicial mind convicted appellant.

CONVERSION OF LIFE IMPRISONMENT INTO 10 YEARS RIGOROUS IMPRISONMENT

Santosh Kumar Gupta

v.

State of Madhya Pradesh,

(2012) 118 AIC 479 (MP)

After confining in his house the appellant committed rape on a minor girl. Delay of 6 days in lodging First Information Report was successfully explained. The evidence of prosecutrix was corroborated by medical evidence and evidence of other family members. The appellant was properly and rightly convicted by the Trial Court, but the High Court converted life imprisonment to 10 years rigorous imprisonment.

ACQUITTAL OF ACCUSED OF RAPE

State of Himachal Pradesh

v.

Suresh Kumar @ Golu,

(2012) 118 AIC 556 (HP)

The age of prosecutrix was 18 years. The prosecution story incorroborated and could not be believed. The prosecutrix was habitual of rape. The doctor examined and gave such report. The semen found on Salwar of prosecutrix was not of accused. Hence, it was held that the accused was rightly acquitted by lower court. The High Court did not interfere in it.

CONSENT OF PROSECUTRIX

Sawali Rajbangshi

v.

State of Assam,

(2012) 117 AIC 456 (Gau)

The initial intention of the accused who had sexual intercourse with informant by promising to marry to prosecutrix was found relevant. The prosecution case that the accused did not marry her because the family members objected. The promise made by accused did not suffer from any misrepresentation of fact. Hence the accused was acquitted.

PREGNANCY OF PROSECUTRIX AFTER RAPE

Suresh Rajbhar

v.

State of Bihar,

(2012) 117 AIC 703 (Pat)

The age of prosecutrix was 16 to 17 years. The appellant forcibly ravished the prosecutrix twice and she became pregnant. The prosecution witness was not consistent. The prosecution also failed to establish its case beyond reasonable doubt. The conviction and sentence by Trial Court was set aside by High Court.

QUESTION OF CONVICTION AND SENTENCE TO ACCUSED

Mukesh Kumar

v.

State of Chhattisgarh,

(2012) 120 AIC 439 (Chh)

The conduct of prosecutrix was unnatural. She did not raise any alarm and make efforts to come out of the clutches of the accused when he was dragging her inside the house. The material witnesses were not examined. There was also serious discrepancies in evidence of prosecutrix. Hence the accused was acquitted.

REDUCTION OF SENTENCE

Bhaiya Lal Pal

v.

State of Uttar Pradesh,

(2012) 120 AIC 675 (All)

The victim was an adult married woman over 30 years. The victim did not suffer internal and external injuries. This was not rape not also gang rape. There was lack of aggressive behaviour on part of appellant. In these circumstances the sentence was reduced.

RAPE ON BELOW 12 YEARS GIRL

Guddu Kumar

v.

State of Bihar,

(2012) 120 AIC 576 (Pat)

In exceptional cases the statutory provision of punishment for offence of rape can be less than prescribed. The discretionary punishment comes into play only when grave offence is committed.

OFFENCE OF RAPE: PLEA OF INSANITY

Jeevan Rana

v.

State of Himachal Pradesh,

2015 Cr LJ 4619: 2016 (1) Cr CL 159

The accused ran away from the spot of occurrence of rape by putting up his clothes when he was noticed by grandmother of victim. It showed that he had known what he was doing. There was no abnormalities in behaviour of accused noticed by the doctor who examined him. Medical evidence failed to prove his insanity. Hence the accused was convicted and sentenced and his plea of insanity was rejected.

RAPE ON GIRL OF 5 YEAR OLD BY FATHER: CONVICTION AND SENTENCE

Runche Damai

v.

State,

2015 (2) JCC 833: 2015 (2) Rajdhani LR 64: 2015 (3) Crimes 651: 2015 (4) Cr CC 508: 2015 (6) RCR (Cri) 773: 2015 (3) AD (Del) 117

One day when the prosecutrix's brother had gone to school, his father and she were at home. Her father removed her clothes and committed rape on her. She felt pain and cried. The evidence was proved beyond all around doubt. The plea of poorness and family burden was rejected. Hence his conviction and sentence was held proper.

OFFENCE OF RAPE: MARRIAGE: NO COMPROMISE: CONVICTION

Pankaj Tiwari

v.

State of Madhya Pradesh,

2016 (1) Jab LJ 23

In case of rape or attempt to rape, the compromise cannot be made under any circumstances since these crimes are against body of a woman. Any compromise between the victim and the offender in relation to offences cannot be accepted or approved such offences are not private in nature and have a serious impact on society. Hence conviction was proper.

RAPE ON TWO MINOR GIRLS: CONVICTION

Vishal

v.

State of Punjab,

2015 (4) RCR (Cri) 617: 2015 (3) PLJ (Cri) 587

The girls being the age of 16 years old, even if there was consent, this was no consent in the eye of law. Though there was delay in lodging of FIR. It was not a defence as it was held as inaction of police as he did not register it. Hence the accused was convicted and sentenced under section 376 of Indian Penal Code.

RAPE: CONVICTION: DISMISSAL OF REVISION PETITION

Jareena Khatoon

v.

State of Jharkhand,

2015 (1) E Cr C 358

The contention of the accused was that the prosecutrix had not deposed that the accused committed rape upon her. As per statement of prosecutrix in FIR that inspite of objection the accused committed sexual intercourse upon her. The witness also stated that the accused committed rape on prosecutrix. Hence conviction and sentence was upheld and revision petition was dismissed.

RAPE AND MURDER: LIFE IMPRISONMENT

State of Bihar

v.

Hemlal Sah,

2014 Cr LJ 1767: 2014 (16) RCR (Cri) 832: 2015 (1) PLJR 337

The deceased girl along with her cousin had gone to clear bowels, the accused came out of bushes, caught hold of deceased's neck, wrapped dupatta around her kneck and raped her. The cousin ran and narrated to the family of deceased. Thereafter dead body of deceased was found in bushes. The prosecutrix found all these evidences as credible and trustworthy. The death sentence was awarded by lower court. But High Court commuted death sentence to life imprisonment.

RAPE ON 16 YEAR OLD GIRL: CONVICTION CONSENT OF PROSECUTRIX HAS NO VALUE

Manohar Lal

v.

State of Himachal Pradesh,

2014 (2) Him LR 1186

Even if there is consent, the act will still be a "rape" if the girl is under 16 years of age. According to witnesses the accused used to give beatings both to him and the prosecutrix and threatened to kill them with a drat and axe it such acts were disclosed to any person. The testimony of prosecution witnesses was found to be wholly reliable. Hence the conviction and sentence of accused was confirmed by the High Court.

RAPE ON MINOR GIRL: CONVICTION

Om Prakash

v.

State of Himachal Pradesh,

2014 Cr LJ 4091: 2014 (Supp) Cr LC 373

The prosecutrix was a young child and was a student of Class V. She was clear, cogent and consistent in her deposition. Medical evidence fully corroborated with the testimony of prosecutrix. The statement of grand-mother of prosecutrix corroborated fully with the version of prosecutrix. The conviction and sentence of accused upheld by the High Court.

RAPE ON A TEENAGER DAUGHTER BY HER FATHER: CONVICTION

Ramher

v.

State (Govt. of NCT of Delhi),

2015 (93) RCR (Cri) 422: 2014 (207) DLT 245:
2014 (140) DRJ 344: 2014 (1) JCC 478: 2014 (3) AD (Del) 436

The Criminal Law Amendment Act, 2012 introduced a new clause under section 372(2) of Indian Penal Code as clause 6(f) to cover cases where rape is committed in a fiduciary relationship. In this instant case the father of teen-aged prosecutrix committed rape upon her. All evidence were proved and the accused convicted with life imprisonment. But the High Court considering the consequence of mother and children, reduced his sentence to 10 years rigorous imprisonment.

RAPE IN TRAIN LADY COMPARTMENT: MURDER: DEATH SENTENCE: RAREST OF RARE CASE

State of Kerala

v.

Govindaswamy,

2014 (1) ILR (Ker) 141

The accused barged into the ladies compartment of a train and pounced on the deceased and after inflicting injuries on her, dropped her from the running train resulting further fatal injuries to prosecutrix. He thereafter jumped out of the train and brutally raped on unconscious victim, resulting her death. Hence death sentence was awarded and the same was confirmed by the High Court.

RAPE ON MINOR GIRL BY SHOP-KEEPER: CONVICTION

Dharampal

v.

State of Himachal Pradehs,

2013 (3) Sim LC 1404

A minor girl was raped by a shop-keeper when she went to shop to buy groceries. The accused closed the door, overpowered her and committed rape. The statement of prosecutrix was consistent, natural and corroborated with other evidence on record. The medical evidence showed the prosecutrix was pregnant. Hence the conviction and sentence of accused was held proper by the High Court.

Part 11

Criminal Pleadings, Petitions and Affidavits

CRIMINAL PLEADINGS, PETITIONS AND AFFIDAVITS

FIR AND CHARGE-SHEET

Model Form of First Information Report (Section 154, Cr.P.C.)

नमूना–प्रथम सूचना रिपोर्ट

Model Form of Charge Sheet

नमूना–आरोप पत्र

MODEL FORMS OF CHARGE

Model Form of Charge under section 34 of IPC (common intention)
Model Form of Charge under section 75 of IPC (enhanced punishment after previous conviction)
Model Form of Charge under section 115 of IPC (abetment of Capital offence)
Model Form of Charge under section 120B of IPC (criminal conspiracy)
Model Form of Charge under section 302 of IPC (punishment for murder)
Model Form of Charge under section 307 of IPC (attempt to murder)
Model Form of Charge under section 376 of IPC (rape)

BAIL APPLICATIONS AND PETITIONS

Model Form of bail application under section 167(2)(a) of Cr PC (when investigation not completed within 60/90 days)
Application for Baii
Additional Bond
Application for Anticipatory Bail
Bail Application under section 439 of the Code of Criminal Procedure, 1973
Application under section 439(1)(B) of the Code of Criminal Procedure, 1973
Bail Application under section 389(3) of the Code of Criminal Procedure, 1973
Application under section 444 of the Code of Criminal Procedure, 1973
Petition under section 317 of Cr PC (inquiries and trial in absence of accused)
Affidavit in support of an application for trial under section 437 of Cr PC (Bail in non-bailable Offence)
Counter Affidavit in the bail application filed under section 437 of Cr PC

DECLARATION OF AN ACCUSED

Declaration of an accused at the time of his release from Jail under section 356 of Cr PC (Notification of address by convict)

CONDONATION DELAY

Application for condoning Delay in filing complaint under section 473, Cr PC (Extention of period of limitation)

PETITIONS

Petition for withdrawal of a case by the party under section 257 of Cr PC (withdrawal of complaint)
Petition under section 205 of Cr PC (Dispensing of Personal attendance of accused by magistrate)
Petition for examination of a witness under section 284 of Cr PC (Dispensing and commission of attendance of witness)
Petition under section 311 of Cr PC (Summoning of persons and witness)

AFFIDAVIT

Affidavit: In Case of Bail Under section 437 of the Code of Criminal Procedure
Counter Affidavit: Under section 437 of the Code of Criminal Procedure
Affidavit in support of an application for trial under section 437 of the Code of Criminal Procedure, 1973
Affidavit: Under section 438 of the Code of Criminal Procedure, 1973
Affidavit supporting an application under section 362 of the Code of Criminal Procedure, 1973

CRIMINAL PLEADINGS, PETITIONS AND AFFIDAVITS

FIR AND CHARGE-SHEET

MODEL FORM OF FIRST INFORMATION REPORT (SECTION 154, CR.P.C.)

Serial No. : Book No. ....

1. District............... P.S......................... Year................ FIR No. .... Date.............
2. (i) Act.. Section...
   (ii) Act.. Section...
   (iii) Act.. Section...
   (iv) Other Acts & Sections..
3. (a) Occurrence of offence Date from...................... Date to..........................
   Time Period................. Time from .... Time to.......................
   (b) Information received at P.S.: Date.......................... Time.................................
   (c) General Diary Refernce: Entry No. .... Time ....
4. Type of Information: Written/Oral
5. Place of occurrence:
   (a) Direction and distance from PS.. Beat No.........................
   (b) Address..
   ....
   (c) In case outside the limit of Police Station, then
   Name of PS,... District...
6. Complainant/Informant
   (a) Name...
   (b) Father's/Husband's Name...
   (c) Date/Year of Birth.. (d) Nationality.................................
   (e) Passport No........................ Date of Issue..................... Place of Issue.......................
   (f) Occupation..
   (g) Address..
   ....
   ....
   ....
   (h) Tel No. ....
7. Details of known/suspected/unknown accused with full particulars (Attach separate sheet, if necessary)
   (1) ....
   (2) ....
8. Reasons for delay in reporting by the complainant/informant ....
   ....
9. Particulars of properties stolen (Attach separate sheet, if necessary).......................
   ....
10. Total value of property stolen...
11. Inquest Report/U.D. case No., if any...
12. F.I.R. Contents (Attach separate sheet, if required)..
    ....
    ....

Serial No. : Book No. ....

13. Action taken: Since the above report reveals commission of offence(s) u/s ....as mentioned at Item No. 2:
   (1) Registered the case and took up the investigation or
   (2) Directed/Entrused (Name of I.O.)......................... Rank....................... No. .... PIS No......................... to take up the investigation or
   (3) Refused investigation due to...
   (4) Transferred to P.S. .... District .... on point of jurisdiction.

F.I.R. read over to the complainant/informant, admitted to be correctly recorded and a copy given to the complainant/informant, free of cost.

Signature of Officer in charge/Duty Officer, Police Station

R.O.A.C. Name...

Rank.................................... No. ....

PIS No. | | | | | | | | |

14. Signature/Thumb impression of the complainant/informant.
15. Date and time of despatch to the Court...

नमूना–प्रथम सूचना रिपोर्ट

(दण्ड प्रक्रिया संहिता की धारा 154 के अन्तर्गत)

क्रमांक संख्या किताब संख्या.............

1. जिला.................... थाना.................... वर्ज़.......................... प्र.सू.रि. सं. .... तिथि...........
2. (i) अधिनियम... धाराएं.....................................
   (ii) अधिनियम... धाराएं.....................................
   (iii) अधिनियम... धाराएं.....................................
   (iv) अन्य अधिनियम एवं धाराएं...
3. (क) अपराध घटित होने का दिन तिथि से............................ तिथि तक...............................
   समय अवधि......................... समय से.................... समय तक...............................
   (ख) थाने में सूचना प्राप्त हुई दिनांक............................... समय...................................
   (ग) सामान्य डायरी संदर्भ: प्रविश्टि संख्या................................. समय...............................
4. सूचना का प्रकार: लिखित/मौखिक
5. घटित होने का स्थान: (क) थाने से फासले एवं से दिशा गशत संख्या
   (ख) पता...
   (ग) यदि इस थाने की सीमा से बाहर हो, तो थाने का नाम.................................. जिला....... ....
6. शिकायतकर्ता सूचनाकार
   (क) नाम...
   (ख) पिता/पति का नाम...

(ग) जन्मतिथि/जन्म वर्ष.. (घ) राष्ट्रीयता...............................

(ङ) पारपथ संख्या.................................... जारी होने की तिथि...

जारी होने का स्थान..

(च) व्यवसाय...

(छ) पता..

....

(ज) टेलीफोन नं. ....

7. ज्ञात/संदेहास्पद/अज्ञात सिद्ध दोषियों का पूरा ब्यौरा दीजिए (यदि आवश्यक हो, तो अलग पृष्ठ लगाइए)

(1) ....

(2) ....

8. शिकायतकर्ता/सूचनाकार द्वारा रिपोर्ट विलम्ब से रिपोर्ट करने के कारण...

9. चुराई गई/सम्बद्ध सम्पत्ति का ब्यौरा दीजिए (यदि आवश्यक हो, तो अलग से पृष्ठ लगाइए)......... .

....

....

10. चुराई गई/सम्बद्ध सम्पत्ति का मूल्य...

11. मृत्यु की जांच रिपोर्ट/अप्राकृतिक मृत्यु केस संख्या, यदि कोई हो...

12. प्रथम सूचना रिपोर्ट (यदि आवश्यक हो, तो अलग से पृष्ठ लगाइए)

13. की गई कार्यवाई: चूंकि उद्र रिपोर्ट मद संख्या 2 पर उल्लिखित धाराओं के अनुसार हुए अपराधों को उजागर करती है:

(1) मामले को दर्ज किया तथा छानबीन शुरू कर दी

(2) नाम...नं. ....पी.आई.एस. नं. ....को जांच आरम्भ करने का निर्देश दिया/जांच सौंपी गई।

(3) जांच/अन्वेषण करने के लिए इंकार कर दिया क्योंकि...

(4) क्षेत्राधिकार वाले थाने...................................जिला...को हस्तान्तरित कर दिया गया।

प्रथम सूचना रिपोर्ट शिकायतकर्ता/सूचनाकार को पढ़कर सुनाई गई उसने ठीक माना कि इसे सही-सही दर्ज किया गया है और इसकी एक प्रति शिकायतकर्ता/सूचनाकार को निःशुल्क दी गई।

थाना प्रभारी/कर्त्तव्य अधिकारी के हस्ताक्षर

नाम...................................

रैंक..................................संख्या

(पीआईएस सं.) | | | | | | | | |

14. शिकायतकर्ता/सूचनाकार के हस्ताक्षर/निशान अंगूठा...

15. न्यायालय को भेजने की तिथि व समय...

MODEL FORM OF CHARGE SHEET

District............................ Charge Sheet No.................................... of 20.... Date .... 20......

Police Station .... First Information Report No................. of 20.... Date .... 20......

Name, address and occupation of complainant or informant	Names and addresses of accused persons not sent up for trial whether arrested or not arrested, including absconders (show absconders in red ink)	Names and addresses of accused persons sent for Trial		Property (including weapons) found, with particulars of where, when and by whom found and whether forwarded to Magistrate	Names and addresses of witnesses	Charge or information: Name and offence and circumstances connected with it, in concise detail and under what section of the Law charged
		In custody	On bail or recognizance			
1	2	3	4	5	6	7

DETAILS OF DOCUMENTS

(To be attached with charge sheet)

(1) No. of Challans ....

(2) No. of Duplicate FIR..

(3) Specimen of Handwriting...

(4) G.P.A. Papers (Photocopy)...

(5) Search and Seizure Report..

(6) Map of Place of Occurrence..

(7) Arrest Memo...

(8) C.F.S.L. Report..

(9) Statement of Witnesses with address and place of witnesses and date (including the I.O.)

INFORMATION SHEET (To be attached with Charge-Sheet)

District..

Dated..

....alias...

.... S/o Shri ....

.... Resident .... Village (Ward) ....

....District...Height..

....

....

....

....

....

....

Inspector
In-charge of Police Station..........................
District..

N.B.—This is admitted fact that the abovesaid person is a habitual offender/ suspicious person.

नमूना–आरोप पत्र

फार्म सं.

जिला .... आरोप पत्र सं. .... दिनांक .... 20 .....

थाना.................................... प्रथम सूचना रिपोर्ट सं. .... दिनांक .... 20 .....

शिकायतकर्त्ता या सूचना देने वाले का नाम, पता एवं व्यवसाय	अन्वीक्षा के लिए नहीं भेजे गए अपराधियों के नाम एवं पते, गिरफ्तार किया गया या नहीं किया गया, फरारों को भी शामिल करें (फरारों को लाल स्याही से दिखाएं)	अन्वीक्षा पर भेजे गए अपराधियों के नाम एवं पते		सम्पत्ति (हथियारों को सम्मिलित कर) कब, कहां, किसके द्वारा पाए गए एवं क्या न्यायाधीश की सेवा में अग्रसारित किए गए	साक्षियों के नाम एवं पते	आरोप या सूचना–इनसे संबंधित नाम तथा अपराध एवं परिस्थितियां सविस्तार से दें एवं नियमानुसार कौन सी धारा लगती है।
		अभिरक्षा में	जमानत पर या शनाख्त हर			
1	2	3	4	5	6	7

प्रपत्र आरोप-पत्र के साथ संलग्न करें

(1) चालान संख्या ....

(2) प्रथम सूचना पत्र की प्रतिलिपि संख्या ....

(3) हस्तलिखित (सुलेख) का नमूना ....

(4) जी. पी. ए. कागजातों की प्रतिलिपि ....

(5) तलाशी और जब्त करने का विवरण ....

(6) घटना स्थल का नक्शा ....

(7) गिरफ्तारी का प्रपत्र ....

(8) सी. ए. एस. एल. विवरण ....

(9) गवाहों के ब्यान, पते और गवाहियों के स्थान दिनांक सहित (थानेदार सहित)

सूचना पत्र आरोप-पत्र के साथ संलग्न करें

जिला...........................

दिनांक.......................

.... उर्फ ....

....पुत्र श्री ....

....निवासी ....गांव (मुहल्ला)

....जिला ....कद

....

....

....

....

....

....

....

निरीक्षक

इंचार्ज थाना...

जिला ....

टिप्पणी–यह विश्वास करने का कारण कि उपर्युक्त व्यक्ति एक अभ्यस्त अपराधी या संदिगध व्यक्ति है, पृष्ठ के अन्तिम भाग में दिए जाने चाहिए।

MODEL FORMS OF CHARGE

MODEL FORM OF CHARGE UNDER SECTION 34 OF IPC (COMMON INTENTION)

I, ...(name and office of Magistrate/Sessions Judge), do hereby charge you.......(name of the accused) as follows:—

That you on....... day of ....20.......at about ....pm/am along with .... (names of other accused persons) committed a criminal act .... (enter the detail of the act) punishable under section 34, IPC, in furtherance of a common intention or you and ....(names of other accused persons) participated in the meeting, (give the details of common intention) and you are guilty under Section ....(mention the section of the IPC), read with section 34, IPC and within the cognizance of this Court.

Accordingly, I hereby direct that you be tried by this court on the said charge.

Date and Seal of Court | Signature of Magistrate/Sessions Judge

.... | ....

MODEL FORM OF CHARGE UNDER SECTION 75 OF IPC (ENHANCED PUNISHMENT AFTER PREVIOUS CONVICTION)

I, ...(name and office of the Magistrate/Sessions Judge) do hereby charge you.............(name of the accused) as follows:—

That you, on ......day of ....20.......about ....pm/am committed an offence punishable under section .... IPC (mention the section) and within my cognizance, that you, the said.............. stand further charged that before committing the said offence you had been convicted on............. of an offence punishable under the section .... of IPC for a term of ....years and the said conviction is still in force and that you are thereby liable to enhanced punishment under section 75 of IPC.

And I hereby dierct that you be tried by the said Court of Session on the said charge.

Date and Seal of Court | Signature of Magistrate/Sessions Judge

.... | ....

MODEL FORM OF CHARGE UNDER SECTION 115 OF IPC (ABETMENT OF CAPITAL OFFENCE)

I, ...(name and office of Magistrate/Sessions Judge) hereby charge you .... (name of the accused) as follows:—

That you on.......day of ....20...., at about ....pm/am abetted the commission of offence by name of the accused of an offence of ....(mention the section of IPC) punishable with death (or imprisonment for life), which said offence was not committed in consequence of the abetment, and thereby committed an offence punishable under section 115 of IPC and within my cognizance.

And, I hereby direct that you be tried by the said Court on the said charge.

Date and Seal of Court | Signature of Magistrate/Sessions Judge/ High Court Judge

.... | ....

MODEL FORM OF CHARGE UNDER SECTION 120B OF IPC (CRIMINAL CONSPIRACY)

I, ...(name and office of the Magistrate/Court of Session) hereby charge you ....(name of the accused) as follows:

That you on ....day of.......20.......at about.......pm/am, agreed with (name of the conspirator) to do (or cause to be done) an illegal act, namely.............(or an act which is not illegal by illegal means) and besides the above said agreement that you did some acts, in pursuance of the said agreement to commit the offence of ...... section of IPC punishable with death or imprisonment for life or rigorous imprisonment for a term of ....years or upwards or a criminal conspiracy other than a criminal conspiracy to commit an offence punishable under section 120B of IPC, and within my cognizance.

And I hereby direct that you be tried by the said Court on the said charge.

Date and Seal of Court — Signature of Magistrate/Sessions Judge

.... — ....

MODEL FORM OF CHARGE UNDER SECTION 302 OF IPC (PUNISHMENT FOR MURDER)

I, ...(name and office of the Magistrate/Sessions Judge/High Court) hereby charge you ....(name of the accused) as follows:—

That you on .... day of............ 20.... at about.......pm/am.......committed murder intentionally (or knowingly) causing the death of .... (name of the deceased) and thereby committed an offence punishable under section 302 of IPC and within the cognizance of this Court.

And I hereby direct that you be tried on the said charge by the said Court.

Date and Seal of Court — Signature of Magistrate/Sessions Judge/ High Court Judge

.... — ....

MODEL FORM OF CHARGE UNDER SECTION 307 OF IPC (ATTEMPT TO MURDER)

I, ...(name and office of the Magistrate/Sessions Judge/Judge of High Court) hereby charge you .... (name of the accused) as follows:—

That on ....day of ....20.......about ....pm/am you committed an offence namely.......with such intention or knowledge and under such circumstances that by that act you had caused the death of ....(name of the victim), you would have been guilty of murder (and that you thereby caused the hurt to the said (victim)), and that you have thereby committed an offence punishable under section 307 of IPC, and within the cognizance of this Court.

And I hereby direct that you be tried on the said charge by this Court.

Date and Seal of Court — Signature of Magistrate/Sessions Judge/ High Court Judge

.... — ....

MODEL FORM OF CHARGE UNDER SECTION 376 OF IPC (RAPE)

I, ...(name and office of the Magistrate/Session Judge/High Court Judge) hereby charge you ....(name of the accused) as follows:—

That on ....day of.......20....... at about.......pm/am you committed rape on .... (name of the woman raped), and thereby committed an offence punishable under section 376 of IPC and within the cognizance of this Court.

And I hereby direct that you be tried by the said Court by this Court.

Date and Seal of Court

Signature of Magistrate/Sessions Judge/ High Court Judge

....

....

BAIL APPLICATIONS AND PETITIONS

MODEL FORM OF BAIL APPLICATION UNDER SECTION 167(2)(A) OF CR PC (WHEN INVESTIGATION NOT COMPLETED WITHIN 60/90 DAYS)

IN THE COURT OF JUDICIAL MAGISTRATE (FIRST CLASS)

at ....(mention the place and address)

Crl. Case No. .... of 20.......

IN THE MATTER OF

.... Petitioner

vs.

State Respondent

(1) That the petitioner............. (name of accused) was arrested................ on day of ....20.......for the alleged offences under ....IPC (mention the section). The petitioner has been in Judicial custody since the date of arrest till date.

(2) That the prosecution did not file charge sheet even after the expiry of 90 or 60 days (mention the exact days till the date of application) under section 167(2)(a) of Cr PC and the petitioner ....(name of accused) is ready and willing to furnish the sureties as may be directed by this Hon'ble Court.

It is therefore prayed that this Hon'ble Court may be pleased to release the petitioner ....(name of accused) on bail and pass such other suitable orders as the court may think fit and proper.

Signature of Accused

....

Place.......................

Dated.......................

Signature of Advocate

....

APPLICATION FOR BAIL

In the court of .... (Metropolitan Magistrate/Judicial Magistrate/ Chief Judicial Magistrate/ Sessions Judge, etc.)

Criminal Case No. ....of 20............

State Complainant

vs.

Accused Respondent

Offence under section .... of I.P.C.

Police Station ....

Sir,

It is most respectfully submitted as under:—

1. That the accused/applicant was arrested by Police/Customs Officers (in case of economic offence) on .... for an alleged offence.
2. That the accused has been falsely implicated in this case and nothing incriminating has been recovered from him.
3. That the accused is innocent and has not committed any offence whatsoever.

4. That the accused/applicant was induced/threatened to make involuntary statement by police/customs officers.
5. That the accused/applicant is permanent resident of ....with his family and there is no chance of his absconding.
6. That there is no likelihood of applicant tampering with the prosecution evidence since the challan has already been filed.
7. That no useful purpose would be served, if the accused/applicant is denied bail, since the complaint has already been filed and no investigation is said to be pending in this particular case.
8. That the accused/applicant is ready to abide by any condition that may be imposed by the Hon'ble court while granting the bail.
9. That the last bail application was moved before this Hon'ble Court on .... which has been dismissed on ....

PRAYER

In view of the foregoing it is most respectfully prayed that this Hon'ble Court may kindly admit the accused/applicant to bail on such terms and conditions as this Hon'ble Court may deem fit and proper in the interest of justice.

Prayed accordingly.

Dated...................... ACCUSED/APPLICANT

through

(Advocate)

ADDITIONAL BOND

Under section 438 of the Code of Criminal Procedure, 1973

1. I undertake to make myself available for interrogation by the police officer whenever asked to do so.
2. I undertake not to induce or influence or threaten any of the persons acquainted with the facts of the case so as to prevent him from disclosing any fact to any of the courts or police officer.
3. I undertake not to leave India without prior permission of the court.
4. I undertake to abide by the terms and conditions of the bail order.
5. I undertake to present myself before the court whenever asked to do so.

Dated...................... APPLICANT/ACCUSED

APPLICATION FOR ANTICIPATORY BAIL

Under section 438 of the Code of Criminal Procedure, 1973

In the Court of Sessions Judge, ...

Criminal Case No. .... of 20...............

State Complainant

vs.

Accused Respondent

Under section .... of I.P.C.

Police Station ....

MOST RESPECTFULLY SHEWETH:

1. That the applicant (particulars about him, his respectability and credibility, status in life and reasons as to why and whose instance he is required by the police).
2. Narrate the humiliation to be caused showing that applicant is innocent and is falsely implicated due to ....
3. That applicant is not named in FIR.
4. That no incriminating articles have been recovered from the house of the applicant and the applicant has been implicated on mere suspicion.
5. That the applicant does not have any past criminal record, the applicant is not a previous convict.
6. That the applicant apprehends that he might be arrested.
7. That the offence is bailable/non-bailable. That the applicant has no desire to evade the due process of law and shall face the trial to vindicate their innocence.
8. That the applicant undertakes not to misuse the bail and he also undertakes to abide by the terms of the bail orders.
9. That the applicant has not filed any other bail application under section 438 of the Code of Criminal Procedure in this Hon'ble Court.

PRAYER

It is, therefore, most respectfully prayed to this Hon'ble Court that this Hon'ble Court may be pleased to direct to release the applicant on bail in the event of his arrest directing the CJM/M.M/ Police Official of the concerned Police Station .... for such amount of money as this Hon'ble Court deems fit to fix.

Prayed accordingly.

APPLICANT

through

Dated......................

COUNSEL

BAIL APPLICATION UNDER SECTION 439 OF THE CODE OF CRIMINAL PROCEDURE, 1973

In the High Court of .... at ....

Criminal Misc. .... (M)................No...... of 20......

In the matter of:

Petitioner/accused..

(Presently lodged in Central Jail Tihar)

vs.

Collector of Customs..

(Application under section 439 (praying for releasing of the petitioner/accused on bail)

To

The Hon'ble Chief Justice and his Companion Justices of the said High Court......

The humble petition of the petitioner above–named:

MOST RESPECTFULLY SHEWETH:

1. That the petitioner/accused was apprehended by the Customs Officers of .... on .... in connection with an alleged offence punishable under section 135 of the Customs Act, 1962 in connection with recovery of 20 gold

biscuits weighing .... gms valued at Rs...................
.... and currency worth Rs. .... from the luggage which does not belong to the petitioner.

2. BRIEF FACTS OF THE CASE.
3. That the petitioner/accused informed the officers that he had no connection with the seized goods, the petitioner was forced, induced and threatened to make involuntary statement by the Customs Officers under section 108 of the Customs Act, 1962.
4. That the petitioner/accused is innocent and has not committed any offence whatsoever.
5. That the petitioner/accused was produced in the court of Ld. Session Judge on .... and bail application moved by him was rejected on ....
6. That the petitioner/accused is a respectable man of the society and he has never come to the adverse notice of any law enforcing authority.
7. That the petitioner/accused is not a previous convict.
8. That the petitioner/accused is a permanent resident of ...... living with the family members and as such there is no chance of his absconding from trial.
9. That the investigations of the case *qua* the petitioner/ accused is over and no useful purpose would be served if the accused/petitioner is denied bail.
10. That the bail application moved before the Sessions Court was dismissed on.......................
11. That the petitioner/accused is ready to abide by any condition imposed by this Hon'ble Court.
12. That no similar Bail application has been filed on behalf of the petitioner/accused in this Hon'ble Court or in any other High Court.

PRAYER

In view of the foregoing it is most respectfully prayed that:

(a) the petitioner/accused may kindly be admitted to bail on such terms and conditions as this Hon'ble Court may deem fit and proper in the interest of justice and/or;

(b) pass any further order or orders as this Hon'ble Court may deem fit and proper in the interest of justice.

Prayed accordingly.

PETITIONER/ACCUSED

through

Dated............................ COUNSEL

APPLICATION UNDER SECTION 439(1)(B) OF THE CODE OF CRIMINAL PROCEDURE, 1973

[Special Powers of High Court or Court of Session to grant bail—

Under section 439(1)(b) Condition imposed by Magistrate to be modified or set aside.]

In the Court of the Sessions Judge at......................

Criminal Misc. No.............................of 20.........

In re:

State ....

Under section .... of I.P.C.

Police Station ....

[Application under section 439(1)(b)]

The humble application on behalf of the applicant most respectfully sheweth:

1. That the applicant is innocent and has been falsely implicated in the case due to enmity.
2. That the applicant's name is not mentioned in the F.I.R.
3. That there was no recovery of any incriminating articles from the possession of the applicant.
4. That the learned Judicial Magistrate 1st Class was pleased to release the applicant on bail on the executing of bond with two sureties of Rs................ each but imposed condition on the applicant, such as:
   (i) the applicant shall leave the town of .... and .... must not enter into the town until the disposal of the case,
   (ii) the applicant should report to the Officer-in-Charge of the .... Police Station twice in a week.
5. That the applicant has been living in the said town with his family for about 10 years and has been earning his livelihood by working in a ....
6. That the applicant will be put to immense difficulties if he were to leave the town so much so that he will be out of work and the members of his family including the applicant shall have to face starvation.

PRAYER

The applicant, therefore, prays that this Hon'ble Court be pleased to set aside the said conditions imposed by the learned Judicial Magistrate and/or to modify them.

Dated....................... APPLICANT

BAIL APPLICATION UNDER SECTION 389(3) OF THE CODE OF CRIMINAL PROCEDURE, 1973

(Suspension of sentence pending the appeal, release of appellant on bail)

In the Court of Shri........Judicial Magistrate (First Class)

State Complainant

vs.

Accused Respondent

U/s .... IPC

Police Station ....

[Application under section 389(3)]

The humble application of the applicant respectfully showeth:

1. That the applicant has been convicted and sentenced by the court in the above case to .... month's rigorous imprisonment.
2. That the applicant was on bail during the trial by this Hon'ble Court and never abused the privilege of bail given to him.

3. That the case is of minor nature and the applicant is entitled to be given the benefit of doubt.
4. That the filing of appeal/revision shall take sometime, and convict applicant shall suffer irreparable loss till he is heard by the appellate court.
5. That the applicant is the sole earning member in his family and he is the only person who can arrange for a proper conduct of the appeal against his conviction above mentioned.
6. That the applicant contested the case during the appeal/trial and intends now to go up in the appeal to file which the applicant requires time during which it is necessary for him to be on bail.

PRAYER

It is, therefore, respectfully prayed that this Hon'ble Court may be pleased to grant bail for the applicant to enable him to file the appeal and get orders for bail from the appellate court.

Dated......................

COUNSEL FOR THE APPLICANT

APPLICATION UNDER SECTION 444 OF THE CODE OF CRIMINAL PROCEDURE, 1973

(Discharge of sureties)

In the Court of ....

Criminal Case No. .... of 20 ....

State — Complainant

vs.

Accused — Respondent

Under Section .... of I.P.C.

Police Station ....

(Application under section 444)

The humble application on behalf of the applicant.

MOST RESPECTFULLY SHEWETH:

1. That the applicant is one of the sureties for the accused .... in the above case.
2. That the accused .... is present in the court today.
3. That the applicant is leaving .... and is not likely to return before the expiry of a couple of years within which he will not be able to exercise proper control over the accused and discharge the responsibility that he has undertaken.

PRAYER

The applicant, therefore, prays that the Hon'ble Court be pleased to allow the applicant to withdraw as a surety and take action as provided by law for the discharge of the applicant from the responsibilities.

Place:

APPLICANT

PETITION UNDER SECTION 317 OF Cr PC (INQUIRIES AND TRIAL IN ABSENCE OF ACCUSED)

IN THE COURT OF ....(NAME OF COURT)

AT.................... (NAME OF PLACE)

Cri. Case No. ....of 20.......

IN THE MATTER OF

.... Petitioner

vs.

State Respondent

(1) That the petitioner ....(name of accused) charged with....... (mention sections of IPC) and his attendance is not necessary for following reasons .... (mention the reasons).

It is therefore prayed that Your Honour may be pleased to dispense with the attendance of petitioner ....(name of accused) for the present and proceed with the matter in the interest of Justice and may pass such other order or orders as this court may think fit and proper.

Signature of Accused

....

Place.............

Date.............

Signature of Advocate

....

AFFIDAVIT IN SUPPORT OF AN APPLICATION FOR TRIAL UNDER SECTION 437 OF Cr PC (BAIL IN NON-BAILABLE OFFENCE)

IN THE SESSIONS COURT OF.......

Cr. Misc. (Bail) Application No. .... of 20.......

.... Applicant

vs.

.... Respondent

Affidavit of ....(name of the deponent) s/o.............(name of the father of the deponent), aged.............(age of deponent), resident of.............(place of residence).

1. That the deponent referred to above is the accused in Sessions Case No. .... of ......20..... which is allegedly for an offence punishable under section 307 read with sections 120B and 34 of the Indian Penal Code.

2. That the deponent is fully familiar with the facts and the circumstances of the case and is competent to depose to the facts mentioned hereunder.

3. That the deponent is not guilty of the offence with which he is charged, and is innocent. He has been falsely implicated in the said Sessions case for having allegedly committed the offence referred to above due to past enmity with the *de facto* complainant who had given the First Information Statement to the Police. The aforesaid case arose out of the First Information Statement referred to above. The FIR dated ....of 20.......lodged by the.............(name of the complainant) at Police Station............. (name of Police Station) was that he arrived at the residence of ....(mention the place of residence of the original complainant), at ......pm/am on the day of......20......., got hold of his collar, threatened to strangulate him and also hit his head with a revolver. A true copy of the FIR has been filed before this Hon'ble Court.

4. That the aforesaid facts stated in the FIR are totally false and concocted and are born out of the figment of the wild imagination of the informant and the Police .... (name of Police Officer) who have registered the crime.

5. That despite the fact that the deponent was arrested a few days ago, no weapon or other material object was discovered/recovered from his person or as shown by him. The memo of arrest which is produced herewith will clearly bear this fact out.

6. That there is no independent evidence from any reliable witnesses to the occurrence and the entire prosecution case is a cock and bull story.

7. That no occurrence of a criminal nature much less like the one alleged against the deponent, has ever taken place.

8. That the deponent is unnecessarily detained and his freedom of movement and action is curtailed on total violation of his fundamental rights.

9. That the deponent is the only earning member of his family who earns out his livelihood as a daily labourer. His big family consists of his aged parents as well. Unless he is enlarged on bail, the petitioner's family will be reduced to starvation.

10. That the deponent is willing to provide two solvent sureties in the event of granting of bail by this Hon'ble Court. He also undertakes to abide by all the conditions this Hon'ble Court deems fit to impose for the purpose of enlarging him on bail. He will co-operate with the investigation and not try to influence any witnesses.

11. That the deponent has not filed any bail application earlier, nor any bail application is pending before this court or any other court.

Verified that the contents of paras 1 to 11 of this affidavit are based on personal knowledge of the deponent and nothing material to the case has been hidden from the affidavit.

Signed and verified at............., on the ....day of.......20....

Deponent

Solemnly affirmed and signed by the deponent, who is personally known to me in my office at.............on this ....day of.......20.......

Place.......................

Date.......................   Seal and Signature of Advocate

COUNTER AFFIDAVIT IN THE BAIL APPLICATION FILED UNDER SECTION 437 OF Cr PC

In the Sessions Court of.............

Affidavit in Cri. Misc. (Bail)

Application No. .... of 20.......

.... Applicant

vs.

.... Respondent

Affidavit of............., s/o ...., aged......, resident of.............

1. I, the above mentioned deponent do hereby solemnly affirm and state on oath as follows:—

2. That I am the Circle Inspector attached to the ....Police Station, ...I am investigating officer in the crime covered by the above case. I am fully conversant with

the facts and the circumstances of the case and I am authorised and competent to file this counter affidavit in the Bail Application of the accused.............(name of the accused).

3. That all the averments in the affidavit of the accused applicant, save and except those which are specifically admitted hereunder, are denied as untrue and incorrect.

4. That the averments in paras 1 to 3 of the affidavit being matters of record deserve no reply.

5. That with regard to the averments in paras 3 to 11, it is respectfully submitted that the same are not true or correct. There is *prima facie* evidence to convict the applicant for the offence with which he is charged. As an investigating officer I was able to recover the revolver used by the applicant from the hidden place in his residence soon after his arrest. The place where the revolver was kept was pointed out by the applicant himself.

6. That further investigation revealed that there was serious dispute between the complainant informant and the applicant and there was civil litigation between the parties in which the complainant (victim) eventually succeeded. The accused was nursing hatred against the victim and he has been telling everybody that he would be doing away with the life of the victim (informant).

7. That the applicant is a person wielding considerable influence among the political circles. He is affluent and there is every possibility of his interfering with the investigation making use of his political connections and influencing the witnesses with his money power, if he is set at large. This will seriously affect the investigation and prosecution of the case.

8. That his remand to, and continuance in, custody till the investigation is very essential for an effective and complete investigation of the case.

It is, therefore, just and necessary that the bail application filed by the applicant be dismissed.

Verified that the contents of paras 1 to 8 of this affidavit are true to my personal knowledge and belief and nothing material has been concealed therefrom.

Signed and verified at............., on this ....day of............., 20....

Signature of Deponent

....

Solemnly affirmed and signed before me by the deponent, who is personally known to me on this.............day of ....20.......in my office at ....

Place.......................

Date ....

Seal and Signature of Advocate

....

DECLARATION OF AN ACCUSED

DECLARATION OF AN ACCUSED AT THE TIME OF HIS RELEASE FROM JAIL UNDER SECTION 356 OF Cr PC (NOTIFICATION OF ADDRESS BY CONVICT)

I, ...(name of accused) s/o..............(name of father of accused), ... village.............(name of village), Thana.................(name of Thana), District............. (name of District), do hereby declare that I shall reside at ....(name of Village) and I shall inform to the ....(name of police station) whenever I shall change my place of residence.

Signature of accused

....

Date.............

Countersigned by Superintendent of Jail

....

Date.............

Attested by the Jailor

....

Date.............

CONDONATION DELAY

APPLICATION FOR CONDONING DELAY IN FILING COMPLAINT UNDER SECTION 473, Cr PC (EXTENTION OF PERIOD OF LIMITATION)

IN THE COURT OF.............(PLACE OF COURT)

.... Complainant

vs.

.... Opposite party

The humble petition of.............(name of complainant) most respectfully sheweth:

1. That the petitioner.. (name of petitioner), s/o.............(name of father of petitioner), resident of ....(name of place of resident), aged ....(years) was attacked by the opposite party about .... hours in night.

2. That some people after hearing the shout of the petitioner intervened in the occurrence and rescued the petitioner from the trap of the opposite party.

3. That the petitioner received serious injuries and his two legs were fractured in the abovementioned attack and hence he remained in the hospital.............(name and place of hospital) from date.......to.......date and because unable to make complaint within the ....prescribed period from the date of occurrence before this Honourable Court as prescribed in ....of Cr PC (mention the section). A medical certificate has been attached herewith petition.

Therefore it is prayed that your Honour may be pleased to extend the period of limitation in the interest of justice.

Signature of Petitioner

....

Place.............

Date.............

Signature and Seal

Advocate

....

PETITIONS

PETITION FOR WITHDRAWAL OF A CASE BY THE PARTY UNDER SECTION 257 OF Cr PC (WITHDRAWAL OF COMPLAINT)

IN THE COURT OF.............(NAME AND PLACE OF COURT)

Cri. Case No. ....of 20....

.... Petitioner

vs.

State Respondent

This humble petition most respectfully sheweth:

1. That the accused.............(name of the accused), aged ....(enter the age) is charged with the .... sections of IPC (mention the sections of IPC) in the abovementioned case.

2. That the accused ....(name of the accused) belongs to the same blood relation of the complainant.

3. That on ....day of.......20.......some people in the same locality themselves intervened in the matter and an amicable settlement was brought among the complainant ....(name of the complainant) and the accused.............(name of the accused) and they both were agreed to withdraw the abovementioned case and finally the complainant is ready to withdraw the case and not to proceed further.

It is, therefore, prayed that this court may be pleased to allow the complainant to withdraw the case from this Honourable court and the accused may be allowed to be acquitted from the abovementioned case.

....

Signature of Complainant

Place.............

Date............. Signature and Seal of Advocate

....

PETITION UNDER SECTION 205 OF Cr PC (DISPENSING OF PERSONAL ATTENDANCE OF ACCUSED BY MAGISTRATE)

IN THE COURT OF.............(NAME OF THE COURT)

AT.............(NAME OF PLACE)

Cri. Case No. .... of 20......

.... Petitioner

vs.

State Respondent

1. That the petitioner ....(name of petitioner) herein submits that a case has been initiated against him under Sections ....IPC (mention to sections) and the petitioner is charge-sheeted under ....Sections of Cr PC (mention the section).

2. That the petitioner has appeared through his counsel on the various dates of hearing.

3. That the petitioner is a very old man of about .... years age and he is unable to attend this Hon'ble Court for every date of hearing.

4. That the petitioner is the neighbour of the complainant and is known to all the witnesses and there is no problem of identification at trial and his appearance in the last trial.

5. It is therefore prayed that this Hon'ble Court may be pleased to grant exemption from personal appearance and may permit him to be represented by advocate .... (name of advocate) and also pass such other suitable orders as this Hon'ble Court may think it fit and proper.

Signature of Accused .... Signature of Advocate ....

Place.............

Date..............

PETITION FOR EXAMINATION OF A WITNESS UNDER SECTION 284 OF Cr PC (DISPENSING AND COMMISSION OF ATTENDANCE OF WITNESS)

IN THE COURT OF.............AT...................(PLACE OF THE COURT)

IN THE MATTER OF

Cri. Case No. .... of 20.......

.... Petitioner

vs.

State Respondent

1. That in the above said case.............(name of witness) is a material witness for the defence.

2. That the examination of ....(name of witness) for defence is absolutely necessary for the ends of justice.

3. That ....(name of witness) is at present residing with her/his son in a distant place.............(name of place) .... miles away from this court. Besides he/she is an old man woman of ....(age), suffering from .... (name of disease).

4. That it will be prohibitive to bring him at any other expensive mode and such may cause it hardship and inconvenience to both accused and witness.

It is therefore prayed that, Your Honour may be pleased to issue a commission to the Chief Judicial Magistrate, ...(name of place where the witness presently resides) or to any Magistrate of first class within the local limits of whose jurisdiction the witness resides for his/her examination.

And your petitioner, as in duty bound, shall ever pray.

Name and address of witness

Place...

District....................................

Police Station.............

Signature of Advocate ....

PETITION UNDER SECTION 311 OF Cr PC (SUMMONING OF PERSONS AND WITNESS)

IN THE COURT OF....................

at....................(mention the place)

Cri. Case No. ....of 20......

IN THE MATTER OF

.... Petitioner

vs.

State Respondent

1. That PWs....................(name of prosecution witnesses), were examined on .... 20.... (mention the date) and the matter is coming up for further prosecution intenses.

2. That PW1 ....(name of witness) is to be recalled for the purpose of further cross examination on the following aspects, namely..........(specifically mention the reasons).

It is therefore prayed that this Hon'ble Court may be pleased to recall PW1......... (name of witness), for the purpose of further cross examination and also pass such other suitable orders as this court may think fit and proper.

Signature of Accused

....

Place.......... Signature and Seal of Advocate

Date.......... ....

AFFIDAVIT

AFFIDAVIT: IN CASE OF BAIL UNDER SECTION 437 OF THE CODE OF CRIMINAL PROCEDURE

IN THE SESSIONS COURT OF ....

Criminal Miscellaneous (Bail) Application No........of 20..........

Applicant:

vs.

Respondent:

AFFIDAVIT of.........................., S/o......................., aged................., residing in ....

The deponent named above hereby solemnly and affirms as follows:—

1. That I am the deponent referred to above and the accused in Sessions Case No............... , which is allegedly for an offence punishable under section 307 read with sections 120B and 34 of the Indian Penal Code.
2. That I am fully familiar with the facts and the circumstances of the case and I am competent to depose to the facts mentioned hereunder.
3. That I am not guilty of the offence with which I am charged and I am innocent. I have been falsely implicated in the Sessions Case for having allegedly committed the offence referred to above due to past enmity with the *de facto* complainant who had given the First Information Statement to the Police. The aforesaid case arose out of the First Information Statement referred to above. The F.I.R. dated.............., lodged by the..................Police-station, was that I arrived at the residence of.............., the original complainant, at..................pm on the.................., 20, ..., and tried to attack him with a *lathi.* A true copy of the F.I.R. has been filed before this Hon'ble Court.
4. That the aforesaid facts stated in the F.I.R. are totally false, concocted and born out of the figment of the wild imagination of the informant and the Police who have registered the crime.
5. That despite the fact that the deponent was arrested a few days ago, no weapon or other material object was discovered or recovered from his person or was shown by him. The memo of arrest, which is produced herewith, will clearly bear this fact out.
6. That there is no independent evidence from any reliable source whatsoever as to the occurrence and the entire prosecution case is a fictitious one.
7. That no occurrence of a criminal nature, much less like the one alleged against the deponent, has ever taken place.
8. That the deponent is unnecessarily detained and his freedom of movement and action is curtailed, totally violating his fundamental rights.
9. That the applicant is the only earning member of his family and earns out his livelihood as a contractor. He has a large family consisting of his wife, two children, two younger siblings and aged parents. In the event of the deponent's continuing status as a detainee, his family will be forced to starve.
10. That the deponent applicant is willing to provide two solvent sureties in the event of being granted bail by this Hon'ble Court. He also undertakes to abide by all the conditions this Hon'ble Court deems fit to impose for the purpose of releasing him on bail. Further, the deponent will willingly co-operate with the investigation and not try to influence any witnesses or hamper any evidence.

11. That the deponent has not filed any bail application earlier, nor is any bail application of his is pending before this or any other Court.
12. That the deponent has never been convicted of any offence before, nor has he been implicated in any crime whatsoever.

Sd./

Deponent.

Verification

I, the abovenamed deponent, verify that the contents of this affidavit are true to the best of my knowledge, belief and as per information received by me by experts and nothing material has been concealed therefrom.

Date........................

Place........................

Sd./

Deponent

Solemnly affirmed and signed before me by the abovenamed deponent who is personally known to me, on this the.................day of..........., 20............

Sd./

Counsel for the deponent

Note: Affidavit to be attested by the appropriate authority prescribed under law.

COUNTER AFFIDAVIT: UNDER SECTION 437 OF THE CODE OF CRIMINAL PROCEDURE

IN THE SESSIONS COURT OF ....

Counter-Affidavit in Criminal Miscellaneous (Bail)

Application No. .... of 20.........

Applicant:

vs.

Respondent:

COUNTER-AFFIDAVIT

I, ..., S/o....................., aged................, residing in..........................

1. I, the abovenamed deponent do hereby solemnly affirm and state on oath as follows:—
2. I am the Circle Inspector attached to the ....Police-station and am the investigating officer in the crime covered by the above case. I am fully conversant with the facts and the circumstances of the case and am authorised and competent to file this counter affidavit in the Bail Application of the accused ....
3. All the averments in the affidavit of the accused applicant, save and except those which are specifically admitted hereunder, are denied as untrue and incorrect.
4. The averments in para Nos. 1 to 5 of the affidavit, being matters of record, deserve no reply.
5. With regard to the averments in para Nos. 6-14, it is respectfully submitted that the same are not true or correct. There is *prima facie* evidence to convict that applicant for the offence alleged against him and with which he is charged. As an investigating officer, I was able to recover the *lathi* used by the applicant from

the concealed place in the very residence of the accused soon after his arrest by me. Further, the applicant himself pointed out the place where the said weapon was kept.

6. Further investigation revealed that there was bitter animosity between the complainant informant and the applicant and there was even civil litigation between the parties in which the complainant victim eventually succeeded. Consequently, the accused was harboring feelings of hatred and animosity against the victim and even went to the extent of threatening to put an end to the victim's life.
7. The applicant is a man of abundant resources and there is every possibility of his interfering with the investigation making use of his political connections and influencing the witnesses with his money power, if he is set free. Granting bail to the applicant will seriously affect the investigation and prosecution of the case.
8. His remand to, and continuance in custody till the investigation is over is very essential for an effective and complete investigation of the case.

It is, therefore, just and necessary that the bail application filed by the applicant be dismissed.

Sd./
Deponent.

Verification

Verified at................on this the..................day of............., 20............., that the contents of the above affidavit are true and correct to the best of my knowledge, belief and information and nothing material has been concealed therefrom.

Sd./
Deponent.

Solemnly affirmed and signed before me by the deponent, who is personally known to me, on this the...................day of..........., 20..............

Sd./
Counsel for the deponent.

Note: Affidavit to be attested by the appropriate authority prescribed under law.

AFFIDAVIT IN SUPPORT OF AN APPLICATION FOR TRIAL UNDER SECTION 437 OF THE CODE OF CRIMINAL PROCEDURE, 1973

IN THE SESSIONS COURT OF.............................

Criminal Miscellaneous (Bail) Application No............................. of 20........

Applicant.

vs.

Respondent

AFFIDAVIT

I, ..., S/o ...., aged........................years, residing in.............................., do hereby solemnly affirm and state as follows:—

1. I am the deponent referred to above and the accused in Sessions Case No. .... which is allegedly for an offence punishable under Section 307 read with sections 120B and 34 of the Indian Penal Code.

2. I am fully familiar with the facts and the circumstances of the case and I am competent to depose to the facts mentioned hereunder.

3. I am not guilty of the offence with which I am charged, and I am innocent. I have been falsely implicated in the Sessions Case for having allegedly committed the offence referred to above due to past enemity with the *de facto* complainant who had given the First Information Statement to the Police. The aforesaid case arose out of the First Information Statement referred to above. The F.I.R. dated............................. lodged by the............................. Police Station was that I arrived at the residence of...................... ...., the original complainant, at............................. pm on the.........................., 20........, got hold of his collar, threatened to strangulate him and also hit his head with a revolver. A true copy of the FIR has been filed before this Hon'ble Court.

4. The aforesaid facts stated in the FIR are totally false and concocted and are born out of the figment of the wild imagination of the informant and the......................... Police who have registered the crime.

5. Despite the fact that the deponent was arrested a few days ago, no weapon or other material object was discovered or recovered from his person or as shown by him. The memo of arrest which is produced herewith will clearly bear this fact out.

6. There is no independent evidence from any reliable witnesses to the occurrence and the entire prosecution case is a cock and bull story.

7. No occurrence of a criminal nature much less like the one alleged against the deponent, has ever taken place.

8. The deponent is unnecessarily detained and his freedom of movement and action is curtailed totally violating fundamental rights.

9. The applicant is the only earning member of his family who earns out his livelihood as a daily labourer. His big family consists of his aged parents as well. Unless he is enlarged on bail, the petitioner's family will be reduced to starvation.

10. The deponent applicant is willing to provide two solvent sureties in the event of granting of bail by this Hon'ble Court. He also undertakes to abide by all the conditions this Hon'ble Court deems fit to impose for the purpose of enlarging him on bail. He will co-operate with the investigation and not try to influence any witnesses.

11. This applicant has not filed any bail application earlier, nor is any bail application of his pending before this or any other court.

Verified that the contents of paras 1 to 11 of this affidavit are based on personal knowledge of the deponent and nothing material to the case has been hidden from the affidavit.

Signed and verified at........................, on the......................... day of , 20.....

Deponent.

Solemnly affirmed and signed by the deponent, who is personally known to me in my office at......................... on this the........................ day of , 20.....

Advocate.

AFFIDAVIT: UNDER SECTION 438 OF THE CODE OF CRIMINAL PROCEDURE, 1973

BEFORE THE COURT OF SESSIONS JUDGE, ...

In

Criminal Complaint No........................of 20.......................

Applicant/Accused

vs.

Opposite Party

AFFIDAVIT of.........................., S/o..........................., aged.....................years, presently and permanently residing in ....

The deponent abovenamed hereby solemnly affirms and states as follows:—

1. That the deponent is the applicant herein and the accused in the Criminal Complaint referred to above. The deponent is well conversant with the facts and circumstances of the present case and competent to swear to this affidavit.
2. That the deponent is a young man of 26 years. He is the Managing Director of one of the leading Multi-national Companies.
3. That the deponent is a very respectable person of his locality and is a peace loving citizen.
4. That on.................., the applicant got married to the..................., D/o......................, now residing in ....
5. That the relations between the deponent and the complainant were not cordial because of the latter's extra-marital affair with the complainant, who has been working with the.................Police.
6. That the deponent objected to such affair of his wife and did not permit her to go out of the house.
7. That nursing a grudge against the aforesaid natural response of the deponent and taking undue advantage of his office, the complainant got the abovementioned complaint registered against the deponent on ....at...................
8. That the said complaint registered against the deponent is absolutely false and incorrect. The deponent is not at all involved in the offence alleged in the complaint.
9. That as a matter of fact, the deponent is a victim at the hands of the complainant, who has conspired with the Police and got the complaint registered.
10. That the said complaint is absolutely fictitious and pregnant with malice.
11. That in view of the abovementioned circumstances, the deponent apprehends that he may be arrested in pursuance of the aforesaid fictitious complaint.
12. That the arrest of the deponent by the Police will cause irreparable loss and injury to the impeccable reputation of the deponent and will also adversely affect his service.
13. That the deponent is a permanent resident of......................, and there is no chance of his absconding in case he is granted bail.
14. That the deponent is not a previous convict and has never been involved in any criminal case before.
15. That the deponent undertakes to abide by any of the conditions that this Hon'ble Court may deem fit for admitting the deponent to bail.
16. That the deponent is ready to produce surety to the satisfaction of this Hon'ble Court.

Sd./
Deponent.

Verification

Verified at................on this the.................day of............, 20............, that the contents of the above affidavit are true and correct to the best of my knowledge, belief and information and nothing material has been concealed therefrom.

Sd./
Deponent.

Solemnly affirmed and signed before me by the deponent, who is personally known to me, on this the..................day of.........., 20............

Sd./

Counsel for the deponent.

Note: Affidavit to be attested by the appropriate authority prescribed under law.

AFFIDAVIT SUPPORTING AN APPLICATION UNDER SECTION 362 OF THE CODE OF CRIMINAL PROCEDURE, 1973

IN THE HIGH COURT OF JUDICATURE AT.......................

Affidavit

in

Criminal Miscellaneous Case No.......................

IN

Criminal Miscellaneous Appeal No.......................

(District.......................)

Applicant...

vs.

Respondent...

Affidavit of....................... aged....................... years, residing in.......................

Deponent.

1. I, the deponent referred to above, do hereby solemnly affirm and state on oath as under:

2. The deponent is the father of the applicant in the application referred to *supra* and he is fully conversant with the facts and the circumstances of the case and competent to swear to this affidavit, and is doing so as authorised by the applicant.

3. A typographical error occurred in the application No....................... referred to above in as much as instead of Crime No....................... it has been erroneously typed as Crime No....................... of the....................... Police Station.

4. When the above application for bail was moved before this Hon'ble Court on....................... this Hon'ble Court granted bail and based on the application erroneously Crime No....................... was given in the Order. The mistake happened on account of an inadvertence on the part of the stenographer of the applicant's counsel and is not intentional.

5. In view of the said mistake, the police is not ready and willing to set the applicant at large.

6. It has, therefore, become necessary to correct the application and also the Order referred to *supra* by incorporating the correct number of the Crime No.......................

7. It is, therefore, expedient and just that the applicant may be permitted to make necessary corrections in Criminal Miscellaneous Case No....................... by substituting Crime No....................... of....................... Police Station for Crime No....................... and also make corresponding correction in the order of bail granted by this Hon'ble Court, as prayed for in the accompanying application.

I, the deponent referred to above, do hereby swear, verify and state that the contentions of the preceding paragraphs of this affidavit are true to my knowledge, information and belief and no material fact has been concealed therein.

Dated this the....................... day of......................., 20.......

Deponent.

I, ... registered clerk of Sh....................... Advocate, High Court of....................... do hereby declare that the person swearing to this affidavit and alleging himself as Sri....................... is known to me from a perusal of the papers produced by him in the case and I am satisfied that he is the same person.

Deponent.

Solemnly affirmed and signed by the deponent before me in my office at.................... on this the.................. day of.................., 20.......

Counsel for the Petitioner.

SUBJECT INDEX

C

D

W

•••